# The Welsh Highland Railway
## Rheilffordd Eryri
## Caernarfon - Rhyd Ddu

© Gordon Rushton V2a 06.12

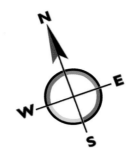

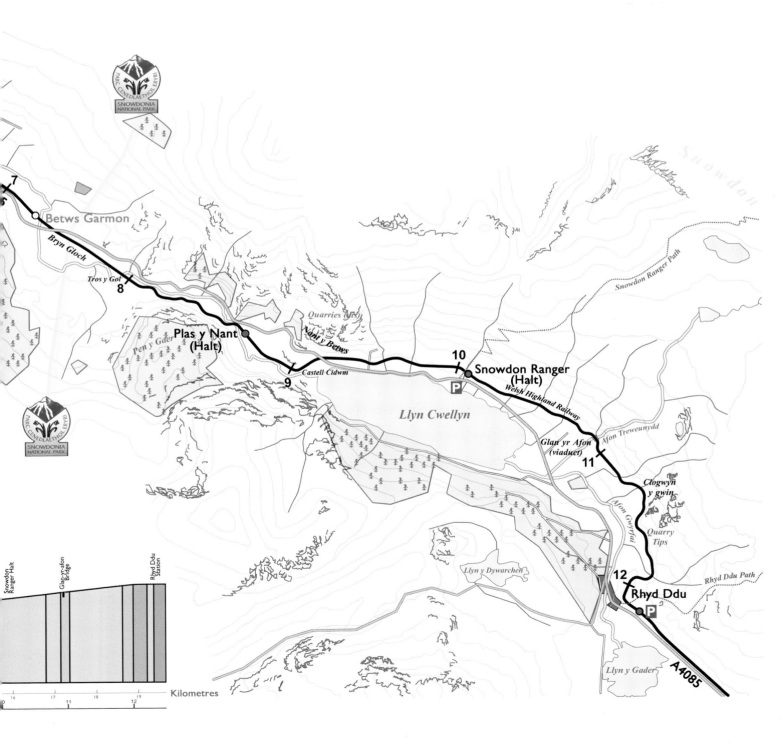

SNOWDONIA NATIONAL PARK
PARC CENEDLAETHOL ERYRI

7

Betws Garmon

Bryn Gloch

Tros y Gol

8

Pen y Gader

Plas y Nant (Halt)

Quarries (dis)

Nant y Betws

Castell Cidwm

9

10

Snowdon Ranger (Halt)

Welsh Highland Railway

Snowdon Ranger Path

Llyn Cwellyn

Afon Treweunydd

Glan yr Afon (viaduct)

11

Clogwyn y gwin

Afon Gwyrfai

Quarry Tips

Llyn y Dywarchen

12

Rhyd Ddu

Rhyd Ddu Path

Llyn y Gader

A4085

Snowdon Ranger Halt
Glan-yr-afon Bridge
Rhyd Ddu Station

Kilometres
16    17    11    18    12    19

# Welsh Highland Railway

# Renaissance

# Welsh Highland Railway Renaissance

## The story of the restoration of the Welsh Highland Railway 1991-2011

# Gordon Rushton

**In memory of Ben Fisher 1963-2009.**
His excellent chronicle and his approval provided the
impetus and the material to create this volume. It is very
sad that he is no longer here to enjoy its consummation.

ISBN 978-0-9571456-0-3 (hardback)

Published by:

**www.adlestroppress.co.uk**

Adlestrop Press
15 Rycroft, Furzton,
Milton Keynes, MK4 1AH


Design & Graphics by:

Gordon Rushton


Maps by:

Gordon Rushton


Printed in Great Britain by:

Amadeus Press
Cleckheaton
BD19 4TQ

# Contents

# Foreword

Richard Faulkner (Lord Faulkner of Worcester) is something of a railway champion in the House of Lords. His appointment in 2008-9, as spokesman for transport in the government whips' office, deputising for Lord Adonis, Secretary of State for Transport, meant that he had to step down from the chairmanship of the Railway Heritage Committee, in order to support the strongest wave of railway revival ever seen. After Labour left office, he became a trustee of the National Museum of Science and Industry, and the President of the Heritage Railway Association. In the House of Lords, Richard raises and deals with matters of particular interest to railways, and also promotes and safeguards the interests of the heritage railway movement. He is co-author of *Holding The Line – How Britain's Railways Were Saved*, whose publication coincides with the 50th anniversary of the Beeching report.

*'Railways will remain safe in the midst of panic; and though times of pressure, severe, hazardous, ruinous pressure, have been felt in this country, and unfortunately must be felt again, yet it will only prove them to be part and parcel of the genuine sources of wealth and avenues for labour, in which this country lives and moves and has its being.'*

That remarkably prescient sentence can be found in John Francis's A History of the English Railway, 1851; substitute "Welsh" for "English", and it describes what those involved in the rebuilding of the Welsh Highland Railway had to go through in the 1980s and 1990s in order to realise their dream.

And what a dream it was! These days the restoration of any closed railway is a long, complicated, and expensive process, even for a great national undertaking like Network Rail. Here the proposition was to restore 25 miles of closed track on a route that had been abandoned for 70 years, where some land had been absorbed into lineside farms and the rest had gone back to nature. It runs through a National Park containing some of the most breathtaking natural beauty anywhere in the United Kingdom. Restoration was in the face of opposition from land-owners, upland farmers, and residents doubtful about the outcome of an influx of tourist visitors, and nervous of real hardship caused by the loss of land and amenity on the farm that was necessary to facilitate heritage steam trains.

Winning the battle was bound to be a monumental challenge for all the railway's supporters, and one would have imagined that an essential prerequisite would be that all the interested parties spoke with a united and consistent voice. But as Gordon Rushton describes with passion and in meticulous detail, that unity of purpose was missing right up to and beyond

the point that the decision was finally taken in 1994 by the Secretary of Transport, over-ruling his planning inspector, to give the job of restoring the railway to the Ffestiniog Railway – the organisation that had sought in 1987 to buy the railway's disused trackbed and hand it over to the county council to prevent the railway's restoration, because it feared a competitor operating into Porthmadog would abstract revenue from their own services.

Initially local sensitivities tended towards introversion. By contrast (and unusually) Whitehall thinking was far-sighted. Later, Gwynedd did think in regional terms, but from an early stage the Welsh Assembly Government in Cardiff was thinking 'national'. Government is often blamed for failing to see the wider context in the longer-term. Here all parties in the Welsh Assembly Government encouraged this railway development, in the hope that it could stimulate the tourist industry as a basis for the promotion of regional prosperity.

As an example, early and late season trains, like the 2011 **Snowdonian** (Porthmadog - Blaenau Ffestiniog, Caernarfon - Porthmadog) in April brought 200 people to Porthmadog and Caernarfon for a couple of nights, and hotels were booked out, restaurants did well and tourist spend was boosted - and it is the attraction of the railway that encourages this additional visitor spend at quiet times. Everyone wishes to see the Welsh hill farmer prosper, and income from tourism, boosted by a new asset like this, makes this process easier not more difficult, offering opportunity for farmers to diversify, with bed and breakfast and offer other attractions to the holiday maker. For traders in a town like Caernarfon, doubling the numbers of long-stay visitors is a real boost.

The opening of the new railway has attracted new business, especially in years where the emphasis on holidays at home has increased. In 2011 visitors to the WHR nearly equalled those to the Ffestiniog

Railway, and numbers carried on both railways went up. Visitors exclaimed how different the two railways are, and many wished to travel on both. Additional 2012 investment at Porthmadog will make this process easier, as trains from each railway will soon be able to be in the Harbour Station at the same time. Access to the beauty spots like the Aberglaslyn Pass and Beddgelert was previously almost exclusively by car. The WHR was objected to for making this access difficult. In the first month of reinstated service to Beddgelert, 7,000 people visited by train - and their cars were parked outside the National Park, in Caernarfon, in a car park next to the Castle. By the year end this number to Beddgelert had risen to 70,000. In the public inquiry, some 5,000 cars were predicted to be reduced from National Park roads as a result of this railway - the number would seem to be higher than this already.

Each of the stages coincided with opportunity in a symphony of glee. The initial proposal came at a time of political change, with the Conservative Party at Westminster about to lose office, when the dogma of the rail privatisation process touched the project. Then followed a keen search for good Millennium projects, and having discovered WHR, the 'centre' protected and encouraged the little railway. Labour, and a devolved Welsh Assembly Government, provided renewed optimism to banish stasis at Rhyd Ddu, and helped the project down the hill towards Porthmadog with a 46 per cent grant, to which well-wishers, and the public's astonishing generosity added the remaining 54 per cent. Once in Porthmadog, an economic crisis kept holidaymakers at home, and filled the new trains to bursting point. No-one could have foretold this outcome or this combination of circumstances - if the project had been attempted even slightly later, it would surely have languished.

Only in Anthony Trollope's 19th century political novels (written at a time of an earlier railway mania) can one find evidence of such intrigue, personal jealousies and rivalries as Gordon Rushton reveals here. He writes as an insider, who saw much of what he describes at first-hand from his position as general manager of the Ffestiniog Railway.

For students of political plotting and of railway history, this book is a treat. Those seeking to learn about how to solve difficult railway engineering problems will also learn a very great deal, as will those who are interested in the labyrinthine planning inquiry process.

But above all, this is the story of a triumph — one that would never have achieved a happy ending without the dedication, devotion and professionalism of scores of volunteers and generous sponsors.

As we turn the pages we should remember the extraordinary contribution that heritage railways make to the national and regional economy. Our attention is drawn to a University of Bangor PhD thesis which revealed that by the normal economic measures, for an expenditure of £10m, one-off, from public (EU) funds, approximately £14m annually would be generated by the joining of the Welsh Highland and Ffestiniog railways.

The value to tourism is enormous. Heritage railways enjoy more support from the public than almost any other part of the heritage sector, with the exception of the National Trust. Whilst historic ships, aircraft and classic cars have their adherents, no other transport mode attracts anything like this level of interest with direct benefit to the tourist economy.

This is an industry which employs 2,000 people directly, engages a further 18,000 volunteers, carries 6.8 million passengers on 15 million passenger journeys, has a turnover of £84 million and contributes a staggering £579 million to the national and regional economy.

These are good times for the railways, and we should all celebrate the success of the Welsh Highland Railway in rejoining the nation's railway heritage map, and by overcoming adversity, disunity and difficulty, to deliver a truly sustainable and popular railway for the 21st century.

Richard Faulkner,
Worcester
January 2012

# Acknowledgements

Of course this story had to be told, but not by the Directors, not officially as 'attributable comment'. This is the independent voice of the people. Ever since we were kids, the Welsh Highland Railway was lying there in a little tragic cocoon of 'might have been'. No one could have planned what happened, unless you believe that scheming dragons at Dinas Emrys eventually decided that they were being disadvantaged, and wanted some of the action. They've now got it, and I should tell you who the human agents were that supplied the inspiration and the information for this book to be written.

The intense interest in the WHR project has supported two, full-time web sites. It doesn't matter whether you prefer the startling blue of Barrie Hughe's Isengard, or the calm yellow of Bangor.ac.uk. The latter was written by the late Dr Ben Fisher, and it is from that site that much of the contemporary information contained in this book has come. The book has taken a great deal of time to write. So I was able to talk with Ben before his sad and untimely death, and to receive his permission to use the contents of the site freely, to offer a permanent record of just what happened, the when and the how. But then that was the measure of the man. If it supported the WHR, you could count on Ben's backing. It is tragic that he isn't here any more, but his work is. And whilst we would much rather have him, his work has been used to allow the book to make what he did more accessible to all.

Another person who must not be forgotten is John Routly, Chairman of the Festiniog Railway Company until 1993. It was he who saw the signs of an attempt to change the status of the WHR trackbed, and determined to take the action he thought best to safeguard the FR's interests. It is likely that had he not done so, then the whole of the WHR would not have been restored.

One must in passing acknowledge Fate. The combination of strife, devolution, determination and a booming economy, have fortuitously combined to deliver the renaissance, which is why those suspicious of such benign augury try to finger the dragons. To have dallied could have spelt doom to restoration on this timescale. The Millennium Grant came at precisely the right time, and flagged the project as 'favoured' at the right moment. Rhyd Ddu was not a place for a railway to tarry long, yet it would have been in danger of doing so had Mr Hart's inestimable efforts in Cardiff, and the availability of grants not found union. So the railway surged forward, and when it reached Porthmadog, the exhausted pot was scoured for that little bit more, which has brought the vital alterations needed to make Porthmadog Harbour Station able to answer the new calls on its services. At just the right moment for the WHR, but the wrong moment for everyone else, the shadow of recession has brought crowds off the beaches of Spain and back to holidays at home. Thus the newly opened railway has surged with traffic. I like dragons.

Mike Hart was the man best to combine the shining parts of such fate into a restored railway. It required formidable determination, and exceptional staying power, to complete the course. Mike Hart has done so, through all the ups and downs, despite considerable personal cost, and he is as aware of the sound of missiles of disapproval passing his ears, as of the feeling of pats on the back. His OBE is public acknowledgement of the general acknowledgement of a job well done.

Less in the limelight, though as much deserved, must be Mike Schumann. Mike cut his teeth on the Ffestiniog Deviation, the successful project to build a diversion for the FR around the Tanygrisiau Pumped Storage scheme, bottom lake. His good fortune was a substantial inheritance, some of which he has disbursed wisely, and appropriately, in favour of the WHR. There is no doubt whatever that Mike's generosity has enabled the WHR project to succeed. He funded the enterprise at key moments, so that like the RAF in the Battle of Britain, the FR rose again, and again, despite its demise being predicted. Of course Mike was sensible enough to enjoy the expenditure when circumstances permitted. Going to buy Garratts in South Africa was fun! And as a qualified civil engineer, Mike was well fitted to play a practical part in the design and build of the restoration. Mike's donations are not public, but they are not secret either. He has decided to treat them as advantages he has that can be shared.

However there were other donors, some who also gave the project even greater amounts of money when it was really needed, notably for Phase 4. Their pleasure was to give but to remain in the background. Whilst that must be respected, it doesn't prevent thanks being offered. The list of items that the WHR project received is considerable. All of the Garratts have, been obtained with gifts, either all or in part.

A prize must go to the men of TCL - you will see them figure in these pages, and then know why. Just occasionally someone says to you 'would this be useful', and it happens to be the key to the puzzle. On this occasion, although the 'reconstruction' idea was misconceived, it was the acknowledgement that FR was trying to reopen the whole WHR that flagged it up as the most likely choice for the job.

Acknowledgement must be made to the County Council in all its re-organisational guises. Once a formidable detractor, as soon as it became plain that FR meant to honour its promises, and had the clout and the wherewithal to do this, the Gwynedd Council did what it says on the box; it sought to do the best for its constituency, when that meant facilitating WHR. GC's co-operation has been, and is still, vital to the interests of WHR.

An indispensable individual, who's particular blend of humour and determination got things going for the WHR on the ground, was Roland Doyle. He persevered against the odds to bring home Phases 1-3. It is he who has gone on from masterful management of construction, to mastermind the vital level crossings, and to pioneer electronic methods of issuing tokens for safe passage of trains along the line. After Roland came Alasdair Stuart and Stuart Mc Nair - what fortune to have such necessary and valuable skills.

The Welsh Assembly Government (WAG) changed the whole catalogue of prospects for the WHR. There has been solid support from Cardiff ever since WAG was formed. This was enjoyed publicly, when the charismatic Rhodri Morgan made one of his visits, and privately, when funding assistance has been made available by negotiation, with advice on how to satisfy the complex criteria. Phase 4 would not have happened without WAG. With their support came the support of the local MPs. As WHR became successful, there was pride in an all-party consensus for this feisty little railway in North Wales. Thus the train in May 2009, opening the railway to Hafod y Llyn, was a pantheon of politicians, all smiling.

And well they might smile, as also to be acknowledged must be Dr Megan Williams, the Bangor University pupil of FR Director Dr Dafydd Gwyn. Her PhD thesis indicated that from the £10m of public money invested in WHR, the enterprise returns to the local economy some £10m annually, and that will rise to £14m when the line is open to Porthmadog.

Who could forget the 64 Co., the people that worked tirelessly to persuade Gwynedd County Council to allow reconstruction, only to find the FR as unwelcome intruder.? They were casualties of unwitting acts that sealed FR into full restoration, against their original intentions, and then of being in a union of the wrong political flavour. Yet they still contributed volunteers and materials to rebuilding the WHR, despite eventually being thwarted in their aim of an autonomous railway.

It may be that their antithesis is Cymdeithas Rheilffoirdd Eryri (CRhE), the FR inspired WHR Society. Kick-started with some funds, they recruited members at great speed, and were momentarily frustrated by the cultural problems of the contractors who could not embrace volunteers. This was got over by the rising excellence of the associated tracklayers' skills. The Tuesday Gang, the Black Hand Gang and the Rest of the World Gang, proved themselves to be so adept at laying track, and dealing with all the connected activities, that they not only laid some 22 miles of it, with loops, but they generated income within the grant structure in acknowledgement of their contribution.

A man of immense value in writing this book has been John Hopkins. He had the foresight to attend public inquiries, and to record the events. These act as a foundation for unravelling what was said and by whom. Not only has he provided a detailed account of otherwise obscure proceedings, together with immaculate reasoning about the minutiae of decision making, he has also battled to make sure that the text, although simplified, takes no short cuts with describing the facts.

On the subject of money and a number of other important skills, this book has benefitted greatly from the help of Andy Savage. Apart from serving as a Statutory Director of the Festiniog Railway Company, we made an unlikely partnership for raising money from public and supporters. The story about how this was achieved is firmly recorded. The outcome approaches £3m, which is not great in comparison with the big donations, but it most certainly is in comparison with the fundraising achievements of other hallmark schemes. Such results count greatly in any political assessment, and perhaps the jewel in this crown is that the area that gave the most per head was Gwynedd! Andy has moderated firmly a fair amount of what has been written, extracting the emotional, and banning the outrageous. Perhaps his efforts have resulted in a more balanced and factual account.

The rest of the FR Co. Directors have shown interest.

*A nondescript picture taken on a dank February afternoon - but this is the symbolic union of the Ffestiniog at Porthmadog, with the WHR, stretching right through to Caernarfon 25 miles away. These are the Golden Bolts that signify 'We've done it!'*

Obviously this book is a celebration; it is not meant as criticism to anyone, more to shine the light of reason upon recent events. In doing so it must seek neither to offend, nor to sensationalise. FR Co. Director Nigel Burbidge has offered firm and fair guidance and forensic corrections. This book is not an 'official' account, but it would be sad if unjustified comment in this volume opened old wounds or had an unfavourable effect, by some biased or unnecessary comment. So it is with care that one must listen to revisionary advice, and comply to ensure fairness; this isn't censorship, it should be good sense. We join to achieve balance in this work, and many have contributed information to try to make it so.

I am of course now in possession of privileged information. Thank you to those who passed it over. It makes it possible to offer the facts, knowing the full story, but it places the duty on the author to be discreet, while allowing truth to govern candour.

There are people with inexpressible patience who read through the halting English of these pages, and then don armour so they may make suggestions for betterment. I unhesitatingly apologise for any bad temper involved. My thanks therefore to Dr Peter Jarvis, and the others who are so persistent, and then insistent, so that the facts may not be glossed over or be squeezed for effect. My thanks too: to Peter Johnson for advice, to him and to others, who have allowed their photographs, and to John Sreeves and others, who have allowed their drawings, to lend weight and character to the dialogue.

The last to be mentioned must be David Allan, now Chairman of the WHR Heritage Group, former Chairman of the 64 Co. His patience, perseverance and fair-mindedness brings the balance needed to this story. He has allowed an insight into both sides during the conflict that flared until restoration of the whole became a promise redeemed.

Whichever way you see it, as time passes, it becomes more apparent that it was not who restored the Welsh Highland Railway that matters. It is the vital fact that it has been restored at all that counts. The WHR now stands as a magnificent tribute to human endeavour - so let us now enjoy it.

There are more, many more people I should thank. And if they do not find their names here, then perhaps I can apologise for the omission, and urge that they move to the cut and thrust of the dialogue and seek them there.

Mike Hart, once remarked that we were better to be history makers than history writers. This enterprise has exampled the fragility of that statement. It is a wry twist of fate, within the knotted ball of events that is the Welsh Highland, that it should be he who does the making, but me who is doing the writing.

**Gordon Rushton**

# Introduction

When the summer sunlight sparkled on the Traeth from a sky of the purest blue, on a day hot enough to make Llyn Cwellyn's dark surface look lustrous and inviting; on a day when ewe called to ewe from velvety cushions of soft green grass, then there was the occasional chance to stroll through a journey of discovery among the ghosts of the old Welsh Highland Railway. This was the time to ponder the fading smoke-stain under a sturdy little stone arch, time to rue the spreading rust on a long abandoned plate girder bridge, and to mourn the desiccated timbers, empty of shining track.. Where the sheep had maintained a splendid lawn, one that raised hopes that all was not lost, then crumbling buildings bordered by encroaching undergrowth offered only renewed despair. All around was grand scenery, flaunting delightful vistas of the roaring tops, with the deep valleys, sunlit in summer, hosting still air and echoing bird calls. And as you walked, the calls were replaced by the gurgling of clear water. All the natural ambience was present that is now seldom enjoyed by those in our towns and cities.

The course of the old railway was clear, and somehow this made it worse. The wonderful places through which it once ran were now unreachable. The imagination ranged to the smell of the fusty compartment, the squeal of flanges, the clicking out of the rails beneath, swirls of lazy smoke from the puffing locomotive, the incomparable views, all lost in time. If the trains were running now, the line of thought shimmered, the view pacing the train from this road would be sublime. And so it would have been, in more than one place, for the route of the Welsh Highland Railway far from lurking among lofty prospects is alluring in parts. It is deliberately visible in the Aberglaslyn Pass; it plays hide-and-seek at Waunfawr; shares the road at Pont Croesor and Porthmadog, and looks like the County Donegal from Pitt's Head to Rhyd Ddu. In other places the magic of the view, devoid of habitation and filled with the majesty of the mountains, had been forgotten, and has only been rediscovered today, now that the track has been put back, and trains are running once more.

No surprise then that wistful glances were so often cast at restoring this jewel of a railway, with its trains in exquisite surroundings, aromatic smoke, and whistles that echo across the hillsides. It was interesting to find that others shared what one had supposed was a private dream of trains returning. They too made little railway scrawls in their schoolboy books. They also speculated on clouds of steam rising up the mountain slopes. No one I knew had ever seen a Welsh Highland Railway train, and that made it more romantic. There were working parties to the FR, and the one in June meant long, long evenings that were sometimes blessed with fair weather. Then people who 'knew' would take you out into the hills, and in the cooling beauty of a Welsh golden evening, you could tread where the rails had been, and imagine what it was like when the Croesor Tramway was delivering slates to Portmadoc, and the WHR train with brightly coloured coaches, took the curve at Croesor Junction to head off into the Aberglaslyn Pass.

There was much cruelty to be applied to any notions that this longed for event might ever happen again. Accidents of fate bound the railway in a legal tangle. The Festiniog Railway Company had a lease that it surrendered, with strange repercussions upon some stock and locomotives. The railway had been left, unused and destitute, in the hands of the Liquidator in wartime, and the track was removed. No statutory abandonment had been made; there were liabilities outstanding, and parts of the trackbed had gradually been appropriated as farmland and access roads. When the War had ended normality had returned, and interest had grown. Uncertainty that anything could be done within reach of the threadbare pockets of those times, to a railway with nothing left, made many draw back. The Festiniog was all there, magnificent, intact, and also derelict. A lesser sum expended here bought glory for sure. The rustic Talyllyn appeared to be saved by generosity and smiles alone. This gentle railway, though brought perilously close to dereliction, managed to keep running, and the tender loving care it received prompted a rapid rescue from oblivion. The Festiniog took much effort and generosity to be saved from extinction. There was a massive and difficult set of problems to be wrestled with for decades in order to safeguard its future. So when one was there volunteering in the early days, there was so much to be done that thought of restoring the WHR was almost heretical. If there was innovation and energy to spare then it ought to be directed to the FR.

For years it seemed that the Welsh Highland had unfriendly dragons guarding its gates. So much was against it that people were discouraged. The Receiver, always assuming he would consent to deal with you, required sums of money beyond imagination to stimulate interest, and was immune to blandishments that seemed to move the patrons of other small, orphaned railways. There was no track, no rolling stock. The Caernarvonshire County Council required road widenings from the trackbed, and this was a serious threat to restoring a railway that had failed and wasted ratepayers' money. There were none of the appurtenances of a running railway; the Festiniog had shed loads of those, and the Talyllyn had steam coming out of their locomotives. So that was where the effort should be directed - and there was so much to be done on these railways just to help them survive.

So bright bands of steel through the Aberglaslyn Pass remained a dream, while the other little railways in Wales enjoyed their renaissance. Lots of us walked along the trackbed imagining, hoping, wishing. Many had obligations to projects that just had to have their attention to survive, but the Welsh Highland Railway was a bit like the Titanic. It was a story that refused to go away, and its absence continued to fascinate. Ultimately, all the other railways were restored, flourished and completed. It became a natural thing for families to ride on the Great Little Trains of Wales. However all interested and expert in such things knew that there was one Great Little Train that had still not been rebuilt. The pressure grew gradually to do something about it. To those 'in the know' it seemed that the WHR restoration project was a hopeless case, mired by a legal tangle that was never to be unpicked. When it became known that the County Council was likely to bid for the trackbed, there was intense speculation. On the one hand the Festiniog was all of a tremble that unwanted competition would result. Others were concerned that the Council would acquire the trackbed as a footpath, and only a little portion would ever become a railway again. The most vocal opinion was that only the Council had the means to unravel the tangle, and that were they to do so, then at least something would be saved.

There was a band of people determined to see the railway restored. In 1964 they had formed themselves into a company to restore the railway. But by 1990 it had not been possible to restore a single inch of track on the original line. This stood testament to the difficulties involved - but suddenly there was movement.

The story of what happened next: the immense row that was caused by Ffestiniog making a secret bid, and then asking the council not to favour competitive development; a leak that revealed the FR Co.'s actions; the pressure this brought to bear on the Festiniog to restore the whole line; the way that the adverse publicity fed the fastest and biggest fund raising campaign ever mounted in railway preservation to that date; the Greek tragedy of how the progenitors only got a siding for their pains, is some of what this book is about. The rest of it - and perhaps the most important part - is of how the largest and longest tourist railway reconstruction ever attempted in the world so far has been brought to fruition. And it's all been done by ordinary folk!

The railway has been restored for a sum of about £28m - for 25 miles this is 'cheap' in railway terms. The economic payback from the grants totalling about 55% is calculated at £14m per year. Traffic has surged on to the new railway and the reports back about what the ride is like gives cause for joy. For years some of the enthusiasts dreamed of taking a ride on the Welsh Highland Railway. In 2011 this became a reality. The last train ran in 1937. The first in the new era ran on 30th October 2010, an absence of 73 years. No one therefore knew what riding on the new WHR would be like. Many of those who dreamed to see the railway restored rode on the first train. It was run for all those who gave regular subscriptions of money to help plug the funding gap. It was easy enough to work out what it would be like riding the bits that could be seen, but the WHR is rather secretive, and it goes into 'virgin territory' for quite a large part of the way. Also the feel of it was quite unknown to all.

The shining faces from that first trip proclaimed the success of the enterprise to all. Years and years ago, the pioneers who restored the Ffestiniog Railway in the 1950s always said that the WHR was the railway that they would like to have restored, as it was so magnificent - but they couldn't. It was just too difficult. and all the railway bits had disappeared. Now the FR bulldozer had flattened everything that was difficult, and the railway was restored. People coming off that first journey told the story. The WHR was indeed magnificent. It's the most scenic railway ride in Britain. The variety of the views, the gliding through tunnels, along ledges above the river, in the forest, under Snowdon to the great fortress at Caernarfon is truly superb.

Now this remarkable job is complete, and such an enterprise proves not only that railway enthusiasts can bring off a cutting-edge £28m project for the pleasure of it, but that the result has a most important helpful economic payback to the region. It is this that inspires - it shows what can be done.

Gordon Rushton
Milton Keynes
May 2012

*The Inspector's Train, a delightful and timeless*
*cameo in steam. Betws Garmon 26th July 2003*

Martins Kreicis

# Chapter 1
## Some history

Ice ages have worn smooth the Cambrian rocks, and ground down the Ordovician volcanoes, leaving a series of smooth shapes rising to a kilometre above sea level. Here is still the highest mountain in England and Wales, Snowdon. Rainfall has filled the cwms and kept soil from the rocky tops. The sea has risen to create great estuaries and make an island of Anglesey. The area is a small, concentrated, Welsh mountain upland of great beauty, studded with lakes and occasional forests. It is tiny in comparison with the mountain vastness of Scotland. Sheep on the land have kept trees to a minimum, confining Sessile Oak to small stands rather than the natural landscape of tree-cover from beach to mountain top. A man-made landscape of smooth green carpets of well-cropped grass abounds, made lush by frequent, soft rains. Conifers march en-bloc in areas planted by man. *Rhododendron Ponticum* wickedly flourishes wherever it can. Planted by the Victorians, spurned today, it sports joyous flowers in June, as if to tempt us to tolerate its alien presence. Roads of modest aspect, but immodest traffic in summer, snake through this temperate glory, but fail to invade. The crags, screes and buttresses of rock confine them largely to the valley floors, and thus this compact, accessible little area of outstanding natural beauty

*The top of Snowdon and the Moon - from Rhyd Ddu - not far apart.*

has an unsullied air about it that we find attractive. Deposits of minerals abound, and so North Wales has long borne witness to the hand of man attempting to wrest treasure from the ground. Thus the Industrial Revolution visited the area, and laid some of it waste. Today the recovery is almost complete, and the giant scrapings, left as witness, offer intrigue to the natural landscape. Yet our attraction to these lovely places brings a new invasion from the modern, industrial revolution. Every pull-off, every car parking space in high summer can have a car in it, with perhaps one cruising by, looking speculatively. The hills bear scars where people walk off the thin soil. The visitors threaten the very thing they have come to see and enjoy. It is time for us to accept the restoration of the railways and their use, not for the removal of

minerals, but for the safe encapsulation of those who wish to experience first-hand the charms of the place.

Yet the human hand in changing this landscape is by no means new. The large, shallow estuary of the Glaslyn promised easy land reclamation. Madocks built a tramway in 1808 when constructing the Cob, to reclaim vast acres of the Traeth for agriculture. It did not quite pan out as he thought, but the great work has more than achieved its promise two centuries on. There were other early railways. The Nantlle Tramway was being used to ship slate to Caernarfon by 1828. The Ffestiniog Railway (FR) used the Cob and the harbour, formed by the scour of the Glaslyn confined at Porthmadog, to bring slates to the sea in 1836. Many more schemes appeared, as the early railroad concept blossomed into a national railway system. Development was unplanned by Government, though competition was tempered by Parliament. However speculation was rife, with dreams of development and prosperity for the Victorians, as promoters proliferated railway schemes. They harboured heightened expectations, many before their time. The North Wales Narrow Gauge Railways was one of these imagined argosies. It was conceived in 1872 as a general undertaking, with lines connecting Beddgelert with Porthmadog, Betws y Coed, Llanwnda and Bryn Gwyn. After paused construction, a reduced version opened between the London and North Western Railway (L&NWR) station of Dinas and Snowdon Ranger, for goods traffic in 1878, and to Rhyd Ddu in 1881, with a branch from Tryfan Junction to Bryn Gwyn. Receipts were uninspiring, and the North Wales Narrow Gauge Railways (NWNG) was run by a receiver almost from the start. Although the railway served a number of quarries, its termination at Dinas, within a short distance of the port of Caernarfon, was a serious disadvantage. Transhipping of all goods to the standard gauge put time and cost into the transits. The promise to connect the NWNG with Caernarfon was never redeemed, and it dogged the railway throughout its life, leading to an early closure. With

*Such wonderful promise of mountains to come. Pont Croesor spans the Glaslyn, but the abutments of the rail portion of the bridge carry no girders. Trains ran here last nearly 70 years ago - but all that will soon change. Cnicht (doing a Snowdon impression), Moelwyn Mawr and Moelwyn Bach arm the horizon.*

hindsight, the optimism that promoters of this railway backwater shone on their schemes to reach Porthmadog, Caernarfon and Betws y Coed seems rash. There was confidence then that cheaply built, light railways, especially narrow gauge ones, would generate traffic and allow agricultural and light engineering development in rural areas. Today we rest on the power of that hindsight to say that the coming of the motor age ought to have introduced realism into the 1922 plan for the Welsh Highland Railway (WHR). Such was the weight of the light railway philosophy in the 19th Century, that others threatened to build railways that competed with the NWNG plans. The Porthmadog, Beddgelert and South Snowdon Railway (PB&SSR) was formed in 1901 under the control of the North Wales Power and Traction Company. This was created to generate hydro-electric power, and looked for every possible user for its electricity; it acquired the NWNG and promoted the PB&SSR. The idea of an integrated power utility and transport undertaking is well known to us today from the now extinct interurban railways of North America promoted by Samuel Insull . Hard times and the First World War

prevented the completion of the planned PB&SSR three-phase, electric railway, but the hydro-electric stations are still there. After the WW1, the NWNG was still just operating. The Power Company had gained control of the FR as well as the NWNG and the uncompleted PB&SSR. The Welsh Highland Railway (Light Railway) Company was formed in 1922, incorporating the NWNG and PB&SSR, with the intention of completing the link to Porthmadog, via the Croesor Tramway, and also of extending to Caernarfon. The former was achieved, the latter was not, and this unattained goal was almost certainly fatal to the WHR interest. Debentures were sold to raise capital, and the Government advanced half the cost of completing the railway in order to mitigate unemployment. McAlpines were the contractors, obliged to employ as many local persons on the contract as they could. The change of plan, from electric to steam traction on the section from the Aberglaslyn Pass through to Rhyd Ddu, had repercussions. The electric locomotives were planned to handle more severe gradients than steam locomotives could. New sections of line had to be added to the partly built formation in great loops,

*Hunslet 2-6-2T Russell, originally of the PB&SSR, in cut down form to fit the FR, steams uphill through the Aberglaslyn Tunnels on its way to Beddgelert. The date is 7th August 1933. Four years before the 'chop' for the WHR.*
**David Allan Archive negative collection WHR Heritage Group**

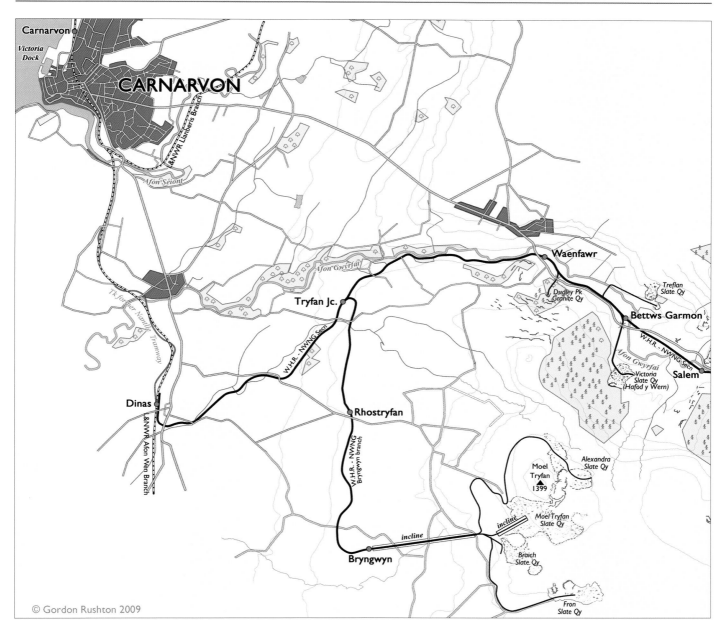

*The North Wales Narrow Gauge promoters could be forgiven for thinking that their enterprise would be blessed with success, serving several quarries, as is shown. The connection with the L&NWR was at Dinas and the 'Branch' was to Rhyd Ddu. They did not run through to the Port of Caernarfon. This probably put paid to their interests - and to those of the WHR as well. Today's enterprise will fare better at the centre of tourism in Caernarfon. The map and spellings are of 1922.*

to increase distance and thus to ease the gradient. The steeper parts, some already built, or part built, were abandoned, though as a steam operated narrow gauge light railway, it was still left with formidable gradients in comparison with its Festiniog cousin. There were also unfinished pieces of the railway that needed to be completed. The line opened in summer 1923, with optimism that tourism was the likely generator of profit. The situation was not good. Even the FR was losing money from the lack of slate traffic following the wartime interruption of traditional trade with mainland Europe, so life was difficult for the new WHR. Although there was a response from the public to the encouragement for tourists to visit and enjoy the scenic splendour of the area, the outcome for the new railway was a disappointment. The tourist traffic in the quantity needed to make sustained profits failed to materialise, and the WHR had a receiver appointed in 1927. Bad went to worse as motor buses robbed the railway of most of its passenger traffic by 1930. The Depression continued the slide in business, with goods traffic reducing to a fraction of its earlier

levels. In 1934 the FR, perhaps grasping at straws in view of its own state, surprisingly took a lease of the WHR. This proved to be an over-optimistic decision, as the increases in business for that year were not sustained, and custom fell away. Traffic ceased on the WHR in May 1937. In 1942 the FR surrendered the lease, but by then the Second World War was in full swing. The scrap drive of the 1940s caused most of the track to be removed by 1941, and there was some confusion over what rolling stock was where, and to whom it belonged. There was no money to fund the abandonment process for the railway, and thus it remained a railway in name only. This was the start of a legal tangle, that both stopped any restoration of the railway until its resolution, and protected the line of route from almost all comers.

The WHR from Dinas to Porthmadog had just 15 years of existence. It was a financial disaster for those who had invested in it, and it burdened the already ailing FR, who had unwisely taken a lease on it. However, in those few years, many people visited and travelled on the eccentric little trains that took over two hours

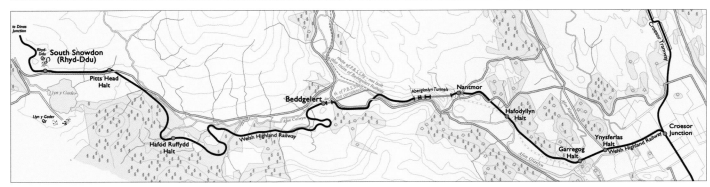

*In 1922 a new section of 2ft gauge railway was constructed by the contractor McAlpine, connecting the Croesor Tramway at Croesor Junction, and the North Wales Narrow Gauge Railways at Rhyd-Ddu. Taken together, this was the Welsh Highland Railway from Dinas in the north, to Porthmadog (then Portmadoc). The new line took advantage of earthworks of the partially constructed Porthmadog, Beddgelert and South Snowdon Railway. The PB&SSR was to have been built for electric traction, (see Appendix 'A') and in consequence had some steeper sections that had to be eased from 1:28 to 1:40, to permit steam working. The ghosted railway (for more detail see end paper map) was standard gauge, the Beddgelert Railway, a promotional scheme of the previous century, that came to grief with the collapse of Overend,Gurney's Bank. The reader may be forgiven for thinking there are great mineral riches in Beddgelert - apparently there are not. There were some distinct outbreaks of optimism in the 19th and 20th centuries over the prospect for railways here, (there was a plan to build the 2ft gauge on as far as Betws y Coed!) and there's a lot more history than this, but there are books and books written about it already, so there is no need for repetition here.*

to run just over 20 miles. Although shorn of track in 1941, the WHR remained a statutory railway. As it had obligations that it could not meet, the Receiver administered its affairs with frugality, and matters remained as they were. Local landowners gradually absorbed the railway if it suited them, using the trackbed as a road, or removing the fences and incorporating the land into their own. There were a couple of sections that the Receiver sold, but undisturbed portions of the trackbed reverted to nature. From the 1950s, little railways in Wales began their renaissance. The FR became expanding and prosperous. It had begun service to Tan y Bwlch in April 1958, and was contemplating restoration to Dduallt. The Talyllyn was carrying passengers, and the Welshpool & Llanfair Railway had restored service over a portion of its route in 1963. Arguably the most beautiful railway of them all was still mouldering, laced up tightly by a legal tangle. Yet the plight of the WHR had not gone unnoticed. There were those who sought to acquire and restore it, either as a whole or in part - but they met major problems from the legal circumstances. An organisation called The Welsh Highland Light Railway (1964) Company Limited (64 Co.) was formed. They suffered many disappointments and false starts, and because of this, they were looked down upon by those with progressing railways in a patronising way. There was a plan to lay track at Nantmor that proved untenable, though the rails lay there until recent times. Some track was put down at Beddgelert, but it could never be extended. They had a plan, set with the local liquidator (Official Receiver - OR) to buy the trackbed for £750 in 1964 that slipped through their fingers - bad news indeed (see Chapter 3). Then the liabilities of the old railway were said to be a million pounds. Problems with the OR seemed to be intractable, and the years went past with little or no progress, whilst other

restored railways came to fruition. Parts of the trackbed were used as a footpath: parts were converted to access roads for adjoining properties; a little was sold, and much was appropriated. By the 1980s it seemed that although the WHR was still a statutory railway, the likelihood of all but a short part of it ever being restored to railway use looked poor. The 64 Co. set up shop in Porthmadog and acquired land from British Railways, upon which they laid track and built station and workshops, as a ready base from which to expand. They courted the county and district councils, in the hopes that with their support, at least a portion of the WHR could be restored, if not the whole. So far the FR had observed the arrival and setting up of a potential competitor in Porthmadog with mild concern, but had taken no action. They had enough to do with the 'Building Back to Blaenau'. The 64 Co. had applied for a Light Railway Order to Pont Croesor, but the FR Co. still saw no threat to their enterprise. However they were now tipped off to do something, as approaches were being made by the Official Receiver to sell the trackbed to Gwynedd County Council (GCC), and the 64 Co. intended to lease sections and expand. The FR Co. Directors made an offer of £16k for the trackbed to the Official Receiver in 1997. This was done anonymously 'to avoid encouraging speculation'. In fact it was also a move to protect against competition, and to avoid a row, as well as avoiding a bidding war. The thinking was that if the 64 Co had to have a landlord, then the FR wanted it to be them - better to control development. There was concern felt in FR circles that if the WHR was restored to Beddgelert from Porthmadog, then such competition could undo much of the hard work that had gone in to the FR over the years. The Directors approached GCC in 1989 in confidence, with a request that having supported the FR for

*Hen Hafod, south of Nantmor, at the end of the flatlands, before the great rise through the Pass. This section had been used for years as a farm access road. The restoration of the railway required the provision of an alternative road. Many similar sites existed.*

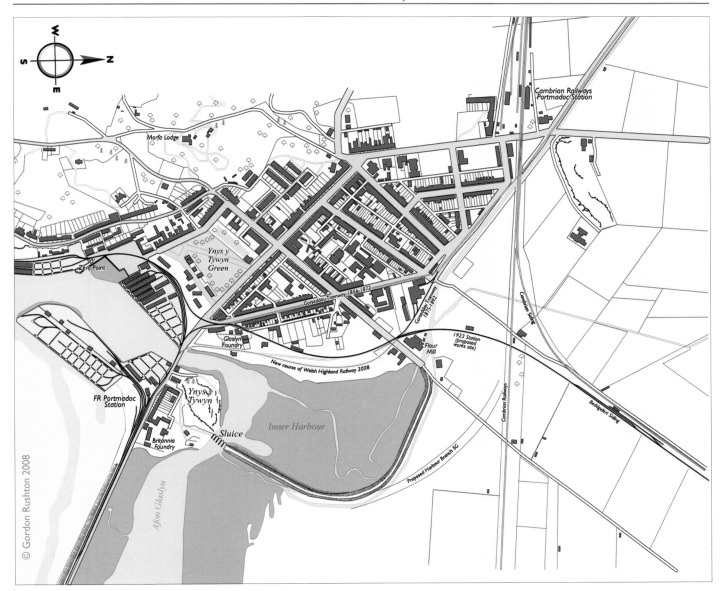

*This is a historical map of Portmadoc, and the changes today reflect the disappearance of the slate trade, and its replacement with tourism, with slate gone from the wharves. The restored WHR is placed for context, but the main emphasis is on the situation as it was in 1922, when the WHR crossed the Britannia Bridge to run up Madocks Street. Not everything shown on the map existed at any one time - but to study this map reveals what a busy place the town once was for the slate trade.*

so many years, perhaps they would look again at supporting a competitor.

The Official Receiver (OR) announced in late 1989 that it was the intention to seek the permission of the High Court to sell the trackbed for £1 to GCC. FR Co. decided to tell 64 Co. who the secret bidder was at the end of 1989, before their anonymity was unmasked. However the 64 Co. had found out about the FR Co. approach to GCC, and they were incensed by what they saw as spoiling action, as well as accusing the FR Co. of only telling them they were bidders when they were forced into the open by the OR. Their Chairman told the FR Co. not to meddle in their affairs, and announced that the 64 Co. were going to be competitors with the FR Co. So from then on, FR understood that 64 Co. were declaring themselves competitors of another railway in the same town.

The strong reaction of the 64 Co. supporters against the behaviour of the FR Co., created strong demands to desist from many quarters. Had the protests taken a more restrained form, then it is likely that the FR Co. would have felt itself able to back down. However the strength of protest forced the FR to be bold in justification of their behaviour. So when a former faction of

the 64 Co., Trackbed Consolidated Ltd (TCL) that believed in the reconstruction of the original 1922 WHR Co., decided to offer the FR Co. the solution that had been rejected again by 64 Co., they accepted. They knew that the Receiver was to apply to the High Court to sell the trackbed to GCC for £1. This was a way for the OR to dispose of a moribund railway to a statutory body that could properly discharge the obligations. Upon acquisition GCC would be obliged to abandon the residuary powers, and after this they would be free to dispose of parts of the trackbed for footpath, cycle path or railway use, as the elected members determined. TCL's gift permitted the FR Co. to attend the Court proceedings as FR Holdings, to apply for a stay of the sale to the County Council, claiming that the FR had a viable plan to reconstruct the original 1922 Company, and so to restore the railway. The High Court found that the FR application was 'wholly misconceived', thus the application for a stay failed. Some felt that the FR Co. had lost. Yet there were perceptive words in the judgement that shaped events. The judge deemed that restoration of the WHR would not be the main aim should the GCC acquire the trackbed, so the sale to GCC was 'stood over', so that ways could be explored in which the residuary powers could be transferred to the FR Co., allowing title to the trackbed to pass to them and so permitting the restoration of the WHR by the FR Co. applying for the necessary powers to put the track back. The start of the process was the application for a Transfer Order (TO). Competing application by GCC, together with the level of objections, made a public inquiry necessary. The Inspector found against the transfer of the residuary powers of the WHR 1922 Company to the FR Co., suggesting it was not in the public interest for the FR Co. to acquire the trackbed. The outgoing Secretary of State for Transport overturned the Inspector's recommendations, and granted the TO to the FR Co. Thus FR Co. was able to acquire title to the trackbed and then to apply for appropriate Orders to restore the section of old standard gauge railway from

*HRH Prince Charles talks to Roland Doyle and Richard Broyd on his visit to the railway on 30th July 2003*
**Photo: Peter Johnson**

Caernarfon to Dinas as two-foot gauge, and to restore the whole WHR section of railway. It took another public inquiry to gain the necessary Transport and Works Order (TWO) and then another to get past the objections of the National Park Authority. The first stage built was Caernarfon to Dinas in 1997. In 2000, Phase 2 was built from Dinas to Waunfawr, 7 miles. From Waunfawr Phase 3 saw the line extended up past Snowdon Ranger to the original North Wales Narrow Gauge Railways terminus at Rhyd Ddu, 12 miles from Caernarfon in 2003. The restoration received support, from public bodies, like the Millennium Commission, the EU, the Wales Tourist Board and others, and from individuals. The line was opened to Rhyd Ddu in 2003, and HRH the Prince of Wales travelled on a special train over the restored section on 30th July. Traffic quickly grew towards 60k passenger journeys in 2004. There was the thought that a long and tedious consolidation would have to be gone

*Palmerston, an original England, FR loco and newly rebuilt Cockerill Garratt No. 87, show the contrast of power between old and new at Harbour Station, standing on the newly reconnected WHR line on 28th February 2009.*

through first. But before consolidation of that 12 miles was achieved, the pressure was on to continue with Phase 4, to complete the railway for 25 miles, through to Porthmadog, to join up with the sister FR.

History suggested that a second application for public funds to complete a project was a chancy affair, and that a pause was

to be expected as the engineering challenges in Phase 4, from Rhyd Ddu to Porthmadog posed greater problems than those encountered so far. The original decision had been to apply for a TWO for the whole line. The reasoning was that meeting the opposition in one lump, and offering the pledge to restore all was the right strategy. When it came to asking for funds in 1995, it was decided that the Millennium Commission would be more likely to look with favour on an application to build 12 miles, than the full 25. This length could never be competed by the year 2000 - and neither was the 12 mile line as far as Rhyd Ddu! Though that was more to do with the public inquiries holding things up. However the time was right in 2004 to hold out for a resumption of restoration. The Government was suggesting that far from rejection, an application for funding would get careful and sympathetic consideration. One person has to be marked for his tenacity in fostering the Welsh Assembly Government willingness to back the project with a grant to make the project possible immediately. Mike Hart OBE did everything possible in his power to persuade them that such an enterprise was worthwhile for the helpful regional economic effect that the restored railway would have.

His efforts were timely. If the project had waited, if the spark of innovation and the sheer persistence he brought had not been there, then the chances of getting support during the 2009 recession would have been almost zero. In 2004, co-operation and support from private and public bodies, and from the general public provided matched funding, so the grant was accepted. Perhaps the early notoriety that the project had achieved now profited the public fund raising effort, spearheaded by Steam Railway Magazine, because so many people had heard about it. The Phase 4 Appeal response was rapid, and beyond that for any other railway scheme to date.

Phase 4 began at Rhyd Ddu and the work flowed steadily towards Porthmadog. Unlike Phase 3, there were not frequent road bridges to rebuild, but instead five large steel bridges needed to be replaced. The Cambrian Coast Line had to be crossed, on the only narrow/standard gauge level crossing in UK. The route crossed into Porthmadog on the Britannia Bridge, occupied by the A470(T) road. These were considerable obstacles to overcome, but there were four tunnels, and miles of substandard embankments, eroded by years of disuse. Phase 4 saw all challenges overcome, with the full 13 miles remaining to Porthmadog being attempted in 'one go'. Civil engineering jobs were mainly put out to local contractors, but the grant terms allowed work by volunteers to assume a cash value, and so the track was largely laid by them.

It has not all gone to plan; the scope of the work was perhaps too great for that. The line was connected with the FR, throughout between Caernarfon and Blaenau Ffestiniog on 28th February 2009. Now adjustments to track layouts and buildings are wanted, to achieve that degree of perfection exampled by the FR. Phase 5 has been devised to deliver a sustainable railway, the quality of operation expected of a world class attraction, and to combine the railways. The acceptance of trains from both lines in Porthmadog Harbour Station is essential and a £1m scheme for a new WHR platform and loop line will achieve this. New carriages, a new locomotive depot and carriage sheds are needed to house the expanded fleets now in service. The stations need to be able to offer the amenities that visitors expect to find. There is still much to do - the railway is by no means finished. Fortunately even in the midst of a depression, an appeal for funds in Steam Railway was able to raise £600k.

The Welsh Highland Railway traverses countryside of great natural beauty, from coast to coast, that is available by train once more for people to enjoy. At Snowdon Ranger, the line is at the foot of the west flank of Snowdon, with views of Llyn Cwellyn. The railway loops down into Beddgelert, an especially pretty village, and enters the Aberglaslyn Pass to run through tunnels and drop on to the Traeth. The views from the train as it glides over the Nanmor and Dylif bridges open out into a big sky, normally the privilege of farmers and the odd Osprey about its business. After the sharp curve at Croesor Junction, the line straightens up for fast running to Pont Croesor. Then the train crosses the Glaslyn again on the eight span bridge, and all enjoy the views across a great expanse, as the line nears the coast. Arrival in Porthmadog offers the experience of crossing the standard gauge Cambrian Coast Line, and finally indulges the passengers with some street running, before joining the route of the FR at Harbour Station. It is a scenic, 25 mile ride in comfortable carriages, that requires the power of the Garratt locomotives, repatriated from South Africa, to achieve. The once derelict railway now see trains again; the newly smoke-stained bridges echo to the rumble of trains, and pacing the train from the road is sublime. The sheep are not in the least bothered; they are enthusiasts for their grass, and haven't the slightest interest in railways. The once empty trackbed hosts trains again; that grass now grows up against the replaced fences, and is banished from the tracks once more. Thousands now gently roll through the spectacular scenery, as the Welsh Highland Railway has resumed business. It really doesn't look as though the line has been to sleep for over 70 years!

*The old **Prince** (1863) was summoned to Beddgelert to add gravitas to the opening of the new Welsh Highland Railway from Caernarfon, to Beddgelert and on through the Aberglaslyn Pass to Hafod y Llyn on 21 May 2009. During the season following, the trains to Beddgelert and through the Pass were most popular, and the Ffestiniog Railway did well too. Home demand was boosted by an economic recession, but perhaps it all augurs well for the future. It was certainly sensible to reopen the railway from Caernarfon - that strategy made all the difference, safeguarding FR from the loss of its traffic.*

*This was the train of dreams - the one we used to imagine we would run up the abandoned railway once we had managed to reopen it. It was schoolboy dreams, as everyone knew that double-Fairlies couldn't run up the steep gradients of the WHR. We dreamed on nevertheless, because in our dreams we <u>could</u> make these things happen. It was no accident therefore that the fund raising tagline was 'Making your Dreams Come True', and no accident either that when the* Snowdonian *did actually run - with its double Fairlies - there were no empty seats. Double Fairlies will go up the WHR - no bother at all.* Merddin Emrys *leads* David Lloyd George *at Beddgelert on 2nd April 2011. This for many was a defining moment - we'd built our railway, now were going to reap the bliss of travelling on it - this offers such creamy satisfaction! But so far, the railway hasn't got to the starting block in the story opposite.*

# Chapter 2
## Let Battle Commence
## 1989-1991

Fortunately FR Society (FRS) member John Hopkins published an account from meticulous notes that he took when he attended the public inquiries that arose from the machinations caused by the restoration of this railway. These excellent records, and interpretations of the remarkable circumstances surrounding the renaissance of the WHR, have provided the foundation for this account. Much of what happened, even in recent times, has become myth and legend, as we all record in our minds our own versions of events. The WHR was surrounded with 'problems' that imposed severe restraint upon its rehabilitation. Here is what was thought at the time:

o     The were legal barriers arising from the extended period of uncompleted liquidation of the 1922 Co. from 1944. As to what legal niceties applied and what did not - definitive answers were elusive

o     The costs of taking legal advice upon these abstruse matters were daunting, taken with the uncertainty of raising funds to deal with contingent items.

o     Each of the local authorities astride the trackbed, had policies that supported their constituents. These were mainly farmers, some of whom had appropriated trackbed. The members therefore warned of substantial liabilities for anyone attempting rescue and restoration of this railway.

o     The risks had to be faced of going formally to law in the Companies Court, which is apt to take a detached view of railway preservation in the light of its over-riding concern for financial propriety,

o     There were uncertainties when applying to and dealing with the Department of Transport and successors over a railway not yet abandoned, but with no track for many years.

o     It was likely that one or more public inquiries with their "political" overtones could be generated, with all the costs

involved

Information was not in plentiful supply. It was not clear why the Official Receiver (OR) was unwelcoming, appeared to treat inquirers as time wasters, and ignored questions, offering no solution to critical problems. When the determined pressed further, they were shown an empty cash drawer, with no promise of a clear outcome. He had no funds; he took no action, and the WHR appeared locked in an impenetrable legal tangle. No surprise therefore that railways with infrastructure and rolling stock in place were the first choices for restoration. When attention was focussed on the WHR it was from those with a more wistful state of mind. The reputation grew that restoration of this railway was hopeless. Those who had dug deeper were sure that even if the track could be put back at great expense, there was still a £1m bill in the background to be paid for liabilities incurred, and the costs involved with all the liabilities ongoing.

In 1961 the Welsh Highland Railway Society was formed, and incorporated into a company in 1964. The view taken by those busy with the backbreaking task of restoring the FR, was of a bunch of hopeless romantics, diverting effort that could more profitably be offered to the FR. After the Welsh Highland Light Railway (1964) Co. Ltd had been formed, members of both organisations reported tales of delay, disappointment and obfuscation by the authorities*. These tales were taken as proof that the Welsh Highland Railway restoration was a hopeless case, as the same obfuscation by the authorities had been experienced

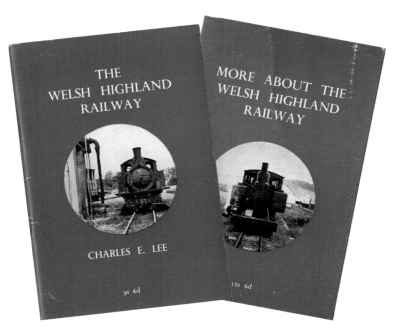

*These booklets were the source of fascinating information and inspiration in the 1960s. Inside was a little railway world that few knew existed - and better than that, if you took the trouble to look, there was the trackbed, just waiting to be restored! But the price of the books to a schoolboy - OUCH!*

---

* For a more exact tale of the 64 Co. 'pre-history' and their trials and tribulations, as well as competing bidders, this can be found, meticulously researched, in Peter Johnsons's Illustrated History of the Welsh Highland Railway : 2nd Edition, published by OPC.

by the FR in its own restoration, and it had been overcome. It would have been nice to join this society, and there was an invitation to be found in the back of the red booklet, but the price was £2-2-0 (£2.10) for an adult and 10/6 (52.5p) for a junior associate (under 18). Unfortunately the Ffestiniog Railway Society cost £1 adult, 10/- (50p) junior, and their guidebook was 2/6 (12.5p). In 1964, I could not afford to join the 64 Co., and neither could my railway-mad friends - and the FR had a running railway that you could work on. Most with narrow gauge interest had heard about the WHR, but booklets at 9/6 and 12/6 were out of our affordability range. On FR working parties, especially during the long, light summer evenings, we went to visit the WHR and other derelict railways, like the Croesor Tramway. There was fantasy about trains storming through the tunnels in the Pass, and squealing round the tight curves, but reality was the Ffestiniog, where that actually happened and you could be a part of it. Thus the 64 Co. was rather written off and forgotten about, eclipsed for the FR supporters by restoration to Dduallt, and then 'Building Back to Blaenau'. In 1982 the FR reopened to Blaenau Ffestiniog, and began to try to improve its image and quality of service. The FR had exhausted itself by the struggle and was trying hard, in the face of economic difficulties in Britain, to make ends meet, and service an extra three miles of new railway, for which there was no hope of corresponding increases in income per mile. The FR had been slowly losing market share for years, in the face mainly of the growth of foreign holidays.

During this time the 64 Co. decided after all the false starts and reverses that it had endured, to set up shop on the old Beddgelert Siding in Porthmadog, the remnant of a failed standard gauge scheme aimed at Beddgelert. This land was not riddled with legal traps, and was simply bought from British Railways, though

*Again, a view of the beautiful and unspoilt Pass of Aberglaslyn*
*Road: politically correct - Railway : politically incorrect.*

not without problems. They laid a short railway, gradually built themselves a workshop, restored the WHR (PB&SSR) locomotive *Russell*, rescued some historic vehicles from the WHR that had been in fields, built some replica WHR carriages, got a Light Railway Order (LRO), and opened for business in 1980 as the Welsh Highland Railway. All of this was well accomplished, and showed skill and determination. But apparently no one either asked or informed the struggling FR about the establishment of a 'competitor' in the town, nor explained the aims of the organisation director to director. They were not at all obliged to do so of course, but it rather set the scene for what happened later. Looking back, the absence of dialogue permitted each side to inhabit their own world of 'make believe', and this (quite common condition in a clash of culture) led to conflict. The lack of contact at the 'top' may have been because a number of disaffected FR volunteers (of which there was a supply) were drawn to them. However, friendly co-operation was established by the volunteers and staff, with a crossover of membership, and several jobs and

services being willingly rendered between Gelert's Farm and Boston Lodge - the neighbours got on together.

The application of hindsight may make one wonder why the 64 Co. didn't steer clear of trouble and start at Caernarfon, or another place, far from any other railway. They had a good relationship with Dwyfor District Council, but had experienced problems with the northern end previously with Caernarfonshire County Council, in addition the Dinas site was not available at that time, so the Beddgelert siding in Porthmadog was the attractive and affordable option.

## The fuse is lit

The 64 Co. had made an offer for the WHR trackbed, and in 1982 a planning application was to have gone to public inquiry, but that was adjourned for a year and later abandoned. However there was a change of front. In mid-1987, the Ffestiniog Railway General Manager, David Pollock, had an approach from Bob MacGregor. Bob was in charge of FR S&T, and looked after S&T for 64 Co. as well. He warned David Pollock that arrangements were in hand for the OR to apply to the High Court to sell the WHR trackbed to Gwynedd County Council (GCC) for £1, a sum in acknowledgement of the liabilities already met by the County Council. Bob MacGregor harboured concerns, as did others, that GCC gave no clear undertaking that they would allow complete railway restoration, partly because elected members had it firmly in their minds that the Aberglaslyn Pass ought not to be sullied with a railway again, and partly because some of their farming constituents would be affected adversely.

The Council's logic did not extend to ways of protecting the environment by reducing traffic on the adjacent motor road. There were no thoughts of restricting road traffic in the Park, or of charging for access, and they were not going to have a railway, despite the traffic congestion in Beddgelert. There was among the elected members an attitude that tourism wasn't real jobs; this persisted long, despite the support for reopening the railway from the Scott Handley report in 1992. Some might have thought that farming received insufficient support and tourism too much, as from time to time it seemed tourism was viewed as a burden and not a boon. Council officers were more realistic and public spirited - but of course it was the elected members that set the policy. GCC also declared intent to use part of the WHR as footpath/cycle track, and there was carefully worded comment about not doing anything to prevent the railway from being re-opened in the future. Yet until 1992 there was no policy of seeking restoration of WHR throughout its length.

The County Council, as a statutory body, was permitted to seek to acquire the trackbed. If the GCC took it over, it was said that it would (as a condition of sale by the OR) obtain an Abandonment Order under the 1962 Transport Act, which

## WHR/FR Development Chronology, in brief

| 1937 | WHR operation ceased | The FR handed the lease back, the railway was derelict and the track was removed in 1941 |
|------|---------------------|------------------------------------------------|
| 1961 | WHR Society | WHR Society formed in 1961 and was later incorporated into the Welsh Highland Railway (1964) Company Ltd |
| 1980 | Beddgelert Siding | The 64 Co. set up shop in Porthmadog, developing a 750 yd demonstration line, a station and workshop to overhaul locomotives and rolling stock |
| 1982 | Building back to Blaenau | FR completes the restoration Porthmadog to Blaenau Ffestiniog, but life is difficult |
| 1987 | Warning bells | FR Co. is warned that 64 Co. is now intending to expand, and that the means is the intention of the Official Receiver to sell the trackbed to GCC for £1. |
| 1988 | FR answering action | FR make a £16k bid for the trackbed, saying later that as 64 Co. have to have a landlord, that FR hope it can be them |
| 1988 | FR concerns | FR Co. ask GCC not to help a competitor, bearing in mind the investment that has gone in to FR; they also told them about the bid |
| 1988 | An LRO | GCC submitted a joint application with the 64 Co for an LRO between Pen y Mount and Pont Croesor |
| Nov 1989 | The OR moves towards sale | OR stated that he intended to seek the consent of the High Court to sell the track bed to the GCC. |
| Dec 1989 | The whistle blows | FR Co. decides to tell 64 Co. about their bid for the trackbed - but the news of the FR Co. 'buy to shut' mission is leaked to 64 Co. before that happens |
| Apr 1990 | Columns of fire | Ken Dicks in 64 Co. Journal 96 objects strongly to FR action, calling for FR to stop meddling and accept 64 Co. as a competitor |
| 1990 | Campaign to force FR to withdraw | 64 Co began a campaign in the railway press, with the ARPS and other heritage railways bodies, to get the FR Co. to withdraw. This was extremely effective |
| Feb-Jul 1990 | TCL offer to FR Co. | WestCo and TCL reached agreement to give FRCo. control of their collective majorities of shares and debentures of the WHR, thus qualifying FRCo. to be a party to any Court proceedings |
| Dec 1991 | High Court action | FR Co applies for a stay of the sale of the trackbed from OR to GCC. They got no stay, but for a different reason than that applied for they got a deferment! |
| 1992 | Competing LROs | Entry of competing applications for a Transfer Order by FRCo. and by a partnership of GCC & 64 Co. |

would extinguish all the railway powers and all future liabilities, but not the current liabilities. Those the GCC had incurred anyway, in repairs at a cost the OR could not meet. GCC would not itself use the trackbed to run a railway, it was perfectly proper for it to 'adopt' a bona-fide railway company to do so - the 64 Co. All of these arguments would later get major ventilation and examination in the public inquiry.

It is important at this point to observe that GCC was attempting to serve the public interest - something they were bound to do. Criticisms in hindsight must acknowledge the concerns of hard-pressed mountain farmers, and remember that CCC had been 'had' before by the 1922 WHR, that promises of its restoration had been current from 1961. Thus critics must pause before condemning their attitude, and remember that the FR's entry, just about to be made on to the scene in 1988, would make matters more complicated for the councillors and officers to divine the right outcome for the public interest, not less.

Bob MacGregor had three concerns which he and others of like mind shared.

o The first was that if the County Council obtained title to the trackbed, this would block restoration of the whole line. The Abandonment Order would extinguish all the residual railway powers, opening the way for claims for adverse possession and compensation. A new LRO would be needed for restoration, and this would meet objections from the new landowners on the trackbed. Compulsory purchase powers would be unlikely, there would be an LRO public inquiry, and purchasing the line back would make restoration unaffordable on the whole line, so forcing the 64 Co. to accept only a part.

o The second was that the 64 Co., would not have the determination, resources and 'clout' to push total restoration through, though they might get a 'short' line, in time perhaps as far as Beddgelert (8 miles).

o The third concern was that a 'short' line from Porthmadog to Beddgelert could compete effectively with the FR, such as to damage its long term viability. MacGregor used this third concern to alarm the FR management, when in fact, by this time the 64 Co. were making private statements that they might never get beyond Pont Croesor - and that perhaps this would not be a bad thing as a springboard for eventual further expansion.

No one from FR Co. chose to go and speak to Ken Dicks, Chairman and General Manager of the 64 Co. about the OR High Court application, and 64 Co. aspirations. Had they done so in advance of any action that they took, FR Co., might have been reassured that the 64 Co. entertained no dangerous, expansionist vision. Careful examination of the state of affairs at this time indicates that quiet diplomacy would most likely have delivered an 'agricultural trundle', perhaps as far as Pont Croesor. There is no doubt that the rapid restoration of the WHR, and its extension to the Castle in Caernarfon, sprang from the fierce conflict that was about to break out.

The matter of the OR's application to the High Court was discussed between MacGregor, FR General Manager David Pollock, and FR Co. Deputy Chairman, Les Smith. He went to John Routly, Chairman of FR Trust and Company. John Routly had not presided over the struggle to save the FR, in order to see it threatened by a competitor. If there was to be another railway from Porthmadog, John Routly believed that FR Co. should be 'in on the act'. So in late 1987 the FR Co. placed an anonymous bid for the trackbed of £16k. It was anonymous for two reasons. FR Co. did not wish to encourage a bidding war - which was a possibility if it was known that FR had bid. The second was that a row would likely ensue, and this was better later than sooner. By making bid, FR could attend the High Court., and as a statutory railway company John Routly believed that the best way to safeguard the FR was to seek to control the trackbed. The £16k figure was the FR Co. estimate of what was needed to top the previous highest bid of £12k.

In September 1988, John Routly decided to go and speak to the County Council about extensions beyond Pont Croesor, and how such activity could adversely affect FR. He revealed in confidence the anonymous bid for the trackbed, and spoke of concerns that WHR would compete with the FR. He reminded the Council that they had contributed money to the restoration of the FR, and thus they could harm their 'investment' if they supported the WHR restoration. Apparently he didn't ask GCC what support WHR would get - however warned of the potential harm to FR. The County Council officers communicated between themselves, and their interpretation of the FR Co's plea is now in the public domain.:

---

### CONFIDENTIAL –WELSH HIGHLAND RAILWAY

Last week the Directors of the Ffestiniog Railway met with the Chairman of the County Council, the Chairman of Finance and Economic Development, the Economic Development Officer and myself. This was at their request and they were unwilling to broach the subject of discussion prior to the meeting.

In the meeting they advised us that they were concerned that any further development by the Welsh Highland Railway would have a serious impact on their revenues. They feel that the tourist market is such that people in general can only afford to pay for one "expensive" train ride during the holiday, and that two competing railway companies will only share the same amount of income overall. They implied that if this were to happen they would have to consider the position of the "unprofitable" sections of their operation such as Blaenau Ffestiniog.

The Ffestiniog Railway Company have put in a bid for the Trackbed of the Welsh Highland Railway. If successful they would be prepared to lease it to the County Council with covenants to prevent any railway development. On the other hand should the County Council be successful in acquiring the trackbed they would wish us not to lease any part of it to the Welsh Highland Railway.

We explained to the Directors that they could not expect us to give any instant reactions to their claims and proposals, and that the officers would need to meet to discuss the issue in its wider context.

I think it would be advantageous for us to meet as officers as quickly as possible, with a view to calling a meeting of the relevant sub-committee to consider the issue.

I await your observations.
(signed)

County Treasurer.

---

Activity had been going on between OR and County Council for a long time, and the GCC had a long, and now favoured, relationship with the 64 Co. Here were the dangers of the organisations not talking to one another at the top. The FR Co. must have been ill-informed about its perceived value and standing with GCC to have acted as they did. It was noble to

seek protection against competition, bearing in mind all the effort put into FR across the years by its staff and supporters, but to do so by bidding anonymously, and then offering to lease back the trackbed with covenants upon it 'against railway development' was surely to invite misunderstanding. The people trying to restore WHR had been working hard since 1961 to achieve their aim. It was fair that FR should seek to protect against competition, but to do so anonymously and 'in confidence' in this way primed a ticking bomb. Talking through the action with 64 Co. in advance would have been a more effective way of avoiding competition. Instead, there was now a latent threat to FR Co.'s reputation arising from the massive risk of exposure and scandal if the confidences were broken.

Surely the warnings from Bob MacGregor alone ought to have indicated that there was likely to be a relationship between GCC and 64 Co. that might mean that sympathy for suggestions of preventing railway development would be in doubt. The the GCC WHR Sub-Committee minutes were in the public domain.

○ In June 1981 the OR had agreed to the sale of the trackbed to the County. This failed, from the Planning Sub-Committee's view that it was not possible to grant 'outline' planning permission for a railway, and that the 64 Co. was not in a position to submit detailed proposals for the whole route. Thus another attempt was pending.

○ In November 1983, the 1964 Co agreed with GCC to a lease of 99 years for the section from Porthmadog to Pont Croesor.

○ In January 1986, a joint meeting between the County Welsh Highland Sub-Committee and representatives of Dwyfor District Council resolved that the trackbed should be held in public ownership. Subject to the viability of the 64 Co., the railway should extend beyond Pont Croesor, and the railway should take precedence over the provision of a footpath and/or cycle-way.

○ In January 1988, the County submitted a joint application with the 64 Co for an LRO between Pen y Mount and Pont Croesor.

There were two truths apparent before the 1988 FR Co. visit to GCC:

**a.** The Council favoured public ownership for the trackbed

**b.** They had chosen as the 'railway' partner 64 Co.

No tribute was paid to the 'public interest' argument by FR Co. asking what provision GCC had made for protecting FR Co. jobs and income from harm from competition. Instead FR Co. indicated action taken to oppose the sale of the trackbed by OR to GCC with hostile intent to railway development. The action ran counter to declared GCC policy.

It is not clear that John Routly understood that FR Co. policy was now counter to that of GCC, and that hostility, resentment and accusations of 'buy to shut' were potential outcomes from the visit rather than protection against competition. The visit remained privileged information to the FR Co. Board, and was not revealed to the staff or to the FRS.

The GCC went on as before:

○ Negotiations continued with the OR, thus in November 1989 they stated their intention to seek the consent of the High Court to sell the trackbed to the County.

○ On 6th November 1989 the GCC, Welsh Highland Railway Sub-Committee informed the 64 Co. that they were ready to go to the High Court to sanction the sale of whole of the original trackbed from Porthmadog to Dinas, near Caernarfon, to the County Council for the sum of £1, so that the Council, in turn, could lease the trackbed back in stages to the 64 Co.

As soon as the OR's application to the High Court became public, the bidders for the trackbed would be revealed. At or about this time the memo of the 'confidential' visit of the FR Co. Officers to GCC was sent to the 64 Co. in a brown envelope. The 64 Co. was aghast to learn of FR machinations, and moved at once to gain help to force FR Co. to withdraw its trackbed bid. FR Co. now appeared, despite denial, to have been forced to reveal its hand, rather than to do so voluntarily. The leak led to accusations of FR Co. dishonesty that appeared again and again to erode the FR's reputation.

John Routly, unaware that 64 Co. 'knew', summed up in the FRS Magazine No. 128 - Spring 1990 as follows:

**1.** *We are in the business of Railway conservation and do not wish to close any railway capable of viable development.*

**2.** *We hope that the FR and the WHR (1964) Ltd can both develop in ways which would complement each other.*

**3.** *We have no intention to sell off any land for development.*

**4.** *We would expect to co-operate with the National Park and County Council in every way to conserve the countryside and help access to it, as we do with the FR.*

**5.** *We see our role as similar to that of the County Council in some respects but, in addition, we have the physical resources and experience of minor railways which can be of benefit on a consultancy basis to the WHR. We would expect to rent part of the trackbed to the WHR and extend the lease to further sections in the light of experience.*

**6.** *We are quite capable of taking responsibility for the trackbed.*

**7.** *We would not wish to take over the management of the WHR. We would expect the management of WHR (1964) Ltd to accept their own responsibility.*

**8.** *We explained the ownership and other constraints on the FR that ensured that no individual could benefit from our activities.*

## The 64 Co. responds

The 64 Co. saw this as a patronising piece of writing, disposing another organisation's hopes and aspirations. It fanned the flames of anger, which eventually spilled out with a passion in the WHR Journal No 96 in April 1990. From then, on any chances of peaceful co-operation receded rapidly. Ken Dicks wrote:

*'Over the Christmas break, I was contacted on more than one occasion by the General Manager of the FR (David Pollock) regarding a meeting between the two of us. This meeting, which took place on 5th January, was to reveal what has now become the latest stage in the trackbed saga.*

*At the meeting, it was revealed to me that the FR were the anonymous third bidder for the trackbed, the identity of which we had been ignorant, despite persistent enquiries, for well over a year,*

*since the bid was first made. I was given a copy of a letter from the Chairman of the FR Board to the County Council Secretary which set out the main points of their meeting of the previous month. In this letter, Mr Routly clearly states that the Officers urged him to reveal their identity as the anonymous bidder to us. This prompted him to contact me, through his GM who was given the job of informing me of the FR's policy on this matter. On conclusion, a further meeting was arranged between us for one week hence when I would endeavour to advise on WHR reactions.*

*I arranged an Emergency Board Meeting for the following Saturday, with the intentions of advising my fellow directors and forming a policy regarding these latest developments. I excluded all Officers from the meeting due to the implications of the matter involved.*

*The results of this meeting are now public knowledge. Your Board resolved unanimously to inform Gwynedd County Council, Dwyfor District Council and Porthmadog Town Council that we confirmed our present policy of supporting Gwynedd County Council's bid for the trackbed. I would meet the FR GM and advise him that "The Board reacted with caution to the information concerning the FR's bid and would welcome further details of their proposals". A Press Release would be issued which would state "We were surprised to learn of the Festiniog Railway Company's bid and we question whether it would be in the interest of either Company for a railway to own the principle right of way of the other. However, the matter of ownership will be decided in the end by the High Court and, meanwhile, we reiterate our support for Gwynedd County Council's bid and subsequent lease to the Welsh Highland". All*

*Beddgelert from the air. This was the place that frightened John Routly - in case someone else got there and this adversely affected the FR's viability!* **Peter Johnson**

*members would be advised of the situation by letter and members on site that day would be told as soon as the meeting ended.*

*The following Monday, I met the GM of the FR as arranged and informed him of the Board's policy and actions, which was followed up by a formal written reply on 19th January. On the 26th January, members of your Board met Officers of Gwynedd County Council, when both parties re-affirmed their resolve to continue with the course of action which they decided at the meeting in November 1989.*

*There have been numerous statements and views expressed through the media, through the railway press and from the FR, and I would now like to take this opportunity to clarify our position. I can confirm that, prior to 5th January 1990, no one in our organisation, to my knowledge, knew that the FR were the anonymous bidders for the trackbed. There had been no contact or consultation on this subject between our Company and the FR prior to this date.*

*Following the formal reply to the FR, dated 19th January, no reply or acknowledgement has yet been received. A letter from our legal adviser to Mr Routly personally, received only a curt reply. There has been no contact or consultation between our Board and the FR since my meeting with their GM on Monday, 12th January.*

*Your Board was unanimous in its resolution to confirm its course of action acquiring the trackbed, i.e., in co-operation with GCC. Your Chairman is in complete agreement with the Board's resolutions and is not in favour of the FR's proposals. I hope that these few statements can counteract some of the statements made by other bodies. So where do we go from here?*

*It is accepted that the disposal of the trackbed rests with the Official Receiver, who must decide which way he is to carry out his obligations. He has taken the course of asking the Companies Court to instruct him in this matter. It is considered by our legal advisers that he will continue in this vein and not take it on himself to sell to the highest bidder.*

*Amongst the FR Board's claims regarding this matter, they state that they are capable of taking responsibility for the trackbed, which I would not consider could be interpreted as meaning the same as that which we understand the OR requires indemnifying against.*

*If the OR continues on his present course of action, a court hearing could take place, which could result in one of two decisions being reached which would enable him to discharge his responsibilities and dispose of the trackbed. They are :-*

*Sell to the body who can best indemnify him against any future liabilities, or sell to the highest bidder who he also considers would have the ability and financial resources to meet all future liabilities.*

*If the former is the outcome, this would probably be the County Council and, if the latter course is adopted, a similar outcome would result, as sufficient finances are available to both the County and ourselves to outbid any other offers. There is however, one other course of action that could be adopted.*

*The FR could withdraw their bid, stop meddling in our affairs and, if (as they claim) their only interest is railway preservation, and that they acknowledge that we are capable of developing a viable railway, let us get on with the job, and when we have overcome the matter and, in good time, accept us as a business competitor.'*

Had this measured response been adhered to later by supporters of the 64 Co., the FR might have been persuaded to back off, yet he does say clearly he is going to be a business competitor - and of course this simple statement confirms John Routly's worst fears, strengthening his hand against his blunder. Additionally, in FR Co eyes, this statement justified the counter action to be taken from then on, against a declared competitor. However there were those who saw the FR as a bullying tyrant, attempting to steal the 64 Co. birthright. It was called a 'shocking attempt', forced into the open by the impending High Court hearing. A friend and neighbour was attempting to own their right-of-way without any pre-discussion, and this left a nasty taste. It was clear to the 64 Co. supporters that the FR had made a hostile move in an underhand manner and that:

*'... if this is how they handle their affairs, then heaven help us if they realise their territorial ambition.'*

These were prophetic words, yet after the Dicks's declaration of competition, the FR mandarins now thought the words were insincere. In truth there was far more to this than they knew. FR Co. were not told that Ken Dicks had had sight of the GCC County Treasurer's letter before he made his statement, as it had been leaked to 64 Co. Therefore the direct statement about not knowing of the FR bid until 5th January in the piece was untrue! Who did what, and how FR found out later about the leak will remain secret - but it had important effects later.

The FR was struggling after getting to Blaenau, and the 64 Co.,

now revealed as a competitor, had set up shop in the same town - they did not expect FR's action. When it came indeed they were shocked, as people they had previously trusted and looked up to were now trying to take them over.

The 64 Co. decided to act vigorously over the Festiniog 'buy to shut' intervention. They broadcast wide their outrage, better to make FR Co. withdraw. David Morgan, Chairman of the Association of Railway Preservation Societies (ARPS), was told of the secret negotiations with the OR, and the meeting with the County Council. ARPS suggested that the FR ought to withdraw its bid. The FR response was not deemed satisfactory, and the ARPS censured the FR Co. in a motion at it's AGM. There were headlines in the railway press. The accusations were blunted by the censure motion being placed upon the Ffestiniog Railway Society (FRS) as member, when in fact it was the FR Co. that had taken the action - thus the Society got the blame, wrongly, for the Company's actions. This nicety hardly changed the atmosphere of censure, though David Morgan was fair enough to hear the FRS explanations as to what the FR Co. were about. This meant that he was aware of the case for the defence, but it doesn't mean that he believed in it!

There were serious and strident calls in the railway press for the FR to desist, notably in Steam Railway Magazine, and a shoal of letters were written to a wide audience, including many prominent people, asking for help to right the wrong, and to put pressure on the FR to withdraw their bid.

This vigorous, tactical counter-action, had a flaw. The intense pressure impacted upon FRS members. They hated the infamy and degradation (as they saw it) emanating from the popular railway press. The adverse publicity was stoked by those supporters of the 64 Co. who were also members of the FRS. One moment the FR was being hailed as hero for restoring its line, the next it was a wicked villain for attacking its neighbour and trying to steal his birthright. It was a campaign mounted to force the FR to withdraw. Some of the complaint was too strident, and the actions of an extreme fringe became counter productive. Some of the interpretations of fact were, shall we say, 'terminological inexactitudes'. The advantages of trusting in a sustained campaign of determined diplomacy were overlooked. The situation became extremely difficult for the FR Co. Board, who entered a state of siege; the heart of the FR was thrust into turmoil. The situation made the FR and its supporters very angry: angry with John Routly for his misjudgment, and angry (unfairly) with GM David Pollock **Note 1** for not reaching accord with the 64 Co., before matters got out of hand; angry with the FRS for blind loyalty to the Company. This anger and the pressure it generated made the FR Co. directors combative - they were cornered.

The Society Chairman was asked for a view by the Company Chairman. He said that he thought restoring the WHR was unwise, but that the FRS would support the Company; this was no time to bicker. If the FR Trinity (Trust, Company and Society) was to mean anything, some careful thinking and close co-operation was needed. There was considerable disquiet within the FRS about association with the WHR, and what that would mean for the future of the Ffestiniog Railway. The conservative case stated that the FR was still recovering from being completed back to Blaenau, and that this was hardly the

---

*Note 1: David Pollock was not to blame for any of this - he was the Board's paid servant, given an impossible task.*

time to enter any expansionist phase, and certainly not the time to have a slugging match with your neighbour that was eroding support in an alarming way. Besides, there had been no planning for involvement with WHR restoration, which was demonstrably 'too difficult', and therefore the policy was unsustainable and lacking funds to succeed.

Elected representatives, such as the local MPs, had become disturbed by the affair. The FR made it a priority to explain themselves to local MPs of all parties, and to any other politician who would listen. Talking to various external interested parties revealed to FR what had been said by others. The basic message of 'buy to shut' was being embroidered. Discussion allowed the obvious inaccuracies to be corrected. The previous policy of remaining silent had only advantaged detractors, and there were now untruths abroad that demanded rebuttal.

A 64 Co. and FRS dual member, Peter Thomason, threatened an action against the FR Co. for being *ultra vires*. It was claimed that the FR Co. could not use its assets to support another railway company, and (incidentally) that it could not operate a tour business, as it was not in accordance with its statutes. An injunction to make the FR Co. withdraw its bid was likely.

The former claim was quite right, though the latter inference was considered debatable. When deciding to 'hit back' at an organisation the choice of action often has unintended consequences. The *ultra vires* problem was easily answered by the formation of Festiniog Railway Holdings Ltd, (FRH) as a subsidiary company of the FR Trust, to conduct such business - and anything else that might be needed. In fact the creation of Holdings was an inspired move, as it offered separation between WHR and FR (as promised); it was most convenient. However the action in bringing the matter to notice from within the membership by a 64 Co. dual member, provoked anger that provided the impetus for hardening further the attitude of FR Co. Board

*Was this really as far as the 64 Co. would have gone? Beyond here and FR had competition concerns.*

and Trust; it made them proceed with determination. Strong anti-FR sentiments, undoubtedly intended to scare the FR off, were fuelling extreme behaviour by 64 Co. supporters. This served to strengthen determination, and to make the FR Co. play harder, as well as encourage support from FRS for FR Co actions.

The brouhaha meant that the FRS members would be unlikely to support involvement, unless there was a significant 'win' for the FR somewhere. The Routly policy was to acquire the trackbed in order to control its development. To do this it needed some fairly heavy statements in justification, about not buying to shut, and a complex explanation over the fact that the 64 Co. had to have a landlord, so why not the FR Co.? The holes in the argument were obvious; it was all rather thin and unconvincing, unless 'competition' came into it, and so that 'nice new landlord' proposal was only self-interest, not altruism for railway preservation. Defeat loomed large at the High Court, but there was an unexpected intervention.

## Trackbed Consolidation Ltd offers a gift

Messrs Lodge, Ewing the Prestons et al. had acquired 23.5% of the debentures and a majority of the shares in the Welsh Highland Railway (Light Railway) Company of 1922. They proposed a scheme of (financial) reconstruction; after taking control they would replace the track, settle any land disputes, and re-open the railway, using the original, existing powers, or if not simply apply for more as necessary. Some had counselled against this approach, as uncertain and unworkable. The Trackbed Consolidation Limited (TCL) and WestCo group were eventually barred from the 64 Co. AGM in 1984, in a manner that they felt called forth comment for its high-handedness and unprincipled unfairness. But reconstruction was not the approved policy of the 64 Co. board. TCL had been asked to desist and had not, and it was apparently felt that their actions might have harmed the delicate negotiations in progress with GCC, who were at last showing clear signs of favourable action at that time. The rejection of TCL then caused unfortunate consequences for 64 Co. now.

In 1990, after a further refusal from 64 Co., TCL and West Co., offered the FR a lifeline and support at a critical moment, that was negotiated by FR Co. Director Mike Hart. The intensity of the anti-FR battering made it possible that the FR could have been persuaded to quit, had TCL not made an acceptable offer. It had been clear since 1989 that the OR was to apply to the High Court to sell the trackbed to GCC. So the TCL gift of control of their collective majorities of shares and debentures in the 1922 Co., qualified FRH to be a party to the Court proceedings. FR Holdings applied to the High Court for transfer of ownership of shares and debentures, and for a 'stay' of the sale of the trackbed from OR to the Gwynedd County Council, applying the following stratagems (*A detailed summary follows this chapter.*):

**1.** The FR and TCL had a viable plan to recover the 1922 WHR(LR)Co from receivership, and to restore the railway to full operation in stages.

**2.** The public good would be better served for the Festiniog Railway Company to take control of the trackbed, and to restore the WHR, than for a county council with manifold priorities to answer, and an untried railway company in association.

Fortunately, FRCo. a sponsor agreed to fund the legal expenses of the application to the High Court. Having already promised not to use FR funds on the WHR (which was *ultra vires* **Note 2**) the way forward was for the FR Trust and Board to commit themselves to the reconstruction of the WHR route by agreeing to lease the 64 Co., the trackbed in stages, for them to run the railway. It was all still a bit thin, but it was the best that could be done by FR Co.

---

**Note 2**: *As a lawyer, FR Co. Chairman Routly knew about* ultra vires - *that the FR Co. could not involve itself in WHR without applying for powers to do so. Perhaps he thought it wouldn't be noticed - but it was!*

Thus armed, Trust, Company and FRS chiefs came together to plan effective tactics in response to the waves of criticism. The FRS and Company Chairmen paired to find some basic points on which to riposte. The former siege mentality had to be rapidly and robustly reversed with some telling counter-strokes. The FR's counter-campaign began with vigorous rebuttals to letters written in, especially from members, and there were a lot of these. The candour and directness caused shock, as hitherto John Routly and his colleagues had been secretive and withdrawn, and so members had believed what they had read and heard in the media. Suddenly, pointed responses appeared, outlining the counter view in an articulate manner. The campaign against the FR's action began to waver - not from the 64 Co., but from the FRS members. All the outward communications from the FR family were co-ordinated. There was resentment that the Welsh Highland name was being used to 'legitimise' the 64 Co. campaign, yet they occupied none of the WHR trackbed. The campaign had now lost it's foundation of morality against the FR's bid by the abandonment of standards of decency that it demanded but did not offer. A 'brand exercise' was begun where the 64 Co. were subtly separated from the WHR title over a period of time. They even used the name to describe themselves, which indicated a want of understanding valuable to their opponents.

## Broadway

The 64 Co. lost their most able and thoughtful diplomat, Ken Dicks, who sadly died after a heart attack on 26th December 1990. This caused an unfortunate discontinuity, but Alisdair McNicol stepped into the breach. It was a difficult job, as in January 1991 there was a meeting between the FR and 64 Co., hosted by Ian Allan at his Broadway hotel.

The 64 Co. people remarked afterwards that there was no apology for the action, no remorse shown about the visit to GCC (an attempt to shut down a 'neighbourhood friendly railway') and so it was perfectly obvious to them that talk of some sort of joint enterprise was deceitful nonsense.

Neither Gordon Rushton (FRS), nor Cedric Lodge (CRhE), the other two FR delegates, knew the details of the GCC 'buy to shut' meeting, - though they knew of the anonymous bid for the trackbed. The 64 Co. delegates never faced the 'opposition' with their knowledge. The reason why it was leaked to the 64 Co. was to give 64 Co. an advantage. By keeping it secret 64 Co. stoked the fires of their own discontent, creating a virulent campaign against FR, filling their heads with the deceit and treachery of FR's action. Instead of facing John Routly with the knowledge of the results of his secret action, it was allowed to cause damage internally, by creating mistrust that stopped any settlement - that was disastrous, and the repercussions stretched for 20 years after.

To John Routly, 'buy to shut', and the anonymous bid were both tactical actions. He had moved on from there, as it had been

explained to him that his actions had been counter-productive, creating overwhelming, hostile correspondence, and a vote of censure. So he changed the policy to try to reach agreement for joint development of WHR restoration, on the principle that to join with the competitor controls competition. To him, the Broadway meeting was about finding that common ground. He didn't apologise for his tactics; in his experience it was far better to 'trade' out of a disadvantageous situation, and see if he could find a way of getting along with this competitors. He was unaware that he was opposite people who knew of his 'buy to shut' attempt and the anonymous bid, and who therefore at least expected apology, remorse, or some expression of reconciliation. There is a problem when a strong, skilled personality centralises power. When they get out of touch they can overlook opportunity by ignoring the obvious. It is the price to pay for strong leadership.

The 64 Co. attendees were the wounded party, full of resentment and outrage - an unwise state of mind for negotiation. It is unexplained why the 64 Co. never said anything about the leak, as had they handled it right, the FR offer proposal would have had to have been much better. Perhaps they were protecting their source within the GCC. Yet FR was able to find out who it was when the leak was revealed. Not only did the 64 Co. team fail to capitalise on the only time when they really had FR at a disadvantage, they failed to indicate to them that if they lost at the High Court, then FR would face humiliating defeat, which 64 Co. would have

*In the FR Co's mind the matter of the WHR was all about who would run trains from Porthmadog to Beddgelert. The FR was wound up to believe that whoever did that held the key to competition. They decided that if WHR was to be restored it had to be them!*

pleasure in administering, in the absence of a good deal now, at Broadway.

This was the only time where tough talk could have frightened FR Co. into offering concessions, or withdrawal. Instead the 64 Co. people allowed FR apparent success, with a relief of the pressure of the censure motion, and no difficult deal demands. After the Broadway meeting, the ARPS withdrew its motion of censure; the one from the 64 Co to the Association of Independent Railways (AIR) did not go ahead, and there was a great deal of favourable publicity to be found in Railway World, as Editor Handel Kardas had been at the meeting. For the 64 Co. there was a lull in proceedings on the run up to the High Court case, and it appears that following the Broadway agreement, the FR Co. was stringing 64 Co. along. The force offered by the knowledge of the leak rapidly diminished, but the distrust it engendered shone brightly.

During the summer of 1991, David Pollock, the FR Co. General Manager, gave way to his successor, Gordon Rushton. The move, like all things FR, was arranged in secret, but since the new GM, previously FRS Chairman, was a specialist in marketing and communications, and had been writing the letter for the FR Co. Chairman, his policy of actually explaining to members what the FR was doing got a boost, and FR supporters' confidence continued to rise as the opposing pressure was countered.

## The Difference between the parties

One should be reminded at this point of the essential differences between the 64 Co. and the Festiniog Railway Company. Misunderstanding, and an underestimation of what they were up against, eventually led to the wishes of GCC, the National Park Authority (SNPA), and all their objections to the reinstatement of the WHR eventually being overturned. GCC had hitherto dominated the struggle to try to rescue and restore the WHR, but this was all about to change. It would be wrong to think that 64 Co. people were stupid, or unenterprising. They were different from FR people, and perhaps in earlier times their scheme was less cheeky than it could have been. The fact that it was now 1991, and the restoration struggle had run for 27 years with no track being laid back on the original WHR, only shows how difficult it is to change the view of an entrenched local authority. The 64 Co. had worked tirelessly to restore the WHR - and they are owed a debt of gratitude for this.

At the beginning of the process, the GCC was confident that it held all the cards. The duty of a county council is to safeguard the interests of the public. Those interests are defined by the elected members, who are brought to account at the ballot box. It is clearly on record that neither members nor officers saw the restoration of the complete WHR as in the public interest. They certainly did not appreciate how the war of words had changed matters - but they soon found out. Neither did the 64 Co. appreciate the strength of the FR's railway mafia - and it should have done. This mighty machine had overcome the most difficult restoration project ever attempted hitherto, in building back to Blaenau. Whilst it was benign and rather patronising in its dormant state, the FR family, once really roused, was relentless, formidable, ruthless, and tough. It was also innovative. This is easy to say now that machine has totally rebuilt the WHR and done everything it said it would - this latency was not so visible then. It is taking hindsight to new levels to expect the 64 Co. to have made peace with the FR after the 'buy to shut' scandal. It just wasn't going to happen, as the leak destroyed trust. This unique set of hostile combinations drove the FR to promise reinstatement, at first via the 64 Co., and then on its own account.

The unique makeup of the FR family holds the key to understanding it. The Festiniog Railway Trust (a charitable trust) holds the controlling interest in the Festiniog Railway Company (a statutory company). The trustees appoint the directors of the Festiniog Railway Company, and they in turn, appoint the General Manager. The FRS has a director exchange with the FR Co., and a nominated Trustee on the FR Trust. The FRS has directors elected by the membership, and a network of groups around Britain, who organise volunteers and fundraising for the FR Co. This Trinity is a strong and flexible structure, well tested in operation. FR Co. is empowered as a statutory company to apply direct to Brussels for EU funds: it could (then) set aside planning permissions in pursuit of its statutory business; FRS is a registered charity; it has over 5000 supporters, and it was used to the ways of Wales, and the local people, who had on occasions in the past been grudging, inhospitable and downright hostile. Thus although foment might disturb the oligarchs, and threaten the support from the FRS, it could not destabilise decision making, nor could any issue affect the 'shareholders', as ownership was vested with these same oligarchs as trustees. The FR was then powerful and stable in a way that the 64 Co. was not, and the County Council was run with the swirl of political realities upon its elected members, who then instructed their officers. A meeting of FR chiefs to plan

their reaction with care was significant. The previous bungling was corrected, and careful thought went into the most successful course to take.

The 64 Co's organisational structure couldn't have been more different as John Hopkins points out:

*"The 1964 Co was registered in 1964 but had its origins in the Welsh Highland Railway Society in 1961 which was formed to rebuild as much as possible of the former WHR. The 1964 Co was limited by guarantee and did not have share capital. Membership was renewable annually and entitled each member to a single vote. It was a unitary organisation which consisted of one legal body to which volunteers and supporters belonged and which owned the land and equipment. Currently, there were 1,300 members of whom some 10% provided active support. A one-member one-vote system controlled the Company and the Board was thus fully accountable to the membership. The operational aspects were controlled through a General Manager and a Works Manager. The task of rebuilding would require the structure of the Company to be expanded so as to raise the capital required. Two subsidiary companies had been formed to assist in this role, Cwmni Rheilffordd Beddgelert Cyfyngedig (the Beddgelert Railway Company) and Cwmni Rheilffordd Caernarfon Cyfyngedig. The management boards of the 1964 Co and its subsidiaries had been strengthened by the addition of a number of experienced business men."*

To be commendably democratic, unlike the autocratic Festiniog, was not always an advantage when it came to matters like this. The significance of these differences of organisation and structure was considerable. The 64 Co. rejected offers from FR Co. to be its landlord, on the grounds that they had long association with GCC, and that if they withdrew, and the land was acquired by the GCC, they would risk exclusion. The FR Co. understood well how new realities could be imposed upon county councils from outside, to make them inconstant partners. It was in their mind to do as they had done with the flooded FR trackbed years before. The FR Co. position sprang from a simple statement, believed by Messrs Pollock and Routly, that he who controls the return fare to Beddgelert and Tan y Bwlch from Porthmadog holds all the cards. Their attitude to the WHR, sparked off by Bob MacGregor, was either 'buy to shut', or 'buy to control'. It was the oldest capitalist rule in the book for staying in business - always deal with your competition. Thus to them their secret bids and approaches to GCC were entirely justified - WHR was competition, indeed this was recorded fact, in writing, from the 64 Co. To the FR Co., who battled the vicissitudes of the last 30 years, the WHR 64 Co. were being naive, and their whining was an act of weakness. The claim that the FR Co. was undemocratic was treated with knowing smiles. They thought that with the FR Trinity, its committees, its volunteer supporters, and its strong management, the record of accomplishments offered favourable comparison with that of 64 Co. Yet they were so very close to being defeated. It was difficult for the 64 Co. to curb an indignant response to this powerful and far-reaching matter. They believed themselves wronged, and deceived by the FR. They had spent money, time and effort in trying to revive the WHR, while the FR was doing its own thing, restoring its railway. They had battled long and hard with GCC, and now, just as things looked like heading their way, the FR was trying to muscle in, to stop them, or at the most generous to 'take them over' by becoming their landlord. Furthermore FR had done so in secrecy, and they were trying to spoil their plans - the 64 Co. thought it was inconsiderate, dishonest, immoral, and unfair.

## Action in the High Court

At this moment in time the FR was still operating under the strategy of the Routly regime that sought comfort from competition. Some FR advisers and supporters stated that it was the 64 Co. who was the 'pretender' to the WHR throne, and that the FR had a valid claim, especially if it cited in addition, determination, and superior resources for restoration; that it should strengthen this claim by adding its track record, to qualify it as the only sure restoration hope for the whole railway, and not only a part.. This misplaced commercialism was the reason why John Routly wasn't too concerned about doing a deal. FR thought that such restoration as they would permit was obviously a safer bet with them. It was however by now clear to FR Co. bosses that accusations of dishonesty, of 'buy to shut', and the attacks upon the reputation of the FR would stand in the way. They had to do the following:

1. Win the High Court application and reconstruct the old 1922 Company

2. Show that they were being fair to the 64 Co.

3. Be convincing in their proposal to restore the whole WHR trackbed.

Mike Hart had joined the FR Co. Board in 1989 and he was urging public disclosure and bold action to restore the whole WHR. John Routly hardly approved of this, it ran counter to the cautious approach. He was for measured risks, only within the strategy of containing competition. He didn't understand the depths of feeling that had been caused outside FR circles. He didn't believe that the salvation of the FR's reputation was something pressingly urgent. To him reconstruction of the WHR from Pen y Mount to Dinas was a large undertaking to offer in pursuit of this aim, but one thought necessary to stay in the game in the High Court. So he did support the case for gradual restoration, but was only happy to do so with checks and balances in place.

After a deferral for FR to prepare its case, the action in the High Court began in December 1991. Things did not go well for the FR. Mr Justice Vinelott gave a complex judgement to a complex case. The advice that the 64 Co. had been given was correct. Stephen Wiggs was vindicated. The reconstruction was not possible, as had the WHR 1922 company not been 'statutory', it would have moved long since to being 'wound up' and then into oblivion. The application for 'stay' failed because FRH could not be confirmed as title holders to the shares and debentures. Transfer of the shares and title to the bonds could not be approved, so there was no legal standing for FRH to accept responsibility for the reconstruction of the 1922 Company, the proposal for reconstruction was wholly misconceived.

This was a stunning blow, wrecking the FR's plans. The Council and 64 Co. were vindicated and victorious, and the FR

*Mike Hart indicates the points at Porthmadog that started it all - always known as the WHR Points, it was a romantic dream to reconnect them.*

was routed. However, there was more 'in the small print' from this extraordinary business, and this revolved around the FR side's stated wish to restore the whole railway as the motivating force for bringing the action. Herein lay the trap for 64 Co. who had 'nailed their colours' to the GCC mast. The two entities at the hearing were Ffestiniog Railway Holdings Ltd and Gwynedd County Council. The judge came to the conclusion that it would be wrong to approve the sale of the trackbed to GCC at this stage, as '*complete restoration of the railway will not be the primary object of the County Council if it acquires the trackbed*'. He then supplied the key to the legal tangle that had beset the WHR restoration for so long. It was open to someone (not the FR Co.) to apply for an amending order for FR Co. to acquire the remaining powers of the WHR 1922 Company, and then to acquire the assets from the OR, and to adopt the liabilities. If successful, the FR Co. would then be able apply for powers to restore the track. The choice was not the Judge's to determine which of the competing claims should succeed. He therefore dismissed the application for a stay, but deferred permission for the sale of the trackbed by the OR to the GCC because FR should be given the opportunity of considering what other courses are available to achieve the ambition of fully restoring WHR's undertaking. He added that it was open for the Official Receiver or Gwynedd County Council to restore their deferred application, (from the OR to sell the trackbed to GCC) should there be no real prospect of FR Co. succeeding in acquiring the powers it needed.

## After the High Court

The 64 Co. supporters read the first part of the judgement as a distinct and clear endorsement of their position; a victory indeed, and they now awaited the banishment of the FR in ignominy from the field of battle. Yet the architect of misfortune for 64 Co. that changed the points of destiny, and handed FR Co. the initiative, was their bond with GCC. That unwillingness to commit to the restoration of the whole WHR offered FR Co. the chance to snatch the crown; 64 Co. was powerless to intervene. The TCL gift that 64 Co. spurned, had offered FR the opportunity to appear at the hearing, with a strong claim that their aim was full WHR restoration. Thus they earned a deferral of the sale - though this was neither the reconstruction, nor the stay they had applied for.

There was no outcome that directly enabled restoration from this hearing. The next hurdle was a Transfer Order (TO) application, to get precedence of negotiation with the Official Receiver; to allow FR Co. take title to the trackbed. This was a public process, allowing objection from anyone claiming that the transfer of the powers affected them adversely.

GCC saw clearly that if the transfer of residuary powers to the Festiniog Railway Company went ahead, this would mean that their plans for roads, footpaths and public access could be lost. Thus, in their view, an FR Co. TO would not be in the public interest. For the 64 Co., the transfer of powers to FR, and their acquisition of the trackbed, would spell doom for independent development plans. GCC decided to apply for a competing TO, citing the 64 Co. as 'railway partner', to allow them to lease and develop such trackbed as was agreed for restoration. There were 13 objectors to the TO application, and with competing applications, the matter was referred to a public inquiry.

The 64 Co. still believed they must preserve the carefully negotiated position with GCC. It seems they could not see why it was that the High Court had made such a judgement. (Mind you it took the FR some time to reason this out.) So the urgent need for a deal with FR to preserve their autonomy was not apparent to them; perhaps their minds were still clouded with the FR's treachery, as in the event of FR Co. winning they would need some insurance. Without a deal they would have none.

It was clear to FR Co. that a strong. policy of restoring the WHR was needed to win. This was driven partly by a need to recover their reputation from by 64 Co. taunts about the 'buy to shut' action, and partly by the emerging vision that there was the prospect of another railway to restore. So far, to FR Co., 'restoration' had meant leasing the trackbed to 64 Co., and this still allowed the fig leaf of moderation of competition to apply, as the expectation was that progress would be slow. Realisation came that a definite plan for something more innovative was needed, and that FR Co. may be able to take the initiative. A public inquiry had to be fought, and as 64 Co. was evidently an unwilling partner, the proposal of acquiring title to the trackbed, and then leasing it back to 64 Co. was considered to amount to a weak case. Something stronger was needed.

There had been a bright idea discussed with FR Co. Director L.J.W. Smith for FR Co. to fund an Abandonment Order (AO). The chief concern of the OR was to avoid liabilities by selling the trackbed to the County Council for £1. His policy was to tell all that if they acquired the trackbed, they must, as a condition of sale, apply for an AO. It is possible that GCC would have accepted this idea in the early 1990s. Then, the adverse possession claims and alternative uses of the trackbed could have made the subsequent gaining of an LRO or TWO to reopen the line all but impossible. An AO would have suited anyone committed to 'buy to shut'. It was the option to seal the 64 Co. into the short, bottom stretch. Now the opposite was true, and the policy was about to swing right round to that of reopening all, and this had a profound effect. Les Smith made sure the idea never reached John Routly.

Within the FR a power struggle was growing as the 'emerging vision' was becoming much stronger. Not only had John Routly's policy been unfortunate, the FR Co. had 'lost' the legal battle. He might well have known the possible outcomes of reconstruction at the High Court, and have known about the value of residuary powers and the advantage of TOs; indeed he took counsel's opinion before acting. However, although any of the parties could apply for an LRO for the transfer of powers, the OR would still go to the High Court, to get permission to transfer assets. John Routly failed to appreciate the implications of the disturbance that had arisen from his protective actions, and at over 70, he did not have the leadership skills needed to go from protection to expansion, and to fight FR Co. policy through a public inquiry. Chiefly there were fears that under cross examination that he might fare badly on the 'buy to shut' issue. He was requested to step down as FR Co. Chairman, and did so with reluctance.

The 64 Co. and GCC had also not anticipated the simple expedient of jumping clear of the legal tangle by transferring the residuary powers. Their strategy was to acquire the trackbed and open it in stages, which indeed might have meant applying for an AO if there was no agreement to apply for powers to reopen the whole WHR. Of course, all along, it had been open to apply for a TO of the residuary powers of the 1922 Co. to the FR Co. or to the GCC.

As the FR strategy was almost the same as GCC, it was necessary for FR Co. to seek some differentiation in order to win the public inquiry. Messrs Mike Schumann and Mike Hart, both FR Co. Directors, together with the FR GM, came to a realisation, when appraising the options, that the only sensible and radical course that would provide that differentiation, and offer the clear choice for robust offence at the public inquiry, was for the FR Co. to restore the Welsh Highland Railway right through from Caernarfon to Porthmadog. Gordon Rushton and Mike Hart put together a business plan. This was the emerging vision, and it required several deep breaths to take in. It threw over the 64 Co. as a choice of partner; they would not be invited to run the railway. Instead, the FR and all its restoration expertise, was to be placed right in the centre of the stage to 'have a go'. All who heard it liked the fierce frontier-like boldness of such a move. If life was going to be made difficult, then let's have it really difficult, with a real challenge, one to grab the imagination and to inspire people. There would be no more pussyfooting, hiding from criticism and accusations. Instead of running 13½ miles of railway, it would be 40 miles. Better still, any argument about moderation of competition would disappear. In this Grand Slam, the line would be restored from Caernarfon to Porthmadog, tapping markets 25 miles away, and growing them slowly, as the line advanced to join with the FR. The Grand Slam would not be offered to the opposition. The project would be placed under new management. No longer 'buy to shut', the new policy was to go nuclear and to 'restore and run the lot'! These requirements for the 'vision' to be made to work, governed actions for the next twenty years:

**1.** New markets needed to be tapped - so the line had to start at Caernarfon and encourage new traffic southwards.

**2.** There needed to be enough traffic to make the new railway pay its way, as well as complement the existing FR. In fact it needed to combine with FR to create a new world-class tourist attraction like the Glacier Express in Switzerland.

**3.** Someone needed to be found to pay for it.

The FR Co. policy was clinched when Mike Hart took over as Chairman from John Routly.

There was an interesting and prescient comment about what was to come at the tail end of the Illusions Shattered piece by Alisdair McNicol, the new 64 Co. Chairman, in WHR Journal No. 104 in April 1992:

*'The County Council have called a round-table meeting of all parties in early April to see if some mutually satisfactory agreement can be reached. Meanwhile, the Festiniog are believed to be considering a planning application over the full 22 miles of the old trackbed. While the two major players are slugging it out, the very least they can do is to consider how our very modest short-term ambition of getting track to Pont Croesor can be achieved - quickly; is that too much to ask? Watch this space.'*

Such a request for consideration comes not from a 'major player', but one pursuing a 'very modest short-term ambition'. It began to dawn with increasing horror that perhaps the FR were indeed doing the unthinkable, and really were intending to restore and run the whole railway, right through to Porthmadog from Caernarfon itself. Indeed they were!

# A review of the High Court action

Anyone who wished to restore WHR had to deal with the problem of relieving the OR from the burden of debt and the liabilities of the old 1922 WHR Co. GCC had offered to pay for the OR to make an application to the High Court to sell the trackbed to them for £1. Ownership of the trackbed would permit a number of public and constituency benefits, one of which was to reinstate some railway. FR Co. had made an application to the Court in opposition to the GCC. They wanted the trackbed solely for the purpose of reinstating the railway. Yet there had been a period of over sixty years of closure, during which time the trackbed had lost its railway context; the land had reverted to landowners, and was used by ramblers and others without challenge.

The outcome of the applications was not a matter for 'yes' or 'no', it required judgement. Mr Justice Vinelott offered a determination of a slightly less direct nature than was expected. He answered matters of law, he declined to choose between competing applications, he chose to treat the matter in a 'transport' context, and he moved the decisions on the outcome away from the Court and into a public forum, with the final decision being made by a government minister. He made no decision on whether WHR should or should not be restored. Instead he set the correct context for the decision to be made in our time.

1. If the OR sold the trackbed without abandoning the residual powers, he could be held liable if the vendee became bankrupt. An AO extinguished liabilities from those residual powers, leaving only common law landowner liabilities in place. As GCC could NOT go bust, GCC was the OR's preferred title holder for the trackbed. The titleholder had to have the means to meet the liabilities - the OR did not. It was generally believed that the liabilities were large - £1m was the guess. It was the GCC who had been obliged to pay for maintenance work on bridges, frontage owners got nothing over the years in respect of WHR liabilities. GCC felt that they were the 'heir apparent' for the trackbed, and that it should be in public ownership. GCC wanted the trackbed to:

i. Get something back for money spent and in respect of the current liability for bridge maintenance.

ii. Use the asset in the public interest, like provision of footpaths, cycleway, road widening, and a tourist railway.

[The GCC considered themselves better able to discharge the liabilities to frontage owners than say the FR Co. For the purposes of the High Court case, 'substantial' current liabilities would become the responsibility of the new title holder, and GCC's liabilities and bridge expenditure outranked the FR Co. bid figure for the trackbed of £16k.]

2. The OR was obliged to seek the permission of the High Court to sell the trackbed to GCC, or he might be held liable by share or debenture holders who felt they had been disadvantaged.. The reason for the £1 proposed sale figure to GCC was for the current liabilities (mostly borne by GCC). Once sold and the issues of liabilities determined by the Court, then the liquidation of the 1922 Co. could be completed.

3. The entry of FR into the High Court case turned 'permission' to sell into a more complex 'judgement' over who should have 'preferred bidder' status with the OR

4. The FRH/TCL intention at the High Court was to attempt to clear the way to settle the outstanding liabilities of the WHR 1922 Co with the liquidator, to ask for shares etc. to be transferred to beneficial owner, thus re-establishing the management structure of the company, and with debts settled, to take the WHR 1922 Co. out of liquidation. Thus the application by FRH (to avoid FR Co. being *ultra vires*) to the court was:

a. the validation of the transmissions of the shares

b. the validation of transfers of shares by rectification of the register

c. the validation of transfers of debenture stock by rectification of the register

d. the application for a stay of winding up the 1922 Co.

5. Mr Justice Vinelott was an 'insolvency' judge, concerned with issues of company law. Paraphrasing the words of the judgement, the absence of a Company Secretary indicated an inability to comply with the prescribed machinery for the registration of changes of interests in the Company's shares, thus the Court had no jurisdiction. It was first assumed by the advocates for the Official Receiver and the WHR that the stock had been properly registered in the name of FRH. The advocate for Gwynedd pointed out that this was not so, and that the Official Receiver had no power to register FRH as the holders of the debenture stock.

Under s.549 of the 1985 Companies Act, the Court may stay a winding up on the application of the Liquidator or the Official Receiver, or any creditor or contributory. FRH could not claim to be a creditor or contributory if the Court could not register them. It follows that the applications a-d (above) had to be dismissed.

Even if FRH could have procured or compelled the registered holders of the debenture stock to apply for a stay, the application would be bound to have failed. WHR 22 Co. had no directors, no secretary and there was no means by which directors and a secretary could have been appointed. If there are no directors, no meeting can be convened to appoint new directors. In the Judgement of Mr Justice Vinelott, therefore, the application for a stay failed. It was wholly misconceived.

It might at first sight seem surprising that the Court should have no power to rectify the register of WHR '22 Co., to enable new directors to be appointed, and to bring back '22 Co. into the world of the living, by a stay of winding up. It will seem less surprising if it is borne in mind that if WHR '22 Co. had been an ordinary trading company, under the Companies Act, it would long since have moved from the catatonic state of a winding up into oblivion. The '22 Co. was in liquidation. It only survived because it was a company created by Order under the 1896 Light Railways Act, with powers, and a constitution governed by the Order and, having been created by this means, it could in appropriate circumstances be restored to life by an amending order. The Judge said that with some degree of hesitation he had come to a determination that it would be wrong to approve the sale to the GCC at this stage. It seemed to him that FR should be given the opportunity of considering what other courses were available to achieve the ambition of fully restoring WHR's undertaking.

He judged that it was open to the Ffestiniog Trust or some other supporter, but not to The Festiniog Railway Company itself, to apply for an amending order under s.24 of the 1896 Act, conferring on Festiniog power to acquire the WHR's undertaking, or to acquire the trackbed following the making of an Abandonment

Order. They could go on to gain the powers needed to re-acquire those parts where title of WHR has been lost, and to restore the track. He said that the complete restoration of WHR's railway would not, it is thought, be the primary object of the GCC if it acquires the trackbed. The choice between competing claims was not, in the judgement of Mr Justice Vinelott, one to be made by the Court. If the necessary orders are sought, it will be for the Secretary of State, and ultimately Parliament to decide whether they should be made. It will be open to the Secretary of State to take the views of all interested parties, to weigh the competing demands of other leisure activities in the National Park, and to direct a public inquiry if necessary.

In the Judgement of Mr Justice Vinelott, the only course which could be taken was to dismiss FR Co's and FRH' application with costs, and to stand over the OR's application. It will be open to the OR or GCC to restore the application, if at any time it becomes clear that there is no real prospect that FR will succeed in acquiring the powers it will need.

During an argument over costs the Judge said that the application for a stay, if it had been more carefully considered, would not have been pursued. It was plainly hopeless and, if it had succeeded, it would be far more expensive than the alternative course of seeking amending orders giving FR Co. a direct right to run the railway.

Perhaps the parties had lost sight of the alternative approach to restore the railway by transferring the powers and applying for 'more'. It seems there was an echo that the spirit of the 1896 Railways Act here that transfer of powers should be for 'railway' purposes.

Note the Judge's comment about the likelihood of the primary object of the GCC not being the restoration of the railway. It was the FRH application to this court that set the agenda for 'full restoration' - from then on that is what the Establishment expected. GCC did not display this aim, and FR did. The 'primary objective' comment negated 64 Co.'s policy of sticking with the GCC.

6. FR Co. advice gained by John Routly from Counsel was that the powers still applied, and the railway could be reinstated. Yet had WHR 1922 Co. been reactivated, it would have been a fountain of litigation, with disputed title to the land, attempts to disallow claims for adverse possession (AP), footpaths, trespass, fencing liabilities et al. The strategy would have been to try to reach accommodation with adverse possession and other claimants. It might have worked, if the argument that the powers still applied had held, but it was more likely to have sparked off legal disputes that would rumble on to everyone's discomfiture for years to come, with arguments stretching back to the wartime sequestration. Whilst the litigation was in progress, there would be no railway built on the disputed parts, and it could not be done by FR Co., as without an amending order, FR Co. would be *ultra vires*. Mr Justice Vinelott was right in saying that it would be more expensive than the alternative course of seeking amending orders, but not perhaps from principal and interest, more by disputes over land title. (The GCC liability for road overbridges was not known at this time.)

7. The outcome was a judgement in law which left subsequent events to be dictated by statutes in place. Future events would be decided by the outcome from applications for Transfer Orders (TO) and Transport and Works Orders (TWO) Powers that applied from the 1922 Co. would be replaced with new ones, gained by the new orders applied for.

i. Application for a TO was open to GCC and to FR. It was not for the High Court to decide who was most suited, and who it should be that took title to the land. This depended on the party that gained the TO, via public inquiry, Ministerial decision, then acquiring the assets, and assuming the liabilities, thus taking title to the trackbed. The TO would allow public objection - the frontage owners and others affected could be heard. It's odd that Mr Justice Vinelott stated that the FR Co. could not make the TO application itself. This seems to be at variance with normal practice, where a railway company may make an application for a statutory instrument that will confer powers on it to run 'another' railway, and thus not be *ultra vires*.

ii. A public inquiry was the equitable means of ventilating all of the issues surrounding the proposal for one or other of the parties to acquire title to the trackbed. It would assure assessment of the suitability of the applicants to acquire/receive the assets, and to accept the liabilities involved, leaving the Secretary of State to decide who it should be, whether he accepted his Inspector's recommendations or not. Bearing in mind that if the logic of the recommendations or decisions was thought to be unsound, the decision could be challenged by judicial review.

iii. The TO would NOT permit the track to be put back. That would require a TWO.

iv. The TWO would do the 'decent thing'. It would reapply for all the powers to rebuild the railway in one go - brand new, no comebacks, OR off the hook. It could also confer compulsory purchase powers (CP) on the successful applicant. CP powers overcame the difficulty with adverse possession, as the powers to treat and enter allowed the railway to be rebuilt, and settlement to be reached in respect of title to the land later if need be if there was a dispute over title to the land. Here the AP claimant assumes the burden of proof of land title, not the CP issuer. Whereas 1922 Co. reconstruction would have placed the onus of proof of title to the land with the Railway Company - before it could reconstruct.

v. A TWO would require mitigation for all those affected by the railway in the long period of closure - this was the 'fairness' element, properly dealt with.

vi. Perhaps best of all for the cause of fairness, the TWO process if contentious, would require another public inquiry to hear the public voice. Thus any who objected would have a chance to say their piece, and mitigation measures could be challenged.

All in all, although it was expensive and uncomfortable, the High Court judgement was a model of fairness.

# A digest of the TCL story*

The value of gaining WHR (1922) Co. debentures had been talked about often, but abandoned because of the problems of tracing the holders. In any legal proceedings, debenture holders are entitled to be consulted, and, in principle, to a share of any financial residue. Thus to be in a position to act in the affairs of the 1922 Co., obtaining a significant quantity of debentures and shares was important. The idea was to reverse the company out of liquidation by settling the claims of creditors and bringing the company back under the control of the shareholders.

There was a divergence of opinion within the 64 Co.. There were those who considered that working with the councils was a surer way of achieving their aims. The leadership was of that opinion, considering that the financial reconstruction route was a dead end. Others thought that the debentures and shares acquisition route offered a more secure outcome than working with councils who were equivocal in their support for a railway.

By initiative, hard work, world-wide enquiries and significant personal expense, persons succeeded in tracing and acquiring the beneficial rights of appreciable debentures and shares which had been held privately since the early days of the 1922 Co. This was a considerable accomplishment. Of the holder of a group of debentures listed as "Bank Nominees Ltd", there was no trace. When the name "Branch Nominees Ltd" was applied the search was resolved quickly. In 1982, Cedric Lodge bought debentures of face value of £9,950 (11.7% of those issued). This was followed a little later by John Ewing's purchase of the £10,000 holding (11.8%) of Sir Robert McAlpine & Sons, the original WHR contractors and builders. These two holdings, of 23.5% of debentures in aggregate, gave the holders a "seat at the legal table" as creditors of the 1922 Co in any discussions of import with the OR, and the right of approach, inspection of papers and of consultation,

After much detective work and long distance negotiation, John Preston purchased what had become the two holdings of H. J. Jack's shares, face value totalling £79,587 (88.4%), a very substantial fraction.

So, three individuals (Messrs Lodge, Ewing and JE Preston), had become at their own expense the new beneficial nominal holders of a majority of shares and significant fraction of debentures. In this radical new situation, they issued a "Statement of Intent". At a three-part, 'tempestuous' 1964 Co Board meeting, the majority sought to insist that these holdings were transferred to the Company's control, free of charge. (Was this perhaps to frustrate any departure from the Board's chosen policy of close co-operation with the GCC?) The demand was refused. Upon the majority of the Board repeating its demands to be given unfettered control of the shares and debentures in question, Mr Lodge and Mr Ewing declined to hand over their holdings and resigned as directors of the 1964 Co. Mr JE Preston had resigned in July 1982.

The widening split hardened markedly at a crucial 64 Co. EGM in November 1983 when the Chairman [Ken Dicks] refused discussion upon the merits of proposals that the Company should act independently of the County, but insisted that the Council's policies be accepted.

---

*\* A Brief History of the WHR, its Antecedent Railways from 1863 and related activities including the emerging interest of the FR Company from c.1986. 2003 Version by John Hopkins. Checked by the late Ernest Preston. This is TCL's view on matters.*

Messrs Lodge, Ewing and the Prestons decided to establish Trackbed Consolidation Ltd (TCL). The members holding WHR 1922 Co shares and debentures in personal capacity exchanged them for shares in TCL. Thus, TCL became the holder of the associated nominal powers with respect to the WHR 1922 Co.

In May 1984 when a few members, now of both that Company and TCL, sought to attend to put their views and to seek the election of a couple of them as directors in order to influence Company policy, the five members principally concerned were informed at the door of the meeting that their memberships of the 1964 Co had been suspended by the Board that morning and that they were banned from the meeting. Some altercation occurred. This compounded existing animosities and, sad to record, the suspensions remained in force until withdrawn in late 1996, some 12 years later, by which time the scene had changed markedly. The conduct of business at the EGM in November 1983, and the abrupt suspensions at the AGM of May 1984, damaged the reputation of the 1964 Co and to its repeated claim of advantage over FR Co. in being 'democratic'. It left in its wake deep seated resentment, and accusations of unfair treatment, which on reflection indicated the triumph of emotion over reason - a feature that surfaced later in this complex affair.

TCL sought to strengthen its holdings of securities and this included offers to buy the debentures of the investing local authorities and the Department of Transport (DoT). However, the local authorities refused all offers because possession qualified them as interested parties at law in the future of the WHR 1922 Co and its remaining assets.

In February 1984, the OR had written to TCL's legal adviser, saying that, as Liquidator of the 1922 Co, he had decided to sell the remaining assets to the County Council, and proposed to apply to the High Court for permission to do so. This news stimulated TCL to undertake a further review of options. Having gained, in the previous few years, powers conferred by control of some debentures, TCL was able to initiate the formal legal proceedings of a Creditors' Meeting, under the Companies Acts, in order to put before all the debenture holders a formal Scheme of Arrangement for financial reconstruction of the 1922 Co to recover it from liquidation. A Creditors' Meeting was convened in July 1984. This involved further significant legal expense, funded by the members, but had the advantage of making it impossible (or difficult, at least) for the OR to go to Court until its outcome was known.

For such a reconstruction to succeed in law, the voting in favour by nominal value of debenture holdings must be 75% or greater. The attitude of most holders among the original investing local authorities was known to be generally hostile, but there was some uncertainty and thought to be a chance of success. However, by the date of the Meeting, it seemed clear that it would not be possible to achieve the necessary vote of 75%.

Underlying all these considerations and moves was doubt upon the legal validity of the transfer of full ownership and powers to the latter-day "purchasers" of shares and debentures. Going to Court to resolve the point at these times would have been a very expensive option of uncertain outcome, so all parties seem to have suppressed their respective doubts and participated in the activities upon the pragmatic assumption that the transfers had indeed been valid.

Those doubts turned out to have been well-founded. Definitive adjudication upon the question came 7 years later in the High Court case of 1991.

A surprise at the Creditors' Meeting in July 1984 was the very late arrival of the DoT representatives, and their unexpected announcement that the Department was to offer its appreciable holding of debentures (£35,774 - 42%) for sale by public tender. The meeting was adjourned.

Following this news of the outcome, the West Consortium ("WestCo") was formed from a sympathetic but quite separate, informal group of members of the 64 Co based in the south west of the Country who had become frustrated with the slow progress of the 64 Co. WestCo agreed to relieve TCL of the financial burden of tendering for the debentures held by the DoT. Their tender of £5,100 for the holding of £35,774 was successful, purchase being completed in January 1985.

TCL and WestCo had acquired in aggregate the beneficial rights of a majority both of shares (88%) and debentures (65%) of the 1922 Co. Later, TCL received legal advice that the chance of success of its case in Court as sponsors of the financial reconstruction would be enhanced if the TCL did not own the securities. So, most of its holdings were dispersed to independent persons.

The Creditors' Meeting in July 1984 having been adjourned before the vote had been taken and the outcome determined, the OR could not go to the High Court to seek permission to sell to the County Council. In January 1986, TCL reconvened the Meeting. It was clear beforehand that the Gwynedd and Meirionnydd Councils remained firmly opposed to any Scheme of Arrangement which might well pre-empt judgement in their favour by the High Court. Their aggregate holding of debentures amounted to 21.2% and, if this was the total of the opposing vote, then the reconstruction would succeed by the small margin of 3.8%.

Dwyfor Council held a crucial 13%, and its consistent policy had been to support restoration of the WHR in view of the demonstrated benefits to its district of the narrow gauge railways as tourist attractions. The transfer of the DoT's holding of 42.2% to WestCo and the "For" vote had given a considerable increase of votes in favour and there was hope that it might be decisive. Unfortunately, at the last moment, Dwyfor was prevailed upon by the other Councils to vote against. So, the aggregated opposing votes of the local authorities was 34%, the required majority of 75% of debentures in favour of reconstruction could not be obtained, and the attempt failed.

Had TCL and WestCo, gained control of and financially reconstructed WHR 1922 Co, and acquired its assets, mainly the trackbed, its published policy was to offer leases of progressive portions of the whole trackbed to the 1964 Co, northwards, for restoration as required. This was better than the limited and conditional prospects offered by Gwynedd. Yet the antipathy remained so deep that all exploratory approaches for reconstruction were rebuffed until overtaken by other events in 1990. Though in themselves TCL and WestCo were unable to force reconstruction through the played a crucial role in the High Court proceedings, and by preventing sale to GCC, an Abandonment Order was avoided thus, the integrity of the whole route was preserved to be restored by FR Co..

Notwithstanding the reverse to TCL's and WestCo's hopes at the Creditors' Meeting, nor the uncertain legal status of their holdings, their combined nominal control over some 65% of debentures gave "clout" in the later High Court case, allowing with FRH to appear. Co. Although the future was uncertain TCL and West Co. developed the policies that FR Co. adopted from

about 1990.

TCL and WestCo stated that they had been unaware that FR Co. had made its anonymous bid till its announcement in early 1990. They had considered it was doubtful whether they could afford to take (expensive) action in the OR's imminent High Court case themselves, to oppose the sale to GCC. However, following the revelation of FR Co.'s bid for the trackbed, WestCo realised quickly that FR Co.'s policy was at least in line with its own aims to restore the whole of the WHR. Initially, TCL was opposed to intervention by FR Co. and it tried once more to persuade 64 Co. to break free of the County Council's policies and the associated uncertainties. The 64 Co. again refused to embrace reconstruction, claiming that there was no chance that it would work.

Following that last refusal TCL after much consideration, decided that FR Co appeared to have the policies most likely to lead to full restoration of the WHR and deserved an approach. Formal agreement was reached in July 1990 by which, upon promise that FR Co. would seek restoration of the whole of the WHR route, TCL would transfer the greater fraction of its shares and debentures to qualify FR Co. as a participant in legal proceedings concerned with the 1922 Co in liquidation.

FR Co. understood how useful it was to be a creditor of the 1922 Co in liquidation, and the position it offered FRH at the High Court hearing. So, the interests of FR Co., WestCo and TCL had come together by July 1990. FR Co. was able via a sponsor to be at the OR's court case, and it was agreed to pursue the reconstruction of the 1922 Co. and ask for validation of the transfer of ownership of shares and debentures by the court.

TCL insisted that first refusal of the shares and debentures should be offered to the 1964 Co., to allow them to pursue reconstruction. 64 Co still refused the offer as they were convinced it would fail. It is the TCL view that had the 1964 Co accepted that offer in principle, and then argued the details to gain advantage, the decade might have turned out very differently.

The FR Co. didn't get its 'stay' of sale, in fact it got something rather better, the suggestion that the best way forward was to apply for a Transfer Order, and then to take title to the trackbed and adopt the liabilities. It got a stay of the sale of the trackbed to allow FRH to seek the TO. Reconstruction of the 1922 Co. was now a dead letter, and it was eventually wound up and sank into the oblivion long predicted for it.

---

*When reading this one must remember the need to accept that the account above differs in certain details with that from elsewhere. There were allegedly some difficulties with TCL legal debts that needed to be overcome to obtain a detailed understanding of their work from lawyers. The questions of the negotiation with FR Co. were handled by Mike Hart. He, having as a result come to a clear understanding of the position, persuaded FR Co. to receive the assets of TCL into FRH, to be able to use them to create a locus to be at the court proceeding - a key event in restoration.*

*It may appear today as though the proposal to take the 1922 Co. out of receivership was a non-starter, as WHR 22 Co. was part way through liquidation - that is what Mr Justice Vinelott ruled. Before the case there was legal opinion from those who believed that the Court could validate the various transfers of the title, and also legal opinion to the reverse view.*

*There can hardly have been any pressing reason to authorise transfers, bearing in mind the advantages of NOT doing so. The attempt to rescue the 1922 Co. from receivership did not fail in concept. It allowed FRH to be in the High Court with a measure that stopped sale of the trackbed to GCC. It established FR Co. as an organisation trying to reopen the railway, and the GCC as an organisation that did NOT have that aim as a primary purpose. The stop on the sale permitted restoration measures to progress that were subject to scrutiny by public inquiry. This was an equitable outcome.*

## Liabilities - a review of the extent of the liabilities in wait for anyone rash enough to take the WHR on. Plus the reasons given for the secret bid.

*'There was no doubt that anyone trying to take on the restoration of the WHR would be immediately bankrupted by the swingeing liabilities that would emerge as soon as it was announced who you were, and that you had taken title to the trackbed'. [the assumed wisdom said]*

This story (or something like it) was trotted out to all who showed interest in WHR, and it might well have been one of these 'don't bother me unless you are serious' anecdotes. Many people looked into what the liabilities were; it was a rather important thing to do, as the railway was in the hands of a receiver. There were it seemed dragons acting as gate guardians; the FR, with quite enough on its hands, and well familiar with the tales of woe emanating from the old days, now filtering in from those who had made more recent inquiry, had little interest in restoring a railway so encumbered.

Of course information flowed about what was happening on the WHR front. FR people knew and went to see the materials and track at Beddgelert in the 1960s, and the rails at Nantmor. It seemed as if there was a plan to link the two points, with a railway through the Aberglaslyn Pass. Ultimately nothing came of it. There were bids on the trackbed, and tales of people trying to gain control of the WHR and restore it like a dark tragedy.

The 64 Co. set up in Porthmadog in 1980, proud of its pioneering achievements and full of zeal for restoration, but they decided to do things in a different way. For them the trackbed was to be acquired by GCC, and the portion/s they needed were to be leased to them. It was the news of the intended sale of the trackbed to the GCC for £1 that spurred the FR Co. into making a bid itself. However, FR Co. felt it prudent to try to find out what the liabilities might be before doing such a thing. John Routly, whatever people might say, was excellent at trying to measure his risk. Thus Chairman Routly asked Andy Savage to use his civil engineering skills to examine the trackbed and assess what liabilities he thought there were accruing. Andy Savage did this, clandestinely, walking his kids along the trackbed on summer holiday. He found the following:

o Most of the railway was fenced, except for those places where the trackbed had been reclaimed into the fields. Farmers had set the fences to suit their immediate needs, and did not claim as the OR had no funds, but if the title changed after a Transfer order (TO), the liability would go with it. Restoration implied fencing the whole property anyway..

o Andy walked the line and carefully examined and noted the condition of all of the bridges. He then met GCC to talk about Betws Garmon Bridge (OB54) and Bryn y Felin bridge (OB173). It had not been disclosed at this stage that in 1934, Caernarvonshire had agreed to adopt the maintenance of the overbridges. When he met GCC, they admitted they had made no formal claim to the OR, and as it was over 12 years since works were carried out, claims were statute barred. Much of work at Betws Garmon (OB54) that was now necessary was caused by the gradual raising of road surface during resurfacing, thus overloading the side walls, so it was a GCC problem. There was a similar difficulty at Castle Cidwm (OB71). It was assumed at that time that liability for the bridges would be with the WHR. For those who wish to restore railways, that is the normal thing, though Mike Schuman et al. were

diligently searching documents of minutes to understand what was 'in position' with liabilities attached to it.

o It was Andy Savage's view that the four steel underbridges (Bryn y Felin, Nantmor, Afon Nanmor and Afon Dylif) were each no longer able to bear the weight of a train. There was no immediate liability for these, but they would require replacement. There was a footpath installed by the National Trust over the Bryn y Felin bridge. It was closed before FR acquired the title to the trackbed. The old WHR truss bridge was removed as soon as it was possible thereafter, to prevent trespass. The steel bridge over the A4085 at Nantmor was fenced off, and was therefore no obvious liability. There was a fatal accident at that spot when a cyclist unfortunately fell to his death on to a fence below. This was not deemed to be at the liability of the FR Co.

Andy Savage estimated the liabilities for WHR to total no more than £15k - but it was most likely to be zero, as GCC determined the works that created the liability.

FR Co. went forward into TO and TWO applications in possession of this information. It gave them considerable courage.

## The Secret Bid

It is interesting to reflect on why it was that FR Co. made a secret bid for the trackbed. Others were bidding, so there was some justification not to encourage an open auction. It was known that one of the bidders had been John Ellerton, who at the time was looking for somewhere to place his 12¼" gauge Réseau Guerlédan Railway from Brittany. He bought the Fairbourne in 1984, but he had bid for the WHR trackbed. It was reputed that there were others awaiting an opportunity. Likewise there was the logic that said that if FR Co. was unsuccessful in its bid, then it could withdraw quietly afterwards. None of this really 'washes'. Circumstantial evidence says that the real reason why the FR Co. made a secret bid was so that the 64 Co. would not find out about it until the FR was ready for them to know. Until such time the bid was speculative.

FR knew clearly that when the OR wanted to make application to the High Court, then all bidders would be disclosed. The rationale for the bid was based on asking the High Court to stay the application of the OR to sell to GCC for £1, and to sell it to FR Co. instead (as the highest bidder). The FR Co. would then give the trackbed to GCC, provided there was no railway development to be made on it. Yet GCC papers show they were confident that FR Co's £16k bid was not high enough to win, confirming that without TCL's help defeat was inevitable.

The FR Co. knew it would be revealed as a bidder. Anyone was free to bid (as it happened the people who weren't were FR Co.; their bid was *ultra vires*). However they did not make their bid until they had assessed the liabilities and found them affordable. The fuss came when 64 Co. was leaked the information about FR Co's GCC 'buy to shut' approach, and that there was a secret bid to go with it. 64 Co. were incensed and the row began..

This was a high-risk strategy pursued by FR Co. Telling 64 Co. that FR was intending to bid in advance would have avoided much of the unpleasantness. It might have been possible to have some co-operation, and it would have avoided accusations on secret bids and 'buy to shut' that so inflamed the situation. Asking GCC to prevent railway development was courting trouble. After the leak, to 64 Co. the flames of conflict roared. With no secret FR bid, no 'buy to shut', would the WHR be an isolated stretch of railway to Pont Croesor, and perhaps Nantmor, or would it have been the rebuilt railway we have today?

**Above:** At Bryn y Felin the WHR runs under the A498 road. It is said that these small roads are 'A' roads as Caernarvonshire County Council was so impoverished in the old days, that they had to ask the MoT to reclassify them so they could get a grant for maintaining them. In 1934, CCC agreed to adopt the maintenance of the WHR road overbridges. For years and years they had been threatening to rebuild the one in this spot. Originally there were 15 places cited where road widenings would take a piece of trackbed - and this it seems was one. In the event the WHR was restored before any work took place. Gwynedd Council took advantage of the WHR advancing reconstruction to grab time/space to rebuild this bridge to more manly proportions whilst they had the chance. That might mean 14 more places to go, but now there's a railway back, so if the rest of the work has waited since 1934, it might be able to wait a bit longer.

**Above:** The trackbed near Snowdon Ranger in 1997. This shot shows that the farmers fenced the line where needed, so acquiring the trackbed did not mean a requirement immediately to fence the railway, but this would have to be done when the line was restored. This wasn't so much of a problem as the cost would be included in any grants received.

**Both Photos: Mike Schumann**

**Left:** The 4 larger steel overbridges were all slated for replacement. This one is the steel truss bridge over the river Dylif. Andy Savage examined all of these and decided that none was fit to bear the weight of a train. There was no immediate liability for any of these bridges, except to bar them to pedestrians. However, this one was the old Pont Dylif, out in the 'wilds', near to Croesor Junction. Note how the embankment has eroded away during the years of dereliction. The picture was taken in 1997, 60 years after closure.

M Holmes
Yalding,
Kent

Dear Sir,

Can you give me one good reason why the Festiniog Railway Company should take over the Welsh Highland Railway's trackbed?

Perhaps the above is an unfair question, maybe you are as baffled by the FR Company's motives as the rest of the Preserved Railway fraternity. Frankly, from all the articles I have read so far, this must rank as one of the most unpopular and unnecessary action of the 1990's. Could the FR Company not put £16,000 to better use than by becoming landlord to a rival railway, surely the most unacceptable liaison that could possibly be imagined?

We in the Society are, after all, subsidising that £16,000 with our subscriptions, donations and volunteer labour. As a Festiniog Railway Society member for 23 years, I will not be renewing my membership in 1991 if the FR Company does not withdraw from this blatant act of empire building. If enough people feel as strongly as I do, perhaps we can make the Company see sense. If, however, I am a voice in the wilderness, I'll just shut up and go away!
I look forward to the July and October issues of the Society Magazine with more than usual interest, knowing they will be honest and pull no punches.

Yours faithfully,

M Holmes,

---

Andrew Morris
Bristol.

Dear Sir,

Whilst writing, I must say I agree whole-heartedly with Nigel Garvey and M Holmes over the FR's secretive action to obtain control of the WHR trackbed. The FR badly over-reached itself concerning the WHR in the 20's and 30's and the arguments about lost opportunities are misplaced. It is a large outlay, with unknown liabilities (e.g., 50 miles of fencing to maintain), and with little real possibility of significant income. A better bet would have been to loan the WHR the money for them to make a bid! Whether or not Porthmadog can sustain two railways is irrelevant; it would clearly support one better, and the FR's prime duty must be to itself. A far more important missed opportunity by the FR is the failure (at a similar cost) to buy Monarch. It is in the field of narrow-gauge articulated locomotives that the FR should ensure opportunities are not missed, and, arguably, should have a monopoly. Whether Monarch were then to be rebuilt for FR use or be retained as an exhibit is another matter, but the former would again be more interesting than another Fairlie.

Yours faithfully,

Andrew Morris

---

Christopher Padley,
Market Rasen,
Lincs

Dear Sir,

Any complex task which involves many people working together - e.g., restoring and running narrow-gauge railways needs, amongst other things, honest discussion of where the project is going and how to get there, and some light relief.

Neither of these is possible if the people involved easily take umbrage. A certain robustness of personality, of give and take, is called for. Honest debate cannot take place if everyone has to tip-toe around other people's extreme delicacies of feeling. Equally, if people insist on taking jokes the wrong way, no one will ever make any, and morose dullness will pervade all.

As a member of the Welsh Highland Railway (1964) Ltd, I can well understand why the FR's bid for the trackbed can be seen as tactless, etc, including by some members of the FR Society. But what matters is the issue, not bruised egos. The bid is there, it needs discussing, it needs understanding

At the very least, it is an original idea as a solution to the WHR's trackbed problem, and has got the subject being talked and thought about. Maybe there is something in it for both railways, maybe there isn't. So, please, let no one pick up their bat and stomp off saying they won't play any more, because they think they, or someone else, has been slighted.

Yours faithfully,

Christopher Padley

---

*Mr Holmes is an example of the numerous, vigorous letters of protest that began to arrive with the Society, as soon as the FR Company's actions became known and protests started in the Railway Press. Such protest was thought by FR to be endorsed and encouraged by the 64 Co. but all they had worked for was being threatened by what looked like a 'shut down' move by the FR upon a competitor. It was the secret bid that caused the problem and at this point the pressure was on to get FR to withdraw their bid.*

*Mr Morris displays an interesting and recurrent piece of concern - that the sad scenes of the late 1930s would be repeated if the FR rebuilt the WHR (or presumably anyone else for that matter). Even after Scott-Handley and Steer, Davies and Gleave reports confirming viability, these fears were paraded. The base was emotion, and for some the facts were discredited by the 'secret' actions. On **Monarch**, Andy Savage and Gordon Rushton bought her, but the FR rejected her!*

*Mr Padley shows that by no means all the letters received by FRS or FRCo. were 'against'. There was latitude and Christopher Padley's letter was an interesting example. Mr Padley is plainly for discussion between the parties.*

## Correspondence and Comment

In November 1990, Ron Wilsdon, a 64 Co. director and Ffestiniog Railway Society member wrote to FR stalwart patron, Sir William McAlpine. Mr Wilsdon 'told the story'. To write as Mr Wilsdon did, one has to be sure of the facts, and although one can offer a spin, a slant or a bias, errant fact is dangerous. The letter is five pages of close-typed prose, unsuitable for quoting in full. He said that as McAlpines were the WHR contractors, that Sir William might have an affinity with the railway. Bad news. Wilsdon was an FR member, he knew that Sir W.H. McAlpine was on the inside, front cover of the Magazine as a Patron. So this appeared to be insincere. He gave a potted history then there were interesting accusations:

*'About three years ago we heard that a third bid (of £16,000) had been made for the trackbed but we were unable to discover who was behind it. We understand that during 1989 the Official Receiver insisted that he must know the people behind this anonymous bid and it was then revealed that it came from the Festiniog Railway Co. The O.R. then told the F.R. to make it known to the G.C.C. who in their turn said that the 1964 Co. must also be informed. Thus the Board of the 1964 Co, first heard of the F.R. involvement in January of this year. Because of the rehabilitation costs, we believe, the Official Receiver wished to accept the G.C.C. offer. However this would mean that he would not be taking the highest bid and as a result he sought a ruling from the High Court.'*

Some of this is naughty. The information about bid and 'buy to shut' was leaked to 64 Co. Yet Wilsdon and 64 Co. Chairman Dicks, both state publicly that the first they heard of the FR bid was when OR insistence forced FR Co. to tell them who the anonymous bidder was. The OR did not insist that FR told 64 Co. about their bid. The OR knew all the bidders, and would reveal the names in the High Court, so FR decided they must tell 64 Co. first. And OR was going to the High Court anyway - FR bid or no. These are either tweakings of the facts by Mr Wilsdon, or plain exclusion. The letter goes to report that the FR staff had to read a 64 Co. publication in order to know what was going on; it alleges that Routly curbed discussion at AGM. He mentions that the FR has given no convincing reason for wishing to obtain the trackbed, except to control competition. He speculates that the FR will develop the WHR from Dinas, and this would render Gelert's Farm useless. The FR was elevating the costs, has had a poor trading year, and expenditure on the trackbed could have a serious effect on the financial stability of the FR, he said. He wonders if the FR Society Chairman sees his volunteers being available to work on WHR, and that he got an evasive answer from him. He tells of the proposed Thomason injunction against FR Co. for being *ultra vires*, and then he says he believes the two railways could exist in friendly rivalry (optimistic after a letter like this). Mr Routly has apparently said that all the criticism is like water off a duck's back to him. At the end he notes that Sir William is a Patron. Of course Sir William sent the letter to John Routly. There was a rather strong exchange on a point by

**WELSH HIGHLAND LIGHT RAILWAY (1964) LTD.**

Reg. Office: Gelerts Farm Works, Madoc Street West, Porthmadoc, Gwynedd.    Reg. in England.    No: 790125

A Company Limited by Guarantee, not having a Share Capital.

From David Allan: WHR (1964) Co.
19.02.90

To Paul Harris, Editor FR GIM Newsletter
Gwfoddolwr y Lein Bach -
The Caervonshire Purchase

Dear Mr Harris,

With reference to this article in the Feb. issue, I am surprised you did not have the editorial courage to report the universally hostile reaction to the F.R. Board's bid for the W.H trackbed.
A copy of our press release was sent both to Mr. Routley and to Mr Peter Johnson, but in case you haven't seen it I am enclosing a copy for your perusal.

We would not welcome the F.R as landlords and we are especially aghast, given the extremely good relations which exist between the two companies, at the secret nature of the bid. Surely in the 2¹/2 years that the bid has been in, someone on the F.R.'s Board should at least have had the courtesy to inform us of their intentions, especially, as from the protestations now being put out, that the F.R Board only want to help.

We can only comment that it is an extremely odd way to help someone by not telling them about it!

In fact the F.R.'s bid, far from speeding things up, has had the opposite effect and had to be taken into consideration by the counsel employed by the Official Receiver in his deliberations. It is even more ironic that both W.H and Gwynedd Council have had to reimburse the O.R in respect of the expense of the Court Hearing which could run into tens of thousands of pounds - no gesture of financial support here from F.R whose secret bid has, in part, been responsible for these expenses being necessary.

No we don't want the F.R. as landlords as we can only hope that the bid is withdrawn as soon as possible so as to enable the normal friendly co-operation between our two companies to be resumed.

Yours sincerely,

David Allan
Director.

*David Allan plays the 'normal friendly co-operation' card but, his Chairman, Ken Dicks, was writing for the WHR Journal No. 96, that the FR should accept 64 Co. as a business competitor. If competition is what the FR was entering, is it normal to tell your competitor what your strategy is? Some puzzled why the 64 Co. thought building a competing railway in the same town amounted to 'normal friendly co-operation', and why does Mr Allan think a court hearing should be supported by a competitor?*

From Paul Harris
28.02.90

To David Allan, Director 64 Co.
Thank you for your letter of February 19th. I was rather taken aback by your comment that I "did not have the editorial courage to report..." Am I to understand that you not only expect me to read your mind, but further to publish the results of that exercise? Is this how your railway's newsletter gathers its material? I am currently transcribing from it, for the F.R.'s Heritage Group, Mr. Jenkins' series of articles on the Beddgelert Railway and I find both that this is very interesting and that it shows a rather more rigorous attitude to research than you seem to advocate. I trust that you have already informed your Editor and his contributors of the news-gathering method that you require. I will be interested to see whether they are sufficiently courageous to adopt it.
More seriously, I am, honestly, sorry to learn that the F.R. Company Board's latest manoeuvres have upset the W.H.R. May I, as tactfully as possible, suggest your rather bad-tempered comment is not a good way of winning friends or favourably influencing people.

Subject to the availability of space etc., I hope to publish your "press release" and letter in the next issue of Gylb/Gim, which is due out in the middle of May.

Yours sincerely,

Paul Harris. BSc., A.R.C.S., PhD., D.I.C., M.Sc.

THE
# FESTINIOG RAILWAY COMPANY
HARBOUR STATION, PORTHMADOG, GWYNEDD LL49 9NF

Ormonde House,
18 St Johns Hill,
Shrewsbury,
SY1UJ

07.01.91

Dear Mr Wilsdon,

Thank you for your letter of the 30 December. I am glad you found my letter revealing, I intend to be even more revealing. I am sure that we can provide fodder for the press by hurling insults back and forth. However this doesn't provide the strong leadership that the people who depend upon us deserve and whilst we are engaged in backbiting, the world has a habit of continuing to pass by. Perhaps we should lay aside the discourtesy that has taken the place of negotiation and plain speaking and examine some of the central issues.

The matter in contention seems to be that the Festiniog has equipped itself to try for rescue of the original company from receivership against your wishes. You do not believe that this is possible and you resent the uninvited attentions of a neighbour because not only do you mistrust our intentions, but you have been made to suffer delay to your own carefully laid plans with attendant extra expense.

The charge is levelled, by others than just ourselves, that your plans were not carefully laid and had great gaps in them, inviting others to join. Anyone is still able to bid for the trackbed and we were encouraged to do so by some of your associates who were, in their view, justly frustrated by the 64 Company's refusal to consider any other approach than that with the County Council. It has been said that had you been more flexible in your approach and less strident in your condemnation, when the FR stood up to be counted, then not only would the FR have been obliged to go away but TCL would never have offered what we see as the crown to us.

So we contend that by your own actions, you have opened the way for someone else to try an alternative approach. The FR has no intentions to manage or run a WHR rescued from receivership, that pleasure would pass to a separate organisation set up for the purpose, one that we would hope you would wish to play a part in.

I don't wish the FR to appear to be smart, smug or arrogant. The reason we decided to act on the encouragement we received was that we believed then and we believe now, that tourism is expanding and that the Welsh Highland has a good chance of succeeding. We think that the FR would be ignoring its duty to the future and deserve major criticism from its supporters, if we had ignored an open invitation to be affiliated to a potentially successful operation.

I wouldn't expect you to agree with the rightness of these views, considering your actions but then it will be public opinion not yours and mine that will be the judge in this affair.

It seems clear that the 64 Company will not be deflected from its decision to progress the plan with the County Council. It is clear to us that the County Council either can not or will not give guarantees about the restoration of the whole line. Rescue from receivership has as its central aim the restoration of the whole line. If you don't back a plan to restore the whole line, then why maintain the pretence that you do - that is surely dishonest?

If you are correct and rescue from receivership fails [and this is within the discretion of the Court] then you will reap whatever rewards the County Council hand to you as your landlord. Should the prophecy that the County Council have no intention of endorsing restoration of the whole line become true, then you will have some explaining to do to the people who have trusted you.

That you should sneer at the FR over rescue and support an attempt to prevent us accepting the gift of shares that you yourselves have rejected, more than once, hardly supports your own demands for fair play. We may succeed in bringing the original company out receivership. Should we not be allowed to have a go at this, since you have decided not to? After all it is we who now have the controlling interest in the original company and this was not achieved by chicanery or sleight of hand - you refused the shares. If we succeed then a sister company to the FR Co. will go ahead and attempt to restore the whole railway. If we fail with rescue then you will have the satisfaction of being right ; we will have the satisfaction of having tried.

If you are wrong and rescue from receivership succeeds, then the rudeness of your campaign against us, your refusal to entertain any other approach than marriage with the Council and the fact that you won't support anyone else trying another approach, will act as deterrent to anyone advocating your involvement with successful full restoration. You ask from time to time where the volunteers for full restoration will come from. I would imagine that the answer lies very much with yourselves. Success breeds more success. A company that rescues the Welsh Highland from receivership and sets out to pioneer a new railway isn't going to need to work hard to find volunteers. Are we so awful that you expose yourself and your members to the risk of the erosion of all the work that they put in just because you cannot bring yourself to enter into sensible discussion with us? Obviously decisions like this must be the preserve of yourself and colleagues on the 64 Company Board but if rescue from receivership works then the wider audience may find your actions in the affair strange.

It must be clear to you by now that we are too determined to be frightened off, even by the most virulent campaign of insult and misrepresentation. We also refuse to be banished in the same way as you despatched those who disagreed with you internally. The carefully cultivated 'battle' image in the press is quite wrong, the FR hasn't any dispute with the 64 Company. We cannot think of anything that you have that we would wish to dispute. The County Council position is quite clear and stated. Apparently it makes no difference if we come to an agreement together with yourselves, the County Council has told us that still wishes to acquire the trackbed, which is entirely consistent with their aims of using vital parts of it for other than little railways! We are, however, quite willing to talk with you, sensibly about the issues, face to face. Don't you think from what I have written that this may be a good idea?

Whatever happens, whoever wins, we all have to live together afterwards. Perhaps we should address ourselves to that.

Yours sincerely,

John Routly.

---

*Read this - it's the most significant entry in this book. It has clear signals of what FR will do in the future. This is not Routly's hand - it is the FR's counter campaign machinery in action. If as a 64 Co. Director you failed to examine its contents, or to assess the position indicated within, you would be extremely foolish. Subsequent events lead one to believe that 64 Co. did not, indeed they may have dismissed its contents. It might have been that the sad loss of Ken Dicks eclipsed the significance of this communication. Their campaign of writing to FR supporters and opinion formers continued, but no one seemed to notice in the 64 Co. camp the two-edged nature of such a policy. Rocket fuel was now being pumped into the FR engine.*

point basis; on 29th November 1990 from Routly, and a barbed refutation of that from Ron Wilsdon on 30th December 1990 in which Wilsdon says:

*'David Morgan has told me that his understanding from a telephone call with you was that you admitted that the F.R. had been compelled by the Official Receiver to disclose its identity and he then insisted that the company notified the County Council, and they in turn insisted that the W.H.R. Board be appraised.'*

Such comment and such an exchange was unwise. Time for John Routly to change tack with a hallmark reply that is opposite, but the Morgan comment would resurface later to do harm.

The Association of Railway Preservation Societies took an early interest in the procedures. Correspondence was more confusing here for a number of reasons. The FR Company was a member of the AIR (Association of Independent Railways), chaired by Ian Allan, businessman, printer, magazine proprietor, and hotelier. He also ran a subsidiary producing and supplying Masonic regalia. Perceptive, astute, street-wise, and attuned to any 'clubby' atmosphere, Ian Allan was a courteous and competent 'fixer'. Thus John Routly was relaxed and comfortable with the FR Co. in this forum. The ARPS was the larger body, containing within the majority of preserved railway societies, and some railways. It was to the ARPS that the Ffestiniog Railway Society belonged. Chairman David Morgan was a lawyer, a paragon of fairness and debate, witty and full of fun, a champion of the oppressed, and willing to stand and debate in any forum.

The ARPS took issue with the FR over the secret bid. Reading David Morgan's letter of 2nd May 1990 to the FRSL (who were the members) explains their involvement with the affair. (Letter overleaf) This is one letter in a long string, and it was at a time that the FR was on the back foot, unlike the letter opposite when it had recovered its poise and was returning fire.

The substance of the correspondence being received, and (partly) exampled by the ARPS letter overleaf is as follows:

**1**. The FR Co. had made an unwarranted and unjustifiable intrusion into the affairs of another railway company.

**2**. In doing so (and following complaint letters and a wave of criticism in the press) it was bringing disrepute to the preservation movement.

**3** The FR Co. was holding up the progress of another railway company and causing it expense.

**4** The other company (64 Co) had carefully laid plans that were being impeded by the FR Co., which seemed to be attempting to frustrate this development by underhanded means.

**5**. The FR Co. plans to take the 1922 Co. out of receivership will not work - it cannot be done.

**6**. If the FR Co. had money to spend on the WHR, then it would be better spending on the FR and not on some external adventure. There was bad feeling that FR Co. had made redundancies and was unjustified making speculative bids of £16k for a trackbed.

The essence of correspondence at this time echoed one or more of these sentiments, and the ARPS had written to FRSL in May 1990 as quoted overleaf, and this made a reference to arbitration by ARPS that FR Co. rejected as 'inappropriate'. On 18th July, David Morgan was back with the mounting concern of the ARPS Council, wanting to know the reason for the bid. The FR was required to make a case. ARPS wanted clarification of the position. The FRSL response was after careful consultation with the FR Co. It stated that anyone was free to bid for the trackbed,

and that the bid was kept quiet:

*'out of a wish to avoid encouraging speculation....and to minimise the hassle which would inevitably arise from such an action. It was by no means clear that our bid would succeed. When it became clear that this was possible, the Festiniog Railway Company first revealed its identity to the Official receiver. Contact was made immediately with both County Council and WHR (64) Co.'*

There were 3 further paragraphs offering reasons for the bid, one as an investment in railway tourism, others in justification; others were joining in. Former FR General Manager, Allan Garraway had a trumpet in August to Gordon Rushton. It was not a helpful intervention to FR interests, written on ARPS headed notepaper, and accusing FR Co. of 'philanthropic platitudes'; he questioned why the FR had made the bid. John Routly wrote to David Morgan on 27th November. It contained a barb about David Morgan being a great friend of Stephen Wiggs, 64 Co. Parliamentary Agents. It accused the 64 Co. of breaking confidences (which might explain why FR communications were all marked 'Private and Confidential'). It revealed the liabilities for the bridges had been quantified, and that they had been grossly distorted. The 64 Co. was accused of personal attacks and of writing to FR Co. sponsors. It ended with a request to Mr Morgan for his views on the matter, particularly about ethical behaviour, and the fact that having given the reasons for the anonymous bid, the 64 Co. were still continuing to 'plug it' as 'buy to shut'.

David Morgan replied with a four-pager on 6th December. There was a clear denial that Stephen Wiggs was a great friend - the Routly barb had not gone down well. ARPS considered the unwanted interference of the FR Co. looked suspiciously like a spoiling tactic, that the bid and the intervention in the court did nothing but bring the whole preservation movement into disrepute. Ffestiniog Travel had been dropped as agents, the Transport Trust would be unlikely to grant or loan money to FR, (but they didn't intend to be involved otherwise). He remarked that there was a huge groundswell against FR, and that a motion to censure FR was to be debated at the ARPS AGM on 26th January 1991.

Yet the whole tenor was just about to change. FR collectively was becoming exceedingly annoyed and irritated about what they saw as the biased nature of the affair. They considered that the reason why there was a groundswell was that the 64 Co. had been skilful at organising a powerful machinery of defensive publicity, designed to coerce FR into withdrawing its bid for the trackbed. Firstly the FRSL Secretary landed a fairly serious complaint on ARPS, questioning procedure for the notice and authority for the Motion of Censure. The claim was that FRSL (the members) had not received the 'repeated requests' for information cited in the motion for the 15th January 1991. Then Gordon Rushton wrote on 4th January on behalf of FRSL with some searching questions broadly along the lines of the letter to Mr Wilsdon, opposite, this time with no confidentiality. John Routly wrote on 5th January with a difficult paragraph for Mr Morgan regarding ethics.

*'I have often wondered how that story which the 64 Company have long promulgated ever started and I found out only this morning in correspondence with Ron Wilsdon. He tells me that you understood it from a phone call you had with me! You must therefore have spread it to others. I did tell you that the OR thought that we should talk to the 64 Company. We would*

# Association of Railway Preservation Societies Ltd

3 Orchard Close, Watford, Hertfordshire WD1 3DU

Telephone: Watford (0923) 221280          Fax (0923) 241023

Please reply to:

*President:*        Dame Margaret Weston D.B.E.
*Vice-President:* Capt. Peter F. Manisty M.B.E. R.N.

Gordon Rushton
Chairman FRSL

2nd May 1990

Dear Mr Rushton

RE: FESTINIOG RAILWAY COMPANY

Further to our telephone conversation yesterday, I thought I should place on record my concern that I am being misquoted on the current dispute between the Festiniog Railway and the Welsh Highland Railway. There are two matters of principal concern the first relates to my initial Involvement and the second relates to my public utterances.

I understand, and I have to say that I did not hear this myself direct, that John Routly has questioned my involvement/interference in Festiniog affairs. May I say right away that I did not volunteer to be so involved; I was first alerted to the problem by a member of the press who wanted my reaction to which I gave none, since I knew nothing of the dispute; the second approach I received was a letter from the solicitors acting for the Welsh Highland Railway who wrote to me and John Routly on 22nd January, when they showed me as being the recipient of a copy of their letter to John Routly. They gave me notice that they wished to raise the matter at the ARPS AGM in January and at the same time asked whether we would be prepared to arbitrate.

The third contact I had in this matter was when I received a telephone call from John Routly on the afternoon of 23rd January asking me to call him before 10 am the following day. This I did, when he pointed out that the Festiniog Railway Company were not members of the ARPS and therefore it was quite frankly none of my business, but as he knew me, he would do me the favour of reading out his letter addressed to Gwynedd County Council on 5th January. He said there was no need to justify their motives to anyone, and if people distrusted them, he could not stop that. I did explain to him that considerable concern had been expressed and that those who had expressed their concern to me made the point that we were somewhat different from normal businesses insofar as we were very largely reliant on public goodwill.

I made it clear to him that I had not pre-judged the issue but stated that we were prepared to act as arbitrators if he so wished, but he made it very clear from the outset that he had no intention of submitting to arbitration, which was fair enough.

At the ARPS AGM, the matter was raised by the Welsh Highland, and a reply was made by a representative of your society insofar as he was able to. I also reported my conversation with John Routly and have to say that I explained that I was more concerned by what Mr Routly did not say rather than anything he had said or written. I did say that we did not have sufficient information to reach any decided view on the position, and furthermore that I had no intention of pre-judging the situation. I did, however, express my concern and say that until I heard of some more reasonable justification for the action taken, the esteem in which I held the Festiniog was somewhat diminished. I have to say that the mood of the meeting was generally very hostile to the Festiniog bid.

I enclose a copy letter which John Routly has written to Mr Wiggs which Mr Wiggs has forwarded to me because of the comments made in the fifth paragraph relating to arbitration. I am quite prepared to accept that your board consider it inappropriate. However, I am not prepared to accept that I have pre-judged the issue by saying "in the same sentence that I did not have the full facts but consider the FR to be in the wrong." I have said that I did not have the full facts and said for that reason, I was not prepared to pre-judge the issue. I have never said that the FR are in the wrong. It is fair to say that I have expressed my concern that the Festiniog have seen fit not to attempt to justify their bid to me.

You will see from this that I have not gone off on my own volition to involve myself in the affairs of other societies and certainly resent the implication that I have done so. The press, the Welsh Highland and John Routly telephoned me, not the other way round.

You did say, Gordon, that perhaps I should state why we take any view if at all. The matter was raised at the ARPS meeting on Saturday on the Bluebell Railway and indeed, if anything, I was somewhat castigated for taking a rather supine view; ie that we had no locus standi in the dispute.

So why do so many in the outside world take a critical view of the company's actions? First, the bid was put in nearly two-and-a-half years ago, or so I understand, and this was made secretly and not disclosed to the Welsh Highland. John Routly admitted this to me and further admitted that it was only disclosed to the Welsh Highland because the Receiver had compelled him to disclose it to the County Council, who in turn had required him to disclose it to the Welsh Highland. I do not personally favour secrecy of this nature in dealings over such a period of time in business at all, let alone in the railway preservation movement.

Secondly, the purpose of the bid is at best obscure. I have heard it suggested, although you have refuted this, that the reason for putting the bid in was to prevent your competitor railway from being subsidised by the County Council. I did feel that at least that reason had a certain logic to it, although I am sure that I could go along with it.

A reason put forward is that you would like a slice of the-action. What concerns me here is the level of rent which it is intended to levy for any railway running over this line. Obviously, a level could be demanded which would make the whole thing totally unfeasible and this would be little more than an obvious nobbling of competition. We are all used to fare wars etc and,what I call open-market competition, but I have to say that I am not in favour of the form of restrictive practice that this would seem to give rise to.

Thirdly, it has been said that the acquisition of the line has been made a goal for the Festiniog with the aim of stopping any further extension by the Welsh Highland or at best allowing only partial extension. I have to say that this smacks of the actions of large cartels and again I feel it is unworthy of a body such as the Festiniog.

I know that there are those who would argue that the suggested practices are typical of big business. I also appreciate that many of our railways are becoming big businesses. However, the prime motivation is, in my view, not the generation of profits for distribution, but to ensure the restoration and continued preservation of old railways and coaching stock etc. I fully appreciate the desire of the Festiniog Railway Company's board to guard its future. It has been extremely successful and you yourself told me that last year's profits amounted to £136,000. All the more power to your elbow!

I think the Festiniog is a superb railway, well run and obviously very successful. I do not believe that they need to stoop to the level of the gutter to ensure future and continued prosperity.

If any of the reasons outlined above are not the reasons for the bid, and the Festiniog Railway Company is able to show good justification for its bid, I would be only too delighted to revise my opinion. However, in the absence of what I consider to be reasonable justification, you must excuse me if I remain unhappy at developments in North Wales.

Yours sincerely,

David Morgan

---

*Hindsight permits comparison between the two letters - to Ron Wilsdon, the confident FR in 1991 (P41), and much earlier, from unbiased David Morgan, to the people who stoop to the level of the gutter in 1990 (above). In all of this, one can detect the gradual dawning on FR that silence was better replaced by clear motives and explanations. For the ARPS it was difficult to penetrate the murk, but one wonders what the point is? It answers the pleas for help from 64 Co, but why not encourage the parties to talk? Eventually there was the threat of a censure motion, but brokering a round-table meeting in an effort of mediation was left to AIR in January 1991. A refusal of arbitration was accepted, but isn't expecting a competitor to reveal plans to a rival unrealistic?*

have done so anyway, without any suggestion, but our going public was our own volition and not required by the OR. This is a small and unimportant detail in the whole saga, but it does make me feel you have not been fair or even handed.'

He went on implacably outlining facts, and the source for evidence of David Morgan's bias. He offered, and David Morgan accepted, the invitation to meet. There was a reply from ARPS on 7th January with three requests:

1. Why was the bid not disclosed to WHR (1964) Limited?

2 What is the motive for the bid?

3. What terms are the FR Co. prepared to offer to WHR (1964) Limited if it is successful? If the letter from John Routly of 5th January applied, what say will the 64 Company have in the running of the railway? In particular who will appoint the directors?

On 15th January 1991 the FR Co.,TCL, FRSL and 64 Co. met under the chairmanship of AIR boss Ian Allan. This meant that the chance to do this had been lost by ARPS, but some confusion was to follow. Despite all that was in motion to satisfy the ARPS, they issued a press release, dated 2nd January. This was unwise, as it opened a window to the charges of bias, as by now the parties were meeting, there was active correspondence in train aimed at achieving satisfaction, there were questions of the ethics of the complainants (and thus the strength of their case) and there was a motion of censure which had aspects of failure to follow proper procedure. The entry in the ARPS Journal 'The Welsh Highland Trackbed Saga' contained information that was

by now rather suspect. However, neither the ARPS nor 64 Co. noticed that the FR had been pushed into a spot where there was but a single course of action available. Following the meeting at Broadway, chaired by AIR on 15th January 1991, the censure motion at Swindon on 26th January was suspended - it was not surprising that this should be so. The motion was:

'This meeting deplores the actions taken by the Festiniog Railway Company:

1 In bidding for the former trackbed of the Welsh Highland Railway

2 For blocking the proposed sale by the official receiver

3 For refusing to give a satisfactory explanation, despite repeated requests, both as to the Company's motives and the terms, if any, which it would offer to the Welsh Highland Railway (1964) Co. Ltd., if such bid is successful. This meeting further condemns the Festiniog Railway Company for bringing the railway preservation movement into disrepute by its actions.'

It is a matter to ponder that facilitating a meeting between the warring factions was not given top priority by ARPS. The explanation may have been that 64 Co. had told ARPS what was in the leak - so they knew about 'buy to shut' If that was so (and it is conjecture) then they may have accepted the David Allan view that by their actions FR Co. wished no negotiation. This was a costly misapprehension, not for ARPS, who only properly reflected their member's interests, but for 64Co., for what followed was stunning.

## Notes of Joint Meeting of FR, TCL, 64 Co. at the Broadway Hotel, Broadway
Tuesday 15 January 1991

**Present:**

Chairman: Ian Allan

| J Routly | FR Co | A McNicol | 64 Co |
| G. Rushton | FRSL | D Allan | 64 Co |
| C C Lodge | TCL | S Wiggs | 64 Co |

Handel Kardas:
Editor, Railway World

The meeting commenced at about 12.15. J Routly was delayed by a motoring incident and did not join until about 13.00.

The Chairman for the day, Ian Allan, opened the meeting by welcoming the delegates to Broadway. He made it clear that there were to be no recriminations, or dragging up the past; he was starting with a clean sheet of paper.

S Wiggs announced that he had prepared some Heads of Agreement, and asked if he could distribute copies. I.A. declined, reiterating: we were starting with a clean piece of paper.

IA explained that the meeting had been called in order to respond to the following:

1. The adverse publicity being directed at the FR Co., as a result of their efforts to take the WHR (LR) Co. out of liquidation.
2. A resolution tabled by the 64 Co. for the board meeting of the Association of Independent railways (AIR) to be held the following day, demanding suspension of the FR Co. membership of AIR.
3. A censure motion by the council of the ARPS for submission to their AGM on 26 Jan (The FR Co. is not a member of the ARPS).

He hoped the meeting would help clear up misunderstandings, and be a forum for constructive decision.

To establish common ground, delegates were invited by the Chairman to state their objectives for the WHR.

Gordon Rushton and Cedric Lodge stated that it was their intention to ensure the WHR was opened throughout its length.

Stephen Wiggs stated that contrary to some reports, the 64 Co. intended rebuilding to beyond Beddgelert.

There followed a discussion of topics of a general nature until about 13.00 when John Routly arrived.

David Allen posed the question as to why did the FR Co. want the WHR. John Routly replied that the leisure industry was expanding and demand for leisure pursuits was rising. The FR Co. was in the leisure business, and the WHR represented an opportunity for long term investment in the type of business in which it had great experience. John Routly maintained that the FR Co. was eminently capable of helping the WHR get started. He saw a partnership composed of FR Co., TCL, and the 64 Co., as the means by which the project would be administered. John Routly asked the 64 Co. representatives what they wanted.

David Allan replied:

1. To control the WHR (LR) Co.
2. To be able to rebuild the WHR without let or hindrance, in their own way, and in their own time.

In reply to DA first point, John Routly observed that they had been offered the shares before the FR Co., and had rejected the offer. These points were not pursued.

64 Co. representatives asked for an indication of how the partnership would be made up. JR replied by outlining the component organisations, illustrated by the following:

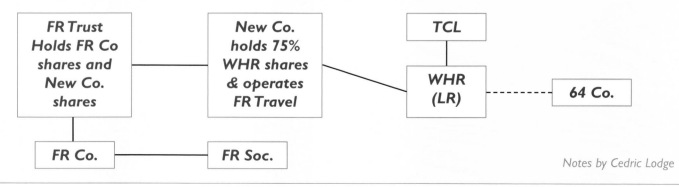

JR pointed out that there was a reciprocal arrangement between the FR Co. and Society, under which each nominated one director to the other's board. In addition there were other points of control between the FR Co. and Society:

1. A Joint Interests Committee
2. Joint Board Meetings
3. An Annual Convention
4. Joint marketing
5. Volunteer functional liaisons

Together these arrangements maintain a very close-knit relationship between the FR Co. and FR Society.

JR emphasised the status of the FR. It was, he said, a volunteer operated railway, supported by full-time paid staff; it was not a railway run by paid staff, supported by volunteers. He expected the same status would ultimately describe the WHR. He saw the 64 Co. taking a similar role in relation to the WHR (LR) Co. He suggested nominations to the board of the WHR (LR) Co. might be as follows:

FR (New Co.) 1, TCL 2, 64 Co. 2, outsiders 2. Ian Allan suggested that 2 directors be nominated by the Gwynedd County Council. Handel Kardas predicted a progressive merging of TCL with the 64 Co.

Alisdair McNicol asked how the railway would be developed by the WHR (LR) Co.

JR replied that it would be by taking the WHR (LR) Co. out of liquidation, rebuilding and operation would be in the name of the WHR (LR) Co. To help get things started the FR Trust would appeal for funds. A volunteer organisation would be required. In effect, the FR Co., with the FR Trust and New Co., would be helping a struggling colleague over a stile. Once established the WHR (LR) Co. would be an autonomous company in its own right, free to set its own pace and devise its own methods of working.

Stephen Wiggs interjected that he would advise the 64 Co. Board against supporting the FR/TCL initiative, as the legal problems connected with the powers of the old company could not be resolved and a new LRO would be required.

John Routly commented that his legal advisers were not quite so pessimistic regarding the validity of the powers, but that this was not the time nor place to debate this particular issue.

SW responded with a tirade of inquisition, insisting that he be allowed to confer with the FR legal advisers, in order to correct their interpretation of railway law.

The Chairman tried to call him to order, but he did not stop until constrained by his associates.

The Chairman commented that there was a far better chance of success if the separate groups were working together. He went on to ask what other options were available.

John Routly outlined the following:

1. Reconstruct the WHR (LR) Co., and form a partnership with TCL and 64 Co. regarding the composition of the board.
2. Purchase the trackbed from the OR and lease it to the 64 Co.
3. GCC purchase the trackbed and lease it to the 64 Co. Under this condition the FR Co. would not be involved.

The 64 Co representatives made clear their relationship with the GCC: during the seven years since the EGM in 1983; great efforts had been expended in gaining the confidence of the GCC. They now believed they had the support of GCC, and were reluctant to surrender loyalty to GCC by switching to the FR. They were adamant that rebuilding the WHR could not be achieved without the support of the GCC. They also expressed confidence in the assurances expressed in the GCC minutes of support from rebuilding WHR.

At the close of the meeting the 64 Co. representatives were asked if they had changed their mind over start item 2, the resolution for the AIR meeting. David Allan replied that they were not empowered to take decisions and must report back to their board meeting on the coming Saturday. Upon being pressed by IA, they agreed the motion should be suspended for the time being, and this was accepted by John Routly.

The Chairman went on to say that he was now able to report to the ARPS Chairman (David Morgan) that all the parties were talking, and that he would recommend the ARPS censure motion be withdrawn. The 64 Co. representatives declined to comment.

Following a short discussion, it was agreed that a simple press statement be composed and issued.

The Chairman thanked delegates for their attendance and for the constructive atmosphere in which the meeting had been held.

*The fascinating part about this meeting was that Stephen Wiggs was right about 'reconstruction'. The problem for 64 Co. was that there had been such a build up of frustration, because they knew by leak of the visit by FR to GCC to request no railway development on the trackbed if FR Co. acquired it. They did not take advantage of that knowledge, to attempt to warn FR Co. of the consequences if the outcome in the High Court was negative for reconstruction. John Routly did not seem to be doing too much listening - he didn't know 64Co. knew about the visit to GCC and the request that was made there. His horizons had now moved on from 'buy to shut', and were aimed at the removal of pressure for the censure motion by reaching agreement on the post-1922 Co. reconstruction arrangements. He was prepared to give ground, but the FRSL/TCL people didn't know about the details of the visit to GCC, so facing FR with that could have gained useful concessions. For undisclosed reasons, 64 Co. said nothing about what they knew, and then agreed to withdraw the censure motion. This was an opportunity lost; in hindsight it doomed them.*

**WHR Journal No. 97, July 1990**
**NOTES FROM THE CHAIRMAN by Ken Dicks (extract)**

The implications of the approaches to us by the FR appears to be that we have nothing to fear from their moves to buy the trackbed and that, if we support them, the matter will be swiftly resolved by their acquiring the land. This, at least, is a questionable assumption. By favouring the FR bid, we would be abandoning our long-standing policy of co-operation with the County Council and of supporting their moves to acquire the trackbed. If we part company from the Council, they are likely to press on with their aim of acquiring the land and, in all probability, will succeed without our help. All this would leave our company in a hopeless position and could result in our being stuck forever at Pen-y-mount. There are those who believe that this is precisely what the FR would like.

It is understandable that, given the present impasse, some of our members are asking whether the policies pursued since 1989 are the right ones. Not surprisingly, the news of the FR bid resulted in an approach to us by Trackbed Consolidation Limited who still appear to believe that they have the answers to all our problems! The message to all these people is this. Despite the delays, our policy of co-operation with Gwynedd County Council offers the surest prospect of success that we could hope for. There can be no question of the Board of Directors recommending any departure from this policy. It must also be understood that the Company has given legally-binding undertakings to the County Council to share the costs incurred by them in the Court proceedings. The Company must not and will not change direction at this stage or otherwise do anything which would breach those undertakings while it would be quite improper for us to bring pressure to bear on the County Council with a view to improving the terms which we have already agreed with them.

**by David Allan**

This statement [situation ?] is now leading to such frustration amongst the membership and Board, not to mention to our partners, the County Council, that I think it is true to say that our collective patience has finally snapped. The "softly-softly, play-by-the-rules" policy has failed and stronger action, much stronger action is called for. Not only is this state of affairs losing us money and losing Porthmadog tourists, but it is also losing local people the chance of employment. Clearly it has to stop. By the time you read this, positive political action will have been taken; pressure will be maintained, and if necessary increased, until the matter is put before the Courts. Meanwhile, on the other little irritation of the FR's bid, a meeting has been held with the Chairman and two Directors of the FR. If the purpose of the meeting was for us to persuade them to withdraw their bid and or them to convince us of their integrity, then it failed on both counts. Further progress is not anticipated.

Let me conclude by reminding you that failure is not a word in the Welsh Highland's vocabulary but that grit, determination and success figure highly. It is these characteristics which will determine our right to the trackbed and our right to rebuild and operate the line to Beddgelert and further.

---

*Ken Dicks avoids inflammatory language whilst putting serious points across. One could believe from this that the GCC is committed to the WHR - it was only in the TO public inquiry that they offered commitment! So loyalty to the County Council might obscure the main aim of getting a restored WHR built in its entirety. The David Allan approach is more robust. The meeting with the FR has failed, and another is not intended. He has a 'right' to the trackbed and they are both sure that the TCL initiative will fail. The question is, as the story moves towards the culmination of the High Court case, why were 64 Co. unable to back more than one horse? David Allan hasn't realised that 64 Co. cannot 'stop' FR. Is the power of the leak gumming 64 Co. in it's 'don't trust them' embrace?*

---

**FRS Magazine No. 129, Summer 1990**
**From the Society Chairman (AJG Rushton)**

**Thank you WHR**

I expect that all of us can put ourselves in the place of the dedicated volunteer at Gelert's Farm who wakes up to find that the stuffy Festiniog is chewing away at the foundations, trying to muscle in on an act that much effort has attempted to make as different from the FR as Clapham is from Croesor Junction! However, from the FR point of view, what we see is the application of straightforward foresight. (Gwynedd County Council have the results of a study that show there is room for two railways in Porthmadog.) In fact, anyone is free to bid for the trackbed; this is not a private affair and if there is narrow-gauge railway 'action' on the doorstep in Porthmadog then the FR would be seen as complacent if it didn't take an interest. Looking longer term, in both camps, hasn't the FR got expertise to contribute to another railway, even if it is only "Boston Lodge at your service"? That the WHR has to have a landlord is apparently not in dispute. It has certainly been made clear by the Company that the FR has no intention of trying to manage or run the WHR. In our view then, there should not be too much to get worried about if the landlord is the FR. There are plenty of those on the FR who would love to see the WHR grow and prosper.

Naturally, the matter was raised at the AGM, firstly by Joe Lloyd and then by Ron Wilsdon, a member who is also a Director of the Welsh Highland. If you didn't think John Routly's answers were convincing (opinion was that they were), then the FR has gone on record very clearly as not being in a "buy to shut" or "stifle at birth" mode. In a world where Councils, however benign, can have their objectives transformed overnight by higher authority, perhaps with the right guarantees available, the FR bid will not be seen as quite the aggressive move that the first reaction to it indicates; the anonymity of the bid seems to have caused more hassle than the bid itself (as is evident from the correspondence columns) and so, in answering questions, John Routly took the opportunity to explain why the FR bid was anonymous. He said that there were those who would misconstrue the motive for the bid and that, since the misunderstanding and hassle were bound to follow, the Board wished to keep this to as short a time as possible. They went public when it seemed likely that the bid might succeed. Contact was then made with the WHR 64 Company immediately.

Passions have been aroused on this issue and, whilst they are so, we shall gain nothing by inflaming them further. The Society Board supports the Company because the action has a broad base of logic and is about the future. One gesture that shows that, beneath the understandable concern and the strength of feeling at Gelert's Farm, there lies a heart of gold, was the visit of *Russell* to the Gala. The genuine thanks from the Chair at the AGM and the applause which followed showed our appreciation.

---

*The 64 Co. reaction made FR people feel extremely embarrassed. Routly and the FR Co. Directors allowed 64 Co. to make the running in telling them that what they had done was wicked and dishonest. 64 Co. never disclosed that they had the news leaked to them before ever the FR Co. 'confessed'. And when 64 Co. declared themselves as competitors, the world had already decided that FR Co. was dishonest and guilty. FR was wrong-footed by not talking to 64 Co in the first place. This piece is trying to recover the situation from 'buy to shut', and reminds members that the 64 Co had to have a landlord - it wasn't able to do things on its own, and secondly the FR is now going on record as not 'buying to shut'. Too late - the damage is done.*

## THE FESTINIOG RAILWAY COMPANY PRESS RELEASE 1990

For some time now, the actions of the Festiniog Railway Company in seeking to acquire the trackbed of the old Welsh Highland Railway Company, in receivership since the early 1940's, have attracted the interest of the media and railway enthusiasts. The Festiniog has been accused of being underhand, of interfering in the affairs of another railway and of acting against the interests of railway preservation. Recent hearsay, portraying as fact, suggests the liabilities upon acquisition will total £1 million! John Routly, the Chairman of the Festiniog Railway Company, who has suffered personal attacks upon his character in the press, tells the Festiniog side of the story.

"We decided to bid for the trackbed of the Welsh Highland Railway for a number of reasons. The main one was simply that it seemed to us a straight-forward investment in railway tourism. Over the years, against great odds and against the advice of many sceptics, we have managed to make the Festiniog Railway the most successful of the Welsh narrow gauge railways. As we have proved that there is potential in restoration, then we would like to be a part of the revival of the Welsh Highland and put the wealth of experience that we have amassed to good use. There have been a number of criticisms levelled at the Festiniog Railway Company with the benefit of hindsight. We have missed opportunities in the past and we see the chance for the Welsh Highland trackbed to be acquired as an action directed towards the future. There is no wish to control the Welsh Highland Railway 1964 Ltd, or to operate train services. Indeed, particular assurances have been given publicly on this latter point. With the FR's involvement, there is an obvious advantage to the Welsh Highland of the availability of expertise".

"We have been accused of unethical meddling in the affairs of another preservation concern, with the inference that we are trying to take away something from the 64 Company and their railway at Porthmadog. In fact, they occupy no part of the Welsh Highland Railway trackbed and anyone was free to make a bid to the Receiver for it. Our bid was kept private to discourage speculation, further bids from other organisations who may have been interested and to minimise the hassle which would have inevitably risen from such action. It was by no means apparent that our bid would succeed. When it became clear that this was possible, the Festiniog Railway Company revealed its identity to the Official Receiver. Contact was then made immediately to both Gwynedd County Council and Welsh Highland Railway 1964 Ltd. The initial reaction from a first meeting with the 64 Company appeared encouraging. However, this was rapidly followed by a demand that we withdraw our bid, and then by public pronouncements (despite requests to treat the matter as confidential) as to the improper intentions of the Festiniog Railway Company. At a meeting between representatives of the two Boards (64 Company and Festiniog Company), the 64 Company was unwilling to discuss the matter, demanding solely the withdrawal of the Festiniog. The Festiniog assurances, made publicly, were brushed aside. The Festiniog was vilified as having acted in an underhand way, so as to put at risk the 64 Company's arrangements with Gwynedd County Council".

"The alternative plan supported by the 64 Company and the Gwynedd County Council, is one where the County Council offers to take ownership of the trackbed for £1 and leases it to the 64 Company. Perhaps it is not well-known that acquisition of the trackbed by this method forces the abandonment of railway powers. Furthermore, there are bodies who have powerful interests in seeking to use a substantial portion of the trackbed as a cycle track or footpath and their aspirations include the section through the Aberglaslyn Pass. They would be free to contest any application for a new Light Railway Order. The County Council has interests to satisfy, other than a narrow gauge railway and no matter what the stated policy may be at present, we have seen recently how Councils' priorities may be re-ordered at short notice. So we think it likely that the 64 Company would be left only with the least interesting section of the railway from Porthmadog to Nantmor. Worst of all, we think that the abandonment of railway powers would destroy the chance of restoring the original Welsh Highland Railway, which should clearly not be allowed to happen.

"An organisation called Trackbed Consolidation Ltd, who had bought shares in the original Welsh Highland Railway Company, broke away from the 64 Company, of which they had been part, because of their opposition to the implications of the County Council's plan. They approached us and have transferred to the Festiniog, free of cost, sufficient ordinary shares in the original Welsh Highland Railway Company to give a controlling interest. This has allowed the possibility of freeing that Company from its long years of receivership, subject of course to the Court's approval".

"Arrangements are being made for these shares to be held by a new holding company being set up by The Festiniog Railway Trust (a registered charity which owns the controlling shares in the Festiniog Railway). Thus, the Festiniog and Welsh Highland will be sister Companies. Trackbed Consolidation Limited and the Festiniog believe this will provide a much better chance for restoring the whole of the Welsh Highland Railway than the County Council's plan".

"As I said before, recent hearsay, portrayed as fact, suggests the liabilities upon acquisition will total £1-million! The facts are quite different. First of all, the bridges were well-built and, in the opinion of an expert witness, the work needed to update their maintenance is well within the capabilities of experienced volunteers. Second, the debts of the old Welsh Highland Company are now expected to be very limited, so the way is reasonably clear to lift the Company out of receivership, provided we can obtain the Court's approval to do this".

"Trackbed Consolidation Limited and the Festiniog Company hope that the 64 Company and their volunteers, who have made a good start in creating a terminus and a short length of line, will continue to play a part in the development of the Welsh Highland".

"We believe that the actions that are now being taken are very much in the best interests of railway preservation. If successful, they will bring back to life the original Welsh Highland Railway instead of allowing an important piece of heritage to become extinct. Restoring such an attractive railway to its rightful place will allow thousands of people to enjoy matchless views from the comfort of a train. In addition, we believe that such activity will add greatly to the tourist potential of the area and provide safeguards for the fragile environment as well".

*Here the FR communications operation is running up to counter the 64 Co. in 1990, well before the High Court hearing and judgement. This is fighting stuff and satisfied many of the FRSL concerns - that was the objective.*

**WHAT THE FR DO NOT SAY.  WHR Journal No. 99 December 1990**
**This Company has issued the following 15-point response to the FR statement.**

1. The FR's explanation does not convince! If their directors are so keen to see the WHR reopened, why is it that most of them have not troubled to join our Company or Trackbed Consolidation Limited, for that matter?

2. The remark by an FR Society director that the aim was to prevent the trackbed from being used for development harmful to the FR has never been explained or denied. Similar statements have been made very recently by another officer of the FR Society. These comments and the conduct of the FR throughout make us suspicious.

3. Other statements from the FR suggest that they see ownership of the trackbed by Gwynedd County Council as a threat to them but do not see us as rivals. What does this mean? If the FR are saying that, in certain circumstances, they could be threatened by what happens on the trackbed, can we be sure that they might not seek to restrict our expansion in future?

4. It is clear that whoever owns the trackbed will incur very heavy actual and potential liabilities, even before the land can be put to good use for railway or other purposes. This is not just a matter of the old Company's debts.

5. Expenditure by the FR on the trackbed will be passed on to us in the form of rent. Conversely, the County Council will accept full responsibility for the parts not leased to us.

6. We are advised that the FR have no power to hold shares in the old WHR Company or to bid for the trackbed or, for that matter, to finance the take-over by the Festiniog Railway Trust which is now proposed. The FR are facing legal action from one of their shareholders who, like many FR supporters, is concerned at the expense and other difficulties which control of the trackbed would involve.

7. It is untrue to say that the Abandonment Order required by the Official Receiver will prejudice the reopening of the railway (see point 8 below). The Abandonment Order will get rid of old statutory obligations which otherwise could cause difficulties.

8. Are the FR aware that the Department of Transport have said that the WHR probably could not be rebuilt under the old legislation? There are several examples in recent years of lines closed long after the WHR, the re-opening of which has required new powers. We are advised that this is so whether or not the line is re-opened by the original owners. The revival of the WHR will need a new Light Railway Order which, as TCL and others have said, can be opposed by anyone.

9. A glaring omission from the FR statement is their failure to say that planning permission will be required to rebuild the line. Revival of the old Company will not avoid the need to obtain planning permission.

10. With points 8 and 9 in mind, we decided long ago on a policy of co-operation with Gwynedd County Council who, if they wished, could probably stop the railway anyway, whoever owns it. The FR are now planning a major court battle to overturn long-established policies of the Council - the elected representatives of the local people - as regards the WHR. Hardly a recipe for good relations!

11. The FR do not control the old WHR Company - it is in the hands of the Official Receiver. All they have acquired - without payment - is a claim over the shares which will not be registered in their name without a court order. It remains to be seen whether the order will be granted.

12. Public opinion is overwhelmingly hostile to the FR take-over attempts which have been condemned not only in the railway press but by the local authorities, local politicians and others. The FR have few, if any, supporters outside their organisation.

13. The FR deny meddling in our affairs. If making an agreement with a splinter group and adopting their policies is not meddling, what is?

14. There is much unhappiness within the FR Company and Society about the bid. Many FR supporters have apologised to us for what their Board is doing and an FR patron has resigned in protest. Moves are being made by members of the FR Society to dissociate that body from the actions of the FR Company.

15. We are first to admire the FR achievements and support the idea of co-operation between the two railways, despite the harm done by the bid, but this can take place without the FR owning the trackbed.

*It is worth using the benefits of hindsight to look at some of the statements. This is a document written for home consumption and it is effective at countering the FR assertion that they are not trying a takeover. Reality is worse than takeover, FR are thinking about restoring the whole railway themselves.*

*The two organisations haven't talked together and so neither is clear on the effects of competition. The question of liabilities are becoming known to FR, but 64 Co. as yet is repeating the conventional view. It is difficult to know if this is because it frightens off competition, or whether as GCC will own the trackbed 64 Co. think themselves safe from liabilities. The Abandonment Order effect hasn't been thought through by 64 Co. The mechanism for their disappointment is contained herein - we see this from the hindsight of the High Court case. The existence of the residuary powers have kept people off the trackbed. The Abandonment Order will expose GCC to landowner activity to regularise their use of parts of the trackbed. Adverse possession may or may not be claimable, but the GCC constituents most listened too are agricultural - this became plain later in the TO and TWO public inquiries. It was therefore unwise to allow the course of action where an Abandonment Order was applied for. It was the surest method of preventing total railway restoration. 64 Co, did not see this as they 'could not'. Wedded to GCC, the County's policies were to be accepted if they could not be changed. 64 Co. never saw the danger that in the High Court, GCC would be labelled as unlikely to have as their main aim the restoration of the railway - they were trying to say that this label applied to the FR! The fixity of purpose, demonstrated in point No.10, halted any pragmatic desire to have a 'just in case' deal with FR Co. This desire was muted by mistrust, strengthened by the leak. Doubt over the granting of transfer of ownership of the 22 Co. shares (and debentures), together with a strong feeling that taking the 22 Co. out of liquidation was most unlikely perhaps led to a failure to see the danger from a Transfer Order - FR knew about this, but thought 22 Co. reconstruction was possible - in any event, they said this to TCL, who provided the means for them to be in the High Court asking for a stop of the sale of the trackbed from OR to GCC for £1. FR Co. did have fall back plans - 64 Co. did not.*

*FR Co. were not meddling in the affairs of 64 Co., they were engaged in an outright attempt to take control of the lot, which is much more serious!*

**THE FESTINIOG RAILWAY COMPANY**
**Background material for the public interest - inserted in FRS Magazine No. 131 Winter 1990/1.**

**John Routly, Chairman of the Festiniog Railway Company, spoke out recently on the matter of the Company's involvement with the Welsh Highland Railway. There are still awkward questions unanswered. The Board of the Festiniog Railway responds here, to counter the effects of misrepresentations from other bodies.**

**Q: Why does the Festiniog want to buy the Welsh Highland?**
A: The FR thinks that the Welsh Highland trackbed has the potential in the right ownership to become a viable tourist line. It sees the increase of leisure and tourism in the future, and believes that, and taking people through fine scenery by rail allows them access to it and contributes to the protection of the environment.

**Q: The FR is accused of muscling in on a smaller neighbour, on someone else's railway. How do you answer that?**
A: When the '64 Company set up in Porthmadog, they didn't feel the need to ask the FR's permission. The FR, at that time, was nothing like the successful enterprise it is today, yet there was no orchestrated campaign against the '64 Company. We therefore adopt the view that it is naive for them to carp at a successful FR's interest in acquiring a stake in what looks promising for the future. We uphold the right for us to act in the interests of our future as well, especially as in our view to do so will favour the interests of the Welsh Highland Railway, although despite promptings from many sides the '64 Company prefer to play ostrich on this point.

**Q: Surely buying the Welsh Highland is taking away the '64 Company's birthright?**
A: No. The Welsh Highland Railway (1964) Company owns none of the trackbed [which the FR wants to buy] and neither does it occupy any of it. It resolved years ago not to purchase the trackbed and to rely on leasing it back from the County Council, who have bid £1 for it. The '64 Company has therefore given up the idea of trying to own the trackbed, they are prepared to accept a landlord. So, we don't see any reason why we shouldn't attempt to acquire it and be that landlord, in the same way as anyone else may. We believe we could do a better job than the County Council.

**Q: Yet your actions have put back the plans of the '64 Company for a year at least and your terms of the lease will be much worse than those of the County Council.**
A: This is nonsense. The legal complexities of the lease, with adverse possession claims, transfer terms etc, will take a great deal of time. The rescue from Receivership plan of ours will probably be quicker. To suggest a short time-scale for any of this would be foolish. As to the terms of the lease, there can be no comparisons since the County Council has not stated their terms and neither has the Festiniog. Anyone who says that Festiniog terms would be worse than County Council is indulging in mischievous speculation.

**Q: You may see a commercial case for your involvement but you are spoiling a carefully laid plan to join with the Gwynedd County Council in acquiring the trackbed. That's hardly fair?**
A: It may be a carefully laid plan but we think it is naive and unworkable. What hasn't been admitted is that their plan will lose the original railway for ever and we will probably not see trains running again over the best bits. It has been the statutory powers held by the original Company that has preserved the trackbed from vanishing for all these years. Our plan is to rescue the original Welsh Highland Railway from receivership and, thus, try to save the whole railway from extinction. Our plan is much harder to achieve and takes more courage than just restoring a little bit and letting the rest die. We couldn't do what we've done without the terrific support we've had.

**Q: You accuse the '64 Company/Gwynedd County Council plan of being naive and unworkable?**
A: I think you have to make your own mind up about whether you believe the County Council can deliver what the '64 Company believe it will. The fact that, as a condition of sale by the Official Receiver the existing railway powers must be abandoned, is the part that hasn't been noticed so far. A planning procedure needs to be gone through before a railway may be run. Since there are parts of the trackbed which powerful organisations wish to be reserved for other purposes, such as cycle track and footpath, we don't think the County Council can deliver on anything other than an agricultural trundle. Furthermore, recently, we have all seen how private railways have suffered through the re-ordered priorities of local authorities.

**Q: But haven't Gwynedd County Council have agreed to lease the Railway back to the '64 Company and don't their articles of association state that they are committed to restoring the whole stretch between Porthmadog and Dinas Junction?**
A: We challenge the '64 Company to show a clear undertaking on behalf of the County Council to lease them the railway between Porthmadog and Dinas Junction. There may be agreements in principle, but no binding agreements at all, no security, nothing tangible. Why do you think the Gwynedd County Council want the trackbed? It is naive to think that is to run a railway! It is the powers that have preserved its integrity along its length over 50 years, and now we see the '64 Company actively conspiring to remove these powers, naively assuming that their actions are going to get them a railway to run on. They will, a little short piece, and the rest will be lost to all of us! There are powerful lobbies that would like to see the trackbed confirmed in other uses. They do not have the emotional attachment that we do to steam engines and trains. Also, there are a number of road schemes that the removal of the railway would make more convenient. If the powers disappear, then much of the Welsh Highland Railway trackbed will be lost forever, since it will be so much more difficult to negotiate the trackbed back into railway use in their absence.

*These are FR 'spin' countermeasures, attempting to thwart 64 Co. 'hearts and minds' success with FRSL members. It achieved its purpose and was never quite countered or equalled by communicators in the opposite camp.*

**Q: Does this mean that if the FR gets control of the Welsh Highland that it will lay the rails back straight away?**
A: It is not as simple as that. First, our plan is to rescue the original Company from Receivership. That in itself is a problem that must be handled through the courts, who have a "discretion". Second, if we succeed in this, then we shall preserve the statutory powers of the original Company and all its land intact. We may then negotiate with those concerned the reinstatement of the railway. However, this has to be done sensitively and gradually. One cannot bounce in after 50 years of dereliction and relay a line without careful consultation with those affected. But our aim is eventual restoration of the whole railway.

**Q: How long will that take?**
A: If you had asked that question about the FR back in 1955, would you have been told 1982 with certainty? Of course not. The answer is, as long as it takes!

**Q: Won't you have £1 million of debts to pay to rescue the original WHR from Receivership?**
A: If we thought that then we wouldn't be acting as we are! That figure is a fable put about by people who are either being malign or who are unimaginatively ignorant. There are debts but we believe them to be relatively small and to be worthwhile in the context of rescuing the original WHR. Our experts have also had a good look at the structures along the line and we recognise them as being soundly built with remedial work to be done which is well within the capability of volunteers.

**Q: Some say you only want the WHR to stop it running or close it down, is this true?**
A: Our record from 1955 is one of far-sighted, hard-working, successful restoration. We rebuilt the FR against the odds and have made it one of the leading tourist attractions in Wales. We are not in the business of petty protectionism. We know you can't stifle railway restoration, there were plenty who tried with the FR and failed to stop us. We think that we can help to restore the WHR. There is no fun to be had in keeping it closed.

**Q: But, if the FR controls the WHR, that will mean all the people who have spent over 25 years struggling to get the line running will be excluded.**
A: The FR doesn't intend to run the WHR. We already have a railway. We are honest in our intentions of sharing the acquisition should we be successful. I think there are those who suggest otherwise and I am sorry about this.

**Q: Who might those be?**
A: Some are so strongly opposed to FR involvement that considerable misinformation has been given and some dirty tricks have been in play. I think that when the truth dawns on the majority that these actions will rebound.

**Q: But wasn't the FR's secret bid a dirty trick?**
A: Hardly. Bidding is still open to anyone. The FR kept quiet from a wish not to encourage further bids, speculation and to avoid the inevitable hassle when our identity became known. Also, we weren't sure at that time whether a bid could be success-ful. When we became aware of possible success, then we told the Gwynedd County Council and the '64 Company as soon as possible.

**Q: Why didn't you get an agreement with the '64 Company, it would have saved a lot of trouble?**
A: We tried. We have our approaches documented. Our first meeting was encouraging. The FR asked for the proceedings to be confidential but the next thing we knew the Press was carrying material accusing us of being underhand. We met again but all the '64 Company representatives would talk about was the withdrawal of our bid and they were impolite about it.

**Q: Why did you arrange a marriage of convenience with Trackbed Consolidation Limited?**
A: TCL came to us with a surprising story. They said they had been a part of the '64 Company at one time and had supported Rescue from Receivership. They thought that the County Council bid was fraught with risk. They purchased a majority shareholding in the original Company. In 1983 (*Compiler's note: May 1984, in fact*), they were ousted from the '64 Company and the Rescue from Receivership plan suppressed in favour of the deal with the County Council. TCL offered their controlling interest to the '64 Company this year in exchange for their adoption of the Rescue from Receivership plan. The '64 Company Board apparently saw fit to turn this offer down, despite knowing about the Festiniog bid for the trackbed and despite not knowing the County Council lease terms or the certainty of restoration of the whole of the line. It seems they didn't even consult their membership about either the offer or their decision! Following this astonishing refusal by the '64 Company Board, and in despair of seeing the whole railway ever being saved, TCL came to speak to the FR. They decided to give the shares to the FR to see the rescue plan mounted. When this became known, the '64 Company associates reported to the Press that the Festiniog Railway Company has no authority to acquire the shares and that an FR shareholder is prepared to take out an injunction to prevent the alleged action of the FR Co outside its powers. It seems to the FR to be amazing that the '64 Company have accused the FR of not acting in the best interests of railway preservation. Not only that but some elements of the Railway Press have been persuaded to write a whole article on that theme! So, our marriage with TCL is more one of love than convenience.

**Q: So do you feel resentment towards the '64 Company?**
A: Actually, we are sorry for them. Those in charge have been so busy defending their corner that they have forgotten the true nature of what they are fighting for. The same amount of energy in reaching a mutually acceptable agreement with TCL and the FR would have achieved far more. Instead, as the extent of the bad feeling they have caused through misinformation, and the fact that they cry wolf against a viable plan for rescue and restoration becomes clear, they may find that they end up with no respect left. It is possible that a significant section of the membership, which has been indicating privately that it approves of the FR/TCL plans, will take action. We have always been pleased to talk seriously with the '64 Company and nothing has changed.

---

*Much was invested in the TCL attempt. This was a high risk strategy, but then the stakes had been raised high, and the FR Co. was prepared to go nuclear, as anger at 64 Co. 'stir' had reached new heights, boosting determination.*

**FRS Magazine No. 132, Spring 1991**
**Editorial - extract**

It is, worthwhile reviewing some aspects of the affair which have upset members. There are those who don't understand the initial secrecy surrounding the FR's involvement. John Routly says there was "no wish to encourage speculators", and you only have to read the 1964 Company's story in Boyd (Narrow Gauge Railways in South Caernarvonshire Vol 2 The Welsh Highland Railway) to understand why he would be concerned. Apart from that, any organisation sometimes has to conduct aspects of its affairs in confidence. Railway companies are no exception.

Why, some say, the WHR, after what happened in the 1930s? Well, the FR has always been interested in this route, even before some of it was built. In 1872 Livingston Thompson was a founding director of the North Wales Narrow Gauge Railways (NWNGR) and the FR was given powers to work the line. Seven years later, the FR was given powers to work the Portmadoc, Croesor and Beddgelert Tram Railway and these powers were also enshrined in the WHR's 1922 Light Railway Order which has yet to be rescinded. The historical interest in the route is not unlike the present day interest although, in this case, it is the prospect of increased tourism which is responsible rather than increased freight traffic. It's hardly surprising that the FR takes an interest. After all, says Peter Jarvis, you can't open a hamburger stall outside Macdonald's and expect nobody to notice. The FR has a marvellous record of fund-raising in support of railway restoration but there are limits; it would be a shame if that expertise were to go to waste and to what better purpose could it be applied than to our near neighbour, the WHR?

The FR shouldn't involve itself in non-FR organisations, say others. Apart from the WHR, this is nothing new either. Two historical examples have just been cited. More recently, in the 1970's, the FR was ready to form a company to take over the Conwy Valley line if BR had closed it. And [FR] Magazine 125 (p. 206) reported the purchase of a travel agency business being considered. There is no rule which says that railways shouldn't involve themselves in other railways and activities, and neither the Society nor its members have ever intimated to the Company that it shouldn't. The FR's major claim to fame is that it is unamalgamated, consideration of which immediately leads to the realisation that most other railways did change hands by one means or another. Of course, there were some things which should have been said which weren't. It should have been made clear that there was no intention to divert investment capital away from the FR and that there was no intention of asking the FR Society to provide either funds or labour to aid the WHR restoration. (And, no, the possibility of being involved with the WHR was most definitely not the cause of the recent redundancies.)

Finally, there was the publicity. The ferocity of this in some quarters has caused most upset, we feel, and [we] can well understand members wondering why they should be involved with an organisation reported in such a way. We can also well understand the Company's thinking. Don't say anything and it can't be distorted. That there wasn't a 'Plan B' has become only too clear, but no reasonable person could have foreseen that Steam Railway would have picked on the affair like a lock-jawed dog with a bone and find it impossible, in this context, to say anything positive about the FR, or even to report the FR's side as fully as it did the '64 Company's. In the February edition, even our brief comment about the magazine was incorrectly reported, and described as an 'attack'. Our 'yellow pages' were completely ignored.

Whilst the press release issued by Ian Allan after the January meeting resulted in Steam Railway News headlining "Peace talks succeed', it had Steam Railway describing the outcome as a 'fragile truce'. Their report included quotes from Ian Allan and a WHR director - none from the FR. We don't know why the magazine has it in for the FR so much that it lowers its otherwise high journalistic standards to report news in such an unbalanced manner. We commend to members the balanced approach of Railway World or the minimalist approach of Railway Magazine.

Talking of magazines, some members were concerned by a note in the WHR's Winter Journal published in January, in which the FR's November press release (see [FR] Magazine No 131, p. 438) was quoted, complete with WHR responses. What caused concern was the introduction to the feature, which ended with the challenge 'If the FR want to give us space in their magazine to put our viewpoint, we will be pleased to hear from them!' What they didn't say is that last July, David Allan - director and co-contributor of the feature, telephoned to ask if he could respond, on behalf of the WHR, to WHR comment in our Summer issue. Approval was given readily. As the Autumn issue was about to go to press, David Allan telephoned again, saying that the WHR had decided to make no comment at that time. He was told then that, if the WHR did want to address Society members in the future, space would be made available. No further approach has been made.

**WHR - Useful Discussions**
The '64 Company met with the FR Co and Trackbed Consolidation Limited (TCL) in January, under the chairmanship of the Association of Independent Railways, a body to which both Companies belong. The atmosphere was cordial. An exchange of views took place between the parties and both agreed to refer to their respective ruling bodies. The exchange amounted to an outline and discussion of the position each company would take under the three scenarios of - success to the County Council or Festiniog bids for the trackbed and rescue of the 1922 Company from receivership. Should the Festiniog bid for the trackbed be successful, then it will be prepared to lease it to the '64 Company. John Routly explained that a new Company, Ffestiniog Holdings, had been created to hold the shares of the 1922 Company. If the court allows rescue from receivership, then the way is free for the 1922 Company to take on the duties of restoring and running the Welsh Highland Railway. The FR Company says that it will be prepared to make space for the '64 Company and others on the 1922 Company's Board.

**ARPS to the rescue**
We really mustn't be disrespectful to the ARPS but they seem to have behaved rather oddly in the recent past. You may have seen reports of a motion of censure against the Festiniog Railway Company earlier in the year. The text is too lengthy to report in full but uses the words 'deplores', 'condemns' and 'disrepute', certainly it contains nothing chummy. A press release was circulated which managed to stir the Cambrian News to echo some mild deploring. Since it is the Society which is the ARPS member, not the Company, we thought it odd that, having written in explanation to the ARPS in August, this action should have arisen without further reference to us. There is a logical explanation for this, but of such complexity that we shall have to meet the ARPS to understand it fully; with luck that meeting will be chummy. At the request of the '64 Company, the ARPS Council recommended, and the ARPS AGM agreed, to suspend discussion of the censure motion, 'to allow constructive negotiations between the parties to proceed in the best atmosphere in the hope that the motion can ultimately be withdrawn altogether'. Perhaps the Magazine might be prepared to hand the blancmange back to the ARPS now?

*The pre-High Court, chatty tenor of the FRSL Magazine was now trying hard to make sure that a clear FR party line was being disseminated to the members. In fact there was a lot of ground to be made up, and the boot was going in.*

**WHR Journal No. 106, October 1992 and 107, January 1993**
CHAIRMAN'S NEWS LINE by Alisdair McNicol - extracts

106

MENTALLY-RETARDED MUTTON DRESSED AS LAMB DEPARTMENT. (Ref. Journal 104 Letters)

Hungry Lion Watchers amongst the Company will be gratified to learn that the Festiniog Railway has not only turned down the chance of sharing a table but has made it clear that its intention was to scoff the lot. Fortunately for us, the County Council promptly slammed the door in their face before they could get the lid off the mint sauce.

Whilst the natural reaction is to say "phew" and gracefully slide down the door to floor-level mopping perspiration from the brow, there is still a ravenous carnivore pacing about out there, and one that has seen an easy lunch snatched away.

The cosy oligarchy that controls all things Festiniog still basks in the top-dog status of its railway amongst the GLTW, but has been left standing by the more dynamic society/plc combinations of the standard-gauge outfits such as Seven Valley Railway. You can bet that they are going to fight tooth, nail and claw to remain king of the castle, narrow-gauge division, and have made it abundantly clear in the past that they take a seriously dim view of competition, particularly the Welsh Highland.

Such then is the background to our current situation. Firstly, however, it is necessary to dispel a few myths. It is not the Festiniog Railway that is the competition, it is a shell company, claiming the expertise of big brother as its unique selling point, largely manned by former members of our own Company.

So, the way is wide open for a cogent counter-argument. Exactly why is the FR's particular expertise applicable to the Welsh Highland? We do not require massive deviations, we do not have to cope with loading gauge more suited to fitting rats up drainpipes than light railway operations, the concept of grabbing control of a moribund company has been shown to be expensively fallacious and, most important of all, we do not have to put big brother's interests first.

So, we have the wide open opportunity to draw on experience across the board to provide the structure that will ensure the future of the Welsh Highland and address its particular problems. We will not enjoy the luxury of being able to raise two fingers to everyone and just get on with the job. First, we have to convince farmers, environmentalists and local communities of all this whilst somebody is huffing and puffing and attempting to blow the house down. Aren't you glad you're one of those really nice people of the Welsh Highland Railway?

AND FINALLY THE GOOD NEWS

Since word is out that the Welsh Highland is going for its stated destiny, i.e., the Welsh Highland Railway, interest has been shown by many whom we thought dead and forgotten, having lost interest or disillusioned. Apologies to anyone whose expression of support, help or just simple exhortations to "go for it" have not received due acknowledgement, but the mail bag is bursting.

What this flags for me is confirmation that our enforced concentration of effort at Beddgelert Siding has allowed some sympathisers to be swayed by sweet talk from people claiming broader vision, purity of purpose, loyalty to first principles. Well then, let us reassert our birthright. It may not seem like it on a wet September Sunday, trying to find a dry corner of the cab to hide in, but we are not alone. The Welsh Highland remains the cause célébre of railway preservation. Massive support can be forthcoming to him who can pull the sword out of the rock.

107

By the time you read this, December 17th 1992 will have gone down in the records as either one of the greatest days in the history of the Welsh Highland or as one of to biggest anti-climaxes. This was the day Gwynedd County Council was due to consider several motions on Welsh Highland affairs, described later in this issue.

Prior to this meeting, Trojan efforts have been made by a small number of people to put in place the necessary documentation in a "last shot" Light Railway Order and Transfer Order that will be crucial to the future of the Welsh Highland Railway. This action was triggered by the depositing of the Festiniog Railway Group's application for a Transfer Order which threatened the joint application previously made by ourselves and Gwynedd for the Pont Croesor LRO.

An emergency meeting of the [County] Welsh Highland Railway Sub-Committee strongly endorsed the strategy being pursued by the Company in partnership with Gwynedd and gave its approval to a much more vigorous approach to the whole matter. In particular, it recommended the granting of our greatest opportunity yet, a lease of the Caernarfon - Dinas trackbed, in anticipation of the joint feasibility study commenting favourably on this.

The only discordant note has been the emergence of a few voices falsely claiming the credentials of the Welsh Highland Light Railway (1964) Ltd in endorsing the attempts by the Festiniog group to wrest control of the trackbed from under the noses of the local community that contributed to its creation many years ago.

For those holding sincere views contrary to the majority and unable to hold their peace, there is one honourable course of action - resignation. Credibility is perhaps a separate issue, but would you believe a Turkey advocating Christmas.

Astrological Prediction :- 1993 may be a difficult year. You will need persistence to overcome someone denigrating your best efforts. Do not worry though, with a little help from friends that long-awaited goal may be yours.

Do not waste time on red herrings, and always remember who your real friends are. It could be a good year for romance.

---

*These two later pieces caused damage. The sinned against were sinning themselves by flinging insults. The 'really nice people' were telling dissenters to resign. For the 64 Co, the sword remains firmly in the rock.......*

## IN BLACK AND WHITE - PART 2 by Dave Allan

In the last Journal, I attempted to summarise the-then position of all three parties involved in the trackbed. The situation is constantly evolving and the following is an attempt to objectively assess the position at the time of going to Press (7th December 1992).

### FESTINIOG RAILWAY

To recap - the FR rejected the compromise offered to them by the County Council. This would have included :-

a) Lease of council-owned, standard gauge trackbed from Caernarfon to Dinas

b) Lease of WHR trackbed from Dinas to Rhyd-Ddu

c) Possible £300,000 of Grant Aid towards refurbishing of trackbed

The FR have now applied for the Transfer Order, anticipated in the previous Journal article. If successful, their order will have the effect of transferring the residual powers and assets of the bankrupt 1922 Company to FR (Holdings) Ltd. These assets include the trackbed. It is understood that there have been several objections to their application.

### GWYNEDD COUNTY COUNCIL

Has held a further meeting of the Council's Welsh Highland Sub-Committee (13th November). This sub-committee approved the following resolutions :-

### RESOLVED

a. To authorise the County Secretary and Solicitor, in consultation with the County Planning Officer to object to the application for a Transfer Order made by Ffestiniog Railway Holdings Limited and the Festiniog Railway Trust.

b. To recommend the Council at its next meeting to make a joint application with the Welsh Highland Light Railway (1964) Ltd for a Transfer Order to authorise the vesting in the Council of the disused Welsh Highland Light Railway and its branch lines.

c. That, if the above mentioned application is successful, to agree in principle, subject to terms to be agreed, to lease, such part of the trackbed between Dinas and Porthmadog to the Welsh Highland light Railway (1964) Ltd as is necessary for the Company to operate a railway along this length and subject also, wherever feasible, to the retention of land for the construction of a recreational route for walkers and cyclists.

d. To recommend the Council at its next meeting to make a joint application with the Welsh Highland Light Railway (1964) Ltd for a Light Railway Order in respect of the trackbed of the British Railways line, between Caernarfon and Dinas Junction.

e. To recommend the Council's appropriate committees and sub-committees to lease, on terms to be agreed, such part of the trackbed between Caernarfon and Dinas Junction to the Welsh Highland Light Railway (1964) Ltd as is necessary for the Company to operate a railway along this length, subject to the retention of sufficient land to allow the retention of a recreational route for walkers and cyclists.

f. To authorise the County Planning Officer to make an application (jointly with the Welsh Highland Light Railway (1964) Ltd if he considers it to be appropriate) for planning permission to construct and operate a railway between Caernarfon and Dinas Junction along the trackbed of the former British Railways Line, including the relocation (if necessary) of Lôn Eifion alongside the proposed railway.

### WHR (1964) COMPANY

Undertaking intensive preparatory work in connection with the joint Light Railway Order and Transfer Order applications.

The LRO application needs to be made before the end of the year in order to take advantage of cheaper costs under existing legislation.

The decisions of Gwynedd Council at their meeting of the 17th December, on the recommendation of the Welsh Highland Sub Committee will be the subject of a supplement to this Journal

## IN BLACK & WHITE - SUPPLEMENTAL by David Allan

### FESTINIOG RAILWAY

On the 17th of December (1992 Ed.) the FR published notices which confirmed that they had applied for further Light Railway Orders.

Both Orders seek powers to build a narrow gauge railway between Dinas and Caernarfon.

The second of these two Orders include Compulsory Purchase Powers which, if granted, would enable them to enforce the purchase of the Standard Gauge Trackbed between Dinas and Caernarfon from the present owners, Gwynedd County Council.

### GWYNEDD COUNTY COUNCIL

On the 17th of December, the full Council approved by the necessary two-thirds majority, the recommendations (b) and (d) reported in the Journal article.

The Orders, which are sought jointly with the 64 Company are :-

i) Proposed Welsh Highland Railway (GCC) Light Railway Order. This Order, if granted, would have the effect of allowing the Official Receiver to transfer the assets of the old Welsh Highland Railway (1922) Company to the Council, including the trackbed.

ii) Proposed Caernarfon Light Railway Order. This Order, if granted, would enable the Council, or its lessee, to construct and operate a narrow gauge railway between Caernarfon and Dinas.

### WHR (1964) COMPANY

The Company now has the necessary legal backing of the Council to jointly promote Orders which, if granted, will enable the County Council to acquire the trackbed and enable the Company to build a railway from Caernarfon to Dinas. Also, if the further Order is obtained, the Company will be able to rebuild the Welsh Highland Railway from Pont Croesor to Dinas.

The significance of this step is immense and has transformed the position beyond all expectations. The Company is now in its strongest position ever to complete its objective - the total rebuilding of the Welsh Highland Railway.

### SUMMARY

There are now six Orders outstanding which are concerned with the rebuilding of the WHR.

These are :-

| No. | Order | Sponsor |
|---|---|---|
| 1) | The Pont Croesor Light Railway Order | GCC/WHR (64)Co |
| 2) | The Welsh Highland Railway (Gwynedd County Council) Light Railway Order | GCC/WHR (64)Co |
| 3) | The Caernarfon Light Railway Order | GCC/WHR (64)Co |
| 4) | The Welsh Highland Railway (Transfer) Light Railway Order | Ffestiniog Railway |
| 5) | The Caernarfon Light Railway Order | Ffestiniog Railway |
| 6) | The Caernarfon Light Railway (No.2) Order | Ffestiniog Railway |

The next step will almost certainly be a Public Enquiry to consider all of these applications. It is not possible to say when the enquiry will be held, save that it will be sometime in 1993.

*This clear summary of the position in December 1992 shows who was doing what. The FR had rejected a GCC compromise - they would; they were beginning to think that success was possible if they kept at it. Broadway was gone.*

# 'Secret' negotiations

Perhaps they were not exactly secret, since the principles were advised to 64 Co. members in a letter of 2nd February 1991. The matter arose from Chairman Ken Dicks's untimely death on Boxing day 1990. Alisdair McNicol took the Chair and wrote out to members shortly after. It was a particularly sensible and realistic letter. He was happy about the publicity the battle with FR brought, and with the censure motion from the ARPS. He reports the start of constructive dialogue at Broadway. It was accepted there that the court was going to decide the future of the trackbed. The FR had apparently escaped the threat of Peter Thomason's injunction, and that there were three scenarios to consider from the court proceedings:

1. The court could agree to 1922 Co. being taken out of receivership
2. The court could order a sale to the highest bidder
3. The sale to Gwynedd could go through.

According to the 64 Co. legal advice the latter was most likely.

It was felt to be advisable to talk with FR Co. to see if they 'apologised' and so were possible to work with, and to see if they had a sensible offer for working together. It was AIR who suggested the meeting should take place, as despite the ARPS motion of censure, there was no sign that FR Co. contemplated withdrawing their bid for the trackbed.

No sure prediction of the court action was possible since FR Co. and TCL had decided to request a stay of the sale to GCC to enable them to reconstruct the WHR 1922 Co. So 64 Co. wanted to know what FR plans were to include them after the High Court. For 64 Co. the meeting was an irritation. Routly talked 'at' them and not 'to' them, and they did not know at all whether FR people knew about the leak from GCC of the Routly 'buy to shut' meeting. They decided not to reveal that they already knew about the 'treacherous acts' of asking GCC to stifle development of WHR. In doing so they passed by the last chance to jolt the FR Co. from its complacency. The Broadway outcome was that in return for a suspension of the Censure Motion at the ARPS AGM, the FR Co. and 64 Co. would look for a means of a satisfactory partnership to restore the WHR. The High Court hearing was set for 11th November, and so there was 9 months in which to find it.

On 15th February John Routly wrote to Alisdair McNicol. The substance in that letter was that GCC did not have railway preservation as the real purpose in making their bid (an uncomfortable truth for the 64 Co.) and that an accord for sharing responsibility needed assurances from 64 Co. that they would assist in achieving the desired result by supporting FR Co. efforts. This was hard; FR Co. were tweaking their tail in proposing a contrary course than that of partnership with GCC. It was deeply unfortunate that either from an attack of misplaced loyalty, or from the deep feeling of mistrust engendered by the leak, 64 Co. would not contemplate even a safety-net deal with FR Co. as no one knew then, but it was precisely this factor that GCC did not have railway restoration as their main purpose that led to a Pyrhhic victory in the High Court.

Alisdair McNicol wrote to John Routly to deny that they had promised active support at the Broadway meeting. In doing so he (the 64 Co,) would have to abandon their long-standing policy of favouring the acquisition of the trackbed by Gwynedd. He said the reason for meeting was to ensure that if FR plans succeeded then the 64 Co. would play a part in the restoration of the WHR. He reminded that the trackbed might pass into the hands of the GCC and presumed that the success of the FR court application was by no means assured, and that he thought this confirmed by FR's eagerness to secure the active support of GCC and the 64 Co. Alisdair McNicol asked for a summary of proposals. He wanted to know the following:

1. The 1922 Board composition
2. How would the offer of two 64 Co. directors on that Board be made legally enforceable?
3. How would the rebuilding of WHR be financed?
4. What role will the 64 Co. have to play if the 1922 Company is revived, other than appointing directors.

He said that he understood that in strict legal terms the statutory powers to operate the line would belong only to the 1922 Co. He wondered about the FR Co. - FRSL model and if that model could be applied to allow 64 Co., who would own the engines and rolling stock, to operate the line.

This letter revealed serious doubts in the 64 Co. minds as to their relevance under an FR (and even a GCC) regime. They were of course vulnerable if FR Co. did a deal with GCC and if FR Co. won the High Court case. They certainly did not understand how exposed they could be in a scenario where FR Co. decided on 'full' restoration with Garratts and 165m platforms - and that was what was being thought about by FR at the time!

The attitude and thinking of the two sides is relevant. FR had shown no remorse, no understanding of what they had done, and didn't seem to care. To John Routly this was 'business'. He was now dealing with a declared competitor. He would do a deal, but only within his structure, and he was impervious to any 'hurt feelings'.

There were several exchanges thereafter, on 28.03.91, from the FR, on 08.05.91 from 64 Co. It looks like the FR Co. were playing 'string along', as not much counted except the High Court judgement, and keeping the ARPS from reapplying the censure motion. It was clear from the correspondence that 64 Co. thought small, with Pont Croesor at the fore, and already thought that their own attitude was of little relevance to the outcome. They certainly were unaware of the dangers of GCC being seen as unlikely to restore the whole railway. Today that appears as potential a danger as the 'misconceived' FR case for restoration.

There was no definition of the 4 points as requested by Mr McNicol. He asked for clarification of the Broadway accord, but didn't get it. 64 Co. tried to suggest that ARPS would be 'back' if there wasn't progress, noting that FR wanted a declaration in their favour, yet had not delivered on a 'deal'. There was irritation about the FRSL Magazine, using the hamburger stall gag. The reply was a frustrating stringalong from Routly; the 'philanthropic platitudes' accusation by Allan Garraway was justified. The insults of the FR magazine bear comparison with the 64 Co. Journal's comment, that FR Co. found unhelpful. Routly reminded that the Foil the Ffestiniog Fighting Fund boxes are still 'out there'. The ARPS threat is countered by Routly's assertion that he has told Morgan in person about his doubts over their real contribution.

There was no movement of 64 Co. away from GCC. The publishing of the Gwynedd Structure plan with no commitment to the restoration of the whole railway caused FR Co. to object, and to note that 64 Co. were opposing it. In truth this was a period when 64 Co. could have been dealing harder. The chance for them to be main players subsequently was lost at Broadway, but theirs was a dilemma. Yet a deal done before the High Court would have had moral substance whatever the outcome.

# THE WORLD'S BEST–SELLING STEAM MAGAZINE

**STEAM RAILWAY**

In 1990 there were three main railway enthusiast magazines, Steam Railway, Railway Magazine and Railway World. Railway Magazine was edited by a Talyllyn man, John Slater, and he decided to stay right away from the WHR controversy, confining reports to short, factual accounts.

Steam Railway was the newcomer, lively, entertaining and journalistic in its approach. The editor was Nick Pigott, a young man, ably teamed with David Wilcock, an experienced journalist, who brought his skills to the railway enthusiast forum. The WHR trackbed saga was an absolute magnet for such a publication. The previously staid reporting of the railway press was gone; the new competitive, brassy approach was here to last. Steam Railway eagerly reported on the FR Co.'s wickedness, with a big headlined story on the secret bid **'Not in the spirit of preservation, Mr Routly'.**

FR Co. did not reply, which was a mistake. It was believed that anything said would be twisted. There was much activity in 1990, and FR considered Steam Railway's reporting misrepresented FR's action, imputing that there was no justification for them. The FR Magazine carried an amusing piece accusing them of not reporting fairly, with comment on **'Scream Railway - the cess press'** that entertained many FRSL members, and wounded the magazine. In February 1991 the Steam Railway news piece reported, **'Now Ffestiniog faces 'disrepute' charge in ARPS censure motion'.** FR thought this reporting too was neither accurate nor fair. To their delight the FR Magazine comments were reported as an 'attack' on the **'Sunday Sport of the railway press'.** Steam Railway commented that if the censure motion was carried, the FR could find itself a moral outcast. It seems to have drawn on comment from David Morgan, the ARPS Chairman who was **'still awaiting answers to a range of questions',** presumably about the FR Co. bid, and the terms to be offered to 64 Co. They had remarks attributed to them about the **'unwelcome interference in the affairs of a neighbouring friendly railway'.** Also mentioned is the request by 64 Co. to AIR to suspend FR Co's membership. On 15th January the AIR had called the parties to a meeting in Broadway - that isn't reported, but perhaps it happened after the press date. It has been long considered as strange that ARPS were preparing motions of censure, and not forcing the parties to talk together - the AIR took the initiative with this action.

Of course the Ffestiniog Grandees tried to say that Steam Railway didn't matter, and should be ignored, but with a readership of nearly forty thousand people it mattered very much. In fact it became quite clear over ten years later just how much people cared, when it was Steam Railway - ever in the van of reportage - who supported and carried the WHR Phase 4 Appeal, that was so successful in raising funds for the restoration to Porthmadog. History repeated itself in 2010/2011 when Steam Railway supported an appeal, this time for Phase 5. Indeed Steam Railway is owed a debt of gratitude in the restoration of this railway, by putting pressure on FR Co. that precipitated the move to restore all, and then by helping the fund-raising effort subsequently.

Railway World was edited by Handel Kardas, who was pro-FR, but was hampered by the FR Co. being so tight-lipped. Railway World did not have the readership of Steam Railway but it was from the Ian Allan family of magazines. In May 1990 Handel Kardas wrote to John Routly complaining that the FR Co. was declining to comment, when others were publishing statements about the WHR affair. As an FRSL member he noted comments at the AGM and asked Routly for clarification. He warned that being silent would lead people to assume that there was something to hide, and this loosened the log-jam and began a useful relationship. Handel Kardas's letter was very strong but well argued. Here was an editor actually making the news - he said he couldn't help FR express itself if it insisted on silence. FR's policy of silence depended on the maxim, 'if you don't say anything you cannot be misquoted'. It was pointed out to John Routly that failing to make any comment was indeed harming FR's interests, yet he declined to change the policy just to favour a publication that was overtly hostile. However, it was pointed out that Railway World was exactly the opposite.

In December 1990, Handel had got the information that he wanted, and formulated the policy of printing factual matters in the body of the magazine, and reserving comment and opinion for the editorial. He reported that he had a large mailbag of comments, but that his contained remarks that of all the magazines, Railway World was the fairest, reporting in an unbiased manner by showing the information received broadly as it was, and reserving opinion for the Editorial. The fact that Railway World was an Ian Allan magazine meant that when the AIR (chaired by Ian Allan) met at Broadway, in the Ian Allan hotel, Handel Kardas was present to record all the details. Thus it was rather well reported in the next Railway World. There was much more of a feeling within the Ian Allan organisation that the right way to handle problems like this was to bring the parties together to broker some sort of accommodation, some sort of deal. Indeed this is what was done. The fact that it didn't last was due to the changing circumstances of events that followed. However, in 1991, Railway World was in at the front of progress; AIR made the settlement and Handel Kardas got the story. From here on in, through the Inquiries and the granting of the various Orders, the press was not in the news-making arena, they were only reporting the news. That did not change until Steam Railway was offered the initiative by FR/WHR for Phase 4 fundraising. Alas Railway World faded from view after Handel Kardas died of cancer in the late 1990s. The magazine eventually shut. Railway Magazine continued under different editors, steadily and reliably reporting the news and gaining readers until it eventually outstripped Steam Railway.

The local press were bemused by the action, not being familiar with railway enthusiast matters, but always up for negative stories and knocking copy whenever it suited them. It was the public inquiries that switched them on to the opportunities for reporting the 'hardships' caused by Welsh Highland Railway restoration, with sympathetic ears tuned to the way that the rebuilding was 'controversial'. In that area, little has changed over some 20 years.

**D**avid Allan was always a major force within the WHR 64 Company. He could be tough but he always tried to be fair, and above all he is pragmatic. He never gave up, and is now one of the active guardians of the WHR heritage, with no legacy of bitterness. The questions of what people felt within his organisation, and his thoughts have not until now been expressed in the light of the events that took place.

**I**nspired by narrow gauge track at Gelert's Farm in 1981, I became a member of the WHR ('64) Co on the spot. My intention was to support, not to get involved – some hope!

Under the able chairmanship of both Bill Brown and Ken Dicks the task of convincing the authorities that the Company was both serious and resolute in its ambition to restore the old WHR had been an uphill struggle. From the formation of the '64 Company success was elusive. The 'big hitters' were involved with other railways that seemed to offer a better chance of reinstatement, so no millionaires came our way.

Disappointment occurred, first in the late 1960s. The company had just about finalised negotiations to buy the trackbed from the liquidator (Aubrey Thomas) when, rather inconveniently, he died. The trackbed then passed into the hands of the Official Receiver, whose vice-like grip was only disturbed as a result of the Vinelott judgement some twenty years later.

Those in authority in the county and district councils pledged their support in private, but in public there always seemed to be reasons, with sincere regret, why they were unable to help us to make things happen, despite the obvious effectiveness of railway restorations around us. We cited the rising success of the Talyllyn, the Ffestiniog, the Welshpool, but to no avail. There were several plans for the reconstruction - one was to start in Waunfawr and build to Beddgelert, we even laid track in the 70's through the Goat cutting which was to remain until the FR completed the task some 30 years later. Alas it was Caernarvonshire County Council who would not venture that critical step of supporting what was to us such a certain winner. They cited fifteen points of potential conflict over the use of the trackbed for a restored railway, and declined to support our proposals for reinstatement. And that was that; back to square one – well almost! The Council did point the company towards the disused standard gauge slate-interchange siding at Porthmadog. I suspect that they hoped that this would make us go away, but instead the reverse happened!

The obduracy of the Official Receiver, with whom the company was now dealing in its efforts to secure the trackbed, was extremely frustrating, but somehow it made us all the more determined – we were not going to be put off by some paid official. We simply would not allow our *bête noir* to frustrate

the Company's ambition. And to prove the success of that determination, we were now operating a service on the little line in Porthmadog that we had created on that disused siding. The company had added to its holding by purchasing Gelert's Farm – which was adjacent to the siding. We now had buildings – farm buildings albeit rather ramshackle - into which we could lay track and store our meagre but increasing rolling stock. We had paying customers, we had a shop and we were voted a member of that exclusive club – The Great Little Trains of Wales. Our line finished on the trackbed of the old Welsh Highland at Pen y Mount – the perfect position from which to extend to Pont Croesor and then to Beddgelert.

We had a firm base, an excellent team, vaulting ambition, goodwill and some funds. It looked set fair. We engaged with the local political scene, we talked to local councillors, we had discussions with their officials, we spoke to the local people, after all Lein Bach was their train - the People's Little Train. Our persistence paid off and we launched a Light Railway Order Application that would have enabled us to complete the second phase of the plan by extending the line to Pont Croesor.

We knew we were late on the scene, with no rich backers, so advancement would be in incremental steps. We were realistic; we had no ambition to conquer the world. We had no wish to offend, or to do other than complement our neighbours the FR. Our organisation was elected by the membership on an annual basis. We had a definite goal about which we made no secret. We attracted individuals that preferred our more informal way of proceeding, rather than the structured and dictatorial approach of our neighbours. Relations with the FR were excellent, and we made no secret of our long-term ambitions, bearing in mind that the reality of our resource base indicated a very long and very slow approach to expansion. Many of us were Ffestiniog Society members, we were a part of that Band of Brothers restoring old railways – or so we thought.

From about 1988 onwards Alastair McNicol and myself were having discussions with Gwynedd County Council officials, which were proving to be less than satisfactory. The basic requirement was clear. For there to be any chance of the WHR ever being restored, there had to be a mechanism for settling control of the trackbed. The Official Receiver had

*This is what the WHR (P) premises on Tremadog Road looked like in the early days, when we were just getting going. The full-barrier crossing on the standard gauge is in operation, and there is some hard standing in our car park, but the shop is a temporary building and there's till a long way to go yet.* **David Allan**

made it clear that he would not sell the trackbed to us. We didn't have the funds to discharge the liabilities that went with it, and he feared that he would simply get it back. The saga became notorious within official circles as the longest running liquidation in his department's history. We had tried every way to remove his barnacle-like grip on this sole 'asset' of the bankrupt 1922 company. We even elicited support from Lord Evans of Claughton, then President of the Liberal party who wrote to him in no uncertain terms, but all to no avail. The Official Receiver was in a 'Catch 22' situation. If he performed acts of ownership on the land, then he invited claims from adjacent landowners in a host of areas. If he did nothing - and he was doing nothing - then vital parts of the route were gradually being subsumed for the purposes of access, for agriculture, for water mains, and so forth. The only protection for this was the tissue of the law that said that Adverse Possession claims could not be admitted that frustrated the statutory purpose of railway powers that still applied. However, as the years rolled on, the argument that it was still a 'railway' grew thinner and thinner, as the last train had passed in 1937, and there had been no rails since 1941. It was not possible for '64 Co. to acquire the trackbed; we had not the resources to do so. We were clearly advised that taking the 1922 Company out of receivership was not a practical option, however good an idea that may seem to be.

The discussions then were centred on Gwynedd County Council acquiring the trackbed and leasing it to us in stages as we progressed. This had been agreed at an EGM, and was clearly a practical way forward. We were trying to persuade them that this option gave everybody what they wanted - as near as can be. If the Council acquired the trackbed - and the Receiver was pleased to expedite this, as he saw clearly that such a statutory body fulfilled all his requirements of disposing of contingent liabilities - then the County Council would be free to lease us agreed sections to restore as a tourist railway. Of course there were some risks to this proposal. We were not masters in our own house, and the council was at the whim of the ever present political uncertainty, and could change its mind at any time. It was a calculated risk, but one that had a very good chance of success. Gwynedd were receptive to the idea that we should

*Russell went over to the FR Gala, in 1990, our pride and joy. She looked good, and much fun was to be had with her - see here she is at Rhiw Goch. However, all this time our hosts had been plotting to try to close us down, and no one said a word. We looked back on it when we knew just what they had been doing, can anyone blame us for being angry? Why wasn't anyone honest enough to talk it through with us first? We were no threat.*

extend from Pen y Mount to Pont Croesor as a first step. It was our hope that successful accomplishment of this part of the plan would generate subsequent stages in restoration. We were engaged in convincing them that designation of the trackbed for leisure purposes, footpath, cycle way and eventual railway, was in the public interest. We were making progress in this regard, and saw acceptance from them of the first step of taking the trackbed into public ownership, and then we sensed unwillingness.

Something was amiss. Although outwardly keen on our proposals, there was a reluctance to commit themselves, and I was becoming suspicious that there was another party involved – it wouldn't have been the first time that this had happened in our history! Somewhere in the darker recesses of my mind, I did wonder if this might have been the FR, but soon dismissed it as fantasy. One day a plain brown envelope arrived in the post, and its contents confirmed my worst fears. It was a copy of an internal County Council memo; there was no covering note, and it soon became apparent that it was a 'leak' designed to alert us to why the talks with the Council were stalling. The memo explained that at a visit from FR Co. Directors to the Council, a request had been made to prevent any 'railway developments' on the WHR trackbed. The memo confirmed that the FR had put in a counter bid for the trackbed, and said that if they were successful they would ensure that the line was not reconstructed, and requested that if the Council were successful, that they too should prevent any further development. The FR had expressed their concern that such developments would have a serious impact on their revenues, commenting "that there was only room for one railway in Porthmadog".

This innocuous brown envelope, with its devastating contents, was the detonator of everything that followed. The reaction was explosive. How could they? The fantastic Ffestiniog, that great example of volunteer railway preservation and reconstruction, whose enterprise and dogged persistence showed what could be done in the face of bureaucratic indifference and opposition. How could a railway of such accomplishment, of such dignity and standing, stoop so low? It was a blatant, covert attempt to close us down. There had been no warning, no concerns expressed about our well known ambitions. We had been brothers, united in preserving the country's railway heritage. That these people with whom I had shared my thoughts on the Great Little Trains of Wales panel, that this paragon of preservation, the company to whom we had just lent *Russell* at a celebration gala, should try to destroy the efforts of our tiny, struggling, embryo line was a betrayal of such magnitude that my faith, and indeed that of the whole company, was shattered.

The board met to discuss a response. The game had changed, the stakes raised, negotiating was not an option; we had to strike back and do it quickly. This was fratricide on a grand scale. This was our Pearl Harbour; this was war. The Ffestiniog Railway was attempting to sabotage the restoration of the Welsh Highland Railway, the project on which we had been working for over twenty years. There could be only one reaction to such an attack – an immediate counter offensive, using the only weapon at our disposal – the full glare of publicity. The board was united, and a non-attributable account was released to Emyr Williams, chief reporter in North Wales for the Liverpool Daily Post. At more or less the same time, a crowded and hushed HRA meeting in London were also given the news.

Later board meetings agreed the FR's action was designed to encourage neither negotiation nor settlement. For negotiation, we would surely have been advised long ago of their concerns. In retrospect perhaps, with the difficulty that GCC was experiencing in declaring for full restoration, a joint approach by the FR and ourselves could have been a practical proposal, but we did not see it that way at the time. So we took action to show the railway world that FR action was treacherous, dishonest, and immoral. We wanted to persuade them to withdraw their bid.

Across Christmas 1989 there was an approach to Ken Dicks our Chairman by David Pollock, the FR's General Manager who suggested that the FR might help us with our plans – but of course it was all too late. We knew what the hidden agenda was, and we neither believed them nor trusted them. The support that came flooding in was overwhelming. The reaction in the railway press was huge, and uniformly unsympathetic to the FR. Our membership had been provoked beyond reason, and the hostility generated was to last for years. The FR's miscalculation had sent the railway preservation world into a convulsion that was to last for a generation.

In the middle of all this mayhem, Ken Dicks, our thoughtful and moderate chairman, died. This was a tragedy. His calming influence, his tact, his discretion, and his ability to see all sides - these gifts were suddenly lost to us.

But now the members were angry, they made their feelings known in no uncertain terms, and the longer the FR prevaricated the angrier they became. Who could blame them, given the turn of events, but the groundswell of furious opposition took

no account of the delicate diplomacy that was necessary to encourage the FR to withdraw their bid.

We met Routly at Broadway, but he talked at us and not to us. There was never enough on offer to convince our members. There was never any contrition from the FR, not then, nor since. There was no regret, no acknowledgement that our aspirations had been dashed, our ambitions thwarted. At Broadway and after, the man who had started this mess with his ill-advised intervention blustered and waffled but made no positive proposal that would meet our goal; there was nothing that didn't seem to have some hidden agenda, real or imagined.

After the High Court, where some of what we thought would happen, did happen, we had little alternative but to go for the nuclear option of a public inquiry. This would decide trackbed ownership once and for all. The result is history, but it added insult to injury. To win the inquiry and have the Inspector's recommendations overturned by the Minister was a bitter pill. A Judicial Review was not something that we could afford, having spent the best part of £100,000 on the inquiry.

Following the loss of the trackbed, my suggestions to talk to the FR and patch up the relationship did not meet with favour from colleagues, and an ill-judged statement was put out condemning the FR in explicit terms for its interference in the affairs of another HRA member. I couldn't see that sniping would help; some attempt had to be made to put the relationship back on an even footing. Our job was to ensure that the FR rebuilt the line, and we would have exerted more influence from being inside the

*The 1942 Peckett 0-4-2T Karen runs round the train at Porthmadog, she's small but fun.*

tent than out. However this was not the majority view; vicious anti FR sentiments continued to be expressed in private and in public. I decided not to seek re-election to the Board.

The Beddgelert Inquiry came and went; I was not a part of this but was pleased when the 1998 Agreement was signed, which went some way to guarantee our place in the overall scheme. I thought things would settle down, now that we could start to build to Pont Croesor and to offer our general support. I re-joined the board, and continued with a series of meetings with Mike Hart which had started well before the 1993 Inquiry. In 1998 I was elected chairman, and continued to have very promising discussions with the new FR chairman, Michael Whitehouse. I have to say that I had a good relationship with both of them – I could never understand the argument that you had to dislike the people with whom you were in negotiation. In order to have a positive outcome, it is essential that the atmosphere between the negotiators is also positive.

I decided to retire from the board at the AGM of 2003, leaving it with FR relations restored to a sound and workmanlike level. The parties were speaking to each in convivial and constructive terms, and the ground was well prepared for solutions - or so I thought!

# Chapter 3
## Public Inquiry
## 2nd November 1993

It was almost as though the third railway mania had arrived in North Wales. Summing up after the High Court judgement, the relevant parties had deposited or applied for the following competing Orders in respect of this little railway:

1. The Pont Croesor LRO     GCC/WHR (64)Co
2. The WHR LRO     GCC/WHR (64)Co
3. The Caernarfon LRO     GCC/WHR (64)Co
4. The WHR (Transfer) LRO     FR Holdings
5. The Caernarfon LRO     FR Holdings
6. The Caernarfon LRO (No.2)     FR Holdings

1. This old Order application was for the run from Beddgelert Sidings, on to the WHR trackbed as far as Pont Croesor. (In line with GCC policy.)
2. The competing Order opposing that of the FR (4).
3. The Order for the railway from Dinas to Caernarfon, to extend the WHR to the Castle
4.. The transfer of powers from the WHR 1922 Co. to the FR Co.
5.. The FR version of the GCC Order in 3.
6. An extension Order, taking the WHR terminus back to the site of the old station in Caernarfon - an application that the GCC claimed would spoil its traffic scheme and superstore plans for the site.

Such a wealth of applications, plus a flood of objections, made quite sure that there was no way that the FR would be permitted to transfer the powers of the 1922 Co to Holdings without challenge. In the face of competing applications from the FR and the GCC for the necessary TO, the Secretary of State called for a public inquiry, and fortunately a sponsor came to the fore, with funds for FR Holdings to sustain the application.

The WHR Transfer Order public inquiry was to be held in Caernarfon on the 2nd-19th November & 16/17th December 1993. John Hopkins attended, and he carefully recorded the events, from which the account in this chapter is taken.

The inquiry was an important opportunity for those against the FR's involvement to put a stop to it. The essence of case against the FR TO application was to satisfy the Inquiry Inspector that the public interest would be best served if the GCC were to acquire the trackbed, and then to make its dispositions as it wished (as it had put on record). The Festiniog claimed that it would serve the public interest better for a railway company to acquire the powers under the Light Railways Act 1896, as upon receipt of them the FR Co. would apply for a Transport and Works Order (TWO) to restore the whole of the WHR from Dinas to Porthmadog, to

supplement those LROs applied for from Caernarfon to Dinas.

If the Inspector found against the transfer of the powers to the FR Co, then the stay on the sale of the trackbed to the County Council would be quashed. The Council would acquire the trackbed, and the FR Co. could not. Feelings therefore ran high, as there was much at stake for those in opposition to the Festiniog's application. If the TO application was lost, the FR's unwanted intervention would be decisively rejected.

Extension into Caernarfon and total WHR restoration were weaknesses to be exploited in the 'other' camp, as this was not a place where the GCC could follow easily; it was caught among a welter of conflicting statements made by elected members and officers across the years. Its disadvantage was that no binding undertaking had been given to restore the trackbed as a railway - and of course, one could hardly expect that from a county council, with its wide spread of obligations. Such promises from the FR Co. left the 64 Co. without clothes. They could hardly argue against restoration - except to say that it was they who should be doing it, and this was not an argument with any force. Instead, there was a general murmur from the forces in opposition that they did not believe the FR's promises. Of course, if the Inspector could be convinced that FR were untrustworthy in the Public Inquiry, then they would be discredited and routed by a decision against the transfer of powers.

Formal objections to the FR Co's application for a TO, of which there were 18 in all, carried common themes, that the Order conflicts with GCC plans to restore the whole railway, stifles competition, and would not be in the public interest. Of course the draft County Structure Plan was deficient in its statements, and this was seized upon. FR Mag 139 carried a Q&A piece of FR propaganda that said (extract):

*What do you think the County Council's plans are now?*
*The draft County Structure Plan says nothing about a railway from Caernarfon to Porthmadog. The railway mentions are wishy-washy, the old tale about Porthmadog to Pont Croesor and beyond towards Nantmor. This is important because it crushes any assertion by GCC that they have loyally supported the 1964 Company through thick and thin to restore the whole railway. History says otherwise. Politicians can be inconstant partners; whilst yours and their interests coincide, then all is well. A puff of political wind and all can change. It may be that the latest plan is more subtle. The GCC own the Caernarfon-Dinas-Afon Wen trackbed. They hope to protect the WHR from our ownership both by leasing the Caernarfon-Dinas to the 1964 Company and by applying for Light Railway Orders with the 1964 Com-*

## Welsh Highland Consolidation

I understand that a group of Directors of the Welsh Highland Light Railway (1964) Ltd have recently made an attempt to call for an EGM of the Festiniog Society and I would like to call your readers' attention to a few points concerning that railway and the negotiations that have taken and are taking place in the matter of the Welsh Highland trackbed. The Festiniog Railway Trust is now the major player in the current negotiations.

First however I must declare my interest since I am Chairman of Trackbed Consolidation Ltd; it is the activities of that company in the past that have made the present position possible. In my privileged position I do have the benefit of information not readily available to most observers and it is with the benefit of this information that I write.

The realisation that there is now a very real chance that we shall, within a fairly short time, see work start on the rebuilding of the Welsh Highland must bring joy to the hearts of all true narrow gauge railway enthusiasts, a group to which the great majority of FRS members must belong, and it is to the credit of the Trustees of The Festiniog Railway Trust that their actions have made this possible.

Some Society members may fear that a rebuilt Welsh Highland may attract some traffic away from the Festiniog itself and this fear is fully understandable. These pessimists should be reassured, however, by the announced plan to extend the Welsh Highland into Caernarfon and to commence rebuilding from the northern end; this will ensure that the Welsh Highland taps a new source of passengers who can be offered a journey comparable in scenic content to that offered by the Festiniog, instead of merely being taken for a ride on the Traeth Mawr.

Although the Festiniog and the Welsh Highland will be in common ownership it is planned to operate them under separate management. This will ensure that neither will ever be able to drag the other into financial difficulties and will make all forms of cooperation possible, and it is unfortunate, to say the least, that these advantages are not seen, or are ignored, by those who direct the affairs of the Welsh Highland Railway (1964) Ltd. Is it that they see their own office more important than the welfare of the Welsh Highland?

The directors of the WHLR have, for the last twelve years, done all they can to ensure that the Welsh Highland trackbed is acquired by Gwynedd County Council and this policy, coupled with the adamant refusal of the County Council to give any binding undertaking that it would preserve the trackbed for a railway, that led to the formation of Trackbed Consolidation. We are now told that the County Council promised the WHLR that it lease to it the whole of the trackbed (if it succeeds in buying it) together with that part of the old Afon Wen branch between Caernarfon and Dinas. Furthermore, a story has been put out that a package of assistance valued at £300,000 has also been promised. However this offer is by no means unconditional and some of us with long memories will recall that it is not the first tempting offer made to the WHLR by the County Council. One wonders if history will continue to repeat itself and if this offer, too, will fade like a mirage, and

if the WHLR directors will continue to be deluded.

It was because of the narrow-minded vision on the part of those in control of WHLR that Trackbed Consolidation Ltd was formed in 1983, immediately upon the conclusion of the EGM of WHLR at which members of that Company were told that they would gain early access to the trackbed if they voted in favour of the board's recommendation to support the acquisition of the trackbed by Gwynedd County Council, and that if they rejected the proposal there was no way whatsoever that access to it could be gained. Those who held differing views were not allowed to put their proposals forward for discussion at the meeting. Such was the antipathy of the WHLR board to free informed discussion that the five who became the first directors of TCL, three of whom had previously been directors of WHLR, were suspended from membership of WHR when the ruling clique realised that they had been nominated for election to the board of that Company. The suspensions were decided upon during the morning of the day the Company's next AGM was held, and news of it was notified to those concerned as they were about to enter the meeting hall. Although the matter has not been debated in accordance with the Company's articles they remain so suspended to this day.

In the light of developments since 1983 it is important to remember that the Welsh Highland Railway and WHLR (1964) Ltd are not synonymous. The lack of vision of those who control the affairs of the latter organisation is increasing the probability that they will never be the same and by their action they are doing a great disservice to WHLR members.

A perusal of the minutes of the County Council's Welsh Highland sub-committee reveals that it only meets when it is necessary to counter a proposal made to further the prospects of the railway, and such is the interest of the members of this small committee that it is not uncommon for several apologies for absence to be sent. Such is the measure of interest in the Welsh Highland in the County Council circles.

It is virtually certain that this latest move by the County Council has been made because the council fears that the FR may succeed where TCL failed. It is almost certainly hoped that the offer will swing public opinion against the FR and towards the WHLR and that as a result the FR will withdraw its plans.

So why should the County Council adopt such a strategy? A close examination of WHR accounts as published shows that the railway operation at the Beddgelert Sidings does not cover its operating expenses. Can anyone seriously believe that this line will generate sufficient funds to cross Pont Croesor, and to extend further along the Glaslyn lowlands before it reaches any worthwhile scenery? The Council clearly believes that the WHLR will fail too.

All members of the Festiniog Railway should be grateful to the Trustees of the Festiniog Railway and its management for grasping the opportunity to restore this highly scenic (and historically important) line; without their actions all other efforts would have had little chance of succeeding.

PONTEFRACT, WEST YORKS                **E.H. Preston**

*Perhaps this letter from FR Mag.138, Autumn 1992 illustrates the point about rebuttal. Of course it is meant to sting. To anyone in opposition to the FR, here is a traitor to the cause, cosying up to the tyrants. Yet the points were being made that innocence in this affair was in short supply - there was more than one side to the story. And the call for the EGM, far from hindering the FR, was a gift that rallied the disheartened!*

pany for the whole line. Of course, the 1964 Company, the ones who have made play of their unwillingness to move from Porthmadog, have been tempted by the sudden promise of the whole railway, to start at Caernarfon and divide their base. They will be faced with the immense task of restoring a 25 mile railway. They have meagre funds, a small membership and will be dependent on the GCC for Eurofunding. The restoration will take years. I do not say they cannot do it but I do say that they will be open to other sudden changes of plan by GCC who aim to own the trackbed and lease it to the restorers.

*It is said that public ownership will be the most beneficial course. What answer do you have to that?*
One of the particular lines of chat of GCC is that the line ought to be in public ownership. This does run through all they have ever said about the WHR. The real question is why they wanted to own the old WHR trackbed in the first place. Not for a railway, that would be in the draft structure plan if it had been really contemplated. I suggest they originally wanted it part for bridge re-alignment and highway improvement, part as foot and

*cycle path. And if the line had been publicly owned since it was dismantled, I have no doubt that this would have happened, and that there would be little if anything left to restore, except perhaps at the Porthmadog end.*

Also in the FRS Magazine was a reproduction of the Ffestiniog Railway's proposals to embark upon an eight million pound project to rebuild the Welsh Highland Railway. It steadily puffed the FR case for restoring the whole railway, with consequent employment benefits, park-and-ride for Caernarfon. Good stuff, it was thought, to have on record before a public inquiry. Support from the FRS was a major issue, as if they were 'against' then this would be seized upon at the inquiry.

The FR was a wonderful, tatty but proud little railway - proud of the uniqueness of the enterprise, proud of the history and continuity of this surviving gem at the edge of Wales, and tatty from having few funds to beautify the railway after the struggle to reach Blaenau Ffestiniog. Over the years its membership had grown older, and had become more conservative in attitude and outlook. So suddenly to find themselves wrenched from their comfortable roles as folk heroes, to be thrust into boiling controversy accused of being dishonest, evil, empire builders, intent on rapine, was a nasty shock - and members resented it. This was made known in a variety of ways, but mostly through wagging fingers that the WHR had brought the FR nothing but trouble last time round, and it would do the same now. There was regular comment that money raised and effort offered for the FR should on no account be expended on this foolish and risky enterprise - a sort of 'not in my name' feeling.

The situation had become difficult. High Court actions, public inquiry - these things were serious and cost big money. It may have been less of a problem had the railway press not been so critical. News of competing LRO applications, bellicose comment from the opposition, and money worries, were bringing matters to a head. There had already been dissent at FR Society AGMs, in 1991 particularly. The nervousness was concentrated upon fears that scarce FR funds would be wasted on WHR. Assurances were given at the FRS AGMs by the FR Trust and FR Company Board, that no money from the FR would be used on the Welsh Highland. The foment was eventually quelled by a combination of a lively response of refutation in written communications, the setting up of the WHR Society, the news that generous sponsorship was being made available, and the opposition reaction against the FR that went too far.

In mid-1992, on the initiative of TCL, the WHR Society was formed with a £4,000 grant from FR-WHR funds, which enabled extensive advertising until membership numbers had grown. (The first WHR Society in 1961, matured to be the 64 Co.). Its first Committee was formed from the Board of TCL: Messrs JE Ewing (Chairman), CC Lodge (Hon. Secretary), JR MacGregor, EH Preston, JE Preston and RF Preston. In September 1994, FR Co. appointed the WHR Society to be its official volunteer support body, the Cymdeithas Rheilffordd Eryri (CRhE), or (in English) the Welsh Highland Railway Society. Apparently the 'role' of official support society was offered to the 64 Co., who said that they did not want it. However, when the WHR Society was set up, and then appointed as the supporting society, this failed to find favour with a number of people who complained about it. The FR Co. was quite clear that a support society was an extremely valuable and influential resource. The first edition of Snowdon Ranger, the CRhE journal was in August 1993.

In FR Magazine 139 (Winter 92/93) there was an interesting letter from Malcolm Hindes, FRSL member and 64 Co. director, replying to the EH Preston letter opposite, and insisting that the forthcoming SGM was not a conspiracy. The irony of Ernie Preston's tale of alleged suppression by the 64 Co. caused wry amusement when compared with Malcolm Hindes' polite treatment by FRS. However he evidently did not see that the manoeuvrings of the FR had placed him in shoaling water. Yes, he was quite right about the reconstruction of the 1922 Co., but the case showed that the FR Co. meant business; the outcome was a deferral of the sale of the trackbed, and the expense was not the FR's. 'Wildly inaccurate mud' of course was plentiful all round. FRCo. needed no mandate, except from the Trust - which it had. It was difficult for a director of 64 Co. to insist on exemption from charges of conspiracy.

Fuzz Jordan, FR Society Chairman's piece in FR Magazine 140 offers the flavour of the moment (see over). Though several months before the public inquiry, it encapsulates the current feeling between the two sides, and reading it now shows how the interlocked FR Family was effective when it worked in concert. The fact that the SGM was called by a requisition that included directors of 64 Co., and that some of the signatories were

# Welsh Highland Railway

## From the Society Chairman

The FR scheme to restore the Welsh Highland seems to me to contain a great deal of good common sense. We have asked the Company to explain exactly what they intend to do and they have done so in the *Magazine*. The scheme does not risk the Ffestiniog Railway, it asks no resources from the Society, it draws on funds given specially for the purpose to the Trust. No one is asked to commit themselves who doesn't want to. It has the evident merit of starting at Caernarfon, a massive source of potential passengers. It is intended to extend in easy stages, as did the FR. The progress made has been swift and steady and the whole scheme has the promise, to me, of being successful.

It has been said before but bears repeating, that we have received assurances from the Company that NO Festiniog Railway Company money will be expended on this project; the only cash used will be that raised by the Trust or the new supporters' organisation, SPECIFICALLY for that purpose. There is no question of Festiniog Railway Company funds being used to rebuild the line. The whole idea is that the new organisation will raise its own funds for its own project.

I am sorry that the opposition are taking things badly. It seems that they have thought small, not big. Nearly thirty years of modest achievement does not seem to have fitted them for the recent rapid change of pace. It is sad that they have felt unable to join with us, despite invitations. It is sadder still that, complementing a barrage of unpleasant press comments, the '64 Company inspired action to hold a Special General Meeting. The motion is hostile to the FR Company and, I believe, is intended to play upon the guilt their press campaign has induced in some of our members. At this stage it is perhaps pertinent to quote the Chairman of the '64 Company writing to his members in their Journal,

*"For those holding sincere views contrary to the majority and unable to hold their peace there is one honourable course of action - resignation."*

The action of the '64 Company members in sponsoring a Special Meeting of the Festiniog Railway Society is in dramatic contrast to this concept.

I am happy to see a band of determined professionals, supported by the FR, backed by adequate funds, plenty of expertise and enterprise, get this railway off the ground and running because, in years to come, I think it can and will complement our own, not only by the two railways eventually being rejoined at Porthmadog but by Boston Lodge and Glanypwll both being able to bid for contracts on a commercial basis, benefitting both railways. I see the fears of risk to the FR have been well satisfied. I shall join the new Welsh Highland Railway Society for the interest and daring of the proposals and I back the enterprise of the FR in championing this cause with all the strength I can muster. I therefore urge you to come along to the Special Meeting and vote down the '64 Company's resolutions.

Fuzz Jordan

---

luminaries in the 64 Co. allowed Fuzz Jordan to comment on the 'action of 64 Co. members' playing upon the guilt their press campaign induced, and to quote the recommendation in the 64 Co. journal for dissenters to resign.

Malcolm Hindes' and his colleagues' intervention was a gift to the FR Co. The SGM resolutions were voted down. It was a PR disaster for 64 Co. who's previously cultivated 'victim' status had been so effective in rallying support. It is doubtful if it had any appreciable effect on the outcome of the public inquiry, but it immediately relieved the pressure from the FRS members - that melted away like the snow in spring.

Between the High Court hearing and the public inquiry, both main camps had to do a bit of careful positioning. The glove on the floor had indicated the requirement for the TO application by the FR Co, but of course GCC also made an application as it would be a very weak position just to oppose FR. GCC could hardly seek to acquire the trackbed and be open to charges that it wanted it only for road widening, leisure use (cycleway, footpath etc.), and only after this the eventual re-establishment of a railway over part of it. They understood consequences of the High Court outcome. Now the lid was off the WHR pot, any unfocused comments would weaken the GCC case to a point of hopelessness, as FR had announced that they were going to 'do the lot'. The GCC competing TO application needed to have a firm foundation. Thus the Council modified the Gwynedd Structure Plan, to give priority to the reconstruction of the railway. This was a rather stunning *volt face*, allegedly brought on by the FR's actions, but it strengthened GCC contention that they were the fit and proper place for the trackbed ownership, to be vested

in public hands. There was an interesting consequence of this action, that will come back into view in Chapter 5. The Snowdonia National Park Authority was obliged by law to adopt the same position in its Draft Structure Plan - and later this cost it dear.

FR Co. had applied both for a TO and for an LRO (two actually) to extend the WHR from Dinas to Caernarfon. GCC did this too - but they evidently thought the position still not robust enough to be sure of a win against FR Co. in the public inquiry. Thus GCC decided, only a week before the opening of the public inquiry into the competing Transfer Orders, that they would back the total reconstruction of the WHR themselves, via the 64 Co. Without this decision, they felt that they would have had real problems in the inquiry. For the 64 Co. it was the culmination of their dreams of thirty years. Yet their joy was muted at the realisation of just why it was that such decisions had been forced upon GCC.

The Caernarfon MP, Dafydd Wigley was brought up to date at one of his constituency surgeries in the Porthmadog Ganolfan. It was admitted that the initial FR Co. actions had been unwise, but were motivated by concerns about the threat of competition. It was explained to him that the FR was resolute in promising to restore the whole line, from Caernarfon. He listened patiently, and asked a string of perceptive questions.

His attitude suggested a local undercurrent of disapproval running in the background to which he was attuned. A public inquiry for something as obscure as a Transfer Order was difficult to understand, and the public view of the outcome did not represent the major component. No one in Porthmadog would readily offer praise to GCC, yet the combination of the FR's

## The First Public Inquiry Chronology

| | | |
|---|---|---|
| December 1991 | High Court FR Holdings | The outcome was a deferment of the sale of the trackbed by OR to GCC to allow the application for a Transfer Order for the 1922 Co. powers to go to FR Co. |
| mid 1992 | Cymdeithas Rheilffordd Eryri | Formation of CRE to be the support society to FR Co. plans for WHR |
| October 1992 | Transfer Order application | FR Trust and FR Holdings made a Transfer order application for the powers of the 1922 Co to be transferred to FR Co. |
| December 1992 | LRO application | Application for Caernarfon-Dinas LRO by FR Co. for which no public Inquiry was required |
| December 1992 | LRO Application | Extension application to Caernarfon-Dinas, from station in Caernarfon to the old station - this was contentious |
| December 1992 | Transfer Order application | GCC and 64 Co made a Transfer Order application for the powers of the 1922 Co to be transferred to GCC |
| 1st January 1993 | Transport and Works Act 1992 | This act became law, thus replacing the 1896 Act, so now LROs were replaced by TWOs, more expensive and more complex |
| 7th September 1993 | Public Inquiry Pre-meeting | This was for the Inspector and the advocates to agree procedure and the likely timescales |
| 12th October 1993 | Proofs of Evidence | All the proofs of evidence of each witness had to be submitted by this date |
| 2nd-19th November 1993 | Part 1 of Inquiry | The main body of the Inquiry with the first visit |
| 16th - 17th December 1993 | Part 2 of Inquiry | Second visit and summing up |
| 20th July 1994 | Inspector's report - Minister's decision on transfer of powers | Inspector recommends 'no' to FR Co., (4th March 1994 - private, internal) Minister not adopting Inspector's recommendation, says 'no' to GCC and 'yes' to FR Co. |
| 14th March 1995 | Transfer Order | Made for the FR Co. |
| early 1996 | Conditional grant | Millennium Commission offers FR Co. a conditional grant for Caernarfon - Rhyd-Ddu |
| April 1996 | Gwynedd Council (GC) | Major reorganisation of local government created the new council, that in July announced support for FR Co. project |
| December 1996 | Debentures transferred | GC transferred all debentures to FR Co. for a nominal sum - the aggregated holdings of 5 local authorities. FR Co. now held 99%, which made things simpler for 1922 Co. matters |
| January 1997 | WH Light Rly Ltd | FR Co. formed to carry out the construction projects |
| 27.03.97 | TWO | Application made Dinas-Port |

anonymous bid, the response of the 64 Co. to the leak, and the subsequent reports in the local and enthusiasts' press, had cast the FR as the villain. The profound silence, and absence of any counter-arguments in response to the 'buy to shut' allegations were taken as signs of guilt. When the information was revealed by 64 Co. to the local press, they eagerly fed on the controversy that had been generated. This reflected strong feeling against the FR, partly because its early inquiries remained unanswered. Despite the prosperity generated locally by FR, the disapproval was fuelled by frequent injections of anecdotal evidence from 64 Co. trying to get FR to withdraw its bid. I well remember the apprehension and guilt I felt as the FR Co's General Manager abroad in Porthmadog. There was the possibility of being verbally abused, and of any look being interpreted as one of disapproval. In fact there was no issue at all in public. Townspeople in Porthmadog were friendly and outgoing - as are North-Walians in general; extremism inhabits the shadows. Later there was a local reporter who would telephone for a quote, and then write carefully worded pieces of innuendo and negativity. But this was easy to deal with; by then the FR was the one making the news, he just never got any exclusives or prime information, but not talking was a self-defeating policy. The disapproval was to have repercussions later on with the TWO, the level crossings in Porthmadog, and the general attitude of opinion formers in the local population. It all sprang from actions in 1989.

Within the FR camp, all gave way to preparation for the impending inquiry. People's minds were taken up with an intense examination of motive and purpose. On a personal note, I was contemplating attending a conference in India about the Himalaya Darjeeling Railway. They wanted some advice and had asked various experts to attend. Historic connections with that railway evidently deemed the FR worthy, as I was invited. Just about to book and take leave, I was spotted by Mike Hart, debarred from going anywhere, and set in a corner to write loads of material for the forthcoming Inquiry. A proof of evidence, timetable, basic budget estimates, a business plan, and so forth, were needed by the FR team, to bring together in a single, credible, expert document, what consultants and various experts had said. This information was required immediately, to be checked and rechecked. It was important that the GM be seen as a reliable witness. Successor Society Chairman Fuzz Jordan got the India job instead, and he has been the DHR's staunch champion and supporter ever since.

The FR Co's Parliamentary Agents, Sharp Pritchard, recommended **Winston Roddick QC** be engaged to represent the FR case. Too late - the GCC had already engaged him. Mr Roddick was a fine advocate, and a fluent Welsh speaker. **Jeremy Sullivan QC** was recommended equally. He was nimble, amusing, an ardent railway enthusiast, and a brilliant advocate. Though, fluent Welsh speaker Winston Roddick QC was seen as something of a prize, the employment of the very English Jeremy Sullivan QC was feared as provocation of local sensibilities. This was stuff and nonsense, and showed the nervous state which the 'contra-campaign' had achieved, but FR supporters were anxious.

**Winston Roddick QC** was from Caernarfon, gained LLB and LLM at University College London, was called to the Bar in 1968, and took silk in 1986. His area of practice included public inquiries, and he had the ability to conduct himself in fluent Welsh. As a locally born expert (from Caernarfon) - he was definitely a most able, articulate and excellent champion for the opposition to FR Co. He went on to become Counsel General for the

National Assembly for Wales, and is now Winston Roddick CB QC.

**Jeremy Sullivan QC** was educated at Framlingham College and Kings College, London, where he gained LLB and LLM. He was called to the Bar in 1968, and took silk in 1982. Described as a planning lawyer in The Lawyer in 1997, he was said to be "a very effective advocate" and "absolutely brilliant in the High Court". Later Sir Jeremy Sullivan PC, he is now Rt Hon Lord Justice Sullivan PC KT, one of the Lord Justices of Appeal.

In 1993, as a consolation prize, Jeremy Sullivan QC came out for a day's entertainment on General Manager's newly arrived locomotive *Sgt Murphy*. This staunch little machine was much used to entertain friends of the FR, and Jeremy Sullivan stated that he now knew lots more about the running of the railway as a result. It was agreed that this was essential training for the rigours of a public inquiry, and only someone unrealistically sensible would call it playing trains.

Both sides needed a Parliamentary Agent, to promote and oppose legislation, to authorise the construction of transport infrastructure, etc., which is what was happening in this case. The FR Co. appointed **Sharpe Pritchard**. Michael Pritchard related with enthusiasm his firm's long association with the FR Co. They were thought to have been involved with the 1832 Act, in William IV's time, and were certainly the FR Co. agents for the 1869 Act. Such continuity was reassuring.

The GCC appointed **Sherwood & Co**. as their Parliamentary Agents. With an impeccable reputation for 'quick and accurate' work, the company was often on opposite sides to Sharpe Pritchard. The 64 Co. was fortunate indeed to have among its members the able, Welsh speaking Stephen Wiggs, billed as 'a solid choice for all infrastructure and transport matters'. Stephen is now a Partner in Winckworth, Sherwood, and at the time took a pretty dim view of the machinations of the FR Co.

The parties in opposition were formidable; the FR side were tense. Two QCs on the books indicated the possibility of a gruelling day for those called to give evidence and be cross-examined. The adversarial system was permitted, though the witnesses were not on oath.

The Inspector appointed to the inquiry was **Mr. J. A. Morgan CBE BSc.** The scope of the Inquiry was defined by the Secretary of State for Transport in the notes of the pre-meeting on 7th September 1993:

**A.** Which Applicant was most likely, and best able, to use a Transfer Order in order to pursue an application for works powers under the 1992 TWO Act.

**B.** Whether it was in the interests of competition, and

*This description is getting rather weighty, so here is an excuse to remind ourselves about railways. This is* Sgt Murphy *as he looked when pressed into service to force poor Jeremy Sullivan to endure first-hand experience of the Ffestiniog Railway in advance of his advocacy.*

hence against the public interest, that the Festiniog and Welsh Highland Railways should be owned by the same or associated company?

**C.** What was the pattern of existing land ownership, and what impact would the railway have on the environment of the Snowdonia National Park?

**D.** Whether an LRO was in the public interest. Was there evidence to show that the WHR should not be re-instated, and that neither Transfer Order should be granted?

The document made clear also that the Inspector could not hear evidence upon government policy, matters of law or claims for compensation.

A significant rider had been added by the DoT in writing to applicants, namely, that:

*"the Secretary of State is likely to be much more concerned with the relative technical and managerial competence of the applicants and in particular with their perceived ability to finance the scheme and make it a commercial success"*

It was made clear that having gained the Order, the successful applicant could then only restore the WHR after acquiring the necessary powers, by means of a successful Transport and Works Order application. Transfer of the powers of the 1922 Co. only conferred the rights to be able to acquire the assets and assume the liabilities of the trackbed from the Official Receiver. This was an area of concern, as estimates of liability had been as high as £1m. Routly was dismissive of this amount - claiming it would be far less. He was right, the extent of liabilities was eventually settled at £15k. The 1922 Company owned the trackbed, except for a very few areas where ownership had been transferred - not by Adverse Possession, as this was claimed as excluded under the statutory railway powers that had never been abandoned. Not included was any of the land upon which the 64 Co. had their short line. They were said to occupy no part of the 1922 Company trackbed. Also not included was the closed former standard gauge line from Caernarfon to Dinas. However the WHR Bryngwyn Branch and some of the Croesor Tramway were included. Title to the land did not extinguish the powers, so any parts of the trackbed, where ownership did not rest with the Official Receiver, would still hold its residual powers in the Transfer Order. To restore the railway, whoever won the transferred powers still had either to acquire title to the land, or to negotiate a lease or wayleave, in order to satisfy the requirements of the following Transport and Works Order application. All of this is written to emphasise the point that the Transfer Order application was merely the first step in a massive legislative journey that the 'winner' was obliged to negotiate. It is not surprising that the WHR had lain derelict for 70 years! However, please note the seamless join between the High Court judgement and the scope of this inquiry, as it makes it easier to understand the outcome from it. At the time this was not noticed in the FR camp, the simpler folk, immersed in the minutiae thought the procedure a large bureaucratic machine. This was not the case.

There were FR Co. board room changes before the inquiry, brought about by the wish not to subject John Routly, the Chairman of Company and Trust, to the ordeals of the cross-examination. John Routly was unwilling to relinquish his post, but the consensus was otherwise. Alas he went with ill grace, muting the well-deserved rewards for half-a-lifetime's service to the FR. It was he not Alan Pegler that was the saviour of the FR (though he was happy for Pegler to wear the laurels). John Routly brought the order and toughness to sometimes emotional and impractical notions at vital moments. He put backbone and good common sense into proposals by railway-enthusiastic colleagues, whose ideas were with the fairies. John Routly had an unrivalled 'old boys' network, and although entrenched in the 1950s way of conducting affairs, the people he knew, and what they brought to the FR was unmatched. It was John Routly who 'sorted' the Deviation legal problems, when the line above Dduallt was flooded, and it was John Routly who was unwilling to permit the threat of unregulated competition from the WHR to go unchallenged. However recent events required a new man. His successor Mike Hart, a flexible, urbane and persistent businessman, sure of the way forward, and not likely to be intimidated, now led the project with vigour.

The Inquiry was held in the Royal Hotel, Bangor Road, Caernarfon. This then ancient and rambling establishment, with deep but in places threadbare carpets and creaky floors, at that time sported the shabby gentility of a county town from years gone by. Indeed, this was the impression that the Caernarfon of recession-torn 1993 offered. It was a town run down and in need of hope. It seemed that the promise of a new railway with incoming visitors, failed to reach the public consciousness. It did later, when a stream of objectors tried to stifle its development. However the Mayor became a staunch ally.

There were seven FR Co. witnesses obliged to submit proofs of evidence to appear in front of the Inspector, to answer questions from their own advocates, and to bear cross-examination from the opposition's advocate.

**For the FR Co these 7 were:**
o Mike Hart (Chairman, FR Co.),
o Hugh Eaves (Financial Director, FR Co.),
o Andy Savage (Deputy Chairman, FR Co.),
o Mike Schumann (Director, FR Co.),
o Gordon Rushton (General Manager, FR Co.),
o Tony Smare (Volunteer on FR Co. and transport consultant)
o Jim Steer (MD, Steer, Davies & Gleave, consultants).

**For the GCC and 64 Co. there were 13:**
o Peter Marston (Chief County Planning Officer)
o TD Heald (County Treasurer)
o D Archer (Assistant National Park Officer)
o Alisdair McNicol (Chairman, WHLR 1964 Ltd)
o TW Craig (Consultant, level crossings)
o David Allan (Director, WHLR 1964 Ltd)
o P Thomason (Financial Director, WHLR 1964 Ltd)
o EA Johnson (MD, Telesis Consultants Ltd)
o JE Jones (Director, WHLR 1964 Ltd)

o David Morgan (Chairman, ARPS)
o TJ Oaks (recent PW Director, Peak Rail Plc),
o Lord Elis-Thomas (Cynefin Environmental Consultants)
o AL Sturkey (Deputy Chief Planning Officer, Dwyfor District Council)

My personal recollection is of a rather trembly pre-meeting with Jeremy Sullivan QC, who briefed us over what would happen. Our worst fears were realised. He would take us on a jolly romp of the wonderful things that were written in our proofs of evidence, happy in the knowledge that our case was indeed gold-plated and standfast. Then the savage beast of the opposing advocate would be unleashed upon us, as in a Roman Circus, for the pleasure of the masses, to flay us with stinging words, to show what miserable, deluded and mendacious, capitalist, empire building lackeys we were. Sullivan seemed full of intelligent caprice. I imagined the piercing, accusatory tones of Robespierre, and that last, fatal rattle of the tumbril, before the glittering blade struck. It was terrifying.

The Inquiry opened with the FR Co. evidence, and Jeremy Sullivan QC trying to make the case that the County, in seeking an Order, could do so only to obtain ownership of the trackbed for no other legal purpose than to facilitate the reopening of the WHR. He drew attention to evidence submitted by GCC that they wished to acquire the trackbed for other purposes, suggested that their applying for a competing order was 'copycat', and that 'public ownership' was not needed to facilitate the reopening. He asserted that the best means of reopening the WHR would be through the vigorous, expansionist and business-like approach of the FR Co. He said that light railway powers should not be conferred on a public body, precisely because there was real risk of conflict with its many other responsibilities, whereas the Ffestiniog was most likely to argue for the railway point of view, to secure the statutory objective - the re-opening of the WHR.

This all sounded splendid, as it was delivered in the flamboyant but convincing Sullivan style. There was some discomfiture showing in the body language of the other side, which gave all heart. It surely couldn't be so bad.

In the next 5½ days each witness in turn was led through their evidence by Mr Sullivan, and the first up was **Mike Hart.** He told the FR side of the story of the application so far. To me it sounded shaky, and sure enough, Winston Roddick QC in cross-examination, got straight on to the anonymous bid, secret approaches, prevention of competition and so forth. He spent the best part of a day in careful cross-examination. It seemed that the FR Co. were being marked out as shysters. There was perhaps a loss of interest when the real outcome of the High Court, and the application for the TO were exhibited as proof of FR Co. intent. The opposition sword didn't then seems so sharp.

**Hugh Eaves** followed Mike Hart, to elucidate the financial record of the Ffestiniog and its success with volunteering. The cross-examination sought to reveal that the FR Co. operated at a loss. The position of a not-for-profit enterprise sustained by volunteer support was defended.

**Andy Savage** explained: the need for really powerful locomotives, Beyer Garratts, with oil firing and suitable carriages, with complementary diesel locomotives; the challenge of the civil engineering to be met, and the suitability of the FR Co. volunteers and management to meet those challenges. The ability to restore the Ffestiniog was compared favourably with the skills needed to restore the WHR. He described how the 64 Co. had been invited to act in a supporting role, but had turned the invitation down.

Mr Roddick concentrated on the difficult crossing of the Cambrian Coast Line, Snowdon Street and the Britannia Bridge in Porthmadog, claiming that the availability of realistic solutions here was important to a credible claim by the FR to restore WHR.

**Mike Schumann** perhaps gave the most spirited and defiant rebuttal under cross-examination. He had outlined the history and achievement of his sponsorship funds, and described the financial undertakings made by himself if the FR Co. application was successful, so that the reconstruction startup phase would be rapid. It emerged, as Mr Roddick revealed in cross-examination, that a meeting with the GCC in September 1993 had been tape recorded without disclosure. FR thought this information was damaging, revealing evidence of chicanery from the GCC. A slight spat by Mike Schumann, where he suggested wilful misconstrual of the 'profitability' of a preserved railway, owned by a charitable trust, and supported by much volunteer support, led to the abrupt end of the cross-examination. We saw it was possible to best this advocate.

**Gordon Rushton**'s job was to present the business plan, and of course I little knew that this gave the opposition the smallest opportunity to counter of all of the witnesses. The cross-examination tried to discredit the high cost-base, but found no purchase on the slippery wall of expertise. There was no one in the opposition who had the FR experience on this ground. This was frustrating for them.

**Tony Smare** did a fair demolition job on the Handley Draft Report's revenue estimates. This was the report of a study commissioned by the GCC that said that the outcome from WHR was likely to be favourable, and without severe environmental impact. It would generate more visitors to Caernarfon and would be better built south, from Caernarfon. Two railways in Porthmadog would compete, and the WHR was likely to abstract 60% of the Porthmadog traffic from the Ffestiniog Railway. Tony Smare concluded that Handley (upon which much of the GCC case was based) had bad flaws in its income forecasts, whereas the FR Co. plan, backed by a study from Steer, Davies and Gleave offered more realistic estimates for restoring and running the WHR.

**Jim Steer** of Steer Davies and Gleave took the stand. He was not a person to 'mess' with, as his reputation and experience was paramount. It was his assertions, backed with estimates, that in traffic terms still hold good today. His recommendation was the opening of the line from north to south, the FR Co. proposal.

This was the last of the Ffestiniog witnesses, and the place at which clarity and understanding gradually withdrew from the proceedings for me and several others. In retrospect it wasn't as bad as was imagined, and Mike Schumann's spirited rebuttal of his cross-examination was entertaining, together with real proof of what looked like GCC shady dealings with clandestine recordings.

*The Inspector made a visit to key locations at the start of the public inquiry on 5th November 1993. Here he is in Boston Lodge, having a point explained by Andy Savage, Director FR Co.*
**John Hopkins**

How little was known of what was passing through the Inspector's mind. Both the advocates played to him - Winston Roddick QC in particular was adept in this respect - casting significant glances when a significant point was highlighted in cross-examination. It seemed to make little impression; inscrutability was everything. Yet in the Inspector's report, there were items marked down that seemed out of place, or assigned undeserved significance, whereas other points were passed over - such are the vagaries of a public inquiry. But the show was only half-way through!

The GCC gave evidence. They began with **Peter Marston**, the Chief Planning officer. He ploughed through mountains of stuff; it seemed to go on and on, as though wearing the Inquiry down through the sheer weight of the information he presented. His was a really difficult task. He was obliged to march through the entire written record of the GCC, and to outline the long history of the negotiations with the 64 Co., through which it was difficult to keep concentration. Goodness knows what it must have been like to construct as a proof of evidence. One quickly understood when listening to the evidence of the opposing side why the sharp minds of Messrs Roddick and Sullivan were necessary. One could sympathise with the plight of the 64 Co., listening to that testimony. Getting the Council to agree to anything firm on leasing a bit of WHR must have been like trying to nail jelly to a wall. First, any agreement to restore some railway was held up to facilitate road improvements, then footpaths. Then, it was leasing trackbed from Caernarfon to Rhyd Ddu, then Dinas and Betws Garmon, then Porthmadog to Pont Croesor - but, of course, it would be better in public ownership! The wickedness of the FR Co. was cited in muted and diplomatic terms - but the arrow found its mark. Astonishingly, in 1992 the resolve appeared from the WHR Sub-Committee to underline their commitment towards the railway, and there was the epiphany of June 1993, when the GCC agreed that there should be a narrow gauge railway between Caernarfon and Porthmadog. The Ffestiniog side wondered what on earth it could have been that set aside the long prevarication, and suddenly caused such purposeful, single mindedness? They knew exactly!

This commentary is not intended to be scathing, as elephants appeared in the rooms of both protagonists. However, if anyone thought that the County's comments were cant, they were perhaps positioning themselves in 'Westminster', because here in 'Wales', such a revealed attitude was considered as sensible and common sense stuff - and the FR Co. was still 'wicked'. Perhaps it was - there was more to come - but at least the County's colours were now well and truly nailed to the mast. Peter Marston agreed in cross-examination that the GCC did consider there were flaws in the draft Handley report. He also admitted to not having considered the relative merits of the 64 Co. and FR Co. cases, being convinced of the ability of the 64 Co. to rebuild the whole line - however he was not able to support his conviction with any documentation to that effect. He stated that he respected the Ffestiniog as a successful operation, and he now accepted the change of the FR Co. from opposing to supporting the WHR. However, he thought that this could easily shift back, but the GCC would support whichever operating company was successful in its application, subject to a feasible plan. (And so they did!)

**Mr D A Archer**, the Assistant National Park Officer gave evidence. As the planning authority within the National Park's boundaries, (from Betws Garmon to the crossing of the Afon Dylif) restoration was agreed as the railway was likely to have small environmental impact, and to bring reductions in road traffic. The authority would insist on a full environmental assessment before giving any planning permission, and they would be against any terminus in the Park. This was good news indeed - but these statements should be borne in mind against the next (TWO) public inquiry, where a certain shifting of minds had taken place in the intervening time.

**Mr Alisdair McNicol** gave evidence next, recounting thirty years of attempts to gain access to the trackbed, outlining that the 64 Co. was a base, with roots deep in the local community, and long-held ambition to rebuild the WHR. He described the delaying interventions by Caernarvonshire County Council. He outlined the joint application for the Pont Croesor LRO with GCC, which awaited County ownership of the trackbed, and explained the Caernarfon-Dinas and Dinas Porthmadog LRO

*Here is the Inspector on the trackbed in the Aberglaslyn Pass, 'inspecting', at the last gasp of the public inquiry on 16th December 1993*     **John Hopkins**

applications, with restoration from both ends. It was a clear, well presented explanation of the 64 Co.'s case, and merited cross-examination. Jeremy Sullivan drew out from the witness the view that 64 Co. did not say they were better than FR Co., but it was working hard to catch up. There was a small disturbance over the suitability of motive power, the lack of large locomotives for the task, and the possibility of the line being worked by diesel - sensational stuff to the railway enthusiasts maybe, but this hardly rattled the cage of the bureaucrats. Also there were some uncomfortable moments over figures which were left to the financial expertise of fellow witnesses.

**Mr T W Craig,** a level crossing specialist cited the problems in transit over the Britannia Bridge and Cambrian Line in Porthmadog, claiming massive expense to achieve it, and technical skills beyond the scope of the Festiniog Railway. The lack of parallels between main and preserved, volunteer-run, narrow gauge railways costs, offered the railway-wise FR Co. advocate some demolition pleasurable for his supporters.

**Mr J E Jones**, a recent addition to the 64 Co. Director fleet, spoke elegantly in Cymraeg, with excellent and skilled simultaneous translation, to exhibit his conviction that a partnership of public and private concerns would best achieve the revival.

**Mr T D Heald**, the County Treasurer described the two FR Co. officials, who had come to him to offer to lease the WHR trackbed to the GCC if their bid succeeded, if the Council in turn would do the same. FR supporters thought this most significant testimony, but Jeremy Sullivan did not.

**Mr Oaks**, a recent Director of Peak Rail testified that Mike Hart had told him that if the 64 Co. got the trackbed, grants and local authority subsidy may allow them to operate the WHR with a lower cost base that the FR, and that the FR involvement was necessary to forestall such competition arising. Mr Oaks endorsed the capability of the 64 Co., and warned of a conflict of interest if the FR Co. also controlled the WHR.

**Lord Elis-Thomas**, a pillar of the local community, spoke in favour of the railway for the benefit of the local economy, but it was his opinion that the trackbed should be owned by the County, and that any long-term management plan should have a strong presence by the public authority.

**Mr A L Sturkey** of Dwyfor Council revealed that the GCC had consistently opposed the reopening of the railway in its entirety, although they seemed willing to see part of it reopened, and that they were more favoured to a long distance footpath along the old railway trackbed. Again it was said that they would support which venture appeared most likely to succeed, but they were of the view that the GCC's policy was most likely to do so. Dwyfor endorsed the view that the WHR be developed from Porthmadog, with its HQ in that town.

**Mr David Allan** spoke of the differences between the 64 Co. and TCL, claiming that they had delayed the restoration operation by 10 years. The major problem was TCL's deep distrust of local authorities, a view not shared by the 64 Co. He held that the misconceived application to revive the old 1922 Company in the High Court confirmed TCL's persistent recommendations were fallacious. This was exciting testimony and he went on to describe the varying attitudes of the FR Co., from secret bids, 'buy to shut', and only now a wish to revive the whole WHR. He explained the constant willingness to talk with FR Co., and that although talks had taken place recently, no partnership had been agreed to date. He was disturbed by the recent formation of a new Welsh Highland Railway Society, with the encouragement of the FR Co., which had given rise to confusion about whether the 64 Co. was still in business. Despite the deplorable behaviour of the FR Co., the 64 Co. was still willing to co-operate on a basis of equality, but he felt that the FR Co. was simply not prepared to tolerate the existence of a competitor on its doorstep which had any degree of independence.

**Mr David Morgan**, Chairman of the ARPS recounted a sorry tale of how both organisations were members, yet the FR Co. would give no answer to a request for an explanation of its secret approaches. Mr Morgan quoted examples of the successful involvement of local authorities, which in his experience had been entirely productive. He declared himself in favour of the 64 Co. application, as having a greater degree of democratic control and links with local communities.

**Mr P Thomason**, the Financial Director of the 64 Co. recounted the financial history of the 64 Co. He outlined the method of restoration by two companies simultaneously, north and south and declared the restoration cost estimation of £9.16m was based on the Handley report, with adjustments for volunteering input.

The last witness was **Mr E A Johnson** of Telesis Consultants, who were preparing a business plan for the 64 Co. They were confident that the 64 Co. were able to undertake the larger project. They too believed that control of both railways by the FR Co. was not in the interests of future visitors.

There were a number of written submissions by various people, some having significance after the event and some not.

**TCL** entered a written submission, setting out the reasons for and the extent of their support for the FR Co. The WHR Society set out their support for Ffestiniog, describing how their membership had risen to 800 in such a short time, and how they were going to assist the rebuilding of the WHR by the FR Co. with volunteer labour.

**Mr Ian Allan,** the Chairman of the Association of Independent Railways (which unlike the ARPS, could count the FR Co. as a member, and included the 64 Co. in its membership) offered a written submission in support of the FR Co. Mr Allan banged the drum on the undesirability of county council support, with its changeable political influence. He was in favour of north to south restoration and was bold enough to point out the small amount of progress that the 64 Co. had to show for all their years of effort. He explained the pitfalls of 'democracy' and the rivet counting that followed. It was a shame that Ian Allan was not able to attend in person as his testimony was powerful stuff, and not something that a partial member of the FR Camp could say - though they thought it!

The Inspector Mr J A Morgan CBE BSc went on an inspection tour on 5th November. He was affable, interested, alert, and asked many questions, but there were no fireworks. He went on a special train on the 64 Co. and examined Pen y Mount and Gelert's Farm. He then went on the Ffestiniog to Minffordd and Boston Lodge.

On 19th November it emerged that FR was holding up the sale of the old Caernarfon Station site to a developer of a superstore. FR Co. had made an LRO application - the GCC were 'wrong footed'. The advocate for the FR Co. reserved his clients position - but it was the first example of FR Co. manoeuvres that could frustrate the until-now all-powerful GCC. The full story is in Chapter 4.

*The Inspector's visit to the 64 Co. site at Porthmadog. He advances next the loco* Russell, *flanked by a rather dapper looking Mike Schumann. The Inspector is looking attentively at everything - he didn't miss much, and evidently appreciated the 64 Co. setup from the favourable comments about democracy in his report.*
**John Hopkins**

There was a late submission of undertaking on 19th November to the Inspector from the FR Co., which was in effect a promise to rebuild the Railway, given certain provisos, like obtaining the trackbed from the OR, together with an offer to sell the land to GCC if after 5 years work has not 'substantially commenced'.

On 16th December, the penultimate day of the Inquiry, a party of a dozen representatives from the two applicants accompanied the Inspector on a tour including Dinas, Waunfawr, Bryn Gloch, Betws Garmon, Salem, Quellyn Lake, Rhyd Ddu, Aberglaslyn Pass, Nantmor, Portreuddyn Farm, and Snowdon Street, Porthmadog. It was a rather fraught day, with feelings of swords suspended on threads. This was after all the key juncture in the WHR saga. If the 64 Co. lost at this point, all they had hoped for may be at an end. If the FR Co. lost, then humiliation, ignominy and competition awaited - it was no laughing matter.

Winston Roddick QC announced in his closing submission on 17th December, a binding agreement between the GCC and the 64 Co. to lease the trackbed to them in return for undertaking to rebuild the railway within 15 years. The 64 Co., had at last got what they had always been asking for.

It is a different story when the creamy, velvety and sweet sauce of hindsight is applied. But at the time there were careful, measured assessments broadcast on all of the proceedings, often uttered in authoritative graveyard tones by many who should have known better. Observers unused to such proceedings were unable to penetrate the significance or otherwise of point and counterpoint. Only with the Inspector's Report and the Minister's judgement delivered much later could the significance of testimony be made clear.

The advocates summed up most impressively. So impressively that even the cognoscenti were unable to assess the relevance and hitting power of many of the points delivered to the Inspector. In his closing submission, Jeremy Sullivan spoke to 41 pages of notes. The basic tenor of his argument was that:

**1.** GCC accepts that public ownership of the trackbed is not essential to facilitate reconstruction.

**2.** The Council's role is an enabler, and they accept that being a landowner is not necessary to do this.

**3.** There is no compelling argument to show why GCC owning the land would enable them to do anything better that the FR Co.

**4.** The claimed advantages of Council access to grants and influence was a more uncertain bet than the FR Co.'s money which is in hand.

**5.** It was suggested that the trackbed vested in the Council would allow them to choose the railway operator. It is not part of the GCC's statutory function to do this.

**6.** There is no minute or other document setting out the reasons why GCC had decided to prefer the 64 Co. to the FR Co.

**7.** The GCC claimed to be fully committed to the entire reopening of the WHR since the mid-1970s. Mr Marston said this, yet not one elected councillor was called. The Council acts by resolution and there are no documents supporting this claim.

**8.** A fair interpretation of Council documents indicated that in fact they wished to gain control of the trackbed in 1974/5 for National Park purposes. Only in December 1992 did all the relevant committees agree in principle to the reopening - subject to a feasibility study.

**9.** The Council was not in favour of reconstruction throughout - this was the Dwyfor District Council's understanding in 1983. TCL broke away from the 64 Co. as they too believed that the accord of the 64 Co. with GCC would prevent reconstruction throughout.

**10.** If the Council minutes were a true reflection of what the Council meant by 'commitment' over the last 20 years, they provided a very clear demonstration why the trackbed should not be transferred to public ownership.

**11.** The documentary evidence emanating from the GCC confirmed the proposition that it was using the 1896 Act procedure as a device to obtain public ownership for non-railway purposes. There was no evidence that the Councillors were ever advised or considered that acquisition by Transfer Order under the 1896 Act had to be justified on light railway grounds.

**12.** There was no assessment of comparable competence between the two contenders to operate the railway. The GCC 'total confidence' in the 64 Co.'s ability appeared to be the product of long association rather than any analysis.

**13.** A comparison of the relative experience of the Festiniog Board and of the Boards of the 1964 Co's new subsidiaries was instructive. Running a short length of siding was not the same as running a railway.

**14** Notwithstanding allegations about the Festiniog's "non-democratic" character, in practice, volunteers were found at all levels in the organisation.

**15** It was clear that in 1988 there was an initial panic reaction by some highly-placed Festiniog personnel. However, it was equally clear that, as time passed, those initial fears subsided, and the Festiniog's attitude became increasingly more positive. In 1992, Festiniog saw the opportunity for starting at Caernarfon when the road scheme was informally abandoned. Mr D Allan gave them credit for that idea. It had subsequently been adopted by the 1964 Co.

**16.** Ffestiniog wished to cross the Cambrian Line and link the two railways, thus enabling through running to Blaenau Ffestiniog. This had been dismissed as a "pipe dream". Provided that the remainder of the proposals were robust, it was desirable to have such a "pipe dream" in the 1990's, just as reaching Blaenau Ffestiniog was regarded, by all save Festiniog, as a "pipe dream" in the 1960's.

Jeremy Sullivan submitted his conclusions. These were:

o The GCC and 64 Co. clearly resented the FRCo.'s recent intrusion.

o The 1896 Act was not there for the transfer to public ownership of railway land for non-railway purposes.

o It is important to distinguish between the 64 Co. desire for a short run to Pont Croesor and the FR's desire to reopen the whole railway.

o There could be no doubt that the FR Co. was the applicant best able and most likely to fulfil the statutory purpose of reopening.

o Whilst the Council had no expertise to choose between rival railway operators, both it and the District Council did have expertise as planning authorities. At this stage, no overriding environmental or other objections had been identified. It would, therefore, be right to make a Transfer Order, knowing that detailed objections may be pursued at the Works Order stage.

After this sterling performance, the FR camp all rather thought it would save time and trouble if they could just have the Transfer Order issued now. However, the might and wisdom of Winston Roddick QC was about to be unleashed on the Inspector, and he made his mark!

**1.** Firstly he came through with a vigorous and convincing rebuttal of what was a major plank of the FR case against the GCC. The written legal submission contended that it was clear that the purpose of the 1896 Act was to enhance the economic benefit of the area served, not merely to construct light railways as an end in itself. He sought to undermine the suitability and likelihood of the FR Co. as the restorers of the WHR between Dinas and Porthmadog. It would be wrong to decide for them on the basis that the FR had a rich supporter. Just because the FR was long established did not mean that starting from small beginnings (as the FR had done) should have less weight. Ability and determination was what counted, and the wider public interest should carry greater weight than the length of time the FR had been in existence. This was hard hitting stuff and was deeply appreciated by 64 Co. supporters, and it seems by the Inspector - the Winston Roddick touch was working its magic; 'good was triumphing over evil'.

**2.** The real power and control was not with the witnesses from the FR Co. side. The FR Trustees were the ones who made the decisions and they were not called as witnesses. None of the key players who made the secret bid for the trackbed were called, and it was critically important. Those persons who would implement the intention to use the Transfer Order to apply for powers to develop the trackbed have not been seen and heard. The question of likelihood needed cogent and uncontradicted evidence on this point, which had not been placed before the inquiry. Mr Roddick contended that the failure to call any Trustees was a self-inflicted wound, as it left unresolved the essential issue

*The Inspector and the unhappy band tramp the springy turf at the Beddgelert Station site. It wasn't much use trying to point score at these events. It was unclear what criteria were being applied, so one was in a state of mild terror.* **John Hopkins**

of those who controlled the applicants. It was unclear what the intentions were of those who controlled the applicants.

This strong, thrilling and frightening response brought a chill to the hearts of the FR side, and the scent of victory to the 64 Co. and GCC supporters. There was however a massive crack in this concrete! Mr Roddick was ignoring the fact that not a single elected member of GCC had appeared as a witness. Thus a similar contention applied on the other side.

**3.** However, he swept onwards to comment on the fact that Mr Steer had no relevant experience of light railways, and was late on the scene. As he was obliged to refer to a colleague; he was voicing the views and conclusions of some other persons. On the other hand Mr Johnson, for GCC looked at the matter broadly, and in sufficient detail for reliable conclusions to be drawn.

From time to time advocates overreach themselves - here was a case in point. Neither Winston Roddick, nor the Inspector evidently quite realised the likely relevance of Steer Davies and Gleave to the conclusions yet to be drawn by the Department of Transport in London.

**4.** Mr Roddick praised Mr D T Morgan of the ARPS in supporting the latent ability of the 64 Co. to restore the Railway. He then played his gifts upon the ability of the 64 Co. to use the Transfer Order to apply for works powers under the 1992 Act, and came to the recommendation that they were both fit to do so, and had the advantage that they could bring the WHR into their station. The idea of bringing the WHR through the town of Porthmadog to the FR Station was a pipe dream.

**5.** He headed into a series of points and counter points when for a time it was difficult for ordinary mortals to follow, however they were probably all telling matters, it was just that the lay audience did not understand them. However, no doubt the Inspector suitably marked his conclusions.

**6.** His final contention was that the likelihood of the FR Co. restoring the Welsh Highland Railway was dependent upon the protection of its own railway, whereas GCC had evolved its commitment in a carefully considered and well thought through manner. (Muted, derisve laughter followed at this point, as the GCC Damascene conversion was as well known as the FR one.) There was now a binding and enforceable agreement to give a 99 year lease of the trackbed to the 64 Co. The FR Co's recent undertaking was not enforceable, and could not be relied upon as other than an expression of present intentions. He submitted that it was fatally flawed. Thus the peals of thunder stilled, and the Inspector closed the Inquiry with affable thanks.

As one who was present, it was not possible at this point to achieve emotional detachment. The arguments against the FR Co. appeared to be incontrovertible. It seemed that they were destined to lose ignominiously, and that natural justice was in

favour of the GCC. Dispassionate examination of the two cases is possible now, only after studying the Inspector's Report and the Minister's Judgement. Hindsight of course now tells us that the analytical stare in Westminster is unlike anything possible locally, and that the ruling government's policies are the ones that are likely to take precedence, unless there is a particular need for a local flavour. At that time FR analysis was that the future looked bleak. To have come thus far and forced the GCC to pledge full restoration of WHR, and then to see FR ejected from the scene would have been 'from frying pan to fire', and a distinct recommendation for having let matters lie at the outset. It was a period of high risk and great unease. Yet matters were hardly different for the 64 Co.- the risk for them was high. They did not give consideration of the outcome of the inquiry finding for FR, and how as a result they could lose their self-determination.

The whole matter of the restoration of the WHR had been brought to white heat by the conflict between the FR Co. and the 64 Co. For those who were not interested in factions, but about the restoration of the WHR, then things were looking up - both parties were now committed. The WHR would be restored.

*How much better it would have been to have your railway presented to you intact, with a nice little engine standing by, with smoke coming out of the chimney. True the Tal y Llyn had lots and lots to do in the 1950s to reach the perfection seen here, but WHR was locked into a legal tangle and shorn of railway assets. TR was lucky. Tywyn: 1st September 2002*

It is worth consideration at this stage in the proceedings therefore just what would have happened if FR had not interfered. The fuss over that interference has closed everyone's eyes to the realities of it.

**1.** The Inquiry showed the equivocation of the GCC to restoration of WHR. To claim that GCC was resolved in the matter is a fiction, as Mr Marston's proof of evidence disclosed.

**2.** It must follow that had FR left all alone, then GCC would have acquired the trackbed for £1 from the OR.

**3.** Political reality would then have been most likely (not certain) to have demanded an Abandonment Order. The reason for this is that the strength of the farming constituents seeking adverse possession would have been stronger in political terms than the 64 Co.'s demand for full railway restoration.

**4.** The *quid pro quo* for this would probably have been co-operation for the 64 Co. to build to Pont Croesor, and possibly onwards to Hafod y Llyn, and perhaps Nantmor.

**5.** Time is now stretching so far into the future that probability is too wide to call that result, but although there would have been some competition with FR it would not have been very great.

**6.** Radical change was not a strong suit of the 64 Co. They had a problem in grasping opportunity, and perhaps this was because they were held back by their democratic practices. Being brutal, it allowed FR to outperform them. So their very presence pursuing their 'short term ambition' does not fill any hearts with hope that they could have surmounted the victorious adverse possession landowners and punched their way through the Aberglaslyn Pass to Beddgelert, Rhyd Ddu, Dinas and Caernarfon if GCC had gained title to the trackbed..

**7.** The Abandonment Order if made would have stymied WHR restoration. As well as the adverse possession threat, the council wanted the trackbed for road widening. At Bryn y Felin, Betws Garmon and St Helen's Rd; flattening the bridges would have made WHR restoration impossible. It is unlikely that 64 Co. pleadings could have prevented those works. Their position as lessees, and promises of advancement in exchange for compliance, would have ensured their silence.

**8.** If FR Co. had done nothing, it is alas likely that railway restoration would have been confined to a short bottom stretch. It was FR intervention that sparked off progress. The moment of glory for 64 Co. was alas Pyrrhic. The massive reaction against FR's intervention provided the fuel for a series of such determined actions that all barriers were pushed aside.

**9.** There is no doubt that the FRHoldings/TCL intervention at the High Court had a more significant role than was allocated at the time. The proposal for the reconstruction of the 1922 Co., misconceived or not was key.

**11.** The key turned because Mr Justice Vinelott held that GCC was less likely to restore a railway than FR Co. was. This got FR Co. a pause in the sale of the trackbed to GCC for £1, and the suggestion to pursue the TO option.

**12.** After the High Court Al McNicol observed with regret that the 64 Co. modest short-term ambition was being thwarted. It may have seemed that a possibility existed of co-operation between 64 Co. and FR Co., but the leak stood in the way.

**13.** The reason why 64 Co. were never able to achieve autonomous restoration in a different way, was that 64 Co. trust in FR was rock-bottom. This accounts for the extremely strong anti-FR reaction, and for the determination not to do deals with FR Co., as 64 Co. thought the FR stance was one where they didn't wish to negotiate.

**14.** In fact this hard stance by 64 Co. led FR Co. to decide to restore the whole railway itself. The strife served to keep the two sides apart, to make sure that relations were sour, and stayed sour. Perhaps 64 Co. failed to see that it was FR Co. action that forced GCC to declare the whole trackbed would be for a railway - something that 64 Co. had been unable to accomplish.

The question now remaining was the outcome of the public inquiry. Would it be for GCC, who now claimed that the whole railway would be restored - **eventually**, because of FR

intervention, or would it be for FR, the private choice?

Looking back to the 1960s, had penetrative legal minds considered a similar remedy to the WHR legal tangle, they may well have considered the reconstruction of the WHR 1922 Co. It could have been possible then. There were officers of the original company left alive, so the share transfers could have been made. It is certain that money would have been needed to purchase shares and settle the debenture holders, and then a visit to the High Court would have been needed, to take the company out of liquidation. Recent opinion has suggested that a further application for powers to restore the removed track may not have been required at that time. The track was taken away in wartime - it's just possible that putting it back may have been countenanced. Even if it had not, it would have been possible to get a Light Railway Order to do it. The vital ingredient missing in those times was money. Indeed this difficulty hampered the Festiniog Railway Society; it did not have any money. One must remember the difference in those days between railways like the Talyllyn, that were still operating (just), and the Ffestiniog, that was not long gone, and was still intact. Compare that and the state of the WHR and all is clear. The Talyllyn, Ffestiniog, and even the Welshpool offered a practical start at a reasonable price. The WHR with an unwelcoming OR, had pressing and expensive problems. There was an immediate demand for money, there was no track, no rolling stock, and no locomotives. Full restoration could not have happened in the 1960s for those very reasons.

*Russell and the Baldwin at Beddgelert Station in the 1930s. All this was soon to end. But could the track have been put back after WW2? A question that has never been answered - as no one had the money to try!* **John Keylock Collection (No.17) WHR Heritage Group**

Even as late as 1993, the elected members, and the National Park Authority, failed to perceive the potential value of tourism from tourist railways, despite the collection of successful railways that were all about them. The elected members were dedicated to agriculture; farmers were a vocal part of their electorate. Therefore it was slightly breathtaking for the FR supporters to hear in the Inquiry of the conversion of the GCC to full railway restoration. However, it was also easy for the conversion of the FR Co. to be attributed to self-interest - because that's what it was! So if the question in the Inspector's mind was to favour the perceived public interest, then the GCC should come out on top. Such a scheme surely needed a county council behind it. To approve the FR proposal needed enterprise. Years after the event, it is still difficult to weigh the various points, the Inspector's report, the Secretary of State letter, the likelihoods, the potential, and the politics. As memories of the inquiry receded, dread of the impending result grew. The answer came in July 1994.

## The Inspector's report

Inspector J.A. Morgan CBE BSc. issued his report on 20th July 1994, and accompanying it was the decision letter from the Secretary of State for Transport John MacGregor. The Inspector found in favour of the GCC . However the Inspector's finding was overturned by the SoS. The FR Co. was to have its Transfer Order, and the residual powers of the 1922 Company were to be transferred to The Festiniog Railway Company enabling it to take title to the trackbed.

The news was stunning; so stunning that I unpardonably commented to the hardworking and exultant Michael Pritchard that FR Co. would do to remember that they had in fact lost the public inquiry. I feared the repercussions of this upon the FR Co., but it was a churlish breach of good manners to make such a comment after the massive amount of work that Michael Pritchard had put in!

The Inspector's Report makes instructive reading, to find out what he thought was important and what was not. His opinion begins in his conclusions. The points weightily raised by advocates upon the 1896 Act came out best for GCC, in that the Act authorised a local authority to become involved with support as the primary motive. He accepted the abstraction of 40% traffic (Steer) and the legitimate concerns of the FR Co. to minimise such a threat, plus it was clear, in his view, that they would, if given the opportunity, rebuild the WHR with enthusiasm and dedication. The Inspector had no doubt that with the recent changing potential benefits of a railway becoming clear, the GCC's prime aim was now to ensure the WHR was fully restored. Though the 64 Co. did not yet possess the managerial and commercial experience of FRCo., it was now, in the Inspector's view, an efficient and well-managed organisation. The evidence indicated to the Inspector that each applicant wished to see the WHR rebuilt as quickly and efficiently as possible.

In the Inspector's view, the rebuilding would offer considerable, long-term benefits to the public in general. It would, however, affect a small number of local residents, who would occasionally be disturbed by passing trains.

The Inspector had already indicated that both applicants appeared to be capable of, and had the intent to rebuild the WHR, and that either could be granted the LRO. He said that Mr Allan, Chairman of AIR, concentrated on the undoubted professional and commercial expertise of FRCo. However, the Inquiry has been examining rebuilding what was a virtually derelict trackbed, rather than a functioning railway. Thus, the Inspector considered that the views expressed by the ARPS were more relevant. (*In his proof of evidence Mr David Morgan instanced successful co-operation with county councils and the greater degree of democratic control within 64 Co.*)

The Inspector recommended the application of the GCC for the following reasons:

o the support of the County, Dwyfor and the Community Councils would be a major advantage in dealing with any planning or environmental problems which might occur,

o a higher level of public grant funding would be forthcoming as a result of the involvement of GCC,

o the 64 Co.'s facilities at Porthmadog should be a considerable advantage which should be further enhanced by the support of Dwyfor,

o the 64 Co. was dedicated to the task of rebuilding the WHR whereas FRCo. had a number of other significant projects in hand which, at times, might take precedence over the WHR,

o FRCo.'s activities were controlled by a small group of shareholders, providing firm and positive control for the commercial organisation which FRCo. had now become. However, the role of volunteers would be significant in the rebuilding, and the Inspector considered that the more democratic form of control within the 64 Co. is more likely to generate the required level of volunteer support.

At this stage the partisan member would be very satisfied with a decision based on such premises - yet the SoS overturned the recommendation of his own Inspector - why? And what were the points of evidence in the Public Inquiry that caused the SoS to differ in interpretation from the Inspector? Sifting through the SoS reasons for his judgement, the points are stated clearly:

**A.** The Inspector had attached too much weight to the role of the County and other local authorities as facilitators of railway infrastructure schemes. The GCC scheme would result in direct local authority involvement and contingent liabilities, and risks being placed on the local taxpayer when, consistent with Government policy, they should be transferred to the private sector.

**B.** It was noted that the large personal financial commitment, together with the 800 WHR Society supporters pledged to restoration, would overcome the 'precedence' that the Inspector cited in his cautions.

**C.** The opinions expressed by the Inspector regarding democracy were supported by no evidence to show that the more democratic form of control within the 64 Co. was more likely to attract volunteers. The support for the 64 Co. on these grounds by the ARPS were counterbalanced by the views of the AIR, confirming from the FR Co. experience that democratic discussions amongst groups of enthusiasts was not conducive to quick decision making.

**D.** The SoS it seemed took issue over the public/private argument, suggesting that there were as many advantages as disadvantages for a private company to undertake the restoration of the WHR. The undertaking given by FR Co. saved the day, as it was cited as guarantee that if FR Co. had not started restoration within 5 years, the land would be offered to the local authority.

**E.** FR Co. have the greater proven managerial and commercial experience, and appear to be more likely to provide the strong and positive project control demanded for such a major undertaking.

With torpedo hits like that the Gwynedd County Council case could float no longer. It was a 'political' outcome, and of course that is a major factor to be taken into account when investing in a public inquiry. None of the SoS's comments found any locus with 64 Co. as they were effectively critical of their culture and methods. Both sides had been answering the inquiries by politicians to find out what the WHR was all about. There has always been an accusation that FR Co. tried to exert influence at Westminster. Indeed information has come to light that there was an intervention, but it was neither proposed nor supported by FR Co. and was perfectly proper. Who it was, what they said, and to whom must remain privileged information for the present. There was certainly an acknowledgement from FR strategists that maintaining dignity and politeness amid the flood of accusations and provocations was the wise course. It was clear that there would be no penalty for acting to mitigate competition. Competition was intended as the following words made clear from Ken Dicks 3 years previously:

*'The FR could withdraw their bid, stop meddling in our affairs and, if (as they claim) their only interest is railway preservation, and that they acknowledge that we are capable of developing a viable railway, let us get on with the job, and when we have overcome the matter and, in good time, accept us as a business competitor.'* WHR Journal No 96 in April 1990.

The Inquiry Inspector's words on this question were:

*'Adverse comment was also made regarding FR Co.'s decision to keep its bid for the track bed to the OR a private matter.........and the Inspector fully understood the concerns and subsequent actions of the directors of FR Co. in their attempts to minimise such a threat.'*

Perhaps more constructive dialogue between FR Co. and 64 Co. would have suited their own case better. However, with today's hindsight, it seems that the stormy and passionate nature of the affair was actually what got the railway rebuilt.

There was plainly someone in DoT with a profound knowledge of railway enthusiast matters. Government frequently knows more than it gets credit for. So if one applies the Westminster dimension of the time, the following interpretation comes through:

**1.** Tourist railways have helpful regional, economic effects.

**2.** FR Co. is one of the more successful and well organised tourist railways.

**3.** This government favours private enterprise - and this private organisation looks enterprising.

**4.** There's a guarantee that if it fails, the land must be handed to the local authority.

**5.** It's not costing government anything - but it may if GCC do it.

**6.** Railway privatisation was enacted on 19th January 1993 with the British Coal and British Rail (Transfer Proposals) Act 1993 So 'private' was the flavour of the time.

**7.** The Conservative majority was only 18.

Reaction to the SoS John MacGregor's ruling was mixed. He had signed the Order on the day he was replaced by Brian Mawhinney MP. This may have been something to do with Prime Minister John Major's problems with his right wing of the party, and his slim majority. The fact that it was MacGregor's last act seemed to cause adverse comment - it is difficult to see why. There seems to have been an attempt to indicate outrage at the decision. If so then it indicated a want of knowledge, as the grounds were clearly given for the SoS decision. The implications drawn from the comments are that the FR Co's 'private' status counted with this government, as did it's size and commercial acumen, and there was no evidence that 64 Co. style 'democracy' was more likely to attract volunteers.

The local press enjoyed the controversy; such stories sell papers. 'Bitter' seemed to be the word of the moment.

o  The Liverpool Daily Post reported that the Chairman of the GCC WHR Sub Committee denounced the decision as political - a strange observation from an elected councillor.

o  Caernarfon's Mayor thought it a worthwhile opportunity, which may show why there has been such consistent support for the WHR from that town.

o  David Allan of the 64 Co. was stunned - so was the FR Co.

o  There was a report that no challenge was to be made to the decision by GCC, despite bitter disappointment. Then the 64 Co. announced that it would not appeal against the decision, and expressed the view that it would be a tragic loss to the whole project if the 64 Co's talented scheme were to be sidelined, and its enthusiasm and energies dissipated.

o  Alisdair McNicol claimed in the Liverpool Daily Post that the long-term development of track would be best achieved by co-operation. He appealed for the past to be 'put behind us'.

In the Porthmadog community in general, the undoubted prosperity the FR brings to the area did not get the public acknowledgement it deserved. Indeed, whilst hosting the oldest independent railway company in the world, the first narrow gauge railway, one of Britain's most popular and well visited tourist railways, Porthmadog advertises itself with a sailing ship. It is interesting to ponder why this is so, with an activity generating some £14m to the local community at its heart. If one asks Great Men of Wales why, they offer indefinite answers, given with raised eyebrows, as though they had not noticed. In the past when there was any contention, the FR Co. kept quiet. It never took its place in the community with ostentation, and put up its supporters for election to official bodies. So perhaps, if there is regret, FR has only itself to blame. The 64 Co. made a feature of their local 'Welshness', and by natural processes the focus for CRhE and the FR/WHR are now deeply rooted within Gwynedd.

Controversy hung about the results of the public inquiry as an unwanted ghost, and it appeared again to haunt a following inquiry, and the reconstruction process - undaunted that almost all the work went to local contractors, and seemingly ignoring the potential economic benefits that the WHR would bring. It was still present on the opening day to Beddgelert in April 2009, when a group with 'white elephant' placards ignored the fact that the trains were full of Beddgelert residents.

The TO was made on 14th March 1995, the end of a process that had taken some 3¼ years. The Order when made, allowed the FR Co. to negotiate between the specified parties for the acceptance of liabilities and the title to the trackbed, and this will be dealt with later.

There was no fellow feeling between FR and 64 Co. Perhaps it was the 'buy to shut' leak that generated such distrust - it exacted a heavy price if it was. Initially 'Talks' with 64 Co. had led only to demands that FR Co. withdraw their bid. During exchanges before and during the Inquiry, there was no contingent discussion to offer 64 Co. insurance against losing. This showed a remarkable degree of 64 Co. confidence after the outcome at the High Court. So, being without insurance meant that when best laid plans went wrong the outcome was grim. Indeed so: the Broadway 'accord' was forgotten - it did not apply now, and with TO, FR Co. would go ahead and acquire title to the trackbed. David Morgan was considered to be tainted by bias; support from ARPS was viewed with disinterest. No one from FR. wished to whisper anything endearing - for them the choice really had been fundamental. Their loss would have enabled a competitor! The 64 Co. course of action to 'tough it out' now excluded them when FR policy changed from 'lease' to 'run'. The FR Co. had said that there was nothing the 64 Co. had that the FR Co. wanted. It seems possible that the 64 Co. did not believe this, and felt that they held in their hands cards that would keep them in play. Alas, it appears from what happened that they did not. Nor after such rough handling did FR believe there was any moral case.

## RHEILFFORDD FESTINIOG RAILWAY

Harbour Station Porthmadog, LL49 9NF
John Nicholson
The Green Party

05.10.93

Dear Mr Nicholson,

Thank you for your letter of 2nd October. I answer its questions directly:

**1. Where will the station be in Caernarfon?**
Ffestiniog originally applied for compulsory powers to construct the station on the North side of town, on the old BR station site. Apparently the planners wish to develop an out-of-town Hypermarket there and have been asking us to relinquish our intent. In addition there is a traffic scheme designed to occupy the railway tunnels under the town, thus the planners wish to relegate the narrow gauge railway to a strip near to the Seiont Bridge. They promise to consider moving the station back towards the town with a Wharf station when some buildings on the Seiont waterfront have been demolished.
Sites we consider suitable would be either at the tunnel mouth adjacent to the Castle, or using the old harbour offices as the station frontage. We can see some discussion will be needed to make sure that the station gets a sensible site.
**Where will the station be in Beddgelert?**
In exactly the same site as it was in old WHR days.
**Where will the station be in Porthmadog?**
This requires considerable discussion. It could be on the present WHR site [by agreement and arrangements yet to be made] it could be at the FR Harbour site [by rejoining the two railways together again]. Time must pass for the site to be decided clearly.
Access to local people for shopping is important and we look to the railway being able to offer a service in this respect. The locations best served will likely be Porthmadog, Caernarfon and Beddgelert in that order.
**2. Will the Bryngwyn Branch be reopened?**
We have no plans to reopen this branch line and have said publicly that any part of the railway not employed as a railway can be set up as a footpath. We would wish such use to be regulated and would favour the job being done by the GCC who are the footpath authority.
**3. Designs of buildings**
Care must be exercised here as the WHR used the vernacular style of `20's corrugated iron'. This may not seem appropriate today but if we were to be historically accurate this is what should be erected in many locations.
The Ffestiniog track-record of building erection and restoration is good. There are many examples of careful and painstaking work to be seen. The same care will be brought to the WHR and local materials, very much in keeping with the context of the stations will be used. Anyone who has any doubts may come to Ffestiniog and be shown a dozen examples of what we have done and are doing.
**4. The proportion of steam trains and the fuel to be used.**
The main-line service will be 100% steam for most of the year. It will make sense to use diesel in the quiet months for half the trains but since the customers like steam so much it

---

2

behoves a tourist railway to run it. There will be a service of rapid diesel trains for the walkers because part of the rationale of the railway is to persuade people to stop cluttering the National Park up with their cars.
We went over to oil fuel to safeguard the forest on the Ffestiniog. We have managed to experiment successfully with a special type of coal firing, one that does not emit sparks, which we may be able to use. The locomotives will be very powerful by narrow-gauge standards and so only coal or oil will be suitable fuels. Our record on Ffestiniog is good and looking at the forest environment of WHR and its steep gradients we shall be careful to make sure that the fuel we use is both efficient and environmentally acceptable.
**5. The ticket facilities for local people.**
On Ffestiniog we offer local people tickets at 75% reduction if they buy a `Residents' Railcard' for £4. This card lasts for 4 years. It is used for recreation and shopping and we have sold a few thousand. I would expect to extend the facility to WHR. In addition we have several weeks per year [mostly in the spring], when residents of Gwynedd and Clwyd can have a trip on the line for £1.50. These weeks are very popular.
**6. Bus/rail ticket inter-availability.**
Ffestiniog passengers can use their tickets on bus by arrangement, in emergency. Most people want to use the train, which is why they come to us. We will consider reciprocal arrangements for WHR and will be pleased to come to arrangements with the bus companies. It may be that we can arrange for bus to act as feeders to the train services, this will be fertile ground for the future.
**7. Supporters and Volunteers**
The Ffestiniog Railway Society is nearly 6000 members strong. They are interested in what is happening with the WHR. We set up a WHR Society [after inviting the 64 Company to fill that role] and now have over 800 members in it. The Ffestiniog Railway runs using some 50% of volunteer labour as well as employing up to 60 paid people. We have managed the mixed workforce with great success and intend to do this with the WHR which has no chance of succeeding without the sort of massive effort needed to propel the FR back to Blaenau. It is the volunteers that allow the Ffestiniog to look after buildings and restore the historic locomotives and rolling stock. All members get 10 free tickets per year and all can buy unlimited `75% off' travel and take a friend at this price.
**8. Design safeguards for the National Park**
We have been working hard to make sure that our railway blends in with the landscape, after all it is man-made and one cannot disguise this entirely.
We can however line the railway with dry-stone walls. We have a professional waller training our volunteers and paid staff to do this with the intent of constructing as much stone wall along the trackside as possible, as well as repairing and maintaining what we have already. We have also been at work to clad the embankments made in the 1980s with sub-soil and to seed it with the `natural' blended seed mixture which one can obtain these days. The results are very satisfying.
We have been observing a policy of cladding new buildings with cut slate blocks so that they blend in with the surroundings and of making sure that the stations have tended gardens, with the effect that we won second prize in the Wales in Bloom Competition in 1993.

---

3

We are gradually upgrading each station up the line to Blaenau and have a major plan to landscape Tanygrisiau and to improve the Blaenau Station area. The same meticulous attention to detail will be put into the WHR. The scenery it runs through is so magnificent that it would be a sin to do otherwise. We have the expertise and the sensitivity to ensure a good job is done and it will not please us at all to have a tatty railway. The impact that a narrow gauge railway can have if carried off sensitively is most helpful. We currently shift up to 2500 people a day on Ffestiniog. The same numbers translated into WHR terms could persuade 1000 or more cars to remain in car parks on the National Park periphery. A large part of our traffic on Ffestiniog is coach parties. They could be loaded at Caernarfon and picked up at Porthmadog, the main road could have the benefit of the coach instead of the narrow road through Betws Garmon and Beddgelert. Wouldn't it be a superb achievement if the WHR removed the need for the road through the Aberglaslyn to be widened?
**9. Footpaths and the WHR**
The standard gauge railway that used to run between Caernarfon and Afon Wen is wide enough for a 2ft gauge railway and a footpath/cycleway alongside. We would therefore see Lon Eifion continuing to offer the recreational facilities it does today.
In the Aberglaslyn where the railway and footpath may run together the footpath will remain. In the tunnels it will be wiser to divert around the outside. There may be a perceived lessening of the amenity here. Perhaps any loss of amenity is offset by the fact that people who walk the stretch tend to leave their cars parked somewhere inside the National Park. If they use the train the chances are their vehicles will be off the roads, outside the Park.
**10. Signalling systems**
It would be traditional to use the standard system with semaphore signals at the approaches to and in the passing stations. I suspect we shall use radio signalling and only have visible signals at Porthmadog and Caernarfon. There is no WHR equipment remaining. The Ffestiniog is now developing a traditional narrow-gauge type of signal which we will be installing on our line. We would use this for the WHR where appropriate.
I appreciate the depth and detail that your questions demand. It shows your interest in trying to make sure that if this railway is restored, whoever does it will make sure it is done creditably. No other party has shown any such interest and I salute you for it. I hope that the answers that have come through demonstrate our wish that if we restore this railway, we shall do so in a way that benefits the community, for if it does not there is little point in going on.
The Ffestiniog exists for the pleasure of those paying to travel on it and for the pleasure of those who pay to work on it. We do have ideals in this matter and they are important to us. We are not out for profit, are owned by a charitable trust, all our directors are volunteers and the money we make goes back into the railway. If you are in doubt about our methods then please come and have a look at the Ffestiniog and judge for yourself.

Yours sincerely,

*Gordon Rushton*

Gordon Rushton
General Manager

---

*There was a great deal of correspondence and discussion going on before during and after the time of the public inquiry. Of course the FR was trying to look credible, but this document is interesting, as it shows how FR were thinking nearly twenty years before the completion of WHR restoration. It shows clearly now that what FR were saying then they meant. Of course matters proceed slowly. Today the railway still does not have a permanent station in Caernarfon (2012) - but then the wharfside buildings at Caernarfon are not yet cleared either, so this is just the grindings of great matters and no reflection of feelings on any side. In the 2010 election the Green Party was still marginalised, but the inquirer received a full answer as the FR publicity machine was determined not to be lax.*

**Welsh Highland Railway Society**
**The Snowdon Ranger No. 6**
**November 1994**

### The Sixty-Four Dollar Question

As Editor I have studiously avoided more than passing comment on the difficult position of the 1964 Company and its members, dedicated to the revival at least in part of the WHR since 1961 when Bob Honychurch started the original WHRS, who now find the WHR likely to be saved in toto by a crusade of outsiders which has, without malign intent, trampled them underfoot. I think "without malign intent" is fair. I joined the old WHRS in 1961 and sent a donation, I was so keen on the idea. A response from Stanley Chadwick thanked me for my support for the project to open "part of" the Welsh Highland. This had the immediate effect of making me feel I had sent the money to the wrong people. Even if force majeure or economic rectitude meant in the end that only part of the old WHR could be opened, this kind of talk was no way to go about setting things up at the outset. Opponents to a new scheme needed to be shown a mailed fist. The decision to spend money and effort on a base in Shropshire, no matter now historic in railway terms, filled me with still deeper gloom and I resigned after a couple of years. The reigning tonality of the WHLR thereafter seemed to be timidity in action and while this happily meant that operations did not after all constitute a danger to the FR, the WHLR did seem to me to have fallen short of the grandeur of thought the Welsh Highland as a greater project seemed to demand. So my feeling about the '64 Company, whose officers and members (apart from those who are also WHRS or FRS members) are quite unknown to me, is not hostile so much as "right thought, but not enough of it". Had I remained a member, I am pretty sure I would be thinking now, "well, well, so in the end the FR pulled all the chestnuts out of the fire for us. We don't get one little slice of WHR, we get the whole shooting match, Councils, Ramblers and National Park notwithstanding. This is over the top." I might even be thinking that if the FR's grand plan fails, we are now likely to finish up with the WHR we always thought was possible and maybe more.
It is my hope that '64 Company members, if not the whole organisation itself, will feel it possible now to join with us in forming the limited-by-guarantee Society and seeing the WHR project pursued with the greatest vigour possible. All its original major opponents have been pacified or turned round and recruited to the cause. Everyone wants the Welsh Highland Railway back, and as successful as possible. It is time for a new start.

Dan Wilson

One question in people's minds was what would be the arrangement with the 64 Co. for the restoration of the WHR, now the Public Inquiry was over? Those bent on revenge, said 'none'. Those with more vision said 'Let's join forces'; Dan's wry comment made the recommendation of a new start. The period post the Inquiry was one of frustrating waiting. There was no smooth machinery that could purr into action, immediately to restore the Welsh Highland Railway in pristine condition. It appeared that the 64 Co. experienced outrage, lack of trust and anger at the result, and a pragmatic sense of reality was hard to find. With hindsight one cannot blame them, it is asking a lot to expect the hand of friendship from those in the lifeboat of the ship you just torpedoed!
The cynical within the FR Co., had worked out correctly, that if the 64 Co. sulked and sat on their hands, all that would happen was that their supporters (the more flexible ones) would move to the other side anyway! However, perhaps one reason why few of the mandarins of the 64 Co. would have anything to do with the Welsh Highland Railway Society was that the founders and Directors were the people from TCL. However, from now the FR put all their energy into restoration and bothered about nothing else but restoration. The competition threat was bested. There was now a new 25 mile railway to build.

## The Watershed

**Now there are a number of clear outcomes that settle matters for all that follows subsequently.**

**1.** The Festiniog Railway Company will now gain title to the trackbed, and must define and accept the liabilities involved. If they do not, then it will be open to the Official Receiver to reapply to the High Court to sell to GCC. This will mark the end of Part 1 of the legal tangle; the trackbed will be out of the hands of the Official Receiver, and that will place the WHR in the position of unencumbered restoration - subject to being able to gain the statutory powers to do this.

**2.** The way forward to restoring the whole WHR to Caernarfon, now lies open. The new Gwynedd Council can hardly oppose the task, as they themselves have applied to do the same. One of the potential barriers to reopening is removed - though we shall appreciate the last gasp of the Sub-Committee, loath to allow the FR to escape with no restriction.

**3.** The problems have only just begun for FR. It may have been 'fun' to suggest the radical reopening of 'the lot', but the commitment will be greater than was supposed.

**4.** The world expects the 64 Co. to be treated with courtesy and fairness. The FR will try to do this, but they will not understand the reaction they get.

**5.** FR Co. must now apply to rebuild the Railway from Dinas to Porthmadog. It cannot stall matters at this point, and fail to apply for the Transport and Works Order needed to perform this task. The pressures of the last few years, and the pronouncements and promises they have elicited have caused three things:

**i.** The FR must build the railway from Caernarfon to Dinas. This it has promised to do.

**ii.** The FR must make a TWO application for the rest.

**iii.** The 64 Co. and others are just waiting to see if the FR reneges, wavers or fails. If it does, the sky will fall in!

**6.** Realisation of the real size and scope of the project is slow to reach the outside world. Once it does there are two things that result:

**i.** There were those within FR Co. who thought that having got to this point, the opposition to bringing this railway back had largely been overcome - wrong! The battle with 64 Co. and GCC has now ended. GC will be supportive. There may be skirmishes with 64 Co. but they are tactical and no longer strategic. There is a shock to come from major objections to restoration. Perhaps WHR had been shut too long; perhaps too many people's interests are affected. Common to all opposers is the failure to see the wider benefits. Common to all proposers is to fail to anticipate the strength of opposition.

**ii..** There is also startling support for the railway - quite unlike any previous project. Not only does it get major funding, it also enjoys massive volunteer support and a huge following of donors, as well as major sponsorships.

**Read on!**

29 Medi, 1994

**HOUSE OF COMMONS**
London SW1A 0AA

Mr Rushton.
Manager
Ffestiniog Railway
Porthmadog
Gwynedd

Dear Mr Rushton,

I write to you since I feel that I have to express the very substantial volume of opinion that has been made known to me over the last few weeks, concerning the Government decision over the Welsh Highland Railway. Quite clearly, the decision by John MacGregor MP has caused a very bitter reaction, and I am afraid that it is polarising opinion in my constituency against the Ffestiniog Railway. Rightly or wrongly, you are being considered as having "nobbled" the Secretary of State and "put a boot in" on the Welsh Highland Railway Company. As you may well know by now, there is in this part of the world a strong feeling of sympathy with any underdog and the Welsh Highland Railway is getting this sympathy massively at present. Equally, I am afraid that the reputation of the Ffestiniog Railway has taken a severe knocking.

I have no idea why the Secretary of State overturned the Inspector's decision, and I realise that you will, no doubt, be pleased that he did. I think it is right that you should know, however, that this decision will not be without its consequences, and I am afraid that has done nothing in terms of public relations for Ffestiniog Railway in the area.

I don't know whether there is any way in which Ffestiniog Railway and the Welsh Highland Railway can find a workable compromise (and possibly the local authorities also) in order to ameliorate some of the bitterness that is now being felt - and expressed to me in numerous letters that I am now receiving.

Yours sincerely,

*Dafydd Wigley*

Dafydd Wigley MP.
(Caernarfon)

---

*There were accusations that the FR Co. was gerrymandering with government politicians to steamroller the local people and get what it wanted. This has always been denied. At the time, the lid had been firmly placed on saying anything at all, for fear that some awful process like Judicial Review would be mounted by fundamentalists to reverse the Minister's decision. It was made very clear that 'chatter to influence' was dangerous. However it was imagined elsewhere that preference was gained by 'behind the scenes', underhand manoeuvres. In fact the progress of everyday events drove what happened, as it was equally possible that the winner had offered the most plausible case. The Caernarfon MP, Dafydd Wigley (Plaid Cymru), was placed under considerable pressure from those against the FR Co. involvement with WHR. There had been concern expressed previously about 'buy to shut' that led to a meeting between Dafydd Wigley and the FR General Manager. Here it was explained what the FR was trying to do. Yet it seems after the TO Inquiry decision by the SoS, the pressure grew stronger. A local MP cannot ignore a clamour from constituents. What had taken place was unexpected by many, and it was the sensible and proper course to ask the FR for an explanation, clarification on what actions were proposed and a compromise settlement. The reply explains in clear terms what the FR Co. intended and why. Subsequently Dafydd Wigley MP, now Lord Wigley, became a supporter of the railway. Later his question in the House of Commons helped to prompt John Prescott's decision on the final outcome of the TWO public inquiry, that had become grounded over issues of falling rocks in the Aberglaslyn Pass. It may be that this exchange began the process of support, as what the FR said made good political and economic sense.*

## The
# Festiniog Railway Company

DRAFT

3rd October 1994

Dear Mr Wigley,

I am sorry to receive a letter from you in such terms. You were kind enough to allot us time at your surgery after we contacted you before the Inquiry. We explained then, clearly, what our policy was and have stuck to it subsequently. It was reported to us from elsewhere that you did not find it possible to support the Ffestiniog Railway's initiative over the Welsh Highland and so we thought you were somewhat against us.

As your constituency covers both Arfon and Dwyfor, you will no doubt be keen to see benefits to both Districts emanating from the restoration of the railway. There is certain to be discontent from a vocal group of supporters of the 64 Company at Porthmadog, since they have just suffered a crushing disappointment. I suggest you have identified yourself with the other side, and will naturally be the recipient of the opposing view. Of course people will say that their competitors have nobbled the arbiters, if they do not they must admit that the losing case was the weaker. With a long Parliamentary experience you are well aware of what can and cannot be achieved by lobbying. To be frank with you we were advised to leave off, otherwise it would be counter productive; we did so. The last thing ever to do is to rubbish a competitor which is why, unless stung by a particular untruth, we generally remain silent. We have expressions of relief and support from people who say that now at least they are sure that the WHR will get rebuilt, whereas previously they felt the project was beyond the conceptual powers or the means of the previous promoters.

The Ffestiniog Railway, majority owned by a charity and employing some 60 people in the neighbourhood, brings in nearly 200,000 visitors to Porthmadog annually. Some 5000 bed nights are generated from volunteers working on the line, many out of season. We co-operated with Dwyfor District in 1993 to generate some 10-12,000 visitors over the May Bank Holiday, and won an award from the Wales Tourist Board for doing so.

At the Inquiry it was clear from two consultants' reports, one adopted by the County Council as policy, that a completed WHR would take some 65% of Ffestiniog Traffic away from it. We saw that the plans advanced for the extension from Porthmadog by the 64 Company expected to employ no one, yet the consultants indicated that a main potential source of traffic would be ourselves. We could see this beforehand, and as I remember explaining to you when we met, our solution was to champion a counter scheme aimed at complementing railways rather than competing railways. The obvious place to start restoration is from Caernarfon, it desperately needs help, and a railway will be an important factor in consolidating tourism in the town. Porthmadog has a railway, arguably the most successful in Britain, certainly one known across the world. Porthmadog is a prosperous town, without the dereliction that is evident in Caernarfon. We hear opinion that tells us that it appears to want a second tourist railway, and by implication deny this to a needy neighbour. We now have the task of ensuring that in ten years or so it will get the second tourist railway, and that when it does so it will add to a healthy Ffestiniog, which all this time has been increasing jobs in order to build the new line. We were at great pains to safeguard the FR; a massive volunteers effort and much public money has gone into it over the last 40 years. Buying to shut is a negative and worthless proposal, and so we became inventive and enterprising, deciding to expand and bring to bear our whole expertise and experience in putting forward a viable scheme that will be successful. We have done this and have won the day. We now intend to deliver.

We recently met the Officers of Dwyfor to explain our plans for the restoration, to tell them that just because the railway was not starting from Porthmadog did not mean that jobs would go elsewhere, and to reassure them that our proposals for the railway included an important link to the Ffestiniog. The link opens new possibilities for tourism and by widening the scope for traffic consolidates both railways rather than forcing them to compete.

Immediately the Transfer Order decision was made known we wrote to the 64 Company, inviting them to join with us in restoring the WHR. After several meetings and much correspondence it has become apparent that they wish to retain their identity, and require us to let them build an independent railway from Porthmadog. We cannot agree to this, if only for the reason that in order to accomplish the massive task of restoring a 50 years gone railway, we have to raise in excess of ten million pounds in ten years. With such a formidable project we cannot have disparate groups, we must form a cohesive whole and put aside separate aspirations in order to work together. If we can reach agreement with them then we shall join together. I fear it will take some time for the bitterness to subside, and accusations of 'nobbling' and 'putting the boot in', given force by repetition, will extend rather than shorten the period.

The reasons why the Secretary of State overturned the decision are well publicised and available for all to see. I include a copy of the letter to the applicants. We were particularly unpopular in Blaenau Ffestiniog when we sought to restore our line taken by flooding for the power station. Now we are part of an SDS bid and looked upon as important in the fight to bring commercial life back to that place.

We are quite clear on our mission to restore the WHR, and I hope that now the decision has been made that you will support what will hopefully be the creation of another 50 jobs, the generation of some 150,000 visitors, and the large number of visiting, spending volunteers. I hope we can meet to talk over what it is we hope to do, because although there is bad feeling at present in some sectors of the community, a boon for all lies there awaiting release. I am sure you will want to know precisely what it is we propose, and how it will benefit your constituents. If you feel any merit in passing on some of the letters for us to be able to comment, then by all means feel free to do so.

Yours sincerely,

*This was the draft response. If you do not find it compelling then you will at least need to acknowledge that all that was claimed in this letter in 1994 has in effect happened. One must ask what sort of distorted information had been fed to the MP for Caernarfon? The main plank of the Festiniog argument was rather than to abstract business from the railway already at Porthmadog, the sensible way forward was to build in new business from Caernarfon, and so increase prosperity for everyone and generate jobs. Compete then becomes complement, and the FR is safeguarded. This letter is clear. It lays out the policy in a comprehensive way, possibly for the first time in a public response. However, there was still a long way to go, and much opposition to overcome.*

# The Welsh Highland Railway - Steam Narrow Gauge
## Monday to Thursday - Summer Timetable
### Caernarfon, Dinas, Rhyd-Ddu & Beddgelert to Porthmadog

| Miles | Station | | Steam | Diesel | Steam | Diesel | Steam | Diesel | Steam | Diesel | Steam | Diesel | Steam | Diesel | Steam | Diesel | Steam | Diesel |
|---|---|---|---|---|---|---|---|---|---|---|---|---|---|---|---|---|---|---|
| 0 | **Caernarfon** | | 09.00 | 09.30 | 09.45 | 10.15 | 11.00 | 11.30 | 11.45 | 12.15 | 13.00 | 13.30 | 13.45 | 14.15 | 15.00 | 15.30 | 15.45 | 16.15 |
| 3 | **Dinas** | | 09.12 | 0942 | 09.57 | 10.27 | 11.12 | 11.42 | 11.57 | 12.27 | 13.12 | 13.42 | 13.57 | 14.27 | 15.12 | 15.42 | 15.57 | 16.27 |
| 7 | **Waunfawr** | | 09.28 | | 10.15 | | 11.28 | | 12.15 | | 13.28 | | 14.15 | | 15.28 | | 16.15 | |
| 8 | B'Garmon | RQ | 09.32 | | 10.18 | | 11.32 | | 12.18 | | 13.32 | | 14.18 | | 15.32 | | 16.18 | |
| 10½ | S'Ranger | RQ | 09.41 | | 10.26 | | 11.41 | | 12.26 | | 13.41 | | 14.26 | | 15.41 | | 16.26 | |
| 12½ | **Rhyd Ddu** | a | 09.49 | | 10.33 | | 11.49 | | 12.33 | | 13.49 | | 14.33 | | 15.49 | | 16.33 | |
| | | d | 09.59 | | 10.34 | | 11.59 | | 12.34 | | 13.59 | | 14.34 | | 15.59 | | 16.34 | |
| 14 | Camp | RQ | 10.04 | | 10.39 | | 12.04 | | 12.39 | | 14.04 | | 14.39 | | 16.04 | | 16.39 | |
| 17 | **Beddgelert** | | 10.14 | | 10.49 | | 12.14 | | 12.49 | | 14.14 | | 14.49 | | 16.14 | | 16.49 | |
| 18½ | Nantmor | RQ | 10.19 | | 10.54 | | 12.19 | | 12.54 | | 14.19 | | 14.54 | | 16.19 | | 16.54 | |
| 23 | **Portreuddyn** | | 10.33 | | 11.07 | | 12.33 | | 13.07 | | 14.33 | | 15.07 | | 16.33 | | 17.07 | |
| 25 | **Porthmadog** | a | 10.39 | | 11.13 | | 12.39 | | 13.13 | | 14.39 | | 15.13 | | 16.39 | | 17.13 | |

### Porthmadog, Beddgelert, Rhyd-Ddu & Dinas to Caernarfon

| Miles | Station | | Diesel | Steam | Diesel | Steam | Diesel | Steam | Diesel | Steam | Diesel | Steam | Diesel | Steam | Diesel | Steam | Diesel | Steam |
|---|---|---|---|---|---|---|---|---|---|---|---|---|---|---|---|---|---|---|
| 0 | **Porthmadog** | | | 09.00 | | 09.45 | | 11.00 | | 11.45 | | 13.00 | | 13.45 | | 15.00 | | 15.45 |
| 2 | **Portreuddyn** | | | 09.07 | | 09.52 | | 11.07 | | 11.52 | | 13.07 | | 13.52 | | 15.07 | | 15.52 |
| 6½ | Nantmor | RQ | | 09.21 | | 10.06 | | 11.21 | | 12.06 | | 31.21 | | 14.06 | | 15.21 | | 16.06 |
| 8 | **Beddgelert** | | | 09.26 | | 10.14 | | 11.26 | | 12.14 | | 13.26 | | 14.14 | | 15.26 | | 16.14 |
| 11 | Camp | RQ | | 09.39 | | 10.27 | | 11.39 | | 12.27 | | 13.39 | | 14.27 | | 15.39 | | 16.27 |
| 12½ | **Rhyd Ddu** | a | | 09.45 | | 10.33 | | 11.45 | | 12.33 | | 13.45 | | 14.33 | | 15.45 | | 16.33 |
| | | d | | 09.55 | | 10.37 | | 11.55 | | 12.37 | | 13.55 | | 14.37 | | 15.55 | | 16.37 |
| 14½ | S'Ranger | RQ | | 10.03 | | 10.45 | | 12.03 | | 12.45 | | 14.03 | | 14.45 | | 16.03 | | 16.45 |
| 17 | B'Garmon | RQ | | 10.12 | | 1054 | | 12.10 | | 12.54 | | 14.10 | | 14.54 | | 16.10 | | 16.54 |
| 18 | **Waunfawr** | | | 10.15 | | 10.57 | | 12.15 | | 12.57 | | 14.15 | | 14.57 | | 16.15 | | 16.57 |
| 22 | **Dinas** | | 09.53 | 10.28 | 10.37 | 11.12 | 11.53 | 12.28 | 12.37 | 13.12 | 13.53 | 14.28 | 14.37 | 15.12 | 15.53 | 16.28 | 16.40 | 17.10 |
| 25 | **Caernarfon** | a | 10.05 | 10.37 | 10.49 | 11.24 | 12.05 | 12.37 | 12.49 | 13.24 | 14.05 | 14.37 | 14.49 | 15.24 | 16.05 | 16.37 | 16.52 | 17.22 |

*Note : At an average speed of 19mph to perform with 5 x 3 minute station stops this was a very ambitious undertaking!*

This was the timetable submitted at the Public Inquiry, and it is interesting to see how much of what was predicted in 1993 has come about today, nearly twenty years later.

1. The frequency of service is not attainable. A 23 minute turnround at Porthmadog is 'difficult' currently, nor will it be easy until Porthmadog Harbour Station is altered suitably. Even then it will be operationally ambitious.
2. This timetable requires 4 sets of carriages. There were not enough carriages to form three sets in 2012. Current aspirations are for a 3 train timetable.
3. Point-to-point timings, to permit a journey time of 1hr 37 minutes, have not been achieved. Although 25mph running was envisaged widely (and the locomotives are certainly capable), so far there is only one stretch likely to be authorised for this speed. This timetable required 19mph average, an that is not possible.
4. It will be possible that 5 Garratt locomotives will eventually be operational. But such a timetable also aspires to a powerful diesel as a rescue locomotive - and that was not yet a fact in 2012.
5. The station list is not what was planned in the 1990s. Portreuddyn has been replaced by Pont Coesor. Camp is known as Meillionen Halt. Betws Garmon does not have a station, but there is a halt at Plas y Nant, near to Salem. There are extra halts at Bontnewydd, between Caernarfon and Dinas, and Tryfan Jct.
6. No Dinas shuttles ever ran.

| Fact versus fiction - today's running performance ||||| 
|---|---|---|---|---|
| Miles | Stations | | 1993 | 2011 | Comment |
| 0 | **Porthmadog** | | 09.00 | 09.00 | |
| 2 | **Portreuddyn** | | 09.07 | 09.25 | Pont Croesor |
| 6½ | Nantmor | RQ | 09.21 | | Nantmor RQ |
| 8 | **Beddgelert** | | 09.26 | 10.00 | |
| 11 | Camp | RQ | 09.39 | | Meillionen Halt RQ |
| 12½ | **Rhyd-Ddu** | a | 09.45 | 10.25 | |
| | | d | 09.55 | 10.30 | |
| 14½ | S'Ranger | RQ | 10.03 | | |
| 17 | B'Garmon | RQ | 10.12 | | not open |
| 18 | **Waunfawr** | | 10.15 | 10.55 | |
| 20¼ | Tryfan Junction | RQ | | | added 2010 |
| 22 | **Dinas** | | 10.28 | 11.15 | |
| 23¼ | Bontnewydd | RQ | | | community request |
| 25 | **Caernarfon** | a | 10.37 | 11.35 | 58 mins more for the journey |

*The journey from Porthmadog to Caernarfon takes 2hrs 35 minutes in 2011, not 1 hour and 37 minutes. It is taking far longer to run throughout the WHR than was ever imagined. Is this a problem? Apparently not, as the passengers seem to love it.*

# Chapter 4
# Phase I Caernarfon-Dinas
# 1992-1997

The case in the High Court, the battering the Council witnesses received at the public inquiry, and the subsequent Ministerial decision in favour of the FR Co., later ensured a respectful audience, even from elected members. However all was not yet plain sailing. When on 20th July 1994, the Minister ruled in favour of the transfer of powers to FR Co., against the recommendations of the public inquiry Inspector, the County Council had been dispossessed of a trackbed which they had hoped they would have control over. They had originally wished it to be a green, long distance walkway, or some other public boon, road widening etc. Any right thinking persons (and of course this excludes railway enthusiasts) would consider it proper that a county council ought to be looking for the best possible amenity from a derelict railway trackbed that ran through outstanding scenery. It was not obvious that the right thing to do was to put a railway back on all of it - indeed this was not considered 'best use' by Gwynedd County Council (GCC) members and officers. The FR was now determined to create a 25 mile railway, from Caernarfon, right through the Aberglaslyn Pass, all the way to Porthmadog, and the FR had manoeuvred itself into a position where it had to do what it said it would do, as after the High Court judgement, there were many waiting to pounce if it did not. This, paradoxically, was despite the fact that the whole struggle had been started by FR to suppress competition - not to create it! The FR Co. needed to apply for new powers to reconstruct the WHR from Caernarfon to Dinas, and from Dinas to Porthmadog. Those affected would have a chance to object to these applications.

The GCC had applied for a Transfer Order, and had been manoeuvred into claiming that their intention was full railway restoration, so they could hardly object to the principle - indeed it was now in the Gwynedd Structure Plan, so there would be

*NWNG Train with 0-6-4T Beddgelert and an 0-6-4T single Fairlie, with all of the carriages, at Dinas, waiting for the 'off' with an excursion in 1893.*
© David Allan Archive - courtesy- WHR Heritage Group, John Keylock

no objection from them. The story of the TWO application appears in Chapter 5. This chapter deals with the first phase of the building, from Caernarfon to Dinas, it was a luxury project.

The railway between Bangor (Menai Bridge) and Afon Wen (Cambrian) ran through Dinas Junction, where the WHR had a station adjacent. The original railway on the patch was the horse drawn 3'6" gauge Nantlle Tramway of 1828. The standard gauge was built in replacement in 1862. There was talk of the 1877 built North Wales Narrow Gauge Railways being extended to the port, like the Nantlle, but it never was. The Porthmadog, Beddgelert and South Snowdon Railway developed similar proposals, but they came to nothing.

A second standard gauge branch left Caernarfon and swung east to Llanberis. There were two lines running under the town in tunnel. They split just before the bridge over the Afon Seiont. The Beeching cuts saw the standard gauge lines closed. The first closure in 1964, was from Caernarfon, to Llanberis and Afon Wen. The second in 1970 was from Caernarfon to Menai Bridge (though it lingered a while longer from the destruction of the Britannia Bridge). The Afon Wen line was a closure frowned upon by hindsight, as there is now talk of reinstatement from Caernarfon to Bangor. The section from Caernarfon to Bryncir was laid out as a popular foot and cycle path called Lôn Eifion in the 1980s. However the trackbed through and under the town, up to the start of the footpath under Segontium Terrace was left unused.

It was determined early by the FR Co. that the restored railway must begin at Caernarfon. It was acknowledged that the weak spot of the NWNG and WHR undertakings was that they never reached this port. Furthermore, the town had but one attraction, the brooding fortress of the Castle, courtesy of King Edward I of England. This had attracted some 400k visitors in the years surrounding the Investiture of the Prince of Wales in

*Looking down from a Castle tower, up the River Seiont at high tide. The WHR runs right, from centre-left. Below is the quay, once served by standard gauge sidings and now a 274 vehicle car park. This is an excellent place from which to start a tourist railway.*

1969. The number had fallen to the 200k mark, by 1990, and people were not staying in the town to spend their money after their visit. A restored railway would have a ready market of people to draw from, as well as providing the town with a second attraction for visitors. More importantly for the FR, there was a clear element of self-protection in the action. Consultants Scott Handley and Steer, Davies and Gleave had confirmed in separate reports that a second railway from Porthmadog would abstract considerable volumes of traffic from the FR. Therefore it made sense to build the WHR from Caernarfon, and to draw on that market, one well out of the FR's main catchment area. The theory was that as the WHR extended southwards from Caernarfon, it would bring traffic with it, growing the local market and complementing rather than competing with the FR. All of this depended on the TWO application powers being won, to allow restoration of the WHR proper, and an LRO application made to acquire powers to build the line from Caernarfon to Dinas would certainly endorse the FR Co.'s determination to honour its promise to restore the whole WHR.

Caernarfon suffered from traffic congestion, despite a relief road built through it. At that time, although the fabric of the town with the massive fortress and mediaeval streets,was potentially a major tourist trap, it was a dispiriting place that looked shabby and run down. Caernarfon was a rather large town (pop. 9,500) to have been dispossessed of its railway; other, smaller towns had not suffered such treatment. It was clear that a tourist railway from Caernarfon would be welcomed.

There was the question of where to site the terminal. The FR Co. considered that the right place would be at the old station,

on the Bangor side of the town. Here there was room to park, and it was a prime spot to catch people driving in from Bangor and from the busy A55 Expressway, about 10 minutes away by road. The WHR trains would leave the terminal to enter the old standard gauge tunnel under the town, with a halt by the Castle, and then proceed along the old standard gauge Afon Wen line trackbed to Dinas. This enlightened plan was the sort of thing the FR Co. had the confidence to propose. As a statutory company, it was not beholden to the County Council to determine this or that. The FR Co. was mindful of the way that all the effort, all the business, all the prosperity it had brought to Porthmadog and the surrounding area over the years, was seemingly ignored.

It was the leaked news that the 64 Co were preparing an LRO application for Caernarfon to Dinas with GCC, and the imminent coming into force of the Transport and Works Act on 1st Jan 1993, that spurred FR into action in mid-October 1992. The base mapping at 25 inches per mile was provided by the Council, and there wasn't time to do a proper survey of the levels, so in best railway tradition the OS bench marks on some of the bridges and four different versions of the gradient profile, together with a catch-all phrase that said the formation level would be within +/- 1m of existing ground levels, was put forward in the FR application.

In December 1992 Festiniog Railway Holdings Ltd., deposited the application for the Light Railway Order between Caernarfon and Dinas, (the Caernarfon Railway) and a second Order (the Caernarfon Railway Extension) between the Castle and the old Caernarfon station site. GCC, jointly with the 64 Co., also made their LRO application for Caernarfon Dinas. These were the last

Light Railway Orders applied for under the 1896 Act, just before the introduction of Transport and Works Orders. The question of who should withdraw one of the competing Orders obviously depended on the outcome of the Transfer Order (TO) Inquiry.

The publication of the Caernarfon to Dinas LRO applications at the end of 1992 naturally produced a string of objections from people living alongside or close to the route. These were dealt with by visiting the landowners and by correspondence, until by the end of 1996 there were only two outstanding objections. The DETR decided these did not justify a public inquiry, and they were dealt with by written submission. (In fact the Order was only finally granted about ten minutes before the first public train left Caernarfon in 1997.)

The Festiniog's action had certainly commanded attention from GCC, whilst the public inquiry cogs whirred in 1993. If they hadn't got the message from High Court and public inquiry that it was a solidly determined organisation that they were dealing with, it went home with the news of these applications.

There was a charming idea to develop the unused railway tunnels as a traffic relief road under the town. This was a cherished plan in action, much caressed by the elected members. They also wanted to develop the old station area

*The track came in from Bangor and Menai Bridge to the north, ran from the station as two separate single lines under the town (now a road), and emerged to split, the Llanberis line heading east, the Afon Wen line south, before crossing the river. The 2ft gauge now starts by the old De Winton works, is joined by the Lôn Eifion footpath, and crosses the river on a steep gradient towards Dinas. .*

The first official word FR had heard of the proposal for a superstore was when Peter Marston stood up at the closing of the Transfer Order public inquiry to say that a major investment in the town, and a £5 million pound sale of council owned land, was being jeopardised by the FR's Light Railway Order extending through to the old BR station site. The application had been made, and the best way forward for the County to get what it wanted was negotiation with the FR to have it withdrawn. There was hardly an atmosphere of cordiality between the parties during the public inquiry on the application to allow FR Holdings to transfer the statutory powers of the 1922 WHR undertaking to the FR Co. The County Council was an objector. Pragmatic as ever, the officers of the Council appeared in the negotiating room, outside the inquiry, to bargain for what they wanted. There was horse trading over the Caernarfon Railway, and despite any conflict within the public inquiry, a working relationship formed. It was obvious that the real interests of the town were well served by the proposals for a big supermarket. It was equally obvious that there was room for a station at some future date. It was clear that the Council was very much set on its relief road - practical or not in the FR's eyes. The Council was willing to facilitate an

and its environs as a superstore - one boon conspicuous by its absence in the area. This was most sensible, a commercial winner; the tunnel was not such good value - a park and ride railway could have been better. The reason for their attention was that the application for the Caernarfon Railway Extension LRO by the Festiniog, would wreck the relief road proposal, and cause major problems to their commercial plans for the superstore. The FR Extension LRO was therefore highly undesirable in GCC eyes.

The FR Co. had got wind of the tunnel proposals only at the last minute before the application went in, which is why the LRO was split, as although FR Co wanted to terminate at the old Caernarfon Station site, they were being cautious in case there was anything in the rumour about development. Or was there a touch of mischief by FR?

alternative. There was also room for a temporary terminus at the Castle, as additional to the double-track formation, there had been a standard gauge headshunt in a vital spot, thus permitting a narrow gauge platform, run round loop, headshunt, space for a temporary booking office, and a small car park. The GCC asked the FR Co. to withdraw the Caernarfon Railway Extension LRO application, for the section of line in tunnel under the town to the old Station site. Mindful that the GCC had been placed in a position where FR Co. were now being 'asked', that prevarication by FR Co. could be seen as obstructing a boon for the town, and that a difficult appeals process (likely to be lost) would be the result of further FR bulldozing, their 'request' was agreed. FRH undertook not to pursue the extension order, unless the supermarket proposal came to nothing. The Caernarfon Railway

Extension Order application was dropped. After the TO outcome the (new) GC withdrew its Dinas - Caernarfon LRO and the FR. first Order went forward, to be made on 9th October 1997. In the meantime, construction of the new Safeways supermarket went ahead, as did the conversion of the unused railway tunnel into a relief road.

The good will of the Council over relocating the Lôn Eifion footpath and cycle way was valuable, as were their good offices elsewhere with the highway authorities and matters of planning with landowners etc. The support of a local authority is essential in matters of this kind, and a working arrangement was forged. The change in attitude with FR had a marked effect on what happened later, when the WHR proper came to be restored. It was clear from the start that working with FR Co. was perfectly straightforward, reasonable, and practical.

Although a temporary station for the WHR was envisaged, it was plain where railway enthusiasts would have liked the proper terminal to be. The old Harbour Master's building, now the HQ of the Harbour Trust, has ' Large Narrow Gauge Terminal Station' writ large upon it. It is a superb official looking, limestone, single-storey, Victorian building of exceptionally fine appearance. Behind is a row of back-to-back, outwards facing artisan buildings, that look rather past their sell-by date. The imagined station is drawn into the map below. However it would probably make more sense was the line to cross St Helen's Road and run along a cleared Seiont Quay to a station. Perhaps at a time in the future, a magnificent station in Caernarfon will be constructed that can cope with full-length WHR trains. However, for the moment, the temporary station has become the resting point for the budding world class railway attraction in Wales. It has the fault that the platforms are too short. A little more length can be obtained by eliminating the small car park, and there is car parking space, with capacity for 274 vehicles along the quayside in front of the Castle. If the

current site is to remain permanently, then a bit of innovation would allow it to prosper, as the town centre is nearby, above the station, and a mezzanine floor with entry to the main square, Y Maes, via Segontium Terrace is a possible 'connective' prospect, but the story digresses.

There were quite lengthy periods between 1993 and 1996, where not very much happened, except planning and talking. It can be seen from the chronology that all went quiet after the public inquiry, whilst its outcome was awaited. There was speculation; there were talks with the GCC over Caernarfon to Dinas, but there was precious little money to spend in pursuit of anything.

Mike Hart and Mike Schumann made an initial visit to the closed railway to Donnybrook and the Alfred County Railway at Port Shepstone, South Africa, to see what equipment was available. Phil Girdlestone, a man with FR ancestry, was managing the engineering operation there. Mike Hart negotiated a provisional order for two overhauled NGG16 Beyer-Garratt locomotives, some wagons and much track materials. Once the Transfer Order was determined, a firm order was placed for the two Garratts, Nos 138 and 143, which were paid for outright by FR Co directors. The initial 14km of track materials were paid for using a loan from Mike Schumann, and George Nissen, also an FR Co director. These loans were subsequently converted into gifts. Mike Hart found and negotiated with Pretoria Portland Cement Ltd for the acquisition of the three Funkey diesels from Port Elizabeth. This was an opportunistic and excellent unplanned purchase at very short notice. Mike says he could have floated them out on the beer consumed with the representatives whilst negotiating the contract for sale. Their purchase and transport was paid from WHR funds, although one was intended principally for use on the FR. (Loco details - Chapter 9).

The period until the outcome of the public inquiry was one of

*Can anyone one see the astonishing merit of this as the WHR narrow gauge terminus? There is a motley collection of buildings behind that have been listed by CADW, when the land could be developed as a magnificent terminus for everyone's prosperity. Mind you, there would be the matter of asking the Harbour Trust to bless such a proposal first! But it is nice to dream.*

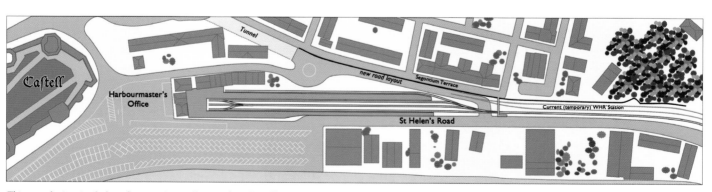

*This was the inspired place for a station in Caernarfon. Equally, it could be on the Seiont Quayside, in a more convenient location with a lot more space, subject to the clearance of the current vacant buildings along the wharf. If ever there was to be an act of faith in the tourist industry in Caernarfon, then a splendid Caernarfon terminal station would be the right statement! It would a crowing glory to a new world attraction.*

## Phase 1 Chronology

| | | |
|---|---|---|
| December 1992 | Caernarfon Railway and Caernarfon Rly Extension LRO applications. | The first was for Caernarfon-Dinas, the second thru' the tunnel to the old BR station site. |
| 17.12.93 | End of the first Public Inquiry | This was for the Transfer Order of the residuary powers from the WHR 1922 Co. to FR Co. |
| 20.07.94 | Inspector's report the Minister's decides | The Inspector said 'no', The Minister said 'yes' |
| 14.03.95 | Transfer Order | The Transfer Order was made on this date. |
| April 1995 | K1 went on display at Y Maes in Caernarfon | Support for the new railway began to appear |
| May 1995 | The Millennium Commission conditional offer. | The MC offered £4.3m - 45% of the cost of project, Caernarfon-Rhy-Ddu |
| June 1995 | Planning Application to GCC | The planning application was made for Caernarfon-Dinas |
| November - December 1995 | Public Consultation | Meetings to reveal the plans for reinstatement of WHR, Dinas Porthmadog, before the TWO application |
| July 1996 | Caernarfon Festival | Funkey 2, overhauled and on Y Maes, named *Castell Caernarfon* by Dafydd Wigley MP |
| mid-1996 | Lease for Caernarfon-Dinas | £999 for 999 years, signed in early 1997 |
| mid-1996 | Dinas Station site | GCC Ceng. moved out, WHR moved on to site, purchase was completed in December 1996 |
| Sep 1996 | Rail arrives | 1,300 tons by March 1997 |
| Sep 1996 | Wagons arrive | SAR hi-sided bogie wagons |
| Oct 1996 | ERDF Grant | Offered £735k to match the Millennium Fund |
| Dec 1996 | Contract let for construction | John Mowlem PLC, Cardiff, £750k |
| 28.12.96 | WHR/CRE staff working on site | At Dinas to recover materials from buildings about to be demolished |
| 06.01.97 | Mowlem start work | |
| 02.10.97 | HMRI inspection | There was a snagging list, but OK for trial running until 30th November |
| 04.10.97 | CRE AGM | Trial running with *Mountaineer*, No. 138 and 5 Winson carriages |
| 09.10.97 | LRO comes into force | The Caernarfon Railway LRO is made on this date |
| 11&12.10.97 | Unadvertised service begins | |
| 13.10.97 | Opening of Caernarfon-Dinas | Performed by Mrs Mair Williams, Lady Mayoress of Caernarfon. |
| 14.10.97 | Public service begins | Ran until winter closedown on 2nd November |

waiting with a fear and ominous dread. If the decision was against FR, then the initiative would be lost and FR would be defeated. Decision day on 20th July 1994 came without warning. As soon as the news became known, there was immediate action at Harbour Station, with the embodiment of well laid plans to move the project forward, although there was dismay at Gelert's Farm. FR now received the freedom to act as it thought fit in pursuit of its strategy. The enormity of the task was becoming apparent, which is why the action had to be immediate.

The next problem for the Caernarfon-Dinas project was to secure the route with a lease, to find the funds to do the job, and to set up a base. The old Dinas station site was occupied by the County Council, Civil Engineer. The old engine shed and works site was owned by the Environment Agency (The National Rivers Authority). Both were persuaded to relinquish their sites, GCC for £175k, the Environment Agency for £80k, buildings included. In the old Dinas yards and station there was the vital storage space needed for materials, as well as the room for the fan of sidings needed for construction and operation.

After the TO announcement, on 20th July 1994, the boring interregnum was made more palatable by the allocation of a part of Minffordd yard as staging post for material purchased for WHR, to be brought to the FR yard to be processed. Several thousand sleepers arrived, together with good quality baseplates, Pandrol clips, and screws. All were surplus from the Channel Tunnel construction railway. Some 30k of the Pandrol clips were bagged, and all the sleepers needed to have their baseplates removed from them. This was the sort of work that keen supporters needed, to show their devotion and determination. During those days it was difficult for some people to stop smiling - and for some occasionally to break out laughing. Cedric Lodge and his colleagues from TCL were central to the FR's renaissance of the whole railway. He worked off his years and years of frustration and unpleasant happenings in Minffordd Yard, safe in the knowledge that some time soon, he would see his precious WHR come back from the dead. No wonder Cedric was a happy man; what pride it gave people to be able to see their efforts translated directly into rescuing the railway - as a result productivity was excellent. Things must have been buzzing, as there was a FR Health and Safety directive that a supervisor must be in attendance at Minffordd Yard when people were working!

Representatives from FR/WHR and 64 Co. met on 4th April 1995, to talk about co-operation. The meeting was encouraging; it was the second of a series planned. A joint announcement was made that was full of hope. The proposed Memorandum of Agreement had (only) 5 numbered paragraphs, and two additional points (and that's always good). It was a pity that the 64 Co. were not persuaded to 'throw in their lot' with the project. Perhaps out of a lack of trust, they wished to remain autonomous. FR Co. saw the only way to succeed with such a big project, was for everyone to join firmly in one purposeful whole. It was impractical to have more than one receiving body for grant funding, and FR Co. were not going to start a railway from Porthmadog, having come so far in the struggle that was by no means won.

The strength of the 64 Co. aspiration encouraged them to propose to build independently, from their base at Gelert's Farm Porthmadog, to Pont Croesor. There was a view held by a small circle of people that if enough pressure was put on FR they would be more likely to concede, to a build out from Pen y Mount, at least to Pont Croesor, and then perhaps beyond. Indeed it was diplomacy by David Allan that succeeded in this regard, but not

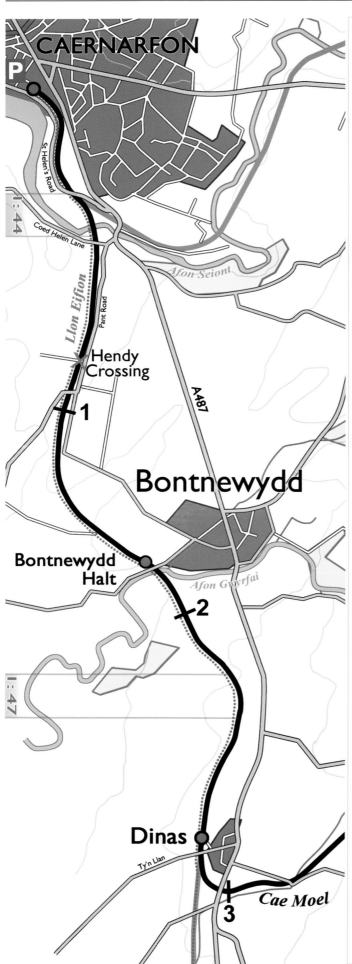

## CAERNARFON TO DINAS - CHARACTERISTICS

Caernarfon to Dinas had been a standard gauge railway with a generous trackbed, laid double through the Caernarfon WHR station site. There was not much significant earth moving work required, as the GCC had created the Lôn Eifion, long distance cycle path throughout the entire length of Phase 1, and had thus 'smoothed the way'. From time to time the old Nantlle Tramway trackbed crosses the formation. The cycle path was moved over to the west of the railway all the way. A gradient begins immediately upon leaving the platform at Caernarfon Station,steepening to a sharp 1:44 over the Afon Seiont. The road junction across the Seiont Bridge was comprehensively rebuilt, fortunately with the GCC co-operation; the way was eased for the WHR and the Lôn Eifion footpath and cycleway.

Hefty gradients on the pull out of Caernarfon ease after the river bridge, and once the old junction with the abandoned tracked to Llanberis is left behind, and the Coed Helen Lane crosses, the course of the line has next an OLC at Hendy Crossing. This minor road level crossing has the unfortunate layout of butting right on to a 'T' junction. This is always potentially awkward for railway level crossings, and it is avoided wherever possible. Not here alas, and the only way the risk assessment would work was for the train to be required to stop, blow the whistle, and if the road was clear, to proceed across at caution. This restriction has since been eased, to allow the passage of trains at 5mph.

The first milepost is passed just after Hendy, and there are a number of accommodation crossings here that occasionally spawn tractors, and call for a fair bit of whistling from locomotives. The line gradually emerges on to embankment at Bontnewydd Halt (opened in 1999) where trains tend to stop rarely. The short, three-span, stone viaduct over the road and the Afon Gwyrfai is now crossed before reaching milepost 2. There are more bridges over this particular river later on in the journey, and some of those had their moments - this is the first and it was solid. Remedial work was necessary to this viaduct, but it was not onerous.

This line was built for standard gauge; Garratts were easily accommodated. The work on this stretch was to: clear the line of vegetation; to reinstate the drainage, repair the infrastructure, lay and compact the ballast bed, and lastly, to lay the track. The first parts were performed by Mowlem. The track was laid by staff with volunteer input, as a precursor to the feats of volunteer tracklaying that grew ten years into the future.

The course of the line curves gently towards the station at Dinas, with dense tree cover on either side. Dinas was chosen as the main depot for the WHR as the space was available. The WHR had terminated here, and the goods yard was bought back from the GCC. A fan of sidings was laid in, a two platform station was recreated from what was there before, and the formation curved east, to join with the original NWNG trackbed. The old loco shed and carriage shed, were bought from Welsh Water and the carriage shed was converted for locos, the old locoshed became a workshop. These first 3 miles became the WHR restoration 'test' railway. When Phase 2 began it did so from where the new track joins the old formation, outside the engine shed, and the line curves sharply to run under the A487 road and to resume its original course.

Note: Actually the WHR is said to be a metric railway, but it is perhaps a somewhat unwilling convert, as no one seems yet able to bring themselves to read speed limits in k/mh or quote boiler pressures in Bar. We shall leave them to their illusions and use miles.

*Dinas yard at the end of Phase 4 has gone back to looking a bit like it did before work started! Watch this space!*

until 1998.

The search for funds to relieve the sponsor, and to get Caernarfon-Dinas built, led to the Millennium Fund, set up by the Conservatives to celebrate the event, and later embraced by New Labour. In short they took to the idea of the WHR restoration. Initial talks were favourable, and led to an offer of a grant of £4.3m in May 1995. It unlocked the application for funds from other bodies like European Regional Development Fund (ERDF). The full story of that and the money involved is covered in Chapter 12.

There had been the move by the GCC Light Railway Sub-Committee in 1994-5, to make the GCC, Caernarfon-Dinas lease contingent upon FR Co. offering the reciprocal arrangement for Pen y Mount to Pont Croesor. This did not advance the Memorandum of Agreement, and if the lease conditions recommended were insisted upon, FR could claim that the judgement of the High Court and the decision of the Secretary of State were being frustrated. Matters moved on when in 1995 the Sub-Committee had made a resolution as follows:

*RESOLVED In the light of the obvious threat to the sum of £4.3 million from the Millennium Fund, that we authorise the County Valuer to lease the land from Caernarfon to Dinas to the Festiniog Railway Company on condition that they use their best endeavours to enable the Welsh Highland Light Railway (1964) Company to build the railway between Porthmadog and Pont Croesor at the earliest opportunity.*

This had been in discussion since a first resolution in November 1994. FR Co. reaction to this was that the such a

condition was unacceptable. The question of the arrangements for 'best endeavours' between FR Co. and 64 Co. was something properly to be left to the companies to settle themselves.

There was a local government reorganisation in Wales in 1996, and the GCC became a unitary authority, the GC, that took Merioneth and Caernarfon council areas under one roof in Caernarfon.

The likelihood of funds allowed the planning application to be made for Caernarfon-Dinas on June 16th 1995, but as the new GC was being formed, understandably process was delayed and planning permission wasn't given until 7th June 1996.

The lease of the trackbed was agreed in principle in mid-1996, with no caveats. It was signed on 19th May 1997, and registered on 19th June 1997, for 999 years lease at £1 per year. The lease divided the responsibilities for the trackbed. The FR Co. took on liability for all underline bridges and the central and eastern fence lines, whilst GCC took responsibility for all overbridges, the major retaining walls in Caernarfon and the western fence line.

In summary we have the following progress by the end of 1996:

**1.** A lease for Caernarfon to Dinas is on offer.
**2.** The Millennium Fund has made a funding offer.
**3.** The LRO stands, and may now be made.
**4.** Planning has been applied for.
**5.** A new unitary authority is in place - GC
**6.** Agreement with 64 Co. is between FR Co. and 64 Co., with no outside influence.

It was now possible for the construction of the section between Caernarfon and Dinas to begin.

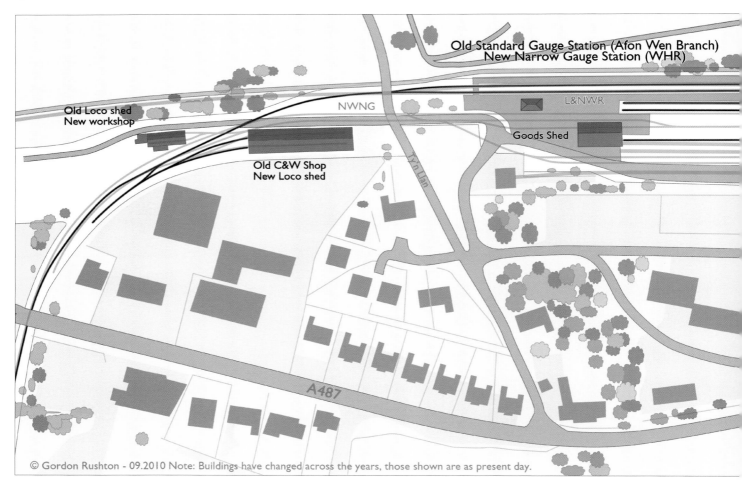

*Caernarfon is cramped, and so the operating base for the northern end is Dinas. The yard was a store for materials needed to build the railway, and a space to lay things out. Red overlay shows approximately where the old NWNG/WHR narrow gauge tracks ran. The green overlay is where the L&NWR standard gauge tracks lay. The plan is not to scale, but it gives an idea of what Dinas used to be like in the old days, and how it has been reconfigured to 'face' Caernarfon today.*

## Construction

The K1, Tasmanian Garratt was liberated from York Museum (NRM) and came to the old station site in Caernarfon on 28th April 1995, and for two days on display at Y Maes in Caernarfon. Still in its works grey livery, it went to Minffordd Yard, to star at an FR Gala, to be celebrated, and then to go to Tyseley on 21st June 1995, to begin its restoration. Its appearance stoked the fires of enthusiasm, and advertised to the greater world that WHR was to be rebuilt, with a new and exciting project. Considerable interest was generated from this exercise..

The ERDF grant came through in October 1996, with sponsorship covering cash flow demands until grant money began to flow. By the middle of 1996 the Dinas station site had become vacant after its purchase. Two major shipments of track and track components from the lifted Umzinto - Donnybrook

*Funkey 2 also went on display at Y Maes in Caernarfon in July 1996 and was named Castell Caernarfon by Dafydd Wigley MP for Caernarfon.* **Ben Fisher's Website**

line in Natal, South Africa, came in from the Docks at Immingham. Some 700 tons was delivered in September, and a further 500 tons came in November. In broad terms, this 1200 tons of 60lb per yard rail and sleepers, offered about 9 miles (14km) of single track. There was certainly enough in the stacks to lay Caernarfon to Dinas.

The first rolling stock arrived. There were 9, high-sided, vacuum brake fitted, bogie wagons, which had been used as convenient containers for track fittings during demolition of the Donnybrook line. As far as the South Africans were concerned, these wagons were scrap. Mike Hart had been pleased to arrange for their use as convenient containers for sending all the components across to UK. They were an absolute Godsend, and were adopted at once, and remain still, both running around in traffic as bicycle wagons, and dotted in odd places holding various bits and pieces

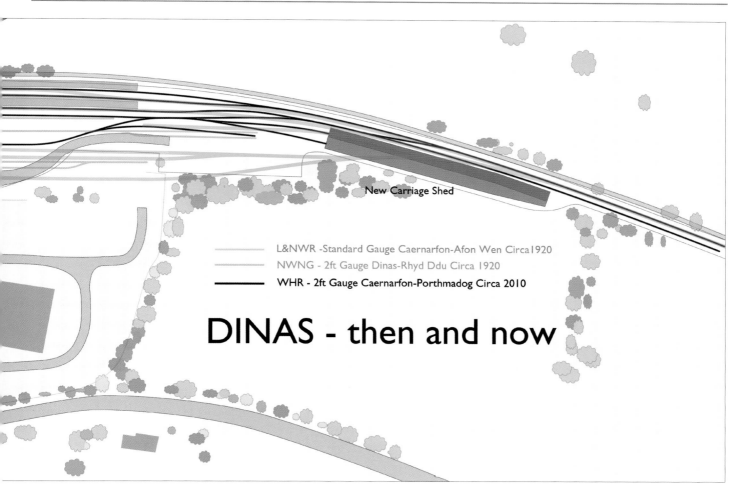

New Carriage Shed

L&NWR -Standard Gauge Caernarfon-Afon Wen Circa1920
NWNG - 2ft Gauge Dinas-Rhyd Ddu Circa 1920
**WHR - 2ft Gauge Caernarfon-Porthmadog Circa 2010**

# DINAS - then and now

of valuable kit. Another shipment of 300 tons of rail reached Dinas in March 1997.

In July 1996, Funkey 2 went to the annual Gwyl Caernarfon Festival. It was named by Daffydd Wigley MP, *Castell Caernarfon*. and speeches were made by Messrs Wigley and Hart to launch the construction project. A shop was rented on the Maes as an information centre, and the glossy, bilingual brochure produced for TWO consultation in 1995 was much to the fore. The intention was being broadcast 'in clear' that the whole of the WHR was earmarked for restoration, and that Caernarfon-Dinas was just the beginning. The October 1996 ERDF announcement was the last link in the chain to permit construction to go ahead. In order better to facilitate construction, and to maintain separation, Welsh Highland Light Railway Ltd (WHLR) had been set up as a subsidiary of FR Holdings Ltd, to

*Left: The surprise arrival of these wagons as boxes for the bits was deeply welcome, as they were fully functioning vehicles - and there weren't any of those. They were put to work, and have been in use ever since, a wonderful gift.* **Clive Briscoe**

*Below: It was sad that to get this stack of rail shown here at Immingham Dock, the wonderful railway from Umzinto to Donnybrook in Natal was sacrificed - but the rail could have gone into the electric arc furnace as scrap, and be a Japanese bread-bin by now, instead of hosting locomotives that used to run over it, in a new setting in Wales. So one person's tragedy is another's fortune. Here was the railway we always wanted in kit form, waiting to be laid. What a wonderful piece of good fortune.* **Clive Briscoe**

act as the legal entity for the reconstruction of the WHR. As soon as the Dinas station area became vacant in 1996, temporary office buildings were set up, and a project team was gradually assembled. Roland Doyle, a Ffestiniog stalwart, restorer of the locomotives *Palmerston* and *Taliesin*, and former Senior Broadcast Engineer of the BBC at Bangor, was appointed as General Manager. Roland's approach to project direction, made him able to manage the multi-directional tasks that arrived in ever increasing numbers for this job.

There was emerging some real railway construction to be done. Those for whom restoring the railway was the longed for aim, moved to the CRhE camp. Those who found union unbearable, held on to the Gelert's Farm culture, and five numbered paragraphs were not enough to prevent the drift apart, and the continuation of hostilities. Those who simply couldn't work together with the mostly 'new' people who formed the CRhE, fell out of the main restoration effort. Of course there were those within the FR camp who really disliked the WHR restoration, and all it stood for. At first the notoriety caused by all the squabbling was their complaint. Then the oft raised accusation resurfaced that reviving the WHR would encourage a rerun of the financial disasters of the 1930s. Even when it became obvious in later years that FR was not losing traffic to WHR, there was a rump of the disgruntled, who would take no pleasure in it, refused to volunteer on it, and they growled disparagingly about it at every turn.

The Welsh Highland Railway Society - Cymdeithas Rheilffordd Eryri (CRhE), had organised themselves into sections of responsibility for the construction work, but the timescale required in which to build the WHR, meant that volunteers could not immediately provide the resources for the effort needed to achieve the full construction to meet that timescale. This was disappointing, bearing in mind the time and skills they had put in, however as the project developed, volunteers found a major place in tracklaying. This was fortuitous, and corresponded well with the skills and time that volunteers could offer. Their expertise grew to such a level that their contribution in every phase of the forthcoming reconstruction was substantial.

*The start of proceedings - high jinks at Dinas, 15th February 1997.* **Eddie Bellas**

*The bridge carrying Coed Helen Lane, with a weak deck. This stout new steel frame does the business. To see the old one, look at the picture section later.* **Ben Fisher**

So, with a view to getting a rapid start, Symonds Travis Morgan based in Colwyn Bay, with whom WHLR was already working under Mike Schumann's direction, sought a contractor for a design and build contract for Caernarfon to Dinas. John Mowlem & Co were awarded the contract, and they appointed Parkman as their detail design consultants for Phase 1.

Over Christmas, 1996 volunteers, led by Cedric Lodge, removed valuable materials from the Dinas North yard, before Mowlem entered the site on January 6th 1997, and their demolition contractor came in to clear the site of the unwanted, brick and steel sheds.

The Funkey diesel *Castell Caernarfon* was delivered by the FR to Dinas on January 14th, and on the 15th there was a press event to call attention to the start of construction. Obviously *Castell Caernarfon* itself was not what was needed to build the railway - it was too big to do the sort of work required from the beginning, and confined itself to minor duties until there was some sensible railway to run on. The WHR is said to have been built by the FR's Planet diesel, *Upnor Castle*, but it was not available until August, as it needed a new motor. The little Hunslet, *Harold* was lent from Boston Lodge in July, as a stand-by, returning to the FR after *Upnor Castle* arrived to take up its duties. Later on the ancient Simplex, *The Colonel,* spent some time at Dinas pottering round as a shunter.

Mowlem needed to clear, fence, refurbish and ready the three miles of railway, to prepare the formation for tracklaying, and to create stations at Caernarfon and Dinas, (Bontnewydd was built and opened in 1999). Once Mowlem's were in, they refused entry to the volunteers, on the grounds of safety risk, and unnecessary hazard to their very tight programme. Although the work was perhaps easier than that of later Phases, since there was a wide formation left over from the standard gauge line that had closed in the 1960s, there was much to be done. The vegetation had to be cleared. The railway route needed to be securely fenced, and for the first three miles the formation was to be shared with the 12½ mile Lôn Eifion cycle path. It was closed for the duration of the contract whilst it was being relocated between Caernarfon and Dinas. (It reopened in July 1997). At Dinas, the cycle path continues on the old standard gauge formation to Afon Wen as far as Bryncir, whereas the WHR turns left on to its own formation towards Waunfawr.

The drainage arrangements needed renewal where necessary; North Wales is not known for its arid climate. The wide formation offered generous access for machines to get in and do the work. The railway from Caernarfon to Afon Wen had been built with bridges for double track, but a lot of the earthworks were on the narrow side in places, and there was an unstable section near to the yet to be built Bontnewydd Halt. There was also spoil to take away, left over from old BR ballast. Clearing the formation for the new railway and widening it out to accommodate the cycle way produced a vast pile of unusable soft material contaminated with Japanese Knotweed, which was left buried deep under a pile, where the formation was wider as a result of the original Nantlle tramway route being straightened.

*If the road scheme had happened much before the WHR got going, this bridge, St Helen's Rd., would have posed great problems!*    **Ben Fisher**

Fortunately for the timing of this project, there were major roadworks on the approaches to Caernarfon that led to the building of a bridge across the formation at St Helen's Road. The 64 Co., had already done some work on lobbying for a rail opening here, but as the bridge had not been designed by the time that WHLR came on the scene, it was possible to specify the width and height and alignment of the opening, to allow Garratts to operate. Other bridge work included the strengthening and waterproofing of two river bridges, Pont Seiont and the three span Bontnewydd Viaduct, over the river Gwyrfai. The bridge carrying Coed Helen Lane had a weak deck that was supported by a steel prop that obstructed the railway alignment. A new one was fitted that offered the required clearance for narrow gauge trains to pass under.

At Dinas Station the wise decision was taken to ignore the old layout, orienting the new to work to Caernarfon. Tracks were laid in the former standard gauge loop, and the platforms were made 195m long, a little in advance of that necessary for the early trains - but then the WHR was looking ahead. The old NWNG yard was cleared, to allow a large materials stacking area, and sidings were laid, including one into the old goods shed. A 12 car carriage

*This big three span viaduct is plainly a standard gauge structure. It carries the railway over a minor road and the Afon Gwyrfai, a waterway to be crossed four times along the restored line of the WHR.*    **Ben Fisher**

shed was erected at the Caernarfon end, and beyond the bridge crossed by Ty'n Llan at the south end, the old NWNG locomotive shed was adapted as a workshop. Opposite, half of the building occupied by the Environment Agency/Gwynedd River Board, on the site of the former carriage shed, was adapted for use as a locomotive shed, with the capacity for two Garratts, and a stores area. Opposite, the old loco shed was converted for use as a workshop and store. The two NWNG railway buildings remaining on the Dinas Station site are now back in railway use. The former station building in particular had suffered from modifications since the railway closed in 1936, and this was restored to one of its many original states, including turned slate ridge stones. The WHR Heritage Group restored the interior of the former waiting room.

The new plan was for the restored formation to make a sharp left turn after Ty'n Llan road bridge, passing through the old standard gauge arch to regain the original NWNG formation. The limit of the new railway from Caernarfon was the bridge under the A487 road to Pwllheli and Porthmadog. The owners of the Y Mount pub on the other side of the road had filled in the deep cutting beyond the road, and were using it as a car park extension. Mike Schumann and myself went to meet them, to airily tell them of the news about the railway's reinstatement. Nothing in any way harsh was said, nor anything very definite; it was got across that we would be most grateful to have our railway back please. At that stage they seemed to accept it - at least there were no recriminations.

There was enough completed formation to start track laying in the Easter of 1997, but Mowlem were still on site as the principal contractor, and did not want 'extra' tasks slowing them down. They were unused to enthusiastic volunteers, many unaccustomed to the way of the construction site. It became obvious that a process was needed to allow volunteers on site with Mowlem's blessing. Roland Doyle arranged a site induction course on behalf of the Railway's own Welsh Highland Light Railway Ltd, (WHLR), who became the principal contractor, so that Mowlem could handle the safety risk. Mowlem completed by July 1997, though discussions over the 'final account' continued on for about a year. However, the work had gone to a local enterprise, and this began a trend that continued throughout the project.

Much second hand equipment had been stored in the north yard: South African rail (in various stages of wear), steel sleepers and fastenings, and baseplates for wooden sleepers. Some 80 or so lengths of track came over ready assembled, but it was found out that prefabricated track is not so easy to lay, yet when some of the trackbed towards Caernarfon became available for track laying, in May 1997, a piece of highly innovative thinking indicated that a bit of mechanisation was needed, better to handle the track panels. A massive, rail-mounted gantry that came to be known as 'The Forth Bridge' was ordered from Winson Engineering of Daventry. The idea was simple enough; prefabricated track panels were loaded on to a pair of wagons behind the massive machine; a travelling gantry

*Dinas car shed 2010 empty, as the vehicles are all out in service. The extension of secure storage like this useful. This is one of the priorities for the Phase 5 Appeal, keeping the carriages under cover protects from weather \and vandalism*

lifted them and laid them in front, on the ground. Obviously something on the large scale was needed, and this grand piece of plant took a while to be constructed in Daventry to the drawing supplied. In the meantime, inventive minds were still running. Little rail mounted trucks with lifting tongs were devised, so that a pair of loose rails could be recovered from 'ready use' in the two-foot, suspended between a pair trucks, and then pushed to the railhead. The rails were off-loaded at the railhead on to rollers, to be advanced and then bolted in place on the steel sleepers, laid out in anticipation. The simple and effective devices became known as the Roland's Rail Mover, or RRM. They had a spring loaded, skid brake, so that if the people pushing should lose control, the brakes would be applied immediately upon letting go of the brake lever. Users were trained always to push these loaded RRMs, and were warned most strictly never to ride on them.

'The Forth Bridge' was delivered to Dinas, and it looked

impressive. It was the sort of machine that would give confidence if you had to lay 2ft gauge tracks across the Nullarbor Plain in Australia. It was loaded up with track panels for a try. When the first track panel was lifted ready, and started on its traverse through the gantry, a loud clunking noise of steel on steel rang out. The first sleeper of the panel hit the gantry's front girder support on both sides. The machine's success as a tracklayer depended on the smooth transit of the suspended track panel, out from under the gantry, to be laid on the formation in front of it. If the panel failed to fit through the columns then the machine was set for a limited future. Faces were pink, but it was evidently the fault of Winson Engineering. They politely pointed out that the machine conformed exactly to the drawing they had been supplied; so it wasn't the fault of Winson Engineering. Further investigation revealed that it was the sleepers to blame. It turned out that SAR made two types of two-foot gauge steel sleepers. WHR had the longer variety, but the drawing was supplied for the shorter ones. The staff struggled to use the machine by passing the track panels through the gantry, tilted over at an angle. The next result was the discovery that time saved by using the Forth Bridge, rather than assembling the track panels in situ with RRMs, unless the track was straight, or nearly straight, was marginal. After laying all the pre-assembled track panels delivered, the gantry was not used again, but was placed

**Above:** *The Forth Bridge stands new in Dinas Yard, hungry for action, and looking mean and fit for purpose. Alas this was not to be.*

**Both Photographs: Ben Fisher**

**Left:** *One of the snags with this machine is immediately apparent. If it's wider than the sleeper ends, then getting past it in places of tight clearance might be a problem - not one that will be apparent between Caernarfon and Dinas. The text above tells more.*

in a corner of Dinas yard and spoken about in whispers. There was no culvert large enough to need an underslung truss, so denied a second career as a bridge, it just stood there, becoming less yellow. Many years later, at the beginning of Phase 4, when steel prices were high, the Forth Bridge was cut up as scrap, and credited against a new rail loading gantry. On the other hand, the process of laying track, accelerated by means of the Roland Rail Movers to the point eventually where the volunteer gangs could put track down at great speed. Because the RRMs were simple, they were also relatively cheap to produce, and thus it was possible to fabricate enough of them to enable track laying to be undertaken at several locations at once. This was particularly important on Phases 2 and 3, where the contractors were working on bridges that blocked access to the trackbed, so tracklaying was not 'linear'. More detail about tracklaying can be found in Chapter 11.

*The site of Hendy level crossing. Formerly it was a fully gated standard gauge crossing just under a mile from Caernarfon. Later the cycleway users had a wicket gate to operate. Seen here before railway restoration, when the track was back and the trains ran, the bad sighting meant that all trains had to stop before proceeding on this restored 'open' crossing.* **Mike Schumann**

There are clouds to the silver lining of grant projects. At the same time as planning and construction for Phase I was occupying people's time, a whole lot of other work was required to be done. There is a great administrative load in projects of this kind, and it is not appreciated just how much paperwork has to be completed before any money flows. Indeed, in order to be grant aided the project has to bid. There might be the ability to reclaim the money spent on this process after the bid has been

gained, but there is a considerable risk involved. The work must be done without any guarantee of success, and huge amounts of activity must take place before the money starts to flow. This was the funding gap that sponsorship was able to cover.

It was clear from the Millennium Commission's grant that there was a requirement to get the application for a Transport and Works Order for the line from Dinas to Porthmadog underway as soon as possible. Hard luck that it all had to run at the same time as the organisation and administration of Phase I, from Caernarfon to Dinas. However, had it not done so, then there was the risk of a long wait between the end of one phase and the beginning of the next, and with a finish date of the Year 2000, time was short. The 'Establishment' was now backing this railway, and the critical path that maintained credibility rested on the building activity and the success of the TWO application. This was all quite a task, with activity running at the same time which will be described in the next chapter about the TWO public Inquiry.

At the same time as they were constructing the Forth Bridge, Winsons gained a contract to make five passenger 'new concept' coaches to a wider WHR loading gauge than FR. The construction of these 12m long vehicles, Nos 2020, 2040-2042 and 2090 was overseen by Boston Lodge. They arrived on extended low loaders in late September 1997, and were craned onto the track in the Dinas North Yard, shunted into the Dinas platform road and coupled together. Once the set was complete, they were carefully taken into the south yard, which was as far as the track went in that direction. The vacuum brakes had not yet been commissioned, and so the only stopping power available was from the Funkey's locomotive air brake. Later that week, the set was pulled out of the South Yard into Dinas Platform so that the vacuum brakes could be commissioned. As Roland Doyle drove the train gently

*Above: The track is down and being fettled, with the borrowed locomotive Harold in attendance, which dates this scene to July 1997. The cycleway and footpath runs alongside all the way to Dinas.*
**Ben Fisher**

*Right: On its way from Windon's Daventry factory, Coach No. 2090 sits on a road trailer in a lay-by at the eastern end of Penmaenbach Tunnel, awaiting delivery to Dinas, on 29th September 1997.* **Roger Dick**

*Above: Dinas Station under reconstruction, with the formation coming together on the firm roadway that was the SG trackbed. Lots to do here, with the station building to restore in early '97.*

**Both Photographs: Ben Fisher**

*Left: Building dealt with, track being laid, and in the background the stack of materials in a much more ordered scene. See how the pile has gone down. The toilet block is gone off the station building, and the railway is returning, June 1997.*

towards the platform, a member of staff suddenly put up his hands with great vigour. This being the universal railway hand signal for 'emergency stop', the locomotive's air brakes were applied fully, and the shock wave passed through the train, de-railing the last carriage bogie. The crestfallen person was asked why he had given the emergency stop signal. He said,

"We've run out of tea bags".

Severe sense of humour failure was experienced by those who had to work late re-railing the coach. However something good came out of it, apart from the renewed supply of tea bags. Upon examination the curve under the derailed coach was found to exceed the specification for maximum twist (rate of change of cant).

The initial track laying process with the Forth Bridge was even less quick than had been hoped, because when joining a track panel onto one already laid, the gaps between the rail ends need to be set accurately to allow for expansion. This meant that one rail would be positioned accurately, but to adjust the other, the fastenings along the whole length of the other rail might have to be loosened to move that rail up to correct the gap. However the track advanced steadily from Dinas towards Caernarfon, and by September 1997, *Upnor Castle* was in attendance whilst the points were laid in at the terminus.

The old standard gauge platforms were reused at Dinas,

*Almost BR 1950s carmine and cream, the Winson saloons, sit in Dinas platform in the early days. The wide, spacious interior and traditional narrow-gauge experience went down well. At that time they were considerably more comfortable than anything running on the FR.* **Ben Fisher**

but the trackbed was raised from the original level, to offer the right height for the narrow gauge trains in the platform. This track was laid with track panels, and a 50 tonne crane, from Bob Francis Crane Hire to lift them in. With the platforms in place, track alignment was simple, because it was offset using the platform edge as the datum, care having been taken to get the platform edge straight and level. There was pressure to get the track down, as the TWO public inquiry for Dinas to Porthmadog was pending, and it was considered advisable to have something to show when trying to satisfy objectors and potential supporters, to emphasise that the FR Co. was in the business of restoring the whole railway.

There were two locomotives, Nos 138 and 143 that had been acquired from South Africa and had been overhauled there to be ready for work. Despite this, Boston Lodge felt that more remedial work was needed on these locomotives, and No. 138 was the first one to be completed. It had been steamed at the FR Gala in its storage place of Glanypwll, Blaenau Ffestiniog. It was stored there as heavy haulage vehicles had a relatively easy entrance into that site to drop and pick up such large locomotives. Garratt No. 138 and ALCO *Mountaineer* came across to Dinas by Allely's heavy haulage, using one of their tri-axle, rear steerable, low loaders, on September 23rd, 1997. This meant that there was now a full train set to be played with, and a real railway for trains to be run on.

Oil fired, No. 138 was lit up and brought into steam. When first driven down Dinas platform road, by Roland himself, the front cow-catcher planed off the top of the up platform edge like a huge planning machine. As all good machinists know that you should never stop a cut half way through, the whole of the platform edge was planed, rather than get stuck part way. The blame was firmly parked with Roland Doyle, who had been responsible for the exact and careful construction of the platform edge and track. However,

*Water for all, the tank put up in 1997 continues to give service, whilst red No 138 turns water into steam. The original siding was taken out and the loop realigned to accommodate the locomotives. This was a better arrangement.*

on checking the track-to-platform edge relationship afterwards, it was found to be perfect. Roland therefore practised a different skill on the locomotive, introducing selected parts to the wonders of the oxyacetylene torch. It fitted after that.

A steam engine water supply was needed in Caernarfon Station. Volunteers had led the recovery and restoration of a cast iron water tank from a gas works. The tank was stored in Dinas yard, waiting for its installation in Caernarfon. Water for locomotives needs to be delivered in quantity, fast - otherwise delay takes place to the train. The tank had to be supported about five metres above ground to give it enough head to deliver the required

*The view just outside Caernarfon Station in March 1997, looking south the trackbed is being cleared of vegetation by the contractor, to await fencing and then a ballast top, so that the track can be laid upon it.* **Mike Schumann**

quantity quickly. At 1kg per litre, 8lbs per gallon, 10 cubic metres of water in the air weighs 10 tonnes and needs strong supports. Consultants designed a 6-leg structure, which was fabricated and installed by D. J. Williams and Son, of the famous Brunswick Iron Works in Caernarfon. They figure frequently in the catalogue of WHR restoration. A wooden frame made from greenheart

was fitted to absorb any irregularities between the top of the steel legs and the bottom of the cast iron tank. A Sunday morning in September of 1997 was chosen to lift the tank into position. The crane was set up in St Helen's road at 06.00, blocking the road completely once its outriggers had been extended. However even at that time in the morning, a crowd gathered to watch the successful lift, all completed by 11 am. The tank was commissioned, filled and has done service at Caernarfon ever since.

In order to run, the railway had first to be inspected by HMRI (Her Majesty's Railway Inspectorate). They visited on October 2nd and 3rd 1997. On the first visit the gradient towards Caernarfon, near to Dinas was being examined, when a pair of Roland's Rail Movers came whizzing past, being ridden on by a member of staff, his long hair streaming in the wind. The senior party present squirmed in embarrassment at this breach of strict instruction, but HMRI did not take it particularly amiss. On the 3rd October 1997, the track from Dinas to

Caernarfon was inspected, using *Castell Caernarfon* and all five delivered carriages. At that stage the loco drivers had virtually no experience of driving the route. On the return journey whilst climbing the 1:53 gradient under Coed Helen bridge, David Thornton, HMRI Inspector, decided to try an emergency brake application. However on the footplate the driver sensing the train slowing, opened the throttle wider to maintain speed on the gradient. It took about 30sec to realise that he had lost all vacuum and should close the throttle. The experiment was repeated, but this time the driver watched the vacuum gauge, and as soon as the pressure dropped he closed the throttle, bringing the train to a standstill in a remarkably short distance - such is testing! A snag list resulted from the inspection, but eventually a trial period of running was approved until November 30th 1997.

There was great excitement at the CRhE AGM, held in the Y Mount pub at Dinas on 4th October, 1997. It was difficult to hold the meeting's attention, as test running was going on across the road. *Mountaineer* was hauling the coaches about, and NGG16 No. 138 was running light. Everyone rushed on to Dinas station to see the train after the meeting ended at 16.00. It ran empty, as it was test running, but the chance to travel on it came after Thursday 9th October, when the LRO came into force. An unadvertised passenger service was run over the Saturday and Sunday, the 11th and 12th October. The official opening of the railway was on Monday 13th October, when the Lady Mayor of Caernarfon, Mrs Mair Williams was introduced by Mike Hart to do the honours, and a posse of dignitarios was present. This was the first in a long line of beanos to celebrate each advance. WHR offers no apology for pushing the boat out when an advance is made. The results are gratifying and have always helped the next stage in the project.

Volunteers from FR were curious to see and work on this new railway, and a core signed up for footplate and guards' training, being rapidly passed out. This did not find universal favour on FR, and one senior staff member was heard to remark that WHR stood for 'Waste of Human Resources'. Nevertheless, new things that happen will excite curiosity, and so it has been with WHR. It was just too interesting to be adversely affected by any bad-mouthing it got. There was

*On 4th October, during test running, a Garratt and 5 cars could be seen steaming between Caernarfon and Dinas. Better still, if you got on your bike, and pedalled furiously, you could pace the train on Lôn Eifion.*
**Ben Fisher Site**

no shortage of volunteers to work the newly opened service until the planned winter shutdown on 2nd November - then there was lots and lots of finishing work to do. The sheer size and majesty of the 2ft gauge locomotives and rolling stock on route commanded attention then and now - but attaining the next stage was a real challenge in 1997. Caernarfon-Dinas settled down to everyone concentrating on trying to run a reliable service, with economy, until the breakthrough became possible on to the old WHR formation. It was hardly cost effective to use huge locomotives on tiny trains, but lots of experience was gained with the operation of Garratts, and the steep pull out of Caernarfon with a locomotive almost cold certainly offered that. It was important to test these locomotives out and to try to understand them. There was nothing to equal the exit from Caernarfon in gradient terms until the later stages of Phase 4.

## Managing the MC Grant

The Millennium Commission grant application was for £4.3m representing 43% of the estimated cost to build the railway from Caernarfon to Rhyd-Ddu, and to equip it with infrastructure and rolling stock. The decision taken was to offer the job to tender and move it along quickly using contractors. Yet the most dangerous part of construction projects are the landmines called 'estimates'. These were necessary to substantiate the grant amount, and to form the basis for the tender for the work. Roland Doyle speaks with feeling about projects that run into trouble, that are frequently found to be overspent. He claims that they rarely overspend, they are almost always likely to have been under-estimated in the first place. When the Millennium Commission grant was approved in 1995, MC related that their management system would be very simple, and would pay out within something like two weeks of a monthly grant application. In practice their paperwork requirements were the most onerous of any grant giving body with which the railway had ever worked. Had this been known at the time another 10% would have been added to the grant application to compensate. There was concern at the time, that if more money had been asked for, the application

*Porthmadog, 2nd October 1995, the handing over of the Millennium Commission cheque for £4.3m to Alan Pegler, Gordon Rushton and Mike Schumann. Wish it had been a lump sum - see text!*
**Peter Johnson**

might have been turned down. However the sum asked for did not have enough built in to allow for inflation between 1995 and 2003. It was beset with problems in that there was not access to all areas to do a full engineering assessment prior to making the initial grant application. It fell to Mike Hart to manage the Millennium Commission application, using cost of construction of the formation using figures that had been jointly developed from the Scott Handley report. This is of course being wise after the event, having gone through it, but although it was easy enough to see what the condition of the line from Caernarfon to Dinas was like, the management was lulled into a sense of false security. As a result there were uncomfortable cost experiences to come further up the line, deep in the undergrowth. The available funds would be eroded in a frightening fashion. The story of that is to come.

Other intense activity was proceeding, particular to the next chapter, during the Caernarfon to Dinas construction period. Mike Schumann and Tony Smare started visiting all adjacent landowners from mid 1995 onwards, as part of the TWO consultation process. Phase 1, Dinas to Caernarfon, was the last railway built in the UK under a 1896 Light Railways Act LRO. A 1993 Transport and Works Act replaced it with different conditions and requirements. This required a vast amount of work for Phase 2, Dinas-Waunfawr and beyond, in advance of the application being made. The hope was that the number and strength of objections received would be so slight as not to warrant a public inquiry - this was only a faint hope as Chapter 5 describes. The brou-ha-ha at the TO inquiry had alerted people that serious attempts were being made to restore the WHR. This had a profound effect on the interests of the 'frontholders', thus they were warned and prevailed upon to take interest, or possibly be adversely affected.

## New Standards Apply

New standards were set for the WHR, to take advantage of the extra width and height of the formation, and to exploit and augment this for the use of SAR Garratt locomotives and the new wider carriages.

**1.** There was a new loading gauge drawing to take account of the size of South African locomotives as well as the restricted size of existing bridges, and the need to make it all compatible with FR rolling stock. Calculating the structure gauge widening required on curves revealed that the FR version had been incorrectly calculated. Before the purchase of South African locomotives could be approved, it was necessary to check that it was technically possible to provide clearances for them through all the bridges and tunnels. Fortunately this proved to be the case. (See the comparative loading gauges, kinematic envelopes etc. in Appendix. 'A')

**2.** New cant tables had to be calculated, to take account of taller rolling stock.

**3.** There was a new low cost approach to construction of passing loops, to avoid the complex and expensive machinery installed on the FR.

**4.** A development of a new standard for all level crossing and the design and approval of Welsh-English signage required approval from four different government agencies - HMRI, Welsh Office(WEFO), GC and SNPA.

**5.** A new standard was developed for rolling stock with all carriages gangway connected, and built to the full WHR loading gauge. At the time this was done the latest view for building carriages for the FR was a wooden framed superstructure clad in aluminium face plywood. WHR preferred a stainless steel, welded tubular frame, clad in aluminium faced plywood. (Now experience with problems due to differential thermal expansion means that carriages are clad in best quality plywood.)

The larger, wider carriages, although the space increase was quite minor, seemed to make a big difference. This was stimulus to the carriage builders at Boston Lodge, to improve the general quality of all the passenger rolling stock. There was a lot of room on the converted standard gauge railway - this was not the case on the NWNG proper. The bigger locomotives forced considerable amounts of work to be carried out at extra cost, and the price for doing this was high. Matters eased in Phase 4 as the railway was wider and there were fewer overbridges, but costs of the application of the standards above, whilst high for the WHR, were to prove to be unaffordable for the FR from Rhiw Plas bridge up to Blaenau Ffestiniog. Thus the dream of NGG16 Garratts working throughout with their roomy coaches has not been fulfilled. Much was learned on Phase 1 that would be invaluable experience for Phases 2 and 3. But first there was the matter of a Transport and Works Order to obtain, and the next chapter describes this and the many objections to be overcome.

*Above: NGG16 No.138, just arrived at Dinas on September 23rd 1997 gets a careful examination. Painted in FR green, it received a coat of a lighter shade in 2001*

**Mike Schumann (upper)  Ben Fisher Website (lower)**

*Right: There was tremendous excitement at the beginning of service. Here were African Garratts working in Britain - wow! The service was only temporary in nature - there was so much still to be done on the three mile railway. Here a train arrives Dinas on 11th October 1997, on the day of unadvertised running.*

# Liabilities - Far from rushing into things, matters were thought through by FR Co, and where necessary research was carried out. An interesting tale has come to light. Was there a 'collusion' aimed at directing the trackbed into public ownership, or confusion within GCC?

Stories of the unwelcome reception on offer to restorers by the Official Receiver are true. There was little reason for anyone in the GCC to love the FR Co. if it was their intention (which it was) to try to gain ownership of the WHR trackbed. The railway aspects of this bothered the 64 Co., but not the GCC. The elected members saw public ownership as the better way to regularise the 'untidy mess'. The 'frontagers' who had incorporated the land into their enterprises, such that some depended on it, had become vested interests. Councillors were properly elected to serve those interests. Whilst there was no change, the pressure for regularising the trackbed legal position was low. When railway restoration was proposed, it was first viewed as impractical. When repeated more vigorously, a protective policy sprang up. Transfer to public ownership, and an Abandonment Order for the land, would be more likely to lead to 'comfort' for the farmers. Claims for adverse possession were little considered, as GCC public ownership policies aimed at safeguarding the agricultural interests were augmented by public interest benefits of footpath, cycleway, and road widening.

The public ownership view was supported by the tale that the levels of liabilities were such that only a county council could stand guarantor for them. The OR favoured this view, and acted partially, as he would only agree to the sale of the trackbed if an Abandonment Order followed (to relieve him from future liability). This is not unreasonable, and here GCC and OR guard against whimsical speculators and tie-in to GCC policy. Ponder for a moment the consideration due to the scheme to restore the 1922 WHR Co. and to re-appropriate the land for a tourist railway. How could anyone expect such a proposal to find favour after such a long closure period and the interests in place?

Brown envelopes occasionally appear to spice the tale. The first was the one about the FR's 'buy to shut' mission to GCC. The repercussions of this 'leak' have been thoroughly explored. Little known about is the second BE. The scene for its delivery was after the outcome of the TO Inquiry was known in 1994. It was generally assumed by the FR Co. that part of the £1m liabilities package was the responsibility for bridges. This was a relevant cost in the restoration. Just looking at the NWNG section to Rhyd Ddu revealed major works. At Betws Garmon, and Bryn y Felin, bridge rebuilding was likely. After the TO inquiry was won, and 'privatisation' had been forced upon a reluctant GCC, there was still the TWO to win, and with it conditions in mitigation that could

be costly. Imagine the surprise when a brown envelope from Stephen Paul arrived, containing all the minutes of the various CCC committees which related to the WHR between 1922 or so and 1944. They had been torn out of copies of the Council minutes that are routinely printed for Councillors. In the minutes were references to the Caernarfonshire County Council adopting the bridges prior to the lease of the WHR 1922 Co. to FR Co. in 1934.

The reason that CCC did this was simple. With the WHR 22 Co. in receivership, the railway had no money to spend on the bridges, but work needed to be done, and CCC would have had to bear the expense by default. However, they could get central government to make a 50% grant towards the cost of the work on most of the bridges by adopting them.

Once the TO decision was confirmed, Mike Schumann took copies of the relevant minutes to a meeting with the Chief of the Highways Department. Highways accepted the interpretation of the minutes, and that was the end of the matter. Right from the outset the Highways were very professional and helpful.

It is likely that sooner or later the minutes would have been discovered, as after the TO Inquiry was settled, both Mike Schumann and Ernie Preston started searching through the minutes held in the Gwynedd archives; the BME saved much time.

The reason why GCC had believed the bridges were not their responsibility might be incomplete research from their archives, and this is borne out by conclusions reached by reading only the minutes of the Light Railway Committee. Further research within the minutes of the other committees delivers the true situation.

It was however convenient if there was an unwitting misinterpretation of the minutes. To be able to claim that the bid for title to the trackbed included money that GCC were owed for bridge repair, ensured that the FR Co's trackbed bid figure was topped by GCC. It also possible that numberless sums in liability and 'compensation' were useful in discouraging bidders and restorers in earlier times.

All changed when debentures, etc. were declared statute barred in the High Court. The Transfer Order proposal (with no abandonment) was a major spoke in the wheel for public ownership. With an Abandonment Order, the residuary powers disappeared, thus every farmer who was using the trackbed long-term might have been able to claim adverse possession under the rules current at that time. The GC Solicitors Dept are reported to have agreed that had they acquired the trackbed, then title to most of it would have been lost by adverse possession claims.

Mike Schumann declares that he was against abandoning the old powers because no one could say what the implications of this action were. Mr Justice Vinelott's verdict offered a TO with no abandonment as the way forward for FR Co. Adverse Possession was countered, and compulsory purchase powers in the TWO minimised difficulty with land title.

*GCC had long put off rebuilding and modernising Bryn y Felin bridge on the A498, south of Beddgelert. They did so after the railway reinstatement, but before re-opening. It was at GC expense, which was helpful to the restoration expenses.*

*It is now the 7th of April 2009 and the railway is about to open through to Beddgelert, so it's 10 cars, double headed. The limitations of Caernarfon Station can be seen, NGG16 No.87 is right up by the top points, and Observation Car Glaslyn is squeezed up to the fouling point at the Castle end. On the left of picture is Lôn Eifion, looking neat and tidy, beyond is tidy stonework and steps by St Helen's Road - nice, mature Phase 1 - but the station's too small!*

## What really happened in Minffordd Yard?

**In Chapter 4 there is a description of how thousands of Channel Tunnel railway sleepers came to Minffordd Yard to be processed for further use. Here is an insight from Cedric Lodge into why this was so, and what happened to the material. It was not, as some thought, for use on the WHR. However, having it was still very useful - why was that?**

Following the initial policy of the FR Co. to attempt to acquire the trackbed of the WHR to ensure it was never used as a railway, John Routly was concerned that wider knowledge of this policy could be detrimental to the revised intention to develop the trackbed as railway. He needed to demonstrate publicly the determination of the FR Co. to rebuild the WHR. Acquisition of the sleepers from the Channel Tunnel gave credibility to the FR's new policy.

This was admirably demonstrated at the first Public Enquiry for the Transfer Order, when FR representatives could truthfully state that track materials had already been obtained and were being processed. It might be said that at that time vast amounts of narrow gauge trackwork material was on the way from South Africa. Thankfully, nobody pressed the point, as the sleepers and their fastenings we had were quite unsuitable for other than a light mineral line. It was clear when one got up close and examined the Channel Tunnel stuff, that the sleepers were untreated softwood, and in the conditions within the tunnel, many had started to rot. They had only been got for a construction railway - which of course was never to be. Tolerable sleepers were sawn up and used as packing for the stack of rail acquired from SAR when it all began to arrive. The fastenings were pressed steel baseplates, with small elastic rail clips (ERC) that looked like Pandrol clips. These might have been of some use to Fred Howes, so we stripped them from the sleepers. The job also provided the fledgling society with a task to accomplish, and this was perhaps the greatest benefit.

I think there were about 10 tons of small ERCs, and it is regrettable these were not made more widely available to other embryonic railways. The Lynton and Barnstaple took some, but Fred Howes was asking too much money for them for the L&B to take more. We were all raring to go, as we had spent so many wasted years being told our policies were never going to work. Now we had got one that was - and we were able to do something. The feeling of freedom was exhilarating; we were actually doing something to restore the WHR. Of course from then on, it only got better, and better and better. We felt great!

**All Pictures Mike Schumann**

### CAERNARFON

**Left:** *The vegetation is cleared the fences are up, the cycle path is transferred at this location to the right of the track, and the ballast bed is laid. All that's missing in this Caernarfon view of 19th May 1997 is the track.*

### Nr SEIONT BRIDGE

**Right:** *In 1995 major road works on the approach to Caernarfon are in progress, on the left the tarmac cycleway on the old Afon Wen trackbed, in the centre-right the old Llanberis trackbed.*

### ATOP SEIONT BRIDGE

**Left:** *In February 1995 this is the Seiont Bridge before any work has begun. The view is looking north towards Caernarfon and the Llanberis trackbed has already split off, to run along the north bank, whereas the Afon Wen trackbed continues to rise to cross the river and reach the higher ground on the south side.*

### WORK ON SEIONT BRIDGE

**Right:** *This is a similar viewpoint as that above - see the stand of trees. Now, in March 1997 the road works are complete, and the bridge in front carries St Helen's Road. Both crowns of the Seiont Bridge arches are here exposed for remedial work (waterproofing). The path will be diverted to the right-hand when the work is finished. After that side is complete, it is where the new railway will run.*

### BONTENWYDD BRIDGE

**Right:** *The cycleway tarmac strip runs across the bridge at Bontnewydd in the centre of this February 1995 view. This is the three-arch crossing of the Afon Gwyrfai 1¾ miles from Caernarfon.*

### BONTNEWYDD BRIDGE - DONE

**Left:** *In 1997, Bontnewydd Bridge is now suitably dealt with, and concrete decking has been poured. Soon the tracks for the new railway will be laid in the narrow strip on the left-hand side. Later the Bontnewydd Halt will be adjacent to this point .*

### COED HELEN ROAD

**Right:** *The bridge over the Afon Wen line carrying Coed Helen Road, is weak. After the railway closed the bridge was strengthened by girder work, as can be seen. There was enough room to fit the cycle path and the new railway under the bridge, but the support had to be moved. So the lattice girder was replaced with a new angle girder support.*

### DINAS OLD STATION SITE

**Left:** *Dinas old station site before work started, viewed from Ty'n Llan bridge - April 1995. The tarmac cycle path is on the left, GCC Engineers on the right, with the old station building centre-right showing where the platform once was.*

## All Pictures Mike Schumann

### GARRATTS IN BLAENAU

*Left:* The FR May Gala 1997 saw NGG16s 138 and 140 on display. 138 was in steam and moving up and down the yard tracks. It was the first time such a large narrow gauge engine had been seen in Blaenau Ffestiniog!

### GLA N Y PWLL LOADING

*Right:* On 23nd September 1997, NGG16 No. 138 is seen at Glanypwll, being loaded on to the Al-leley's low loader for the trip to Dinas at Caernarfon. Push supplied by FR diesel Moel Hebog.

### 138'S FIRST STEAMING - DINAS

*Left:* The scene at Dinas, when having been delivered with FR 2-6-2T Mountaineer, No 138 was put into steam for some trial running. Mountaineer, the spare steam loco, in grey livery, saw little use and was returned to the FR in the late Autumn.

### 138 & ALL THE STOCK

*Right:* In 1997, during the brief period of running in 1997, October 13th until November 2nd, locomotive NGG16 No. 138 runs towards St Helen's Road Bridge on the down grade in to Caernarfon, with the full 5 coach train, at that time all the coaches the WHR possessed.

### CAERNARFON STATION

**Right:** The track reached Caernarfon from Dinas at the end of September 1997. Here is the end of the ballasted strip, with the headshunt track yet to be laid. There are no temporary buildings yet and the wall is still being rebuilt.

### ROLAND RAIL MOVERS

**Left:** Two Roland Rail Movers at the 'head of steel' near St Helen's Road, whilst locals come and go on the neighbouring Lon Eifion foot path and cycleway.

### THE FORTH BRIDGE

**Below:** The Forth Bridge at work, here approaching St Helen's Road Bridge on the outskirts of Caernarfon. Behind are flatcars of supplies - more panels. Behind these is Upnor Castle, the locomotive that built the WHR.

### TILTING TRACK

**Left:** Alas this was the problem with the Forth Bridge gantry as a labour saving device. The sleeper length used for the track on WHR was of the longer SAR standard, Sadly the Forth Bridge was made to the drawing supplied for the shorter length. Hence to get the panel through the gap, it has to be tilted. Roland Rail Movers were found to be easier to use and you could get round them. in the restricted spaces.

## The Welsh Highland Railway - Caernarfon - Rheilffordd Eryri          1998

### SERVICE 1 Timetable :
### 4 - 10 April, 16 April - 23 May, 30 May - 28 June, 19 Sep - 8 Nov

#### Caernarfon to Dinas

| Miles | | | | | | | | | | Bold type indicates Caernarfon Departures with Return Service |
|---|---|---|---|---|---|---|---|---|---|---|
| 0 | **Caernarfon** | | **10.30** | **11.30** | **13.00** | **14.00** | **15.00** | | 16.00 | |
| 3 | **Dinas** | | 10.45 | 11.45 | 13.15 | 14.15 | 15.15 | | 16.15 | |
| | | | | | | | | | | |
| 3 | **Dinas** | 10.00 | 11.00 | 12.00 | 13.30 | 14.30 | 15.30 | | | |
| 0 | **Caernarfon** | 10.15 | 11.15 | 12.15 | 13.45 | 14.45 | 15.45 | | | |

### SERVICE 2 Timetable :
### 11 - 15 April, 24 - 29 May, 29 June - 18 Sep

#### Caernarfon to Dinas

| Miles | | | | | | | | | | | |
|---|---|---|---|---|---|---|---|---|---|---|---|
| 0 | **Caernarfon** | | **10.30** | **11.30** | **13.00** | **14.00** | **15.00** | **16.00** | **17.00** | 18.00 | |
| 3 | **Dinas** | | 10.45 | 11.45 | 13.15 | 14.15 | 15.15 | 16.15 | 17.15 | 18.15 | |
| | | | | | | | | | | | |
| 3 | **Dinas** | 10.00 | 11.00 | 12.00 | 13.30 | 14.30 | 15.30 | 16.30 | 17.30 | | |
| 0 | **Caernarfon** | 10.15 | 11.15 | 12.15 | 13.45 | 14.45 | 15.45 | 16.45 | 17.45 | | |

¾ **Hour return trip - Adult Return £3.00, one child free (additional child £1.50) - Senior Citizens £2.25**

# Rheilffordd Eryri
# Rheilffordd Ucheldir Cymri

## What was the reasoning?

The question of what to call the railway surfaced from time to time. It was conceived and operated as the Welsh Highland Railway in its day, and has always had that name in English, receiving the normal 'Lein Bach' or 'Lein Bach Beddgelert in Welsh. FR wasn't bothered about trying to claim the name Welsh Highland Railway exclusively, but 64 Co. sought to register it as a trademark. This was a damp squib, as something in general use so long is a doubtful candidate for exclusive use. The 64 Co. wished to be differentiated from FR in stamping Welshness upon their enterprise. For differentiation 64 Co. used a long Welsh direct translation, Rheilffordd Ucheldir Cymru, entirely accurate but hardly euphonic. Asking around, the Welsh reaction was not partial to this. So searching for romanticism, FR ventured Rheilffordd Eryri, as the only adjacent high ground was Snowdonia, and that's where the railway went. However this has mellowed to become Rheilffrydd Ffestiniog ac Eryri (The Ffestiniog and Welsh Highland Railways.)

Whatever name 64 Co. might have wanted became difficult when the WHR (Caernarfon) grew and spread. People came to the 64 Co. site, expecting Garratts and a big ride, and when that didn't happen some were miffed. The process got no better over the years, as the public will insist on using the term Welsh Highland Railway as a general description. It was a problem for WHRL to differentiate itself from the main line WHR in a satisfactory way. Today they do offer something quite different and quite excellent and now they are the Welsh Highland Heritage Railway and this switches the visitor's lights on!

# Traffic Figures

## How did the service do?

| | | |
|---|---|---|
| 1999 | 27,949 | Caernarfon - Dinas |
| 2000 | 33,387 | August open to Waunfawr |
| 2001 | 32,789 | |
| 2002 | 34,827 | |
| 2003 | 50,679 | August open to Rhyd Ddu |
| 2004 | 58,563 | |
| 2005 | 48,459 | |

These figures are bookings, and can be multiplied by a single/return and number of adults/children factor to make them 'passenger journeys'. It's much of a muchness as long as like is compared with like.

The FR figures at the same time averaged 130k bookings, with a variation of 4k between highest and lowest years. So the WHR did not take traffic from the FR.

See Chapter 12 about the financial affairs of the WHR and its effect on the FR.

Caernarfon - Dinas was accepted as being lossmaking at the time; it was a very small railway. The fare was only £3, and the locomotives were very large. However, as a practice for what was unfolding, it was most valuable experience, and a good indication to all of future intentions.

### Pictures - an apology

The quality of pictures in this chapter is distinctly less than we are now used to. Nothing to do with Ben Fisher and Mike Schumann's excellent composition and shooting skills, it's just that we are all now pampered by the 'wonderful world of digital'. So the apology is that technical advance has been so great since 2000, that the 1990s pictures aren't that good. Sorry - it gets better as the book goes on!

# Chapter 5
# Dinas - Porthmadog TWO
# The Second Public Inquiry 1997

Well before Caernarfon to Dinas was underway, with funding, and the trackbed was under the control of the Festiniog Railway Company, the action needed to gain a Transport and Works Order (TWO) under the Transport and Works Act 1992 was being taken. The Order would allow the track to be put back on the railway from Dinas to Porthmadog. Permission to put the track back on the WHR seemed such a little thing, but the process to gain a TWO to permit the work was long and bureaucratic, and it had to be gone through correctly. The 1992 legislation imposed significant, new, stricter conditions, requiring longer time to implement, at greater cost than the previous Light Railway Orders.

It was necessary to decide whether to apply for TWO powers from Dinas to Rhyd Ddu, or to go for the whole lot, including the perhaps contentious crossing of Cambrian Coast Line and Britannia Bridge in Porthmadog. It was clear that application to the Millennium Commission for funding should be as far as Rhyd Ddu only - the timescale for building the whole railway was impractical, and such an application would risk losing all. But the question of how much TWO to apply for was risk laden. Boldness won - it was decided to apply for the whole route, and to take all the flak in one go. These were wise decisions, and their correctness has been borne out by events.

It is clear now that the swiftness with which FR moved was most helpful. It appears from circumstantial evidence that the detailed effects of the TWO powers were not clearly comprehended by all. This had repercussions 11 years later, when the track was being built across the town of Porthmadog, and the town council had a problem with trains running across Britannia Bridge.  The Gwynedd Council (GC)were well informed and helpful.  Other major players were not yet well informed, but soon became so. The FR establishment required more people to deal with the extra work imposed by the TWO activity. On 1st November

1994, Tony Smare joined the team, to co-ordinate and manage the bid for the TWO.  He was well versed in consultation and working with local authorities, having managed the TWO bid for the Leeds Supertram, and he was also a lifelong FR supporter. Tony well knew what effective  prior consultation was needed to reduce the number of objections to the proposals.  The process leading up to the formal application, made  on 27th March 1997, had begun immediately after the Secretary of State's decision in favour of the Transfer Order in the autumn of 1994. The team in support were Mike Schumann,  John Hopkins, Peter Johnson, and assistant Maddy Chester.  These folk were supplemented by others at various times including FR Co. Board members, FR management, (HR, Financial) and others.

Messrs Sharpe, Pritchard, Parliamentary Agents had been instrumental in guiding FR Co through the complexities of the application for the Transfer Order, and again were vital to this next task.  They knew and explained what a complex process gaining one of the new TWOs was likely to be, and offered advice on the steps that needed to be taken. They outlined the barriers to entry to anyone wishing to apply for a TWO. It is not a process for the faint of heart.  The application also requests a direction from the Secretary of State that planning permission for the scheme be deemed to be granted, saying:

*'Application has also been made to the Welsh Office for a certificate under Section 19 of the Acquisition of Land Act 1981, in respect of public open space. The proposed reinstatement of the railway is supported by the Structure Plan prepared by Gwynedd County Council, the local planning authority which existed until the establishment of its successors, Gwynedd Council and the Snowdonia National Park Authority in 1996. The planning statement of the National Park, the recently-deposited Eryri Local Plan, supports the principle of the railway.'*

A TWO application is dry stuff.  You have to deal with :

o  Any environmental benefits and disbenefits resulting from

*Castell Cidwm 9th June 2001 - can we have our railway back please?*
**Ben Fisher Website**

| Dinas Porthmadog TWO - Chronology | | |
|---|---|---|
| 01.01.93 | Transport and Works Act 1992 comes into force | Act replaced the Light Railways Act 1896, radically changing the requirements in order to apply for statutory railway powers. |
| 20.07.94 | Transfer Order Inquiry outcome | The SoS for Transport decided in favour of the transfer of the WHR 1922 Co. residuary powers to FR Co. |
| autumn 1994 | Compilation of TWO Application documentation begins | FR Co. starts the process required to submit a TWO application for Dinas to Porthmadog, to 'put the track back' on WHR |
| May 1995 | Millennium Commission Grant | Millennium Commission made a conditional offer of £4.3m to restore WHR from Caernarfon to Rhyd Ddu |
| Nov 1995 | Public Consultation | The publication of the brochure (opposite) signalled the start of intensive public consultation |
| 27.03.97 | TWO Application Dinas-Porthmadog | The FR Co. applied for the TWO to restore the WHR track from Dinas to Porthmadog - including the cross-town link. |
| 05.06.97 | Public Inquiry announcement | SoS decision announced to hold a public inquiry on the TWO application by FR Co for Dinas to Porthmadog |
| 09.10.97 | LRO comes into force | The Caernarfon Railway LRO is made on this date |
| 13.10.97 | Caernarfon-Dinas, The Caernarfon Railway | Opened 13th October 1997 by Mrs Mair Watson, Lady Mayor of Caernarfon |
| 28.10.97 | Inquiry pre-meeting | This meeting took place in the Arfon Area Offices |
| 09.12.97 - 28.01.98 | Caernarfon Public Inquiry No. 2 | Public Inquiry upon FR Co's application for the WHR Works Order in the Arfon Area Offices, Caernarfon |
| 12.01.98 | The 1998 Agreement | A legally binding agreement was made between the Festiniog Railway Company and the Welsh Highland Railway Limited, concerning the construction and operation of the WHR |
| July 1998 | SNPA Planning Inquiry | Change of Planning Policy TR 16 to oppose the WHR |
| 03.02.99 | OR transfers Trackbed | The TO of 1995 completed it's last duty as the outcome of the 1993 Inquiry, when the land was transferred on this date from OR to FR Co. |
| 03.03.99 | SNPA Inspector report published by Welsh Office | The report was favourable to the reinstatement of WHR |
| 07.04.99 | John Prescott Letter | Deputy prime Minister gives approval of TWO Application, subject to rock stability problems being solved in Aberglaslyn Pass |
| 30.06.99 | TWO made in letter from SoS 28.06.99 | TWO came into force on 21.07.99 - there was now no bar to FR Co. restoring the historic WHR from Dinas to Porthmadog. |
| Nov 1999 | Phase 2 | Work starts |

the construction and operation of the proposed railway, including implications for traffic congestion, footpath closures, and the adequacy of the proposals by the Festiniog Railway Company for mitigating any adverse environmental impacts or effects.

o Any socio-economic benefits and disbenefits resulting from the scheme, including public safety aspects, and the adequacy of the proposals by the Festiniog Railway Company for mitigating any adverse socio-economic impacts or effects.

o Any effects of the scheme on agricultural, residential, recreational and other property interests.

o The justification for granting compulsory acquisition powers applied for, weighing the effects of those powers on private interests against the wider public benefits claimed for the scheme.

There is a massive amount of work to substantiate the above which manifests itself in a Draft WHR Order of 37 pages of detail.

The Explanatory Memorandum contains 6 parts comprising 40 Articles conferring powers, like Part II, Works, Article 6:

*'Enables the Company, in constructing and maintaining the works, to deviate from the lines or situations shown on the deposited plans or the levels shown on the sections deposited with the application for the Order.'*

There are 5 Schedules showing details, like Schedule 5:

*'Land of which temporary possession may be taken or use made:*
*A schedule of 59 small parcels of land of which temporary use will be required for various purposes, e.g., bridge repairs, modifications to access tracks to adjacent land, footpaths to be diverted, drainage works, etc.'*

There is no doubt that when applying to restore a railway, the precise place where it is to be put must be determined with confidence. So items like this are not to be trifled with, they must be settled.

There is a 600 page statement :The Environmental Statement; it was produced under sub-contract by Posford, Duvivier. Just to give the flavour of this tome, from a non-technical part, here is a small section:

*'Construction impacts and mitigation measures*
*The main potential adverse nature conservation impacts relate to habitat loss, disturbance or severance, for otters and badgers, breeding and wintering birds, and bats. Although some of these represent major to moderate impacts, all can be reduced to minor adverse residual impacts through the effective implementation of mitigation measures. These include restrictions on construction works, adhering to Environment Agency (The Agency) guidelines, and ongoing liaison with specialists, in particular, the Countryside Council for Wales ("CCW").*

*Moderate adverse but localised visual and landscape disturbances can be reduced to minor adverse by adopting mitigation measures to control the extent and appearance of construction areas.*

*There are potential moderate adverse impacts on recreation, associated with the construction process. These may affect walkers, anglers, canoeists, horse riders, campers and youth hostel visitors. Impacts can be reduced to negligible/minor adverse impacts by effective implementation of a range of mitigation measures which include appropriate phasing of works, advanced warning of works, liaison with appropriate which manifests itself on a bodies, temporary diversions, and appropriate signage.'*

The list is fatiguing in iteration but is needed to convey the magnitude of this undertaking. Such a massive exercise serves in a number of ways:

1. You don't get into this unless you are really serious about building your railway, and have got major resources lined up for it.

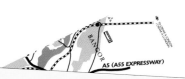

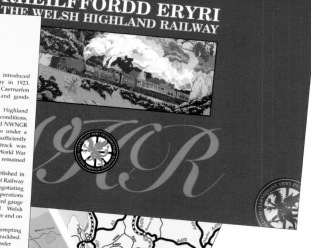

## RHEILFFORDD ERYRI
### THE WELSH HIGHLAND RAILWAY

## IN THE BEGINNING

The historic town of Caernarfon's first rail link opened in 1828 as the narrow gauge Nantlle Railway which passed through the hamlet of Dinas. Its horse-drawn services primarily carried slate, the raison d'être of most North Wales railways. It was replaced in 1867 by a standard gauge line which closed in 1864; its trackbed forms the first stage of the new Welsh Highland Railway.

Charles Spooner, engineer of the famous Ffestiniog Railway (FR), in 1872 proposed an impressive network of North Wales Narrow Gauge Railways (NWNGR). One line succeeded and adopted the NWNGR title - the line from Dinas junction south to Rhyd Ddu. It was completed in 1881 to its terminus, then known as South Snowdon.

In 1864 another horse-drawn tramway had been established on a route north from Porthmadog. It served Cwm Croesor and provided the basis of several attempts at establishing a tourist railway to Beddgelert, which even in 1866 was a popular centre. Works eventually took place to establish this link under the aegis of the Portmadoc Beddgelert and South Snowdon Railway (PBSSR) of 1901 which also adopted the Croesor tramway. The steep gradients of the partially completed works assumed the operation of electric locomotives - several are believed to have been built around 1905 but were never put into operation.

The first World War caused final abandonment of South Snowdon services in 1916. After the war the local authorities prompted the revival of the Beddgelert proposals in a merger of NWNGR and PBSSR interests to create the Welsh Highland Railway (WHR). The WHR

and the FR were then jointly managed and services were introduced between Dinas, Porthmadog and the Ffestiniog Railway in 1923. Unfortunately, due to lack of capital, proposed extension to Caernarfon was never achieved so the inconvenience of passenger and goods transfer at Dinas remained.

The under-capitalised Welsh Highland Railway operated in difficult economic conditions, primarily using what remained of the old NWNGR equipment. A Ffestiniog Railway rescue under a 1934 lease failed to recover the situation sufficiently and the railway closed in 1937. The track was recovered as scrap metal for the second World War effort but the trackbed and structures remained intact.

A preservation society was established in 1961 and became the Welsh Highland Light Railway (1964) Ltd. After numerous attempts at negotiating access to the old trackbed, it established operations in 1980 on a short section of former standard gauge trackbed near Porthmadog. Restored Welsh Highland rolling stock can be seen both here and on the Ffestiniog Railway.

In 1987 the Ffestiniog Railway took the initiative in attempting to break the deadlock on access to the original Welsh Highland trackbed. In 1995, after a Public Inquiry, it succeeded in obtaining a Transfer Order enabling it to purchase the assets, liabilities and powers of the old Company. The Festiniog Railway Company is now progressing the opening of the new Welsh Highland Railway between Caernarfon and Porthmadog.

## CYFLAWNI'R CYNLLUN

Mae Rheilffordd Eryri'n cael ei datblygu gan Gwmni Rheilffordd Ffestiniog, fydd yn llunio strwythur gweithredu ar wahân ar gyfer y rheilffordd. Fe fydd y rheilffordd newydd yn cadw cyswllt agos â chyfundrefn bresennol Cwmni Ffestiniog oherwydd y budd a all ddeillio o rannu'r brofiad a'i adnoddau. Gwerth y trefniant hwn yw profiad hir Rheilffordd Ffestiniog o adfer rheilffordd, a'i throi, gan gynnwys gwaith adeiladu newydd, yn fusnes llwyddiannus gyda throsiant blynyddol sy dros £1 miliwn. Cwmni Rheilffordd Ffestiniog fydd yn berchen ar wely'r cledrau rhwng Dinas a Phorthmadog a rhoddir les hir iddo gan yr awdurdod lleol ar y rhan rhwng Caernarfon a Dinas.

Mae'r Cwmni'n cydnabod yn ddiolchgar y gefnogaeth y mae wedi'i derbyn yn barod oddi wrth gynrychiolwyr y gymuned leol ac oddi wrth amryw gyrff cyhoeddus sy'n bleidiol i ddatblygu'r rheilffordd ac fe groesawyd cefnogaeth oddi wrth Gynghorwyr y Sir a'r Ardaloedd a'r Cymunedau. Rhoddir cymorth i hyrwyddo project y rheilffordd gan amryw, ac yn arbennig gan Siambr Fasnach Caernarfon.

Amcangyfrifir y bydd cyfanswm cost sefydlu Rheilffordd Eryri tua £25 miliwn. Mae rhoddion a chyfraniadau gwirfoddol eraill wedi rhoi hwb sylweddol ymlaen i'r project a bydd yn gymorth i sicrhau y gorffennir y cam cyntaf o Gaernarfon i Dinas. Bydd derbyn grant o £4.3 miliwn o Gronfa'r Mileniwm yn helpu i ariannu'r rhan gyntaf gan gynnwys yr estyniad hyd at Ryd Ddu. Fe fydd cychwyniadau eraill fel dyroddi cyfranddaliadau a grantiau gan yr Undeb

Ewropeaidd ac o ffynonellau eraill yn helpu i orffen y pecyn ariannu. Disgwylir y caiff cyfraniadau o'r sector preifat eu denu o ganlyniad i'r cyfalaf cychwynnol sylweddol o ffynonellau'r sector cyhoeddus a phroffil uchel y project.

Cefnogir y project hwn gan Gymdeithas Rheilffordd Eryri sy'n cynhyrchu cylchgrawn chwarterol darluniadol ac yn trefnu gweithgareddau lleol a rhanbarthol a hir yw'r gyrchfan ar gyfer ynni gwirfoddolwyr. Am wybodaeth am aelodaeth a materion eraill a wnewch chi sgrifennu at:

Cymdeithas Rheilffordd Eryri,
Blwch Swyddfa Bost 1590
Caernarfon,
Gwynedd

Gellir cael rhagor o wybodaeth ar ddatblygiad y project cyffrous hwn ac ar unrhyw fater sy'n ymwneud â Deddf Cludiant a Gweithfeydd oddi wrth Gyfarwyddwr y Project. Fe fyddai Cadeirydd y Cwmni hefyd yn croesawu ymholiadau a mynegiadau o ddiddordeb gan gwmnïau neu unigolion a hoffai gymryd rhan yn y project. A wnewch chi ysgrifennu os gwelwch yn dda at:

Cwmni Rheilffordd Ffestiniog,
Project Rheilffordd Eryri,
Gorsaf yr Harbwr,
Porthmadog,
Gwynedd
LL49 9NF

Mae cynlluniau a mapiau o'r cynigion i'w gweld yn y cyfeiriad uchod yn ystod yr oriau swyddfa arferol (teleffon 01766 512340).

## THE MARKET STRATEGY

...arfon, the initial terminus of ...way and the most important ...via the recently upgraded ...55 Euroroute expressway ...n.

view the splendid scenery of the Gwyrfai valley and Snowdon. Walkers, climbers and cyclists can be expected to make use of the intermediate stations and halts. Hotel and camping businesses, not just in the immediate vicinity of the railway, will start to notice direct benefits. An hourly service using two trains with buffet facilities is expected to operate in the high season, similar to the Ffestiniog Railway. A coach connection from Rhyd Ddu through Beddgelert to Porthmadog is planned. An extended timetable from Easter and up to October, using heated carriages, is likely to be operated to attract out-of-season visitors.

Completion between Caernarfon and Porthmadog enables the Welsh Highland Railway to form the basis of a new public transport network to protect the environment of the National Park. The network is intended to include the Ffestiniog Railway, Sherpa bus services from Beddgelert and Conwy Valley trains from Llandudno. Timetables will reflect the Swiss style of co-ordination and through ticketing. Park and Ride opportunities will be addressed in conjunction with the National Park and local authorities. Through trains to the Ffestiniog Railway are anticipated, some offering dining facilities. The Welsh Highland timetable will generally be hourly between 9am and 4pm. Some trains will complete the journey in about 90 minutes while others will call at local halts. The complete railway will provide a useful transport facility for local people who will be offered fare concessions, as on the Ffestiniog, through a residents railcard.

## LOCOMOTIVES AND TRAINS

Powerful steam or diesel locomotives will ensure efficient operation of the relatively long steeply graded Welsh Highland route. The Beyer-Garratt articulated locomotive is ideal for such terrain and an opportunity has been taken to purchase from South Africa some of the last locomotives of this type - which were built in Manchester. The Ffestiniog Railway owns the earliest of these locomotives, it operated in Tasmania and is now being restored for use on the Welsh Highland after being on display at the National Railway Museum.

The first Beyer-Garratt, known as K1, was built in 1909. K1 has an 0-4-0+0-4-0 wheel arrangement and weighs 33.5 tons. The South African NGG16 locomotives, built in 1958, weigh 61.4 tons and are more powerful but being of 2-6-2+2-6-2 design impose lower axle loadings on the track. The first diesel locomotive for the Welsh Highland, manufactured in South Africa by Funkey and equipped with an almost new 350HP Cummins engine, arrived along with one for the Ffestiniog in October 1993.

The NGG16 is 30% more powerful than the K1. It can haul trains of more than 15 carriages weighing up to 275 tons at speeds of 25 miles per hour. The onerous Welsh Highland gradients of 1 in 45 and 160ft radius curves can easily be negotiated. It carries 1800 gallons of water which allows operation from Caernarfon to Porthmadog, without a water stop. Like most Welsh Highland locomotives, the NGG16s will be oil fired to improve operating efficiency and avoid fire risk in the forest.

Passengers will be able to enjoy the comfort of modern corridor carriages, very similar to the latest Ffestiniog carriages. Carriages will be designed to provide panoramic views, heating will be installed and toilet facilities will be available. Access will be provided for disabled people. A full buffet and dining service will be possible. Some open and 'tourist' carriages are likely to be available initially and for peak summer services. Wagons, surplus from South Africa, are being delivered for construction and track maintenance trains and for conversion into specialist vehicles.

While a new railway is being created the past will not be forgotten, examples of the original carriages and locomotives will be used for special heritage events.

The first two NGG16 locomotives will be available for the start of Welsh Highland services and K1 should be available well before extension to Rhyd Ddu is achieved for the Millennium. Options on a further three Beyer-Garratts will cover anticipated future requirements. It is expected that 24 carriages could be required for Millennium services and about fifty when the line is completed to Porthmadog. Orders for new carriages will be placed for progressive delivery and may be manufactured locally. Ffestiniog Railway locomotives and carriages will be able to operate on the Welsh Highland and the larger Beyer-Garratt and Funkey locomotives will be able to operate as far as the Ffestiniog Railway's Boston Lodge works.

*Here are some extracts from the WHR brochure produced in 1995. It was designed by David Grosvenor, who did a very elegant job. The text was in Welsh and English and it explained a lot, almost all of which has been faithfully followed. Copies of this brochure were sent to all elected council members and officers, and to other relevant people likely to be affected. It was handed out at the consultation meetings and was available to visitors at the public displays maintained (one in the FR Museum -Goods Shed- at Harbour Station for example). Reading it now is convincing - at the time like many brochures of its kind, it was thought to be baloney by those opposed..*

**2.** Although the casual observer might think that much of this is a mix of hot air and red tape, it is now the law, and it has to be done.

**3.** It is really expensive, and in value for money terms probably doesn't stack up - however, this is what people had to do to get this railway.

**4.** Having done all this, having come through: the little flag wavers, the amateur objector, the grudge-bearing detractor, doesn't stand a chance. 'Coming through' however meant that the application would have to be strong enough to surmount another public inquiry. Winning this is the price for gaining Establishment support.. For those objectors that do not like your proposals, their remedy is firstly at the public inquiry, and then in the courts, at their own expense.

All of this is trial by paper - it is bureaucratic machinery that grinds exceeding small, however, it is designed to allow public concern to be exhibited and to 'mitigate' hardship. At the end of it, every conceivable objection is likely to have been aired and it is why the process takes so long.

The Caernarfon Railway LRO was not made until October 1997 - so the railway was being constructed with conditional approval. The Millennium grant application came through in May 1995, with a conditional offer that included Caernarfon-Dinas but, also just under 50% funding for the Railway as far as Rhyd Ddu.

In May 1995 the downside risk was looking frightening:

**1.** No LRO for Caernarfon -Dinas (came 09.10.97)
**2.** No ownership of Trackbed (came 03.02.99)
**3.** No lease for Caernarfon-Dinas (came mid-1996)
**4.** Conditional offer on funding - but big gap (ERDF offer for Caernarfon - Dinas came Oct -1996)
**5.** No guarantee of permission for Dinas-Porthmadog
**6.** Growing opposition to the restoration

It was all shaky, yet what was to follow was to be worse. It has already been observed that this operation was not for faint hearts.

Aside from concerns over the risk that the project might collapse, there was the ongoing concern that if fundraising, permissions and applications for orders were not skilfully co-ordinated, then there could be crippling gaps in activity later, leading to loss of skilled workforce and general demotivation. The only way forward was to act strongly on the points that were open, as progress

in the area of preparation for the TWO application would have payback later, and would strengthen resolve and reputation.

There were points that were quite clear in support:

**1.** The Transfer Order public inquiry was won, indicating some 'approval' from the centre

**2.** The Millennium Commission was supporting the project and giving it publicity, again suggesting backing for the scheme

**3.** Supporters had rallied, being suitably enthused about reports of impending Garratts, and the forthcoming start of construction of Caernarfon - Dinas

**4.** There were immediate funds made available to do the job.

It was decided that the draft Order would be prepared by Peter Johnson. Peter had much experience of the wording of various pieces of railway legislation. He was familiar with terms and layouts, with articles, schedules and all that goes to comprise the details of such a document. Thus he volunteered for the job, and he and Tony Smare co-ordinated the massive effort needed to make the TWO application. This required the draft Order to be submitted, and at the same time to answer the Applications and Objections Procedure Rules Document. Messrs Sharpe, Pritchard, Parliamentary Agents managed and guided the job, under the direction of Mike Hart. It was all to take about two and a half years to put together, starting from autumn 1994. This was an unsure and very long process, with no guarantees. Everything had to be anticipated some way in advance.

It was necessary to have a complete survey of the route, and this was completed by John Sreeves, who after excelled in bridge design work featured later. Mike Schumann and Tony Smare dealt with the landowner contact and correspondence. Mike Schumann produced the plans for the Application ( TWA), which

*Above: The trackbed at Nantmor. Vacant for years - apparently abandoned, so it was used as a footpath, and some were even shown on maps. 'This'll never be a railway again' was the general assumption. It was a pleasant ramble; you parked your car and strolled along the trackbed, (away from the camera) through the old tunnels and up along the side of the Afon Glaslyn. What could be nicer - travel by train?*

*Left: The vacant trackbed rises towards the camera, out of the Gwyrfai Valley, and curves in behind, towards Rhyd Ddu Station. This view, looking north in 1993, shows the remarkable state of preservation of the old railway in certain places after 56 years of abandonment.*

**Left:** *In the middle -distance, the wall is the bridge parapet of the railway passing under the A487. The whole of the emerging part of the cutting is filled in. The pub car park runs close to the erstwhile cutting edge. The restoration of the railway would affect these people, as they had possession of the land, and this needed to be bought back, and the fill taken out down to trackbed level.*

**Both Photos: Mike Schumann**

**Below**: *This dark picture is taken from the A487 bridge, looking down the old cutting, towards Dinas Station shows how much work needs to be done to restore the cutting to use. we should be in no doubt today that in 1997 this was a formidable undertaking, as this barrier was at the starting gate - there was far, far more - and almost no money to do it with.*

of course had to include identifying all culverts, bridges, crossing, and determining where access was required, for construction purposes over other peoples land. The long sections, showing the vertical alignment were surveyed and drawn by John Sreeves. Mike also drew the outline of all new structures, in order to obtain outline planning permission. All of this activity was going on at the same time as planning the Caernarfon-Dinas railway and dealing with objections to the Caernarfon Railway LRO.

GC accepted in advance of the TWO Inquiry that the definitive footpaths shown on the railway trackbed had been created in error. It was agreed with them that the easiest way of modifying the definitive footpath map was to use the TWO as a means of extinguishing them. The alternative methods available to GC were very time consuming. (Even at the inquiry the Ramblers Association accepted that the railway trackbed should not have been made a public footpath.) GC officers were helpful, recognising that working with FR Co. made sense, and willingly assisted discussion of their part in the myriad items needed to facilitate the TWO process. Some of the stuff was straightforward, some was anything but, as elected members had their foibles.

As the potential new owners of the trackbed it was necessary to consult with all those affected, to meet with adjacent landowners, and to talk about the plans to reinstate the track. This process offered clear pointers as to what might be expected, both in the level of objection to the Application, and in the nature of the objections that would be made in the likely event of there being a public inquiry.

Right by the start of the old NWNG proper, at Dinas, the pub owners on the A487T had filled in the railway cutting next the bridge and were using the extra space created for car parking. When visited they were polite and attentive, and FR people were very nice too. However, nothing could disguise the bad news. Others didn't take this so well. Farmers had removed fences and merged the old railway into their fields. Some were using the railway as access to property, either for entry or for servicing their land. It was very inconvenient if the trackbed was to be removed from them - and this opened the way for opposition to form against the whole restoration scheme. A small proportion of the land had been sold by the Receiver (OR), and this was not within the FR Co's power to enter. Compulsory purchase powers can be applied for in the TWO, but these are not granted without

good reason. The TWO applicant must attempt to come to an agreement with the landowner. Quite often this is achieved satisfactorily, normally after money has become involved. Enough reasoned objections against the proposals lead to a public inquiry. When it was possible to come to an agreement with a landowner, then this was one potential objector removed from the list. Those who were against might not say so to one's face - few encourage personal conflict. The results were unclear, and even those most helpful face to face had the right to lodge an objection later.

The FR Co. view was that the railway had not been abandoned, and where there were issues of severance and other perceived disturbance, these needed to be met in order to satisfy an objection - and not all were satisfied. There were a very few cases where landowners felt that they had won the rights to the strip of land by adverse possession. Failure of the title holder to exercise any acts of ownership on land, occupied by another for a period of ten years, might permit a claim for adverse possession, if registered and recorded correctly, and provided such claim does not obstruct the statutory purpose. The adverse possession rules (FR Co. claimed) do not apply to an extant railway - and as WHR had never been abandoned, it was a railway without track. The powers couldn't be extinguished without an Abandonment Order; the track couldn't be restored without a TWO.

Of course the law offered a remedy for those resentful of the denial of their claims. If they objected, and the TWO application was thrown out at any resulting public inquiry, the new landowner would be left with little option other than to regularise their claim. The situation was that maybe the logical thing for a trespasser to

*Right: The trackbed is difficult to pick out in this view near Castell Cidwm, it had been incorporated into the field, that it had spilt anyway when the NWNGRys were constructed. There was opposition in this spot, and it never improved. For any railway enthusiast, this was what they had always dreamed of. It was not a dream shared.*

**Both Photos: Mike Schumann**

*Below: This is the view, in the field, looking along the trackbed to see where the railway once ran. An extremely dim view was taken of the field being split once more. It was considered here, and in many other places, that the railway was long gone - and should stay that way.*

do was to ignore offers, lodge an objection and turn up at a public inquiry looking for a better deal. The general FR solution was to talk softly, and to try to mitigate the effect of railway restoration, to offer alternative access, without any admission of liability.

There were a number of 'implacables' who were not in favour of having a railway at all. Some were against as it would cause them hardship, and some imagined the loss of amenity and the creation of disturbance would be unbearable. The spectre of animals being driven mad in the fields, of wildlife being slaughtered wholesale, and everywhere being invaded by noise and enveloped in smog from the engines eventually arose. It was the same set of 'leave me alone' emotional arguments that met the Victorian railway builders, minus the threat of the air being sucked from one's lungs during the passage of the train.

Whilst landowners, especially farmers, and those using the trackbed for access, faced commercial consequences that could be dealt with by offers of alternative access, environmentalists and residents were usually dissatisfied on a point of principle, and objected with no intention of being persuaded to the contrary. An examination of the logic of many of their objections shows that few acknowledged the potential beneficial economic effect of this railway to the locality. Engaging in conversation on the subject with this type of objector tended to meet conspiracy theories or perhaps just plain, well rooted ignorance, that asked for no light of reason to be shone upon it. On the other hand, utilities normally place widespread objections to schemes that affect them, and the long length of the railway meant that considerable dialogue with MANWEB, British Gas, and Welsh Water was needed to satisfy the many problems that arose. Even then, there were residual

problems that caused the objection to remain, in order to place the promise of a remedy on public record.

Consultation required documents. There was a leaflet, (flyer) produced in thousands, and distributed in 1995 by Royal Mail, to everyone in the postcode areas surrounding the railway. They were used freely and reprinted to include dates of public meetings. The glossy red brochure was used for those directly affected, and as a general promotional tool; publication costs were partly recovered by sale to those interested in the project.

The TWA rules require the submission of an Environmental Statement. Numerous environmental experts on noise, atmospheric pollution, etc. had to be retained to advise and act as witnesses. Of interest was research developing from early tests on the FR, to sample the sounds of a Garratt hauling a heavy load up the just opened section to Dinas. These established benchmarks for the noise of trains, a significant item included in the objection of a number of people concerned at the disturbance likely from the restored railway. Tables with interesting data are given in the Inquiry proofs of evidence included later.

TWA Rules and guidance make clear that there are those who **must** be consulted and, not so clearly, those who **should** be consulted. The Order applicant has to make sure that every relevant person and body has been consulted, if the Application is not to be tripped up at an inquiry. So the applicant has to 'get out there and find everybody' - a job largely done by Mike Schumann and Tony Smare. In November 1995 the consultation was proceeding with rapidity, and a series of public meetings were held. Personal recollection of a gathering at the School at Rhyd Ddu is of a polite and quiet meeting, of explanation, with a number of questions at the end. The difficult bits tended not to emerge at the public meetings; it did not feel as though there were any burning issues - those emerged more gradually after.

Having the red, glossy brochure was very helpful, as it showed how serious the FR Co. was in wishing to restore the railway, and it gave a public face to some of the community benefits that would result. Inevitably, to supporters, the brochure is meat and drink, and to detractors it is mere propaganda. To the general population of the disinterested and the unconvinced, it has little meaning, but it went down well in Cardiff and Westminster where opinion counted very much. After the public meeting, one could form the view that all was well. This was often not the case, as objectors might decide not to opt for public confrontation,

*Left: Snowdon Ranger is a beautiful spot, above Llyn Cwellyn, with a level crossing over the farm road. The trackbed is here being used for access - and has been for years. There is a footpath routed via the railway and shown on definitive maps! To put the railway back means satisfying objections at this and every other spot.*

**Both Photos: Mike Schumann**

*Below: The trackbed rises steadily to run through the site of the old Snowdon Ranger Station. The building on the right is the old station building - not available - and the YHA Hostel is conveniently sited behind the clump of trees. A replacement Halt was intended for here.*

instead to lodge objection, and to appear at the public inquiry, and this was their right.

The TWO Application went in to the DETR on 27th March 1997, accompanied by a cheque to the value of £80,000. The Draft WHR Works Order, was 37 pages long, and subject to amendment, would become the fully-legal WHR Works Order. It had to encompass in sufficient, enforceable, legal detail all the matters concerned with rebuilding the railway adjacent to, or through, the properties of some 50 individual owners or concerns, with six level crossings over public highways - one of which was Britannia Bridge, Porthmadog - authorising a couple of small diversions, diverting some footpaths, safeguarding the near environment, operating the completed railway, etc. It had to refer to and/or observe some 24 principal Acts and Orders that refer to FR and antecedents, plus other railway and general legislation. Not only must the Order give FR Co. legal powers to allow the railway to be constructed and operated, but the responsibilities of the railway proprietors to act within all relevant law must be specified, and injury to legitimate public interests had to be protected. An Order in which there was some legal weakness could be a source of disagreement, expense and frustration on both sides for many years.

Upon the submission of the Order there was a six-week period, during which objections and representations by any other party could be made to the DETR. It was upon the basis of the objections received that the Department, formally the Secretary of State, made the decision on whether a public inquiry should be held. At the same time as the Order was submitted, the event had to be announced widely, and sent specifically to all the parties affected.

At the end of the 42 day period there were 350 letters of objection and 20 letters of support (later to rise to 403 letters of objection and 443 letter of support by 23 January 1998) Objections at this stage were the formal and necessary preliminary, to either a proposed appearance at the Inquiry or at least, presentation of formal written evidence of some detail. There was also the option for FR Co. of entering negotiation with the objector with a view to getting the objection withdrawn.

To give a clear picture of the breadth of objections within the 350 letters, they can be categorised as follows:

o  farmers, land owners, highland shepherds,
o  private residents and informal local communities,
o  local non-farming businesses. e.g., hotels, public houses, local

traders, tourist attractions,
o  walkers' and other associations, e.g., the Ramblers Association, Snowdonia Society,
o  an adjoining narrow gauge railway company at Porthmadog (WHR Ltd),
o local authorities with planning powers, GC, Snowdonia National Park Authority,
o  local authorities without planning powers, those affected
o  Community and Town Councils,
o  other national bodies concerned, e.g., the National Trust,
o  the Highway Authorities, Welsh Office with GC as agent,
o  other  utilities and services, e.g., BT, Railtrack, Welsh Water

Some of the objections overlapped; many held serious problems for which there was no easy remedy if the railway was going to be rebuilt.

On 5th June 1997, the Secretary of State for Transport announced a public inquiry would be held into the Application. A pre-meeting was scheduled for 28th October, with the Inquiry beginning at the Arfon Area Offices Caernarfon, on 9th December 1997. The FR Co. advocates chosen were Mr Rhodri Price Lewis QC, Senior Counsel, and Mr Russell Harris QC, Junior Counsel, both were Welsh speakers, both were specialists in Planning Law.

The Caernarfon Railway, Between Caernarfon and Dinas opened on 13th October 1997, and with the TWA still to be determined, onward construction effort, the funding and everything else would have to remain on 'hold' until determined. The Inquiry itself could not be rushed. The delay to the building process onwards from Dinas was until 21st July 1999, some 21 months. Celebration in Rhyd Ddu for 2000 looked unlikely.

# The Inquiry:

**If what follows is tedious, treat it as a record of events.**

## The case for the granting of the Order*

**Mr Price Lewis QC** put a written legal submission to the Inspector to pass to the DETR for consideration. His plea was that if adverse possession was claimed, compulsory purchase would clearly be necessary in order to allow the restoration of the line.

**Mike Hart, FR Co. Chairman** outlined the plan for re-constructing the Welsh Highland in stages from Caernarfon towards Porthmadog, move the FR from being a major Welsh tourist business to a significant world attraction.

The reconstruction and equipping of Welsh Highland throughout was going to cost about £20 million, of which about half would be spent in creating the Caernarfon to Rhyd Ddu section, planned for opening in the year 2000. Over 60% of the money for the line to Rhyd Ddu had been secured through the Millennium Commission, various Welsh Office funding agencies, and significant gifts from supporters. Volunteer labour would cover a significant part of the total projected capital budget and reduce the actual planned cash cost. Since the Secretary of State decided the competing TO applications in favour of FR Co. in 1995, various efforts had been made to co-operate with the 64 Co. but to date, agreement had not been found. Under the WHR TWA, it was planned that the main Porthmadog boarding point for Welsh Highland passengers would be at Harbour Station. It was believed that the Porthmadog to Blaenau Ffestiniog railway, of which much is also in the heart of the National Park, shows how a railway can be established and maintained that both blends into, and becomes a part of, that landscape.

The construction of the first phase of Welsh Highland from Caernarfon to Dinas was now largely completed, except at the stations. It was understood that the work done, and the way the project had been handled, had been to the satisfaction of the local authority and seemed to have the support of the majority of the people in the area.

**Tony Smare, WHRL Project Manager** explained the context of the WHR restoration in terms of the communities it would serve, how it would be funded, and how many people might be expected to use it. His own experience helped to ensure that the Environmental Impact Assessment was thorough. Local consultants, Posford Duvivier had produced the Environmental Statement which indicated moderate or minor effect, with a few beneficial impacts recorded. Property matters were strongly influenced by the Transfer Order made by the Secretary of State in 1995. This limited issues over property to a few sites where deviations or extra land was required. Equally, there was potential for releasing surplus land, and there was an example already of such a case. Because the railway had been out of use for many years, some adjacent landowners believed that they might have a case for adverse possession of railway land, but the Company was advised that such claims were unlikely to succeed. The Company

was concerned to see so many letters of objection arriving after it had advertised its Order application. The fact that around 70% of the letters explained that the objector was not opposed in principle to restoration was reassuring. There had been much concern expressed about the effects of big locomotives but anyone who had seen the locomotive operating out of Caernarfon should be reassured. The problems anticipated by walkers were addressed by the section of the Environmental Statement entitled 'Recreation'. There were differences of view regarding the status of footpaths, but the Company had improved and re-advertised its provisions, so that alternative routes were identified in virtually all cases. Clearly, the farming community would be affected by the return of the railway. It has been his objective throughout the consultation period to identify what provisions or mitigation measures could overcome the concerns of people, particularly those living or working near the railway.

Tony Smare was in constant demand over the Public Inquiry period, to be cross-examined by objectors, he was involved in many out-of-session negotiations.

**Alan Heywood, FR Co. General Manager** explained the great economic benefit to the neighbourhood from the presence of the Ffestiniog Railway (FR), as visitors to the railway stayed in the area, and FR used local suppliers for its goods and services. For example, much of the £135,000 per year supplies for catering outlets was spent locally, whilst the Company's £70,000 printing budget was spent with printers in Porthmadog. The FR was accepted as part of the national transport infrastructure by British Rail's successors. The FR Residents' Railcard scheme, for those on the electoral roll in North Wales, allowed travel at one quarter of the normal fares, thereby, helping those who regularly use the train. Approximately 3,000 cards were currently in use.

The number of customers using the trains for access to the National Park for other purposes (e.g. walking) was likely to increase. Similarly, customers staying on caravan sites and elsewhere within the Park would be encouraged to use the train to reach the coast at either end of the line. These customers were likely now to use cars for such journeys. Unlimited travel rover tickets would be available at a price which was little above the price of one full return journey. His own experience of using such tickets in Switzerland suggested that, once purchased, the train was used for all journeys for the duration of the holiday. If local bus operators agreed to join the scheme, which experience suggested they would, the tickets would become even more flexible and even better value.

The timetable was based on an average speed of about 15mph and a maximum of 25mph. Garratt articulated locomotives were oil-fired to avoid risk of lineside fires. Because they were powerful locos operating well within their capabilities, they would not work hard, and were extremely quiet in operation. A sample Summer timetable for a complete service from Caernarfon via Porthmadog was comparable to the existing level of service on the FR, both in frequency and in the length of the operating day. The proposal to connect the two lines was extremely important, both for the customer's and the Company. A large number of journeys would be broken in Porthmadog where catering establishments and shops would benefit. Mr Heywood said his Evidence showed that the existing FR operation brings substantial benefits to the towns of Porthmadog and Blaenau Ffestiniog, not only to the tradespeople of the area but also to many individual residents who benefit from the comprehensive transport, information, and

---

*\* Note: This account, and the pages that follow reporting the TWO Public Inquiry are drawn from **John Hopkins's** account, and I am grateful for the excellence of his work, and his permission to use it; some is heavily précised. Ed.*

Merddyn Emrys *at Tan y Bwlch on a down train, 06.07.2010. Alan Heywood was trying to get across the expectation that as Tan y Bwlch was used as a 'stop-off point' for people using the FR, then intermediate stations on the Welsh Highland Railway must also enjoy the benefits in like manner. That indeed it would be more so, as there is reason for visiting Beddgelert in its own right - it is a famous place. Furthermore, that people who do visit Beddgelert (and other places like Rhyd Ddu) in this way are likely to use the train in the National Park and not their cars. Hence there will be an environmental benefit.*

ticketing services provided.

**Mrs M Williams, Lady Mayor of the Royal Town of Caernarfon** said that this railway was a venture which was bringing life back to the local community, life which had lately been blighted by the lack of interesting local activities. It was very encouraging to note that in the three weeks the line opened this Autumn, it generated over 18,000 single journeys. As in most towns in Wales, unemployment is a great worry, and Mrs Williams was confident that the WHR restoration project would help to alleviate Caernarfon's problems by providing employment and job opportunities which had already begun. The interest arising would ensure job creation for young people. The re-opening of the three-mile, first stage of the Welsh Highland Railway, from Dinas Station to Caernarfon, had already created great interest among the young people of the Town. Family parties and many schoolchildren had enjoyed outings on the trains, providing them with both new ideas and new experiences.

**Miss AL Goodall,** speaking on ecology had been employed as a consultant ecologist since 1989, and since 1995, had been Managing Director of ESL (Ecological Services) Ltd. In that capacity, she managed the ecological baseline surveys and impact assessment for the WHR between Dinas and Porthmadog.

The proposed scope of the assessment was circulated to the Environment Agency, the Countryside Council for Wales (CCW), Arfon Borough Council, Cyngor Dosbarth Dwyfor, the

Snowdonia National Park, the North Wales Wildlife Trust and the Royal Society for the Protection of Birds. She spoke to a detailed list of mitigation measures. A consultant ecologist will be appointed throughout the construction phase. Duties will include:

o examination of working plans and drawings for potential impacts, and provision of best practice advice for each activity and on timing of works,

o liaison with statutory and concerned voluntary bodies, provision of advice on design and siting of bat roost boxes,

o supervision of all works for which a potential ecological impact is identified, and setting up monitoring procedures,

o co-ordination of the activities of specialists.

**Mr M Laming**, speaking on agriculture was familiar with the proposals for the WHR and conducted all interviews with the farmers who were affected, potentially some 30 in total. This work went to make up the ADAS report which has previously been supplied on a confidential basis to the NFU, and was annexed to his main evidence. The main issues arising out of his report were:

o access across the railway,

o use of the railway trackbed,

o disturbance of livestock, and

o maintenance of water supplies.

The measures proposed for mitigation are as follows:

**1.** Reconstruction of farm crossings, provision of new gates and fences, and relocation of crossings wherever feasible.

**2.** Existing under-passes or sheep-creeps recommissioned

unless the landowner specifically does not require this.

3. Bridges repaired and, if reconstruction was necessary, this would be to [meet] improved standards. The provision of new gates, boundary walls and fences would relieve some farmers of future capital and maintenance costs.

4. Livestock feeding areas would be provided on hard-core access routes to crossings, which would be widened as necessary. Livestock refuge facilities would be achieved in a similar manner to livestock

*Caernarfon always supported the WHR and the Lady Mayor, no less, took the stand to champion the cause, saying the blighted local activities needed something interesting with ideas and experiences.*

feeding areas. Commitment had been made to the provision of alternative access to residential property isolated by the reinstatement of the railway. Where the use of the railway as an access track or link was essential, access would be provided by an alternative to maintain current land use.

Noise tests had been conducted recently which demonstrated that the noise from WHR trains would be significantly less than measured in earlier tests on the FR. Evidence was presented by the expert witness on noise that there was no basis for concerns related to lambing, as this occurs when a less frequent train service operates. Access to water for livestock will be maintained either by assuring access to the river or by providing or improving an alternative water supply.

The FR Co. conclusion was that no farms were likely to suffer commercial hardship as a result of the WHR restoration.

o no farms would be forced to alter their business, and

o there would be no need for substantial management changes on farms.

**Mr K Heeley** gave evidence on the Porthmadog, Britannia Bridge level crossing installation. The installation would be a tramway crossing with standard road traffic signals at each end of the Britannia Bridge and signals for trains would be in the form of prescribed tramway signals. It would be necessary to control movements at the road junction to the Harbour Station (Harbour Drive) with traffic signals. The use of traffic signals provided positive control and a clear understanding of the system by road users. Closed Circuit Television (CCTV) would operate to provide a monitoring

*Britannia Bridge, Porthmadog, looking 'east' in 1997 before the tracks. It is tranquil as it is out of season. The point to be urged about the tramway crossing was that it would not make congestion worse in the high season than it was 'now'.*

and safety facility for movements across the Bridge.

To allow a train to pass over the bridge required general traffic to be stopped. For the train to clear, it had been estimated that main road traffic would need to be brought to a stand for 92 seconds. During periods of peak congestion in August, there was already extensive queuing on the A487 on the approach to Britannia Bridge. In a westbound direction, 'moving queues' might often extend to the turn for Portmeirion, a distance of some 2.5 kilometres, including in excess of 300 vehicles. The rail impact would be marginal and could not be said to significantly increase queuing and congestion. After train operation, when the signals cleared, westbound vehicles would have a less congested run having been held at the signals, creating a clear section downstream.

The anticipated impacts were based on a worst-case situation, i.e., peak-hour, August traffic flows with maximum train length. For most of the year, the effects would be markedly less than this. Then whilst some vehicles would be halted during the operation of the crossing, this was not likely to increase congestion significantly.

**Major (Ret'd) CB Holden,** one of HM Ex Railway Inspector, spoke on safety considerations. Before the railway could be opened for traffic, it would require approval under the provisions of the Railways and other Transport Systems Regulations 1994. Approval could only be given if the railway fully satisfied the safety requirements set down by the Inspectorate. The proposal was to cross the Britannia Bridge, with the railway running as far as is practicable from the kerb of a footway. The railway between Harbour Station and a point north of the Motor Museum at Snowdon Street should be regarded as a tramway. This would mean that the road crossings in this section of the railway would be treated as road junctions having a tram-phase within the road traffic signal controller. If there were to be an undue blockage or slow clearance of a road junction, the train would be required to stop and could do so. He considered that this operating method would provide the greatest possible safety and would be acceptable to HMRI.

In general, the normal form of protection for accommodation level crossings would be outward-swinging gates opened and shut by the user. All owners of crossing rights will have to be reminded of their obligations under the 1845 Act to keep gates closed except when the crossing is being used by vehicles, animals, or people on foot.

It was his expert view that the operating speed of the railway will be such that the sighting distances of approaching trains will allow foot crossings at stations to reach the platform

The signals at an AOLC (flashing alternate red lights) prohibit the passage of emergency vehicles, whereas traffic lights (and tramway signals) may be passed in the red phase at the drivers' discretion. It was later decided that AOLC installations should be made across the Cross Town Rail Link.

**Mr PE Marston** gave evidence on planning. He stated that the proposal was entirely consistent with Planning Guidance (Wales) Planning Policy 1996, issued by the Welsh Office. The proposal was also in accordance with the Development Plan which comprised the Gwynedd Structure Plan and the Local Plans for Arfon, Eryri and Dwyfor. Therefore, there must be a presumption in favour of its approval. The Company had applied for deemed planning permission, but had given a legal undertaking to submit details of all buildings, to restore original boundary walls, to undertake environmental monitoring, to establish working groups as a forum for discussion, and to safeguard public rights of way. This undertaking provided the safeguards that would normally be provided through planning conditions.

The proposal did not prejudice the establishment of a strategic network of national or regional recreational routes. The impact of the railway on the rights of way network was minimal, having regard to the Company's undertakings, the Deposit Plans, and the Notices of Application to Stop Up a Footpath or Bridleway. The project would provide an important transport link for visitors into the National Park in accordance with Government and the SNPA policy.

As the formation of the railway was largely in place, the impact of construction, infrastructure and operation of the line would be minimal, given the mitigation measures proposed. The development would create both direct and indirect jobs in an area of high unemployment. The railway would bring economic benefit to the region and, in particular, to Caernarfon, Porthmadog and Beddgelert, through increased visitor numbers, greater visitor expenditure, increased length of holiday season, increased bed-space occupancy, and improved community facilities.

**Dr D Laxen,** gave evidence to the Inquiry on air quality. Dr Laxen was responsible for the air quality assessment carried out for the Environmental Statement prepared on behalf of the FR Co. Pollutants that needed to be considered were nitrogen oxides (of which nitrogen dioxide, $NO_2$ is the pollutant of concern), sulphur dioxide, $SO_2$, fine airborne particles, (commonly called PM10 , )

### Table 1. Pollutant Emission Rates used for assessment

| Pollutant | Beyer Garratt Locomotive (g/km) | Deisel Locomotive (g/km) |
|---|---|---|
| NO₂ | 2.4 | 9 |
| SO₂ | 4 | 2.3 |
| PM₁₀ | 1.7 | 0.12 |
| CO | 6 | 1.4 |

and carbon monoxide CO. Consideration had also been given to potential nuisance from dust during construction and odours during operation. The Beyer-Garratt was a more significant emission source, and to ensure that the worst case was dealt with, that formed the basis of his assessment.

Given its rural setting, with prevailing winds from the west and southwest bringing clean Atlantic air for much of the time, it was not surprising that existing air quality was good along the entire length of the route. Since the original Environmental Assessment, the Government had published its National Air Quality Strategy, which set out new air quality standards and objectives (Table 2). These were unlikely to be exceeded in this part of Wales.

Sensitive locations were places alongside the proposed route where people would be exposed for significant periods of time. These would be mainly residential properties of which there are 49 within 25m of the line.

### Table 2. UK National Air Quality Strategy Standards and Objectives

| Pollutant | National Standard | National Objectives 2005 |
|---|---|---|
| NO₂ | 21ppb annual mean | 21ppb annual mean |
| SO₂ | 100ppb 15min mean | 100ppb 99%le ‡ |
| PM₁₀ | 50 µg/m³ run 24h mean | 50 µg/m³ 99%le * |
| CO | 10ppm run 8h mean | 10ppm highest run 8h mean |

‡ 99.9 percentile of 15-min. means
* 99 percentile of highest daily running 24-hour means

Dust was the principal air quality impact that might arise during the construction phase causing a nuisance potentially if present in sufficient quantities. The main mitigation measure was damping down of the ground or any dusty materials being handled. The ultimate control measure would be to cease dust raising activities if there were exceptional conditions.

The emissions from the Beyer-Garratt, while on the move, would have a negligible effect on air quality 10m from the track. Concentrations would be well below the air quality health standards and low enough to be of no significance for vegetation. The Environmental Health Officer for the former Meirionnydd District Council had reported no complaints from the public about air quality alongside the existing Festiniog line. Similarly, the Environmental Health Officer for the former Dwyfor District Council had reported no complaints for the existing station at Porthmadog. There were, therefore, no grounds to expect air quality complaints during the routine operation of the WHR.

Emissions from the locomotives would have an odour associated with them, which will probably be noticed on occasions by people close to the track. This was unlikely to represent a nuisance, as it would last only a very short time as the train passes, and be infrequent.

Concerns had been raised by a number of the residents of Britannia Terrace, within 25 metres of the line, about the proposal for trains to pass close to their houses. The original proposal that the trains might halt there for up to 10 minutes had been modified to ensure that they did not halt routinely, but would wait out on the Cob for clearance to cross the bridge. A busy road ran in front of the houses, which were just 3m back from the kerb. This road carried around 15,000 vehicles per day. It was well known that traffic emissions contribute to soiling, with black oily particles coming from diesel vehicles. He had carried out studies that had shown soiling rates were roughly doubled alongside busy

| Table 3. The effect of the proposed WHR on pollutant concentrations at Britannia Terrace - 2005 | | | | |
|---|---|---|---|---|
| Assumptions in the table below: Road Traffic - peak hour 1,254 vehicles/hr, two way, 3% HGV, 12 mph Rail Traffic - One train per hour each way on 70% days per year | | | | |
| Pollutant | Predicted Conc'trations Road | Road & Rail | Nat Objectives 2005 | Timescale |
| $NO_2$ | 17.1ppb | 17.3ppb | 21pbb | annual mean |
| $PM_{10}$ | 29 µg/m³ | 30.6 µg/m³ | 50 µg/m³ | see Note 1 |
| $CO_2$ | 2.41ppm | 2.42ppm | 10ppm | see Note 2 |
| Note 1: 99 percentile of highest daily running 24-hour means Note 2: Highest running 8-hour means | | | | |

roads. He had calculated the concentrations which would arise at Britannia Bridge, and assumed that the trains would be travelling very slowly at 6mph, with the northbound train stopping for up to 1 minute before crossing the bridge.

Northbound trains at Nantmor would be running up a gradient and working hard, hence emitting more pollutants. However, this would be balanced by the southbound trains, emitting less than normal. Exposure at the properties close to the track would be short-lived, as the trains would be moving past at 10-20mph taking 5-10 seconds to travel 50 metres. They would not be stationary near to these properties.

One of the residents had noted that smoke and sulphur dioxide hang over Beddgelert when coal fires are lit. This would be a far more significant source of air pollution and nuisance than the short duration of emissions from the trains, which were running on low sulphur oil, unlike domestic coal which was a high sulphur fuel.

**Mr K Ratcliffe** addressed the Inquiry on the noise and vibration effect of the restored railway.

Mr Ratcliffe had been involved in a programme of noise and vibration measurements with the Beyer-Garratt, the ALCO and the Funkey diesel locomotive [at a site on a gradient near Dinas Station in October 1997].

He had studied the Statements of Case of Objectors and prepared the answers to questions relating to noise and vibration. Many of the points were site specific but some are general, for example, the impact of noise in the open areas of Snowdonia. He had dealt with this in comments on the objection by the Snowdonia National Park Society.

Many of the objections to the proposals were based on an assumption that the Beyer-Garratt locomotive would create more noise than the smaller ALCO type, but it had been shown that both the Beyer-Garratt and the Funkey diesel locomotives were significantly quieter than the ALCO. Noise levels would generally meet the recommendations of the World Health Organisation and those given in the Planning Guidance for Wales with the

*Apparently the ALCO was noisier than a Beyer Garratt when on test - a result that surprised no FR enginemen! To some this locomotive expends much of its energy on making a noise, but it must be said that here was an occasion when the ALCO was actually useful.*

exception of those at some properties which were at a distance of 10m or less from the railway and/or are close to halts, bridges or cuttings. The levels specified in the Noise Insulation Regulations would be met at all properties. Noise control measures which should be considered included alternatives to the use of train whistles, the reduction of squeal caused by wheel/rail interaction on bends, vibration isolation of rails, especially on bridges, and the maintenance of track and wheel smoothness.

**Mr JK Steer, Highways and Economics** said that he had given evidence on the business planning aspects of the WHR project to the Light Railway Transfer Order Inquiry in Caernarfon in November 1993. Since then, Steer, Davies, Gleave has undertaken several commissions on behalf of the FR Co. during the course of the project.

He explained that the railway would have a beneficial impact on the local economy through the creation of jobs, both during construction of the line and when the line was in operation. The FR Co. estimated that around 30 workers would be required during each phase of reconstruction. The reconstruction of the Caernarfon to Dinas railway drew largely upon the local labour force. Once the whole railway was fully in operation, at least 24 permanent and 9 temporary staff would be employed. The estimated employment benefits to the local economy during the construction phases would be worth around £0.4 million per year and during the full operational phase, a further £0.6 million per year. Around 8,000 volunteer days per year would be generated by the railway, worth £125,000 per year to the local economy when the railway was in full operation. When fully open to Porthmadog, the railway was expected to attract in the region of 250,000 visitors per year, around half of whom were expected to be new and additional visitors to the area. The value to the local economy, he estimated, would be in the region of £3.6m per year with a further £0.6 million per year being redistributed around the North Wales area. Around two-thirds of the benefits would be expected to accrue to the Caernarfon and Dinas areas.

The railway represented an opportunity for visitors to leave their cars outside the National Park. This could occur at Porthmadog in the south and Caernarfon/Dinas or Waunfawr in the north, from where people could travel into the Park by train. Such a policy supported the SNPA's stated aim to develop a comprehensive approach to the management of transport and traffic in the National Park.

Currently, there were in the region of 6.5 million to 10.5 million visitor days per annum spent in the Park, with over 92% of visitors arriving by car. National Road Traffic Forecasts suggested that traffic on rural roads could increase by 30% by the year 2011 and by as much as 60% by the year 2031. As a consequence, the role of the railway in bringing people into the Park by train was expected to increase in importance as traffic growth adds further pressure on the countryside; he estimated that in the region of 5000 car trips [journeys] per year could be 'transferred' to the railway.

A feature of the railway is that it passes through locations where holiday-makers stay, notably Beddgelert, camp-sites at Beddgelert Forest, and Betws Garmon, and the Snowdon Ranger Youth Hostel. For such people, the railway would offer an opportunity to travel to Porthmadog, Caernarfon, and Beddgelert. The Environmental Statement recommended that the WHR should offer special, attractively priced, multi-journey tickets for people staying in the vicinity of the line, and with such measures in place, he believed that the railway could result in journeys which would otherwise have been made by car being made on the railway instead. The existing FR Residents' Railcard scheme offered heavily discounted fares to local residents. Expansion of this was anticipated, and should help ensure that the WHR plays a useful role in providing for the travel needs of the local community, as well as appealing to visitors.

Overseas visitors might consider accessibility by public transport when making decisions on their holiday plans or itineraries. Specific opportunities to link visits to Caernarfon with an attractive leisure rail trip through Snowdonia, could be an attractive proposition and might help encourage overseas tourists to arrive and travel through the area by public transport.

The Environmental Statement indicated that the adverse impacts relating to construction traffic can be kept to a minimum, by restricting HGV movements to appropriate roads and, in the vicinity of residential properties in Beddgelert and Porthmadog, by limiting the hours during which construction traffic can operate.

*Access to places open for 50 years would suddenly be barred, thus mitigation measures were expected - but these are not possible everywhere.*

The main increases in traffic flows are confined to trunk roads outside the National Park, and predominantly on the approaches to Caernarfon. In percentage terms, the highest increase over current peak hour traffic volumes is 7% and, in some parts of the National Park, he estimated that traffic volumes will fall slightly. A concern raised by a number of individuals and organisations was that, during the period that the railway terminates temporarily at Rhyd Ddu, additional traffic would be attracted into the National Park from the south to board the railway there. He believed that the risk of this can be minimised by the provision of shuttle bus services from outside the Park during this stage.

It was the policy of Snowdonia National Park not to provide additional car parking space unless:

*"planned as part of a traffic management scheme or as an integral part of a new (or extended) visitor attraction"* Eryri Local Plan, Policy No. TR13

In this respect, he believed that there was no requirement to provide additional spaces within the National Park, as the traffic relief benefits outlined earlier would offset any increased pressure to park at places such as Beddgelert. Car parking at Caernarfon and Dinas would be met by a planning requirement to provide 150 new spaces associated with the granting of planning permission for the Caernarfon to Dinas section of the railway. This provision was judged to be adequate for the needs of the railway. In Porthmadog, he estimated that fewer than 50 additional car parking spaces would be required to cope with peak parking requirements. This figure would be accommodated within the proposed car park extension at the gasworks site in Porthmadog.

The following benefits were estimated:
1. Economic benefit from construction: £1.6m over 4 years
2. Economic benefit when opened: £4.2m per year; £1.4m per year while at Rhyd Ddu
3. Reduction in car trips into the National Park, 5,000 vehicles per year
4. Reduction origin car trips within the SNP: 6,000 vehicles per year

**Cllr G Owen for Gwynedd Council** was the Chairman of the Council's Highways and Engineering Committee, and Vice-Chairman of the Eryri Railway Sub-Committee. He was also Vice-Chairman of the Llanwnda Community Council, whose members have also instructed him to inform this Inquiry that they are in full support of this project.

He had been personally involved in prolonged discussions on this particular project for a number of years as Vice-Chairman of the Light Railways Sub-Committee of the former Gwynedd County Council, between 1989 and 1996, and subsequently as Vice-Chairman of the Eryri Railway Sub-Committee from 1996 to date. The fact that over 9,000 people travelled on the train between Caernarfon and Dinas during the three weeks it was in operation, indicated how it had fired the imagination of local people and attracted their interest and support.

The preparatory work, track laying and other auxiliary work was carried out with the minimum of disruption. The cycle track, known as Lôn Eifion, has been greatly upgraded by FR Co. and is in a much better condition now than it ever was. New entry gates to the fields have been provided for the local farmers, and badger flaps for wild life. As far as the first three miles of railway track is concerned, the Company has carried out its obligations and fulfilled its promises to the full. As Chairman of GC's Highways and Engineering Committee, he saw great benefits ensuing to the whole area from the extension of the railway track from Dinas through Waunfawr and Beddgelert to Porthmadog.

Surely, at a time when there is a great deal of discussion on in-

***The FR at Tanygrisiau****: it was interesting that the FR had been re-established to run from Tanygrisiau to Blaenau Ffestiniog in close proximity to people's houses. It did so with little fuss and bother, and the dry-stone walls had all been either faithfully rebuilt or provided new by groups of volunteers who had trained themselves for the purpose out of the pleasure of doing so. Of course John Tower's testimony (overleaf) was backed up by the actuality of what he said being proven fact. This somewhat diminished the effect of objections to WHR reinstatement on disturbance grounds.*

tegrated transport, a narrow gauge railway within the Snowdonia National Park could, when completed, reduce the use of cars and encourage more visitors to use the train.

The only industry on the increase and flourishing is tourism. The railway development in the direction of Porthmadog, would be of great benefit to the tourism industry in this part of Gwynedd, an immense boost to the economy of the area.

In conclusion, he wished to draw the attention of this Inquiry and to present as evidence, a letter sent by the Assistant Secretary and Solicitor of the GC to the Project Manager of the Millennium Commission in support of the bid for Millennium Commission funds by FR Co., dated 26th November 1997, that date being two weeks after the SNPA Planning Committee moved into opposition to the WHR:

---

### Welsh Highland Railway Project

I understand that the Snowdonia National Park Authority has indicated its opposition to the above project and its intention to appear at the Public Inquiry as an objector to the scheme as a whole. Following consultation with the Chairman and Vice-Chairman of Gwynedd Council's Welsh Highland Railway Sub-Committee, I am authorised to write this letter in support of the bid for Millennium Commission funds by FR Co. I trust that the following will assist you in any consideration of the funding of the project.

The Caernarfon to Dinas phase, now the subject of the Caernarfon Railway Light Railway Order 1997, has proved a great success in the short period for which it has been operating and has already made a significant contribution to the economy of the town and surrounding area. It would be appropriate to indicate that this phase of the project has 100% support from all the Caernarfon members of Gwynedd Council. It is important that work on completion of Phase 1 between Caernarfon and Dinas takes place during the winter months so that the line is fully prepared for commencement of the 1998 tourist season.

Gwynedd Council has already given its public support to completion of the project and a written agreement is now in place between the Company and the Council regarding the removal of nearly all the Council's objections to the detailed proposals of the scheme. Indeed, the only objection which remains to be debated at the Public Inquiry is the crossing of the A487 at Britannia Bridge Porthmadog, which has raised concerns regarding the impact on traffic congestion at busy times of the day. This is a matter which will be resolved at the Public Inquiry following consideration of detailed evidence.

A substantial majority of Gwynedd Councillors support the scheme which also has the support of Mr Dafydd Wigley, the MP for the project area. It is worth making the point that Gwynedd Council are the only directly elected and, therefore, publicly accountable members for the whole of Gwynedd and that the authority has duties and responsibilities stretching from Caernarfon to Porthmadog (including the National Park area). It is important for the Commission to maintain its support for the project as a whole and particularly with regard to the release of grants for Phases 2 and 3 as soon as the powers are in place following the Public Inquiry.

The WHR Project is the most significant Millennium Commission project in North Wales and there would no doubt be some political ramifications if the Commission were to withdraw its support from a project, the first phase of which has already been completed to the satisfaction of the local authority.

*This is the view from the A4085, near to the Clogwyn y Gwin entrance. The farm land runs up on the right, on the flanks of Snowdon, and the railway is elevated; height that NGG16 No 138 is surrendering as it runs downhill with a train. This is the piece of Heaven that was to be sullied by the nasty railway. Pity about the installed slate tip, but then why should logic be admitted to any of this - the railway caused the slate tip last time round - it was certainly odds-on to do more mischief if it was allowed to rise again. Note overleaf the objections to change.*

**Mr Kyffin Williams OBE PRCA RA** I had considered the proposals of the Transport and Works Order. Given my knowledge of the landscape, of the previous running of the line and of the proposals presently before this Inquiry, I cannot see how the re-introduction of the railway could cause unacceptable harm.

I bear in mind particularly that the greater part of the railway infrastructure needed to run the line is already an established part of the landscape. It is also relevant to remember that the passage of a train through the landscape is transient, by definition. In my opinion, the passage of a train through the landscape will not detract from its beauty. Indeed, in rural areas, roads and railways can on suitable occasions assist in one's appreciation of the landscape. This is the case here. The sight of a train making its way through the landscape is, in my opinion, likely to enhance the charm of that landscape, both in short and long views.

**Mr J Williams, Bontnewydd** There is no doubt that, if the Order is granted, the railway will be of sociological benefit to a deprived area. It will create additional jobs and the local traders will benefit from tourism. It will encourage people to use the train rather than their car. The supporters view with concern the Snowdonia National Park Authority's decision to oppose the reconstruction of the old Welsh Highland Railway, after having approved it in three separate committees. Their statement in the draft Eryri Local Plan supported the proposed development. No rambler likes to lose any footpath but, in this case, [the National

Headquarters of] the Ramblers Association is opposing the railway on the grounds that footpaths on the trackbed and through the tunnel at Aberglaslyn are to be lost. It must be pointed out that at no time have these paths been shown on the definitive maps and, when I walked the area from 1947 to the mid-1950's, entrance to the tunnel was barred.

**Mr J Towers, Penrhyndeudraeth** A number of people have been worried by the threat of noise, smell and dirt from a steam train passing close to a house. The front of my home is less than ten feet from the [FR] trains as they pass, and the trains do not disturb us at all, not even the cat. The house is painted white, and it remains clean. Washing dries in the garden and it does not collect dirt. We hear a rumble as each train passes and, if I notice, I use it as an excuse to get myself a cup of coffee. The local children enjoy it. I think the little boy opposite learnt the names of the engines as his first words. The railway is a benign neighbour, and any who have their doubts are welcome to call on us when the trains are running, to see and hear for themselves. The Aberglaslyn Pass is a very special problem. There has to be a walking route through this pass and the road is not safe for pedestrians. The south end of the existing right-of-way [the Fisherman's Path] takes you to the very best of the scenery, and I am surprised that the Ramblers have not been clamouring for years to make this route easier. The route through the tunnel, though having its own special excitement, simply misses the view.

I have walked on quite a number of paths in other parts of Britain which have been improved using modern methods and they really do succeed in meeting a need without creating an eyesore. So, I have no hesitation in supporting the improvement of this path. The suggestion that this railway could be built somewhere else is sheer nonsense. An interesting railway passing through fine countryside is what is being proposed, in the area which is the birthplace, the historic home, of narrow gauge railways, as much part of the local heritage as slate and castles and mountains.

## The case against the granting of the Order

All the Proofs of Evidence are summarised, and any notes of expansion, clarification or comment are added in italics at the end of the summary.

**Mr AG Roberts:** Whenever road widening schemes were contemplated within the Park in order to facilitate easier communications for local people, they met with strong opposition. The Secretary of State for Wales had recently turned down a proposal to improve the A5 Trunk road that passes through the National Park, also, farmers who wished to construct farm tracks were often refused consent by the Park because they considered it would harm the landscape. It was only right and proper, therefore, that the Railway Company should be treated likewise and that Government Departments should be consistent in their decisions. He urged strongly that deemed planning consent should not be granted as the proposal would inevitably be a scar on the landscape of this sensitive area.

It was of some comfort to the local farming community that the SNP's Planning Committee voted unanimously at their meeting on 12th November to object to and oppose the Railway Company's proposal.

**Mr ER Hughes, North Wales NFU :** In many instances, the livestock move over and/or along the old trackbed at varying but frequent times during the year. There were machinery movements equally frequently over and/or along the former trackbed. Should this trackbed be recommissioned as a tourist railway, the effect on many of these farms would be major.

Whilst some would look at the macro-economic strategy, and quickly reject the low economic viability of a relatively small number of farms in Mid-Gwynedd as statistically unimportant, to the individual farmer who might find himself in that category as a result of the emergence of the railway, the effect would be catastrophic. Such could not survive on seasonal tourism alone.

The resolve of FR Co. to establish a like-railway on the former WHR route between Dinas and Porthmadog often took the form of unannounced visits to farms, trespass, aggressive and provocative attitudes by Directors and Senior Representatives of Festiniog Railway Company, who had no regard to local character or language. On or about 21 December 1995, NFU members directly involved in this section received a circular letter from FR Co. indicating that amongst the consultees, "the National Farmers Union were generally supportive of the scheme". This was a totally inaccurate statement to make, was without foundation, mischievous and designed to mislead.

Mr Hughes appended a letter received from Mr M Schumann, Director of FR Co., which demonstrated the type of correspondence received, and also demonstrated the provocative attitude this Company had employed. Meetings did not occur owing to inappropriate date selections, or the unwillingness of farmers to put up with provocative individuals 'representing the Company' who were uninterested in the farmers' views and unwilling to withdraw their re-establishment proposals.

### Dr WD & Hon. Mrs E Harper, Clogwyn y Gwin, Rhyd Ddu: The proposed Welsh Highland Railway would run across our farmland for half-a-mile taking in approximately two-thirds of an acre. The total rail track will take some 130,060 sq metres of farmland.

The WHR last operated in 1937, the rails were removed in 1941. Since then, the land has become an integral part of the farm, and ownership has been acquired through long use and adverse possession. The trackbed has been farmed without let or hindrance, and without permission of 'the owner'. The owners of Clogwyn y Gwin, past and present, have had open and peaceful physical occupation and control of the half-mile of trackbed for over fifty years.

The farm stands in a superb, unspoilt and quiet part of Snowdonia. The farm is 1,100 acres in all, and 1,050 acres lie above the WHR. We own, manage, treat and breed from a flock of 950 Welsh Mountain ewes, with 200 retained ewe lambs. With the harsh conditions on the mountains, all our lambs sell as stores. Access within and around the farm is also crucial. The trackbed is important for feeding the stock in winter and for moving animals and machines around the farm. Most farms along the track are classified as "severely disadvantaged" (Grades IV and V), any taking of this marginal land, and any disturbance would have extremely damaging effects. The farmhouse and buildings are quite close to, but below, the WHR.

The ADAS report, included in the Environmental Report, stated that the effect on our farm will be "moderate adverse", but this assumed that the trackbed did not form a part of the farm. Farming practice is very different from sixty years ago. The trackbed is vital to the farm and its loss will cause significant problems in managing the farm and moving the sheep. This is made clear

*The WHR was unpopular with the owners of Clogwyn y Gwin, pictured here from the train they so wished would never be rebuilt. It was interesting upon the sad demise of Mrs Harper that the subsequent sale included the proximity of the railway as an asset. It merely confirmed what the criteria for 'normality' actually was.*

in the report of Jones, Peckover submitted by the NFU. If the railway is built, it will be necessary to open and close gates often - with two gates to open outwards each time, there will always be the danger of stock straying up and down the line, especially in winter with the enthusiasm of the sheep for their winter feed. It is the farmers who are the conservationists and guardians of the mountains. The sheep on the hill provide a living, but they also preserve the environment because the land is grazed and kept in good order. The traditional scenes of wandering sheep quietly grazing the mountains, as they have been doing for hundreds of years, is exactly what the tourists want to see, particularly in the summer when lambs, like snowflakes, cover the mountainside. The unhindered future of all farm businesses is essential to the whole of Snowdonia, as well as important to those of us who live off the income.

Obviously, the farm will be affected by construction and maintenance works. The water supply comes from the mountain crossing underneath the trackbed, there is a danger of this becoming polluted. The drainage can be affected and land become waterlogged if the drains are poor, causing flooding and bogs. Sheep might (and will) escape onto the line through fences, over low stone walls or by walking over the grids or barriers that have been suggested. Living amongst the precipices, the Welsh Mountain sheep are notorious for jumping and circumnavigating any obstacle put before them. FR Co. has agreed to reinstate the stone walls, but I believe that the cost on our farm alone will be substantial, and the cost might require a low standard of work. The cost for all the walls along the route, built to blend in with the landscape, will certainly be a major expense.

In addition to the agricultural effects, the WHR the line will pass close to our house and the noise, vibration and smoke will be considerable. The Beyer-Garratt engines are large and they make a considerable noise, they will intrude often and loudly into the peace of the area. This valley is renowned for its outstanding natural beauty with very little modern intrusion.

The environment in this area is especially important. We have very rare flora and fauna which could well be affected by the railway, and certainly these cannot be enjoyed by people in carriages being taken along the route at up to 25 mph. There has been little mention of the hundreds of well-established trees that will have to be cut down along the whole length of the trackbed.

The application to the Millennium Commission refers to the WHR as "a vital link" between Porthmadog and Caernarfon, but this is not true; with much more public transport and many more cars, I have not met anyone here who would be using the train.

The viability of the project and many other factors have not

been spelt out. I emphasise my concerns for Rhyd Ddu which is intended to receive passengers from the half-built line by the end of the year 2000. Rhyd Ddu is a tiny village with only a pub. There are no shops, no chapels, no entertainments and there is great concern as to what the passengers will do when they disembark and spill out on to the road. In the WHR brochure, it states that "a coach connection is planned from Rhyd Ddu through Beddgelert to Porthmadog", thus increasing an already dangerous highway problem for the villages.

The WHR make great play on the 'regeneration' of Caernarfon and the 'local employment' theme. Blaenau Ffestiniog, one end of the Festiniog line has not been regenerated, just the opposite. There are very few local full-time employees on the FR, only two of whom speak Welsh. The Railway's claim that the line will be as in the old days is not true. Originally, the building of the railway (NWNGR) from Dinas junction to Rhyd Ddu was to carry slate from the two adjacent quarries, plus the one here on Clogwyn y Gwin. There were only four trains a day, each engine pulling just four wagons. The proposed WHR will have hourly trains, pulling up to fifteen carriages (a total weight of 275 tons). We are applying for adverse possession of the trackbed.

*(This is hardly well considered or even researched stuff. It is more like a collection of half-truths and hearsay, with a contemptuously imperial dispatch of any prosperity for Rhyd Ddu. But the Hon. Lady was such that all nodded sagely and moved on. There were no rebuttals, no contra-attacks. However irritating such inaccurate prating might seem, stern advice was given against vigorous responses. Any froth was allowed to speak for itself. The nonsenses were as self-evident as the truths.)*

*This is the poor Rhyd Ddu, intended to receive passengers in a tiny village with only a pub. Yet somehow the pub is thriving, there is a cafe and other businesses that welcome the railway's visitors, plus the loo, that does great business when trains are in. All pronouncements were listened to gravely.*

**Messrs E & G Williams, Llwyn Onn & Bron Fedw Isaf - Evidence presented by Mr AG Roberts, Agent:** Whilst the whole length of the disused track had always been grazed, it provided a very valuable link between different parts of both farms which are generally farmed as one unit. The farms had been adapted in order to make use of this valuable asset with gates and fences fitting in to the overall pattern. The objectors had, however, sold off the old station building near Snowdon Ranger, and this had now been adapted and extended as a residence and occupied for many years.

The water supply to Bron Fedw Isaf farmhouse and buildings was abstracted from a watercourse at a point some 3 yards downstream of where it crosses under the railway. The risk of pollution from construction work, etc, was quite worrying.

Severance affected both these holdings quite severely since :-
**a.** both holdings were already severed by the A4085 highway,
**b.** the access to the farmhouse at Llwyn Onn would be crossed by the railway. This was at a very dangerous point in the

road which had a very steep gradient on the uphill side of the crossing. Also, the sight-lines from the downhill side were poor and dangerous. There was a stone building close to the crossing. The crossing might have been adequate in the days of horses and carts but it did not meet present day requirements.

**c.** When the flocks of either Llwyn Onn or Bron Fedw Isaf were gathered, some part would have to be brought over the railway line.

**Mr JC Owen, Cwm Cloch Isaf, Beddgelert. Evidence presented by Mr AG Roberts, Agent :** There would be no access over the river from the farm buildings and yard to the better land situated to the southeast of them. At present, access was gained over the concrete bridge near the farm yard. If the Order was granted, this would become part of the railway track. Access would therefore be lost for stock movements machinery and on foot for shepherding.

The proposed track would pass within 30 metres of the farmhouse and, because the railway would meander through the lower part of the farm, a considerable length of track was within 200 metres of the house. With the numerous crossings and proximity to the proposed station at Beddgelert, the noise of the train and whistles would create an almost intolerable disturbance to the house, yard and immediate surroundings. Most of the stock handling and feeding was also done in this vicinity.

The lower fields and the most valuable part of this farm would be fragmented by the meandering route of the railway, seriously affecting the use and value of the lower land. These fields were of immense importance to a hill unit of this size because of the lack of reasonable quality, sheltered grazing. The day-to-day management problems involved in moving stock were innumerable. Furthermore, when the stock on the hill was gathered, the whole

*At Cwm Cloch the access over the river was duly provided in mitigation. It so happens that this piece of railway is one of the most remarkable in Britain - so the trains that run are highly celebrated. This was a job for the diplomats. As the railway is there now, the process was successful.*

flock would have to be brought over the railway twice, at two crossing points, to bring them to the farmyard, which was where the sheep handling pens are located. There would be a further two crossings when the flock was returned to the mountain.

If the Order was granted, the following works were essential to alleviate some of the effects:

**Bridge over Access.** This was located near Pont Alyn. The main concern here was that it be of adequate width and height to cater for modern-day agricultural machinery, stock, lorries and delivery wagons.

**Gated Crossings.** There would be two of these on the farm access, one near the farmhouse and one in the planted area just to the west of the house. These should be 4 to 5 metres wide with provision to stop stock wandering up the line, and with warning lights fitted for the farmer to operate when crossing

the sheep flock. This was essential with a flock of up to 3,000 to cross at some times of the year. It was going to take from 15 to 30 minutes for this number to cross, and any train must therefore stop.

**Handling Pens.** To reduce the number of times stock have to cross these two crossings, a new sheep handling set-up ought to be built to the west of these crossings. These would then serve the bulk of the land at Cwm Cloch.

**Water Supply.** An adequate and free supply of water needed to be provided.

**Access Bridge.** A suitable means of access over [the stream] Nant Cwm Cloch and situated somewhere opposite the yard needed to be provided to the land south-east of the buildings. This would need to be 4 to 5 metres wide to cater for modern machinery and also of sufficient strength to bear their weight. Also, a further gated crossing 4 to 5 metres wide is required to link the area to the remaining land to the south-east of the buildings.

**Sound Insulation.** With the proposed track passing so close to the house, this substantial farmhouse needed to be insulated for the effects of the noise, as Highway Authorities do with new road schemes.

**Boundaries.** These would need to be stock-proof and maintained by the Applicant with them being liable for any stock that do find their way on to the line.

**Beddgelert Station.** This land had been grazed by my client for many years and he claimed adverse possession. Adequate boundaries needed to be provided that ensure no trespass on to the farm land by the public that visit the station.

**Mr JR Williams, Portreuddyn, Tremadog, Evidence presented by Mr AG Roberts, Agent.** The former trackbed had been incorporated into the fields and grant-aid was paid by the Ministry of Agriculture towards the cost of undertaking this work. The proposal would sever the 81 hectares of land situated on the south side of the A498 and some 60% of this block would be on the far side of the railway to where the new farm buildings had been built. Dairy herd movements would involve four daily crossings of the line with some 125 dairy cows each time. Silage harvesting involves crossing the line some 50 times daily with a tractor and trailer. Slurry disposal would involve frequent crossing of the railway. In winter, an overland pipe was used and the effluent pumped. Obviously, such a pipe could not be laid over the railway track.

Fertiliser applications during the growing season would involve frequent crossings. I have submitted a copy of a letter from an Agricultural Consultant employed by ADAS and who had concluded that the effect of the proposal on the holding would be "considerable". This must throw severe doubt on the Environmental Assessment prepared on behalf of FR Co. who commissioned ADAS to prepare the agricultural assessment. In that report, they considered the overall effect on the holding to be merely "moderate adverse".

## Messrs I, B & E Jones, Bryn Gloch Caravan Site, Betws Garmon.

The owners had invested heavily over the years to bring the site up to a high standard. The proposed over-bridge would be off-putting to anyone that turned into the site, particularly those towing tourers. It would certainly not add to the rural and pleasant appearance of the park, and its construction would involve felling and the severe lopping of some mature trees. The proposal is to have the track in a deep cutting which will mean that customers will be looking down on to any passing trains.

The prime reason people travelled to stay in rural parks such as Bryn Gloch is for the peace and tranquillity of being in the country. All of that will be lost with a railway passing through the park with the resultant noise, fumes and vibration. The character of the site will be changed. Most of the customers travelled from the cities of the Midlands to caravan parks such as this with the sole purpose of getting away from trains and cars.

The railway will introduce a major hazard element to the site. At present parents feel comfortable to let their children wander at will. This might no longer be the case, and the odd ball will inevitably find its way on to the line with the consequent risk that attempts would be made to recover it. The proposal will distract from the facilities available on this site. Furthermore, most tourists had a fixed budget for their holiday, hence, it was difficult to see how the overall expenditure in the area will increase. The railway proposal was another seasonal and tourist-dependent business. What this area needed was permanent all the year round jobs.

*The reception area at Bryn Gloch caravan site, Betws Garmon, in July 1995. It was a mystery why the owner was such a trenchant objector to the WHR revival, when the biggest camping site in the area, down the road, got a station! Bryn Gloch made serious and prolonged objection and so there is no station.*

The proposal would leave the house, shop, restaurant, play area, etc, severed from the main site area situated to the west of the railway line, this would deter potential customers, who would have reservations about coming to a park that involved crossing a bridge,

The site will be injuriously affected. Were the owners to put in their brochure that there was a railway running through the site? You would not blame anyone for being put off by this thought. The owners would prefer if the railway track were level with the ground on either side. Installed barriers would need to operate automatically, with suspended barriers to deter anyone crossing underneath when they were in operation. Any crossing would need to be six metres wide to allow a two-way flow of traffic to pass by.

## Mr AL Pym, Rural Resources Ltd, for Objector Clients

Mr Pym said that he appeared on behalf of Miss Pott and Mr Stevens (Betws Garmon), Dr WD and the Hon Mrs E Harper (Clogwyn y Gwin), and Miss J Entwistle (Nantmor), all of whom were objectors resident along the route.

The Company had failed to produce evidence that the funding for the project can be arranged. The papers on which they have relied to support their contention are not in the public domain. Forecasts of revenue and expenditure and the details of the railway had not been explained. The Environmental Statement suggested that the economic benefits of the employment of full-time and volunteer labour would be significant, while the impact of the expected visitors would be modest, but this was based on very general assumptions which did not match the evidence submitted to the 1993 Inquiry.

The WHR would be another railway in North Wales competing in a crowded and ever more demanding market, which was made up of enthusiasts and of others for whom any railway will be adequate. The Festiniog Railway was the most successful and only two other railways carried more than 100,000 people [per annum]. The Festiniog line was very well known and had unique qualities, but it had had to make economies and changes in recent years. The WHR was intended to be the best, but it would only succeed if it drew visitors from other attractions in North Wales. In 1993, FR Co. admitted that 30% of the traffic would join the completed WHR at Porthmadog, taking 40% of the Festiniog's custom. The benefit of building the WHR would be limited. The Wales Tourist Board did not focus on preserved railways in its strategy for growth, which was based on promoting activities which extended the tourism season, provided greater choice, and did not damage existing operations.

There was no evidence of the ability of FR Co. to fund the scheme. The grants relied upon for Phase I had not all been secured. The WHR would be ring-fenced, but the financial arrangements were not clear, and the economic threat to FR Co. remained, along with the liability to repay loans totalling £903,000 in 1995 and 1996. These matters were important because the Company had to show that it had taken all relevant matters into account, and that it had the necessary funding to meet all the costs. The application did not demonstrate that this was the case.

The Company had not shown that its service would be of value to local residents. Buses were widely available and cheap, meeting the needs of people for much of the day, for all of the year, and at a reasonable price. When Phase I was built, the traffic problem would be worse because the coach link to Porthmadog would increase the chaos in Beddgelert, and encourage visitors even more to bring their cars into the National Park.

Mr Pym submitted that the Company had not proved that the construction and operation of the railway was in the public interest. It was of interest to railway enthusiasts. The railway would damage other tourist attractions, other businesses, existing communities, local facilities, Porthmadog town, and the enjoyment of the National Park. The special character of Snowdonia should be preserved not threatened, and the requirements of the National Parks and Access to the Countryside Act 1949 should be observed. Priority should be given to the protection of the environment and to the social and economic interests of the local communities. Some people might benefit from the railway but this would only be at the expense of the greater number who enjoy this quiet part of Snowdonia as it is today.

Mr Pym said that none of his clients could understand why compulsory powers should be given to railway enthusiasts and damage the interests of those who live or work along the route. The Company was seeking to acquire the power to dispossess owners with legitimate claims of ownership through adverse possession, and ignoring the owners. This was not right. The application should be refused on the basis that the social and economic benefits had not been proved, and that there was a requirement to conserve and enhance the natural beauty, wildlife and cultural heritage.

For the benefit of the public and of the National Park, the Secretary of State should be invited to consider the use of his powers to revoke the spent statutory powers of the Welsh Highland Railway Orders to ensure that the trackbed remained as now; in use by farming businesses, a part of the wider landscape and available for recreation, primarily for walkers.

It was clear that there were many claims of ownership based on adverse possession along the railway line. Whilst not concerned with matters of law, the 1993 Inspector noted these claims, and indicated that they should

*Fourteen years later, on 14th April 2012, the Fisherman's Path ramblers are taking pictures of the train full of 'trippers' and an open topped bus full of gongoozlers is holding the cars momentarily to enjoy the view. This 'seasonal' traffic is rather more widespread than supposed, as it all started in February half-term. Has the public interest been served?*

be resolved by careful and sympathetic negotiations. Since 1993, the Company had met with the owners of property along the route but it had never admitted the validity of such claims. The Company relied on the acquisition of the trackbed from the Official Receiver, by agreement or compulsory purchase, and the transfer of the original undertaking under the 1995 Transfer Order to provide it with a "railway". The Company had ignored the claims of ownership or access by saying that it was not possible to claim such rights along the route, because those rights would frustrate the statutory purpose and that was not allowed in law.

It was not true to say that these rights frustrated the purpose. The railway did not exist and could not exist without the grant of an Order to permit its construction and operation. The original powers to build and operate the railway had been exercised and were spent. The Transport and Works Act 1992 defined a "railway" as a "system of transport employing parallel rails". The

parallel rails were laid and they were used for a time, but they have been removed and there was no existing authority by which they can be put back.

The trackbed was nothing more than land which was formerly a railway but, in the absence of a formal abandonment order, it was still subject to certain legal controls. It was not the acquisition of rights (of ownership or of way) which frustrated the statutory purpose. It was the lack of any statutory authority itself that prevented the reconstruction of a railway along the route. Accordingly, the claims of ownership and of rights of way are not barred by statute.

The Company had clearly stated that it admitted no such claims, saying that no owner could establish a private right of access along the route and that no person could acquire ownership of any part of the route. But the Company was unsure. This uncertainty was highlighted by the wording in paragraph 1B (2)(a) of the draft Order which stated that "All private rights of way or alleged private rights of way over land subject to compulsory acquisition under this Order shall be extinguished". Why did it say "alleged" if it was sure? The making of this Order, without modification, would confer the power of compulsory acquisition on the Company. This would put many individual claimants in the position of having to prove ownership in the courts before claiming compensation for the taking of their land. Given the importance of the land to such owner-claimants, the question of ownership should be resolved before the Order was granted. The assessment looked at the need for crossing points and the rebuilding of drains, boundary walls and services but it did not take any account of the impact of the loss of the trackbed itself. . This had meant that the need for replacement tracks and hard-standings had been ignored. The question of "who owns the trackbed" was fundamental to the resolution of this Order. Because the claims had never been admitted by the Company, there had been an absence of "careful and sympathetic negotiations" and "sensible discussion". This was not intended [under the Law] and it was not right. If it was felt appropriate, the compulsory power should apply to him to resolve legal constraints in the disposal of the trackbed, although the OR was himself an objector.

The application was itself based on the assumption that the OR did own the full and free title to all the land set out in the schedule. Mr Pym said that the principles which he had addressed relate also to the law on the acquisition of public rights of way. The Company had said that GC were wrong to include certain rights of way along the line on the Definitive Map and that GC could not accept any further claims for the inclusion of additional rights of way on the making of any application based on long use. The legal principles about statutory purpose had been used but, given that they did not arise in this case (if at all), there was no bar to the establishment of public rights of way through long, uninterrupted and unhindered use of the trackbed. At Aberglaslyn, for example, the substantial use made of the trackbed for over 50 years was sufficient to warrant the inclusion of the trackbed on the definitive map. Accordingly, this application should be considered on the basis that the rights of way were established so that adequate and proper alternative routes were provided if the application was granted.

_Let all those who wish to reopen a railway gain a fine and complete gasp of the law surrounding such matters. Here is an impressive spray of legal grandstanding in an attempt to defeat the TWO initiative. If you are ill-informed in response you could lose! But what Mr Pym really fears for his clients is the shift of the proof of title if CP powers are conferred - this the FR Co. knew well - it's why they asked for them! To know more look at The Legal Tangle Appendix 'A'._

## Mr B Davies, Cob Records, Porthmadog; _(An Objector who, to a degree, had come to terms with the prospect of the reconstruction of the WHR but who, entirely reasonably, wished to protect his long-standing family business.)_

The whole of my warehouse, directly opposite the shop premises, is included in the scheme so that it could be bought by the Festiniog Railway Company. We have been prepared to negotiate with the Company to limit the effect of the Order. I thought that I had succeeded but have received no formal undertaking to that agreement. As it stands, if the Order is granted, the law will allow FR Co. to take the whole of my warehouse and I will have no power to prevent it.

We have tried to be as helpful as possible to permit the WHR to be built (if it must), and not being obstructive at all, whilst also having to safeguard our own interests. Mr Smare comments in his letter of 28 January 1997 "

' _Mr Davies has adopted a helpful attitude … ''._

From the outset of this matter, we have offered FR Co. an opportunity to take part of the building, and rebuild space equivalent to that which is taken, if any part of the building is justifiably required.

_In the event, FR Co. and Mr Davies reached a private agreement during the Inquiry with Mike Hart as the negotiator, and Mr Pym announced that Mr Davies wished to withdraw his evidence and objection._

_This instance illustrates the utility and effort of reaching such agreements in time to reduce the matters of contention which the Inspector must consider for his report to the SoS._

## Summary of Evidence by Mr AL Pym on behalf of Miss Entwisle: Miss Entwisle lives at Bryn y Bont, one of three properties immediately beside the trackbed at the site of the proposed level crossing in Nantmor village.

The loss of the path between Beddgelert and Nantmor would oblige people to use the Fisherman's Path, but that is narrow,

_Mr Davies of Cob Records had a point! FR had coveted his Cob Records store, left of centre, behind the station. They had failed to buy it when the Madoc Estate was up for grabs, and now it was in the way. The only mitigating measure was to knock off the front, and add to the back. It took time to reach a settlement, but one was reached._

uneven, and very close to the river in places. While the surface could be improved, no details have been given. Concrete, stones and timber could be used to make the path better but this would affect the character and the appearance of the valley while the Path would not be suitable for everyone. It would not be fit for the elderly, cyclists, or push-chairs nor would it provide access at all times. It is not sensible to contemplate the Fisherman's Path as an alternative to the trackbed. From the Fisherman's Path, walkers will have to join the A4085 for quite a distance or turn up through the woods and the National Trust car park and then join the road for a shorter distance. There is no pavement alongside the road. People should be able to walk safely, and away from traffic, particularly as many people will want to continue to walk in this area.

The road in Nantmor climbs steeply into the village from the A4085 and is dangerous. There is a double-bend immediately below the proposed crossing and visibility is very poor. With the railway crossing the road, the passing would be more difficult and traffic would need to use the area of road below the crossing where some improvements are to be made. The Company has said that this will be an open crossing with lights and a "bleeper" to give warning of each train but the design is another uncertainty. This is important for those who live in the immediate area and for the planning authority because Nantmor is a Conservation Area.

The building of the WHR will also generate traffic problems because it will attract people who will park on the roads and watch the trains pass through Nantmor and the Aberglaslyn Pass. It is difficult to see how such problems can be avoided unless legal parking restrictions are imposed but the placing of yellow lines on the roads would be entirely out of keeping with the village and the Conservation Area. If the railway is built, there will be an inevitable change to the character of Nantmor and this will cause significant harm to both the local community and the character of the National Park.

The railway will also have a direct effect on Miss Entwisle who regularly opens her garden to the public for charity under the National Gardens Scheme. It is the combination of her garden in its quiet setting with views to the south and west which make Bryn y Bont so special, adding to the enjoyment of some visitors to this National Park.

The Company has said that a Halt could be provided at Nantmor if the residents want it. Recently, a village meeting unanimously rejected the idea.

The construction of the railway will have an effect on the wildlife. At present, the trackbed provides a different environment from the surrounding countryside for plants and animals which will become inaccessible to people. The wildlife is enjoyed by many who walk quietly along the track and this is particularly the case to the south of Nantmor. There are few opportunities to enjoy such a range of wildlife on a safe, level and pleasant walk and the building of the railway will destroy this.

The Bryn y Bont property will be affected by the noise, smoke and vibration caused by the trains. The engines will be pulling hard to bring the 12-15 carriages up the slope. It is likely that a whistle will be used to confirm the approach of the train and the noise will be very intrusive. There will be vibrations which could not only affect the structure but also cause discomfort and inconvenience to anyone inside. The engines will burn diesel oil and generate fumes and smoke. These effects might be severe if there is a Halt in the vicinity, with the stopping, standing and starting.

**Mrs K Caldwell, for Residents of Nantmor Village:** When the original railway was built in the 1920's, the village consisted of fourteen houses on a hill above a farm. The railway ran below it through open country. Today, the village, designated as a Special Conservation Area, has trebled in size, spread down the hill, and the trackbed now passes through it. The level crossing will be a danger to children and a source of road accidents. It crosses the road halfway up a steep and twisting hill, hidden by a 90° bend. Trains will emerge from a deep cutting directly on to the road. FR Co. are proposing an open crossing with warning lights.

Within the village there is no official play area. Children play on the road. Children will play near the crossing, or run down to see the train when they hear one. School children run down to the bus stop. With children playing at or near the crossing, or venturing up the line, sooner or later one will be injured or killed. It is unrealistic to say that children must not be allowed to go near the crossing. Children have little sense of danger and will do unpredictable things. Children will always behave like children - this is a fact of life. We don't want it to be a fact of death. FR Co. say sheep will be prevented from going onto the track by cattle grids, as if sheep matter more than children. On every envelope we receive from the Ministry of Transport is the message "KILL YOUR SPEED NOT A CHILD". Trains also kill, especially at level crossings.

There will be accidents to road vehicles. Open crossings always mean risk from system malfunction, drivers' frustration or foolishness. At Glan y Pwll on the Ffestiniog line where visibility is far better than at Nantmor, there have been several near-accidents. The only safe solution will be a manned gated crossing. This is what FR Co. have installed at Penrhyndeudraeth, where there is a similar combination of 90° bend on a rising hill.

The village does not want a Halt at Nantmor. This was voted for unanimously at a village meeting. It will be a source of nuisance and no benefit to residents, who will not use it. Trains

*'The village does not want a halt at Nantmor'. This was voted for unanimously at a village meeting. 'It would be a source of nuisance and no benefit to residents, who would not use it'. When the railway came it seems there was a change of heart.*

will be seasonal, expensive, and the terminus too far from the main shops. Any use of the Halt will be by trippers and people coming to photograph trains. Many of these will come by car and expect to park. There is a serious lack of parking for residents and more cars will be a major nuisance and, parked near the crossing, an obstruction.

The rock faces along the line adjacent to the village are unstable. The passage of 61ton locomotives and 275ton trains would risk dangerous rock falls. The possible solutions will be to concrete the cliffs as at Tremadog or to blast out large volumes of rock. The first would be an impossible eyesore, the second an unacceptable intrusion to a village.

The railway line is uphill from Porthmadog. Locomotives will be working hard as they climb. They will be audible from Hafod y llyn, very loud as the line skirts the village, and most unpleasant for residents close to the track. The nuisance will reduce property values. There could be damage to property from vibration. Tests carried out for FR Co. are misleading. To use a locomotive of half the weight pulling half the load on a different geological location with a measuring device 25 metres from the track is no way to assess the effects at Nantmor. The line from Porthmadog runs parallel to and immediately below the village. Exhaust fumes from locomotives labouring uphill will be carried by the prevailing wind directly across the village at ground level.

This is not a reconstruction of the defunct Welsh Highland Railway but one which will run trains of length and weight approaching many main line trains. Present standards of judgement should not be suspended because some commercially hopeless railway was cobbled together seventy years ago. The existence of its abandoned trackbed is irrelevant.

The Railway Company's trippers' cash will go mainly to the Company for fares and for those other services provided in competition with existing trades-people. The tourist industry benefits most from those who stay for several days. These spend substantially over a spectrum of tourist facilities. The new railway will not entice more visitors of this sort for its trippers will be drawn from people already staying in North Wales or from day visitors.

The viability of such a railway is doubtful. If it is built and cannot sustain itself, who will come to the rescue? Further grants from charities at the expense of more worthy causes? Ratepayers who did not want it in the first place? Or will it go bankrupt again? The increased number of restored railways has led to a degree of market saturation. The FR found passengers diminishing and had to resort to fierce marketing to keep numbers up. Extra attractions such as "gourmet meals" to woo passengers who find riding on a steam train and looking at scenery too boring.

*A proof such as this was very much better left alone. It's inconsistencies spoke for themselves as a 'normal' objection.*

**Mr A Heason, Nantmor:** We object to the Order. The proposed routing of the railway passes through a rock cutting and emerges at the boundary of our property. This route is the only means of vehicular access to our garage and for transporting goods to and from the property that cannot practically be transported manually. This access route has been used by us and by previous owners of our property since (and before) December 1, 1959, without let or hindrance.

We have a letter, dated June 12th 1978, from the Chairman of the WH Light Railway (1964) Ltd stating - " …on wishing to relay track … we will make provision or alternative access for the owner … to his garage".

In a letter received from the Project Manager of the WHR, dated January 22 1997, we are told:

*"Reopening the railway will … prevent any other use of the … trackbed. (We) have not been able to identify any practical alternative (for you)".*

*(The case of Mr Heason was rather wider than this. He had written a letter to the press to reveal a danger in the Pass. You will see the full text of this and subsequent events at the end of the chapter - and it is an interesting story. The letter was not entered as part of the proof of evidence, it was apparently handed to the Inspector on the site visit at the end of the Inquiry when the Inquiry was 'closed', thus its implications were not raised and discussion of its contents was denied the affected audience.)*

**Mr & Mrs R Brown, Beddgelert:** When the resurrection of the WHR was first mooted, we were concerned about its impact on the environment of the Aberglaslyn Pass. The more we have discussed the scheme with others, and the more we have focussed on its likely impact on Snowdonia, the more we have come to believe that its alleged benefits have been exaggerated, while the harm it will do to those using the former trackbed will be very great.

*The 'train players' apparently reinforce rather than lengthen the tourist season. Yet this scene in September suggests otherwise. Objectors it seems did not do serious homework, and prejudice of course suppresses contradiction and logic. The WHR was an 'irrelevance', creaming off summer bus traffic it was said. This isn't true.*

We are not lawyers but we find it incredible that a group of train-players can lay claim to an abandoned trackbed sixty years after the previous commercial venture failed. There is such a thing as common sense and indeed common law. The world is very different now from sixty years ago. In particular, sections of the abandoned trackbed have been obliterated while others are used intensively by farmers, walkers, horse riders and so on. A fundamental change of use has long been established. It is inconceivable that planning permission will be given for anything like this today.

We were told by friends that FR Co. people propose to have an open, unmanned crossing. We simply couldn't believe that anyone could be so grossly irresponsible, given the number of children playing in the area during the summer.

We wish to elaborate on a point relating to the noise of the trains. The situation will be worse than we first thought because of the effect of the ravine-type nature of the Pass in containing and reverberating sound. A similar effect occurs around Beddgelert due to the surrounding hills. Indeed, the sound problem could be quite serious around Beddgelert, as the train meanders considerably on its approach. This will also make the whistling associated with such trains particularly tiresome.

We have stated that there is no pavement on the road between the Bryn y Felin bridge and the Aberglaslyn bridge. In fact, there is a short section which lulls walkers into a false sense of security just before a narrow and twisting bend. Our conclusion that this overall section of road is dangerous for walkers is unchanged.

We do not deny that there should be benefit to FR Co., not least from the fact that 90% of construction costs is projected to come from public funds. This must be mouth-watering to a prospective Plc. And Caernarfon might receive a much needed boost from the terminus, though the Dinas section to some extent already provides this (that is, when the trains are running).

However, we remain very confused about the alleged economic benefits to Snowdonia. We are also not sure that the following points have been taken into account :-

o the fact that a significant proportion of total railway revenue is projected to come from non-ticket sources, i.e., the benefit to the local economy, especially in the National Park, might be small,

o the fact that the area is littered with seasonal scenic railways,

o the manner in which the railway reinforces rather than lengthens the tourist season,

o the adverse impact on bus services of creaming off some of the summer trade

o the adverse impact on walkers who have lost some of their traditional routes.

A public transport facility which aims to reduce car traffic should have at least three crucial features. First, it is available throughout the year. Second, its timetable is such as to encourage a wide range of users, including commuters. Third, its fares offer a substantial economic incentive to forego the comfort and flexibility of the car. None of these features are present in this case. The WHR will be essentially a peak-season tourist attraction, with a limited service mid-season and none at all from November through mid-March. Based on the Porthmadog - Ffestiniog timetable of the Festiniog Railway Company, only for 6 weeks in the year would the first train start before 9 a.m.

The vast majority of passengers using railways, such as the WHR, do so because they want to ride on a scenic railway. Those looking for alternative transport to the car will find bus routes which run all year, catering for commuters as well as tourists and locals, with fares light-years below those envisaged for the WHR. The WHR is an absolute irrelevance. Indeed, it could undermine a far better existing system of public transport if it creams off some of the summer bus traffic between Porthmadog and Caernarfon.

The Applicant's statement of case claims that the railway will relieve existing and future traffic congestion and parking problems at Beddgelert. We have not met anybody who believes this. It is claimed that the railway will attract 125,000 new visitors each year, many of whom will arrive by car. The essential point is that Beddgelert would be the access point for those arriving via the A5, and the A470 from the south for those who do not want to visit Porthmadog. These are two very busy routes, especially in the season. Furthermore, the National Park is strongly opposed to the creation of extra car park spaces for day trippers. There is a serious possibility that railway visitors will displace other tourists at peak season.

*This was so negatively 'anti' that it did some good to the WHR case. Some statements were provably, and obviously incorrect. In the first 9 months of Beddgelert station's opening 70,000 people visited BY TRAIN. In 2011 the visitor predictions were met! So time has not been kind to this testimony. This looked like naked NIMBYism, and was taken as such.*

**Ms E Carrog, Bontnewydd:** The argument of FR Co. that there will be advantages in transport for local people falls down completely. It could be argued that it will be impossible to find any occasion where there will be any advantage in time, cost and regularity of travel for local people.

Much was made of the possibility that the railway will be a convenience. For similar reasons, there's no likelihood of this. Where there is a need for a service between the camps on the side of the road to Beddgelert and either Beddgelert, Caernarfon or Porthmadog, the local bus services and Bws Eryri are very experienced in offering any service that pays its way. There is no possibility of the railway being a convenient manner of travel for visitors in the

*Buses, widely available and cheap - and empty? These are provided at taxpayers' expense - OK. Is it really being said that a coach link to Porthmadog will increase the chaos in Beddgelert, and so encourage more cars? Odd thinking; one would assume that people take the train for leisure transport, and that this ties in with coaches?*

simplest meaning of transport, of going from one place to another, without there being an element of tourism in it.

I believe that a small steam railway is a tourist attraction. I myself have been several times on most of them and have written about them many times. I always speak highly of them as an attraction. Why then am I against another railway? Having been connected in many ways with tourism in Wales for 26 years, including time on the Council for the Tourist Board for North Wales, I am of the opinion that the number of similar attractions in this part of Wales is more than enough for the numbers of tourists and the short season that most of them come to stay. Note should be taken of the differences between what FR Co. tells the public and the people of Caernarfon on the one hand, and their plans about which they talk to their supporters on the other. I draw attention to a quotation which says that FR Co. hopes to follow the order of the building from Caernarfon to Dinas drawing on

local labour but, when Mike Hart writes to the railway supporters, he " … thanked members for their help and support in getting this phase of the Railway to its present state of completion." He went on to describe plans for the extension beyond Dinas and his expectation that in future use greater use would be made of volunteers and direct labour than contractors. In "membership notes", Robin Higgs [a Director of the WHR Society] says "With the rebuilding of the WHR well under way ... this ... brings into sharp focus the increasing need to attract more money and more volunteers, both for the physical work of reconstruction and to the operating side." The picture is very clear; the priority of the Company is not to create jobs for local people, but to get the work done free by enthusiasts.

Many things have been kept secret by the Company and we had to drag the information from them. The most important hidden matter was its dependence on income that did not come from the income of travelling in the train. [There was] no public mention before it was drawn from them during the Inquiry that a shop and eating-place will be needed that would contribute extensively - between 57% and 25% on the Company's own figures - to come from sales outside the sale of tickets.

Caernarfon traders had the impression that the train will bring them more business as an extra attraction that will tempt people to go into town. Instead, what comes to the fore is something very different. The Company want the right to have their own shop and cafe located by the parking ground and as near as possible to the foot of the castle in order to grab customers to spend in the shop and cafe of the train. These are the very visitors who will usually go into the centre of town to spend.

A number of Caernarfon business people are angry after realising that this Company does not plan to help Caernarfon. They see that FR Co. has the intention of helping themselves to money for food, drink and gifts instead of letting it go to the original businesses that have been getting it heretofore.

The Company will draw the cream away from other businesses in Caernarfon, and the fact that they tried to conceal this for so long has raised great opposition among traders who have come to understand recently the real intentions of the Company.

The assertion that half the visitors will be new ones or additional to the district is the most shocking and baseless assertion in all the documents of the Railway. There is nothing to support that assertion despite my asking a question on this point to Mr Steer. After listening to everything, I've come to the less shocking conclusion that the attraction of Caernarfon to the Railway are the people that Caernarfon attracts in their thousands already, and the railway wishes to profit from them. If the venture were established as a further attraction, it will be in competition with every other attraction within a circle of 30 miles of Caernarfon, Rhyd Ddu, Beddgelert and Porthmadog. This will include a very great number of the attractions of North Wales and the Tourist Board is of the opinion that there are sufficient attractions here already.

Public money will be a help in starting up community businesses, as has happened successfully in some of the Valleys of the South, with the aim of enabling people to create proper jobs throughout the year with the emphasis on paying salaries to local people. To be very blunt, it will be a subsidy for outsiders to play trains. They already have one; they do not need another, and they're in danger of losing both by being greedy.

*The results from the railway have proved the error of these cruel criticisms in a decisive manner. The alleged assertions were that 'big business' exploits volunteers, that jobs were being taken from local people. 'Proper jobs throughout the year' insinuates that tourism jobs are not 'proper'. Yet isn't agriculture seasonal too? The problem was that cream was in short supply in Caernarfon. The Mayor thought WHR would bring some by attracting visitors to stay longer. FR folk had been instructed not to react to Ms Carrog's comments, believing they would speak for themselves. Perhaps a refutation of Ms Carrog's Proof, to expose the misunderstandings (feasible in the inquiry by cross examination) would have given satisfaction - as the Inspector did find the benefits of WHR at best marginal. Counsel said no.*

*There followed a considerable body of evidence from the Ramblers Association and the Snowdonia Society, which repeated many of the objections already recorded. The Snowdonia Society though, had some interesting comment of which there are extracts are given below.*

## The Snowdonia Society:
The Environmental Statement warns that noise levels in a number of nearby houses could exceed WHO guidance limits, and calls for more tests on the Beyer-Garratt locomotive. The Society regarded traffic as a crucial issue at the Inquiry. There is a growing awareness of the threat which unbridled car-use posed to many of Britain's National Parks. According to figures from the Draft Eryri Local Plan, in 1994 between 6.6 and 10.6 million visitor-days were spent in the Snowdonia National Park, and 91% of these visitors arrived by private motor car. The National Park Authority acknowledges in its the Deposit Eryri Local Plan that it must work in conjunction with statutory bodies and agencies to develop policies which reduce the damage to the environment of the predicted growth in traffic.

In general, public debate in the run up to this Inquiry, some supporters of the railway have suggested that the reopening represents the only way of avoiding massive traffic growth in the area. While not entirely surprised, the Snowdonia Society was extremely concerned to read in FR Co.'s own Environmental Statement that the reopening is in fact likely not to reduce traffic

levels, but to increase them. The Society's fear has been that the railway will in effect be a linear theme park, attracting extra traffic to the area, rather than the "vital transport link", as described by the Millennium Commission up until September 1997. It is perhaps significant that, by 21st October 1997, the Millennium Commission had chosen to amend their description to a "valuable transport link". On the basis of these concerns, the Society entered into negotiations, following which FR Co. made a number of concessions. We believe it was important that the thrust of these be incorporated into the Order.

However, the Society will certainly wish to see more done to ensure that the reopening alleviated traffic growth, rather than accentuating it, and more attention paid to how the line could better serve the everyday transport needs of the local community. We had hoped that FR Co. might be willing to make a commitment not to construct any new car parks within the National Park, but they have been unwilling to make such an undertaking. If FR Co. were confident that the effect of the railway will be to allow people to visit the Park, whilst leaving their cars outside it, then surely they should have no difficulty making this concession.

**Mr A McNicol, Chairman WHR Ltd::** WHR Ltd must concentrate on securing a long term future. FR.Co. failure to consider WHR Ltd's site as a southern terminus cannot be justified in view of the Inspector's and SoS's consideration of alternative terminus locations at Porthmadog, and of the potential of WHR Ltd's site following the Transfer Order Inquiry [of 1993], and changed circumstances since the previous SoS's decision. The limits of deviation should not extend over WHR Ltd's running lines. A second station at Pen y Mount is not necessary. Railway powers, as identified by the limits of deviation, need only be granted as far south and west as is necessary to enable a satisfactory link to be made between the two railways, and should not extend outside the limits of deviation identified in the Draft Pont Croesor LRO. WHR Ltd is prepared to offer its site as a permanent southern terminus and depot. It believes it is more suitable than any alternatives. FR Co. has not provided any evidence that there is a market for through travel between their existing and proposed railways. The justification for the link is operating convenience. If a station close to Llyn Bach is FR Co.'s intention, then it should be included in the application. The cross-town link will have major severance effects in an environmentally sensitive and congested part of Porthmadog.

FR Co. has not indicated that the existing arrangements for moving stock between Dinas and Boston Lodge are unsatisfactory. It has not quantified any savings or other benefits which might be attributable to the link. It would be premature to grant consent for the link in the absence of comprehensive traffic management proposals for Porthmadog and funding guarantees.

*Cae Pawb from the air. One WHRL target was the Cross Town Rail Link - to try to quash FR's connectional aspirations. This was obviously self interest, such that it was commented upon.* **Peter Johnson**

**Mr T Sherratt, Vice Chairman WHR Ltd:** As soon as conveniently possible after the SoS for Transport's decision as to the Transfer Order, the Board of the Company met to consider the situation on the 23rd July 1994 and resolved unanimously as follows:

1. the Company welcomed the SoS's desire to see the rebuilding of the whole WHR as quickly as possible.

2. the Company felt that this objective can best be achieved by co-operation between FR Co., the 1964 Company [now WHR Ltd] and the Local Authorities.

3. the Company's major contribution to date has been the existing operation in Porthmadog and to make the best use of this, we must be able to extend northwards as quickly as possible.

4. the Company will dedicate its skills and expertise, as acknowledged by the Inspector, towards the expeditious rebuilding of the WHR.

5. the Company will continue to run its current railway in Porthmadog, improving, upgrading and vigorously marketing this operation.

Mr Sherratt made informal contact with Mr Hart on a number of occasions. In early August 1997, he received a personal letter from Mr Hart which indicated that he was worried about the strength of opposition to the proposed cross-town link in Porthmadog, and was concerned that the effect of this could be to require the cutting back of the Transport and Works powers to Rhyd Ddu. He wished to come to an arrangement for the use of the Company's terminus, so that the cross-town link could be downgraded to use for [rolling] stock exchanges and the like, rather than for revenue-earning traffic. This is a matter of key interest to the Company, whose sole purpose in acquiring its site in Porthmadog was to establish a suitable southern terminus for a railway to be reconstructed on the trackbed of the former WHR.

Mr Sherratt said that he attended a meeting on 19th August 1997 at Dinas. Notes were taken at the meeting by Mr Hughes. The notes were formulated into a written report, endorsed by all four of the Company's representatives, which was put to a Board Meeting on the 30th August 1997.

*The proof goes on at length to describe in tedious detail the dealings between the two companies. One speedily forms the view that the cogs did not engage when they met. In the end the 1998 Agreement was made and WHR Ltd withdrew their objections.*

**Mr DM Meller, Porthmadog:** This application includes deemed planning consent, but contains no details of the above facilities or any others (such as workshops) which it is acknowledged will be required. It would appear that the application does not comply with the local plan, and that deemed planning consent should not

be granted.

The traffic assessment fails to assess the traffic generated by people wishing to photograph or watch the trains, but not to travel on them. The anticipated transfer from road transport to rail seems extremely optimistic in view of the cost differentials involved. Such transfer would need to involve input from the planning and other authorities to provide park and ride (or similar) services which would require operational subsidies to ensure viability. These facilities would be subject to planning approvals themselves and, given the doubts which must surround such proposals, any mitigating effect should not be considered in assessing the impact of this application.

I am concerned that the Applicant's procurement methods might not encourage environmentally sensitive design and construction. I am concerned at the lack of information relating to the details of the work to be carried out on historically important structures and the lack of information on boundary treatment and other mitigation measures. It would appear that the ES has been prepared too quickly, and with inadequate resources. I am concerned that similar inadequate measures might be used in overseeing the actual construction work.

One of the main advantages put forward by FR Co.'s supporters during the early stages of their involvement was that the scheme would not draw on public funding. In his decision in 1994, the previous SoS made much of the suggestion that private investment would be more likely to support FR Co. than a mixed public/private sector project. This application, however, includes a funding statement showing that only 5-10% of the cost is to be privately funded. FR Co. have given no indication that they have made any attempt to attract private funding for the project. There has been no suggestion of a share or bond issue or any of the other means usually employed to raise money for heritage railways. It is unacceptable that public money should be used to fund a privately-owned development when no attempt has been made to obtain private funding in accordance with the spirit of the previous SoS's decision.

I am deeply concerned by the proposed demolition of the existing Waunfawr station building. This was built by the NWNGR in the 1870's, and is the most complete of the original wayside stations. It would appear that modifications to the proposals could be made which would allow the building to be preserved. I am concerned that the proposals with regard to other structures, such as bridges, have not attempted to preserve as much as possible of the original. I am concerned that, although FR Co. is now indicating that stone walls will be built, within five years of the opening of each section, which would mean that some sections will be a construction site for several years. I suggest

*It is true that putting WHR into Harbour Station was a quart in a pint pot. Yet for all the manoeuvrings of WHRL to stop CTRL, 64 Co. were not offering to pool their assets, so there was never going to be agreement to using Tremadog Road. Anticipating this, FR Co. went on to get the connection it wanted, and then to run trains over it.*

that all such construction work should be completed before any section of the railway opens.

The proposed "cross-town link" through Porthmadog would have an unacceptable adverse effect on the town's residents and visitors. As well as the extremely disruptive crossing of the trunk road, the scheme would disturb a peaceful footpath, disrupt the town's largest car park, cross another road on the level near two existing tourist attractions, remove a second section of footpath and divert a third. This disruption is unjustified when an alternative station site exists. I would only wish to point out that if FR Co. were to make a serious effort to come to an agreement with WHR, an arrangement could be made for use of this station, which would avoid the need for the proposed railway south of the existing WHR station at Pen y Mount, thus avoiding the disruption to the town mentioned above.

I have given details of the excessive clearance of trees, the obstruction and unauthorised diversion of a public footpath, a lack of adequate concern for public safety or convenience, and the insensitive design and construction with regard to railway heritage between Caernarfon and Dinas. I have given examples of several errors, omissions and other inadequacies in the published documents. The fact that these have been identified in the course of a relatively cursory examination gives rise to concern that these documents have also been prepared in haste without adequate attention to detail.

The Draft Order authorises FR Co. to borrow up to £10m. I am concerned that such extensive borrowing might place at risk the input which has been made by volunteers over the years. Other railways have experienced difficulties with much lower levels of borrowing. I would suggest that a much lower figure would be appropriate.

It is extremely unfortunate that in six months since making my objection the Applicant

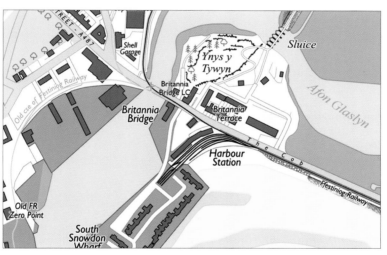

*This is the contentious part of the CTRL - the crossing of the A487. Mr Cochran was unhappy about the proposals. Whatever the plan, it wasn't until later that the Bypass plans came to fruition, so although the AOLC was accepted as part of the TWO, the congestion problem has now gone away.*

has not contacted me to overcome my objection or reassure me regarding my concerns. I am not alone in this. This omission demonstrates the Applicant's disregard for public concerns.

*Mr Meller's status and views were well known to FR Co. In the customary introductory declaration of relevant personal interests to inform the Inquiry, Mr Meller stated that he was employed by "a local Highway Authority", with involvement as a Senior Engineer in major road improvement schemes. He did not mention that the Authority was one of the major parties to the Inquiry, Gwynedd Council, nor that as a private interest he was a Director of WHR Ltd, and had been so for some time. Thus it was left open to FR Co., in a lengthy rebuttal of his evidence, to place Mr Meller's relevant additional interests on public notice.*

*In his proof, Mr Meller took many opportunities to subject FR Co. to criticism, both on highway grounds, and on matters closely concerning WHR Ltd. In his Proof particularly, he criticised the case*

*for the CTRL in Porthmadog, pointing out that a preferable potential southern terminus for the restored WHR existed at Beddgelert Siding, Tremadog Road, the business site of the Company of which he was a Director!*

*In his conclusions, his first preference was that the SoS should not make FR Co.'s WHR Order in any form. Yet it must have been long obvious that if FR Co.'s Application were to be refused, there was no foreseeable prospect of a further application to the same end by any party! It was anomalous that a long-standing member of WHR Ltd, of which the sole formal aim for nearly 40 years has been the restoration of the WHR, should testify thus - it pointed to short-sighted partiality, and indeed it seems that this is how it was taken.*

*In cross-examination Mr Price Lewis for FR Co. was able to draw from Mr Meller an admission that he had not thought fit to join the Welsh Highland Heritage Group, which had been established some months earlier precisely to care for the heritage that he claimed was being placed at risk by FR Co's plans. Indeed, Mr Meller admitted ignorance of the Group's aims, its Journal, and how to join it. In July 1998 Mr Meller was appointed as Chairman of the Board of WHR Ltd. In view of the divergence of approach between his evidence and the legal agreement reached between FR Co. and WHR Ltd, the effects of this appointment were awaited with interest.*

*However, in the weekly "Steam Railway News" of 19th March 1999, it was reported that Mr Meller had withdrawn his own, personal objection to the FR's TWA application in a spirit of reconciliation, in order to further the growing co-operation between the WHR Ltd and the FR.*

*In retrospect the spirit of reconciliation wore thin with those in FR who believed that the testimony revealed expressions of self-interest..*

## Welsh Office Highways Directorate,

**Mr AC Cochran** In September 1996, Festiniog Railway Company (FRC) approached Welsh Office Highways Directorate regarding their proposals to run a railway along a section of the A487 trunk road near Britannia Bridge, Porthmadog. The Directorate's view of these proposals was that, given the traffic problems already existing on the trunk road, the proposed railway crossing and traffic signals would cause additional unacceptable delays, disruption and safety hazards to trunk road users.

The A487T crosses the Glaslyn Estuary on The Cob embankment, which it shares with the Ffestiniog Narrow Gauge Railway. The Cob is privately owned and vehicles are required to stop at its eastern end in order to a pay a toll. The carriageway width between the masonry walls along either side of this 1.25 kilometre long embankment is only 5.6-5.8 metres. Delays occur frequently due to the collection of tolls and narrow carriageway, which can cause queues to extend along High Street in Porthmadog. The problems can be exacerbated further when congestion within Porthmadog causes west-bound traffic to back-up onto The Cob.

Traffic on the trunk road would be stopped to allow a train to cross over Britannia Bridge. This could occur twice an hour during daylight hours throughout the summer when trunk road traffic volumes are at their highest, but possibly less frequently for the rest of the year. Congestion frequently occurs in the vicinity of Britannia Bridge at peak times and it can take several minutes to clear queued traffic from the bridge. For signals to control rail/road traffic safely, trains would have to remain stationary at the 'crossing' until all road traffic had been cleared. Depending upon the speed of the train, the time taken by a train to cross the road could be in excess of 2 minutes. The actual delay to trunk road traffic upon each train crossing could be several minutes longer than this.

The traffic signals proposed by FRCo. would need to be placed on each side-road junction within the area of the 'crossing' in addition to being placed on the trunk road. This would be necessary in order that all road traffic could be stopped for train movements and then allow its phased release afterwards. Between train movements, the signals would be required to control access to, and egress from, the side-roads. These signals would be relatively complex in view of the number of side-roads in the vicinity of the 'crossing' and the need to cater for pedestrian crossing movements and train movements.

Due to the proposed frequency of train crossings, these signals would need to operate as full time signals, and would cause additional congestion to trunk road traffic above the existing situation, even at times when trains are not running. Side-road traffic, outside the limits of the 'crossing', would be likely to experience additional delays due to the increased congestion on the trunk road. Further congestion and delays to traffic is likely to lead to additional driver frustration and, as a consequence, an increase in accidents beyond the

*In Manchester trams and traffic appear to work quite smoothly, with little contention and no apparent congestion. Mr Cochran appeared in cross-examination to be unfamiliar with the operation of city tramways. Notice that the tram crossing is simple traffic lights (with a tramway aspect). Porthmadog later got an AOCL.*

limits of the proposed railway crossing. The proposed running of trains along this section of trunk road is likely to add to the existing conflict within the area of the railway crossing and increase the potential for accidents, including those involving pedestrians and cyclists.

*It appeared in cross-examination that Mr Cochran was not familiar with the extensive experience of operation of tramways in 5 places in Britain. Mr Cochran admitted that the safety concern related not to the fact that the link was on a bridge, but was caused by the simple juxtaposition of the railway sunk into the road as a tramway. It seems there was confusion over the status and signalling arrangements. He accepted that the body concerned with safety of the crossing would be HMRI, and that they had confirmed that a safe and secure crossing of the Bridge could be achieved.*

*The effect of the crossing would be to hold the traffic by traffic-controlled signals to allow the bridge to clear, and to allow the train to*

*cross. The existence of queues at peak times means that closure of the bridge would result in a gap "down-stream" into which held cars would flow and recoup lost time, particularly those "town bound". In fact we can see now the problems over delays have not proved to be serious, but the rails in the road did cause problems for cyclists for a short period. Those concerns were addressed between the construction and operating phases, and this is described in the section on the CTRL in Chapter 8.*

### Snowdonia National Park Authority - Dr KD Bishop

The Government's policy on major development in national parks has two elements: a substantive test which states that major development should not be permitted save in exceptional circumstances, and a procedure which must be followed in assessing compliance with the first. Exceptional circumstances have been defined by the Government (HM Government, 1990) as relating to proven national need and a lack of alternative sites.

No case has been advanced that the reconstruction of the Welsh Highland Railway is to fulfil a national need. Furthermore, in my opinion, it would be very difficult to argue a national need. There are already seven existing tourist railways within, or in close proximity to, the National Park. There is no evidence that these railways are unable to satisfy existing demand or that there is great latent demand for this type of tourist experience.

Whilst accepting, by definition, that there can be no alternative site for the reconstruction of the Welsh Highland Railway, this does not constitute an 'exceptional circumstance' as the two elements of the Government's definition are additional: there must be a national need and a lack of alternative sites.

*Dr Bishop was innocently able in his delivery, however, it did not conceal the facts that:*

*1. A major change of policy had been taken by the Authority, from supporter to objector.*

*2. The reasons for this were not made clear.*

*3. The person giving evidence was neither an Officer, nor an elected member of the Authority.*

*Whilst Dr Bishop spoke eloquently of 'quiet enjoyment', he was unaccountable for the policies of the SNPA.*

*Shortly before the Inquiry, though not then widely known, the SNPA had reversed its earlier clear support to the WHR to one of total opposition. The matter came fully into view only in July 1998 when the SNPA Planning Public Inquiry opened (as described later). The Authority's omission seemed disrespectful both of the public interest and of the position into which it put the Inspector in his duty to advise the Secretary of State upon the whole matter. It is of note that, at the end of Dr Bishop's evidence and cross-examination, the Inspector indicated to the Authority's advocate, Mr Evans, that he would appreciate further enlightenment upon the reasons for SNPA's then recent, abrupt and total reversal of policy to assist the purposes of his report to the SoS. Effectively, the advocate was unable to add more than that "a thorough review had been undertaken" in a few words of courtesy which added no clarity to this important question.*

**National Trust - Mr RA Cuthbertson MBE:** The Trust's Aberglaslyn Estate comprises in excess of 400 ha (1000 acres) all of which has been declared inalienable. The old trackbed of the WHR runs through the heart of the Snowdonia National Park, including the outstandingly beautiful Aberglaslyn Pass. The National Trust believes that reconstruction and subsequent operation of the WHR would significantly damage the existing landscape. The National Trust accepts that mitigation measures can be adopted to reduce the impact, but considers that the residual impact will still be severe and unacceptable.

The passage of railway engines and carriages will be intrusive as will the railway infrastructure. Signage, boundary walls, fences and the appearance of bridges, stations and halts will, no matter how sensitively designed, detract from the natural beauty of the National Park. The Environmental Statement considers the impact on farmers of the loss of access along the trackbed for stock and vehicles and the loss of hard standing. The mitigation measures propose the provision of alternative access tracks and additional hard-standings. Details of these works are not available, and it is feared that they will have considerable adverse impact on the landscape which has not been addressed in the Environmental Statement. We believe that reconstruction of the WHR has the potential to increase vehicular traffic at "honey pot" sites such as Beddgelert and Aberglaslyn, adding to congestion and landscape detriment. We fear that many tourists might choose to begin their journey from Beddgelert, so as to enjoy the most scenic part of the journey without purchasing a full ticket.

The Trust believes that the noise produced by passing trains will be intrusive and conflict with the purposes for which the National Park was established in accordance with Section 5 of the National Parks and Access to the Countryside Act 1949.

The trackbed through the Aberglaslyn Pass is heavily used by pedestrians. A survey by the Ramblers Association registered 1,268 walkers in a single day (8½ hours) on August Bank Holiday Sunday 1997, peaking at 231 between 2.00 and 3.00 pm. The average was 149 per hour at the north exit of the long tunnel. Parts of the trackbed through the Pass, although used by the public over many years, are not currently registered as statutory rights of way. The National Trust supports the application by the Ramblers Association that these routes have acquired the status of rights of way. The old trackbed between the villages of Beddgelert and Nantmor is accessible to walkers of all abilities and is unique in the opportunities for public access to the countryside that it offers. If the line re-opens the only alternative is to divert walkers onto the Fisherman's Path.

The Fisherman's footpath runs below the trackbed close to the river. It is informal and unsurfaced, accessible only to fit and able bodied walkers. Discussions have been held with the Railway Company and National Park regarding works to upgrade the path. However, the route could only be made to a standard equivalent to the trackbed if significant engineering improvements are carried out which are incompatible with the natural beauty of the Pass. The National Trust believes that some upgrading can be completed without serious detrimental impact on the landscape; however the route would then only be accessible to able-bodied walkers. This would deny the pleasures of open air recreation to many less able visitors each year.

Steep scree slopes rise above the trackbed between the tunnels and the Aberglaslyn Pass. We fear that noise and vibration created through passage of the trains will increase the risk of rock falls. This issue has not been addressed in the Environmental Statement. We fear that measures to prevent rock falls such as barriers and catch nets on the slopes would be intrusive and seriously affect enjoyment of the natural landscape.

*It is an interesting point that the railway is criticised for the potential generation of car traffic on one had, and then for removing the walking amenity from 1,268 walkers in a single day. Yet no details are given of what means the walkers used for access - it wouldn't have been by car, would it?*

*The cross-examination of Mr Cuthbertson was interesting. Although Mr Cuthbertson had claimed in Evidence that the Committee now opposed the reconstruction "in principle", as recorded above, he admitted in cross-examination that, until recently, the Trust accepted that the reconstruction would take place because the SNPA and Gwynedd Council supported the WHR. So, the Committee decided not to oppose but to seek mitigation measures where it thought appropriate. The Committee's officers negotiated with FR Co. on that basis, and a draft agreement was at an advanced stage. However, upon learning that the SNPA was proposing to withdraw support, the Committee reviewed the matter in November 1997 and realised that it should oppose "in principle" more actively and openly. Further, he admitted that this decision was ratified at a meeting later that month in "Any Other Business" without prior announcement to the Committee members, and on the basis only of an oral presentation by an officer. No written report or justification based upon study in depth was presented before the vote was taken.*

## Winding up the Inquiry

Mr AL Pym was of the opinion that the majority of the benefit of WHR will be outside the National Park while the real burden of the railway will fall within it. That was a prescient comment. Perhaps the key thing the FR Co. advocate Mr Price Lewis QC had to say was that Mr Hart thought that the WHR would be a service which other National Parks world-wide would look upon with envy. It is submitted that this is no exaggeration. He also submitted that the WHR would bring substantial economic advantages to the area. In fact the evidence given by the FR is unremarkable; it is what it is. The reason why it is unremarkable is that most of what they said has come to pass afterwards. On the other hand the strength of feeling of the objectors perhaps led some to be emotional, and much of what they said depended less on the force of facts, thus it has not come to pass as predicted. There have been instances where the railway brought inconvenience, and that is a matter of balance, to be weighed against the 'good' that came with it. There were emotional charges against the railway that were left unchallenged, largely because they were clearly extreme, and discredited the objectors. There were those who objected out of personal interest, seeking by their strength of feeling to avoid change; one cannot blame them.. The level and point of the objections were clear in indicating to the FR Co. where they should tread warily. It endorsed the policy of generous mitigation.

There was much nodding of the heads about 'quiet enjoyment', but the elephant in the room was the full car parks inside the Park from those 'quiet enjoyers'. Train passengers came by car too, but their cars remained outside. Convenient blindness continues on this subject over a wide area of activity. This might seem unfair, or odd, but voters come by car and politicians are not always brave.

*The Fisherman's Path was a spectacular walkway through the steepest and most rocky part of the gorge, that over the years had been allowed to decay, robbing ramblers and walkers of a delightful experience - though hardly 'quiet enjoyment', since the river was roaring alongside, drowning the noise of the motor road. Instead, people had been obliged to walk through the old railway tunnel. Today, now reinstated, the Fisherman's Path offers a thrill on foot rather better than walking the tunnel. That's finer (and safer) by train. So perhaps now the tourist has the best of both worlds.*

It was thought by many, that a railway was an excellent way to allow large numbers of people to enjoy the scenery of the Park without spoiling the very thing they had come to see! Could the same be said of 'ramblers', or cyclists? A walk up Snowdon might offer a rather sanguine view of that subject, where in more recent years the damage is exampled of people's fooitfall killing the sensitive vegetation..

Following the decision of the National Park Authority to object in principle, the National Trust resolved to shift its position to an objection in principle. The National Park considered the question of quiet enjoyment, and it was within the Aberglasyn Pass that the greatest concern was raised. The only definitive path which took walkers through the Pass was the Fisherman's Path, against the water's edge. The river roars as the white water pours through the narrow defile. The passage of two trains an hour above was unlikely to hinder quiet enjoyment of this. The authority's stance was inconsistent with its own policy on tranquil and quiet areas of the Park. It identifies such areas in the Eryri Local Plan and says :

> *'In some instances, the National Park Authority may seek to regulate traffic movements altogether and promote access into some areas by foot, cycle, bus or train only.'*

*The SNPA had managed to get itself into an anomalous situation that either required clear explanation of why it had shifted position, or failing that, a withdrawal to its previous stance of supporting the WHR. There were problems in store for the future with the new policy.*

## The Inspector Visits Track Bed Sites

On Thursday and Friday, the 29th and 30th January, immediately following the closure of the Inquiry, the Inspector undertook visits to sites requested by parties to the Inquiry. The objecting farmers between Betws Garmon and Pitts Head had placed replica signs at each crossing in order to demonstrate their impact on the landscape. There must have been at least twenty. At a distance of 100 metres or so, they did have visual impact, as is their purpose, of course. However, viewed along the length of the main valley from Rhyd Ddu, they became almost unnoticeable! In the event, the signs put in place were far smaller and less objectionable.

As an aside, at most stops during the Inspector's accompanied visits, one or more objectors gathered to point out features of a particular locality to augment written evidence presented in the Inquiry, as was their right. At one of these, an exchange went roughly thus:

Objector to the Inspector: " ... and the railway people are going to make major, unwelcome changes in this beautiful spot."
Railway representative to the Inspector: "No, sir, we are not proposing that."
Objector to railway representative: "Are you not proposing to cut down that mature tree and fill this hollow with concrete?"
Railway representative to Objector: "No."
Objector to railway representative: "That's the trouble with you railway people. You never give a straightforward answer."

# SNPA Planning Inquiry

## Background

As has been pointed out earlier, SNPA withdrew support for WHR reconstruction. This was not the sort of thing that could be done without notice, but it did happen quite suddenly in October 1997. It was considered strange when Dr Bishop, a consultant appeared before the TWO Public inquiry as an objector to speak for SNPA. He revealed the major change in SNPA policy. It became clear eventually from public papers, minutes of meetings, etc, that the proposal to withdraw the support of WHR reconstruction from the Authority's policies was instigated and driven by a very few individual members, and was contrary to the advice of its officers.

These actions to withdraw support were embarked upon formally at the meeting of the Authority's Welsh Highland Railway Panel on 23rd October 1997, at which only two members were present (one of whom was both its Chairman and an Objector), plus 3 senior officers. The reversal of policy was confirmed by the more weighty Planning Committee on the 12th November 1997, (shortly before the opening of the inquiry). The Inspector at the TWO public inquiry continued to accept new evidence well into the proceedings. It follows therefore, that the Authority had ample opportunity to prepare and present evidence by a witness chosen from any of the members who was determined to bring about this radical change of policy.

The single witness put forward by the Authority was Dr Bishop, a consultant. The Authority's change of view was driven entirely by the elected or appointed members Dr Bishop could not be considered to be an effective witness for the purpose of offering an adequate public defence of the actions. Only a responsible member of the Authority could do that, and such a witness did not appear.

GC upon its formation in 1997 updated its Area plans for Caernarfon and Porthmadog, placing therein supportive policies for the WHR. Snowdonia National Park Authority (SNPA) as the local planning authority within the Park, replacing the Gwynedd County Council, drew up the Eryri Local Plan. In accordance with the usual procedures, the Deposit Version of this had been published in July 1997, and it had supported the restoration of the Welsh Highland Railway. Indeed it had a duty to agree with the Porthmadog and Caernarfon Area Plans of the GC and officers of SNPA were negotiating a detailed agreement with FR Co.

SNPA members decided to change policy TR16 at the Park Authority's Welsh Highland Light Railway Panel on 23rd October 1997, when the officers submitted a draft agreement which sought to resolve FR Co./WHR matters of concern to SNPA but the Panel's Minutes record:

> *Resolved: to express concern about the [FR] Company's apparent lack of consultation with the farmers who are affected by the proposal, the possibility of the railway not proceeding beyond Rhyd Ddu, the effect of additional traffic in the National Park and the loss of the railway track to walkers in Nantmor and Aberglasyn.*

At the more senior SNPA Planning Committee meeting on the 12th November the officers submitted a similar report. The agenda continued the earlier stream of support by recommending the Committee to enter the proposed agreement and to withdraw the Authority's objection to the Railway Order.

But the Planning Committee also rejected the recommendation of its officers and, according to the Minutes, resolved:

> *1. To note the contents of the Minutes of the WHR LR Panel*
> *2. Not to complete the draft agreement*
> *3. To maintain the Authority's objection to the proposed Order on the basis of the railway's significant detrimental impact as a major development on the natural beauty of the Park and on the opportunities for public enjoyment of the special qualities of the Park.*

The next item on the agenda was a resolution to exclude the Press and Public.

This change placed the Eryri Plan in conflict with the Gwynedd Structure Plan. This situation (apparently against the advice of the SNPA Officers, but in accordance with the wishes of the elected members) was said to have come about by interesting means.

For those that like narrow gauge steam railways, and that might apply to nearly all who read this account, the idea that there should be fundamental opposition to such a sensible, logical proposal as restoring the WHR is distressing. The reaction might be to dismiss opposition, or to laugh it off, but for those affected by WHR it was serious. A dead railway coming to life, right in the middle of one's land, was not likely to be accepted passively everywhere, no matter how logical the revival might seem to be.

Just like the idea to restore the railway was energised by those with the determination and the means to do it, and that meant initially two or three people, so the opposition too was critically affected by small numbers of people. One in particular was The Hon. Eleanor Harper. She was the daughter of Lord Woolley of Hatton (Cheshire), past president of the National Farmers' Union. English to the core, a nursing sister in Wirral and a magistrate of Ellesmere Port, she and her husband bought Clogwyn y Gwin, a 1000 acre farm on the slopes of Snowdon. A woman of exceptional spirit, Mrs Harper was determined to get stuck in to run the farm There was no stand-offishness in this Welsh speaking farming community when Mrs Harper struggled determinedly to make the farm work. The neighbours all rallied round out of respect for her hard working resolution. They helped her succeed, and she did. The old trackbed ran near to the farm, circling round it on a higher level, as it descended, past the massive slate tips of the old Glanrafon Quarry, across the Clogwyn y Gwin land. The railway's embankment had been there for more than a century, so not much new was likely to block farm working. However, Mrs Harper took against the restoration plans for the railway for its uninvited intrusion, and she did so on a major scale. Her passion was such that she allegedly spoke with force to Cllr Dafydd Thomas Chairman of the SNPA Planning Committee about the scandal of the WHR, such that he persuaded his elected colleagues to reverse the policy of the Authority. This might be something of a tall story, but then you might not have met the Hon. Eleanor Harper. As a lady of immense respect and standing, she also apparently persuaded someone to from the National Trust Committee to urge the Trust to oppose the WHR as its duty. These might be anecdotes of doubtful provenance, but apparently they are 'in character' However, it is noticeable that those just as determined, but of a less emotional disposition, (perhaps with things to lose of a more substantial nature) concentrated on mitigation measures, and achieved a satisfactory level of remedy. There were repercussions from the lobbying actions of the Hon. EH that offered unintended consequences - not at all what was expected. The SNPA suffered what can only be described as a wreck for its sudden change of policy, and a section of the NT left behind it a feeling of mistrust from major policy changes accompanied by little or no consultation.

The changes to the Eryri Local Plan had to be consulted ,and the FR Co. discovered that Policy TR16 now read against the development of WHR. They decided to organise opposition, and the FR Machine got up a full head of steam, so that there were 5,000 objections against the change. SNPA attempted to rule that the objections against the substitution of the anti-WHR policy be bulked together as one, but this move was quashed. The matter was called in for public inquiry, so as if it wasn't enough, the restoration of the WHR entered yet another public inquiry - the third! The description below is sourced from John Hopkins's excellent RE/WHR Recent History publication, with additional material by Dr PN Jarvis.

## The Inquiry

The inquiry opened on 14th July 1998 presided over by Inspector **Mr J Davies.** The first three days were devoted to the proposed changes to the WHR proposals, and the Inspector made it clear that this was not to be a repeat of the earlier TWA inquiry. He said that matters must be confined to the question of the planning policy for the land-use of the track bed of the WHR.

The FR Co. Advocate was **Mr R Harris, QC,** and FR witnesses were:
**Mr P Marston (Planning),**
**Mr A Heywood (WHR Management)**
**Mr B Morgan (Agricultural Consultant).**
A Counter-Objector appearing (in favour of the WHR) was:
**Mr J Nicholson (Green Party).**

The SNPA's Advocate was **Mr A Evans, QC**, and SNPA witnesses were :
**Mr GI Huws (Chief Officer of SNPA)**
**Dr KD Bishop (Consultant).**
Objectors (against the WHR) were:
**Miss J Entwisle of Nantmor,**
**Mrs E Carrog of Bontnewydd**
**Mr JR Williams of Portreuddyn,**
**Mr R Brown of Beddgelert,** the last three persons being members of Gwarchod, appearing with the Inspector's approval via Mr Williams' own objection.

**Mr Marston** As a witness for FR Co., had the advantage of some 30 years' experience in planning matters in Gwynedd, latterly as Chief Planning Officer, and direct personal knowledge of WHR matters since 1969. He was able to give a comprehensive review and criticism both of the planning position at which SNPA had arrived and the manner ("quality") of each stage of decisions in reaching that.

**Mr Heywood** and Mr Morgan supported the FR Co.'s case in their respective fields.

**Dr Bishop** For the SNPA, showed his customary erudition in considerations affecting planning in National Parks. He argued that in proposing to withdraw support to the WHR, the SNPA had adopted an entirely responsible position in seeking, as its first

accepted duty, to conserve the beauty, tranquillity and wildlife of the Park.

**Mr Huws,** as the Authority's Chief Officer, had a good background of experience and present responsibility in these matters and sought in his Proof to defend the Park Authority's actions on similar grounds. However, in cross-examinations, **Mr Harris for FR Co.** was able to identify significant weaknesses in the Authority's new position on three main grounds :-
**1.** The reversed position in which SNPA had now placed itself was not in conformity with the extant Gwynedd Structure Plan (1993), a non-conformity which violated legal requirements,
**2.** The reversal had been made without presentation or consideration of any new or justifying evidence, and
**3.** The content of the Position Statement of 29th April 1998:

*'The SNPA will safeguard the entire length of the track bed of the disused WHR against any development which would prevent its use as a pedestrian and cycling route'.*

had been put forward without the mandatory public advertisement and consultation, and well after the publication of all the other proposed modifications in the preceding February. If SNPA persisted with the modification, in accordance with normal required procedures, and objections were received in due course, yet another public inquiry would become necessary and that would be nonsensical.

**Mr Nicholson** gave evidence in favour of the WHR on behalf of the North Wales Green Party and a group called "Protect Our Footpaths".

**Miss Entwisle** gave her objection to the WHR based on her residence immediately adjacent to the Nantmor Level Crossing, her knowledge of the opinions of some of the many walkers who used the track bed thereabouts, and of the likely disturbance from trains passing her extensive garden alongside the track, which she opened frequently to visitors in aid of charity.

**Mr Williams's** position contained a difficulty for him. As noted in his evidence to the TWA inquiry, the railway would impinge upon his dairy farming business which straddled the track bed. His farmhouse was within the National Park on the A498 main road near Tremadog. Unfortunately for his position at this inquiry, the road formed the boundary of the Park and his farm land of concern was not within the Park. The Inspector ruled that he had no powers to consider the problems of the juxtaposition of Mr Williams' land and the WHR track bed, but could hear any objections which he wished to make on general grounds.

**Ms Carrog** gave general evidence against the WHR. Among other points of objection, Mr Brown had compiled a list of the many trees which he claimed would have to be felled, but this evidence was strongly rebutted for the greater part by **Mr Marston** by reference to the limited structural envelope of the railway.

There was an interesting moment when the prominent local councillor and Chairman of the SNPA Planning Committee clashed with the Inspector. **Cllr Dafydd William Thomas** (who had refused to take the stand), sought the Inspector's permission to ask questions of a witness. The Inspector told him firmly that, since he was not a registered objector or counter-objector, he had no status at the inquiry other than as an observing member of the public, and his request was refused.

Under cross-examination from **Mr Hopkins, Mr Huws** revealed that the SNPA had not thought fit to consider and set down formally its policies to accommodate the needs of disabled persons, whereas FR Co. had done so.

In respect of the recent Position Statement announcing the proposed change of policy to support conversion of the track bed to a footpath and cycleway, **Mr Huws** admitted in cross-examination that it had not been publicised within normal guidelines and that no consultations had taken place, not even with adjoining land-owners. Nor had SNPA informed the Welsh Office as it was expected to object!

**Mr Harris QC**, observed that, whatever its nature, details of any response from the Welsh Office might well have assisted the Inspector. **Mr Huws** also admitted that the quality of the decision-making process had been poor. Indeed, when Closing for SNPA, its Counsel, **Mr Evans,** admitted that the decision-making process (since October 1997) *"had not been in accordance with best practice"*.

In Closing for FR Co., **Mr Harris QC** said that the sudden withdrawal of support to the WHR had been made without evidence or justification of any kind. Therefore, the reversal was much worse procedurally than being merely 'not in accordance with best practice'. As **Mr Evans** admitted for SNPA in the circumstances, such actions of a public body were unreasonable and, therefore, **Mr Harris** submitted, 'unlawful'. This was striking language to use in a public forum. He suggested that it might

*'A scheme dependent on bringing in volunteers from outside the area is of no benefit to the local culture.' The large number of Welshmen within this group of volunteers would take rather strong and vocal issue with such a contention.*

be an appropriate case for the Secretary of State for Wales to exercise his powers to call in the proposed changes for his own determination.

Discussion of Policy TR16 was completed by the inquiry on Thursday, the 17th July. The Inspector made accompanied site visits in the locality of the WHR the following day. The inquiry ended and all withdrew to await the decision.

*There was much excitement in the FR camp at the end of this inquiry, as it seemed as if what were to them the 'forces of darkness' had taken a significant wrong step, and that for the first time in the long and exhausting legal battle to restore the WHR, the 'opposition' was on the run. The 5,000 objections managed by FR, and the alleged suppression attempt that was unsuccessful was the first indication that things indeed may be going their way. The Inspector's report was eagerly awaited. If this was 'won, then the battle for restoration had one less hurdle to jump.*

## Formation of Gwarchod

Gwarchod (Guardian) was established after the closure of the Caernarfon - Porthmadog TWO inquiry in January 1998, when a number of people known to each other from the public inquiry came together to form it. Some had gone to the inquiry already against the scheme, others to learn more about it. By the end of the inquiry, and in the subsequent weeks, there was more discussion between people and in the Press. Some became hostile to the scheme as more information about it became public. A meeting was held in Rhyd Ddu and from this a working party was set up to oppose the plans. Thus began Gwarchod.

Although it served as a focus for opposition to the restoration of the WHR, the aims were to rather wider.

To guard and defend:
o the future of agriculture in Snowdonia,
o the well-being of local businesses,
o the rights of walkers of the old track,
o the natural beauty of the area,
o wild life.

The membership included a cross-section of people:
'Farmers and others whose livelihood depends on the land; those who were brought up in or have chosen to move to the tranquillity of the countryside; some who live in nearby towns and who enjoy the beauty of the area; some who depend on tourism for their livelihood and see the commercial dangers to the area if the Festiniog Railway Company's plans are allowed, resulting in an ever-decreasing share the tourism cake into small pieces; some who believe that it is a waste of public money to develop yet another tourist train attraction, when there are seven already in the Snowdonia area, in addition to the great number of other extra attractions developed in the area in recent years and some who believed that a scheme so enormously dependent on bringing in "volunteers" from outside the area is of no benefit to the local culture, bearing in mind the Festiniog Railway Company's record, which shows that creating work for local people is not on the priority list of this company.'

**'You are welcome to join Gwarchod if you agree with the aims of the Society.'**

Gwarchod had been formed after expiry of the deadline for submissions to the SNPA inquiry. So, in the period before announcement about the outcome of the TWA inquiry, they felt that it should make a late submission, and this was accepted by the Inspector. There was no cross examination of the evidence. Gwarchod was a voluntary society, with the following officers:

| | |
|---|---|
| Chairman: | **Richard Williams,** |
| Treasurer: | **Eurig Jones,** |
| Researcher: | **Richard Brown,** |
| Agricultural Spokesman: | **Edgar Williams,** |
| Press Officer: | **Eleri Carrog.** |

## Recommendations of the SNPA Inspector, March 1999

**i.** delete Policy TR16 and replace it with the following new policy :

*"The NPA will safeguard the track bed of the Welsh Highland and Corris Railways and will not permit any development which would prevent the reinstatement of a railway along either of these two routes. The NPA will permit the establishment of a recreational route alongside the Welsh Highland Railway track bed or within reasonable proximity to it.*

*In the event that it can be demonstrated that the Welsh Highland Railway cannot be reinstated in a manner consistent with National Park purposes, the NPA will safeguard its track bed for use as a footpath and cycleway."*

**ii.** include reference to the contents of applications and conditions relating to ancillary development in the text and revise the text as necessary to reflect the recommended new policy;

**iii.** revise the Proposals Map to define the areas of land to be safeguarded by Policy TR16 for the reinstatement of the Welsh Highland and Corris Railways.

By March 1999, there had been three public inquiries, an exhausting, vexatious and expensive process that was sapping the vitality of restoring the WHR. The outcome of the first was in progress, but of results from the key TWO inquiry, there were none. Supporters of reconstruction of the WHR therefore received Inspector's recommendations with profound relief, squeezing some much needed encouragement from the SNPA outcome as it was difficult to believe that the SNPA Inspector and the SoS would arrive at contradictory conclusions. One might think one knows what the outcome will be, but until it has come out, uncertainty acts as an ever-present spectre.

In the issue of Steam Railway News of 12th March, a short article appeared entitled 'Inspector's report boosts Welsh Highland hopes', and 'The National Park Officer's report to the Authority concluded with the recommendation that the Inspector's report and all the proposed modifications it contains are accepted by the Authority. It is said that the Authority's official reaction determined to write to the SoS in continued protest against the WHR. It was reported informally later that the Committee debated the 15 pages of their Inspector's Report referring to the WHR for two hours and dealt with the remaining 185 pages in half-an-hour. The wording of the Eryri Local Plan that was adopted is as follows:

## *Eryri Local Plan*
## *Adopted November 1999*

### *Narrow Gauge Railway Lines*

*14.93 The National Park is fortunate in possessing five tourist railways. The Ffestiniog, Corris, Snowdon Mountain, Talyllyn and Bala Lake railways provide popular visitor attractions predominantly during the spring and summer but with the exception of the Ffestiniog line, they do not link other parts of the national railway network.*

*14.94 There are probably sufficient tourist railways in the National Park to provide for present visitor* requirements *although the NPA and Gwynedd Council are still committed to the reinstatement of the Welsh Highland and the Corris Railways. Unlike other tourist railways the Welsh Highland will eventually provide a valuable link in the county rail network to Caernarfon. Its developers, the Festiniog Railway Company, have also proposed to market the route as a Park and ride service bringing visitors into Beddgelert and the southern and western side of the Snowdon Massif by train from towns outside the National Park. It has even been suggested that the railway could carry a certain amount of freight e.g. timber, slate and building materials and relieve the need for road improvements along the A498 and A4085.*

*14.95 The NPA consider that the reinstatement of the trackbed of the former Welsh Highland Railway as a narrow gauge railway should be undertaken in a manner which would permit, where it was appropriate to do so, parts of the trackbed to be used as a recreational cycle and walking route. Where it is not feasible to use the trackbed for this purpose, the Authority will work with the railway company and relevant landowners to develop this leisure route on suitable land either adjacent to or in close proximity to the railway corridor.*

*14.96 The NPA will need to carefully consider proposals for station buildings, car parks, cafes, etc. associated with the reinstated railway to avoid conflict with other planning and visitor management policies. The Festiniog Railway Company will be expected to submit a comprehensive statement of how these facilities will be provided along the length of the whole route prior to consent being granted by the NPA, for any part of them.*

*The livid scar of the wicked Welsh Highland Railway, slashes its way across the virgin landscape of our beautiful Snowdonia. You'll be hard put to see it as most of it's been there for over 100 years and the rest for 70 odd! The view off the top of Snowdon is almost due west, with Llyn y Gader centre-left, Llyn y Dywarchen further right and Llyn Cwellyn extreme right. Garn overlooks the scene and one can see right down the Nantlle Valley to Llyn Nantlle Uchaf and Penygroes. The ridge in the foreground is Llechog and below us is Cwm Clogwyn. Behind Llechog can be seen the Glanrafon slate tips, encouraged by the NWNG when it was a real railway, and supported jobs for slate quarrymen.*

## What happened to the footpaths?

It was one thing as a neighbour, to take advantage of a vacant trackbed left for over 50 years, and another to establish a right-of-way along it. Definitive footpath maps showed parts of the WHR as a public right-of-way. Alas the FR Co. was unable to accommodate footpath and railway on the trackbed, as had been done on the wide ex-standard gauge formation between Caernarfon and Dinas. The FR Co. claimed that the Highways Act 1980 indicated that such claims for rights-of-way were invalid as the statutory body was prevented from pursuing its statutory purpose. In 1999 when title of the trackbed was transferred, the FR Co. notified the authorities responsible that their rights-of-way claims for footpath were invalid. Locations were just north of Rhyd Ddu and around the short tunnels. Unfortunately inclusion on the Definitive Map, even erroneously, legally establishes the public rights-of-way, and so they had to be removed, or diverted, through the TWO process. GC as the footpath authority carried out the action as contained in the Order.

## Mr Heason's concern

An issue had been raised in the TWA inquiry by Mr Heason from Nantmor who used the trackbed to get his car to his garage. Unfortunately the restoration of the railway would mean that this option was no longer available to Mr Heason, and there were no reasonable actions that could be taken in mitigation. However Mr Heason stated that he had written and obtained permission to use the trackbed as an access route to his garage. Indeed he did, as when he showed the letter of qualification, it was from and signed by the 64 Co. It did not go down very well with Mr Heason when it was pointed out by FR Co. that this organisation, had no locus on the trackbed.

Mr Heason, a qualified geologist, became aware that there were loose rocks in the Aberglaslyn Pass, that had in his view now assumed the level of a potential danger,. He believed this would be exacerbated when subject to the coming vibration from passing trains. Mr Heason apparently wrote a letter originally to send to the newspapers, and passed it to the Inspector after the close of the inquiry, during the visit on 29/30 January 1998, so it was never debated, and commented upon at the inquiry.

*Letter dated September 1997*
*Dear Sir,*
*On the morning of Monday, 16 January 1995, a boulder of rhyolite detached from the cliffs directly above the northern entrance to the long tunnel in the Aberglaslyn Pass and fell a vertical distance of approximately 100 metres/300 feet, tearing branches from substantial oak trees during its passage and breaking into two pieces as it fell. The largest piece, weighing an estimate 1000 kg/1 ton, landed directly on the track bed of the old Welsh Light Highland Railway and was winched to one side by National Trust workers. It lies there today.*

*I invite the directors of the Festiniog Railway Company, who are proposing to open a passenger-carrying railway which would pass directly below these cliffs, and over the point of impact described above, to use these columns to inform the public of their views on the following six points :-*

*1. Are they aware of the rock-fall described above?*

*2. Are they aware that the cliffs at this point, which are about 50 metres/150 feet high, rising nearly vertically above the lesser-angled trees and talus slope below, are loose-bound and shattered, principally as the result of weathering? Experienced rock climbers who have moved amongst the cliffs describe them as being, in many places, "like a tottering pile of twenty-ton paperback books". A cursory visual examination from the nearby road will confirm this.*

*3. Do they agree that the operation of railway trains will transmit significant vibration into the ground ahead of, during, and after passing these cliffs? Shear (S) waves and compressive (P) waves will travel at a measurable velocity through the solid rhyolite? This is a compact rock which is readily subject to shear failure along incipient fracture lines. Although the amplitude of vibration will decay according to the inverse square law, it will continue indefinitely until a cohesionless discontinuity is reached.*

*4. Because this vibrational energy will travel regularly to and through the unstable sections of the cliffs, do they agree that there is the possibility that significant detachments will occur? There is proven precedent that even a comparatively small 1000kg/1 ton boulder has hit the track bed at a speed conservatively calculated at 125km/77 miles per hour.*

*5. Can they realistically reassure the public that these cliffs, on National Trust Property, can be stabilised so that there is no reasonable chance of future rock falls?*

*6. Will they please confirm that their public liability insurers are aware of the nature of the above points?*

*Yours faithfully,*

*Alan P Heason.*

Despite the closure of the inquiry the Inspector nevertheless rightly felt that the nature of the letter and the problem it described was such that the SoS should be informed. It is unexplained as to why it was that if the rocks came from NT land, and impacted upon OR land (the trackbed), neither of these bodies took preventive action at the time described in Mr Heasons' letter, in 1995 - nor did Mr Cuthbertson in his Proof of Evidence for NT, make mention of the fact that NT personnel removed a 1 tonne boulder that had smashed into the ground three years before on a public footpath. It's a mystery, and a pity that the matter was denied ventilation at the inquiry.

After Mr Heason's letter

came to official notice, the obvious thing was that the footpath had to close (by FR Co. who would shortly have title to the trackbed) to protect the public from this danger, whilst the threat was averted. This might have been an unintended consequence, and no one told the now safeguarded but excluded walkers. This action had a crushing effect on the aspirations of those many ramblers evidenced at the inquiry. They were suddenly barred from the trackbed, and if the TWA was favourable this would relieve the reconstruction of the Pass section from potential protests.

## The DETR ruling on the rocks

The eventual TWO letter from John Prescott came on 7th April 1999. It contained within, the statement that on 3rd February 1999 the OR had completed the transfer of the land held by him to FR Co. The letter held the recommendations from the Inspector, and the Secretary of States's judgement to make the Order conditional. Before the Order would be made, the potential for rock fall in the Aberglaslyn Pass must be attended to.

Action that could have been intended to impede the restoration of the WHR had instead stopped access to all those who used the trackbed on foot. Now the railway was to be allowed, subject to the problem of rock fall being attended to. It all looked rather bleak, but this was a short term view. In time the Pass would be open to hundreds of thousands by rail, and ramblers would have an improved Fisherman's Path.

A clause in the SoS letter said:

**7.1.** *The applicants are now invited to arrange for a survey to be undertaken, by a suitably qualified person or persons, of the rock faces in the vicinity of the Aberglaslyn tunnels. The specification for the survey, and the name(s) of the person(s) to undertake the survey, should be agreed in advance with the Snowdonia National Park Authority or, in default of agreement within a reasonable period, with the Secretary of State. Following the carrying out of such a survey, the applicants should consult the Snowdonia National Park Authority over a scheme for implementing any remedial works arising, before referring back to the Secretary of State or to the Welsh Assembly if by then it is operational - for a decision on the application for the Order and planning direction*

*The rock fall danger- was a most serious concern to the interests of restoring the WHR The DoT could not be seen to allow the matter to pass. There was a flurry of activity - but the unintended consequence was the prompt closure of the footpath!*

Does the wording *'in default of agreement within a reasonable period, with the Secretary of State.'* seem to anticipate the possibility of prevarication by the SNPA, with an offered escape route for FR Co? Indeed SNPA began what looked suspiciously like a game to delay its considerations, to force the decision beyond the expiry of the SoS's powers on 30th June, so that the matter would come before the emerging Welsh Assembly.

The SNPA planning Committee of 28th April

agreed the appointment of Ove Arup to survey the site. Arup found no problems which 'cannot be overcome'. Their report was passed to SNPA on 19th May. It was placed before the SNPA Planning Committee on 9th June 1999. Cllr Dafydd Thomas was the Chairman of this Committee. FR Co was keen to obtain a decision as soon as possible. SNPA was aware that FR Co. felt much frustration, as they were to meet the SoS on the 10th June, and were claiming to have fulfilled all his conditions.

SNPA's position was that democratic methods took time, that more engineering and geological advice was needed. SNPA must have a proper report, and had not had time to agree the position; the officers needed more discussion, then more discussion with FR Co. was required. The Chief Executive Iwan Huws recommended that no final decision be made at this meeting, and it was expected that a full report would be brought to the Authority at its next meeting on 24th June, and that this would make it a matter for the new Welsh Assembly from the cut-off date of 30th June 1999.

The question was raised whether the Committee could have a presentation from Hyder, their own consultants? SNPA has to be very careful and must take the right steps. It was said that a wall two metres high is proposed in the Aberglaslyn Pass, and planning considerations were involved.

Matters came to a speedy head when the Millennium Commission, already terse from public inquiries causing delay, saw the aspiration of the project fading, to build to Rhyd Ddu by the Millennium, so that there was something to be celebrated. They understood that no work had been done beyond Dinas, and the expectation of nine-miles of railway being built in a year were diminished. They therefore wrote a stern letter, threatening to pull the funding if there was no favourable decision. Whether Mr Huws found the threat of the loss of £4.3m of funding helpful in accelerating the decision making powers of the committees in his Authority is not recorded. However the decisions were taken for him. On 28th June, John Prescott made the Order to come into force on 21st July 1999. The various reasonings of Inspector and SoS are laid out. The following extract is of note:

**1.** Adverse possession claims are a matter for the Lands tribunal and/or the courts, and that CP powers for the land specified in the Order would be within the provisions of the TWA.

**2.** The SoS agrees that the economic benefits of the scheme would arise mainly outside the Snowdonia National Park, and that the railway is not a national necessity. But he considers nevertheless, that the scheme would be in the national public interest.

**3.** The SoS agrees with the Inspector's conclusions relating to the economic benefits of the scheme, especially in the Caernarfon area, and the contribution the railway would make to a reduction of traffic in the Snowdonia National Park and to access to the Park for visitors who would otherwise be unable to enjoy it.

**4.** The SoS agrees that the train and whistle noise would have an adverse effect on the quiet enjoyment of the Park. He notes and accepts the Inspector's conclusion that the overall environmental impact from railway noise would be no more than minor adverse.

**5.** The SoS agrees with the Inspector's conclusion that the effects of the project on tourism and on the local economy would be largely beneficial.

**6.** The SoS accepts that the proposed accommodation works and mitigation measures relating to the farms affected by the reinstatement of the railway would still leave 8 holdings experiencing a moderate adverse impact, and 17 a minor adverse impact. He accepts that all of the farms should be able to adapt to the altered circumstances without major changes to farm management, although he recognises that additional manpower would be required on some of the farms for the movement of stock across the railway.

**7.** The Inspector's overall conclusion is that, there were insufficient benefits to the Snowdonia National Park and its economy to outweigh the adverse effects and the weight of objections. The SoS accepts that in determining whether to make the Order and grant deemed planning permission, he should consider the relevance and application of published Government policies; he has concluded that the proposed railway can be authorised in the particular circumstances of this case without compromising or undermining these policies.

There's lots more on this (In John Hopkins' publication) - but the above are the example conclusions chosen.

## The Aftermath

Poor Mrs Harper died in 1999, and the invading railway was built, much against her will. There is a poignant aftermath of the story, illustrating an outcome hoped for by the FR Co. In 2005 the 1000 acre farm of Clogwyn y Gwin was on sale at £750k, with the hope (but not the stricture) that it would remain a farm. The Daily Telegraph Property Section stated:

*'The farm is in the Snowdonia National Park, and parts of it have been designated a National Nature Reserve. The Welsh Highland Railway Company runs steam trains along the edge of the land. Parts of the lower pastures have Site of Special Scientific Interest status.'*

Oops! The train is suddenly an asset?

After it was all over for inquiries and challenges, there was a sad postscript to the career of Cllr Dafydd William Thomas of Penmorfa, former Chairman of the SNPA Planning Committee, who was a Plaid Cymru member on GC, representing the Dolbenmaen and Beddgelert Ward. According to reports in the Daily Post and the Western Mail, in November 2001 he was arrested by North Wales Police, in connection with alleged offences relating to a complaint made by GC about housing grants. He was eventually convicted of fraud in 2002 and given a nine month jail sentence, suspended for two years.

The end of this chapter finds the fight to restore the Welsh Highland Railway has been through the High Court twice, and through three public inquiries. Two of these saw the Inspector's recommendations overturned, with comments that the Secretary of State was 'wrong', yet in the SNPA planning inquiry it was apparently the Inspector who was 'wrong'. It seemed like few had any good words to say about it in public - there was such a fuss, and such strong local feeling expressed. The cost of all this was prodigious, but it was part of driving the railway through - this was a mandatory consequence of all those years of closure, so there was no point in complaining. The objectors were made of as stern stuff as the railway restorers. They believed that reintroducing a railway was a rather 'cheeky' trick to take advantage of a doubtful sliver of law for a frivolous purpose - in comparison with the general struggle that they were obliged to contend with. Thus they were not going to agree - and it wasn't over yet!

# THE 1998 AGREEMENT

**THIS AGREEMENT** under seal is made the 12th day of January between:

**(1) FRC: THE FESTINIOG RAILWAY COMPANY** whose business office is at Harbour Station, Porthmadog, Gwynedd
**(2) WHRL: WELSH HIGHLAND RAILWAY LIMITED** whose registered office is at Gelerts Farm, Madoc Street West, Porthmadog, Gwyned

## W H E R E A S

1. FRC are a Statutory Railway Company and on 25th March 1997 made an application for an Order pursuant to the Transport and Works Act 1992 in respect of a railway line from Dinas to Porthmadog and known as The Welsh Highland Railway.
2. WHRL supports the said application and the rebuilding of the Welsh Highland Railway to the extent and on the terms set out herein.

**IT IS HEREBY AGREED:**

### 1. Interpretation
A. The terms "FRC" and "WHRL" include their subsidiary companies and businesses and their successors in title.
B. "WHR Order" means the Welsh Highland Railway Order the application for which was lodged by FRC on 25th March 1997 with the variations made by FRC up to the date hereof.
C. "The Inquiry" is the Inquiry to be held by direction of the Department of the Environment Transport and the Regions (the Department) in respect of the application for the WHR Order.
D. "Track Construction" means clearing the site of the track bed including fences, drains, bridges and crossings and laying track all to the standards required by and the final approval of the Department and its successors in title and Her Majesty's Railway Inspectorate (HMRI) and includes complying with all planning and other conditions in the WHR Order or otherwise and the obligation to maintain and keep in repair the track to the same standard requirements and approvals.
E. "Porthmadog WHRL Station" means the Porthmadog WHRL Station.
F. "Rule against Perpetuities" - All future rights shall be commenced within 80 years of the date hereof.

### 2. Support by WHRL
WHRL supports completely the rebuilding of the Welsh Highland Railway by FRC and therefore the application by FRC for the WHR Order. WHRL will be represented at the Inquiry so to declare.

### 3. Support by FRC
FRC supports completely the construction and operation of the portion of the Railway from Pen-y-Mount to Pont Croesor as hereinafter set out retaining all ticket receipts until clause 6 applies.

### 4. Withdrawal of Representations and Objections
In consideration of the terms of this agreement WHRL withdraws all of its objections to WHR Order except its objections to the compulsory purchase powers on WHRL land.

### 5. Action after grant of WHR Order
A. FRC will proceed to enter on and acquire the land and other rights authorised by the WHR Order within three months of the granting of the Order.
B. FRC will proceed with Track Construction from Dinas to Waunfawr as soon as possible and after this work is completed WHRL will proceed with Track Construction of the Section from Pen-y-Mount to Pont Croesor as soon as practicable.
C. If WHRL so requests FRC may agree to let WHRL to carry out Track Construction from Pont Croesor for a further section or sections of the Welsh Highland Railway.

### 6. Action after Track Construction completed between Dinas and Pen-y-Mount
A. WHRL heritage trains would have guaranteed access over the whole route subject to HMRI approval on the following basis :-
i) Train crews are passed out by FRC for operation over the line.
ii) Paths for such trains are compatible with commercial requirements and any requirements imposed by outside bodies.
iii) Fares received from such trains will be paid to FRC but FRC in return will pay for the use of locomotives and rolling stock.
iv) FRC will also pay a proportion of the receipts to WHRL for use of the line between Porthmadog WHR Station and Pen-y-Mount by those trains.
v) WHRL retains in full the proceeds from all sales and income (other than fares) received at WHRL's shop and cafe at Porthmadog (WHRL) and catering/sales on these trains.
vi) The legal responsibility for operation of these trains over FRC tracks rests with the FRC.
B. FRC's trains can, if necessary, terminate at the Porthmadog WHRL's Station subject to payment of access charges to be agreed.

### 7. Use of Name "Welsh Highland Railway"
On completion of the line, the whole route will be known as Welsh Highland Railway. In the interim, the FRC's section will be Welsh Highland Railway (Caernarfon) and the WHRL's section will be Welsh Highland Railway (Porthmadog). It is acknowledged that publicity for the 1998 season is already underway but subsequent publicity from the date of this agreement will carry the new form of words.

### 8. A. Cross-town link
WHRL will support the cross-town link from Pen-y-Mount WHRL Station to Porthmadog Harbour FRC Station as described in the WHR Order and the plan to operate through FRC trains.

### B. Grant Applications
WHRL will not compete with FRC for grant applications.

### 9. Resolution of Disputes
If there is any matter herein or arising out of the relationship of the parties which is in dispute or cannot be agreed then either party may refer the matter of dispute or non agreement to a mediator or failing agreement to the Chairman (or his authorised deputy) of the Association of Independent and Preserved Railways.

### 10. Heritage Facility
Following the date of this agreement, the FRC and WHRL heritage groups should be brought together to develop a "rails to Porthmadog" heritage facility at Gelert's Farm, Porthmadog.

### 11. Joint Committee
A joint steering committee shall be formally constituted on a regular basis as a means to better communication between the two Companies.

### 12. Support
By reason of the terms of this Agreement and to enable the Welsh Highland Railway to be rebuilt WHRL supports the application by FRC for the WHR Order.

SOURCE: http://cms.whr.co.uk/about/ffr-agrmnt/98-jan-final.xhtml [WHHR Website : 20.12.2010]

## The whys and wherefores

Whilst the TWA Inquiry was in full flood a formal Agreement was signed between WHR Ltd (64 Co.) and FR Co. dated, 12th January 1998. This Agreement arose out of a Memorandum of Understanding made on 30th November 1997, at a meeting with A. Heywood (FR GM), T. Sherratt (WHRL), W.R. Cutler (FR Co.) and G. Hughes (WHRL Company Secretary). The WHRL were looking for a means of achieving their aim of building to Pont Croesor, and of being able to run their trains on the completed WHR. The FR Co. had been advised to ensure that there were no objections from another railway company at the TWO Inquiry. This encouraged their willingness to offer consideration to an item that was of such importance to the WHRL. As the inquiry was underway, the Agreement needed to be completed quickly. It seems that the two parties did not come to an agreement that would safeguard their position in the long term, by including a renegotiation clause to deal with changing events and to handle disputes.

The document was tabled before an EGM of WHRL on 21st February 1998, with a motion to endorse the actions of the Board in entering into a binding agreement with FR Co. The WHRL Board members explained that it was drawn up under much pressure, arising from the inquiry, which was entering its final stages at the time. Those within WHRL did not dwell on questions of the validity and status of the Agreement. There were

| WHRL EGM 21 February 1998 Total number of votes cast : 405 | | | | |
|---|---|---|---|---|
| **Votes** | **For** | | **Against** | |
| **Meeting** | 41 | 10% | 53 | 13% |
| **Proxy** | 301 | 74% | 10 | 2% |
| **Sub-total** | 342 | 84% | 63 | 16% |
| | | | | |

405 votes cast, of which 342 (84%) were 'ayes'. On the face of it the Agreement seemed to be an endorsement for co-operation, in exchange for the withdrawal of objection to FR Co. restoration plans, with the implication that co-operation, and some sort of partnership would likely grow. The overall vote was dominated by the proxies. There was an expression of dissatisfaction by 53 members who voted against, a modest majority of the 94 present at the meeting. Since those who had turned up were the 'activists', external analysis would register the result as 'unhappy'.

Problems arose for FR Co. almost immediately after signing. Later, when FR Co. completed to Waunfawr, and WHRL were able to begin construction to Pont Croesor, there was not enough latitude in what had been agreed. Each side accused the other of breaches, either as failure to acknowledge the letter of the Agreement, or even as a substantial breach. The 1998 Agreement was not able to span the march of events.

## Circumstances and comment

Neither signatory understood the import of the Agreement to the other party when they signed. WHRL considered that the Proof of Evidence of Mr Mellor was given in the Inquiry as an individual. Mr Mellor was a WHRL Director, so it was taken by FR as proof that WHRL could not deliver what they had promised. Thus one deduces that FR did not value the Agreement. The interpretation of action over acquiring land was affected by the TWO grant of compulsory purchase powers. Perhaps FR Co. never explained the change, as it confused WHRL, who later talked of breach of the Agreement. FR Co. at first accepted failure of WHRL to build to Pont Croesor philosophically, whereas WHRL included the land issue as a cause of that failure and accused FR of being at fault.

The amount of cash needed to build to Pont Croesor was £700k. One wonders what commitment WHRL thought they were taking on before they signed the Agreement. One can only account for this if WHRL thought that their timescale for building was long, or if they entertained the view that FR Co. had no intention of completing WHR - a strange delusion by that time. Perhaps it was a surprise when FR Co. served them notice to treat/notice to enter on 14th May 2004?

The explanation suggested by the facts in hindsight is that FR Co. was totally absorbed in getting the WHR restored. If WHRL was unwilling to offer it's assets and support to a unitary body dedicated to WHR restoration - the only effective way forward in FR eyes - then FR Co. had little interest in supporting an autonomous organisation that in its eyes contributed nothing of value. Thus FR Co. actions were palliative. They were solely focussed on rebuilding WHR and FR did not ponder long on the future of WHRL.

## The Clauses

**Clause 2:** Using the word 'support' is open to interpretation. FR Co. was battling for TWO; support would mean something quite different if they got it. This clause fits the case short term, but is imprecise for the longer term when it says 'supports completely'.

**Clause 3:** FRCo. did 'support' the construction of the railway from Pen y Mount to Pont Croesor. It was a chunk of railway to be built free, and in the rather strained financial climate this was helpful. The fact that 'supports completely' was not defined (in **Para 1 Interpretation**) allowed both sides to claim that the Agreement was not being observed. Alas the Agreement is not clear enough in who is responsible for doing what. The inexact substance of this Agreement led to fall-outs, grumbles and failure to execute.

**Clause 5:** Here the 'proceed', 'possible' and 'practical' caveats were undefined. There were items of significance like available funds, and adverse possession claims to be overcome as practical bars to progress. **5A** for example was affected by the CP powers granted in the TWO. These were time conditional, and Notices were served when the contractors were ready and able to begin work.

**Clause 6:** Allowed points of detail to obscure undertakings to reach agreement in the light of subsequent events. If the obligation for WHRL to construct to Pont Croesor was to generate a duty for FR Co. to permit 'WHRL heritage trains..... guaranteed access', then what was written failed in its aims through lack of clarity over what it meant.

**Clause 7:** Clarified the name to be used was Welsh Highland Railway, yet dispute over the use of the name resurfaced in subsequent public accusation.

**Clause 11:** The Joint Committee never figured much in the decision making process.

*There is a section on building to Pont Croesor in Appendix 'B' that takes matters further on in time.*

## NFU Judicial Review

On 24th November 1999, the National Farmers Union went to the High Court of Justice to apply for Judicial Review on the grounds that the actions of the Secretary of State were *ultra vires*. They asked the Court to quash the decision to make the 1999 Order, and the direction granting deemed planning consent for the railway.

This was certainly not in any way chummy for WHR. Its struggle looked as though it might have been for naught. The basis of the challenge was that the SoS has misconstrued paragraph 99 of the Planning Guidance Wales Planning Policy ("PGWPP"). Applications for major developments in National Parks must be subjected to rigorous examination, and should be demonstrated to be in the public interest before being allowed to proceed. The Inspector holding the inquiry had found that the proposed benefits of the scheme in terms of traffic management had not yet been explored. He concluded that no strong national need for it had been demonstrated. He recommended against making the order. The SoS decided not to accept the Inspector's recommendation. He accepted that work needed to be done to assess the potential of the railway for road traffic reduction. He was, however, prepared to regard the potential for traffic management as sufficient to justify a departure from the Inspector's recommendation. The issue was therefore, whether the SoS had properly construed the requirement in paragraph 99 of PGWPP, that development in a National Park be demonstrated to be in the public interest before being allowed to proceed, and whether it is sufficient if the development might potentially be in the public interest, even where that has not yet been established.

The judgement was as follows (précis):

o The first thing to be borne in mind about this submission is that it is not for the courts to apply their own interpretation of a planning policy, as they would with a conveyance or a will. The meaning of a planning policy is something which is, in the first instance at least, for the decision-maker, such as the SoS.

o A similar approach has been adopted in a number of other cases. It is therefore, only if the decision-maker adopts an interpretation which the policy words are not reasonably capable of bearing that the courts will intervene.

o In arriving at a judgement on whether it had been shown that the railway proposal was in the public interest, the SoS was entitled to take into account all relevant planning considerations, so long as there was some evidence before him relating to any particular consideration.

o There was evidence in the present case, albeit not spelling out quantitative forecasts of further traffic reductions, which dealt with the potential benefit in question; and it is not argued that there was no evidence on which the SoS could have arrived at his conclusion.

o Once it is established that the SoS was entitled to take this factor into account, the weight to be attached to it was a matter for him as a decision-maker.

o It is to be observed that the Inspector did not regard this factor as being irrelevant or non-existent, but merely as one to which he was not prepared to give great weight. The SoS was entitled to attach greater weight to it.

o I conclude, not only that the Secretary of State's approach to the interpretation of this policy was within the range of reasonable interpretations, but that his approach was a sensible one. He was fully entitled to take account of that further potential in his overall assessment. There is no misinterpretation or misapplication of policy in his decision, and the decision in question and the order are not *ultra vires*. In those circumstances, it follows that this application must be dismissed. Leave to appeal was refused.

Even now, in the letter that the disappointed NFU wrote to its members, there was 'mystery' that the inspectors 'decision' (not recommendations *sic*) were overturned. Had they not been reading the outcome of the proceedings? The reasons were explained with no mystery at all. The NFU had made a mistake with their application (by not sending it to the right place), yet, the Judge decided to exercise his discretionary powers to correct and validate the NFU's application, well after that event. Presumably, this was in the interests of general justice, to avoid the possible injustice to an 'aggrieved person' of rejecting the application upon relatively minor technical grounds, and to avoid giving grounds for further appeal. Yet apparently the proceedings were still full of mystery for NFU.

However, this last action signalled the end of litigation, of public inquiries, and the project was released from uncertainty. For 55 years the restoration of the WHR had been trapped in an awful legal tangle - now it was free. It was time to dream of Garratts running through the Pass of Aberglaslyn; it was time to hear in the mind the clatter of narrow gauge wheels on standard gauge rails, as the train crossed the Cambrian Coast Line; it was now safe to imagine the squealing of flanges on the curve of the Britannia Bridge, and to picture the train curving into Porthmadog Harbour Station. Full restoration of the WHR was to become a reality.

There was a fantastic feeling of relief, that one day a narrow gauge train would steam up the line to recreate all those black and white photos of the 1930s in colour. For those with a more practical bent, those who had for some considerable time been looking under the blocked road bridge at Dinas, with a malign glare at the rubbish packed in there, it was now time for the real struggle - building the railway. There was a proper Project Manager, Roland Doyle, full of keenness, just waiting to go. There were many contracting firms in the locality who would be delighted at the work. There was money available from the Millennium Commission, there was lots to do The real adventure was now ready to begin, as this was going to be a Herculean task.

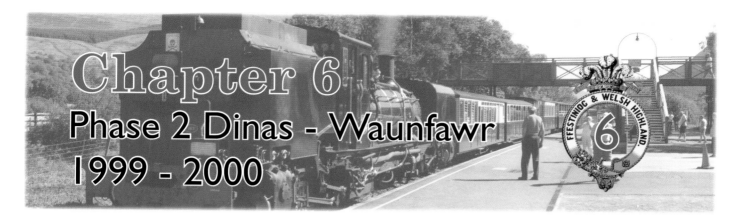

# Chapter 6
# Phase 2 Dinas - Waunfawr
# 1999 - 2000

Waiting characterised much of the time in this early period of WHR rebuilding history. The TWO Public Inquiry had been only one of the ordeals for the restorers to endure. At its end in January 1998, it was known that results from such events take time to appear. The restorers entertained themselves by preparing the Caernarfon to Dinas section of the WHR for full season opening in April 1998, and the strategists tasked Symonds, consulting engineers with the preliminary design work for extending the railway beyond Dinas. The Snowdonia National Park inquiry in July 1998 kept people's minds occupied. The outcome of that particular entertainment was easier to predict from what was said within the proceedings. It was felt that the lack of reasoning for the abrupt change of Snowdonia National Park Authority (SNPA) policy would take more explaining than was offered. There was nothing to report until February 1999, when the transfer of title to the trackbed between Dinas and Porthmadog came through. This instantly encouraged a flurry of activity. The land now became the legal responsibility of the FR Co. and the cost of the transfer of the liabilities was the princely sum of £1. This was the same price as the Official Receiver (OR) offered to Gwynedd. Almost immediately disaster struck, when a mountain biker died from a fall from the Nantmor road underbridge. Although the FR Co. was not held responsible, a secure fencing-off of all underbridges and tunnels, not already barred to entry, was immediately prompted. The OR was happy, he was 'off the hook', protected by the Transfer Order (TO). Part I of the plan had run smoothly. If the railway Transport and Works Order was refused now, FR Co. was secure from competition, as no one could restore the railway without FR Co. as the landlord. Mike Hart and Mike Schumann were not satisfied with this. No one in FR Co. was interested in 'buy to shut', they wanted a 40 mile

railway starting from Caernarfon and were extremely determined about it. There was activity to prompt for a decision so work could begin.

On 3rd March 1999 the verdict was given on the SNPA Inquiry. The Inspector rejected the SNPA changes, and the Minister endorsed this. On 9th March the SNPA Planning Committee accepted the recommendations of the Inspector, but several members wished to protest to the DETR. Though of course 'without prejudice' from DETR, this favourable decision was taken as a pointer that something similar would be offered for the TWA. Dafydd Wigley MP tabled a parliamentary question that revealed that the Minister had got the Inspector's report on 22nd April 1998, and that the average time between receipt and decision by the Minister was between 12 and 13 months. Dafydd Wigley MP was 'doing his stuff' for the WHR in making sure the light did not go out from under the decision making pot! Indeed on 30th June 1999 a letter was received from John Prescott, giving a conditional 'yes', reporting that the Inspector had found that in his view the benefit was mainly outside the Park, but that the decision could be looked at either way. John Prescott had decided to grant the Order, provided the rock problems in the Aberglaslyn pass were remedied. No one in FR Co. thought that this presented a problem, and so they commissioned Ove Arup, nationally recognised expert consulting engineers to report on the hazards and to define a solution..

*To tarmac 195m of platform creates a huge amount of hard standing. This had to be done, and here is a view of Dinas at Superpower on 08.09.06, with K1 waiting on the up road. The effect of a surfaced platform on coach interiors is immediate and decisive - they stay almost clean!*

The villagers of Bontnewydd said that they would like a halt, some ¼ mile from the centre of the village. This was opened in May 1999, and FR Co. was delighted to show how enlightened people became when they got their railway back. It was perhaps a bit of showmanship, aimed at Nantmor - and in time it was effective. Phase I was not yet signed off, and so a list of work 'fixes' had to be completed during the interregnum, like surfacing

*Cae Moel bridge at Superpower in 2006, construction is long gone, and the railway is looking mature as Garratt NGG16 No. 138 steams past with a mixed train. In the distance the cutting emerges from under the bridge under the A487(T) that needed to be re-excavated; in the foreground is a bridge that offered much challenge with a wayward stream that did not wish to be confined. It all looks as though it's been running here for years - well it hasn't!*

the platforms at Caernarfon and Dinas for their full lengths, tamping the track, sorting water arrangements at Caernarfon, commissioning the Dinas loco shed in the South Yard, and building the carriage shed in the North Yard.

There remained a great deal of opposition to the WHR. Not perhaps on the scale of the normal world, at against say a bypass, or a motorway, but the negative comment was upsetting, and surprising for all those with rose tinted glasses that think the whole world loves little trains. Some of what was said in opposition was untrue, provably so. It was suspected that comments in the press were fuelled by disaffection, and this might be true, as local press comment was strangely negative in relation to the potential positive benefits to the community. However, this did not mean that the popular case for re-establishment of the railway was lost. The strategy to get all the fuss over in one lump, and then to be free to tackle the challenging work of the restoration, was the right one. The switch in policy of the Snowdonia National Park Authority Members perhaps gave a clue to the depth of feeling in some quarters against the railway. It seems that their decision to alter their previous policy sprang from the pressure against the WHR from within the farming community.

It is fitting at this point to acknowledge that the determined and enterprising approach paid off. Had a softer, or an incremental approach been adopted, there would have been problems of such magnitude that full restoration would have been unlikely. It was right to apply for funding to do half the job (as far as Rhyd Ddu) but it would have been wrong to apply for a matching TWO to that point only. Some of the matters had long lead

times so immediacy was in the air. There had been no pause in the effort in this respect since the TO had been granted. The pressure that gaining Millennium and ERDF funding put on public bodies was great but unseen. Local chiefs might have affected not to notice, but this was not the case in the seats of power at the centre. It was a tremendous strain on the FR to do all this, and to lead the reconstruction work, indeed the team was tiny! But those in the FR Co. believed that to retain the initiative, applying maximum pressure was the only course. This couldn't have been more different from the methods previously applied by the 64 Co., of consensus and steady progress. FR Co. mandarins knew from experience that such a struggle requires risks, much energy, prolonged working at full stretch, influence, money and luck. It strained the organisation badly; however, eventually success was achieved, but not without setbacks.

It seemed that certain elements within SNPA were hoping that the coming of the Welsh Assembly, and the transfer of the decision making powers to Cardiff would see a change of heart, if they could just delay the Aberglaslyn rocks outcome for long enough. The Millennium Commission intervened, stating that unless a decision was made before 30 June 1999, permitting the development to which they had pledged funding, then the grant would be withdrawn. On 28th April 1999, days before the transfer of power, the Minister, John Prescott, announced that the Order would be made. Once John Prescott had announced his decision in the summer of 1999 it was only the NFU challenge that prevented work starting. There was considerable pressure from the Millennium Commission to get things moving, and it was

## Phase 2 Chronology

| | | |
|---|---|---|
| 28.01.98 | TWO Public Inquiry | Inquiry finishes |
| March 1998 | Dinas-Waunfawr | Design work begins |
| July 1998 | SNPA Planning Inquiry | Change of Planning Policy TR 16 to oppose the WHR |
| February 1999 | Transfer of Title | Trackbed transferred to FR Co., who now assumes legal liabilities for land |
| 03.03.99 | SNPA Inspector report published by Welsh Office | The report was favourable to the reinstatement of WHR |
| 07.04.99 | Decision of Minister | The Secretary of State for Transport decides in favour of the application for the Transport and Works Order made by the WHR, subject to resolution of rockfall in the Aberglaslyn Pass. |
| 30.06.99 | Decision of Minister | Order will be made subject to amendments as above. |
| 21.07.99 | Transport and Works Order | The order comes into force. At last the Dinas-Porthmadog WHR may be restored. |
| 24.11.99 | NFU goes to High Court | Application for Judicial Review on the grounds that the actions of the Secretary of State were *ultra vires*. Application refused - see previous Chapter. |
| November 1999 | Work starts | Contractor Mulcair begins work on A4085 overbridge at Waunfawr Station on the first contract, bridges from Waunfawr to Tryfan Junction |
| January 2000 | More work starts | Mulcair begins work on second contract from Tryfan Junction back to Dinas |
| 2nd April 2000 | The first track laid on the old WHR proper | The CRhE North Wales and Black Hand gangs laid the first main line track panels out from Cae Wernlas Ddu |
| May 2000 | Works in progress | The landslip area gabions and stoneworks reach completion |
| July 2000 | Tracklaying | Track laid continuous from Dinas as far as the ballast stockpile half-a-mile short of Waunfawr Station. |
| 07.08.00 | Opening | Still much to do, but service starts |
| 09.09.00 | Waunfawr Station | Loop completed and brought into use on this date. |
| September 2000 | Waunfawr loop and platform | These came into use in September 2000. Until that time reversal of trains was required by means of a diesel |
| 21.09.01 | HMRI confirmation | HMRI gave formal approval of the line Dinas-Waunfawr. |

realised that the landowner of the trackbed was entitled to clear a route and fence it, even without either planning permission or the TWO finalised. Thus Achnashean Contractors cleared the basic trackbed, and began fencing the line from Dinas to Waunfawr. A contract with Digital Mapping Surveys of Conwy for a topographical survey allowed detail design of the works to be undertaken, contract documents to be drawn up, and tenders to be sought.

The judge found against the NFU, thus at the end of November 1999, 62 years after the closure of the WHR, the FR Co. was in the position of having no further legal obstacles to its reinstatement. Contracts could be signed and work could start.

The 1998 Agreement, meant that the 64 Co./WHRL now had the chance to build the railway in the south that they had wanted for so long, as soon as the WHR in the north was built as far as Waunfawr. They had accepted that their construction would not begin until after Phase 2 had been completed, yet there did not seem to be the 'buzz' around Gelert's Farm that one may have expected after the 'shackles' had been released. They had accepted that WHRL[Note 1] 'supports completely' the rebuilding of the WHR by FR Co. But what does 'supports completely' mean as an influential sector of the membership was against it? The fact that the task of rebuilding the majority of WHR had been taken by FR Co. could not be altered. It seems likely that the lack of trust issues of 'buy to shut' inhibited any asset share or close co-operation. There were tales that moderates became uncomfortable with a feeling of conflict and dissatisfaction, and those for whom total restoration of WHR meant most, were drawn to the organisation that looked most likely to accomplish this. It is a sad fact that the failure of WHRL to apply the buccaneering spirit to restoring to Pont Croesor, (see Appendix 'B') meant that from now on they had less and less bearing on the WHR restoration critical path. There was valuable co-operation in some of the phases of construction, but it never managed to integrate the two organisation, sadly.

After the TWO came into force on 21st July 1999, the NFU judicial review meant that work did not start until it was settled. However, thereafter, the FR pressed on with full force, goaded by the Millennium Fund - there was no 'foot dragging'. The second phase, Phase 2, was only one mile longer than Phase 1, but the nature of the task could not have been more different. The derelict trackbed was confined by its narrow loading gauge. There was a considerable difference between the Phase 1 trackbed, designed for possible double track, standard gauge railway, and this one, a 600mm narrow gauge railway, built 'economically'. The start point was blocked by a large filled in cutting, drainage was generally bad, there was an area suffering from landslip both above and below the formation, and a need to lower track through bridges, some with errant aquatic circumstances. The cost was going to be a difficult target to meet at around £2m, £500k per mile(result £776k/mile). However work started in November 1999, with OB42 (**OB30.14**), the A4085 road overbridge at the north end of Waunfawr Station. In this month the three steel river bridges (Afonydd Glaslyn, Nanmor and Dylif), that had been declared no longer fit for purpose, were demolished to stop people walking over them.

**Note: The red figures in text and picture captions give the kilometric measurements from Caernarfon '+20'**

**Note 1 Please avoid the potential confusion between WHRL: Welsh Highland Railway Ltd - ex 64 Co. WHLR : Welsh Highland Light Railway - FR Co. construction Co**

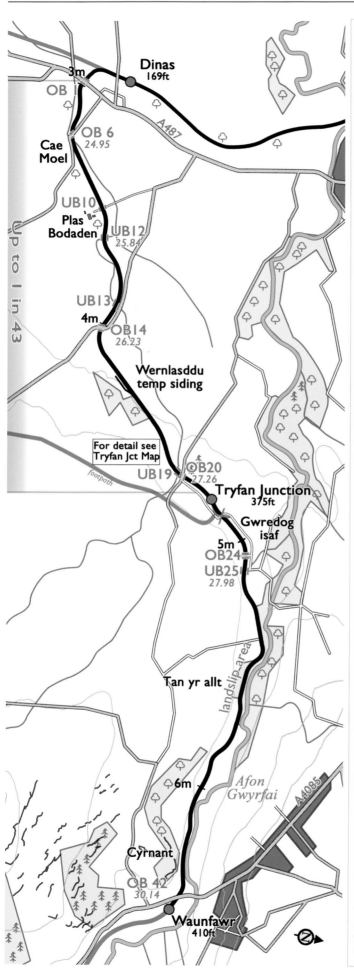

## DINAS TO WAUNFAWR CHARACTERISTICS

This was not the most scenic bit of railway by the time it came to be restored. It was running in lush countryside, away from everywhere and everything. After passing under the main Pwllheli road, the railway suddenly climbs at gradients of 1:43 until regaining the valley of the Afon Gwyrfai, not visited since Bontnewydd. On this first section the engines work hard. There are two further road bridges, one to Rhos Tryfan and the other to Tryfan Junction. This was the busiest section of the old WHR - if any part could be said to have been busy. There's a charming run along the Rhos Tryfan road from Plas Bodaden, with nicely transitioned curves, and a 20 mph racing stretch, but the railway is confined by high cutting sides. The gradient eases at Tryfan Junction, a lonely place but by no means bleak. The Bryngwyn Branch (now a footpath) went off here, and there is a station building under restoration. Trains from the quarries came through here in their way to transhipment at Dinas. The Halt has been reinstated, and there is an open level crossing with regular movements of horses and riders from a nearby stable. This is a very pleasant place, hard to find, interesting to photograph, and up a very narrow dead-end road.

The gradient eases after curves towards Gwredog Isaf and the route rises steadily to the river Gwyrfai. For the last mile-and-a-half of Phase 3, the railway runs adjacent to the river. This has had an effect, as for a half-mile or so the land is susceptible to slip. Further on, the railway approaches the river closely enough for there to be large stones in the bank to curb its excesses. For the run in to Waunfawr, the railway is right on the edge of the river, and for some this is one of the most beautiful stretches of Welsh Highland Railway, verdant and unspoilt.

The railway shoots under the A4085, Beddgelert road bridge and climbs into the station, now a wide, island platform. This is the first crossing point after Dinas, and as the temporary terminus; for a short while it had its moment of glory. Trains may or may not pass there, according to varying timetables. However, the gain in height (169-410 ft) means that locomotives need water, and a generous tank was placed at the end of the up side platform.

The station by good fortune has an excellent pub on site. This establishment did a roaring trade when the WHR terminated, but even now it is such a pleasant place to visit, that people come by train and by car. Waunfawr Station manages to be most welcoming. This may be because of the extremely attractive wooden footbridge, that leads the visitor from the car park above the station, and hidden from it offers access to the platform or to the river meadow beyond. There is a small campsite adjacent to the station as well, and a farm with clucking hens. All of this leads the visitor to appreciate Waunfawr as a pleasant and peaceful place to visit at the edge of the Park.

The construction of this stretch was on a learning curve for the railway builders, as the nice, wide, ex-standard gauge formation of the first three miles, with the difficult bits done by specialist contractors, suggested that restoring this railway wasn't too much of a challenge after all. If that was anyone's view, then it was rapidly dispelled by the experience of a narrow, overgrown bit of walled real-estate, with large volumes of water adjacent, ready to wash over the tracks at the least provocation. Phase 2 was more arduous than Phase 1, and the demand of the time deadline for it to be done quickly, and within budget, sat uneasily with the requirement to do it well.

## The Start of Phase 2 Construction

The most prudent course was to divide the work into discrete parts and contract those bits that would best be done by buying in expertise appropriate to each:

1. Clearance and Fencing (one contract)
2. Bridges (two contracts and some in-house work)
3. Culverts, drainage and earthworks (one contract)
4. Tracklaying (Welsh Highland Light Railway Ltd)

No1 was simple enough. It went to Achnashean Contractors Ltd., of Llandygai, a local firm. This was to clear overgrown areas of the trackbed tougher than those offered in Phase1. On part of the line the view of where the railway ran was blocked by thick vegetation. The first job was to clear a vehicle-sized route to allow access to the various sites for safe working. The job proceeded with the removal of the vegetation, followed by fencing. It had to be decided (with the help of experts from the Gwynedd Council) which trees were to be retained or felled outside the structure gauge. The shape of the railway became apparent, and the structures to be restored, and the access to do it emerged rapidly with the conclusion of this first contract.

There were some six NWNG overbridges, five underbridges, and many drainage culverts under the track to be dealt with. The trackbed had to be lowered one metre under four of the bridges, to give clearance for NGG16 Garratts, and a lesser amount for the others. The bridges were underpinned, and the approaches were regraded, in order to offer a smooth transition. There were some problems where drainage and bridges combined; these are dealt with individually in the text later. Two contracts were awarded for the bridges. The first was between Waunfawr and Tryfan Junction, the second from Tryfan Junction to Dinas, and both went to Mulcair Ltd., of Caernarfon. This was a more difficult railway restoration operation than Phase 1.

Jones Bros of Ruthin were awarded the contract for rebuilding the trackbed, refurbishing/replacing all culverts, providing all the sidelong drainage, and finally ballasting the trackbed, ready for track to be laid. The trackbed over the entire section was soft, and required thousands of tons of slate waste to provide a surface suitable for dumper trucks to pass, let alone establishing the rail formation. The stabilised formation was finally coated with a layer of rolled slate waste, supplied from the Hafod y Wern quarry close to Betws Garmon, and then granite ballast was added from the Hanson quarries at Penmaenmawr,

ready for track to be laid on the top.

The track was laid by WHLR Ltd. staff, along with two volunteer WHRSL track gangs. Symonds, Consulting Engineers of Colwyn Bay, provided a resident civil engineer based at Dinas to act as a link between WHLR and the contractors on a day-to-day basis, whilst Mike Schumann was the director responsible overall for specifying the works.

Although at Dinas the A487 road had been widened after the railway had shut, the bridge (OB1 - **OB24.61**) had been extended in the original style. The deep cutting, right through and under the road, had been filled in under the bridge in 1988, where the land had been sold to the Y Mount Pub. Over the years, much detritus and fill had accumulated, and that had to be removed. As the floor of the re-excavated cutting was to be lower than the original, gabions were used to stabilise the sides, and to ensure the land take was no greater than the original. On the Dinas side, a sewer pipe bridged the cutting at too low a height for trains to pass underneath, and a complicated, 150m long, trenched pipe diversion was required to remove the obstruction.

During this 'gala' beginning of the extension, some 30,000 tonnes of fill were removed from this cutting. Mulcair did the construction work. Once the bridge was fully exposed on the Waunfawr side, before the underpinning work could commence, it was necessary to inject cement grout into the walls to stabilise them, as they had suffered from water washing through. Because of the time taken to clear the cutting, OB1 was one of the last bridges to be lowered and underpinned to accommodate NGG16 locomotives in Phase 2. A concrete deck was cast, the cutting was ballasted, and tracklaying out from the yard began in the first week of July 2000. This particular job took time to complete, and it meant that Phase 2 construction was not 'linear'

*Above: The track curves out of Dinas station, past the loco shed and into a deep cutting leading to the A487 bridge (OB1). Standing on the far side of the engine shed, you can see that clearance work has begun, and the headshunt is out to allow the trench for the sewer pipe to be dug. There was a lot of work at the beginning of the Phase 2 route.*
**Mike Schumann**

*Left: The finished OB1 (**OB24.61**) bridge and trackbed, taken from the Waunfawr, side. Note the tallness of the bridge and the level of the fill from the 'tide marks' on it. Excavation to drop the trackbed to its current level was from about the level of the top of the gabion (right). Note under OB1 the gabions on the far sides and it can be seen why 30,000 tonnes of fill had to come out!*
**Mike Schumann**

*Left: This is the view of OB6 (**OB24.95**) back towards Dinas was taken in February 2000, when the floor of the bridge had been excavated and the stream had been diverted to its own culvert. An invert was cast to offer a new floor with clearance for Garratts. This was just one of a series of major works on bridges*

**both pictures by Mike Schumann**

*Below: The jungle has only just been pushed aside to see, at the end of the cutting, OB14, carrying the Rhostryfan road across the WHR. This bridge was one that CCC paid to rebuild in 1933. This time the WHR had to pay for alteration. The state of the trackbed in these parts needs major attention. More illustrations opposite show the extent of the work.*

from Dinas.

Only a short distance further on is Cae Moel, OB6 (**OB24.95**), the bridge carrying a minor road to Rhostryfan over the railway. The NWNG had built the bridge with girders under supporting the railway through the bridge-hole, with a stream underneath. There were two problems, the first to contain the stream, the second to lower the track to accommodate Garratts. The contractor came up with a cheaper solution than the consultants. That involved diverting the stream through a new culvert under road and railway, then lowering the railway into the space recovered from the bridge, to increase the headroom.

Beyond OB6, the Company purchased two fields either side of the line, to avoid the cost of providing a crossing between the two. One was used for the Jones Bros ballast stockpile, the other was for planting replacement trees lost by building the railway. From Cae Moel towards Wernlas Ddu the line runs straight, on low embankment, with fields on either side of the line. The railway passes Plas Bodaden Farm and UB10. A little further on at UB12 and again at UB13 (**UB26.01**) a small stream is crossed. Built originally with dry stone abutments with twin girder and multiple rail decks, it had initially been planned to replace both structures completely. However after full site clearance, which

enabled a proper site inspection, it was decided to refurbish the abutments with mass concrete backing, and to provide new concrete decks in both cases. After UB13, the Rhostryfan road runs parallel with the line for a short while, and rises to cross the railway on bridge OB 14 (**OB26.23**). This concrete bridge was one that Caernarvonshire County Council rebuilt in 1933, when the WHR was on its last legs. Stephen Paul one day handed Mike Schumann an envelope with all the CCC minutes relevant to the WHR, which he said he had found on a market stall. These showed that CCC had adopted the bridges in 1934, and when presented to the Highways Dept. in 1996, they accepted that they were responsible for them, and that has been the status quo ever since. However, they were not obliged to pay for this work. On OB14 a small amount of excavation was required to achieve clearance, and a concrete invert was cast to carry the track and to brace the abutments. The work revealed that the foundations of the widened bridge had been very badly built. On the bridge top there was more work.

South of this bridge, a small stream smelt of sewage, and as a result of road drainage it was now prone to flooding on to the railway formation at times of heavy rain. Lowering the railway formation made it worse. The solution was a parallel diversion of the

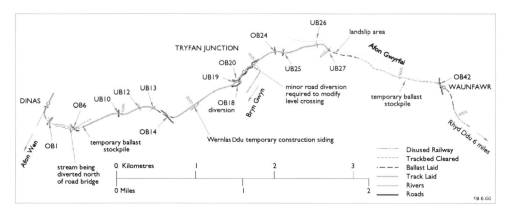

*Left: This is one of the working maps for the time, placed on Ben Fisher's web site to keep all up to date. It shows that in June 2000 the trackbed had been cleared through OB1, as far as Cae Moel, where the track began. This ran as far as OB14, and was interrupted. It then ran on to UB27. Clearance had then been achieved to Waunfawr, with a small bit of track laid there. Plenty was going on, with work on the bridges, diversion of road at Tryfan Junction, the ballast being laid through the landslip area and a temporary construction siding at Wernlas Ddu.*

**John Sreeves**

*Left:* The track moves steadily closer, with the metal sleepers laid out level and the rollers set up to receive the rails from the RRMs. The bridge is UB 13 (**UB26.01**) and behind the hedge on the right is Rhostryfan Road behind the hedge, and behind the camera is the run-in to Wernlas Ddu.

*Right:* Here is the bridge OB14 at Wernlas Ddu in original 1993 condition, with the jungle only just banished. This bridge was rebuilt by CCC after WHR closure. You can see that the trackbed needs considerable lowering to allow a Garratt to pass under. Soon the excavators will be in to do that work. Few trains ever ran under the original; the next ones will be for construction not demolition.

*Left:* The excavation under bridge OB14 has been made. The Acrow props are doing their bit, as the digger outside is there to get on with making the correct transition in the gradient in the trackbed, to even out the dip.

*Right:* The track has been laid up to the bridge in a graceful curve, in this view of Wernlas Ddu. Loco and wagons sit on the straight that head north-east to Cae Hên. After sixty years the track is now back on this bit of the Welsh Highland Railway.

*Left:* UB 19 precedes OB20; behind the bridge, to the south, is Tryfan Junction. The two bridges are complete in this view on 13 April 2000, with the extra footing in the invert reflecting the extra height needed for Garratts.

**Both Pictures: Mike Schumann**

*Below:* Gerald Fox examines the old NWNG station building at Tryfan Junction emerge from years of undergrowth. The building looks too far gone to be saved, but that's not what the WHR Renaissance is about. This building was restored by volunteers who worked at it until the job was completed in 2012.

stream for about 25m, until it could safely pass underneath the railway to rejoin its original course. At Cae Hên, just beyond the house at Wernlasddu, a field was rented to serve as a base for the contractor Mulcair, and afterwards as a base for tracklaying. About 3km worth of rail, some 300 tonnes, was eventually stockpiled in this place, and it was used for ballast deliveries. A temporary siding was laid in March 2000, and Cae Wernlas Ddu became a base for *Upnor Castle*, with a temporary engine shed, for wagon DZ1424 (SAR hopper), and sets of Roland Rail Movers. Other machines arrived on site later, and track was laid out from this site, firstly by the CRhE North Wales Group, and then by other volunteers in April 2000. By May the track was almost to Tryfan Junction, two miles or so from Dinas. A new road was built at the end of Cae Hên to replace that which used to cross the long demolished OB18. There was a substantial underbridge to refurbish at UB19 (**UB27.23**) and gabions were installed to strengthen the slope left on one side of the line. Once the access road was in, Jones Bros laid the first ballast on Phase 2 towards Cae Wernlas Ddu, and then the work moved steadily to Tryfan Junction. The line climbs all the way up this section, at an average gradient of 1:48.

A little road leaves the A487(T) at Bontnewydd and runs its narrow, curvy way to an eventual dead-end. The road crosses the railway on bridge OB20, and after, it branches to serve farms with names like Cae Hên, Tyddyn Gwydd, and Erw. The road to Tryfan Junction Station turns sharp left off the bridge, and drops down into a pretty lane that leads to a little railway heaven. Mulcair had started work on the rebuilding of this bridge in January 2000. The narrow approach made it impossible to get a sizeable lorry to the site, so the area was not used for storage of either ballast or rails. The junction was made with the Bryngwyn Branch,

*Left:* On 10th September 2006, NGG15 Garratt No. 143, in black, returns to Caernarfon with a mixed train on a Superpower Weekend. The pleasant country setting of Tryfan Level Crossing (**LC27.52**) makes it a good place to watch trains, if you can find the turning for the narrow lane at Bontnewydd to reach it by car. Or of course you can now go there by train and leave the car in the car park.

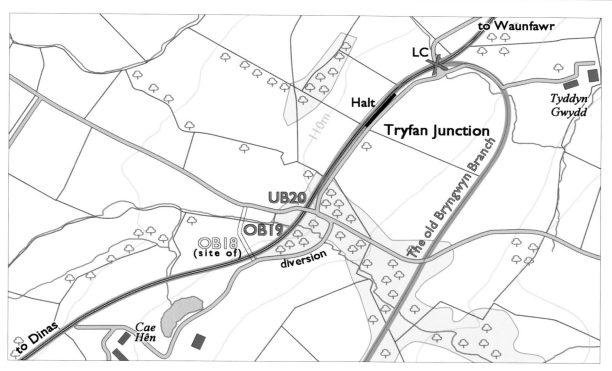

*Left: This was once a busy place, important to the old NWNG. More traffic came from Bryngwyn Quarries than down the main line. The red line shows the old NWNG layout, a loop with crossings across and back, facing Waunfawr. New Tryfan Junction isn't a junction. It has a level crossing, for which track alignment had to shift a little, it is a steep climb up to the station, but a halt has been added as there are some pleasant country walks, and one will be up the old branch.*

that rose to substantial slate quarries at the top of an incline. The bridge OB20 required work to lower the trackbed, and the parapets were rebuilt in original style. A concrete deck for the track was cast, and traditional stone walling was erected instead of the more normal fence. The bridge work was coming to an end in March 2000, ready for track to reach the site in Apri,l and to be laid through in June 2000. A small deviation from the original course was required for the level crossing roadway at Tryfan Junction, to make a 90° angle with the track. The area was made into a quiet and extremely attractive place to watch trains. The station site was overgrown, and when this was cleared, the ruined building was revealed for the first time in many years. The plans to restore the building waited until the railway got running again; in 2012 CRhE has completed much of this work. In 2010 a halt was re-established on the site of the old station, to allow access to the Bryngwyn branch, owned by FR Co. and now refurbished by GC and Llanwnda Community Council as a footpath..

There are places where remedial work is superseded by the need to offer works in mitigation. At Gwredog Isaf, about five miles out of Caernarfon, two bridges giving access to farms were rebuilt to reflect the practical needs of modern agriculture. After the public inquiry the agreements and the promises made in mitigation had to be redeemed. At Gwredog Isaf, substantial modifications to two adjacent bridges, one over and the other under the line, were required. The overbridge OB24 (**OB27.88**) was too narrow for vehicle access to the farmer's fields. The masonry arch of OB24 was removed, to leave just the piers. A new deck was cast in situ with a higher, shallower

*Above: Fortunately, Mike Schumann made a careful appraisal of the line and its structures before work started. This is OB24 in March 1998, showing the formation as it was. The text describes the extensive work undertaken here, but what a hopeless scene this looks, eroding the whimsical romance of those who dared to think the WHR could ever run again. Yet look below.* **Mike Schumann**

*Right: The works on OB24 (**OB27.88**), Pont Hyll, are complete in this photo taken on 10.03.2000. The viewpoint is facing Waunfawr, the opposite to that of the photograph above. The deck is widened and the parapets are faced with local stone. The yellow brick arch of the NWNG has gone in the name of practicality.* **Mike Schumann**

*Right: UB 25, as it was. Its arch offered restricted access and therefore the Railway agreed to rebuild it to more generous proportions, which also complied with current regulations, permitting a safety cab fitted tractor or emergency vehicle to negotiate the bridge hole.*

**Both Pictures: Mike Schumann**

*Below: The result, though of much greater use, looked like it would win no prize for beauty. However, painting and the restoration of wing walls, and buttresses in the local stone recovered from the original bridge, soon put matters right, and the whole affair became a boon to the landowner.*

profile. The modified OB24 has an unusual, asymmetrical pattern to the arch, dictated by the site. The concrete side walls of the roadway were built to the highway parapet height that is now required for all new road-over-rail bridges. The side walls were dressed with local stone, that was expected to weather rapidly to match the remaining original stonework.

Further along the track towards Waunfawr, an underbridge (UB25 - **UB27.98**) that gave off the track from Tryfan Level crossing to serve Tan yr Allt Farm (below the hill), had an opening that was too low for tractors with safety cabs, or for emergency

vehicles to pass through. The original NWNG underbridge was stripped of its arch, which was replaced with concrete beams. This immediately offered increased headroom, with increased width to the height of the new beams. It satisfied the mitigation measures, and met the new standards imposed on reconstructed bridges. Though the new structure might not have had the grace of what it had replaced, later the exposed beams were painted black and the wing walls, copings and buttresses, were built back in matching stone to restore their traditional appearance.

There were two cattle underbridges in this area, Aspinall's, UB26 and UB27 (**UB28.62**) to give the beasts water access. It had been proposed to rebuild UB26 to modern clearances, but it was cheaper to provide the farmer with a piped water supply.

The line takes up position on the south side of the river and keeps a varying distance from the Afon Gwyrfai all the way to Waunfawr. There are numerous curves required in order to follow the course of the river, and the south side suffers from instability over a 200m length, such that landslides had taken place

*Left: UB 27 was a simple enough stone-beamed bridge that submitted to refurbishment without any complication.*

*Right Upper: The tendency of the slope down to the river to slip over the railway, especially when the ground was saturated, called for digging out to restore the formation, and then the addition of gabions to stabilise the ground, hopefully for many years.*

*Right Lower: This remedial work was necessary at more than one place along this rather unstable, short section, between Tan yr Allt and Cae Goronwy. The track is being put back past Tan yr Allt in 2002.*

**All photos Mike Schumann**

during the time of closure, as drainage had been allowed to fail. It might have been better to deal with this stretch in the summer, but Millennium Commission timescales were pressing. The hillside above the railway was restrained with two tiers of slate faced, rock-filled gabions, and a generously sized drainage system to carry away the water. At (**28.25**) two locations gabions were also required below the railway to hold the formation in place. This work required many tons of rock which had to be

*This is LC16 an accommodation crossing at Cae Gornonwy, nearly six miles from Caer-narfon. This bit is near to the Afon Gwyrfai, just past the landslip and it is not thick with growth - pictures from really overgrown parts were more difficult. But this is what the line looked like before any work started.*
**Mike Schumann**

with this requirement the consultants had specified a concrete slab under the railway track to act as a prop between the two underpinned abutments, but separated from them by a 12mm thick by 300mm deep strip of PTFE on either side - running the full length of the bridge opening. This was going to be a difficult detail to build, so that it stood some chance of actually working as the designers intended. A sump was dug adjacent to the bridge with a pump to lower the ground water. Even so, as the first

brought in dumper trucks from Waunfawr. To make this possible the very soft formation was strengthened with copious quantities of slate waste. The last stretch to Waunfawr is very beautiful and this is exclusive to train passengers, however faced with evidential flood marks on the railway formation, the decision was taken to raise a significant length of trackbed by up to 450mm.

## Waunfawr Station

OB42 at Waunfawr Station (**OB30.14**) carries the A4085 across the railway. It was the first overbridge to be underpinned by Mulcair, to provide clearances for the Garratts, and this was difficult. The ground water level was just below the existing formation level, and the sub-soil was sand and gravel, with some clay. To complicate matters, the Highway Authority had demanded that the weight of the train should not be transferred to the bridge foundations. To meet

excavation under the bridge abutment was started, the water poured in together with much sand. This looked like a project that could easily end in disaster. However the Mulcair site agent was master of the task, and soon had everything under control. This bridge took six weeks to underpin. The Highway Authority design restrictions were removed when it was pointed out that the transient ground loading from the train was only a small percentage of the permanent load under the abutments

The NWNG Ry station suffered damage at the hands of evacuees during World War Two, and was subsequently allowed to fall into ruin. Sadly, restoring it was out of the question, as funds were running low from the increased expenditure necessary for the works so far. A major volunteer task at Waunfawr was carefully to dismantle and catalogue what remained, for future rebuilding. Following removal of the remains of the building, work proceeded with levelling the site, and installing ground

*Right Upper: OB42 was a wide, skewed bridge in comparison with the other NWNG structures, and it had to be reconstructed with no interruption to the A4085 road traffic above.*

*Left: The propping by heavy girders made sure nothing 'moved' whilst the depth required was dug out and a new invert was cast. Of course the line had to be suitably graded either side to make a smooth transition. The work is done in this view of 07 March 2000.*

*Right Lower: Another example of one of the nice NWNG station buildings - but removed! This one will eventually return in a spot on the new platform. View taken in 1992.*
**All photos
Mike Schumann**

water drains.

The station site has a large car park, shared with the Snowdonia Parc Hotel. Whilst the railway terminated at Waunfawr the pub did good business, and got a name for friendly service and good food and drink. When the line went on to Rhyd Ddu, its reputation was not lost, and many call in there for lunch or refreshment. Indeed Waunfawr is still sold as a 'short' destination. The large car park, shared with the hotel, gives on to a high-level wooden footbridge. This imposing structure

*Behind NGG16 No. 143 on a down train can be seen the magnificent footbridge, leading from the car park on the right, with middle stairs to the island platform and a span over the loop down side track, leading to a footpath.*

shed technology, one has a loo. When the stone building is back, Waunfawr will be even more of a gem than it is now. A basic layout opened to traffic on 9th September 2000. The loop was not completed for use until September 2000, right at the end of the season. Until that time the steam engine came off the train at the entrance to the station, so that a diesel, waiting locked into the siding, could come out to pull the train into the station, and then the steamer coupled back on to the

came into passenger use in September 2001. It lets down on to the platform, as well as providing access across the line to a footpath and camping ground on the other side. It confers the air of a large country station upon the place. A capacious water tank has been installed, similar to that at Caernarfon. The 400ft uphill pull from Caernarfon of just short of seven miles, is enough for locomotives to need to take wate, for the next five miles on to Rhyd Ddu. At the Rhyd Ddu end of the station, there are excellent vantage points for photographers, who can see the locomotives taking water and then departing, as well as snapping crossing trains running in on the down side. A path leads to an accommodation/ footpath crossing, and this allows disabled access to the station. Two buildings are on the station, created with FR Co. garden

train to return to Caernarfon. The HMRI sign-off was not until September 21st 2001, ten months after construction started, as there was an extensive snagging list to work through during the year. The trains ran the following year to massively increased loadings, demonstrating the popularity forecast by the project promoters. However the growth was impeded by restrictions placed on entry to the National Park by an outbreak of Foot and Mouth disease in Anglesey. It was noted that the relatively lesser agricultural income was safeguarded, yet massive tourism income was surrendered! This had considerable adverse economic effects, but then at that time the railway had not yet demonstrated its popularity.

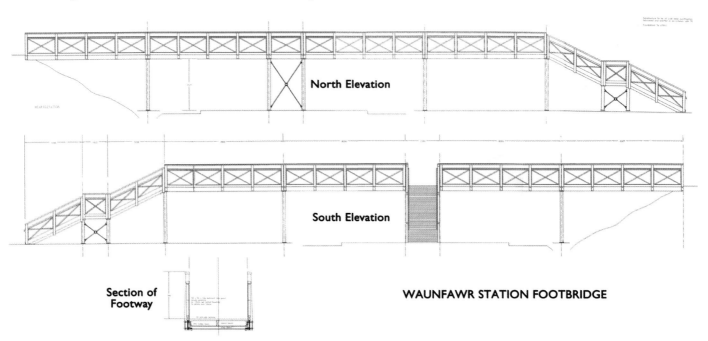

**North Elevation**

**South Elevation**

**Section of Footway**

**WAUNFAWR STATION FOOTBRIDGE**

*This remarkable structure is unexpected at this place, and of course is an accident of topography. The large car park behind the Snowdonia Parc Hotel gave on to the Railway at a high point, around the sensible centre of the platforms. Porthmadog trains take water here, and there are train crossings, so a high point is a natural vantage point. A small set of concrete steps leads up to the bridge, which is set high enough for trains to pass freely under. The bridge gives safe access from car park to platform, and serves the camping ground beyond. It also offers a superb vantage point from which to enjoy trains. But this structure is particularly magnificent in delightful wood, with delicate shapes - there is nothing remotely like it on the Ffestiniog or Welsh Highland Railways, although Tan y Bwlch station footbridge is close.*

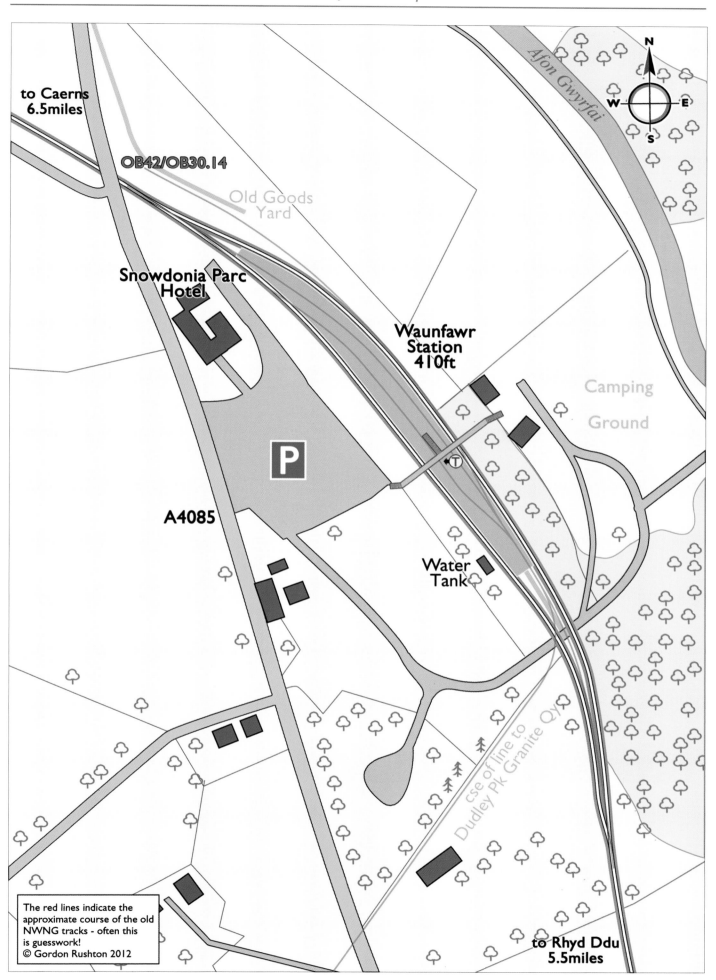

to Caerns
6.5miles

OB42/OB30.14

Old Goods
Yard

Snowdonia Parc
Hotel

Waunfawr
Station
410ft

Camping

Ground

P

A4085

Water
Tank

cse of line to
Dudley Pk Granite Qy

to Rhyd Ddu
5.5miles

Afon Gwyrfai

N
W   E
S

The red lines indicate the
approximate course of the old
NWNG tracks - often this
is guesswork!
© Gordon Rushton 2012

Consultation with those who lived along the line was never going to be easy. People had become thoroughly used to the idea that the railway was long gone. It was three generations since the little trains had last chuffed up the hill. Plus, the whole Welsh Highland had existed only from 1923 until it was torn up in 1941. Many artefacts remained but the land had almost lost its railway context. How do you explain to a landowner that the land is again needed for trains? A Welsh hill farm is real work - and you were proposing to use it primarily for leisure. Tony had to get that concept across!

The route was well preserved between Caernarfon and Dinas. Standard gauge trains ran until 1964. South of Dinas the tracks had been removed after 1941. The LRO for this section contained no compulsory purchase powers but none were needed, as the former standard gauge trackbed had been acquired by Gwynedd County Council from British Railways, and a cycle path was laid along it. Thus the boundaries were all intact. As the formation reflected land acquired in the hopes of twin track, there was no shortage of room, and no land ownership concerns. As any problems were those over the cycle path, we could settle that with Gwynedd Council (GC). As the 'deal' included refurbishment of the path, there were few problems that could not be solved by discussions within a single body, the GC.

Onwards from Dinas. restoration required a TWO, and to get that there was an obligation for discussion of a far higher level. Outsiders to any farming community have to learn quickly about local practice. In this locality politeness and hospitality come first when people agree to meet with you. We needed to catch on to the proper and expected code for welcome and response, as of course it is different nearly everywhere. We had to understand the civilised requirement for taking tea and having general discussion that was a necessary formality before business. It may have been thought that the language complicated matters, but it did not. Some who had grown up with, and spoke Welsh at home and in the community in the normal course of life, were proud to have learned but were slightly shy of their English language in such a formal context. My northern accent, slang and culture helped. People wanted to talk directly, to exchange views, and to feel that they retained their interests in their own hands, so the idea of a Welsh translator was unnecessary. The ability to behave in a polite and friendly manner was the first hurdle in the negotiation, as even if the most cordial discussions led to an objection, people would offer respect for your views and expect this to be returned. Later, some notes of discord entered the proceedings, almost always by outside agencies.

A number of landowners received benefits from improved access and secure boundaries as a result of the reopening project, but the effects of an outside body wishing to change the status quo of over 50 years can cause trouble. Even the opening move, however politely it is put, has overtones of potential discord - telling someone that the land they have been using ever since they can remember is not theirs, and will be taken away from them, is a difficult call. It's not the same as the electricity company wanting to put up poles, or the gas utility needing to dig a trench. And the purpose for which we wanted the land back did not find general favour, as the objections to the TWO eventually revealed. To the hill farmer, who's life was certainly not easy, hardship suffered to facilitate day trippers (if it was put in that way) had little to recommend it. So it was possible for the pessimist landowner to approach matters with a strong wish for you to go away and leave them in peace. As we were not going to do that, then in certain areas the likelihood

*Above: The bridge across the Afon Gwyrfai at Bontnewydd before the WHR got going shows the space for twin-track standard gauge, and the cycle path in the middle. There was no shortage of room here.* **Mike Schumann**

*Right: Near to Snowdon Ranger the trackbed is still evident and is used as useful access to fields. The railway powers, never abandoned, were relied upon as protection when taking the land back. Compulsory powers were available if someone had tried to claim title, allowing the railway to be built, with the argument on title consigned to the Lands Tribunal.*

for disagreement was great.

The statutory system invites objection rather than support, and landowners concern for their own security can obscure that of benefit to the general community. Some see their role as an objector which encourages a costly, and time consuming, thorough examination of the project. Public and affiliated bodies offer a further forum for landowner objection. Large organisations like the National Park, County Council, National Trust, and Ramblers Association, have both supporters and objectors in their organisations, and see a role in ensuring a thorough debate. Although most Councils, and some of the farming Unions did not object to the Order, those that did caused consequent demand of resources on both sides

The National Farmers Union (NFU), which had been advising it's members since the WHR closed, focused objection to reopening the railway from those with properties adjacent or crossed by the trackbed - the frontagers. The NFU became active when the Ffestiniog started the process of obtaining a Light Railway Order, to open the first section along the old standard gauge trackbed. Here most concern was raised by a farmer served by the Hendy level crossing, but there was little difficulty elsewhere. The NFU had about 15 members amongst frontagers; others were members of the Country Landowners Association (CLA), and a few were members of the Farmers Union of Wales (FUW). The NFU's regional office in Ruthin, with whom we negotiated, took the lead by arranging a December 1995 meeting for all concerned, and the CLA arranged a first meeting in March 1996 for its members.

There are few residential frontagers to the WHR, as farming dominates the route, with cattle on the lower sections, and sheep farming in the hills. The FR Co., TWO consultation process required the team to visit individual frontage landowners, to identify their boundaries, and to try and understand their needs. We were nervous about this process, but if they agreed to meet with you, then most were co-operative during consultation period, and measures to mitigate the effect of reintroducing trains were identified and often agreed, even though many were reluctant to see the return of trains.

One could agree to differ, and some maintained their objection, perhaps as an 'insurance'. No one was difficult or aggressive; that would generally emerge from those who refused to meet with you. Being courteous, clear and direct always paid off, and if you

could get in to meet them, then even the difficult cases would acknowledge where they stood, and might discuss mitigation measures, though still with objection. The TWO consultation requirement did not demand 100% agreement; it did require everyone affected to be clear on the proposal, its purpose, and some offer of necessary, relevant measures in mitigation of problems caused.

Some of the trackbed between Dinas and Waunfawr remained within its original fences and walls, although fences and a bridge had gone at one farm where a new access route was offered. Original fences or highway boundaries contain the railway much of the way south from Waunfawr. Householders at places like Cei Hywel, and Bryn Afon, had no vehicular access when trains previously operated. After WHR closed, when the trackbed was derelict with no one using it, they had seized the opportunity to employ it for access. The mitigation commitments offered new permanent access to such houses, and there was generally no request for householder contribution. This may in some cases have allayed deeper objections, but the initiative seemed only marginally appreciated. These were cases where for the most part, the preferred mitigation for the householder would be to be left in peace!

Clearances for modern farm machinery were improved at two bridges still used by farmers, just south of Tryfan Junction, but this did not inspire them to contribute or withdraw their objections.

Attempts were made to ease attitudes through various meetings and initiatives, like taking a younger farmer behind the scenes on the FR. A general hardening of attitude however accompanied the continuing negotiation stages, perhaps reflecting a situation where the few objectors gain standing in

*Above: FR Trustee Robert Riddick stands on the trackbed south of Pont Cae'r Gors, where the Forestry Commission used the trackbed for access roads, but were willing to offer compromises to assist the restoration, provided their access was still possible.*

*Left: The problem for Bryn Afon at Salem was that restoration of the trackbed negated any access by road - as they were dependent upon the trackbed for this. Sensible mitigation measures provided new road access, and an accommodation crossing. This was what the TWO requirements demanded.*

a close community when few are willing to express their support.

Efforts to appreciate landowners' difficulties continued; many had never seen the railway in operation, and worried about the effect of litter from the trains, gates being left open by visitors, etc. Discussions helped to alleviate such concerns, and farmers would chat easily about their families and the future, with perhaps mention of their offspring's greater interest in university study, and a career away from farming. Here was a window on a disappearing world, where the upland farmer still remained as a historic bridge to long ago. The strength and purpose of the people we met, and their unfailing courtesy, left a feeling of obligation on our part to offer the best mitigation measures possible to minimise the impact of the railway returning.

Bridges needed reconstruction at various locations for example at Cwm Cloch, Beddgelert, giving the opportunity to improve clearances for local farm and other traffic. Suggestions that farmers share the cost of reconstruction to reflect their betterment through improved access found no takers. A substantial new replacement bridge at Bryn Gloch, Betws Garmon, secured good access for the caravan and campsite which had developed over the years when the railway was closed. Sadly the attraction to tourists of the railway was not acknowledged, and negotiations were extremely difficult.

Residents of two properties in the Salem area, who had no vehicular access, until they started using the trackbed after the railway closed, benefited from alternative vehicular access routes through mitigation, and a new footbridge retained access to a secluded property. It was difficult to reassure a farmer of both sides of the railway, where fences had been removed near Llyn Cwellyn, and crossings to the farm buildings became an issue. As the route climbs towards Rhyd Ddu, around Bron y Fedw, and Clogwyn y Gwin, its walls and fences become the boundary where sheep cross between the upper *ffridd*, summer grazing, and lower farm land. The return of trains meant that gates here and elsewhere had to be opened, sometimes by a farmer without an assistant who wanted to cross the line with his stock. Additional works offered included underpasses and holding pens at Clogwyn y Gwin. Understanding of cross-line activity, which was sometimes exaggerated, was improved by personal site inspections, including one where the farmer kindly loaned his shepherd's crook.

Issues were quickly resolved south from Rhyd Ddu, on land which is within Beddgelert Forest. The landowner was co-operative and even discussed possible rail haulage of forest products and shared road construction techniques to help railway construction. Benefits of rail service for visitors to the large forest campsite were clearly recognised here, and this resulted in the construction of the busy Meillionen Halt.

*Work in Mitigation* - the two ARMCO bridges, Pont Pugh (OB57.26) and Pont Williams (OB56.83). These structures allow unimpeded crossing of the line, and offer a refuge for livestock during flood.                                   **Simon Melhuish**

The house nearby at Ty'n y Coed depended on using the derelict trackbed for access. The problem was discussed and resolved by providing new access through the forest all the way from Meillionen, and installing a private crossing, but the WHR restoration still prompted ongoing antagonism

Site visits to the Cwm Cloch farm above Beddgelert with its level crossings were surprisingly well received, and the constraints of the railway were accepted, perhaps helped by our offer of improved clearances in the design of the new underbridge, just above the station, that ensured that the passage of agricultural machinery remained possible.

One person in Nantmor was concerned that land that they had occupied during the period of closure, which was alongside but not within the limits of the proposed Order, would be reclaimed through the project. Such concerns could lead to more general objection including encouraging the local community to declare opposition, like against the halt at Nantmor, or perhaps driving attempts to try to derail the whole project.

Cattle and silage activity on the Traeth approaching Porthmadog suggested supervision of crossings by railway staff at peak times, but in the end was accommodated by special bridges offering access and flood refuge for stock.

Negotiations proceeded with all the organisations interested in the prospect of the return of the WHR. Agreement was reached with the Country Landowners Association and others, resulting in the withdrawal of their objections. Gwynedd Council, although generally supportive as the railway was included in the Structure Plan, retained an objection regarding the highway crossing in Porthmadog, about which there was nervousness. The Snowdonia National Park Authority, the National Trust, the Snowdonia Society and the Ramblers Association, entered into discussions that looked like agreements would be reached. The National Trust and the National Park withdrew before reaching agreement and appeared in objection at the TWO Inquiry. Indeed there was a second inquiry about changes to the Local Plan, that resulted in the SNPA having to reverse its decision to stay in line with the County Structure Plan. The National Farmers' Union retained its TWO objection throughout, declared itself dissatisfied with the SoS's ruling on the TWO Inquiry, and mounted a Judicial review in the High Court which failed.

The experience of working with Mike Schumann and the team to deal with the TWO application was unique in my experience. I have never negotiated with so many courteous and helpful people in my life before. Some of the proceedings were indeed character forming, but my respect and admiration for the people living alongside the railway grew to new heights. I wouldn't have missed it for the world. ■

# Chapter 7
# Phase 3 Waunfawr - Rhyd Ddu
# 1999 - 2003

**M**uch of the railway built in 1875 was waiting as a viable candidate for restoration without major infrastructure replacement, even when squeezed through the narrow gap in the hills between Betws Garmon and Castell Cidwm, occupied by the Afon Gwyrfai. One might have expected an abandoned 125 year old railway to have been swept away following sixty years of disuse, but it was not. It was clear that restoration would not be cheap, but it was feasible. The original underbridges were all there, but the assessment showed the remedial work would include extensive reconstruction of the abutments and strengthening of spans. All the overbridges required raising for Garratts. There was a pressing need to get on without delay, as the year 2000 target had already been missed.

Unfortunately, sober assessment revealed that there was not enough money to complete the railway right through to Rhyd Ddu. To reveal this publicly (apart from the glee caused to detractors) would likely lead to the curtailment of the railway at Waunfawr. So a discreet silence was maintained, while savings and other sources of funding were sought with energy. Until they were secured, it was prudent to apply the strictest economy measures to the work. A casualty of this policy was the Waunfawr station building, not one of the better preserved of the derelict NWNG station buildings, and in an inappropriate place. It was demolished and the stone was stored, pending rebuilding later.

The work for Phase 3 was broken down into discrete contracts. It made sense to contract out bridgework for example, but not for more simple remedial work on the trackbed. Those 'easier' portions were taken on by the Company and its volunteers, those more difficult by contractors. The contracts were awarded within geographical areas along the trackbed. Roland Doyle appointed a Civil Engineer both to run the direct civils projects on a day to day basis, and to act as resident engineer for outside contract work; also, Posford Duvivier (Caernarfon office) were retained as civil engineering consultants. Mike Schumann was Engineering Director.

Of five and a half miles of route in Phase 3, contractors undertook 3 miles, and WHLR undertook 2½ miles. WHLR hired the labour and plant needed to do the job, and used volunteer support. Grant aiding fortunately recognises volunteer support, and there is a credit for it - a most useful bonus.

o Contract 3a ran from Betws Garmon station site through Bryn Gloch caravan park, to just short of the river crossing at Cae Hywel (Pont Tros y Gol) UB56.

o Contract 3c-1 ran from UB56 inclusive, past Betws Garmon village and Plas y Nant to Castell Cidwm, OB71, inclusive.

o Contract 3c-2 was for Glan yr Afon Viaduct UB95, and for Rhyd Ddu Station.

All of these were given to contractors. On the other hand:

o Contract 3b ran from Waunfawr to Betws Garmon station

o Contract 3e-1 ran from Castell Cidwm overbridge to the Glan yr Afon Viaduct, exclusive.

o Contract 3e-2 ran from Glan yr Afon Viaduct to Rhyd Ddu.

## Contracts: Contracts for Phase 3 were let as follows (refer to map following for geography):

| Contract | From | To[1] | Location | Designer | Planning 'Super | Main Contractor |
|---|---|---|---|---|---|---|
| 3b | 5.8 | 6.95 | Waunfawr - Betws Garmon | Symonds | WHLR | WHLR |
| 3a[2] | 6.95 | 7.9 | Betws Garmon - Cae Hywel (Pont Tros y Gol UB56) | Posford Duvivier | Posford Duvivier[3] | Jones Bros |
| 3c-1 | 7.9 | 10.15 | Cae Hywel - Castell Cidwm | Posford Duvivier | Posford Duvivier | Jones Bros |
| 3e-1 | 10.15 | 12.55 | Castell Cidwm - Glan yr Afon | WHLR | WHLR | WHLR |
| 3c-2 | 12.55 | 12.7 | Glan yr Afon Viaduct | Posford Duvivier | Posford Duvivier | Jones Bros |
| 3e-2 | 12.7 | 14.2 | Glan yr Afon - Rhyd Ddu North | WHLR | WHLR | WHLR |
| 3c-2 | 14.2 | 15.2 | Rhyd Ddu Station | Posford Duvivier | Posford Duvivier | Jones Bros |

1. From-To measured in Kms. 2. Contract 3a was started by Triact but handed over to Jones Bros.
3. During the course of the contracts Posford Duvivier, whose head office was located in Peterborough, divested itself of its Caernarfon office by a management buyout, and the new company created became Datrys Consulting Engineers. Datrys were contracted by Posford Duvivier to provide consulting engineering services to the WHLR on their behalf. Subsequently Posford Duvivier were themselves taken over and absorbed into Royal Haskoning. These changes had major, adverse effects on the progress of Phase 3.

*Looking northwest, down from the lofty height of Snowdon, Yr Wyddfa. Way into the distance the Menai Strait, and the starting point of Caernarfon. On the left is Llyn Cwellyn, with the route of the NWNG/WHR rising from the near shore, from Castell Cidwm at the far lake end, to Bron Fedw Isaf at the far left end. The railway gains height, heading for the 'pass' at Pitt's Head; you can make out the line of vegetation bordering the line, left.*

Any railway engineer has a dilemma if circumstances dictate the close following of a river valley. Whilst the river has done the work in cutting through the upland, it can so easily turn from friend to foe.

C E Spooner, who surveyed the NWNG, was obliged, on the grounds of sense and economy, to follow the Afon Gwyrfai Gorge on from Waunfawr. The rainfall in the area is relatively high, and the river is given to flood after 24 hours of heavy rain. Peaceful co-existence is the aim in order to surmount the cleft in the hills at Salem, and to emerge into the Nant y Betws near to the shores of Llyn Cwellyn.

C E Spooner did this well, limiting the gradient, and employing his famous masonry walls to buttress the railway against the river - but it has to be three-times crossed.

There is a problem on the course of the line after it traverses the last of the hogsback girder bridges on the final crossing of the

*Derelict trackbed with bridge, and a potential mitigation problem for the residents of Pen y Gaer that was fixed. The concrete structure is a Blacker Bombard mortar emplacement, from when the Germans were expected, but not as tourists.*     **Mike Schumann**

Afon Gwyrfai, at Plas y Nant. The trackbed to the south suddenly dips into marshy ground for a short distance. The railway was built level originally across this marshy ground but the earthworks have repeatedly settled and have been built up only to settle again. Since reconstruction of the railway started at least 2.5m of fill have been placed on the embankment only to settle again to leave a dip in the alignment The railway does not recover until through the A4085 bridge at Castell Cidwm. The trackbed is also threatened with inundation through this bridge, and at times of prolonged rain the water can rise over the rails. This is character-forming for drivers, and acceptable if shallow and taken slowly. It might seems odd on the NWNG engineered by Mr C E Spooner that there is a 'soft' patch like this. Spooner engineered for a 4½ tonne axle load and left other soft patches. There is one just north of Waunfawr where the trackbed has been strengthened over a

## Phase 3 Chronology

| | | |
|---|---|---|
| 02.11.00 | Removal of old bridge, UB 51 at Betws Garmon | An old landmark, this original, hogsback, NWNG girder bridge was taken away |
| Mid-October 2000 | Betws Garmon clearance | The clearance of vegetation began as preparatory work and the formation was temporarily fenced |
| November 2000 | Aberglaslyn Pass work | The condition of the TWO required remedial work to be done, it began in November with shotcreting |
| February 2001 | Foot and Mouth Disease outbreak | This halted and then hampered work for months |
| March 2001 | Aberglaslyn Pass work | The works were completed during March 2001 and the contractors moved off site. This unlocked the start of works on Phase 3 within the National Park Boundary. |
| Easter 2001 First track | First track goes down | The 'process' was sufficiently advanced for the Black Hand Gang to lay track up to the bit parallel with the A4085, just south of Waunfawr at 7m from Caernarfon |
| April 2001 | New rail goes to Waunfawr | 400 lengths of 30kg/metre rail in 18 metre (59'1") lengths were stacked in the station yard. |
| October 2001 | OB 53 A4085 Bridge at Betws Garmon | The Council took the opportunity to replace this weak bridge at this time, with a wide concrete structure. Track was not laid through it until June 28th 2003 |
| November 2001 | Tracklaying | Track stopped at the north end by OB 53, but work was taking place in stages from Rhyd Ddu south. |
| February 2002 | Bryn Gloch | Worked started, and lasted until July 2002, when the bridge OB54 was opened. |
| June 2002 | Salem | Trackbed work was taking place at Salem |
| July 1st 2002 | Tracklaying | Head of Steel from the south reached Glan yr Afon, it would rest there a fair while. |
| 05.06.03 | Pont Betws Garmon, UB 51 | The completed girders were lifted into position and settled on their bearings, thus completing a major connection for the WHR. |
| 17.07.03 | Tracklaying | The Phase 3 railway was connected throughout. |
| 26.07.03 | HMRI Inspection | The Inspector's Train ran on this day, examining part of the Waunfawr to Rhyd Ddu section. |
| 30.07.03 | Royal Inauguration | Prince Charles rode the train from Waunfawr to Rhyd Ddu, transferring from Car. 24 to locomotive *Prince* at Snowdon Ranger, from where he drove *Prince* to Rhyd Ddu. He said 'I'll tell my Mother she should come and visit you' - and she did! |
| 18.08.03 | Public service begins | The opening day - the WHR is now halfway restored! |

100m length with many tons of slate waste. The reason for the Castell Cidwm diversion is snug in history. The authorised route ran along the roadside, a little to the east, though the current trackbed is within the limits of deviation. Ever anxious to save on costs, the authorised route would not have been a cheap way to get past Castell Cidwm, and indeed there was a temporary terminus south of the bridge, indicating perhaps a want of funds. Apparently, sources state, there was a 'little local difficulty' with the landowner, that forced the builders to the riverside. Thus the restorers had some 'wonky' railway to deal with. Not a surprise, and a small problem in comparison with what was to follow on the Rhyd Ddu - Beddgelert section.

Beyond Castell Cidwm, the long flanks of Snowdon are approached carefully, the trackbed rising prudently up the contours, seeking the path of least resistance, until the Afon Trweunydd has to be crossed on the Glan yr Afon Viaduct. The NWNG objective was to breach the pass at the lowest practical height, and sink gradually to Beddgelert and beyond. The best way of doing this was a steady progress to Rhyd Ddu, which at 627ft represented the optimum route. This meant crossing the streams descending from the west flanks of Snowdon; the deep defile was unavoidable. The rocky approach to Rhyd Ddu also necessitated some wide sweeps. Here were concealed some nasty surprises in the later stages of Phase 3 restoration, caused by NWNG penny-pinching.

There was a planning stipulation that work couldn't start in the National Park until the Aberglaslyn rock fall problems were stabilised. The Park boundary runs through Bryn Gloch. For that reason the £285k contract for this work was commissioned in winter 2000/2001, at the start of Phase 3. Another problem was that site access made it impossible to build quickly unless linear construction was dropped, and work proceeded at several sites at once. This offered logistical problems.

## Contract 3b Waunfawr to Betws Garmon

Phase 3 work started at Betws Garmon, on the old station site. There was no intention to reopen the station there. Waunfawr was near, and if there was going to be a halt, it would be better at the caravan park at Bryn Gloch. However, of that place, the story of the difficulties experienced are related later in the panel by Roland Doyle.

The quickest of the contracts to be completed on the Phase 3 section was 3b, from Waunfawr to Betws Garmon, by the WHLR itself. Mike Bradshaw, previously Site Agent for Mulcair on the Phase 2 section, was employed by WHLR to manage the work, and to engage the necessary work force and sub-contractors. First the undergrowth had to be cleared, and this was done by scraping with a tracked excavator. Just looking at that almost offered as much fun as you can have to a volunteer, who from previous experience might have though they were going to have to drive a spade to do the job. Marking out the trackbed and fencing was done by specialist Achnashean of Llandygai, who had undertaken the clearing and fencing for Phases 1 & 2. On top of the scraped area was placed a compacted layer of crushed slate, aimed at preventing damage to the trackbed by contractor's vehicles.

The old Betws Garmon station site was cleared as a base for construction of bridge UB51 (*UB31.59*), Pont Betws Garmon. The crushed slate waste ensured a roadway that allowed easy

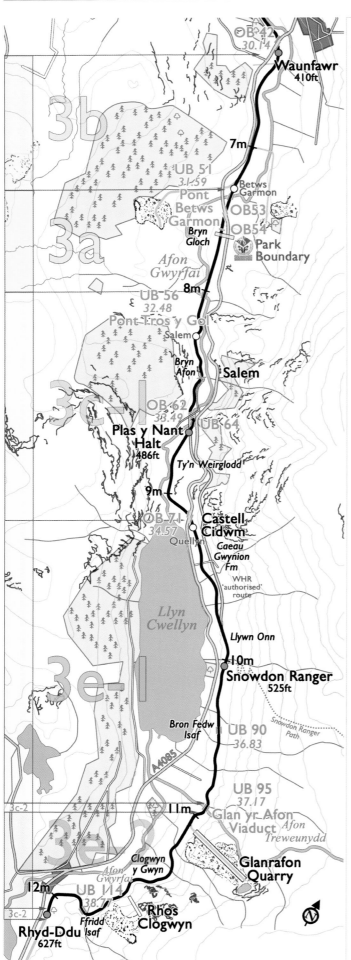

## WAUNFAWR TO RHYD DDU CHARACTERISTICS

If Dinas to Waunfawr had been an unremarkable bit of railway, then this was needed to warm up for this next stretch. In the five miles to Rhyd Ddu there are four river crossings. Three, cross the Afon Gwyrfai on the iconic NWNG standard girder bridges. Of these bridges, all were considered repairable, but OB53 was replaced with a second-hand bridge with a wider span. The fourth river bridge, over the Afon Treweunydd, is the Glan yr Afon Viaduct, the largest span on the line.

The departure from Waunfawr in pleasant farmland is heightened by joining the A4085, with only a hedge and a wall dividing the two. splendid movies may be taken of the train at this point, and cars can be seen pacing the train along this stretch. Relations with the Afon Gwyrfai are close, and after the raver has turned under the railway past the site of the old Betws Garmon Station, the line crosses under the 4085 carried over the railway on a large rebuilt bridge, and runs through the Bryn Gloch caravan park. Welsh Water's drinking water processing site is passed before the Afon Gwyrfai is crossed again on a rebuilt NWNG hogsback girder bridge, Pont Tros y Gol, 8m from Caernarfon.

The line rises past the old Salem Halt site and enters the gorge of the Afon Gwyrfai. It curves on a stone embankment, with the river below, crosses it for the final time and runs through Plan y Nant Halt, skirts the river at Ty'n Weirglodd and crosses under the A4085 at Castell Cidwm, just over 9 miles from Caernarfon.

From here on the line runs through farmland, rising steadily with the Llyn Cwellyn below and the bulk of Snowdon ahead. The contours are steadily cut as the railway climbs to Snowdon Ranger, a halt that has a YHA youth hostel below and a wonderful path up Snowdon that crosses the WHR at this point.

In the 5¾ miles from Waunfawr to Rhyd Ddu, the railway rises 227 feet and as Rhyd Ddu is neared there are sharp curves. The countryside is open for the last three miles, and there are sweeping views below above Snowdon Ranger, as the line has gained some height. There are also splendid views upwards of the flanks of Snowdon.

At Glan yr Afon the most impressive structure is crossed. The 93'6" (18.5m) viaduct span is completely hidden by foliage, but after the crossing, splendid views down become available as the line traverses Clogwyn y Gwin, and curves sharply under Ffridd Isaf, from where the energetic can get superb views of the train. The final curves are negotiated into Rhyd Ddu Station, 12 miles from Caernarfon.

In the long period of the railway's slumber, station buildings decayed: at Waunfawr, the station building has been demolished; at Betws Garmon it is a shell; at Snowdon Ranger it is a dwelling, which doesn't form part of the current railway; at Rhyd Ddu there is a public convenience. The new station at Rhyd Ddu was built east of the old, leaving the car park that has been established on the old station site. As both Waunfawr and Rhyd Ddu passing places were equipped with loops, then temporary shelters were considered desirable. Betws Garmon, Salem, and Quellyn, have not been reopened, but both Plas y Nant and Snowdon Ranger have been re-established as halts.

No steep gradients are met on this section of railway, and most of it was constructed by C.E. Spooner for 4½ tonne axle-loads. Some work was skimped. The locomotives were small, so the infrastructure now has been made capable of running 8 tonne axle-load Garratts, at a cost.

*Right:* The sylvan piece beside the A4085 was one stretch of road eagerly awaited by the movie fraternity. The track going back was greeted with glee. One day you would be able to pace a Garratt here and photograph its intricate workings. Indeed now it is possible. **Ben Fisher**

*Below:* Tracklaying on Phase 3 proceeds beyond the level crossing at the entrance to Tan y Ffordd farm at May Bank Holiday, 2001, with the North Wales Gang at work. **Ben Fisher**

*Below:* It was though this was UB51, it is in fact UB56, Pont Tros y Gol. The photograph remains here to show what state the old NWNG bridges had got into by this date (1995). UB51 was removed, and taken to Dinas to be stored. A bridge of wider span replaced it. UB56 was refurbished, as is reported later in the chapter. **Mike Schumann**

*Below:* Before the bridge UB56 was removed, the cross-beams can be seen. There is strength in them, but not enough for an 8 tonne axle-load, needed for restoration. The wrought iron main beams show a remarkable lack of corrosion. The same was true for UB51. **Mike Schumann**

access for machinery. By the end of December 2000 there was crushed slate waste along the whole 1.1km length of the contract.

Every culvert under the railway had to be renewed, and these were designed to use a precast forebay slab that was produced at Dinas. At Cyrnant, near to Waunfawr was a ballast dump, with supplies ready to lay. It was decided to get the track down on this section as soon as practicable for two reasons.

**1.** The track at the Waunfawr end would allow some storage space for wagons adjoining the running railway, and this was most useful.

**2.** The track to Betws Garmon old station site was needed to replace UB 51, the Afon Gwyrfai railway bridge.

By mid-March ballast was in place on the first stretch beyond Waunfawr, and the first lengths of track were laid for Phase 3. The Black Hand Gang pushed on rapidly, getting the stretch along the A4085 laid over the Easter Weekend 2001. The ballast was also being laid back from Betws Garmon towards Waunfawr. By mid-May the gap between the two sections was small, and tracklaying would soon join up. By the May Bank Holiday track had reached the Tan y Ffordd farm level crossing. By late June track was continuous from Waunfawr to Betws Garmon and there matters halted for a great deal of time. The problems to be dealt with were the Afon Gwyrfai underbridge UB 51, the flood relief openings, UB52, the A4085 overbridge, OB 53 and the Bryn Gloch site and overbridge OB 54, as well as a 19" water main through the opening of UB53. These would all take a considerable time to sort

*Left:* This is the 'cut and shut' part of the operation. On the right a 1.143m slice has been removed from the right-hand beam, to match the other lying on its side. **John Sreeves**

*Below:* The kit of parts as delivered to the WHR, standing on two SAR flats in Waunfawr, waiting for Castell Caernarfon to shunt them to the railhead, right by the old Betws Garmon station, **WHLR**

*Below:* Adjacent to the old Betws Garmon Station site, the kit of parts is unloaded and assembled into the bridge structure. Then it will be painted and ready to drop in to position, **WHLR**

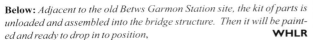

*Below:* The massive DEMAG crane, needed for its reach, is gently lowering the completed and painted UB51 into the bearings prepared for it in its abutments. This barrier, once complete will allow the track to link up the valley to the head of steel. **Roger Dick**

out. In fact the track could not be laid through here for another two years. Such discontinuity was an unavoidable nuisance and certainly made planning and logistics more difficult and the job more expensive.

## Contract 3a Betws Garmon to Cae Hywel.

The description is linear, but the timescale is not.

The three NWNG hogsback, plate girder bridges over the River Gwyrfai (UB51 - Pont Betws Garmon, UB56 - Pont Tros y Gol and UB64 - Pont Plas y Nant) are distinctive enough to have been enjoyed as icons of the WHR. What might not generally be known is that the bridges, 52ft 3ins (15.9m) long, are made from wrought iron. And although they were thought to date from the building of the NWNG in 1875, it was tempting to think that their construction is earlier. These bridges look as though they are standard gauge bridges, rather light ones, that date from the 1850s, but for this speculation to be true, there ought to be evidence of previous use from holes on the bridge, and there is none. Two of the bridges have been overhauled and strengthened to see further service, but UB51 (**UB31.59**)

at Betws Garmon (famous for the Mr Chad style 'WOT NO RAILWAY?' graffiti) has not. The requirement for a longer span meant its replacement - not on grounds of age and condition. Its beams are in Dinas yard awaiting further deployment (does WHR need a turntable perhaps?). They were removed by Triact on 2nd November 2000, and by mid-January the new abutments for the wider river bridge were under construction. A nearly new bridge was found in Yorkshire, but it was a skew span. It was purchased

*Below: The rebuilt Pont Betws shows a large structure of reinforced concrete, clad in cut slate and looking very nice. But of course very nice was also very expensive. The normal slate cladding is going on here, as elsewhere. This invariably improves the appearance of modern, concrete structures. It was all at GC expense.* **Ben Fisher**

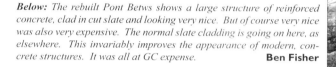

from Network Rail in March 2003, at well below the estimated cost for a new steel bridge. John Sreeves schemed the alterations needed to convert the bridge into a straight span. Each of the four beams was 18.2m long. A length of 1.143m was cut from the excess end of two and added at the other end of the other two beams, to bridge the river gap of 16.8m. The cut measurement allowed full design strength, as the detached pieces and added pieces had to coincide with the stiffening pieces in the webs of the beams, set at 1.54m intervals. It all worked, and the extension of the main beams, and the modifications to the cross-beams, was completed by 25th April 2003 in the Whiteley Engineering Company's works. The bridge then had to be shotblasted, painted with primer, and new rail-bearing beams manufactured, before being sent to Wales to be delivered on May 13th, 2003. The components were offloaded into rail wagons at Waunfawr Station, and taken up the line as far as possible - to the old Betws Garmon Station site. The crane then lifted each component from the rail wagons and the structure was assembled. This work was completed with 22mm bolts, later replaced with high-strength, friction grip bolts, that were precision torqued to make the right assembly. Having assembled the waybeams, the mesh walkway

was added, and the bridge was painted in grey. Work on the abutments was needed to set the bearing plates, and to create the short concrete plinths. The plinths were at each end, to support the waybeams upon which the track would rest. Team Wylfa was hard at work painting on May 31st, and when all was done the final lifting operation was made on June 6th 2003. The 35 tonne span demanded a very big crane to place it across the river, as it had to be able to jib-out some way in order to do this. A giant, thousand tonne capacity Demag telescopic road crane came in to do the job. It weighed 200 tonnes itself when all its gubbins were fitted. When this was done, late in the Phase 3 timetable, the track could be connected right up the valley.

Triact had rebuilt the adjacent flood spans in 2001, UB 52 (**UB31.64**). The Gwyrfai does a bit of meandering at this point, as it is the first bit of valley out of Llyn Cwellyn that offers any lateral space. In common with many rivers, it looks quite innocent on a summer's day, limpidly idling its blue water contents northwards. However, when the rains begin in earnest, it is not to be underestimated. Thus the flood relief channels were restored, and the embankments either side were excavated to ground level. A new internal deck was poured as a load-bearing structure. The stone pillars remain, and the stone abutment walls were restored, so externally it looks as though not much happened - and that is as it should be. There was a lot of engineering and much expense that went into the short stretch at Betws Garmon over the Afon Gwyrfai, the flood spans and under the A4085.

The A4085 follows the Nant Gwyrfai and crosses the trackbed for the second time at Betws Garmon. The bridge, Pont Betws (OB53 - **OB31.74**) was weak and old, and over time had been outclassed by the traffic that crossed it. This was one of the

*(continued on page 173)*

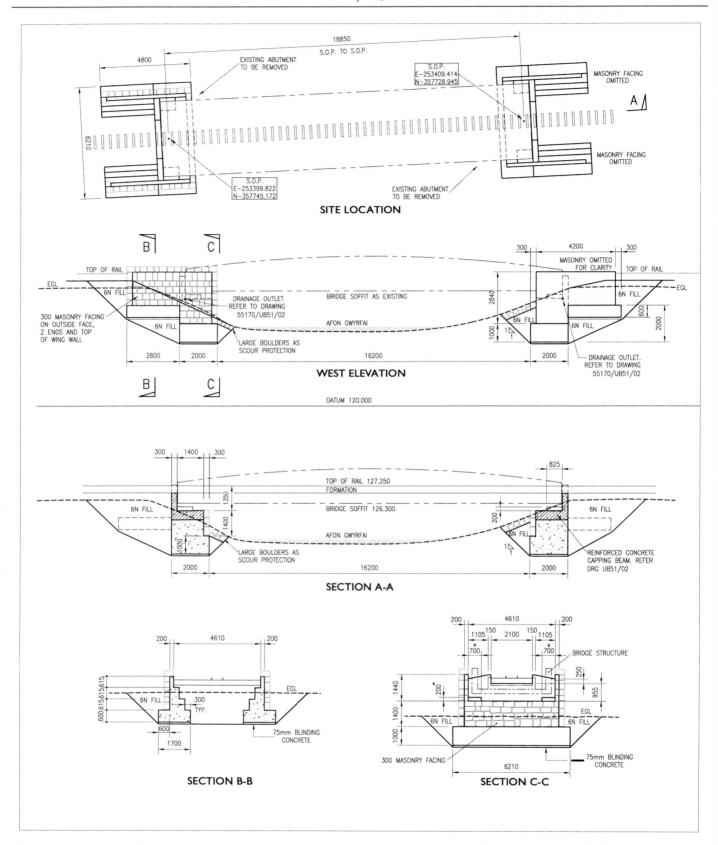

This was a bridge designed by Graham Cole to replace the 14.6m hogsback NWNG standard bridge, to give a clear span of 16.2m across the Afon Gwyrfai. It would have replaced the existing iconic bridge, and been built by an apprentice training school near Darlington. Project delay ruled that option out and commercially built it was too expensive. Of course it would have looked very nice, and it was a hogsback replacement design - but it was not to be. Why was a new bridge required at all? The old one could have been refurbished - the other two were. The span was increased by 1.6m to reduce the upstream water level at times of maximum flow, and thus to prevent flooding of the lowered formation under OB53 The adjacent flood spans at UB52 were also reinstated. Thus it is hoped that flooding of the railway formation at Betws Garmon will not be a problem in the future.

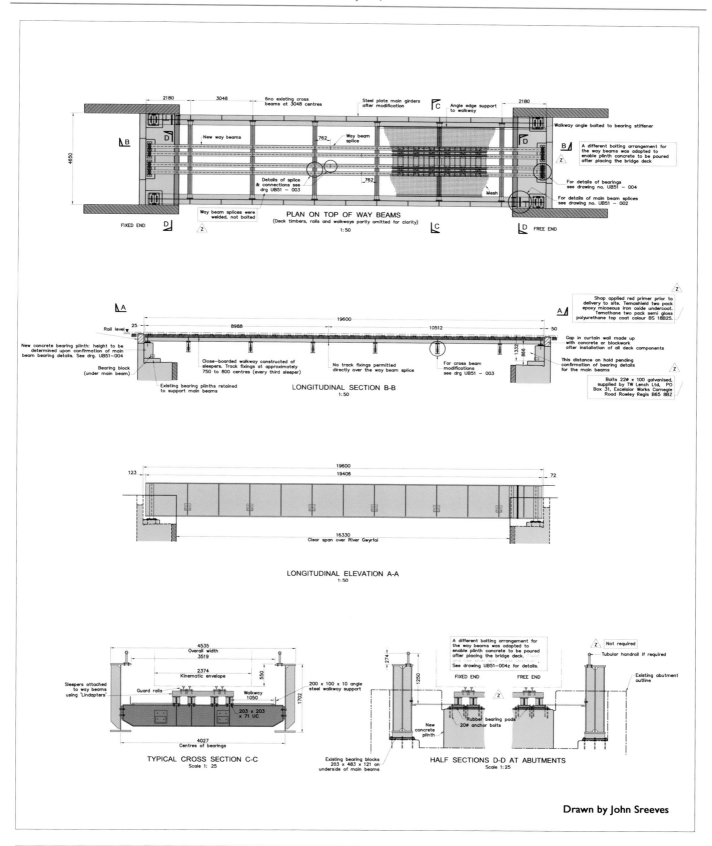

**PLAN ON TOP OF WAY BEAMS**
(Deck timbers, rails and walkways partly omitted for clarity)
1:50

**LONGITUDINAL SECTION B-B**
1:50

**LONGITUDINAL ELEVATION A-A**
1:50

**TYPICAL CROSS SECTION C-C**
Scale 1:25

**HALF SECTIONS D-D AT ABUTMENTS**
Scale 1:25

**Drawn by John Sreeves**

*Fate plays strange tricks, as if the original NWNG standard bridges actually were not second-hand, obtained from a standard gauge railway, then this bridge certainly had that pedigree. It was discovered by Mike Hart, out of use in the Civil engineer's yard in Rotherham. It was a skew bridge, and therefore was uncomfortable in a location only suitable for a parallel bridge. Yet the problem with Graham Cole's beautifully designed new bridge was that alas it was too expensive. This Cinderella of a bridge was worked upon to provide a substantial structure of the correct span, for an affordable price. So, a rather modern intrusion over the Gwyrfai, embarked on a second career, lengthened, and carrying 2ft gauge trains instead of standard.*

**A**berglaslyn Pass was resisted for the passage of the railway. One concern was a deemed risk that rocks from the steep slopes above could plunge on to the trackbed, with danger to life. Thus action had to be taken to stop that. Remedial work was required in the tunnels, and along the trackbed. The National Park was the organisation that needed to be satisfied that the rock stabilisation work had been carried out properly, restricting any WHR restoration work inside the Park until it was done. When stabilisation was complete, then the works to restore the railway authorised by the TWO could begin. The rock work was carried out early in Phase 3, and completed by March 2001.

**T**he outcome of the public inquiry was a ministerial ruling that took proper notice of expert advice and local concerns, that trains passing through Aberglasyn ought to be protected from rock fall. It was obvious to even the meanest understanding that the slopes up to the heights above the Pass were steeper than any practical angle of repose for self-respecting rocks. So, if railway supporters were whispering darkly about conspiracy against restoration, then they were in error. The Afon Glaslyn had been steadily eroding away its confines as rivers do, and if someone comes and puts a railway in the way, then they had better mind the consequences when years of frost and rain loosen surface rock that then naturally submits to the forces of gravity.

It was a condition that remedial works on rock stabilisation needed to be done in the Aberglaslyn Pass, before any reconstruction was permitted within the boundaries of the National Park. The railway restorers knew that a short distance after Waunfawr, just across the river at Betws Garmon, was the furthest that could be built to before tackling this rather expensive job in the Pass, priced at £285k. The Millennium Commission would not pay for this - it was not included. The money had to be found from donations to the project.

Accordingly the work was scheduled post the opening to Waunfawr in September 2000. The stabilisation job was to ensure that no rocks were likely to fall on to the trackbed in front of the large masonry wall that stretched from No.4, Twnel Hir, to No.3, the short tunnel. The height of the wall needed raising by one metre, and above it stout metal posts with 'catch-wires' needed fixing, to provide an effective barrier to any rocks that slid or fell away from above. Consultants Ove Arup oversaw the work, which was carried out by Colin James (Rock Engineering Ltd) of Porthmadog, a much respected local company. Road access was necessary, and this meant the embankment over the Cwm Bychan bridge south of Twnel Hir needed attention. There was a physical examination of the area above the tunnels, and removal of rocks that were an obvious danger. Staging was put up and the heightening work was carried out.

**Above:** *This was what the fuss was about. One can be deeply concerned about the effect on a train of such a fall. In truth, careful examination reveals no impact crater - but it is undesirable and needs to be prevented.* **Roland Doyle**

**Right:** *A view through the two tunnels, No.2 in the foreground of 32 yds, and No.3 behind of 10yds. Work needed to be done on these, and in the 306 yd, long tunnel, and it made sense to do that work at the same time as the stabilisation.*

**Left:** *The shotcreting and rock-bolting work necessary to discourage rock fall from within the short, 10yd, No.3 Tunnel is shown here. Is it fanciful to assume that the extra loft in the centre was to accommodate the twin wires for the three-phase overhead, electric supply for the 100hp, PB&SSR locomotives that it was expected would growl up through the Pass with two carriages in tow? Nice thought, but actually the tunnel has been made a bit bigger for today's trains.* **Ben Fisher**

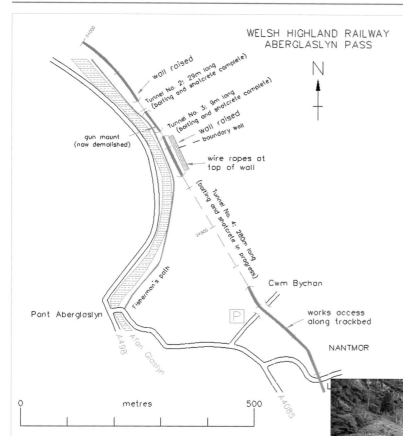

WELSH HIGHLAND RAILWAY
ABERGLASLYN PASS

N

wall raised

Tunnel No. 2: 29m long
(bolting and shotcrete complete)

Tunnel No. 3: 9m long
(bolting and shotcrete complete)

wall raised

boundary wall

gun mount
(now demolished)

wire ropes at
top of wall

Tunnel No. 4: 280m long
(bolting and shotcrete in progress)

Fisherman's path

Cwm Bychan

Pont Aberglaslyn

P

works access
along trackbed

A498

Afon Glaslyn

NANTMOR

A4085

0        metres        500

**Left:** *John Sreeves's contemporary map of the area shows what work was necessary in the pass, and is dated 26th February 2001. The wall was raised in two places, and years after the work the stone has weathered, so one cannot see what is new and what was there previously. The tunnels needed rockbolting and shotcreting, to make sure that the roofs and sides remain stable. As untreated, bare rock, there was opportunity for ice formation to gradually loosen pieces of rock which would fall - more irritation than danger, but much better secured. There was a concrete mount for a Blacker Bombard Mortar, dating from WW2 - similar to that next the bridge at Plas y Nant. This base was relocated. The long tunnel had lights installed to make vehicle access and walking safer. Considerable amount of rock removal and some digging out was needed within the 308yd Twnel Hir, to restore it to the right level for ballast to be put in and track laid on top. Before any of that happened, the Dŵr Cymru water main needed to be removed - and that took place in 2006.* **John Sreeves**

**Below:** *To extend the high masonry wall upward by one metre, the contractor, Colin James Ltd., was obliged to prepare the site so that road vehicles could get in, make it secure so walkers could not get in, and erect scaffolding so that the top of the wall could be easily reached. It was then heightened, and large beams were embedded connected by wire ropes, to impede any falling rocks, preventing them from reaching the track.* **Ben Fisher**

It was also necessary to rockbolt other areas of potential instability in the area around the trackbed. In Tunnels 2, 3 and 4, shotcreting and rockbolting was carried out, such that these would be ready to receive track when it was laid some years after.

Another set of work was the removal of the water main. Welsh water had given the OR an undertaking that should the railway ever be rebuilt, the main would be relocated at their expense. This work was not begun until October 2006, nearer to when the track was due to be put down.

The 'unofficial' footpath was relocated so that there would no longer be any temptation to use the railway, and the cost of reinstating the alternative Fisherman's Path was shared with others. The bridges had been considered by FR Co. to be unsafe, and were taken out in 1999, thus shutting off the walking route across the Afon Glaslyn, except by the long way round, via Beddgelert. It was decided, with the support of the local agencies of government, to install a footbridge, parallel with the railway, crossing the Galslyn at Bryn y Felin. Planning permission was granted by the Snowdonia National Park Authority in mid-October 2000;

both the SNPA, and landowner the National Trust agreed to contribute to the cost of the footbridge, in partnership with the FR Co. Other contributors were the Countryside Commission for Wales, the Environment Agency, and Beddgelert Community Council. The construction contract was let to local contractor Colin Jones (Rock Engineering) Ltd. The bridge reconnects a popular circular walk from Beddgelert, and is accessible for wheelchair users. In February 2003 contractors finally moved in to start work on the footbridge.

*The beams of the Bryn y Felin footbridge are in place on 10th April 2003, and two popular walks will be possible as soon as the footbridge is completed. A definitive footpath will be re-established in this well-liked place.* **Tom Bowen**

**S**ometimes our enthusiasm for cute little railways runs away with us, and perhaps difficulty ought to have been expected on a wider scale when trying to restore the WHR. After all there had been two public inquiries, and the railway was seen as being wicked and foreign by a number of people in the area. Yet perhaps one could be forgiven for thinking that a nice caravan site, right by the boundary of the Snowdonia National Park, would welcome a potential surge of long-term business. Roland explains otherwise.

**I**t was assumed that a pleasant little halt would be provided for the Bryn Gloch caravan campers, who would be pleased to use the restored railway to travel back and forth, leaving their cars in the car park. The rosy intention of restoring the line was to bring prosperity to the area - something often promised by supporters of the scheme. The bile of those not charmed by the thought of trampling hordes of tourists could be understood, but the implacable opposition of someone thought likely to gain much from the railway was hard to grasp. Perhaps it was the element of compulsion, or just that smug little smile and mildly patronising air worn quite unintentionally by people who are convinced they are doing good. Or perhaps it was because we were thought to be strangers? In trying to achieve vacant possession of the land, in the case of Bryn Gloch, the railway became badly unstuck - it took two years!

Bryn Gloch is a caravan and camping site about a mile south of Waunfawr. It straddles the trackbed (or is bifurcated by it – depending upon your viewpoint). The Bryn Gloch business had developed over many years, creating many obstacles to any potential WHR restorer. The original overbridge within Bryn Gloch had been partially demolished; it had been replaced by a level crossing of the trackbed. An agreement existed whereby the trackbed through Bryn Gloch would be lowered, so that the new bridge arch would be low enough not to impede the delivery of 40' caravans. Also, the camp site wanted to hide the trains as much as possible from the customers, rather the reverse of elsewhere! The remains of the old bridge had to go, but an 11kV overhead electricity line passed dangerously close to the top of the old arch. If one ignored the warning signs and fence, and climbed on to the old arch, it might have been possible to touch the 11kV line (but only once). It was too dangerous to attempt the demolition of the old bridge due to the proximity of this overhead electricity line, so it had to go first. A very useful Power Distribution Engineer, was asked to come to site to give his expert opinion on the situation. Imagine his surprise when, looking further into the camp site to trace the route of the overhead line, he discovered that it went with dangerous proximity over the roofs of some 8 or so static caravans.

The caravans weren't there when the line had been installed a long time ago. Apparently permission for entry was not possible to divert the overhead line. Our Engineer said that if this stratagem persisted, then he would have no option but to shut off the overhead line, which also fed power to the entire camp site.

*The wonderful world of Bryn Gloch - an aerial view*

**Peter Johnson**

"What gives you the right to do that?" the question was asked.

"The Electricity Act of 1989" was the reply.

It was essential to check that the planning authority and the landowner believed that the FR owned the trackbed. So a visit was arranged to the planning office in Caernarfon. Recent planning applications which had been submitted from Bryn Gloch were examined. The land ownership map clearly showed that Bryn Gloch did not have title to the trackbed, and that there was awareness of this. However, there was a planning application allowing increase of the maximum number of 40' static caravans allowed on the site to 14. On the filled-in part of the old railway cutting, currently stood caravan no. 15. To restore the trackbed this van had to be removed, as well as several hundreds of tonnes of soil upon which it stood. The new Transport and Works Act Order gave permission to build a new hard standing on Bryn Gloch land, with the view to moving caravan 15 on to it - one more step towards vacant possession of the trackbed. Having discussed this with the planning authorities, a snag came to light: Caravan 15 was currently not on Bryn Gloch land, and so didn't count as one of the quota of 14 caravans. It had planning permission to be on railway land because this had been obtained by default (it had been there for more than 10 years unchallenged). However, if it was moved it off railway land and on to Bryn Gloch land, this would be in breach of Bryn Gloch's planning consent, since it was one caravan in excess of the maximum allowed.

One could be forgiven at this point for feeling faint and wanting to go home - but there is more, all normal complications to restoring this cute little railway. It was thought that the TWO Act gave the FR Co. power to move the caravan onto the pad, but no, it just gave the powers to build the pad. To provoke matters further, caravan 15 was currently on railway land in the Arfon planning authority, and it was wished to move it onto the newly constructed concrete pad, some 30 metres away. This happened to be in the Snowdonia National Park Planning Authority area. Dealing with two authorities at once is not easy! Eventually, (having taken advice) it was decided that the construction team did not have the expertise to move the caravan. Thus the site was offered some money to do it. This was accepted; the van went, never to come back, and the FR Co. breached no planning consents because they didn't move it. The caravan was anchored down in its new location, at its 4 corners, using anchors to the site's design.

The planning authorities had spent about a year or so wondering how to resolve the offending caravan No. 15, when nature solved the problem for them. A storm in the February of 2001 whistled down the Waunfawr valley, picked up caravan 15, ripping all 4 anchor chains from the ground, and dumped it on to an adjacent car. The car was allegedly owned by the family staying in the caravan, but thankfully they were out on foot for the day. This happened two weeks before the camp site was due to open. At first we were asked to compensate for the loss, but eventually the claim came to nothing. The FR Co. was invited to view the wreckage (now burned out in an adjacent field) but this offer was declined.

Part of the diversion of the 11kV overhead line was planned to be underground, adjacent to the site's store, and out to the base of a pole next to the main road. To save money, the trench was dug with a hired-in mini-excavator with a qualified driver. In fact there were several big items of plant on hire within Bryn Gloch for use on the cable diversion. Unfortunately, due to the ground being sodden from a night's heavy rainfall, the mini excavator, which was straddling the trench, ended up at a precarious angle with one track actually in the trench. It would have tipped over, but one of the buildings stopped it. Having sorted things out with the HSE, it was just needed to recover the plant and get it all off-hire to save money. Unfortunately, permission to enter the premises and recover the plant was refused. Legal advice indicated that the police couldn't do much about it, since it wasn't a criminal matter. It was suggested that a representative from the plant hire company was persuaded to attempt to recover the plant. If there was a refusal to give the plant up to this person,

then a theft would have taken place, and the police could be involved to enforce a sensible outcome. This plan worked well, the police did a great job; the plant was recovered and superficial damage to the building was repaired.

It was now obvious that the Bryn Gloch site was going to continue to be difficult to handle, and a new approach was needed. Access via the trackbed from the Waunfawr direction was not possible, as the old road overbridge was too low to get plant beneath. Access from the other end had not been secured either. It was decided to set up an adjacent Tros y Gol work site, since this was required for the next bridge, UB56, and items beyond. The contractor, Jones' Brothers (Ruthin), moved into the Tros y Gol work site, since they had won contract 3C. They were given the earthworks contract in Bryn Gloch as well. Andrew Aikman, Jones' Bros. Site Agent said that they had much expertise in dealing with landowners, and would like to negotiate with Bryn Gloch, to take all the earthworks plant through the Bryn Gloch main gate. It was something of a surprise to hear that Andrew had been successful, and no fee was needed. They planned to move all the plant in on the following Monday morning. Then there was a phone call from Andrew mid-morning on the Monday, to say that all the plant was queued up on the main road waiting to go in to Bryn Gloch as entry had been declined unless a cheque for £20,000 was forthcoming for access. Andrew Aikman was gently reminded that they were on a fixed price contract, and so any arrangement was between him and the site, and should not appear on any invoice to us. The plant was returned to the work site at Tros y Gol. Later that week, the contractor built a haul-road along the railway, and gained access to the Bryn Gloch section by means of the track bed from Tros y Gol. The ransom strip had been circumnavigated.

Japanese Knotweed was found to be growing strongly on railway land between the two parts of Bryn Gloch. Jan Woods, who looked after the environmental liaison amongst many other roles, discovered that the Japanese Knotweed either had to be dug up and taken off site, where its astonishing regenerative powers mean that it gets treated a bit like nuclear waste, and disposal is therefore expensive, or

*A distressed digger - sadly there seemed to be a bit of a problem about getting it back. See text for solution.*
**Roland Doyle**

*Japanese Knotweed - the not is that you may NOT permit it to grow on your land. Disposing of it is a problem, as the text outlines.*
**Roland Doyle**

*Left: The old Bryn Gloch bridge, isolated and derelict, could not be lowered and widened economically for its new role. The only sensible course was to demolish it and begin afresh. The results are rather good, even if they did cost a mint of money.*

**These three pictures Roland Doyle**

*Below: The new bridge had to be a substantial affair, that's the name of the game with bridges. Seen in this elevated view OB54's shuttering is in place for the L/H side abutments, which have already been poured in March 2002. The centring for the arch is in place and in due course this too will be poured. The photographic vantage point is well above the eventual track level.*

*Below: Here is 'Son of Bryn Gloch', OB54 in all its glory nearing completion in May - a substantial structure. Cladding of the concrete exterior in local slate is taking place and the hallmark yellow brick of NWNG arches has been restored (but in new bricks). So when one thrums past this point in one of the comfortable WHR coaches, roaring through the arch in a moment, spare a thought about the large amount of work that had to be done here in 2002.*

it must be buried at a depth of 5 metres. Digging a hole 5 metres deep was not possible, so it looked as though it would have to go off site at a financially prohibitive rate. At the same time, spoil was mounting up in the Tros y Gol worksite. This was detritus, material taken from the top of the trackbed. It looked as though that too would have to go to a licensed tip at great expense. We were about to excavate the Bryn Gloch cutting, which producing even more spoil. Jan came up with a plan which tied all of these problems together with a neat solution, saving a six figure sum. This was to tip the spoil on top, making a mound at least 5 metres high. That Knotweed mausoleum is now slumbering between the two Bryn Gloch bridges.

During the battle of Bryn Gloch, the adjacent landowner consumed four land agents. The first fellow from Porthmadog was a gentleman, pleasant but firm and usually fair. He had the

job of responding to our CPO notice. The first response is basically to register the landowner as a potential receiver of compensation. What was riposted was a claim for £260,000 compensation. This was rather strange, since in the CPO process a landowner is normally compensated for his loss after the land has been taken, on either a permanent or a temporary basis. One component of a CPO compensation claim is that of Injurious Affection. This is the damage, in financial terms, caused to a business or individual by the development being built with CPO powers. Yet the new business needs to be established before any effect on adjacent businesses can be measured. Our Land agent, Simon Simcox, knew the subject very well. It was his judgement that the first year that any form of Injurious Affection could be measured was a year after the Foot & Mouth outbreak of 2001. Bryn Gloch was in the middle of the affected zone, and so business would have been seriously affected in the Foot & Mouth outbreak year, such that in the following year, Injurious Affection would have appeared to be negative. A new CPO claim came in for £60,000. Our land agent asked to see Bryn Gloch's accounts, with a view to claim verification, but was refused. Apparently, the claim was not pursued.

Offers had been made to build a small halt platform for the customers, but it seemed that the idea was considered to be abhorrent. Other similar reactions have long since been reversed in other locations. However I should imagine that those against were not very pleased to see their campers waving enthusiastically at the cute narrow gauge trains, which eventually passed smoothly and undisturbingly though the site. Perhaps the time will come sometime soon to resurrect the Bryn Gloch Halt scheme? ∎

famous '15 places' that were objected to by Caernarvonshire County Council (CCC) in the old days, where the WHR trackbed was wanted for road improvements, and coming on this dreadful old bridge, it was easy to see why. Without the WHR restoration, the bridge would have been knocked down, and this would have been a flat stretch of A4085. Gwynedd Council (GC) took the opportunity to widen the existing bridge abutments and to install a new road deck. GC Highways Dept had been shown the abstracts of the minutes, by which CCC adopted the bridges, by Mike Schumann, after the TWA Order was granted, and therefore after the FR had accepted ownership of the trackbed. They accepted their liability. Work on OB53 was at their charge and was in progress in early November 2001, with a scaffold bridge for pedestrians, and traffic lights for the road. Obviously there was no railway to hamper the work, but it took until June 2002 to lay the roadway across the newly constructed bridge deck. It was a roomy piece of roadway by any standard, and the railway underneath received the reinstatement of the original cast iron beam by De Winton on the Caernarfon side, though not now load bearing, suitably painted with the letters picked out in white. Some trackbed lowering was done through

the bridge opening, and the OB53 (*OB31.74*) drainage system was completed at the same time. This allows rainwater to drain properly into the river, via drains under the trackbed through the bridge. This work was done by Jones Bros, together with other finishing jobs in the vicinity, as one of the final tasks to complete their contracts in Spring 2003.

It was likely that this area of the railway could have been scuppered in its reinstatement had it lain idle for much longer; the rebuilding of OB53 had been urgent. OB54 was next in the Bryn Gloch caravan site, lying across the WHR trackbed, a little further on. Although the proprietors were aware of the ownership situation of the land, it was clear that the presence of the railway cutting and the bridge were a nuisance. It is understandable then, given the obvious, long term abandonment of the trackbed if cuttings were gradually filled, and land was used for 'putting things on'. As time advanced the railway was gradually disappearing. This little stretch of a mile of old railway, with two water and two road crossings could easily have blocked WHR total restoration, had the FR not pursued the project with vigour at the time that it did..

Bridge OB54 (*OB31.87*) original NWNG bridge at Bryn Gloch was demolished. Greater clearance was needed for Garratt locomotives, and the old bridge had already been bypassed, because of the impossibility of getting caravans across it. Work started at Bryn Gloch in February 2002, with the intention of trying to minimise disruption to the tourist season for that year. The weather was not kind, it rained a lot, nevertheless work proceeded quickly. The new bridge is a taller structure than the original. Almost all of this height lies below the caravan park's ground level on either side, and it was arranged to offer only a modest hump to road vehicles crossing. The obtrusiveness of the railway at this point has been reduced to a minimum.

*Above: OB54, the demolished western approach ramp shows in this photo of 19th February 2002, that this bypassed and partly demolished structure was too steep and too narrow to be of any use to the caravan site. As it was too low for Garratts, the only solution was to demolish it and begin again. Even the decorative brickwork in the arch could not be used again - it was a throwaway bridge.*
**WHLR - Jan Woods**

*Above: By 1st March 2002 the rebar forest grows, concrete pouring is taking place, and the diggers work shows how much excavation was needed in order to place this bridge. The view looking south.*
**WHLR Jan Woods**

*Left: A view in the same direction just two weeks later shows the rapidity of progress. One abutment is poured and the shuttering is off; the shuttering for the other is in place.* **WHLR Jan Woods**

*Right: This is a bit of a joke - but actually, it is a wonder the WHR land is left there at all. However, what is in this little corridor, right by the Cwellyn Water Treatment Works, and next to the Bryn Gloch camp site, was certainly not enough to build a railway on, and was not as much as was owned by WHR either. So all this was changed when the fencers arrived.* **Mike Schumann**

*Below: The Roland rail Movers grasp the next pair of rails ready to be laid, but that will be far away, down at the end of the straight at the Bryn Gloch site, in this view of 25th August 2002. This track is going to have a bit of a wait. The picture below shows it just about to be extended, as the bridge UB56 is almost ready - and that's in March 2003!* **WHLR**

*Below: The track was part laid from the Tros y Gol site, that had road access from the A4085, back to the Bryn Gloch site on 10/11 August 2002 and finished later. There was no connection with the Caernarfon end of the railway until July 2003. It was irritating that track was laid and then had to remain idle, but the way that the bridges rebuilt on different timescales caused the project to be disjointed was a major planning and logistical imposition. When the Tros y Gol bridgeworks are completed, in rear of this view of 28th March 2003 - which will be soon, the track will head south towards Salem and Plas y Nant.*

But it was necessary to dig deep for the new bridge's foundations leading to deepened approach cuttings. This involved lowering the trackbed through the site of the old bridge, and its approaches to match the new levels in the area. The trackbed lowering work had to wait until the bridge was replaced, as the caravan site would have been disrupted even further by severing the access roadway that had been made to avoid the old bridge. OB54 (**OB31.87**) was in use from July 12th 2002. The track came through the area in September 2002, but this section of the railway then lay isolated and unused for almost ten months, until connected over the finished Afon Gwyrfai crossing UB51 in July 2003.

Jones Bros of Ruthin were working on the trackbed southward from Bryn Gloch from 7th January 2002. It was all part of the 3a contract, that ended at Pont Tros y Gol, UB56 (**OB32.48**) at Cae Hywel, some 8 miles from Caernarfon and 4 miles from Rhyd Ddu. After emerging from the cutting at Bryn Gloch the line levels out, to a gentle climb, with almost no curves, for a half a mile or so, until beyond the third crossing of the Afon Gwyrfai at Pont Tros y Gol. On the eastern side of the railway is the extensive Cwellyn Water Treatment Works, serving north west Wales. Water is piped from the Gwyrfai at Plas y Nant and processed here for drinking. The water main was located under the trackbed from just north of the treatment works, through OB54 and OB53 after which it went into an adjacent field. Over most of this length the railway was moved to one side and lowered leaving the pipe in the cutting side. Only at OB53 was the pipe just below formation level. However it was made of

steel and was corroding in the acid water, such that Welsh Water could foresee the time when they would need to replace it or risk a burst with serious cost implications. They chose to renew the pipe on a different alignment.

This was the place that got the blame for an outbreak of Cryptosporidium in 2005, when 231 people were affected. It has since been extensively upgraded by Dŵr Cymru (Welsh Water), at a cost of £13m. Apparently the presence of the railway acted as a constraint upon the construction. This goes to show that urgent work of this nature would have unhesitatingly taken what railway land was necessary, had the railway been left 'undefended'.

The trackbed here had been left rather narrow, but the fencing contractor sorted that out. Thereafter the Tros y Gol site was used as a road access to Bryn Gloch when needed, and when the Bryn

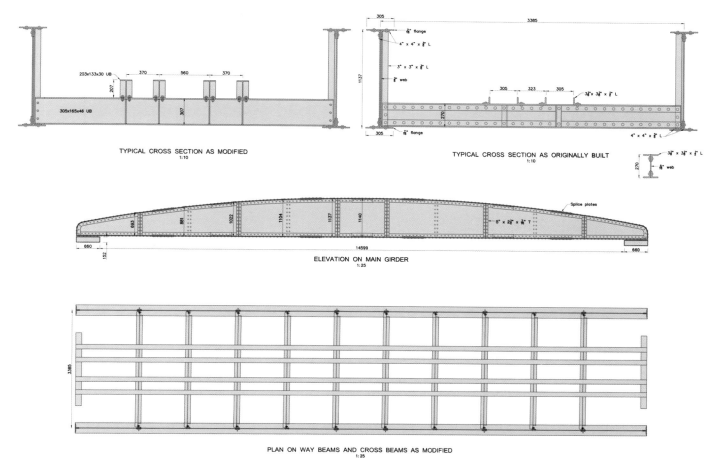

TYPICAL CROSS SECTION AS MODIFIED
1:10

TYPICAL CROSS SECTION AS ORIGINALLY BUILT
1:10

ELEVATION ON MAIN GIRDER
1:25

PLAN ON WAY BEAMS AND CROSS BEAMS AS MODIFIED
1:25

**Drawing by John Sreeves**

*Above:* Pont Tros y Gol, UB56, was removed from place, parked on the north bank of the Gwyrfai, then the original cross members were replaced, whilst thorough de-rusting and repainting of the beams happened. All was then reassembled, painted and placed back in its original position on suitably improved abutments

*Below:* In situ on 28th March 2003 the suitably overhauled bridge, now awaits track, so that it may, support Garratts. This much weight probably exceeded anything previously carried - though after an overhaul like this, it is perfectly capable of bearing it. This wrought iron beamed bridge from the 19th Century has been around for some 140 years, and now it's waiting for a new adventure!

*Right: The bridge has been lifted out and placed within easy reach on the north side of the river. Work is going on to remove corrosion and to paint the bridge, then the new cross beams will be inserted and the new waybeams will be added.* **WHLR**

*Below: The overhauled Pont Tros y Gol is lifted fom its berth on the north bank of the Afon Gwyrfai, to be lowered into the rebuilt abutments prepared for it on 24th March 2003.* **WHLR**

Note: Our impeccable Welsh correspondent states: 'The name Tros y Gol is not right. Trosgl the location is correctly 'rough ground' not Tros y Gol, as this would make no sense - literally 'over the Gol' - the river here is the Gwyrfai. The wrong name has arisen from a typo at some time or other.'

*Below: On 26th April 2003 the view south shows neatness arriving in force. A couple of lengths of track were laid across the bridge, and sleepers are laid out on the fresh ballast, ready for the track to be laid towards Salem . The continuous sleeper decking can be seen, together with the walkways. There is no hint of the massive amount of work that has taken place, it's becoming just another railway bridge.* **WHLR**

Gloch bridge job was finished, the trackbed was levelled and dressed with crushed slate, then rolled. Of course the bridge UB51 (the last Gwyrfai crossing at Betws Garmon) acted as a barrier for the track crossing onward until June 2003. However the track was laid on this isolated stretch in August 2002, across the Bank Holiday weekend. It remained an isolated section, but was extended to connect both of the two NWNG hogsback girder bridges to be refurbished. From Pont Tros y Gol, UB56, to UB64 was in the next contract. The rail connection was not made with Waunfawr until the completion of Pont Betws Garmon (UB51) in 2003.

## Contract 3c-1 Cae Hywel to Castell Cidwm.

The description is linear, but the timescale is not.

The odd thing is that after the recovery of the WHR rails in 1941, the bridges remained; presumably the Ministry of Supply just wanted the 'easy to get' steel. This left three NWNG hogsback girder bridges at Betws Garmon (UB51), Pont Tros y Gol (UB56) and Plas y Nant (UB64). They became something of an icon for the WHR - probably because people tended to photograph them as remnants after the track had gone. The beams were the same for each bridge, and they are each made from wrought iron. As has been described, one of the bridges (UB51) was replaced with a longer span, and has been retired. All WHR bridges have been overhauled and upgraded to take the 7 tonne axle loading of the Beyer-Garratts ($K1 = 8t$).

UB56 (**UB32.48**) had been used for access by a resident whilst the railway was in long disuse. A replacement roadway across a ford was therefore provided for access. In fact this was most useful, as it allowed maintained communication from bank to bank when UB56 was under restoration. The bridge was taken out of position and placed on the north bank, so that it could be accessed more efficiently for the work that was needed. The beams were cleaned and painted. All 10 cross beams were replaced, with their webs increased from 270mm to 307mm, and four steel waybeams (along the bridge) were added, with webs of 207mm. The abutments required renewal, and new concrete ones were constructed. The contractors piled to protect the sides from the river, and across the Christmas - February period of 2002/2003, the abutments were completed with stone cladding. On 24th March 2003, the work was advanced enough for the

*Everyone knows the 'Land of my Fathers'' stuff that passionate Welshmen enjoy in their cups, and they really mean it - which is good. For all railway enthusiasts this is surely the equivalent - it's Grand Sentiment, and it shows we care about things? If everyone knew how much it meant to see this sight of the valiant and ancient little Prince of 1863, puffing gently up the slope to Salem, with the train carrying Her Majesty's Inspector of Railways (26.07.03) they would understand what fighting for the restoration of this railway was about. It hadn't been over long since the last steam train, just 70 years or so - and it really meant something to see it.*

bridge to be craned back into position on its new abutments.

The wooden sleepering across the bridge is continuous. Mesh steel walkways were added. The spans were strong enough to take the extra dynamic load of Garratt and Beyer-Garratts.

During November 2002, whilst the bridge was taken out for refurbishment, track had been laid southward. When the bridge refurbishment was completed, a couple of lengths of track were laid across it in early April 2003. The connection was made in the week beginning 23rd June 2003, and this allowed rails to be brought up by train from Plas y Nant, to tackle the connection across UB51 at Betws Garmon. Phase 3 was not a smoothly flowing and continuous project, work proceeded at numerous locations at one time, and this sometimes made life difficult.

The engineering work on this section of about one mile, between the third and the fourth crossing of the Gwyrfai, took the line on a rising trajectory, passing by the hamlet of Salem to enter the Nant y Betws, through a narrow gap at Plas

y Nant. There are some short climbs at around 1:60, but nothing to alarm a serious mountain climbing engine like a Garratt. Along the A4085 at Salem, there is a splendid view across the road, the river and the velvety grass in a field, of the trackbed rising up the hillside to disappear round a sinuous curve. It's the sort of sight in which the narrow gauge specialises; it was a place where you would discover others, and in muted conversation agree that they too longed to see a train. The FR doesn't really do 'train in the landscape' in the same public fashion. Somehow it is a very private railway. Yet you can hardly miss the Welsh Highland here at old Salem. Alas those that had lived in peace in Bryn Afon, opposite Salem, with their public footpath over the laminated wooden Gwyrfai bridge, needed to have another access. Their road access was along the trackbed, and that was taken from them by the re-establishment of the railway. This was part of mitigation, and the Salem Quarry was briefly re-activated, to obtain the

*Above: Salem Quarry was re-opened by the Railway to create space and supply fill for a new access road that had been promised in mitigation to a householder next to the track.* **WHLR**

stone needed to build a new access road alongside the railway, and then an accommodation crossing was made, to return the road to its original course. The access road for Bryn Afon is quite a long one, it reaches a gated exit that gives on to the A4085 via a discreet minor road near to bridge OB62. The minor road joins the A4085 on its way to Castell Cidwm, and is but a thread on the map. that gives access to the dwelling at Penygaer, and one would hardly know that it is there. It rises over the railway on Pont Cerrig y Rhyd, OB62 (**UB33.49**). Today the old NWNG bridge is back in rail use, with the underneath of its arch being tickled

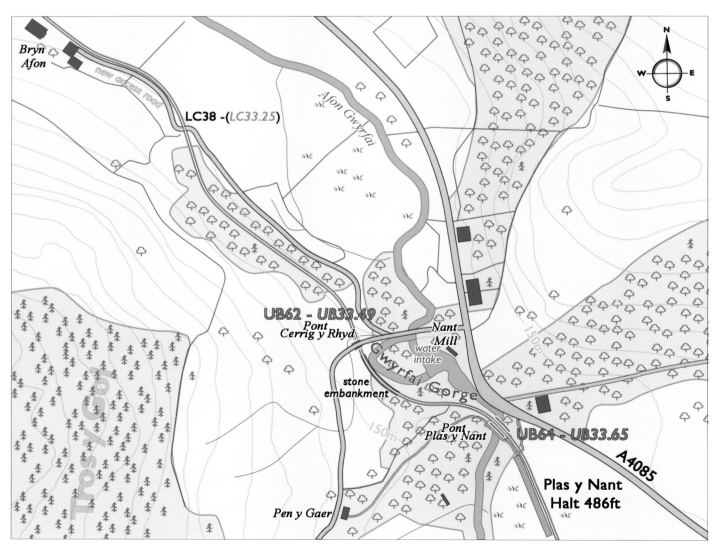

*Left:* *The bridge UB 64 in 1997, with fragments of the timber way-beams still in place. The main beams were sound, but it was necessary to do a great deal of other work which cannot be seen, and cross members and waybeams required replacement.* **WHLR**

*Below:* *The bit that could not be sen in the view above, was the depredations of the Afon Gwyrfai over the years. This needed attending to, and the job was done by jacking each end and propping it 'in the air', whilst new abutments were constructed. This is the northern end looking a bit precarious.* **WHLR**

*Below:* *On 17th November 2002, the south end of the bridge is in a state of suspension whilst new abutments are made. The flood span openings were rebuilt and the centre support was recreated. A coffer dam is in place on the abutment.* **WHLR**

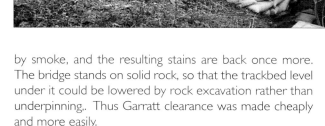

*Below:* *The job is almost done, and it is nearly time for the track to be reinstated. Note the walkway and extension bridge pieces for access to Pen y Gaer, another mitigation measure.* **WHLR**

by smoke, and the resulting stains are back once more. The bridge stands on solid rock, so that the trackbed level under it could be lowered by rock excavation rather than underpinning,. Thus Garratt clearance was made cheaply and more easily.

The line rises for a short way at 1:60 on the south side of the bridge, it curves away from Salem towards Plas y Nant, and passes through some of the most intimate and connected sections of WHR route. In the Gwyrfai Gorge, the railway is fitted in close proximity to river and road, all occupying the gap in the hills. The railway curves sharply from the bridge on to a stone embankment that carries it along a bend in the river some way below. This embankment, perhaps more properly stone wall, had in part been undermined by river erosion, and had to be restored. Opposite at Nant Mill, is the weir from where the water supply is piped down to Cwellyn Water Treatment Works from a pool that can be glimpsed from the train. The line curves on to solid ground for a short stretch, and then runs on another wall, over a hogsback girder bridge, out of the narrows, and into the Nant y Betws.

Repairs to the stone embankments around Nant Mill might have been straightforward, but the logistics of the restoration of UB64 (**UB32.48**) meant that it was more practical to overhaul the bridge in place, so it was hoist on to supports to keep it clear of the works going on around it. Both abutments had to be replaced, and the flood relief openings needed to be reconstructed.

Starting in July 2002, the whole job took just under a year before trains could run over it, . The consultants had planned to stitch the old abutments together with stainless steel dowels, but this turned out to be impractical. Two months after the contract should have been finished, they produced an alternative solution, leaving the contractor to work into the winter months on this job.

*On 28th March 2003, a view from across the Afon Gwyrfai, up to Bryn Afon, from the public footpath. The residents (rightly) are concerned about their privacy, as the footpath does not lead up to the intriguing gate - that is private - instead it traverses the field diagonally, and crosses the line further down. Disruption to this area was on a scale not witnessed since the WHR was removed in 1940. The track has now been put back, after all the fuss. Bad news ahead though, it might go quiet for a while, but do they know they are next to a celebrity railway? In the future this will mean disruption on a regular basis. For supporters, the railway is being reinstated into a delightful, rural cameo. For detractors, the tourist railways have clouds to their silver linings!*

*The railway experiences another of its sudden turns of 'mood' here in its progress from Caernarfon to Rhyd Ddu. It has just been shoehorned between river and rock on a stone embankment. At Plas y Nant it crosses the Afon Gwyrfai for the fourth and final time to run uphill, south, out of the clutches of the narrows at Salem, and under the big sky of Snowdon. After traversing bridge and flood spans, the line passes through Plas y Nant Halt, and heads for the flanks of Snowdon, with the dark waters of Llyn Cwellyn on its western side. From here onward the train glides through big views as well as beautiful scenery. 28th March 2003.*

All pictures were taken on 28th March 2003; this is a view of the work on the trackbed at Castell Cidwm. The Castell Cidwm Lakeside Hotel is an 18th Century fishing lodge on the shores of Llyn Cwellyn, a short way westwards, down the road behind the camera. The picture was taken from bridge OB71. In the distance the embankment stretches back towards Plas y Nant; the far curve is on the river bank near to the shallow Ty'n y Weirglodd (Meadow House) cutting, and beyond is the boggy ground before the widened area for the loop and the halt. There are drainage works visible in the picture, and well there might be, as this is a place that can flood after rains. The trackbed in the picture is all but level at this point.

The trackbed stretches under Castell Cidwm bridge (OB71) and on into the distance across the land of Caeau Gwynion Farm. Hereabouts was the temporary terminus of the NWNG, and a halt, though there do not appear to be any remains. If the original course of the line was to avoid the boggy ground and run to the east (left) of here, then the cost would indeed have been high for this. In the far distance, are the flanks of Snowdon itself. The scraped earth cutting sides hide the considerable works needed to restore the railway - they will soon green over. This bit was expensive.

*On 30th April 2005, NGG15 No. 143 moves smoothly on to Plas y Nant Bridge with the afternoon train from Rhyd Ddu to Caernarfon. The bridge looks fine, testament to the excellent job that was done here, and proving beyond doubt that the ancient structure is perfectly capable of taking 62 tonnes of Beyer-Garratt. The bridge, with attendant lay-by on the A4085, happens to be a star vantage point on the railway, it guarantees an 'Ahhh' photograph every time, in either direction.*

Temporary supports were placed underneath both ends of the bridge, and coffer dams were constructed to allow work to take place on abutment replacement and strengthening.

The Afon Gwyrfai does not have a straight run through this bridge opening. The river turns to pass under the railway, and over the years of closure, without any regular maintenance, the existing abutments had been damaged to the point where replacement was the better option. It was important to do an excellent job in this difficult location, and the new abutments and flood relief openings were constructed in reinforced concrete, faced with stone, to replicate the visual appearance of the old bridge. During the removal of permanent supports, for a while, the bridge stood on its temporary supports, shorn of any connection. This created a rather odd sight.

There were minor crises with a full river, but not on a massive scale. The coffer dams did have to be pumped out on occasions when the river rose, but this did not cause any serious delays. The abutment repair and replacement work was completed by the end of the year 2002.

The hogsback bridge required the replacement of its

***Above:*** *Roland Doyle inspects the almost finished bridge on 30th March 2003. Note the access walkway for Pen y Gaer.*

***Left:*** *The Plas y Nant Bridge flood spans, for when the Gwyrfai becomes full of water.*

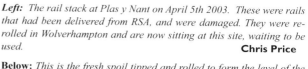

*Left:* The rail stack at Plas y Nant on April 5th 2003. These were rails that had been delivered from RSA, and were damaged. They were re-rolled in Wolverhampton and are now sitting at this site, waiting to be used. **Chris Price**

*Below:* This is the fresh spoil tipped and rolled to form the level of the trackbed. The view toward Cwm Planwydd, on the other side of Llyn Cwellyn shows the course of the line running straight to Ty'n Weirglodd. Alas this pristine state would not endure, the trackbed has sagged since. **Jan Woods WHLR**

*Below:* Jim Comerford's view down of the whole area shows the shallow Ty'n Weirglodd cutting and curve, with the Lakeside Hotel, Castell Cidwm in the distance. **Jim Comerford**

crossbeams, as well as new waybeams. The wrought iron crossbeams were replaced by ones of steel, and four new rolled steel joist waybeams were placed on top, angled to allow the track on the bridge to curve. To replace the crossbeams a suspended scaffolding floor was built, and this work took place through January 2003. There were extension beams fitted to permit a walkway to be hung off the upstream side of the bridge. This was to facilitate an access by foot to the nearby Pen y Gaer dwelling, and was a mitigation measure. When the bridge was seated back on to its abutments it sat slightly higher than in the past.

On March 15/16th 2003 a volunteer working party gave the bridge its first coat of paint. The temporary track laid on the bridge was made permanent on July 24th - commissioning allowed the Inspectors' Train to pass on 26th July 2003.

The story on the line elsewhere was operating to a different timescale. On 12/16th March 2003, the Head of Steel was still not across UB51, Pont Betws Garmon. Tracklaying from the south from Rhyd Ddu was progressing past the old Clogwyn incline, not yet approaching the Glan yr Afon Viaduct, though the trackbed was cleared and fenced from Plas y Nant, to the south, through Snowdon Ranger. Pressure was strong to get the railway

finished - it was a Millennium project after all.

The remainder of contract 3c-1 concerned reaching Castell Cidwm bridge, OB71 (**OB34.57**) and achieving the headroom needed to take Garratts. The first work on this contract had started in at Plas y Nant in October 2002 with the establishment of a ballast dump on the south bank (east side) of the Gwyrfai. Just beyond the bridge, the Pen y Gaer access footpath crosses the railway. Extra land had been acquired here, in order to construct a passing loop, and the Plas y Nant Halt was made later on the western side of the railway. History in this area has already had a mention. Spooner had determined the original course as running eastward of that built - indeed that was the authorised route. It looks like he wished to avoid boggy ground and risk of flooding. Yet the NWNG was built direct to a temporary terminus at Castell Cidwm. Whether economy dictated to the contractor construction by the direct route is not known, but there is a deviation here within the Limits of Deviation. Though cheaper to build, it is a difficult place for a railway as it is on a bog, which when the reconstruction environmental survey was conducted indicated some rare plants. A compromise was reached, to widen the embankment to take two tracks, and enough material was added to remove the existing dip. The embankment settled essentially to its original level. When repeated, the same thing happened again. Investigative soil mechanics found nothing solid in the first 7m below formation level, with a small portable probe rig. Thus, the embankment was left to settle. There is therefore a railway with a dip in this area.

Mike Worthington and the Friends of Plas y Nant, a former Christian Endeavour Holiday Home, got together to raise the funds to build the halt. It took them two years, but the target was hit and the Plas y Nant Halt opened for business on 15th

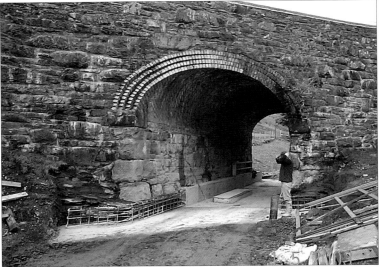

*Left: The first part of the underpinning on a slight curve has been cast, and the rebar is in place for the support to be cast on the north side of the bridge..* **Roger Dick**

*Below: This deceptive and neat scene on the south side of Castell Cidwm bridge conceals three months of work. The cutting sides are being neatened to a finished profile not far from that of the original.* **Roger Dick**

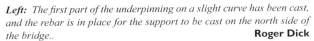

*Below: The last rail length was placed into position at Castell Cidwm on 17th July 2003. The fishplates were bolted together in appropriate weather, making the rail continuous from Rhyd Ddu, all the way to Caernarfon.* **WHLR**

26. 3. 2003

*Below: The rails are now continuous from Caernarfon to Rhyd Ddu, though there is still much to be done. Here on the north side of Castell Cidwm Bridge (OB71) the drainage works and the specially made baseplates can be seen. The baseplates allowed the track to be positioned lower on the invert, thus reducing the amount of loft needed.* **Jan Woods WHLR**

May 2005. The Home closed in 2007 but the replacement hotel plugs the little station on their website. The siding has gone.

The level of the water in the Afon Gwyrfai is not very far below the level of the land on which the embankment was constructed. The risk of flooding is present under Castell Cidwm bridge. The estimated expenditure for Phase 3 had been around £4m. With all the costs rising, the later parts of Phase 3 were becoming difficult to fund, and to make matters worse, the nature of some of the contracts made them take longer than was hoped. Castell Cidwm was full of challenges and contributed to these problems.

OB71 was the final NWNG road overbridge needing to be dealt with. There are no further road bridges over the railway until Pitt's Head. The bridge at Castell Cidwm takes the accompanying road, the A4085, across the railway to the west side, where it stays, running along the shore of Llyn Cwellyn, right up the valley, past Rhyd Ddu, until Pitt's Head. The track under OB71 had again to be lowered to provide the necessary headroom for Garratt locomotives. It was decided that the best way of dealing with the work at this point, was to dig down and place a concrete invert to connect the two abutments and to

keep them stable. However there were flooding complications that had a great bearing on the work.

This area beyond the bog lands at Plas y Nant does not rise much as it crosses the fields below Ty'n y Weirglodd. There is risk of slow drainage to the Afon Gwyrfai in spate, but there is worse. The OB71- **OB34.57** bridge hole was drained by an open ditch about 200m long, leading to a culvert under the railway, and then

**Left:** *A nice day for 'pegging out' through Caeau Gwynion Farm. The warm October sun streams down on distant Snowdon, with its hat of cloud . Soon the fencers will come to enclose the land and the return of the railway will have begun.* **Roland Doyle**

**Below:** *It's a wet spot under Castell Cidwm bridge. The sun's still shining (just), the fences are now up and the vegetation is coming down. This spot needs efficient drainage and there is work to do to clear the cutting. This is the site of the 1877 terminus of the NWNG and later Quellyn Halt\* of the NWNG* **WHLR**
*\*Not Quellyn Lake - that was renamed Snowdon Ranger, to match the hotel*

**Below:** *In the same place, from November 2001, it is now June 2002 and the little strip of compacted ballast is creeping down the hill towards the bridge. The railway is returning.* **WHLR**

area is still subject to occasional flooding during prolonged and heavy rain. As the drainage is improved, the water level falls more quickly, and problems now seldom appear. However, the Castell Cidwm job took 6 months and cost a lot of money.

## Contract 3e-1 Castell Cidwm to Glan yr Afon.

The description is linear, but the timescale is not.

The next section from Castell Cidwm to Glan yr Afon Viaduct (UB95 - **UB37.17**)was in a new contract area, 3e-1, for which the principal contractor and planning responsibility lay with WHLR. Once through Castell Cidwm bridge, the last overbridge on the NWNG, the route climbs steadily at 1:90, crossing the contours one by one. It's not steep; the rate is about 50ft every mile, but the rise is good for the view. Work on preparing the trackbed up to the workbase established at Snowdon Ranger, 10 miles from Caernarfon, began in May 2002, as foot and mouth restrictions were ending. The trackbed was in reasonable condition in this area, in contrast to that later between Glan yr Afon and Rhyd Ddu.

The farmer at Castell Cidwm was not happy at having the railway as a barrier across his land, but due process had been observed. The fenceline was derived from surviving artefacts, and from the 1916 OS Maps, upon which was marked the original land ownership. The fences were erected, the accommodation crossings re-established, and the vegetation removed. Along the section the civil engineering works required varied greatly from place to place. Drainage had to be re-established with efficiency, thus all culverts needed reconstruction. Excavations were wanted in cuttings to remove the accretion of years of neglect; gabions were placed where needed. Walls required reconstruction; embankments eroded by wind and rain needed

by pipe to the river, under the farmers field. In times of flood the river water backed up to the roof of the culvert under the railway. The poor drainage from this bridge hole is compounded by the fact that the adjacent farmer has a four inch pipe under his field that discharges vast quantities of water into the cutting during times of heavy rain. There were difficult ground conditions on this site. Solid rock impeded the lowering of the approach on the northern end, and made the excavation of the drainage ditch more costly and longer to execute. Attempts at underpinning the bridge, as had been done previously, failed due to the fact that the bridge was founded on compacted, waterlogged sand which flowed out as the water was pumped away. A water main had to be relocated deeper, below the track, and this required a deep trench on the southern side. So, the excavated lower approach trench was developed into a neat reprofiling of the cutting on either side. A concrete floor was laid in under the bridge, and in order to minimise the amount of drop needed for the track (and to minimise the effects of flooding), the rails were not placed on sleepers. Instead they were attached to steel baseplates that were bolted directly to the concrete floor. Some 60 holes were needed for this; the baseplates were fitted, and the track was screwed to the baseplates on 13th July 2003. The

**Left:** *Taken by Jim Comerford above Snowdon Ranger on 31st March 2003, this view down the Nant y Betws shows clearly how the track writhes up the slope from Castell Cidwm, past Caeau Gwynion farm and on to Snowdon Ranger station below.* **Jim Comerford**

**Below:** *The track has reached as far as it can get to the bridge OB71 at Castell Cidwm in this view of 29th March 2003. Inside the rails are those waiting to be laid. They will be picked up by Roland Rail Movers and laid as soon as the ballast is down and the sleepers are laid out.* **WHLR**

**Below:** *The tracklayers' train chugs in to the temporary depot at Snowdon Ranger behind Taxi 2, pulling Rail Movers behind it. This view is from May 2003, during the tracklaying on the one mile section to Castell Cidwm.* **WHLR**

to be restored, and the movement of livestock had to be facilitated by accommodation crossings. The railway gradually re-emerged in a way that is rare on such a scale, from south to north.

At Snowdon Ranger there was no loop or pointwork planned for the site, just a halt. There is a YHA hostel on the A4085 below, a very short walk away. In addition, this is the place where the Snowdon Ranger Path starts up Snowdon. In June 2002, drainage works were done, and in August the ground was built up for platform and shelter. By the end of May 2002, after clearing and scraping the formation, the rolled slate waste was laid south along the grade from Snowdon Ranger to Glan yr Afon, the end of Contract 3-e1, and then north to Castell Cidwm. Ballasting then started from the Castell Cidwm end, and together with the laying out of bundles of steel sleepers, reached Snowdon Ranger farm crossing by October 5th, 2002.

Rail was to be laid in both directions from Snowdon Ranger, and thus a considerable rail stack was established from February 2003. A container to act as locoshed for *Dolgarrog*, the track loco, was parked there, facing south. The container was later turned for the north tracklaying. Tracklaying south started on 2nd February 2003, towards Glan yr Afon, and was completed in the second week of April. Tracklaying north from Snowdon Ranger began

on 12th April, and was within sight of Castle Cidwm by May 10th, although the join-up through to Waunfawr was not until July. At Snowdon Ranger itself a 3 phase, 11kv electricity transmission line had to be buried before the earthworks could then begin for the platform. The gap between the two sections remained open until the halt platform was completed, in May 2003, with tarmac laid and a concrete plinth for a shelter to be built subsequently.

By June 2003, the rail stack was clear and ballast was laid in the gap, which received its rails on the weekend of June 21st/22nd. After adjustment, the focus for tracklaying switched to the gap in the track at Plas y Nant, in the north. When connected, the whole pace was tidied up, and supply trains began to run. However it was not until 2009 that the Snowdon Ranger shelter appeared, funded by CRhE. This was an example of the excellent garden shed technology, perfected for the WHR.

Beyond Snowdon Ranger there are a couple of underbridges as the line rises at a steady 1:90 around gentle curves, climbing through the contour lines to gain the height needed to reach Rhyd Ddu. The railway passes above Bron y Fedw Isaf, and there is a footpath that comes up from the A4085 road, crosses under the railway, and rises straight up the hillside to meet the Snowdon Ranger Path up Snowdon. At UB90 (**UB36.83**) the existing small sheep creep was rebuilt with width and height to accommodate walkers, and the neighbouring farmer's all-terrain vehicle. New mass concrete abutments were created, shuttered with walls built from the stone on site, and then topped with an in-situ reinforced concrete deck to carry the ballast and track.

From Castell Cidwm to the site of Jones Bros Contract 3C-2, at Glan yr Afon Viaduct, the count of structures and crossings to be dealt with was: ten accommodation crossings, two occupation crossings, two public footpath underbridges, two bridges over

*Is it the Langkloof with a train on a ballast working? No, it's the WHR on 14th September 2003, soon after Rhyd Ddu opening, with NGG16 No. 143 at Snowdon Ranger, descending, with the shimmer of its exhaust across the flanks of Snowdon and the slate tip of Glanrafon behind.*

streams, many culverts, sidelong ditches, and French drains that all needed reconstruction.

Glan yr Afon Viaduct UB95 (**UB37.17**) spans the fast flowing Afon Treweunydd, 50 feet below. The bridge is an unremarkable plate girder, single-span of 93' 6" (28.5m). Yet of course it is the largest and most imposing bridge on the line from Caernarfon to Rhyd Ddu. At least it would be imposing, except that it is hidden today from all sight below by trees, so it can neither be seen from any distance, nor is there any view of consequence from it. The years of neglect had done it no favours. This was a long and expensive remedial process.

The two wrought iron main beams had survived with little corrosion, despite the lack of paint protection. They supported 20 steel crossbeams, which were seriously corroded. The large wooden waybeams, bolted to the crossbeams had mostly rotted away. The two main bridge beams were judged to be fit for further use, with strengthening, but the expansion bearings had seized and these needed repair and strengthening.

*The recently completed Snowdon Ranger Halt in September 2003, as the Funkey diesel locomotive* Castell Caernarfon *hauls a train through bound for Rhyd Ddu. As finished there is a bare platform, connected by footpath to A4085 road and Snowdon Ranger hostel nearby. It will be a while yet before Snowdon Ranger gets a shelter - these things take time.*

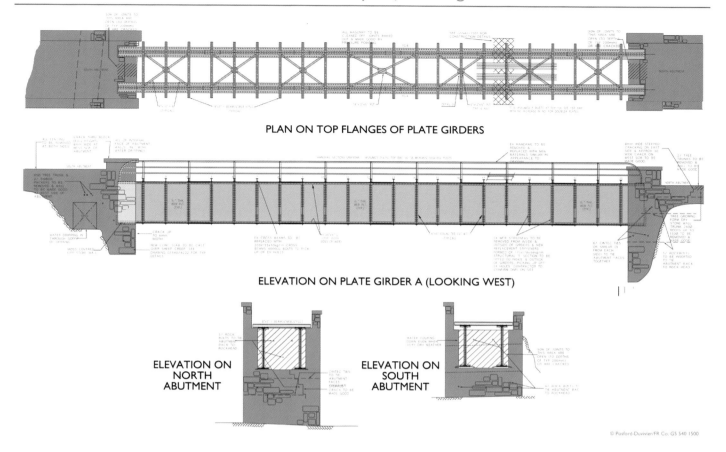

PLAN ON TOP FLANGES OF PLATE GIRDERS

ELEVATION ON PLATE GIRDER A (LOOKING WEST)

ELEVATION ON
NORTH
ABUTMENT

ELEVATION ON
SOUTH
ABUTMENT

© Posford-Duvivier/FR Co. GS 540 1500

*This is a drawing of the unrestored Glan yr Afon Bridge. The text contains the description of what was done, and the illustrations show it.*

The cross-bracing was replaced, additional web stiffeners and stronger diagonal braces were added, materially strengthening the structure. The crossbeams were replaced and four steel waybeams were bolted on the top. A continuous wooden sleeper deck was placed on the waybeams, and both running rails and check rails were installed. On the outside, as the bridge is 8ft wide, mesh walkways were affixed, as on the other metal bridges. New three-rail handrails were also affixed to uprights attached to the ends of the crossbeams. The southerly abutment had suffered from disintegration below one seized bearing and required repair, but otherwise repointing was carried out to restore the abutments to a serviceable condition.

To facilitate delivery of items to site, the trackbed was prepared and completed to the installation of sub-base right up to Glan yr Afon. The first job was to erect scaffolding; this was character forming, and performed by a local contractor in the second week of July 2002. The old timbers were removed from the bridge. Once the scaffolding was in place, everything could be accessed. Brunswick Ironworks were at work manufacturing

***Above:*** *Glan yr Afon Bridge on 12 July 2002. The scaffolding is in place, the wooden waybeams have been removed.* **WHLR**

***Left:*** *The unrestored bridge moulders away, hidden from sight by the trees. It's hardly safe to cross, yet as the railway is in liquidation it is left to rot. Immediately FR Co. accepts liability, things have to change!* **Ben Fisher website**

*Left: Between the girders and below the upper layer of scaffold planks, behold the cross bracing, to be strengthened, and see the web stiffeners which were duplicated.* **WHLR**

*Below: The completed job, with the old tamper hiding its modesty in the trees, about to cross the finished article. It all looks very solid now, in comparison with the picture on the previous page before work started. The bridge has maintained its noticeable end to end camber.* **WHLR**

the various parts needed. They made the new vertical stiffening pieces in the webs of the main beams, and they were in place by mid-January 2003. There was no money available to paint the bridge so a sponsor funded the work, to make use of the installed scaffolding. By May the painted structure had its crossbeams in place, the waybeams and deck were added, and by mid-June the bridge was complete, with the track laid across it by June 19th - but with the check rails still to add. On 20th June the gap with Snowdon Ranger was closed and works trains could access the whole section, from Rhyd Ddu as as far as Plas y Nant.

Two available resources were valuable. Between Castell Cidwm and Rhyd Ddu the services of engineers from both Carillion and Network Rail were made available. The nature of the project offered the opportunity for useful experience to be gained in a railway context. The exchange was mutually beneficial.

There is a theme of exchanges like this running through the FR/WHR story. Getting it right offers real opportunities. For the student or starter, narrow gauge experience on a proper,

professionally run railway, that has most of the problems of the big railway, but doesn't have trains hurtling by at 300kmh is really useful. The potential of the goodwill effect on FR/WHR of NR staff trained in this way is of course extremely important.

## Contract 3e-2 Glan yr Afon to Rhyd Ddu (North)

The description is linear, but the timescale is not.

Contract 3-E2 began on the southern side of the Glan yr Afon bridge, about 11 miles from Caernarfon, and ran the final mile into Rhyd Ddu, excluding the station. WHLR took this contract. This section, built between 1878 and 1881 had been built whilst NWNG was impecunious, and so they had forsaken attention to drainage. So attention had to be paid

*Above: Glanrafon with one of Humphrey's machines excavating from the pile of crushed slate waste that will be spread on the trackbed to protect it from contractors' vehicles.* **WHLR**

*Right: Looking the other way, down towards Llyn Cwellyn at the site of the sidings at Glanrafon. The shell of the distinctive old NWNG building may be seen.* **WHLR**

**Above:** *NGG 16 No. 138 in green heads 5 cars past Ffridd Isaf crossing UB114 on 8th September 2004. This vantage point, accessible with effort from Rhyd Ddu, offers a glorious vista of a down train climbing the gradient to Rhyd Ddu.*

**Left:** *UB114 Demolition begins. There is much work to be done here to dig out both sides of the abutments, so that they may be widened for a vehicle to pass under, September 26th, 2001.* **Roland Doyle**

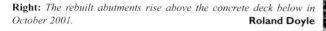

**Right:** *The rebuilt abutments rise above the concrete deck below in October 2001.* **Roland Doyle**

**Left:** *In January 2002 the shuttering from the bridge deck concrete has been removed, the track is across it, and handrails will soon be fitted. It's has similarities to UB90.* **Roland Doyle**

*Left:* This metal gate (taken in June 2001) became guardian to the construction site, at the south end of Phase 3.    **Ben Fisher**

*Below:* In foul weather on 25 October 2001 this lorry is loaded with rails for the rail stack.   The big erratic rock, Graig Rhwygo Blwmar, is still there. The rails now run on the right (east) side of it. Roughly translated 'Knicker Ripping Rock' it was used by the local children as a slide (one side has a smooth incline which would be a magnet even for children today if they could get at it).   The girls in the 1950s of course did not have the protection of trousers, as the boys did, and consequently ran the risk of torn undergarments!    **WHLR**

*Below:* Dogarrog, *a most useful Simplex diesel locomotive preparing to assemble the tracklaying train at Rhyd Ddu North in June 2003. This locomotive was kindly loaned by the energy company Innogy and performed the sort of excellent work in it's natural setting that it was designed for.*    **WHLR**

to that. There are seven accommodation crossings in the section, a public footpath crossing, two small bridges over streams, a sheep-creep (UB114 - **UB 38.77**), and a bridleway/occupation crossing outside Rhyd Ddu.

A large pile of slate waste was delivered to Glanrafon sidings, the wide spot in the trackbed where the Glanrafon Quarry incline landed, and where there were at one time sidings for slate traffic. This was gradually laid out in a layer on the trackbed as protection from contractors' vehicles. It had the advantage of the flat plates of slate 'interlocking' to give it strength.

The Glanrafon area was one to get early attention, and suffered in the 2001 Foot and Mouth

outbreak, when people were allowed back on site but only under careful supervision, and wearing expensive bio-suits.

This was the section past the dwelling of one of the most vociferous objectors to the railway at Clogwyn y Gwin (wine crag), but there were few problems from that source.  Towards Rhyd Ddu (black ford), on the curve at Ffridd Isaf (lower meadow) there were drainage works, and  the cattle-creep in the vicinity UB114 was opened up to be a vehicle accessible road. Tracklaying on the section came from the north between Christmas and New year of 2001/2002 but only to the works at UB114.  In order to widen the sheep-creep, as for UB90, the railway formation had to be removed right down to the backs of the abutments, so that they could be widened. A concrete foundation slab was poured, the new abutments were constructed, utilising the stone from the old abutments to face the new works, and to provide a shutter for the mass concrete fill behind. Then a reinforced concrete bridge-deck, in the form of a trough was built across the gap, and the ballast laid in it.

The track lay fallow to the north until June 2003, when it advanced to the Glan yr Afon (river bank) Bridge and then later in the month became continuous

*This view from Rhyd Ddu car park, looking south is along the approximate course of the old line. The new station is through the trees on the left of the picture. Beyond the trees ahead, is to be the coach lay-by.*    **Ben Fisher**

as far as Castell Cidwm (knave's castle), ready for the big join-up in July 2003.

The works at Rhyd Ddu, terminus of Phase 3, started way back in mid-May 2001, and were affected by the Foot and Mouth Disease restrictions. There were a number of changes that had been determined to Rhyd Ddu, to embrace the alterations that had taken place in the years of closure. A car park had been laid in the former station area, and the old station buildings had been demolished. A toilet block had been built, much needed by those who streamed into this commodious car park in the National Park in their cars, to tramp up the slopes of Snowdon, and to walk in the beautiful hills around. It was therefore decided to 'shift' the station site east a few metres. An island platform was decided upon, along the Waunfawr (large heath) model.

There was no need to complicate matters at Rhyd Ddu, the site sat high to the immediate land around it, so a foot crossing at the platform end was quite good enough. However, with down gradients all around, a generous facility for thirsty locomotives was required. Large water tanks were provided at each end of the station. It was obvious that some sidings were needed, if only for maintenance, and two were planned - there is probably room for more if ever wanted. There was talk of the provision of a stone station building, and even the stone shelter from Llanrwst

was considered at one stage but, WHR Garden Shed technology is as effective for less money, and there was a lot more railway to be built. The car park is fee paying, there are bus stops served (sparsely) by the S4 Sherpa bus, and a coach lay-by was provided.

Contractors Jones Bros started in mid-July 2002, from a base at the southern end of the site. At the northern end, marshy ground had to be consolidated and built up. By mid-August, work had moved outwards to the northern end, where it is crossed by the path up Snowdon, and to the southern end, beyond the car park and site compound. By the August Bank Holiday 2002, excavation had reached its full width across the site. By the middle of September 2002 the principal earthworks were almost finished, and ready for construction of the platform. At the northern end of the site, a new line of fencing and gateposts were being installed for the path up Snowdon, following the station boundary. Tracklaying started at the southern end of the station on January 10th 2003. Tracklaying progressed northwards towards the gap at the level crossing leading to the Rhyd Ddu North site. The set of points previously at Rhyd Ddu North was moved into its permanent position at the north end of the station loop at the start of April, as seen below prior to full assembly. On May 18th volunteers connected the northern point, to the part of the loop line laid in February.

There were new gates on both sides of the line for vehicular traffic to farms and dwellings, and a separate pedestrian crossing just to the north, with gates with both lever and latch releases. The loop was completed in the final volunteer push, immediately before opening; on August 14th sleepers were laid out by Team Wylfa for the headshunt, crossover and part of the siding, ready for rails to be laid over the weekend; the pictures below taken on Saturday 16th show various stages of this work.

The last rail in the Rhyd Ddu siding was laid at 17.00 on 17th August; the station came into public use the next day, on Monday 18th August 2003.

**Above:** *In August 2002 the excavation of the Rhyd Ddu Station site was nearing completion. The area of rolled clay right-of-centre was prepared for a permanent station building. Somehow, even ten years later, other priorities have prevailed, as there's still nothing there yet.* **WHLR**

**Above:** *On 12th October 2002, looking south. The levelled ballast bed curves into the station on the eastern side of Rhyd Ddu Station platform and the sub-base is almost ready for the same on the other side.* **WHLR**

**Left:** *On 25th March 2003 the track has been laid into the station, and the ballast train has been placed in position ready to work north. Note that the western platform face has not been put into position. The cash was being spent very carefully at this stage in the restoration.* **WHLR**

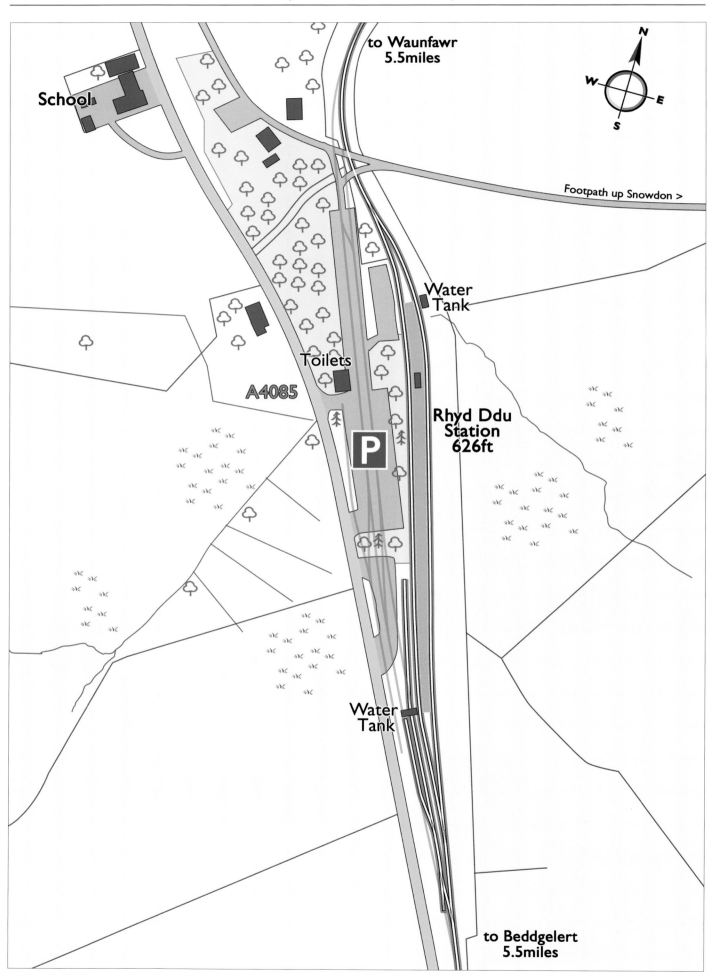

to Waunfawr
5.5miles

N
W   E
S

Footpath up Snowdon >

School

Water
Tank

Toilets

A4085

**P**

**Rhyd Ddu
Station
626ft**

Water
Tank

to Beddgelert
5.5miles

# Phase 3 Commentary - it wasn't plain sailing!

A clash of cultures was inevitable in a project like this, where a grant body, contractors and volunteers must co-operate. There was a major learning curve for everybody to try to deliver the railway on time and to budget, but to find that procedures designed to protect the taxpayer proved to be counter-productive was particularly irksome. A 'drop in the ocean' to some had massive significance on a little railway through the mountains, where every penny counted says Mike Schumann.

After the railway was restored as far as Waunfawr, we realised that we would not have the funds to complete it to Rhyd Ddu in the way that we had planned it. We had some money of our own, raised from supporters, and the Millennium Commission (MC) grant, but all other significant sources of grant money, like ERDF, had dried up in anticipation of Objective 1 funds becoming available. The MC had expected us to complete the restoration to Rhyd Ddu by the year 2000. We had over-run that deadline because of the delays in our permissions to build. The MC had already issued warnings in 1999, over the time it was taking the Minister to determine the TWO, caused by a hiatus created by SNPA. Now there was the ever present threat by the MC of curtailing the project at Waunfawr if we didn't get on with the job of restoring the remaining five miles to Rhyd Ddu.

Making any public admission that funds were short would have made life even more difficult; it was an invitation to have the project stopped. If we managed to restore the railway as far as Rhyd Ddu, then its completion to Porthmadog would become inevitable; if the project stalled at Waunfawr, it might never get any further. So we had to take stern action ourselves to drive the restoration through to Rhyd Ddu or risk termination.

Expenses had to be cutback. We felt obliged not to restore the station building at Waunfawr, a bitter disappointment. We decided that only the minimum work could be afforded for stations like Rhyd Ddu, where the most basic terminal necessary for getting the railway into operation was provided. We were also sure that we could improve the cost performance of some of our contractors. The use of heavy equipment in one location had caused damage to the formation that required expensive repairs. A way forward, using lighter equipment was seen as having a potential financial advantage.

Events played their part in causing us problems. The timing of contract 3a was lengthened first by the decision of Gwynedd Highways to rebuild and widen the A4085 main road bridge, OB53, and then by Welsh Water's decision to reroute the 18" main that ran under the railway formation through this bridge, rather than accept us rebuilding the railway on top of it. Diversion of the water main was delayed by the outbreak of foot and mouth disease, so that after building new abutments for UB51 the contractor was occupied on other contracts, causing it to have to be relet with more delay.

There were however some conditions upon the methods of working that seemed counter-productive. To rebuild the section from Waunfawr to Betws Garmon Station, just short of UB51, a site agent was employed by WHLR, to manage a direct labour force. The job was done well but it was no cheaper per kilometre than by our preferred contractor. Up to this point all the design work was undertaken by negotiated contract by the most competent consulting engineers in the district available to us. The MC were unhappy about this, and wanted the Phase 3 consultant selected by competitive tender. We asked for quotes, and the consultant who quoted the lowest price got the job - it was a different establishment from that we had been using. The cost of obtaining closure with the previous contractor were high, and the quality of the new consultant left a lot to be desired. This led to serious delays, errors on site, and work being done twice. Some critical bridge work drawings were only produced by the consultants after the job was programmed to be completed. There was a change of consultancy management whilst contract 3C and 3A were in progress. This was unhelpful to getting timely and accurate work that led to designs arriving weeks later than expected, and then they contained flaws. In one case a modern version of what already existed was submitted, without appreciating that a considerable amount of excavation, reinforced concrete, and stone cladding could have been eliminated. Had this been accepted the costs would have been much greater. As it was, further delay was added in, and this amounted to the same thing.

At Rhyd Ddu, although the track layout had been fixed for over six months, tracklaying was obliged to begin before the supply of the MOSS alignment data. When it did arrive, it was wrong, showing the northern entry to the loop provided by a set of right hand points with a 1:4 crossing. Considering all loops are entered by left hand points with a 1:9 crossing this caused more delay and interruption to the smooth running of the work. Where variations in the MOSS alignment were requested, because the alignment provided did not fit the existing formation, the response was months in production, so that track was laid without proper data purely to keep the job moving forward.

Alas, many of these last category of problems had to be laid at the door of the insistence upon inflexible and unwieldy procedures designed to safeguard against irregularity, instead of a simple audit. That these irritating and unnecessary proscriptions, should cause failure and extra expense, and that the extra expense should be deducted from the very project it was meant to expedite was extremely frustrating. The outcome demonstrated that 'cheapest' and 'best' are by no means in alliance. The outcome upon Phase 3 was that restoration was delayed further and the costs overran. This was not what was wished for, but we did get to Rhyd Ddu, and beyond. ∎

*At Rhyd Ddu, Welsh Assembly Government First, Minister, Rhodri Morgan, declares the works for Phase 4 open, accompanied by FR Co. Chairman Michael Whitehouse, 1st August 2005.*

# Chapter 8
## Rhyd Ddu - Porthmadog
## Phase 4  2004 - 2011

When the Ffestiniog Railway (FR) managed to reopen over the full distance between Porthmadog and Blaeanu Ffestiniog in 1984, it had to endure life for a while with a fairly crummy outfit, valiantly attempting to improve its 'game' and to make good the railway it had just built. This process took from 1984 to at least 1990, and then the battle for the WHR was taken up. However with the WHR renaissance, arrival at Rhyd Ddu was different. The railway was well constructed, and although there was an excusable shortage of money, there was a general expectation that the newly restored part of the WHR would trade its way out of any difficulty it was in.  You can see from the table below what actually happened; the old NWNG terminus at Rhyd Ddu was evidently not a place to tarry.  Unlike Blaenau it had no natural focus, no slate mine, tourist attraction, no town, no standard gauge branch line to feed it.  There was a car park, a pub, a loo, and the highest mountain in England and Wales; never enough to succour a hungry railway, and it was the same for the NWNG and the old WHR. Of course, shining the harsh light of reality on a tourist railway fuelled by railway

### WHR Bookings: 2002-2006

| Year | Bookings (k) | Comment |
|------|--------------|---------|
| 2002 | 34.8 | Still at Waunfawr |
| 2003 | 50.7 | Rhyd Ddu from Aug |
| 2004 | 58.6 | 1st full year at Rhyd Ddu |
| 2005 | 48.4 | Excitement wanes |
| 2006 | 47.2 | Oh dear! |

*Note: the extension to Rhyd Ddu was a 58% increase in mileage.  The bookings increase of 69% in the first full year was therefore creditable.  For it to fall to 39% in the next full year, and further again the following year did not bode well for Rhyd Ddu as a permanent terminus. [Not that this was ever intended.]*

enthusiasm, reveals that this was building and opening a railway to a set of bufferstops on a remote hillside.  Someone else not far away had already gone to the trouble of building another to the top of the adjacent, celebrity mountain,  so the WHR would face commercial difficulties with Rhyd Ddu if it was intending to remain there as a long-term destination.  The FR Co. Board was clear in its wish to move on, and get the railway restored back to Porthmadog, but there were a number of important hurdles to be overcome first.

An agreement was made early with the National Park Authority, in advance of the TWO application, that before the railway was completed right through the SNP, no intermediate terminal

Note:  The red figures in text and picture captions give the kilometric measurements from Caernarfon '+20'

would be operated, apart from Rhyd Ddu. There were two areas of Snowdonia National Park Authority (SNPA) nervousness: the first was that motor traffic would be generated; the second was that FR Co. might never complete to Porthmadog.  This was an early discussion, before Caernarfon - Dinas was completed, when there was reasonable doubt in people's minds about whether FR Co. would have the means and the determination to fulfil the whole project.

Beddgelert is a desirable place that people want to visit. It is exceedingly pretty, with a delightful narrow bridge near to the confluence of the Afonydd Glaslyn and Colwyn, and streets flanked by attractive cottages in vernacular styles.  Most who flooded to this Snowdonian centre did so by car - the streets were lined with them on a summer's day. There was concern that extending the car park would be inappropriate, and the Authority handed down the condition that the Railway may not terminate, even temporarily before building through, as this would generate too many parked cars.  This might be viewed as strange today, bearing in mind that people travelling to both Waunfawr (opened 2000) and Rhyd Ddu (opened 2003) did nothing of the kind; passengers preferred to leave their cars in Caernarfon, outside the Park, and to take the train in. However, despite this condition, requiring much money to be expended before any could come back from new services, the SNPA sensitivity had to be respected.

The SNPA follows a set of policies, driven by legislation, to which the Authority is bound to adhere [The Environment Act 1995, The Town and Country Planning Act 1990 and others]. The Eryri Local Plan must harmonise with the Gwynedd Structure plan, and the Authority's elected members are charged with interpreting the sometimes woolly wording into a coherent policy, ubiquitous to the Park.  In the three years after the dust had settled from the conflict of the TWA, and the SNPA public inquiry, the WHR had been extended to Rhyd Ddu.  During that time there was no conflict with the SNPA. The 'north' boundary of the National Park is OB54 (**OB31.87**) at Bryn Cloch; the 'east' boundary is the Afon Dylif (**UB52.63**).

Discontinuous restoration as in Phase 3 was undesirable; Phase 4 must be a linear project to the Park boundary and beyond. There were four river crossings to be bridged, numerous stream underbridges, three road bridges - two over, one under; there were two large 'cattle bridges', and a road required in mitigation; two crossing places were needed, one with watering facilities, both with stations; there were many level crossings.  The civil engineering was challenging, with filled in cuttings, disappeared drainage, thin, wasted embankments, steep gradients, sharp curves, and four tunnels.  If that wasn't enough, then there was the Cross Town Rail Link to consider, along with the crossing of the Cambrian Coast Line.  No wonder detractors looked smug,

*(continued on page 202)*

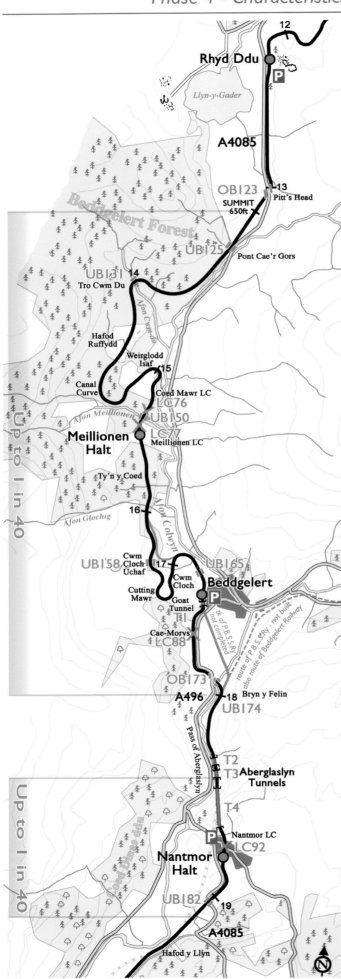

## RHYD DDU - HAFOD Y LLYN CHARACTERISTICS

Rhyd Ddu was the end of the NWNG, and the line onwards was not built to the same standard, and PB&SSR construction had begun with steep gradients arranged for electric traction. To overcome gradients too steep for steam traction, in 1922 WHR built extended loops to reduce the ruling grade to 1:40.

The open mountain scenery along the A4085, on the section just outside Rhyd Ddu, is delightful. Above is the great bulk of Snowdon; to the west the sun sparkles off Llyn y Gader, and it is a place where the train can be paced by car, before the railway darts under Pitt's Head bridge and reaches the summit of the WHR, Y Copa at 650ft /190m.

This is hardly a Himalayan achievement, but the huge open vista and mountain bulk cause the requisite numbers of 'oohs' and 'aahs' from the passengers. The Summit, is at the top end of a tough section northbound, of 4½ miles of line, right up from the Aberglaslyn Pass. When travelling uphill from Beddgelert to Rhyd Ddu, the climb through Pont Cae'r Gors below the Summit calls forth satisfying noises from the locomotive. This section combines sharp curves and a steep grade to make it the most engine unfriendly railway in Britain. To handle a paying load requires powerful locomotives such as Garratts.

Along the side of the line there are long sections of forest, but as the trees are seldom close to the trackside, this part of the journey offers open mountain views and shady glades, a most satisfying experience in both directions. Downhill, the broad sweep of Tro Cwm Du, and the changes of direction round Canal Curve, and through Weirglodd Isaf, are scenic masterpieces. Although ever with trees, this railway does not transit a green tunnel like others, and the gentle pace of progress allows enjoyment of the vistas - long may it remain so.

It so happens that one of the largest caravan and camping sites in Wales grew around the abandoned trackbed. Thus the railway restoration runs through an already installed market. Meillionen Halt was provided to serve the site. The difficult take-off on the gradient, with a heavy train travelling uphill at times of poor rail adhesion, is pleasure for all but the train crew managing the locomotive.

Below the Halt, between Cwm Cloch Uchaf and Beddgelert Station, is the great Cutting Mawr. The line actually dips south of Beddgelert Station at this point, curving twice through 180°, to face south when entering Beddgelert. This is a spectacular piece of railway, arguably the most individual feature on the entire system. Alongside, the run-in to Beddgelert is the 1:28 abandoned grade of the never completed, electric PB&SSR.

Beddgelert (17½ miles from Caernarfon, 7½ miles from Porthmadog) is one of the most sought after destinations in Snowdonia. The village acts as a major traffic generator on the line. The Goat Tunnel (T1), below the station is 42yds, and below this point is the celebrated Pass of Aberglaslyn. This riverside stretch of line allows the passenger the most delightful sylvan views from a narrow gauge train in Britain. There are: a crossing of the Afon Glaslyn, several little tunnels, and superb views down into the white water section of the river. The 306yd long Aberglaslyn Tunnel (T4) is a reverberating and smoky thrill when travelling uphill. The river-view section is very short, and people on the adjacent footpath always wave. Events on this railway are 'quick-fire', with views both narrow and wide.

Beyond the Pass is the tiny halt at Nantmor and a steep embankment on a curve with the A4085 road below. At Hafod y Llyn the line is almost level, and between here and Porthmadog, the character of the railway is quite different. The northbound direction is designated Down, the southbound Up.

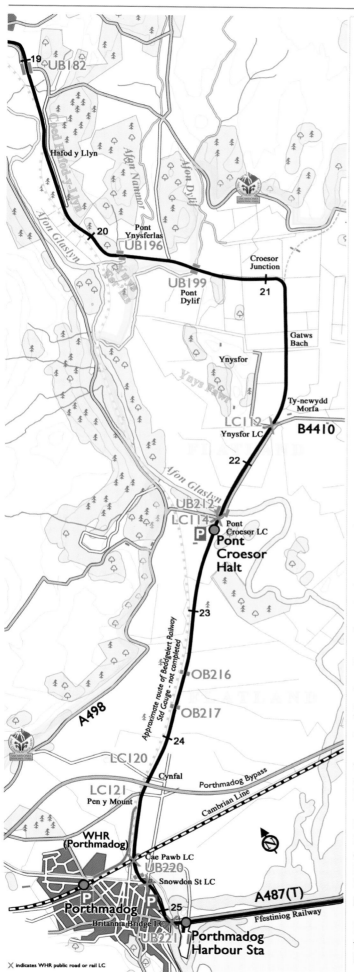

## HAFOD Y LLYN TO PORTHMADOG CHARACTERISTICS

The termination of the gradient section after crossing the A4085 below Nantmor is sudden. The whole nature of the railway changes. Between here and Porthmadog the line has fewer curves and (for 2ft gauge) moves at a rapid pace. Here is Pont Ynysferlas, another truss bridge, over the Afon Nanmor, with an intriguing public footpath attached to it, and a little further on is Pont Dylif, the third in the series of WHR truss bridges designed by John Sreeves.

Croesor Junction, 21 miles from Caernarfon, is a junction no more. The 1864 built Croesor Tramway is now a grass track, and the WHR executes a long curve changing direction through 90°. This area gradually emerged from the Glaslyn Estuary to become farmland when Maddocks built the Cob from Porthmadog to Boston Lodge, and already the mountains seem far behind. Apart from the odd rock 'island' like Ynys Fawr, the land is flat, and the railway has been restored on the little embankment that keeps it above the seasonal Afon Glaslyn floods.

The Croesor Tramway, was the first railway here, built to carry slates mined in the Croesor Valley, high in the hills, down to the ships at Porthmadog. In 1922 the WHR was built along its course, and has been restored to do so again.

Looking north the mountains, with the spectacular peak of Cnicht, dominate the view on this open stretch. It is the longest, flattest run on the system, and was described by historian JIC Boyd as an agricultural trundle. This unimaginative description is confounded by the bright, open vistas of the Traeth. The B4410 is joined at Ynysfor level crossing, to run toward Pont Croesor, a wide, eight-span bridge over the Afon Glaslyn, accompanied by the road that forms a level crossing at right-angles, next to the Pont Croesor Halt. Here there is a loop line to cross trains, and large car parks for the railway and the RSPB Osprey Centre.

The line continues across the flatland, past the old Portreuddin site, and past an area of trackbed that was removed and incorporated into a farm, and thus was recovered to be restored as railway. Also running parallel is the remains of the part-built, standard gauge, Beddgelert Railway, which was intended to reach Beddgelert, but never did. Its earthworks are visible at certain sites up the Glaslyn Valley. The line now passes under the new Porthmadog Bypass, a road fervently wished for, and now provided.

Part of this Beddgelert Railway formed the Beddgelert Siding, which is now operated by the WHHR, and their trains may be seen on the west side of the reconstructed WHR. After the WHHR Pen y Mount terminus, the WHR crosses the Cambrian Coast Line on a flat crossing. This is the only 600mm across 1435mm main line crossing in Europe, and one of the few in the world. Clattering over it is intriguing, and signals the start of Cross-Town Rail Link, through the streets of Porthmadog, leading to the Harbour Station..

At the Snowdon Street Level Crossing, the new course of the line leaves the old, to skirt the car park and the Inner Harbour. It passes the Shell filling station, and enters a 50m radius curve, to take up the centre of the A487 road on the Britannia Bridge, before passing the old Goods Shed into the loop line at Porthmadog Harbour Station, which has been rebuilt with two platforms. The 25 mile journey from Caernarfon is complete.

As Harbour Station hosts both Ffestiniog and Welsh Highland Railway trains, perhaps a FR double Fairlie will replace the Garratt, to haul the train onward 13 miles to Blaenau Ffestiniog. This is now the longest heritage railway in Britain.

**P**aul Lewin a Ffestiniog stalwart, born and bred, was appointed to be General Manager of the FR/WHR undertaking in 2003. He had to launch the WHR into its expansion from Waunfawr to Rhyd Ddu, a five-mile increase, and there needed to be someone in Phase 4 to manage the scope of the construction in a practical and economic manner, and then to operate the railway that had been expanded from 12 to 25 miles long. This was Paul's task, with the minor one on the side of running the Ffestiniog Railway too.

**A**rriving on the railways at the end of Phase 3 it was an urgent necessity to get that railway open. Bear in mind that this was almost to double its length, to exceed the existing Ffestiniog Railway - so it was quite a task. There was a time when we felt we had to test the railways operating ability with a train. It was clear that this railway still needed to have work done on it before all the operating glitches could be eliminated. What was available had to be within our own capacity, as contractors' fees were now out of reach.

It was a surprisingly short time before the rather hazy prospect of extending the railway to Porthmadog became a funded reality. The experience we had gained between Caernarfon and Rhyd Ddu, convinced us that there needed to be a greater involvement with the 'Operators' during the construction stages over the scope of the work. Almost always this process was making the right

*Out on test, crossing UB51, to see if the Phase 3 railway works. Doing this soon exposes any weaknesses that need to be corrected.*
**Dr Ben Fisher**

choice in terms of balancing current and future expenditure. Does one spend freely now to make sure that speeds of 20 mph may be achieved, or does one do a basic job now, at a cheaper price, and improve matters later when the railway is running? This is all good in theory, but the difficulty about large engineering projects is matching the assumptions with reality. Innocent looking items reveal unavoidable expenses upon closer inspection, sometimes from the application of seemingly reasonable but inflexible rules.

UB125 (**UB41.20**), a.k.a. Freddie's Bridge is an innocent enough bridge over a culvert, near the Summit of the WHR at Pont Cae'r Gors. It conceals a great deal of thought leading to an unsatisfactory solution. The bridge is engineered just fine, except that it has caused an operator's problem. This is the breast of the 4½mile ramp of 1:40 gradient up from the Aberglaslyn Pass. Those engines that have the power to ascend this formidable gradient do so better with a little speed in hand. Alas Freddie's Bridge imposes a restriction of 10mph. It also causes a limp descent of the gradient in the Beddgelert direction, allowing time to escape from the timetable. The 10mph cannot easily rise much; the curve at this point demands increased cant to permit the speed limit to be eased. Alas this cannot be,

as the bridge was built subject to a National Rivers Authority restriction on the depth of the culvert. As that restriction means that the culvert is already nearer than one would wish to the minimum depth from girder to cill, to contain flooding in times of heavy rain, and the bridge may not be lowered. Yet if the cant is to increase, to raise the speed, lowering is what needs to be done. It would all cost too much, so a 10mph is in force instead of a 20mph . This is minor in its own right, but it all adds to increase the transit time.

As the line approaches Meillionen Halt, through the campsite, there are two level crossings, Coed Mawr (**LC44.31**) and Meillionen (**LC44.39**). The location numbers show how close together they are. Each is an Open Level Crossing (OLC) and carries a 5 mph speed restriction. Their proximity means that the train is obliged to roll at reduced speed all the way from the start of one, until the train is on the other. Were they further apart, as soon as the locomotive has crossed the crossing, then line speed would be resumed. In this case, a considerable period of time below the natural line speed is needed for the transit of both crossings, and again, it prolongs the journey time.

So the proposal for Phase 4 was that I should act as the moderator for the scope of the project. When problems such as these came up, my role was to broker the compromise between the perfect combined engineering and operating solution, and the minimum cost, basic railway. It was possible to spot things that a relatively modest spend made during construction would lead to an enhanced performance for the operating railway. Doing this was fine when the grant money was pouring in, and the job was proceeding apace. I must have walked between Rhyd Ddu and Beddgelert 50-100 times, bearing in mind that I wore out a pair of deeply tough walking boots, supposedly made to stand such punishment. However, the job got more challenging when the money thinned and everyone was seeking savings. Between T'yn y Coed and Bron Hebog (**LC45.70**) there were two problems that illustrate the compromises that had to be made, and what the effect has been on today's running. Getting a perfect base for the trackbed here, and laying smooth and well supported track proved to be difficult. Yet it was necessary to complete the route to Beddgelert and get the line open to traffic, so only so much of our rather scarce resources were available to priddy this more difficult area. As a result it was not possible to maintain the 15 mph speed here, and it was necessary to impose a speed restriction of 10 mph. The crossing at Bron Hebog was put in as a gated accommodation crossing over the private road/ public bridleway that meets the railway at this point. The gated crossing was cheaper, but the frequency of the gates being left open will probably suggest a change to an OLC, and this may impose a speed restriction of 10 mph. One cannot win!

The original 'ideal' timetable for the WHR assumed an average 19 mph speed, with five, three minute stops. Today the journey takes 58 minutes more than was assumed in that ideal case, and the reasons for that are mainly at the door of the many speed restrictions that had to be imposed for practical reasons during construction, but which we are gradually eliminating as time passes.

The HMRI wished to have but one point of contact for liaison on this railway. As the person charged with defining the scope, and as the likely operator of the railway after, the job fell to me. Thus when we had exhausted our arguments to the point of agreement with the construction people, it was down to me to present the proposals to HMRI to get it passed. This made sense, as when the railway came to open, I was familiar with its foibles through and through. This

*Alas, a storming ascent of the final piece of 1:40 up to Pont Cae'r Gors is rendered a muted chuff by the speed restriction over Freddie's Bridge at the top of the climb. No 87 passes the 10mph limit board on 30th June 2011.*

*LC77 (**LC44.39**) looking towards LC76 (**LC44.31**). At 80m apart the crossings are rather too close, so the speed has to be moderated between the two - it all takes minutes out of the timetable, extending the transit time.* **Dr Ben Fisher**

meant that the experience could be translated into practical operating instructions, and we could get off to a rapid start when trains were permitted to run.

Whilst commissioning the line to Rhyd Ddu, the experience and the lessons needed to be fed into a training plan for Phase 4 and the full 25 mile line. Train crews had rapidly mastered the run to Dinas, but Rhyd Ddu, with two train sets in operation on a good number of days, was a major step change. The exercise revealed a need for some 150 staff members to be competent for the full line, when Phase 4 was complete, and all had to meet the requirements of the HMRI safety submission. And we were going against the grain. On the National Network,

level crossing numbers were tumbling - we were increasing them, and we were adding an unique rail/rail flat crossing at Cae Pawb. We intended regular operation up and down 1:40 gradients, of long heavy trains with Beyer-Garratts - much more difficult on Phase 4 than with the lighter trains we had on Phase 3. Thus training the crews to a high standard was critical in order for the railway to be able to open.

There was also a locomotive problem, as at the time we needed them most, both Garratts Nos 138 and 143 would be coming up for their 10 year overhauls. Thus began the engineering achievement of No. 87's overhaul at Boston Lodge, where generosity, help, hard work, and expertise won, and No. 87 has run 30k trouble free miles since its return to service, allowing Nos 138 and 143 to be overhauled in their turn. Here must be mentioned a quiet revolution that has had many consequences. Oil firing was introduced in the Garraway era to reduce the risk of forest fires on the FR. In fact it turned out to be cheaper than coal and easier on staff and locomotives - though not without its problems. In the 'noughties' oil became prohibitively expensive, with swingeing price increases - we were obliged had to look at coal again, especially with Garratts burning oil in such quantities Fortunately experience with the excellent Lempor-Girdlestone exhaust, we were able to burn coal with complete safety, and massive cost savings. Yet one of the consequences of this, and the need for us to look our best as a major emerging visitor attraction, was the need to spend some pennies on having the carriages cleaned by paid staff.

The longer journey times of the WHR impress upon us the need for excellent rolling assets, with food, comfortable seats, clean loos, and well informed and polite staff on board. There have been many changes made to make this so, and it means that in the future we need to invest wisely in the Sustainable Railway, as the 40 mile asset that has been created has the potential to reach world class standards. The Phase 5 Appeal is heading us in that direction, meanwhile the restored WHR is bringing home the extra prosperity we hoped it would. ∎

## Phase 4 Chronology

| | | |
|---|---|---|
| 18.08.03 | Public service begins from Caernarfon to Rhyd Ddu | The WHR is now halfway restored! Mr Hart searches for funding. |
| 08.09.04 | WAG Phase 4 Funding - Cheque Ceremony | Dr Brian Gibbon, Deputy Minister for Economic Development handed over a cheque at Waunfawr. |
| 23.09.04 | Phase 4 First Sod - Rhyd Ddu | Dr John Prideaux and Mike Schumann cut the first sod for Phase 4 at Rhyd Ddu, with Mike Hart and Roland Doyle. |
| early 2005 | Clearance began | Work started between Rhyd Ddu and Pitt's Head, with Achnashean Fencing. |
| 01.08.05 | WAG First Minister Rhodri Morgan visits the WHR for the official start of construction | Rt Hon. Rhodri Morgan AM visited the WHR, riding on NGG16 No.138, being photographed for the press with some of the local contractors at Rhyd Ddu |
| August 2005 | Phasey Construction start work | Trackbed refurbishment is in progress from Rhyd Ddu Station, and in particular on the difficult job at Pitt's Head. |
| September 2005 | G.H. James Cyf Starts work | Trackbed refurbishment began downhill from Hafod Ruffydd, and put work in hand in Canal Curve. |
| November 2005 | Rail and sleepers | Track materials arrive at Dinas, in the North Yard, in a giant stack |
| early-June 2006 | The Head of Steel is at Copa - 13m | The track reaches the Summit, Pitt's Head is complete |
| 18.08.06 | The Head of Steel is at Afon Cwm Du - 14m | The track arrives at the McAlpine Bridge, UB131, Afon Cwm Du |
| November 2006 | Cae Pawb | Track installed for crossing the Cambrian Coast Line |
| 24.03.07 | Subscribers' Train - 16.5m | Subscribers' Train able to run as far as Cutting Mawr. |
| 31.08.08 | Traeth Mawr -24m | The Head of Steel arrives at Traeth Mawr |
| 28.02.09 | Golden Bolt | Track continuous, Caernarfon to Porthmadog |
| 12.03.09 | Cae Pawb | The first train across the Cambrian was *Vale of Ffestiniog* and ECS for Dinas. |
| 07.04 09 | First service train to Beddgelert | Service to Beddgelert, taking dignitarios from Caernarfon, and then local people for a free ride. |
| 30.10.10 | First through trains, Caernarfon to Porthmadog | The two subscribers' trains ran between Caernarfon and Porthmadog |
| 31.10.10 | The Tracklayers' Train | The first FR train through from Port -Rhyd Ddu. *Taliesin* and *Lyd* together. |
| April 2011 | **WHR reopens** | **At last - the railway is back in service.** |

with 'they'll never do it' expressions firmly in place.

It was clear that achieving the second half of the line, from Rhyd-Ddu to Porthmadog was going to be difficult and expensive. Thus, having got to Rhyd Ddu in 2003, there was a general assumption that a fair period of time would be needed to consolidate the traffic growth, bearing in mind that the extra length of railway made it nearly the same as the FR, which required three train sets to operate it. When the second full year at Rhyd Ddu saw numbers fall 10k, and the third fell further, the pressure came on to operate the new stretch of railway economically, with two sets. Determination to extend did not falter, as it was clear that 'new markets' really were being tapped, and that FR was not competing with itself at all, but that growth needed extension.

## The Funds and the Preparation

The TWO had been applied for the whole line, from Dinas to Porthmadog, because it made sense to do it that way. The application for the grant from the Millennium Commission was made from Caernarfon to Rhyd-Ddu, as it was never thought that the Millennium people would 'buy' a 25 mile line 'in one go', and that there was zero chance of getting such a thing finished by the year 2000. That was quite right, and it proved impossible to build the Phase 3, 12 mile railway project on time and within budget with so many 'unknowns'. The WHR experience left a deep impression on the Millennium Committee, so that they subsequently insisted on all permissions being in place before they agreed to any funding. There would be no more cash from that source; so where was the money to come from to reach Porthmadog? Old favourites like ERDF and Minimising the Problems of Peripherality, (an EU set of funding initiatives for member states on the westward edge of the Union) became more difficult to get, as in 2004 the EU was about to expand to 25 member states, and to enter into places where Wales looked rich by comparison. The general feeling was that Wales had had its share, and that now it was time for the east European countries to have theirs, as they joined as new EU member states. The idea of beginning a 'one shot' extension to Porthmadog without 'grant' funding was not practical - it looked like it could be a long wait at Rhyd Ddu.

Mike Hart had established friendly relations within the Welsh Assembly Government in Cardiff. He found them logical, supportive, and helpful, and though a substantial funding package took him over 2 years to negotiate, matched funding also had to be found in order to get FR Trust and WAG approval to accept the funding package. It was necessary to prove that the FR Co. was doing exactly what it said it would do. And while there were those FR Co. staff members who were disappointed that Caernarfon to Rhyd Ddu had settled in to a steady level of 45k bookings per year, this was an astonishing figure for Rhyd Ddu; it had not abstracted traffic from the FR, (nor from the Snowdon Mountain Railway, that generated about 125k bookings per year), and the WHR traffic was making a noticeable contribution to the local Caernarfon economy. Cars were not flooding into either of the railway car parks in the National Park, and the 12 mile WHR was generally unobtrusive. In fact it was doing what railways generally do, transporting sizeable numbers of people to and from their destinations, without fuss.

For WAG and the Welsh European Funding office (WEFO) to agree that a tourist initiative, such as extending the railway to Porthmadog, was eligible, and had their approval for EU funding, required their consideration of a massive application package

*Dr Brian Gibbon, WAG Deputy Minister for Economic Development handed over a cheque at Waunfawr for £5m, as the grant contribution to Phase 4. Of course it was a little junket, but these are good for business - both government and press like them. From right to left the grandees are; Mike Schumann, FR Co. Director and Trustee, Dr Brian Gibbon from WAG, Dr John Prideaux, Chairman, FR Trust, Roland Doyle General Manager WHR Construction Ltd, and Michael Whitehouse, Chairman FR Co. In front are the children from Ysgol Waunfawr, let out as extras! 8th August 2004.*

of supporting documentation. However, the deciding factor to deliver a grant was that the package submitted (by Mike Hart) must demonstrate to them that the economic return to Wales was worthwhile.

The total cost of Phase 4 was carefully estimated before any submission for grant, and this was £10.766m. It was determined this was eligible for just under 50% funding from European Union Objective I funds, and it was indicated by WAG/ WEFO, after consideration of the application, that £5.2m could be made available. So the question arose over how to find the matched, balancing amount. For a start there were those who were prepared to offer individual sponsorship - under the condition that

*Later in the day of 8th august 2004, Drs Gibbon and Prideaux do their stuff for the cameras and lay out steel sleepers in the direction of Porthmadog.*

they remained anonymous. That was amazingly generous, as the amounts involved were in the millions, and it made the project possible. However, there was still a gap.

There was a need to demonstrate public support for the project, especially against the thin but persistent warble that the whole things was a white elephant, and contrary to the interest of residents. Public support was demonstrated with a public subscription scheme fronted by Steam Railway. The speed and quantity of money that flowed in to the project set a record that has so far not been beaten to date. Perhaps it was the notoriety of the early days of the project, when FR Co. was accused of bully-boy tactics, and 'buy-to-shut'. Whatever it was, the public subscription promise accrued steadily, and there was a good reaction when the same appeal went out in Railway Magazine. Thus the funds to rebuild the railway between Rhyd Ddu and Porthmadog quickly became available - far in advance of timescale anticipated. The detail of the WEFO grant application and the funding battle are expanded, with the full story to be read in Chapter 12.

There was a symbolic cheque ceremony on 8th August 2004,

*Delyth Pritchard offers WAG First Minister Rt Hon. Rhodri Morgan AM the biscuit, on the occasion of the launch of Phase 4 construction on 1st August 2005. This was only fair, as Mr Morgan had given the WHR cake with a fat cheque for £5m, and such support was excellent in making sure that the project was seen with favour by the 'centre' at Cardiff. The band-waggon was rolling with a 'march Cymraeg priodol' - it could not be ignored. The project had proven returns to the community.*

a private 'first sod' ceremony on 23rd September 2004, and a visit from WAG First Minister, Rhodri Morgan on 1st August 2005. The funds were secured with sufficient confidence that construction could be started, way before most people ever thought it possible.

That it happened at all was down to Mike Hart's determined pursuit of the funds, through WEFO, through private individuals, and by encouraging a fund raising team that succeeded in the public arena. Now there was a band-wagon rolling, and there were endorsements in public from national politicians, and thus more of an atmosphere of approval. Of course some still did not get the message locally, thus the press, ever sure that the negative sells papers better than the positive, still referred to the

*Back to the construction office, as Welsh Highland Railway Construction Ltd takes over, under General Manager Roland Doyle.*

WHR as 'controversial'. Political support melted dissent, and the largest subscribing county in the Phase 4 Appeal list was of course Gwynedd. Most importantly, it was now clear to the restorers that the people wanted the railway; the detractors were not the majority, and opposition sprang mostly from fear of change. That

felt good, and offered an injection of self-confidence.

Whilst there might have been visits and celebration, the massive activity of design and planning that was necessary before work could start went on. The new company set up to replace Welsh Highland Light Railway Ltd for Phase 4 was Welsh Highland Railway Construction Ltd, with General Manager Roland Doyle in charge. This was activated from one day per week to every day, based in the Dinas construction office. The organisation for Phase 4 was able to be more canny, as it drew on the experiences of Phases 1-3. The Board of WHRCL adopted the overall management of the scheme, and all looked for ways of keeping expenditure to a minimum.

**1.** Consultant engineers did the detailed design work. Local surveying companies were employed to undertake topographical surveys of the route. Their 'output' was a detailed digital map of all salient features within the boundary fences of the original track bed. The drawings of crossings, culvert headwalls, etc were done on CAD for local contractors to build.

**2.** Full advantage was taken of the expertise of skilled

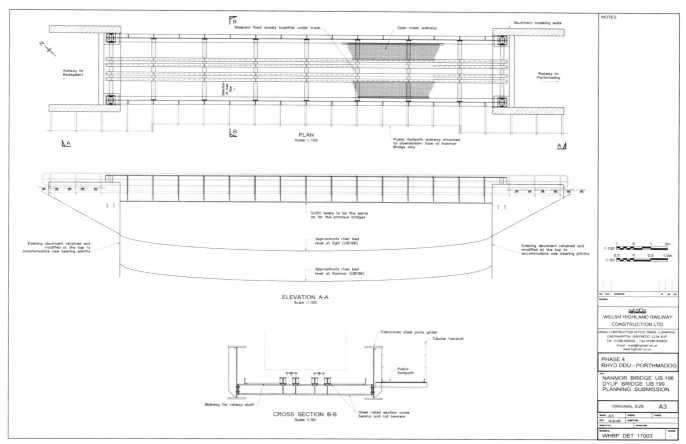

*This is an example of what went in for the planning stage of Phase 4. Accomplished though the design may be , it is a matter for celebration that the bridge was not built to this design. Instead John Sreeves recreated a facsimile of the original truss bridge, but with the faults of the 1922 original removed. You will see this further down the chapter. There are three, just as there were in days of old.*

volunteers who had arrived to assist the restoration effort during the previous periods of construction. Some examples of these generous individuals are: John Sreeves, who led the work on bridge design and Roger Dick who was formerly the supervising engineer working for Mott-MacDonald, employed by the Millennium Commission.

**3.** Roland Doyle and Peter Marston produced the Planning Application drawings, and drew on a team of in-house volunteers like Stuart McNair. The sum-total of all the savings accrued by the use of skilled volunteers was in the region of £300k, which would otherwise have been handed out in consultants' fees.

It was a massive task that followed the topographical survey, completed in early spring 2005. Precise specifications were drawn up, section by section, for the civils and earthworks contracts to be let. Exact details of diversions were also finalised with the utility companies, and with Network Rail, over the arrangements for the Cae Pawb crossing of the Cambrian Coast Line. Exact specifications were prepared for submission to the local authorities in respect of changes to structures, and the Gwynedd Council (GC) and SNPA were consulted on a regular basis for this work. In June 2005, Arup Rail were appointed as consultants to turn the engineering designs into detailed specifications for the work between Bryn y Felin and Hafod y Llyn (extended gradually to Traeth Mawr and CTRL). It was decided that all the tracklaying would be done by volunteers, and details are in Chapter 11.

Now was the time that the TWO really came into its own. The FR Co. used powers conferred by the Transport and Works Order (The Welsh Highland Railway Order 1999) to issue compulsory purchase orders during June 2004 on land over which there might be any doubts about ownership. If any AP

claimant could prove that they held a valid title, then the matter switched to the negotiation of a purchase price; meanwhile the railway was built without let. This was indeed the 'best' way for the restorers.

Meanwhile Achanshean Fencing Ltd of Llandygai were getting on with their contract for fencing, awarded on 17th December 2004. Access to some spots was a problem, until they had drained three waterlogged sites: Pitt's Head (late Garraway's bath); near to Hafod Ruffydd, and near to Cwm Cloch Isaf, just up from to Beddgelert Station. The state of the trackbed constructed by the 1922 WHR company was not good, and bore little resemblance to the 'as built' drawings for the Board of Trade. The TWA maps were used for planning purposes, augmented with elevations and sections etc where necessary. The clearance enabled the topographical survey, to design the horizontal alignment. Whilst the survey work was in progress, all sites were checked for rescuing any special creatures or plants. Nothing of special interest was found - naturally if there were any dragons, they would have remained very much out of sight. The only rare, visiting species was *Enthusiastus Ferrocarriliensis*, but soon they became quite common.

## The Track and the Construction

There were changes to the track components for this phase. It was decided to use steel sleepers with elastic rail clips (ERC). The detailed track description, and the way it was laid by means of staff and volunteers, is worthy of expansion in its own right, at risk of duplication, thus an account is given in Chapter 11. New S30 30kg/m rail came from Poland, enough rails and fishplates were delivered in September and October

*Left: Pitt's Head bridge under the A4085, a mile on from Rhyd Ddu. Aka: Garraway's Bath. This arose from the nasty wetness that had meant several lengths of track were recovered in 1958 in very damp conditions, as the drainage had deteriorated over the years of closure, and water flowed here from the bog. Access to this spot was a problem for the topographical survey, until the water level was made to go down.* **both pictures Mike Hart**
*Below: Pitt's Head Bridge in 1990, looking south towards the Summit, along the old WHR trackbed, shows the rather difficult task awaiting the restorers. It was also overgrown - however putting a powerful bulldozer along there soon sorted things out.*

*Below: This is Cwm Cloch in 1990, 17 miles from Caernarfon. Access to this part of the trackbed wasn't easy. Trackbed like this was a problem, and worse, the ownership was in dispute in several areas.*
**Mike Hart**

Most of the preparation had been completed and all that remained to be done now was the simple matter of building the railway. However there was an important matter to attend to.

Work to finish Rhyd Ddu was needed, to turn what had been a minimalist terminus into a through station with passing loop. The extension of the previous station yard, was made available as the new layout was moved eastwards. This overflow car park was surfaced with grass-grid and tarmac, as was the pedestrian route to the platform. The second platform face had to be constructed, a turning-in point was needed for coaches, platform lighting and a waiting shelter were needed. Two water towers were wanted, the track layout needed refashioning, and then converting to right-hand running. There was a bit of earthworks, some ballast laying and siding recovery, and then the south end points were laid with the sidings running north, ready to serve the Phase 4 works trains.

2005, to complete the WHR. Most of it went to Dinas, ready for movement by rail to where it was needed, though some went to Pen y Mount for the extension to Traeth Mawr, and for the expected continuation to Pont Croesor, and some went to Minffordd for the FR.

Some 21,000 steel sleepers and 84,000 ERCs were ordered from Royal Forgings, an Indian company based in Kolkatta. All of these had also been delivered to the depot at Dinas by the end of November, 2005. A 2 tonne capacity gantry crane was installed in Dinas North Yard in January 2006, to handle the rail and materials, that were to be shipped out on rail wagons adapted for the purpose. Most of the yard central area was a rail stack.

The trackwork was begun in December 2005, and the last of the South African materials were used. Onwards from the loop points, the track was then laid with the new materials. The tracklaying of the loop was completed on April 2nd 2006, and the sidings were fenced off from the main line. Separation was required be-

*The railstack at Dinas, with enough new Polish rail in stock to complete the WHR, all waiting for use, suitably pre-drilled, taken on 1st October 2005* **WHRCL**

*Left: The south end water tank, erected some time previously, has just received its first coat of paint, in this view of 04.02.07. This tank straddles one of the south-facing sidings - and so is a very classy railway feature!*

*Right: This is the last point south of Rhyd Ddu, that gives access to the sidings, and provided separation from the operating railway. The stop-board (with white cross on the back) on the tracks in the distance, and stop block marked the boundary. North of it are the loop points themselves. This spot is about where the course of the original WHR links up with the new deviation for Rhyd Ddu station.*

tween the operating railway and the new line for works trains. The wooden platform shelter was erected on March 26th 2006 as the first example of FR/WHR garden shed technology. A four-lever frame was delivered, with the intention of installing fixed signalling for the sidings, in readiness for the time when trains would run through.

## Pitt's Head to Pont Cae'r Gors

Restoration towards Pitt's Head Bridge, OB123 was relatively straightforward. Contract 4A-1B was let to Phasey Construction of Porthmadog on July 4th 2005.

There was culvert UB120 to reconstruct, in the manner of Phase 3. By the end of September, the trackbed was receiving its sub-base of rolled, crushed slate. The section was ballasted on October 28th with a small 'paver' - a machine normally used for laying tarmac or sub-base. Unfortunately a tracked version was never found. Tracklaying began from the Rhyd Ddu end, with the new materials on December 30th.

GC did some work on the Pitt's Head Bridge. It is the only masonry overbridge on Phase 4, and it already had the clearance necessary for Garratts and modern WHR rolling stock to pass beneath. The problems were with what lay below. A river was occupying the trackbed, at Pitt's Head, and under the bridge there was a lake most of the year. The difficulty was in reordering the drainage system, to enable the trackbed to be recovered. That lay under a good deal of detritus which had to be removed, and works put in place to ensure that it could not return to create problems for the future.

The water had to be directed to a culvert under the road, whereby it was conveyed down to the Llyn y Gader,

*Above: The track creeps out, on to the finished formation, with the new materials on 22nd January 2006. Winter can be wet and very cold up here, but there's a railway that needs to be built!*

*Right: On 9th September, only eight months later, Palmerston chuffs past on newly laid track with a demonstration train, hauling Mr Hart's Armoured Simplex, complete with the gentleman himself. The ordered scene, just approaching Pitt's Head, is in contrast to the images opposite. A neat little railway has emerged from the dereliction.*

**Left:** *Achnashean contractors clearing the overgrowth from the Pitt's Head site on 20th February 2005. A temporary drainage channel has been excavated and the large amount of water is generating a stream through the site as Garraway's Bath drys out* **Peter Johnson**

**Below:** *The pegs are in, the stream still flows, in this view of 5th September 2005. The eastern ditch has been excavated, and the cut slate retaining wall will be built resting in it, with the ditch in front, lined. The trackbed is clearly in view once more.* **WHRCL**

nearby on the west side. Clearance was followed by excavation to reach the proper base level of the trackbed. The work here had first started in the 1900s as part of the failed PB&SSR scheme, and the route was a forest tramway in World War 1, until being incorporated in the WHR in 1922. Now, two ditches were dug either side of the trackbed on the north side. A cut slate retaining wall was built to secure the embankment, which had its slope regulated to a dependable gradient. Both ditches were lined, and the drainage water was led to an enclosure feeding the long drain under the road at the bridge end. At the other end of the ditches, there was an outlet to the culvert UB120 (**UB40.46**). Thus the whole area rapidly became free of water and will stay that way. It was however, an expensive and long drawn out process. The tracklayers reached the north end of the site in mid-May 2006, and were through the area by early June. Remedial work was necessary to the drainage works in September 2007, caused by scour of fine material behind the front faces from full drainage ditches and a lack of fall.

Proper drainage soon solved the 'bog' problems in the Sum-mit Cutting. Slotted drainage pipes carried the water away, downhill, through the bridge and into the new drainage system. Geotextile was laid, with crushed slate waste on top. Ballasting started from Pont Cae'r Gors and was complete by 2nd February, 2006. A stepped drain was installed, to direct the flow-off from the adjacent pasture into the new slot drainage system installed. After the track was laid, and when the trains began to run, the whole site looked so neat and tidy, one would never associate the area with the awful mess that was there before.

The section from Summit towards Porthmadog had a number of interesting features. One was UB125 (**UB41.20**), known as Freddie's Bridge, just before the 1:40 gradient towards Beddgelert. It is shown in detail in the drawing by John Sreeves. Groundwater levels are high, there is a lack of freeboard, and not enough cant for 20mph. It should be possible in the future to apply solu-

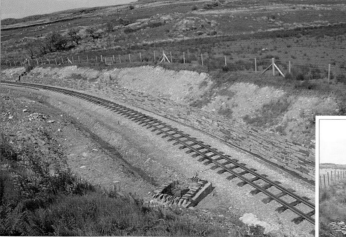

*Above: Looking north from the parapet of OB123, as the track had reached the bridge, the retaining wall, and the two ditches and the enclosure on the west side have been completed, in this view taken on 10th June 2006. With drainage and batter the bank is safe.*
**Ben Fisher**

*Right: A 3rd December 2005 view south from the bridge, with the abutments of the 1900 PB&SSR farm accommodation bridge that was never built. The geotextile sheet can be seen, together with the crushed slate top, the drains are out of sight.* **R Bradley**

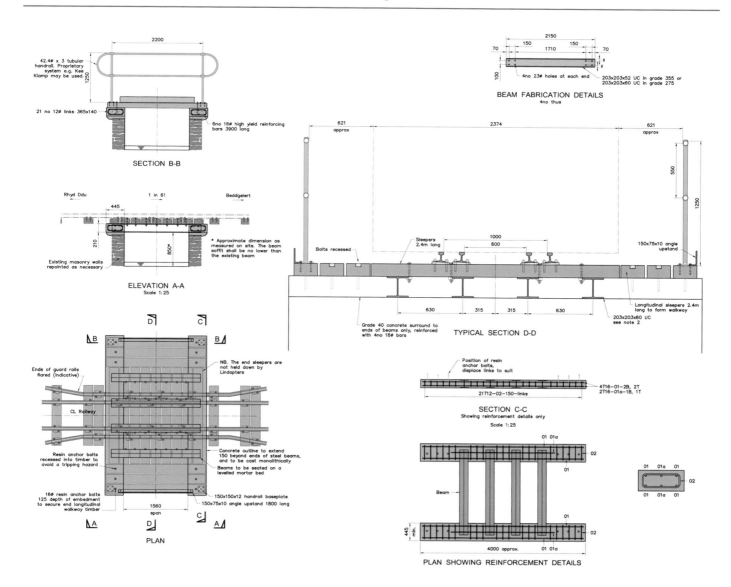

tions to this area to raise the speed. Beyond UB125, at the lip of the 1:40 gradient, there was a bridleway to rebuild as a gated crossing, LC70A (*LC41.16*), that gives access to the forest. The roadway had been levelled out during the years of closure, and the cutting's steep, soily sides had gradually migrated to fill it with muck over the years, so that the by the time restoration came about, the cutting itself was quite shallow. Contractors, Morrison carried out

*Above: This is the distressed state of UB125 on 20.03.05, just one rusty girder left out of two. Serious reconstruction was needed.* **Ben Fisher**

*Right: UB125 is shown in context, you can see the sleepers in the centre of the photograph taken on 8th September 2006. The view is looking north, as the new track curves round towards Summit Cutting.*

*This is a 1:36 slope down from Pont Cae'r Gors on 22nd January 2006, looking south towards the cloud covered flanks of Moel Hebog. It's wet underfoot and either it has just rained, or very soon it is going to rain. All the muck has been dragged out of the cutting. Uphill it's quite a big slog for locomotives to climb . The slot drains will have to be drilled through rock. Care has to be taken to secure the steep embankment sides from encroaching in the future. Geotextile and the crushed slate top are to come. The reason why the photograph is in - apart from the grand but melancholy scene - is because those sleepers in the foreground are left-over remnants from the original Welsh Highland Railway. This was the original line's 'top'. It was a pleasure to see it before it was swept away by today's new railway.*

*Left: This view south before any excavation of the cutting was made on 19th February 2005. It shows what the place was like before work started - fairly dire. An important component of the work was the reduction of the incline of the embankment batter (slope).* **Ben Fisher**

*Below: The bridleway at Pont Cae'r Gors was downgraded to a pedestrian crossing as the timber lorries could not negotiate it. Dolgarrog stands with some track materials, whilst activity goes on down the hill. The evidence is all around of how much work has been done at this location, in this view taken on 15th July 2006, some 17 months later than that above.* **Ben Fisher**

work at the foot of the cutting in Summer 2005, on behalf of Scottish Power/Manweb, relocating a power line.

Part of the problem in this area was the underlying hard rock, which had defied all attempts, except by explosives, to create the channels needed to provide adequate drainage to stabilise the cutting walls.

The original sleepers had been laid on the floor with little or no ballast underneath, unsound at the time, and unacceptable today. The original construction of the cutting left a lot to be desired. The lack of drainage led to the gradual infill that had been experienced. The cutting sides have been 're-graded' to reduce their slope angles to aid stability, and the drainage channel was cut out of rock on the forestry side of the fence to capture surface run-off, and to carry it away from the cutting face, avoiding the build up of ground water in the slope. The track was on this section at the end of July 2006.

At the bottom of the cutting, the Forestry Commission wanted a crossing over the railway to create a new internal road, to compensate for the lorry problems created at the Pont Cae'r Gors crossing, and this was made with the designation LC70A (**LC41.20**). From this point the Forestry Commission had taken over the trackbed as a forestry road, as far as the accommodation crossing at Hafod Ruffydd. Thus the way onward was well consolidated from a good many years of use, apart from a small area of slippage, and damage from water erosion near to LC71.

*(continued on page 220)*

*Above: The measures required to prevent the movement of the bottoms of the sides were in action in this photograph of the cutting taken on 25th July 2006. The Head of Steel had reached part-way down the 1:40 incline. The tracklayers awaited the rock-busting here that would establish adequate drainage and let the cutting become stable.* **Ben Fisher**

*Right: The hard rock under the cutting meant that in order to install proper drainage, to prevent the cutting deteriorating again, a rock-buster had to be used. The 1922 Co,. failed to do this.* **Peter Johnson**

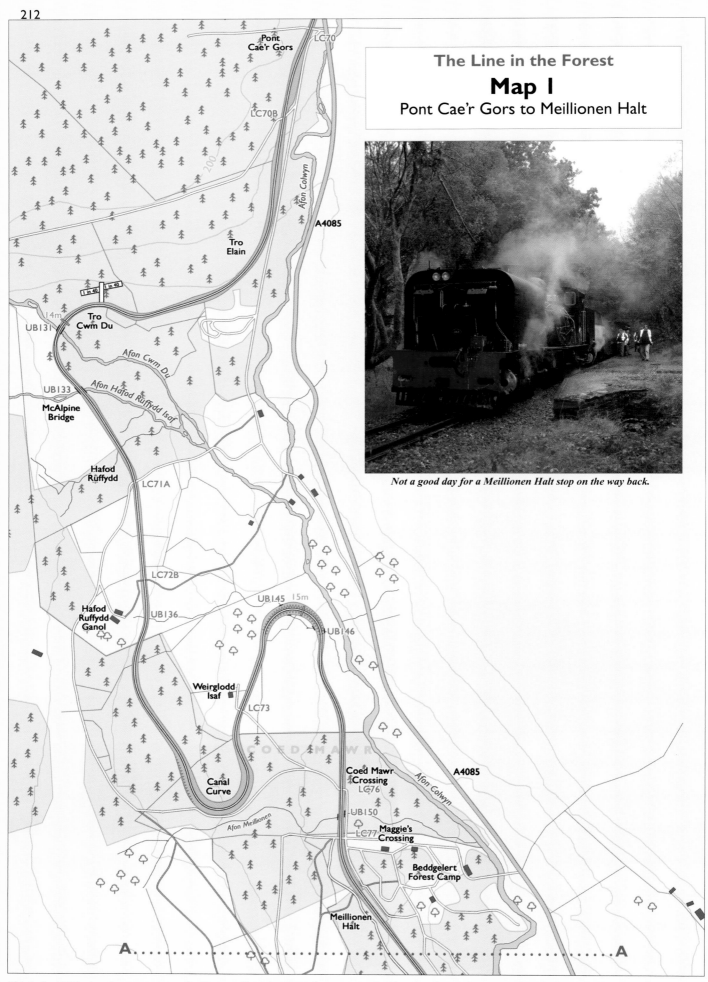

**The Line in the Forest**
# Map 1
Pont Cae'r Gors to Meillionen Halt

Pont Cae'r Gors

LC70

LC70B

Afon Colwyn

A4085

Tro Elain

1 in 40 | 1 in 40

14m

UB131

Tro Cwm Du

Afon Cwm Du

UB133

Afon Hafod Ruffydd Isaf

McAlpine Bridge

Hafod Ruffydd

LC71A

LC72B

UB145 15m

Hafod Ruffydd Ganol

UB136

UB146

Weirglodd Isaf

LC73

C O E D   M A W R

Canal Curve

Coed Mawr Crossing

LC76

A4085

Afon Colwyn

Afon Meillionen

UB150

Maggie's Crossing

LC77

Beddgelert Forest Camp

Meillionen Halt

A .................................................... A

*Not a good day for a Meillionen Halt stop on the way back.*

*This is the 'hidden' section, some was under Forestry Commission roads, some was abandoned and unused. The gradient is 1:40, though this does vary a certain amount. On a wet day the driver's heart sinks when an uphill passenger requests a stop at Meillionen Halt on a heavy train.*

The Line in the Forest
**Map 2**
Coed Mawr to Beddgelert

*The uphill grade is at about 1:40 right through Beddgelert Station, round the punishing curve to Cutting Mawr and beyond. Avoiding the red 1:28 sections of the old PB&SSR (now abandoned) meant that extra distance was needed to ease the gradient back to 1:40 for steam loco working. Views and sounds are sublime.*

***Above:*** *The crushed-slate top disappears towards Coed Mawr and Hafod Ruffyd, Ganol, the white house in this view of 8th April 2006 from LC71A (**42.54**). On the centre-right Weirglodd Isaf can just be glimpsed on the centre-left, behind the tree branch.*

***Below:*** *Canal Curve (**43.30**) became flooded. It looked impenetrable until some hours with machines made it otherwise. There was a contract 'junction' here, though with the same contractor, so for a short while this bit was dug and drained, but the curve continuation was not.* **Graham Whistler**

*Above:* The same view from nearly the same place (as left), from a train running on the finished track. Open carriages are popular whatever the weather; this was 'overcast-cool'. These views from the train are magnificent, and there are better than here by far. The house in the centre is Weirglodd Isaf.

*Below:* On the same day, 1st July 2011 the train, hauled by oil-fired NGG16 No. 138, has now run to Cwm Cloch Isaf, and will soon enter Cutting Mawr at 17 miles from Caernarfon, circling round into Beddgelert, and the start of the Aberglaslyn Pass. The railway is blending in well five years after construction.

**A**lasdair Stewart ACSM Dip CSM was a true 'Ffestiniog Kid', growing up in the area, and being a part of Kids Week in the 1990s. The FR and its ways were second nature. He went off to Camborne School of Mines. During Phase 4 he joined with Stuart McNair, a well experienced FR veteran, to make a formidable team to surmount the problems of getting the WHR Phase 4 restored at a price that could be afforded. For Alasdair, the experience was such that he is now one of the UK's youngest and most qualified engineers in the heritage railway field.

**P**hase 4 of the WHR reconstruction was divided into sixteen geographical 'contract sections' between Rhyd Ddu station and Traeth Mawr (Pen y Mount to Pont Croesor was to have been undertaken by WHR 64 Co., though in the event they only rebuilt as far as Traeth Mawr.).

Section boundaries were based on convenient access points to the trackbed, and varied in length and engineering complexity. Each section had several phases of work – an initial contract to fence and secure the site, an initial clearance 'strip', and a final build contract; though in practice some sections had the latter two phases combined into one operation.

Contracts were let in accordance with ICE 6th Edition form of contract for the ground works. Some projects were let as minor works contracts, separate from the main body of the rebuilding contract, such as the preliminary rock stabilisation works at Nantmor, and the construction of the reinforced earth embankment at Nantmor. In the case of the embankment at Nantmor, this was let to G H James even though their tender was slightly higher than that received from another contractor, but it was felt that the risk of having both contractors accessing the track bed simultaneously from the road crossing in Nantmor would have been a greater risk to programme than the cost saving. Also, James had won the next section down to Hafod y Llyn, where the bulk of the material removed from the original embankment was hauled to (most of the fill was used to form the widened formation for the loop and 'station' site.). We had experienced some delay on the Aberglaslyn section when some rock stabilisation work was taking place whilst James were on site – the stabilisation work was by direct employment – we successfully avoided this problem elsewhere by bundling all the work identified into the main contract that was being performed by the principal contractor, and allowing them to appoint the sub contractor. Other minor contracts were let on the basis of a letter based on an agreed estimate of the scope and value of the work, against bills of varying complexity and detail, and were subject to final remeasure.

Generally speaking, the approach worked well. It took some time to convince all that we were even-handed when we first

*'Can we have it a bit wider at the base please?' Weirglodd Isaf embankment, on the sharp curve. This was one of those interesting jobs where a dose of realism on the ground upped the costs that had been anticipated.*
**Alasdair Stewart**

involved external quantity surveyors to administer the contract to 'widen' and re profile the batters in Cae'r Gors cutting. After initial awkwardness, we settled into an open book sort of arrangement though, it was never formally called that, but such candid displays dispersed any suspicions over trust.

Consultants we had appointed were beginning to demonstrate that they couldn't cope with our needs, and there was a wish for diplomatic separation when dealing with the Forestry Commission. They were being rather disturbed by the railway coming back to cause major disruption in a somewhat customer sensitive environment. It would have been unwise to risk clashes of interest and personality, so it was felt better to allow everyone to maintain professional distance. It is easy to forget how personally everybody involved in the restoration of the railway viewed the job, and how likely it was that we would generate feelings of resentment from mass enthusiasm, unless this aspect was kept under careful control.

A difficulty we had to master (personally through Phase 4) was juggling the availability of funds between those things that had to be done, and those we had aspirations to do. This seemed simple on the face of it, as long as the detail wasn't allowed to take over. Part of the problem was of course the one you are actually paid to manage, and that is to control the costs and still to meet the standard -this concentrates the mind. By having an itemised bill of quantity, it was easier to adjust the costs to the optimum, either at the time of committing to placing an order, or shortly afterwards. The difficulty was anticipation of the outcome with pin-point accuracy - which of course was not possible on WHR restoration! With a railway nearly seventy years gone, one has to learn the hard way. The first section from Rhyd Ddu to Cae'r Gors was done confidently but with a bill that revealed many items that should have been in it at the beginning as matters progressed. These had to be added later in an *ad-hoc* way. The danger then was that any lapse in the observance of instructions by the construction company or the contractor would lead to a dispute at the time of the final reckoning.

We learned well, as the contracts from Beddgelert down

to Traeth Mawr were much better controlled, but of course an increase in the scope of work, post the award, was deliberate and necessary. Matters inevitably became technical, and in some areas like Weirglodd Isaf embankment, subsequent work cost us more than the Board's expectation, after a good dose of realism on the ground upped the costs.

The McAlpine cost estimate was helpful, and very useful, but the realities of the cost of restoring innocent looking culverts, and the difficulties involved in accessing long narrow sites from restricted points, still skewed the best of estimates. Although the exercise balanced out over the whole of Phase 4, it offered anxious moments when used as a budgeting tool for any individual section. Certain things were outside our control, and the rising price of fuel in 2007 was an unhelpful addition to the costs for all materials that needed to be delivered by road..

The Beddgelert Station restoration was ambitious, and aimed rightly to provide the most important, intermediate commercial centre on the WHR. The costs had to be trimmed to keep the price to within that affordable. This inevitably caused compromises that are being lived with subsequently, as in the event, virtually everything taken out has been provided. Although this was at the cost of increased administration and supervision by WHRCL, frustration about this is part of the game. The section between the upper Cwm Cloch level crossing and Bryn y Felin kept to the forecast, though this was still higher than the board had hoped.

*In the Pullman are two out of the three, Alasdair Stewart and Stuart McNair in the mud hut. Together with Owen Duncan they took on the problems of WHR Phase 4, determined to manage the engineering as near to the price and quality that they possibly could. They met many challenges along the way. We have all noticed that the railway got built! These guys were those most instrumental in seeing it through to the end.*

Our presence was justified to know and understand the people who were acting as consultants, and the contractors and their workforce. We solved problems in conjunction with them whilst it was still practical to affect the outcome. Chris O'Connor was the Clerk of Works, and his presence was a boon; a constant presence that ensured implementation of the decisions that had been agreed, so that when matters strayed from the predicted path, immediate judgements in correction were available. If the end costs had been known at the start, restoration would probably not have taken place.

On a day to day level, most of our time at Dinas between summer 2006 and the completion of track laying in 2008, was spent on track alignment work. Little of the WHR is plain, straight track. If the alignment is not spot-on through its sinuous curves and sharp bends, there is a constant danger that the kinematic envelope will be breached. Maintaining correct track alignment consisted of site surveys, followed by interpretation and the preparation of the data. Then the straights, transitions, and curves, were drawn to fit the formation, and the design could be set out on the ground. Stuart McNair and Owen Duncan mastered the task together with Ray Cooper. All of us in the 'Mud Hut' had experience of using proprietary software

for similar types of work, with mixed results; we thought that it would be better to produce our own hybrid technique. The raw survey data was plotted as 'strings' on AutoCAD drawings overlying the track bed survey – we found that in most areas one side or other of the formation would suffice, but where there were tight curves, short transitions, and/or fixed obstacle points, we picked up details on site, on both sides, and where we thought the centreline 'should' have been. Plotted onto the plan, a 'best fit' would usually appear – sometimes more easily than others. A little Excel spreadsheet was then used that would model the curve we were looking for. The 'model' would then be dropped into the CAD drawing, and tweaked as necessary before co-ordinates data could be generated for setting out purposes. Usually we went for 10m centres on plain line, and circular curves, but set out at a much greater frequency in the transitions.

Every curve from the Pitts Head to Porthmadog had to be redesigned before it could be set out and laid. On average it is fair to say that at least one man-week went into the back room efforts to keep ahead of the track laying teams. The trackbed surveys that had been carried out prior to our involvement were not good enough for exacting alignment design purposes, especially as boundary fences had not been installed, post survey, in exactly the right place. The edges of the old formation were not identified, and the subtleties of the way the railway curves, in parallel with the contours, were not present. In a couple of areas the survey followed more recent road vehicle tracks! Fortunately the vertical alignment was not so difficult, with the exception of the Goat Tunnel (T1, *T47.15*).

There were enough straights or circular curves that took the pressure off, enough to allow us to maintain sanity – between the real problem areas like Cwm Cloch, T3, the Nantmor end of the reinforced earth embankment, and Parry's Pig Farm/Afon Nanmor. Although this may seem to have been a labour intensive method of achieving a correct alignment, the track was laid in the right place, first time (with one or two exceptions) which helped keep the motivation of the volunteers at a high level, as well as ensuring that we got, and continue to get, the best service from the track materials used.

The experience of working with someone so experienced and skilled as Stuart McNair, with such tolerance and such a sense of humour was a privilege. It added immeasurably to the sum of my experience personally, and both of us experienced the glee of remembering that this really was the legendary Welsh Highland Railway that we were bringing back to life. Our joint exhilaration of experiencing the first train is well remembered, as is the experience of working in such a good, co-operative, motivated, and able team. ■

**M**ike Hart wasn't just the guy who got the money for WHR, he managed the restoration of it from concept to completion. This meant a lot of things, like working flat out for years, endless driving between Yorkshire and Wales, and having two full-time jobs. Managing WHR restoration wasn't always a bed of roses, and Mike had to be really tough to make things happen. He battered on, realising that little railways have to be grown-up businesses to have any chance of success. Such steely determination won two prizes, a restored railway and an OBE.

**W**hen I joined the Board of The Ffestiniog Railway Company in 1989 the Welsh Highland Railway project was in its infancy. Work had been going on for a while in an attempt to acquire the trackbed of the Railway from the Official Receiver, so as to put the FR Co. into a position where it could control the line's future destiny. It was at my very first FR Board meeting that I floated the proposal for the Company to reconstruct the line itself, expressing the view that by rebuilding the line in stages, starting from Caernarfon, new markets could be found for travel on it, and the FR would not be harmed from competition. Thus, the FR Co. project to reconstruct all of WHR was born

The Board asked me to work alongside John Roulty and lead the WHR project with that aim. Within a few years John retired from the FR Co. Board, I was appointed its Chairman, and continued to take the lead with the WHR project, both as the FR Co. Director responsible, and as Chairman of its subsidiary, WHR construction companies, WHLR and WHRC.

The enthusiasm for a new railway was infectious, and soon we were exploring ways to inject new FR thinking into WHR, and came up with a concept based around long trains hauled by large, NGG16, South African Garratt locomotives.

While it had been a relatively easy task to persuade colleagues to accept such a set of dynamic proposals, it was a less easy task outside, within the area of the County Council and the railway enthusiast community, on whom we would need to depend for support. The outcome of the High Court case helped to move us forward toward the eventual acquisition of the line, and started to demonstrate to the world how FR was serious in its intent. The late Justice Vinellott's directions helped point us along a course that led to a public inquiry on the Transfer Order, that brought FR Co. title to the WHR trackbed. The vigorous and imaginative ideas for creating a new tourist attraction struck a chord with the Establishment, as the Order was eventually granted. This meant that FR could restore WHR, provided it could find the means to do so.

The Millennium Commission were looking for keynote projects. Careful consultation with colleagues suggested that we may manage Caernarfon to Rhyd Ddu, but building to

*Mike Hart with Bill McAlpine when the FR Trustees were making one of their visit to FR/ WHR. They have just been looking at the infrastructure depot at Minffordd, which was then being adapted for service to both railways.*

Porthmadog would be too much to expect by 2000! Gordon Rushton and I put an impressive bid together for funding, and the reception was welcoming. The Millennium Director came for a day's visit so we could show her the Railway, and she made encouraging comments. In due course, the Millennium Fund offered £4.6m for Caernarfon to Rhyd Ddu.

We were able to use that joyous news to lever an application the European Regional Development Fund, for a further £750k, boosting the funding to 45% of the total cost. This, together with financial help from Mike Schumann and others, permitted Caernarfon to Dinas construction to start.

If you wanted a quiet time, then this railway was not the one to choose. The TWO inquiry was in its final stages but construction beyond Dinas, to Rhyd Ddu could not advance an inch without the decision from the public inquiry, that took ages to arrive from the Minister, John Prescott. The Millennium Commission could see the awful delay that was taking place to their by now hallmark project, and they were beginning to become impatient. The pressure went up as conditions were placed on the Order from potential rock fall dangers in the Aberglaslyn Pass, and after these had been cleared up, problems arose with the National Park Authority that led to another inquiry. It was a time filled with difficulty, massive risks, and still the team had to be positive in dealing with the tasks needed to keep Caernarfon to Dinas running.

The rock-work had to be done in the Aberglaslyn Pass before any railway could be constructed in the National Park. None of this was funded by the Millennium Commission grant, and so the FR Trust had to pay for it. Fortunately, after a disappointing start the Garratts gave good service and performed well. There were no great surprises between Dinas and Waunfawr, and the surge in business when it was opened, offered hope for the future, as patronage on Caernarfon Dinas, though nice for Caernarfon, was hardly enough to live on. Immediately the railway was open to Waunfawr, construction began towards Rhyd Ddu. Here life began to be difficult. The large amount of bridge works meant that the railway did not have easy access for supplies. This was expensive and difficult, requiring the team to solve constant logistical problems to build the railway. It had to be done in bits, and they couldn't all follow in geographical order - which made movement of supplies and equipment really difficult, and sometimes made things very expensive. Next, the number of unpleasant surprises rose: bits of bank that needed much more stabilisation than at first thought; abutments that did not just want pointing, they needed rebuilding; stone embankments that were not stable, and would not take the loads imposed with Garratts without a great deal of unexpected work.

The railway reached Rhyd Ddu in 2003 but it was a major struggle. We were obliged to strip costs out as we went. In the end the project required an injection of £300k from the Trust to reach completion, but a visit from HRH Prince Charles, the Prince of Wales made sure that the opening got off to an excellent start, and traffic figures rose steadily to endorse our work. It was time to move on.

European Union grant money is isolated from political influence, and civil servants ensure impartiality, and adherence to tight funding rules. The Welsh European Funding Office appraise potential EU grant projects, and were vital in promoting enterprise. WHR's application for grants coincided with a period where bold Welsh Government officers were promoting innovative projects. The amounts requested were at the maximum government intervention rate of 50%. We were able to show rapidly increasing numbers; we were doing precisely what we promised we would do. Thus I was able to negotiate a package of grant funding for the 13 mile extension to Porthmadog. Again, the estimates of cost resulted in a fixed figure grant. This was dangerous, from the nasty surprises that rebuilding little railways could bring, but, it was not a place for faint hearts. If we believed in our policy then the only way forward was to take the risk and go for it.

The offer for Rhyd Ddu - Porthmadog was £5.2m grant for a £10.8m project. The challenge was now to find the remaining £5.6m. Our saving grace was the great generosity of our private sponsors who made charitable gifts to the FR Trust of £5m - this was what made it possible. However, this still was not enough, and volunteer tracklayers, the Phase 4 Appeal, and the efforts of CRhE filled the gap. The FR Trust sanctioned the go-ahead, the grant was accepted, and the WAG politicians came up to endorse the start of the project at Rhyd Ddu, with all the contracts for the work going to local firms. The management structure chosen for the Phase 4 was different to Phases 1-3, but this didn't stop the little hidden items appearing to make our funds disappear - it was relentless. No matter how good the management is, the intractable engineering project will always get through. The story is told of these in the book, but the effect was again to knock away some of the bells and whistles. This time however there was a very difficult challenge for which there was no easy solution. Sensitive of the threat

of increased road congestion, we had felt bound to agree not to start service to Beddgelert until we were through to the National Park boundary. Thus we were obliged to build nine miles of railway before we could get anything back for it. The sad part about this was that when we ran service to Beddgelert in 2009, 70k people travelled from Caernarfon in the first year, and they all left their cars outside the park.

Extras raised the cost of Phase 4 to £15.2m. Another £1m was forthcoming from grant bodies; the Phase 4 Appeal had raised £1.5m more than estimated, and the rest was made up from increased traffic receipts, further generosity from private donors, and massive volunteer activity. This was a real roller-coaster ride, as it was a real problem to differentiate between costs that needed to be controlled, and items that had to be paid for if the railway was going to be restored.

*Mike stands next to* Palmerston, *(that he subsequently donated to the FR) on the occasion of the first steam train over the CTRL, so that the FR Trustees could examine it in detail. The train is at Llyn Bach on top of the unconnected points there. 29th September 2009.*

The WHR opened in April 2011; nearly 100k bookings were made, and the income was as much as the Ffestiniog. The original strategy for WHR was borne out by the figures - FR traffic was not damaged. The construction of WHR has been with money raised for the purpose, and has not affected the development of FR. There is no doubt that WHR has relieved FR of a slice of overhead costs, equally that WHR is currently generating a large surplus that can be ploughed back into is development. The 1990 Strategy for WHR was entirely successful, and is now complete. The two railways complement each other.

More is needed for the new strategy of the Sustainable Railway, for new coaches, loco shed, terminal etc., to welcome the future. The Phase 5 appeal has raised significant funds in the middle of an economic downturn. It has match-funded the £1m grant from the National Station Improvement Programme to widen the Cob at Harbour Station, to provide two platforms.

WHR restoration needed a team of people with the expertise between them to make it happen. The ten year period by chance spanned an era of enlightened government policy, in the middle of an economic boom. Our strategy had enough elasticity to see the project through. It took account of the need to be able to show real economic advantage to the localities they serve. We see how a recent study estimates that the completed railway is bringing a much needed £14m visitor spend into the area and we now have a wonderful new railway to be proud of that complements the existing Ffestiniog line.

What a delight it has been to have been given the opportunity of leading the project delivery team from inception to completion, and as WHR approached completion, to have received the OBE in the Queens New Year's Honours list for my, and the whole team's, part in that..

We got this one right, and it stands as an inspiration to all others. I am proud to have served. ∎

## Pont Cae'r Gors to Meillionen Halt

The interesting thing around Pont Cae'r Gors was that few people were aware where the railway used to run, and even on driving the forestry roads, it was still confusing. The section from Beddgelert Station all the way up via Cwm Cloch, Meillionen Halt and Hafod Ruffydd was obscure, and nothing much could be seen from the A4085 road between Beddgelert Station and Pont Cae'r Gors. After rebuilding it has become clear that this four mile stretch of 600mm gauge railway is not only unique in the British Isles, it is also the most challenging and remarkable piece of railway in existence in Britain. It is much more akin to narrow gauge lines on the European mainland - it has no relations here. The reason for this lies in its electric origins. The three-phase PB&SSR electric locomotives were to be expected to climb a maximum gradient of 1:28, with only two or three coaches. The WHR when it was built in 1922 (as cheaply as possible) took over the unfinished PB&SSR trackbed and had to find a way of easing the ruling gradient to 1:40, for steam operation. This demanded the serpentine extension at Cwm Cloch that now delights us, offering manifold mountain views that cannot be snatched from

*On 18th August 2006, the first of the trains with pre-rolled rail for the tight curves of the WHR forest section is paused near to Tro Cwm Du, to detach* Upnor Castle *preparatory to pulling the rails off the wagons.*    **Graham Whistler**

the road. This section rises from 176ft at Beddgelert, over four miles to 651ft at Pont Cae'r Gors. That is an average (straight line) gradient of 1:45. During the years of closure, those parts of the line that were not used by the Forestry Commission and others as access roads became overgrown, and the already rather sparse drainage generally failed.

The section from the Pont Cae'r Gors cutting to south of Hafod Ruffydd was contracted out to G.H. James Cyf. and they rectified the formation from their work base at the site of the old Hafod Ruffydd Halt.

At the Rhyd Ddu end of the 1:40 up to Cae'r Gors is Tro Cwm Du (Black Valley Curve), and two stream bridges: the first is UB131 (**UB42.16**), over the Afon Cwm Du; the second is UB133, over the Afon Hafod Ruffydd Isaf (Upper Griffith's Farm River). The McAlpine Bridge (UB133 - **UB42.31**) was tackled in February 2006. It was not in good condition, and incorporated bits of earlier construction buried below the 1922 formation. There was over a metre of top-fill on the bridge; this was stripped off to expose the deck, which had holes right through it. New concrete needed to be cast on the eastern face and on the deck. The task was complete by the start of June 2006, and then the neighbouring UB131 was tackled over the Afon Cwm Du. Similar problems were met, with the addition of concrete side walls to be clad with sawn slate, better to retain the top-fill and ballast. The work was completed and the formation was in position by 14th August 2006. Track was laid down the hill for the first time with pre-curved rails, and by 18th August, the Head of Steel was at Tro Cwm Du, and reached the McAlpine Bridge by 3rd September. By September 26th the track was past Hafod Ruffydd (LC71A - **LC42.54**) and was on its way to the first of the famous looping curves at Weirglodd Isaf.

The bog at Canal Curve (**43.33**) was first tackled in

*Above: UB133, the McAlpine Bridge, over the Afon Cwm Du is seen stripped of its top, ready for repairs to be made to deck and ballast retaining walls. The shuttering is in place for the east wall to be poured. There are holes in the concrete deck that extend right through. Just another of those nasty little surprises on this section of railway that the restorers came to expect and love!*    **WHCRL**

*Right: The photographer has kindly climbed down to give us this unusual view of UB133 - the McAlpine Bridge, showing the ballast retaining wall finished in cut slate. The occasion is the Rest of the World Gang carrying out fencing work at UB131 and UB133 on July 13th 2008.*    **S. Melhuish**

**Above:** *This view is taken on 6th November 2005 of the morass at Canal Curve, looking east, the opposite direction to the picture on Page 214. The track curves to head in the opposite direction, towards Weirglodd Isaf. A short length of original contractors track was found here, under the 1922 formation - it looked like Croesor Tramway materials.*
**Ben Fisher**

**Right:** *On 12th October 2006, slightly less than a year after, a photograph taken from a few paces away, shows the track being installed on this site. Careful study will show the slot drain headed for UB140A, to deposit its water, and note the Forestry Commission 'dam' is reinstated - but as a temporary bund with less harmful effects in prospect as drainage has been installed.*
**Jane Ewing**

January 2005. One of the good things about the line in the forest was that the Forestry Commission roads gave access to the trackbed, so moving in machinery was not a problem. The reason for the flooding of the trackbed at this point, was poor drainage. The soft ground here was almost as bad as at Plas y Nant.

After Achnashean had done the fencing, G.H. James Cyf. moved on to site in September 2005 to begin the drainage, rebuilding, and restoration work on the formation. The drainage works, seen in the adjacent picture, were most important; the water was led away in the concrete troughs of the slot drain, and fed into cross drains, of which there was an extra one added almost on the apex of the curve (UB140A). When the water level fell, the trackbed was scraped back to the old ballast level, (where found)then a crushed slate 'top' was laid and compacted (in the normal way) before the track ballast was laid on to that.

The Forestry Road drops direct to Coed Mawr Crossing, (**LC44.31**) while the WHR formation continues off the curve to complete the 'S' and maintain 1:40. UB145 and UB146 needed to be rebuilt on the curve. The picture of UB145 (**UB44.47**), shows what happens over a long period of time if no maintenance work whatever is done on bridges. The channel was excavated to restore the waterway, and to allow enough flow for the stream in spate. The abutments were repaired, as required, and a new concrete deck was tailored for the top; crushed slate was added, and ballast was laid on top of that. Both these two short bridges were ready in time for the track to be laid over them, on 4-5th November 2006.

One snag that was dealt with a little later was the narrowness of the embankment at this point. It was

**Above:** *The faithful* Upnor Castle *standing on newly laid track, just above LC73, the crossing for Weirglodd Isaf, which may be seen just behind the locomotive cab, on 15th October 2006.*
**J.Ewing**

**Right:** *The state of UB 145, on 6th March 2006. On the cusp of the curve of the trackbed from almost north turning back to south, this spot is some 15 miles from Caernarfon. The stream and the trackbed must be parted. A new bridge is required. The job was done by the time* Upnor Castle *was helping the track to move forward in October.*
**Alasdair Stewart**

**Left:** *Road turned back into railway, and had to be duplicated. This is the deck of the new road bridge over the Afon Meillionen on 30th October 2005, built alongside the old road bridge, which became the rail bridge UB150.* **Ben Fisher**

**Below:** *Working Dignitarios of the Permanent Way Institute, on a weekend inspired by Andy Savage and Fred Howes. The persons are L-R: Andy Savage (President), Phil Bull (Vice-President, England), Bob Gardiner (VP, Scotland), Fred Howes (VP, Wales) and Andy Franklin (Past VP, Wales).* **Andy Savage**

under-engineered in 1922, and a widening scheme to add topsoil to the embankment, to permit train evacuation, was embarked upon, to be completed by March 2009.

Whilst the railway through Coed Mawr (big wood) and across the Afon Meillionen (Clover River) slumbered in dereliction, a caravan and camping site, owned by the Forestry Commission, and run by their commercial offshoot Forest Enterprise (re-absorbed in 2004), grew to exploit the area. It invested roads to access the various camping 'cells' of the site. Therefore when it came to restore the railway, there was a road across the site to be made back into railway, there were two level crossings, a river bridge, and a station to construct, as well as re-routed roads in mitigation. Management of the 1km stretch was subcontracted to Datrys of Caernarfon, and work started in mid-October 2005.

The Forestry Commission were very long-suffering, but the deal had been done a long time ago, and they were getting a major tourist railway as transport and entertainment for the campers and caravanners at the end of it. If they wanted to sport 'green' credentials, then this was a real 'leave the car on the site and go by train' opportunity, unequalled by any other site elsewhere. There was considerable disruption as the various features were established, and there was a wish to get the work completed by Christmas 2005. UB150 (**UB44.35**) over the Afon Meillionen did not require its deck replaced, which made life easier. The river bridge required a 650m road next to the trackbed, with two 90° level crossings.

By late March 2006 Meillionen Forest Camp Site halt platform was constructed, together with a slab for the building. This came later, in 2009, and used the admirable GST

*UB156, over the Afon Glochig at Ty'n y Coed on 1st May 2006 where road is again about to be turned back into rail.* **Peter Johnson**

(Garden Shed Technology). The platform got its tarmac in April 2006. Sleepers were delivered to the site in late May 2006, and were stored either side of the level crossing (LC77).

The track was laid over the weekend of 25th-26th November 2006. It just so happened that worthies of the Permanent Way Institution came to do some tracklaying, something more difficult to achieve by this date on the main line railway, but a practical weekend proposition on a 600mm railway.

## Meillionen Halt to Beddgelert

You could not see that WHR had moved unobtrusively onward in the woods, with the track laid on the Ty'n y Coed (house in the wood) section during the early part of January 2007, almost as far as the bridge over the Afon Glochig.

The contracts for the next section, from UB156 to LC86 were divided. The first part went to G.H. James, and from there to Pont Alyn (UB165) was performed by W.Hughes of Llangefni. James had established a base next to LC82 (**LC45.70**) in July 2006, and moved in to scrape down the trackbed to the original ballast, place a compacted, crushed slate top, and then cover that with fresh ballast, ready for the track to be laid. The Afon Glochig Bridge, UB156 (**UB45.17**) required replacement.

The existing bridge of two parallel girders spanning the stream was therefore removed. The abutments were strengthened and a concrete deck was added, so that ballast could be laid on top of it, with the track on top of that. This was by now a standard bridge arrangement for the WHR restoration. This bridge was a 'neat and tidy' example of what was achieved, and of course the concrete and the stone walling will weather to blend in with its surroundings.

By mid-August, the trackbed scraping was done and drainage works were in hand. UB156 rebuilding meant that access was not possible from the south, thus the ballasting work had to wait until UB156 was done. The bridge was finished in late October; the ballasting was completed right down to LC82B (*LC45.70*) (Cwm Cloch Uchaf) by the end of January. The track was on the section

*UB158 (**UB45.71**), over the Afon Nant Cwm Cloch on 18th August 2006, shows Hughes's men preparing the deck shuttering for pouring.* **Graham Whistler**

*Right:* *The upper end, wing retaining wall has been poured, in this view taken on 16th December 2006, and the shuttering is in place, ready to pour the second section. This was heavy work for such a small bridge, but then the Afon Nant Cwm Cloch was quite able to behave as strongly as the name sounds grand, and this needed prudent defences. The tracklayers' hopeful piles of sleepers show they await completion of the works.*    **Ben Fisher**

*Below:* *LC82 (**LC45.70**) on 18th February 2007, with a vehicle heading in to Cwm Cloch Canol. To the right of the vehicle there was a slip that needed to be remedied. The track arcs across the bridge, on its way to the damp depths of Cutting Mawr. The north wing-walls have now been added to the bridge.*    **Ben Fisher**

and approaching the crossing by the first week of February 2007.

Hughes got on with rebuilding UB158 (**UB45.71**), over the grandly named Afon Nant Cwm Cloch (Bell Valley Gorge River). At the start of the great looping piece of 'gradient smoothing' formation that swept the WHR south of Beddgelert Station was the crescent-shaped Cutting Mawr, UB 158 needed to be

complete before access and track could advance beyond the good access road at adjacent LC82. The bridge was not easy, in December 2006 it was decided that the drystone retaining wall on the downstream side needed to be replaced with something firmer - which meant concrete. This structure was a pest, as in January 2007, similar, shorter wing walls were added on the other side of the bridge, whilst the tracklayers waited uphill, at about 16½ miles from Caernarfon. By mid-February 2007 the track was across, and the formation stretched on down the sharply curved grade towards Cutting Mawr.

Further down the formation, at LC83, the crossing at a track leading in from Cwm Cloch Canol allowed access to the curve whilst UB158 was being restored. Thus by August 20th 2006, rapid progress had been made with scraping down the trackbed, and its consolidation. In September the ballast was spread north to UB158. At the same time, Cutting Mawr was being tackled, first by Colin Jones (Rock Engineering) Ltd of Porthmadog, who used a cherry-picker to remove loose rocks. At the end of October, when the scaling work was complete, drainage works began, using channel sections. Cutting Mawr is a sort of narrow gauge Olive Mount Cutting, with towering vertical walls. It had got wet and full of detritus, and of course perhaps the drainage works done originally were tailored to fit the rather shallow

*Above:* *This was the alternative access LC83 to the trackbed between Cutting Mawr and the UB158, exploited whilst the bridge was being rebuilt, it allowed the ballast to move north to be ready for the track coming south. Picture taken on 1st September 2006.*    **R. Kirk**

*Right:* *Peter Johnson's classic picture of Cutting Mawr, showing the depth of the excavation, now clear of accumulated debris, but understandably damp. Taken on 08th September the view is up the 1:40 gradient towards Caernarfon, a little under 17 miles away. All the loose material has to be removed, then drainage works may begin.*    **Peter Johnson**

*Left: Cutting Mawr on 17th March 2007, with the track gang absent from their labours for a while. The drainage channel is already doing its job, to keep the cutting free of water. Dolgarrog sits on a pair of Roland Rail Movers, and Conway Castle is at the mouth of the cutting with the mess van. When the gang returns, the Head of Steel will advance, on SAR sleepers to allow gauge widening.* **WHRCL**

*Below: This was a complex series of engineering works. The WHR formation was used by the farmer for access, but the bridge needed replacement for further duty. This required a new invert, thus the stream was pumped round it. To provide access a pipe bridge was built. When the railway bridge was complete the pipe bridge was dismantled, and an accommodation bridge was built over the river.* **Ben Fisher**

pockets of the promoters. Certainly the excavations on the west side, followed by the installations of troughs, together with concrete works designed to seal those in, is a quality job, designed to be effective if the drain is kept clean. The effect is immediate, and together with the ballast, Cutting Mawr has become as dry as the climate in Wales will permit. By the second week of March 2007, the track was into Cutting Mawr at **46.00**. At this point, the line is circling round, south of Beddgelert Station, to achieve the required height by maintaining a 1:40 gradient over the required distance. After Cutting Mawr, the line emerges on to embankment, to describe a large 'S', crosses the Afon Nant Cwm Cloch once more, along with the adjacent access road at LC86, curves back past the old PB&SSR, 1:28 abandoned formation, and continues the descent towards Pont Alyn and Beddgelert Station.

UB164 (**UB46.42**) required a new invert under the Afon Nant Cwm Cloch, which had to be pumped by to provide the conditions for this to be done. By October the bridge was complete, ready for stone cladding. Another bridge had to be built in mitigation for the loss of the trackbed as land access. These were quite complex works, where a pipe bridge gave temporary access until UB164 was complete. By April 2007 the works were substantially finished, and ballasting and crossing timbers on LC86 were followed by tracklaying over Easter 2007. On the lower section,

where the track sweeps back in an eastward curve towards Pont Alyn, machines had cleared the way, the drainage works were done, and a rolled slate top was added before the ballast was laid. Tracklaying around this final bend took place around the end of April 2007, bringing the line to Pont Alyn, UB165 (**UB46.70**), and the entrance to Beddgelert Station, where another set of

*Above: The formerly blocked formation around the eastward sweep of the descent through Cwm Cloch Isaf, showing the arrangements for drainage, a geotextile sheet harbouring ballast. Note the PB&SSR formation, rising at a more rapid rate that the WHR* **Peter Johnson**

*Left: See the sweep of the track, fresh-laid around the curve in this view of 25th May 2007. Peter was standing on the PB&SSR formation, and you can see the abutments of the bridge of an accommodation crossing (LC87), for which special drainage works have been made. Arrangements for rain are a major preoccupation for this railway, it is not in short supply.* **Peter Johnson**

**Right:** *The view on 22nd January 2006 looking north, across the top of UB167, showing the wasted embankments, partly caused by a 'minimum cost' construction in 1922. The PB&SSR formation here did not trouble to spare the climb, so the 1922 Co. were obliged to shave embankments and bridge works to constrain the gradient to 1:43. The view of the unrestored northern exit to Beddgelert is a bit different than the view of the re-engineered railway below.* **Ben Fisher**

*Below: John Ewing stands at the temporary scaffolding railing, looking north across Pont Alyn, UB165 at the new cap on the other side. This bridge was widened and the deck was raised. You can spot the consolidation necessary upon the embankment opposite. The embankments were thin to start with and the years of closure had not improved them.*

complexities had to be overcome. The Cwm Cloch section is a difficult one for locomotives, but a very good railway was restored there. In addition, there are working farms that had to have unimpaired access provided, both to get in and out from the main road, and to reach the fields. The WHR had been used for this during the years of closure, and so alternative accesses were appropriately provided in mitigation of its restoration.

Pont Alyn bridges a bridleway; it is not a public road, and there is no public access for motor vehicles. The WHR entry into Beddgelert crosses the bridleway, and the Afon Nant Cwm Cloch (for the third time). The station is on a much larger scale than previously, and a great deal of work had to be done. The opportunity was taken to widen Pont Alyn by two metres, better to accommodate farm equipment. The old entrance to the station was no longer available for use by road vehicles, though accessible by foot. Thus a new private access was made under Pont Alyn, with a left turn under the station site through UB167, an accommodation bridge. The loop had to be longer than previously, thus the top-end trackbed needed to be wider. This meant

widening UB167, and the embankment in this area, which also required strengthening. A water tank was installed at the north end, and the loop was fitted with automatic trailing points. The two lines split below UB166, and the platform begins opposite the water tower, after the crossing of UB167. A gabion allows higher ballast levels, to maintain the gradient through the station. Platform buildings were provided soon after opening, and the footings were placed for a commodious main structure on the eastern side of the tracks. A small siding was provided on the western side, with a sharp curve required to reach the original pit; this siding was later cut back. The large water crane near the platform end can be swung to either platform, but of course the loop is right hand running. At the southern end of the station, there is a foot crossing for passenger access, then the line enters a cutting leading to the 47 yard Goat Tunnel. A footbridge, OB168 (**OB47.05**) Oberon Bridge, takes a footpath across the cutting before the tunnel entrance.

Pont Alyn, UB165 (**UB46.70**), at the north of the station, was completed by the PB&SSR as an arched bridge. The plan for the PB&SSR led to a steep exit at 1:28, up to the top of Cwm Cloch Isaf. This bit of trackbed was completed, and can be followed today, as it curves out of the station on to an embankment, and swings right into a cutting. It was all too steep for the WHR, so to reduce the gradient to 1:43, a flat deck was placed on the bridge in 1922 and the route went via Cutting Mawr. The deck was removed after WHR closure. The south abutment was replaced in reinforced concrete, for a wider deck. An electricity pole route was placed underground, down the side of the UB166 south abutment by November 2006, as otherwise it would have been foul of the trackbed at various points in the area.

Hughes were the

*Pont Alyn looking suitably impressive after its rebuilding. The south abutment had to be replaced, the north required a new capstone, and with the nice, smooth concrete beam across the top, all looks delightfully trim. Contrast it though with its cousins, the Bridge to Nowhere and the footpath to Cwm Bychan at Nantmor, other PB&SSR constructions.*

*Left: Note the additional width of UB167 and the temporary road access to the station site from Pont Alyn. The bridge now has its deck, and further down can be seen piles of earth that will be used to widen/strengthen the embankments. This was the occasion of a site inspection by Great Men on 24th March 2007.*

*Below: Fifteen months later and the station is largely complete. The large water crane, carefully positioned to be unobtrusive, yet to offer sustenance to locomotives either side stands on an immaculately tarmacced platform. The short emergency siding is installed and the track has wooden sleepers, as befits a station. In the distance permanent platform shelters have been erected. Beddgelert is being acknowledged as the Jewel in the Crown of the WHR.*

contractors for the main works, and they were on site in December, to create an access route for vehicles right through to Bryn y Felin. Though UB167 had a missing deck they were able to access the trackbed via the entrance at Pont Alyn, and to get on with site clearance, drainage works, and preparing the embankments. Work on UB165 began in December 2006 with the demolition of the south abutment. In January the abutment foundations were dug, and the first footings were cast. In February the new abutment was cast, and when the shuttering was removed, backfilling restored the embankment to level. On the north abutment part of the 1922 concrete cap was replaced, and the new cap was cast by 23rd March, leaving the way for the casting of the deck by the start of April 2007.

The adjacent PB&SSR road/rail bridge over the Afon Nant Cwm Cloch (UB166) was in good condition, so much work was not needed, although a gabion was laid upon it to allow the track ballast be to be elevated. The bridge carries the private access track to the station as well as the railway exit northbound.

The trio of northern end Beddgelert bridges includes UB167 (**UB46.79**). The deck had been removed, however the embankment here had to carry the platforms and two tracks, so it was far too narrow. The new standard platform length for WHR is 195m. At the southern end of the site, the Goat Cutting limited the placement of the loop points. Both abutments were cast by March 3rd 2007 - the place was a hive of activity. Twelve days later, and the new, widened deck was cast; the bridge had ballast, handrails, and track on it by May. At the same time the embankment strengthening work was taking place, for about 100 metres each side of UB167, and by mid-July the repaired section was

greening over with the native planting on it to blend into the landscape, honouring the pledge to 'touch the site lightly'.

There original station entrance, by the side of the Goat Hotel, could only be used as a footpath. This was solved by installing a private road access under UB167 for service vehicles. Public access was achieved by constructing a footpath and wheelchair incline from the adjacent public car park. Garden shed technology provides the temporary shop and a temporary building houses the loos. Browser's Book Shop funded the platform shelters. A replacement 'tin' lamp shed is now where one used to be, but the curve in the track to the pit was too sharp, so it was cut back.

The first passenger train back to Beddgelert was on 7th April 2009. The locals got the offer of a free ride, to try out the new trains; it was full. The moment service began to Beddgelert - to everyone's surprise - traffic poured in from Caernarfon. Some 7,000 came in the first month, 70k in the first year; thereafter it remains a popular destination - and the same from Porthmadog. It will be up to the Phase 5 Appeal to expand the 'basic' railway into the grand station that this jewel in the tourist crown deserves.

*NGG16 Garratt No. 138 coasts into Beddgelert Station with a train from Caernarfon. The locomotive is about to take the right hand road into the loop. Ahead can be seen the platform - quite welcoming. It's the building for receiving passengers that needs to be built - waiting room, cafe, shops and loo. In 2012 these are not permanent structures.*

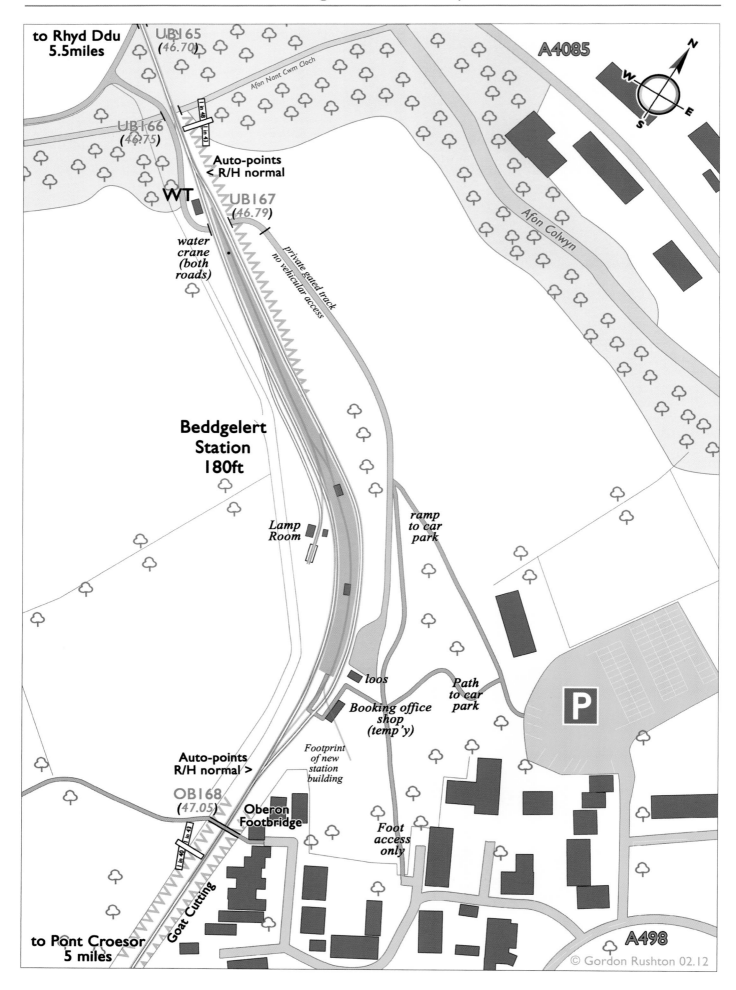

to Rhyd Ddu
5.5miles

UB165
*(46.70)*

*Afon Nant Cwm Cloch*

A4085

1 in 48

1 in 43

UB166
*(46.75)*

Auto-points
< R/H normal

WT

UB167
*(46.79)*

*Afon Colwyn*

*water
crane
(both
roads)*

*private gated track
no vehicular access*

**Beddgelert
Station
180ft**

*ramp
to car
park*

*Lamp
Room*

P

*loos*

*Path
to car
park*

*Booking office
shop
(temp'y)*

**Auto-points
R/H normal >**

*Footprint
of new
station
building*

OB168
*(47.05)*

1 in 43

**Oberon
Footbridge**

*Foot
access
only*

1 in 40

Goat Cutting

to Pont Croesor
5 miles

A498

© Gordon Rushton 02.12

## Tunnel No. 1 to Bryn y Felin

At the south end of Beddgelert Station, the 1:40 gradient continues through the 38m Goat Tunnel, No. 1. (**T47.15**) Upon emerging, the line avoids the old PB&SSR 'Bridge to Nowhere' and sweeps round a sharp 53 metre radius curve to extend the distance, to avoid steep gradients, to pass under the A4085 and cross the Afon Glaslyn a little further south than was originally planned.

The cutting leading to the Goat Tunnel was heavily overgrown, wet and steep. The reservoir trough for the former Goat Hotel water supply had fallen onto the trackbed, and water discharged down the cutting sides in wet conditions. This water was directed from its concrete trough into a pipe and thence into the drain. The drain was put through the tunnel in an open trough and ran rapidly away down the 1:40 gradient, keeping the cutting dry. The tunnel works were mostly complete by March 2007; rockbolting, shotcreting, and removing all the loose rock to be found in the tunnel was needed. The track was laid through in May but the test train experienced clearance problems. Work was required to increased the clearance. This could not be got by cutting away

*Left:* Looking north on 7th April 2007, Easter Saturday from on the Goat Tunnel. This accounts for the neat trackbed, blocked to frustrate vehicular excursion, devoid of clutter or machinery. Note the Oberon footbridge (OB168).     **WHRCL**

the roof; it is just too thin. So the track and all the ballast was taken out of the tunnel. Some loose rock under the ballast was taken away, and the ballast put back. The wooden sleepers were replaced with steel, to achieve the level required to offer the designated clearance. Alas, after this, the drainage channel was then too high, and had to have 100mm cut from the troughing to clear the structure gauge. The track work was completed by mid-July, on a very carefully adjusted alignment.

The line curves sharply after leaving the tunnel, and crosses LC88 (**LC47.36**) to Beddgelert Cemetery; it then curves back again to run over two large culverts, UB171 and UB172, carrying vigorous run off water from the hillside above. These needed to be rebuilt. Two large pipes were buried under the trackbed and terminated in a headwall, adjacent to the track, with a drain beyond. The wall was then stone clad.

A 1:50 gradient is maintained as the line curves southwards, past the only known Hornbeam tree in the National Park, behind a private dwelling toward the Afon Glaslyn. The A498 comes close alongside, and then climbs to cross the railway. OB173 (**OB47.92**) at Bryn y Felin (Mill Hill) was an old bridge, not thought suitable to continue to bear the weight of modern traffic. It had been a candidate for rebuilding for some time, and had there been an Abandonment Order, it would likely have been made level, onto the formation, with the bridge removed, to become one of the blocks to WHR reinstatement. With liability for overbridges with GC, they decided that this was the opportunity rebuild OB173, before the WHR reopened for business.

The railway runs out from under the road bridge on to the river bank, and crosses the Afon Glaslyn over a girder bridge. This bridge was constructed new for the task.

*Above:* Steel sleepers at the north exit of Tunnel No.1. This allows the track to lie lower, and you can see that the trough-drain sides have been trimmed by 10cms to give width clearance for rail vehicles, from the lower track level.     **WHRCL**

*Below:* These are the big pipes at UB171/2, to safeguard the formation against large amounts of water coming down from the hillside in times of flood. This sort of job had to be done everywhere on WHR and as it is not so glamorous, it is hardly mentioned.     **Roger Dick**

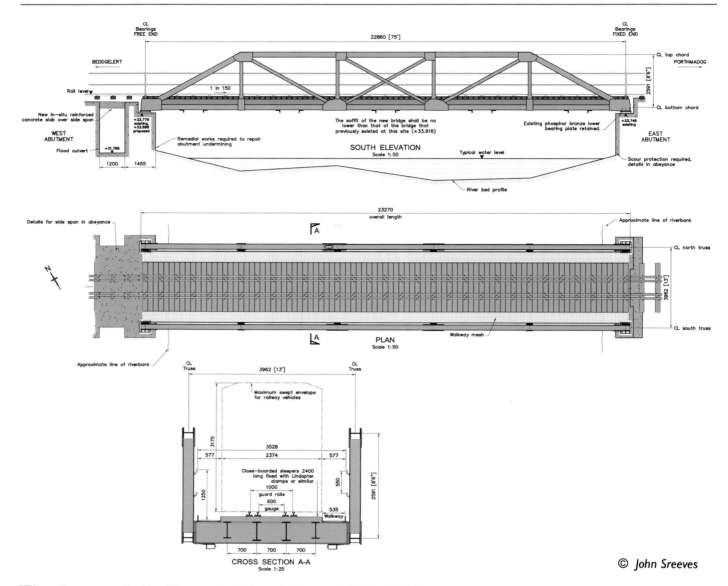

© *John Sreeves*

# The Bryn y Felin Truss Bridge UB174 (UB47.98)

The Welsh Highland Railway contractor, Sir Robert McAlpine & Sons, in 1922, installed three truss girder bridges to span the Afon Glaslyn, the Afon Nanmor, and the Afon Dylif. Today these are at, 18 miles, and between 20 and 21 miles from Caernarfon respectively. Bryn y Felin Bridge was the 1922 WHR Company route. The PB&SSR would have crossed the river further up, and risen at 1:28 to use the 'bridge that leads to nowhere' across the A498 road, as on the map above, right.

When the railway came to be reconstructed, unlike the North Wales Narrow Gauge, hogsback girder bridges, none of the three truss bridges was fit for further service. The webs in the girders had not been fitted with drain holes, and none of the structures had been painted, despite the recommendations of the Inspecting Officer and the Board of Trade. As a result, corrosion had taken place over the years of dereliction with fatal effect. All three of these 75 foot bridges had to be scrapped. The distinctive look the bridges brought to the Welsh Highland Railway had been remarked by many, thus volunteer, chartered engineer John Sreeves designed their modern replacements in the same style. Only one of the old bridges was ever visible to all the world at large, that over the Afon Glaslyn at Bryn y Felin, near to Beddgelert, 18 miles out from Caernarfon (UB174). Of course, at the entrance to the scenic and famous Pass of Aberglaslyn, it is very much in the public

*The Baldwin approaches Bryn-y-Felin bridge in old WHR days.*
**WHR Heritage Group**

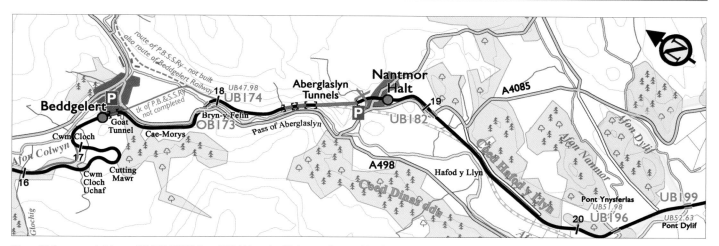

*Three 75 foot truss bridges - UB174, UB196 and UB199 and a 30 foot girder road bridge - UB182, all new. This is heavy engineering by any standard.*

**Map © Gordon Rushton**

eye. All interested in the WHR knew the old bridge. So there are well known photographs of the structure. Restorers all get a feeling of self-fulfillment from recreating a scene lost to time. John Sreeves's design makes this possible, as the delight of the diligent work on restoration allows today the assembly of original equipment, and the recreation of scenes from times past. It was not as easy in the old WHR days to see the Afon Nanmor and Afon Dylif bridges from the trackside, so they do not figure in the records with such regularity, given the relatively short period that the railway was open. Today there is the Bryn y Felin Road bridge and Afon Glaslyn footbridge, and another vantage point from a walkway for a public footpath on the UB196 (Pont Ynysferlas)

crossing the Nanmor, so the contemporary scene will be better recorded.

At Bryn y Felin the Glaslyn uses the full space underneath the bridge, and the flow is brisk. Thus substantial abutments were required, with scour protection from the rushing waters. Remedial work was needed, as the pier on the west side (uphill) was scoured out over approximately one third of its plan area, and had to be underpinned. A four-foot, reinforced concrete link-slab was provided on the uphill side, to span the flood opening between the pier and the west abutment. Rivers are subject to rapid changes in level when heavy and prolonged rains fall. Thus the Afon Glaslyn can become a raging torrent, and the 1.2m wide flood culvert was thought to be a necessary precaution. The uphill abutment was raised by six inches deliberately, to offer a slight (1:150) gradient, to assist the drainage of rainwater from the trusses. The existing east side bridge bearings, dating from 1922, were reused; the new bridge had been designed with the exact dimensions to enable this to occur. The bronze upper surface of the old bearings was not badly corroded. A liberal coating of rail fishplate grease was applied to ensure free sliding movement for expansion, and a rubber pad cut from a conveyor belt was laid over the bearing to allow for small irregularities in planarity.

Invitations to tender for this Afon Glaslyn river bridge

**Above:** *On 18th May 2005, the first truss of the Afon Glaslyn bridge at Bryn y Felin takes shape on the floor of Brunswick Iron Works in Caernarfon. The 76ft span lies on its side, all carefully marked out as it is steadily added to.* **Peter Johnson**

**Right:** *This detailed view of an end of a completed truss was taken a little time later on 1st of June 2005 in the paint shop at Brunswick Iron Works. It shows the part welded, part bolted construction - though the bolts look like the rivets of the original bridge. The white paint has been applied over red, to reveal any cracks in the welding of the bearing foot and webs.* **John C. Sreeves**

*Bryn y Felin main girders were faultlessly installed on site on 11th March 2006 . This was the first of three truss bridges. The two spans were placed on the bearing pads, and bolted to the transoms. The waybeams were then fitted, and a sleeper deck was added later to allow road access.*

were sent out in the third week of July in 2005, and tenders for the bridge, with options for Nanmor and Dylif were being appraised in early September. Like nearly all the work on WHR, the contract was let to a local firm, D.J. Williams and Sons, of the Brunswick Ironworks in Caernarfon in October 2005. They were already familiar with the WHR, having performed contracts in Phase 3. They tendered for all the metal bridges in Phase 4 and won. They set about construction in their Caernarfon works, delivering the first bridge for installation in March 2006. Construction used modern techniques, part welding, and part bolting. The fitted bolts have heads that look like rivets, with a special tool needed to perform the tightening of the nuts. The result is an

*The big crane squeezes along trackbed with only just enough room to spare The waybeams are on the ground awaiting fitment.* **Peter Johnson**

appearance strikingly similar to the original bridge trusses. The longitudinal and cross members were all bolted together at William's works in a trial assembly, to make sure everything fitted together, and the whole bridge was then taken to site as a kit of parts.

UB 174 (**UB47.98**), the bridge at Bryn y Felin was placed in

position on Saturday 11th March 2006. The convoy arrived in the morning to bring the trusses to join the transoms, cross members and longitudinal waybeams that had already been delivered to site. The mobile crane had manoeuvring space made for it from a dumper load of material already laid. It drove into position below, using the lay-by cunningly left for construction. Fortunately it fitted under the road bridge, on the railway trackbed, and so it was able to position itself in the ideal place to lift the spans from above, and then place them in position on the abutments. The large lorry with the spans loaded on to its extended trailer had come in from the Tremadog end. It berthed temporarily in the lower lay-by, that was coned off for the purpose, minimising disruption to traffic. It was called forward after the preparation work was completed for lifting. The road was closed briefly by closure notice, then the crane lifted the two trusses bound together from the lorry's extended trailer, and put them on the ground by the bridge, ready for placing. The transoms were located by crane on to the new bearing plates on each

*NGG16 No.138 hauls a train up through the Pass, rounding the sharp curve and running on to the Bryn y Felin bridge. The neat, asphalted paths below are public footpaths, replacing the informal walkway on the trackbed. The speed limit for this section is a steady 10mph.*

abutment. The spans were split, gently lifted, and lowered into position on the abutments, then bolted to the transoms.

At the very moment of criticality, with the first span suspended over the river, a party of canoeists came into view, happily paddling with the flow and threatening to pass under the dangling span. No one had thought to guard against canoeists on such a very cold morning!

Apart from this, the placing of the trusses went extremely smoothly. The efficiency of the operation was such that the road closure period was kept very short on the A498. After the placement of the trusses, all the other components were added with the aid of the crane, on Sunday 12th March 2006, and bolted together to complete the bridge.

All components had already been painted in the workshop in optimum conditions of temperature and humidity, and to reduce as far as practicable any working over water, which could well have demanded expensive staging. Further painting work was needed on site to repair small areas of surface damage caused during transit and assembly. However, to avoid a patchwork appearance,

*This view north up the Pass, taken between Tunnels 3 and 4, shows the height of the railway above the water, caused mostly by the rapid drop in the river.*

where remedial work had been carried out, the whole bridge got a quick once over, and the sleeper decking was added a month later.

The completion of the bridge then acted as the access to the trackbed for work to be done. Vehicles entered from the lay-by and were able to cross the Glaslyn, avoiding awkward transit through the tunnels further down.

## Through the Pass to Nantmor

The curve leading off the Bryn y Felin bridge, to align the railway with the Pass of Aberglaslyn just happened to be the second sharpest on the railway, after the 50m radius lead off the Britannia Bridge in Porthmadog 7 miles away. There is a 10mph speed restriction from here all the way through Beddgelert to the top of Cwm Cloch. The negligible gradient on the bridge steepens to 1: 50 towards Beddgelert and then to 1:40, with minor variation all the way north to Pont Cae'r Gors (Bog-bridge field). In the other direction, heading towards Porthmadog, further in to the Pass the gradient eases;

**Right:** *This repeat photo from above Tunnel No.2 shows the hefty wire and post guards against loose rocks - look above the tunnel, atop the big wall..*

**Below:** *The period 'estate', metal post and wire fencing was a feature of enclosures created in the 1920s. Fragments of it could be seen about the WHR section in places, distressed and rusty. To see something akin brought back in the 21st century is pleasing on the eye. It is durable, but will probably rust eventually like its predecessor, become slightly mis-shapen, and generally add character. Just a detail, but a nice one.*
**Ben Fisher**

it is 1:370 for half-a-mile, and then even rises for a short while, before levelling in No. 2 Tunnel, dropping at 1:100 in the short No. 3 Tunnel, and then just before the long No. 4 Tunnel (T4 -**T49.10**) the normal 1:40 down grade resumes. The river level appears to be a long way down at this point, because the Glaslyn drops rapidly into the Pass, to form its white-water section. This iis a part of the trackbed that was much loved by walkers and ramblers. Many who adored the WHR and wanted to see it restored walked this stretch, through the two small tunnels Tunnel No.2 (32yds), and Tunnel No. 3 (10yds), before entering the long Tunnel, Twnel Hir, No. 4 (306yds), and then emerged walking back into the open where the magic immediately departed.

The problem of the trackbed becoming a definitive footpath had been overcome. The Fisherman's Path was gradually reinstated, more thrilling by far, it was however a bit more difficult to negotiate on foot. Yet it had been pointed out that the railway was dangerous, and subject to potential rockfall. The unintended consequence of that was its immediate closure - a potential source of future problem for FR Co. was extinguished at a stroke! However, there was work that had to be carried out to stabilise and secure the vulnerable public from the potential of falling rocks. This was under the aegis of Phase 3 in 2001, but there was no budget for it, and as it was done outside the Millennium Commission grant then it was the FR Trust that had to find the £250k needed to pay for it. The stabilisation and remedial work already done on the tunnels meant less work was needed on the restoration of the railway through the Aberglaslyn Pass. However there was the requirement for the refurbishment for tracklaying, as soon Dŵr Cymru (Welsh Water) had completed the removal of the 18" water main that ran in the eastern border of the track from Bryn y Felin through T4. This was the largest of those works placed on the 'closed'

**Above:** *This was by no means an easy stretch, even though the trackbed might have looked in good condition from its use as a footpath. Culverts and sheep creeps were often roofed over with a stone slab. This was not judged to be Garratt proof, and it was wiser to replace them with modern materials. This is what is happening on the stretch of embankment leading to Tunnel No. 2*              **WHRCL**

**Right:** *It was recognised that it would be wise to provide an additional pair of flood channels under the formation, immediately south of Bryn y Felin, thus UB174A was formed.*              **WHRCL**

*Left: Civil engineering technician Owen Duncan wields the load/ structure gauge in Tunnel No. 3 (**T48.85**), on top of a sleeper, to get the right height, and note the sleeper marked with a yellow line to show the centre of the formation. This was sensible practice led by experiences in Goat Tunnel No.1 (**T47.15**), when indeed, the anticipated clearance was not found, and had to be recovered.*
**Ben Fisher Site**

*Below: This is a view taken in the other direction inside Tunnel No. 2, (**T48.77**) showing the sleeper bundles laid out on the new ballast, ready for tracklaying. The gang approaches the mouth of the tunnel, with the Head of Steel following close behind. This picture was taken*

trackbed for convenience, in the knowledge that in the unlikely event that the railway would be restored, it must be removed. Work started on this after the installation of Bryn y Felin rail bridge, when access to the trackbed was made available by road from the Nantmor end, as well as from the lay-by at Bryn y Felin. The work proceeded through November 2006, until completion in mid-January 2007. The trackbed now needed to be taken to ballast condition, and G.H. James secured the contract, from Bryn y Felin through to Nantmor Village, starting on 16th April 2007. There was a lot to do: there were culverts and sheep creeps north of the tunnels, embankment repair works, removal of the old water main, the provision of additional flood channels, and then the ballast to be laid.

When building the PB&SSR, the use of large, solid slabs of stone to bridge sheep creeps and culverts was thought to be adequate. It was considered more prudent to replace the beams with modern materials when it was easy to do so, rather than to leave them in situ and deal with a failure under traffic.

The civil engineering work had already been done in the tunnels, but it was necessary to recheck the clearances. They were a little tight in places, and the check established how much of the fill needed to be taken out of the tunnel floor, so that sub-base could be placed, at precisely the right level, ready for the ballast top. The water main had been encased in concrete through the tunnels (and

elsewhere). This all had to be broken out and removed. Tunnel 4 (**T49.10**) was clear by May 6th 2007. By August 2007 the ballasting was completed through all tunnels and tracklaying into the Pass began immediately afterwards.

The change of scenery out of the Pass is abrupt. The line passes under a bluff in Tunnel No. 4 (306 yds) and emerges into a nondescript cutting, crosses the bridge over the track to Cwm

*Above: The PB&SSR constructed this bridge, UB177 (**UB49.29**), is cousin to 'the bridge to nowhere'. It was in good condition and required little work before trains were restored to run upon it. Underneath runs the footpath up Cwm Bychan.* **Ben Fisher**

*Left: Above UB177 is the embankment on the 1:40 falling gradient towards Nantmor. This embankment had to be extended, first to accommodate road vehicles, as this was the only road access into the Pass until the Bryn y Felin bridge was decked after installation. The embankment is said last to have had track on it during the filming of the Inn of the Sixth Happiness, 20th Century Fox 1958.*

*Right: Nantmor Halt and crossing seen basking in May sunshine in 2010. The Halt had been dedicated to the Late Dr Ben Fisher and was just on the cusp of beginning to tempt people who left their cars in the nearby car park to take the train.*

*Below: An FR Trust visit to WHR on 24th March 2007: Chairman Dr John Prideaux on the left, and Mike Hart OBE on the right, walk down the trackbed to see and discuss the work to be done to remedy the thin embankment at Coed Gelli'r Ynn. Below is the A4085 and the gentlemen are discussing precisely how to ensure that embankment and road never meet.*

Bychan, passing the car park. This is UB177 (**UB49.29**), a bridge built by the PB&SSR, and apart from the thin embankment, this bridge was in good condition. Between the two tunnel mouths, Nos 3 and 4, the stiff 1:40 gradient resumes. After crossing a stream emanating from Cwm Bychan, at UB178, the railway now crosses the road into Nantmor village, after passing through a short cutting that had the detritus removed, and its base lowered to conform with the new road level on the crossing. In March 2007 Ray Jarvis Pressure Pointing and Grouting scaled loose

rock to ensure it was safe to allow the main contractor to prepare the track and ballasting. Beside the open level crossing (LC92 - **LC49.50**) was Mrs Entwistle's house, and adjacent, in 2010, was constructed Nantmor Halt, after a community ballot of the villagers held in 2007 that was 32 :11 in favour. The halt was built by donations made in memory of and dedicated to Ben Fisher, the originator of the website that made this book a practical proposition.

The line runs straight for a while after the halt and level crossing, until Coed Gelli'r ynn. The curving embankment at that point follows the A4085 road, and was too thin for the loads required. The embankment needed raising, and widening at the top, to 3.3m for the formation, but with no further spread at the base, which was limited by the road. Reinforced Earth Technology was employed, to use graded fill, wrapped in geotextile, seeded with native species of plants. This was a big job and the main contract was let to G.H.James Cyf., who began to excavate in mid-June 2007. The actual rebuilding of the embankment did not start until the end of July. In the middle, culvert UB181 (**UB49.76**) a slate box, was protected by a reinforced concrete slab. Layer after layer, the embankment was built back up steadily to the required height.

The work took until the end of September 2007, and on October 8th the sleepers were laid out on the fresh ballast, ready for tracklaying, as far as the new bridge over the A4085. The seeded embankment (**25.18** Cei Newydd) grew over rapidly afterwards, despite winter.

*Above: This was a repair open to the restorers but not to the builders - it is a new technology. It was a costly way to build up an embankment to take the weight of a train - but it had to be done. The embankment edge stretches out and curves to the left. The grade markings show that there is still some way to go.* **WHRCL**

*Right: The red Garratt, NGG16 No. 138, descends with a train at a distance of 19 miles from Caernarfon to Porthmadog on 1st July 2011. The remedial works at Gelli'r Ynn are maturing nicely, and the embankment remains firmly in place, despite the provocation of trains along it.*

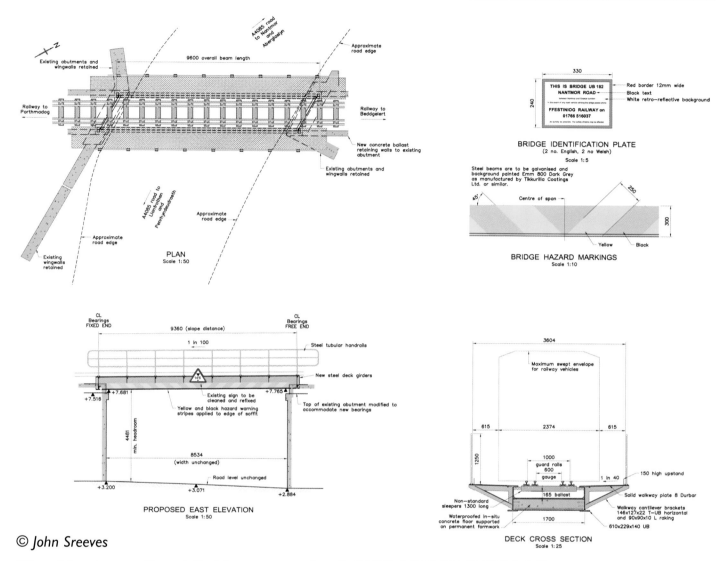

PLAN
Scale 1:50

BRIDGE IDENTIFICATION PLATE
(2 no. English, 2 no. Welsh)
Scale 1:5

BRIDGE HAZARD MARKINGS
Scale 1:10

PROPOSED EAST ELEVATION
Scale 1:50

DECK CROSS SECTION
Scale 1:25

© John Sreeves

# The Nantmor Road Bridge, over the A4085, UB182 (*UB50.00*)

When travelling out from Porthmadog it might seem slightly strange that for 6 miles the WHR has run on the flat, and at Hafod y Llyn, it seems suddenly to change its mind, and heads rapidly upwards, with a ruling grade of 1:40, much of the way to Pitt's Head, a further six miles away. But that is surely part of its charm, as it was an 'electric' railway converted to steam. The first major hurdle the ascending trains come to is the bridge over the road from Penrhyndeudraeth to the Aberglaslyn Pass, the A4085. To achieve the 4.5m headroom offered by this bridge, the line rises from the level, at the last possible moment. Anyone old enough to remember the restoration of the FR, will also recall this living reminder of the faded glories of the old WHR, apparently lost and gone. The old bridge remained after closure, and you could drive under and tell people about the old railway that ran through the Pass. (Not that they would ever listen.) You could walk over it as well, as a wicket gate was thoughtfully provided. In the Beeching years, track and all metal bridges seemed to disappear quickly after railways closed, but this one was reassuringly present - it encapsulated our hopes. It was therefore a mild shock one day, to drive over from Penrhyn and suddenly to come across a vacant space, where once that bridge stood. It had been evidence of the 'this is still a railway-ness' of the old WHR. When the old

bridge was removed on Sunday 6th November 2005, it was a sudden notice that a different regime had arrived, the one of clearance for reconstruction. The approach to the bridge UB182, was different than for the river bridges. There was no need to use it for construction traffic; adequate access to the trackbed was readily available on both sides nearby. The old bridge needed replacement, with the 4,5m headroom maintained. John Sreeves, who designed the bridge takes up the story:

*"The former bridge consisted of two riveted plate girders at 1.3m centres, each 9.6m long, and spanning 8.5m between abutments. The beams were linked by transverse pressed steel troughing, which supported longitudinal timbers to which the rails were directly fixed. This arrangement enabled the rail heads to be level with the top flanges, and derailment containment was provided by two angle rubbing strips attached inside the beam flanges. Whether this would have been effective in deflecting wheels without damaging the bridge itself is open to conjecture! Timber walkways were provided either side of the main beams, supported by cantilever angle brackets.*

*In common with the other bridges dating from 1922, the steelwork was never painted, and had reached an advanced state of corrosion. Riveted plate girders have many corners and crevices where water can be retained, and there was significant loss of section in most areas. Repair by welding or bolting on new plates was considered but*

**Left:** *"That's where the old WHR trains used to run.........." This is the view from childhood of the mysterious bridge, over which once ran the romantic, lost little railway. The chances of getting a satisfactory answer were nil - no one knew anything about it, and in the Beeching years, closed railways were common and railways were considered to be old fashioned.* **Roger Dick**

**Below:** *The old bridge, across the road at Nantmor, waiting in vain for trains that never ever came again. Alas the rust has gone too far to save the bridge that was never painted, and spent more time vacant of trains than it ever did with rails and a regular service across it!* **Roger Dick**

such a job would be difficult and achieve only a limited life extension, as well as needing a lengthy highway closure. We concluded that a new bridge would be cheaper in the long run, so the old deck was unceremoniously removed on 6th November 2005, this being the last remaining example of 1922 steelwork on the railway.

Replacement options were likely to include pre-cast concrete or steel beams, there being a need to bridge the gap with a minimum of traffic disruption. A ballasted trackbed was desirable to avoid the maintenance problems associated with direct fixing of rails, but to raise the rail levels would have interfered with the gradient profile. It became apparent that a trough form of deck would be necessary, similar to that which existed previously, to enable the track to be positioned between rather than on top of the beams, supported by a transverse structural floor. Furthermore, steel was preferable to pre-cast concrete to keep any increase in dead weight to a minimum.

The abutments are very narrow, with tapered sides. Any increase in deck width would result in the bearings having to be set further back to ensure adequate support, thus requiring deeper and heavier beams. To minimise this effect it was decided to use short non-standard timber sleepers 1.3m long, these being just adequate in length to carry the guard rails. The main deck members are universal beams 610 x 229 x 140kg/m set at 1.7m centres. This spacing is only a little wider than before but sufficient to accommodate ballast around the ends of the sleepers, and only minor modifications were needed to the abutments to accommodate new beam bearings.

The transverse floor linking the two main beams consists of a reinforced concrete slab, supported by permanent formwork and

*The new Nantmor UB132 span at Brunswick Ironworks on 23 October 2006.* **Ben Fisher**

bonded to the girders by studs. An alternative steel 'battle-deck' was considered, but a complex fabrication would have ensued to link the two beams with sufficient rigidity, as well as creating potential corrosion traps. Concrete is simpler to construct, and the extra rigidity obtained has the advantage of mitigating any damage sustained in the event of a bridge bash by an over-height road vehicle. The weight to be lifted by crane is 18 tonnes, but this is still less than it would have been for a single wholly pre-cast concrete element.

Cantilever walkways and handrails are supported by angle brackets either side, to replicate the appearance of the original bridge. For durability the walkways are steel plate rather than timber, and do not need to carry construction traffic. An edge upstand was added to comply with current safety standards.

All structural members are galvanised to give long life corrosion resistance, and the inside of the deck trough was fully waterproofed before being filled with ballast. To aid drainage, a gradient of 1 in 100 was introduced instead of being flat, as previously, and the bridge was completed by the addition of black and yellow 'wasp stripes' painted on the outer beam faces."

All of that thought and expertise was required to sort this bridge - and that was only one of the structures on the 25 mile restored railway!

Brunswick Ironworks had been successful in tendering for the contract for building the new bridge, and they built it in their works, so that it could be lifted into place as a single item, fully constructed, including the concrete infill to permit the track ballast to be continued across it.

*The UB182 test lift to make sure all is well before adding the walkways*

**Peter Johnson**

elsewhere, as the road was a firm foundation for lifting. However a closure notice for the road under the bridge was obtained for the day of Sunday 29th October 2006. The lorry with its 18 tonne load was dispatched from Brunswick Ironworks in Caernarfon. There was a snag. The walkways with their supporting brackets, and the handrails, were too wide to be transported attached to the span. These were brought separately. Prudence dictated a test lift to check general fit, and the span was then fitted with its brackets, handrails

After the old spans had been removed from site, the abutments were found to need minor works, for which temporary traffic lights, the bane of all drivers on North Wales's narrow roads, were required. However this was a set that WHR enthusiasts did not curse at! It was a work where the new span had been designed to fit neatly into the spaces left by the old.

Installation of the thirty-foot span of UB182 (**UB50.00**) was rather easier in terms of access than at some locations

and walkway plates, except those parts needed to be omitted for the purposes of the lift. The lift and fitting went well, and the span was down, on its pads by 14.00, after a minor adjustment at the northern end, where the footing of one handrail had to be cut away. After installation, bolt and base plate grouting works were done, followed by the addition of concrete masking and the curtain and ballast walls at the ends.

The bridge opened for road traffic on 29th October 2006.

*The installed bridge being inspected by Great Men on 24th March 2007, the embankment remedial works are awaited before track.*

*Right: On 18th March 2007, CH James Cyf's men were repairing the riverbank with big rocks that were carefully concealed with willow roots. Beyond the digger the trackbed is a streak of green. To the right of the 'modur barcio' is the road from the A4085 to Hafod y Llyn Farm* **WHRCL**

*Below: The view south, down from the A4085 bridge shows the sudden rise of trackbed necessary to clear the road below it. At this time, 24th March 2007, there was still much work to be done to prepare the trackbed for the track to be laid.*

## Hafod y Llyn to Pont Croesor

**B**etween the Nantmor Road Bridge and Hafod y Llyn, the gradient falls at 1:40 and then eases to 1:70 before flattening out at the river's edge. Erosion was a problem here as rudimentary piling showed. The years of closure had made matters worse, plus there was the complication of an Otter Holt. Widening was required to achieve modern angles of repose, by expanding the base to make the sides less steep.

A roadway from the A4985 leads down to the trackbed, which the farmer at Hafod y Llyn Isaf used for access for years. It was decided to establish a depot here, exploiting the road access to the adjacent A4085, and the space between the river and the rocky hillside, which was enough for a siding and later a temporary loop line. Despite there being a Hafod y Llyn on the FR, this name was applied. This was to be the temporary terminus until Pont Croesor was ready in 2009. A halt was created, to be used (normally) for staff purposes, and the area around was available for storage of materials for the construction. A construction of a replacement road was required in mitigation, and that was part surfaced in tarmac by GC.

The Afon Glaslyn is no longer turbulent at this point, but it had worked away over the years, eroding the gentle bend near where the trackbed changes from level to steep climb. It was necessary to repair the river bank, to put in place big rocks to protect against further erosion, and then to disguise the rocks with willow trees, who's roots will provide biological reinforcement, as well as enhance the sylvan scene in years to come. This was all done in mid-March, 2007 before the other work, and before the fish spawning season of the famous Glaslyn Salmon. Repairs to the little culvert UB187 (**UB50.49**) at Gwâl y Dwrgi were also included in the work. The job was completed by September 2007.

The the repairs at Coed Gelli'r ynn embankment were completed in October and so the track was able to approach the A4985 bridge. C.H. James Cyf, the

*Above: The raised embankment is the old, empty, WHR trackbed between the Afon Nanmor and Afon Dylif. The surveyors marks are up, and all will change radically, shortly. 4th February 2007* **WHRCL**

*Right: This view shows clearly the crushed slate base, with the machine for spreading the ballast on top for the track to be installed. Alongside is the road to Hafod y Llyn Isaf Farm. Taken on 21st December 2007.* **Ben Fisher**

contractor, was engaged in the systematic repair of the UB182 (**UB50.00**) approach embankment and by November the widening and raising work was done, with soil cladding being added. Then the crushed slate was laid and consolidated with vibrating rollers, with ballast laid on top. It was in early November that the ballasted trackbed was handed over for tracklaying, offering the volunteer gangs a clear run as far as the Afon Nanmor Bridge, Pont Ynysferlas.

The boundary of the National Park is at the crossing of the Afon Dylif, some 700 yards beyond. The trackbed was needed for access, and so for reasons of practicality, Pont Dylif was installed first, and it will be described next. Once the railway was reconstructed as far as the National Park boundary at Pont Dylif, then service could begin from Rhyd Ddu to a suitable intermediate point. This was chosen to be to Beddgelert first, and then to Hafod y Llyn, to take in the Aberglaslyn Pass.

*The trackbed below Hafod y Llyn loop was formerly the access to Hafod y Llyn Isaf Farm. The new road access lies on the left of the trackbed, which has it's fresh ballast all prepared, and the bundles of sleepers just waiting for the next tracklaying working party. That was not far away, as the photograph was taken on 21st December 2007.*

Service began in May 2009, whilst construction was advancing to Pont Croesor where service to that point would begin in 2010. As a preview: From the foot of the A4985 embankment, the railway runs for six miles, almost level all the way to Porthmadog. The view opens out, as the railway travels east to join with the old Croesor Tramway. On the way to Porthmadog there are three major bridges, crossing the Afon Nanmor, Afon Dylif, and Afon Glaslyn, with a flat crossing of the Cambrian Coast Line, and four public level crossings. The whole of this flat section is raised on a shallow embankment above the area enclosed by the Cob. This precaution prevents the seasonal inundation of this land that was formerly the estuary of the Afon Glaslyn. The line remains between 2 and 4 metres above datum, rising to the higher figure as it approaches Porthmadog. It is this flatland section that will be covered next..

*Just round the corner from Hafod y Llyn Isaf, where the road ends, the Afon Nanmor flows. The 1922 Company had built a truss bridge across the river, just like the one at Bryn y Felin. John Sreeves's design was employed here, and across the Dylif, 700 yds further south. This bridge, now Pont Ynysferlas, has a footpath across it, and so a walkway was installed. Brunswick Ironworks built all these bridges. Pont Ynysferlas trusses were put in position on Saturday 17th March 2007. A timetable dictated by the adjacent Osprey, that could have been disturbed by the high jib of the crane. Picture taken 24th March 2007.*

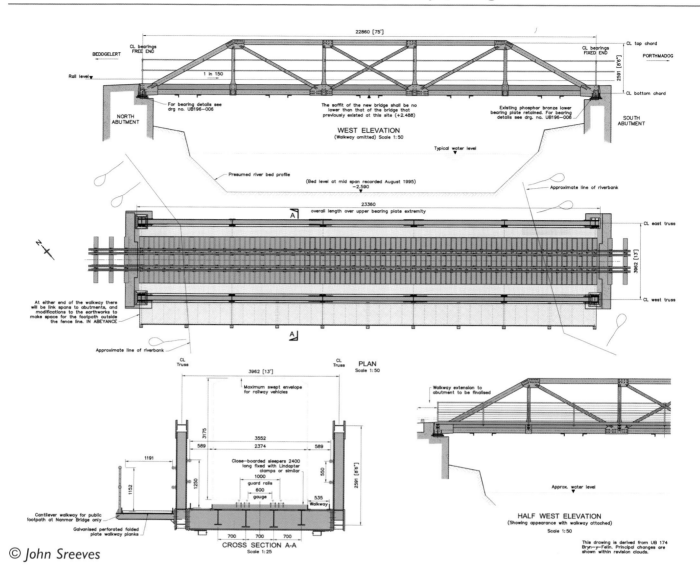

© *John Sreeves*

# The Afon Nanmor and Afon Dylif Truss Bridges UB196 and UB199

urther on down the trackbed towards Porthmadog are the bridges across the Afonydd Nanmor and Dylif. They are between 20 and 21 miles from Caernarfon, and are within sight of one another, only some 700 yards apart. The bridge UB196 (**UB51.98**) crosses the Afon Nanmor and UB199 (**UB52.63**) crosses the Afon Dylif. The previous structures were prudently removed for replacement shortly after the acquisition of the trackbed in 1999. This did cause some concern to local farmers when it happened. The railway had lain unused since the removal of the track in 1941. There had been no railway activity on it; the whole enterprise was

moribund and the track derelict. Thus here, as elsewhere, if the farmers could make use of the trackbed, the better to access and service the land, they did so. The area is remote, and access is by farm track and public footpath.

Abutment work had been done on the bridges in 2005. In the same way as for the Bryn y Felin bridge, both Nanmor and Dylif bridges had their northern abutments raised by six inches, in order to ensure that rainwater would drain from the trusses. The fittings of the original phosphor bronze bearing pads were refurbished, and locating studs were fitted for the transoms.

The lack of road access required that the more

*Both the bridges were removed in 1999. The empty abutments of the bridge over the Afon Nanmor, taken from the Porthmadog side on 22nd February 2006.* **Bruce Brayne**

*Left: On 3rd March 2007, the embankment beyond the bridges is being progressively widened and made up to height by fill brought from a dump at Croesor Junction. This view is on the trackbed from Croesor Junction, towards Pont Croesor.* **John Peduzzi**

*Below: On the north side of the Afon Dylif, clearance has taken place, the trackbed was consolidated for heavy vehicles to deliver the Nanmor bridge without damage, and the machines have moved off to perform drainage works in this view of 24th March 2007. The track will come in February 2008.*

southerly bridge over the Dylif was needed as a means of accessing the Afon Nanmor crossing, thus Pont Dylif was installed first.

There was an added complication at these two worksites. For some time there had been much celebration that a pair of Ospreys (*Pandion haliaetus*) had chosen a nest site nearby in 2004. These were the only Ospreys breeding in Wales, and they are such grand and rare fish-eating raptors that their welcome by the RSPB amounted to celebrity status. It was thought that the disturbance of building a railway nearby might convince these discerning birds that this was a bad place to breed. Both the trackbed and bridge sites in the vicinity were within the exclusion zone, and so construction activity was not allowed while the Ospreys were on the nest from the end of March to the end of August. The project was therefore time constrained, to erect both Dylif and Nanmor bridges before the end of March, the Osprey deadline. This had to be 'put up with' as these birds were a great tourist draw in their own right, and there was no proposal that trains could not run in the future during the Osprey season.

Test assembly of the (UB199) Dylif bridge, took place in Brunswick Ironwork's premises in October of 2006, and the third, bridge (UB196) was in an advanced state of fabrication. The problem was how to get the trusses into position - in particular that for the Afon Nanmor.

It was impractical to bring the vehicle carrying the trusses via the roadway past the Halt to Hafod y Llyn Isaf Farm. The north route via Nantmor was impractical because the corner from the Porthmadog-Beddgelert road, over the Glaslyn road bridge would not permit an extended trailer to cross the river. The route the other way, via the A4085 and Pont Garreg Hylldrem was difficult too, and this left the only practical access for the tractor and extended trailer as along the WHR trackbed from

the level crossing (to be) at Ynysfor, a distance to be travelled of nearly two miles. So the whole of this part of the trackbed had to be made ready, and Pont Dylif (UB199) had to be erected before Pont Ynysferlas (UB196).

Work started here before the riverbank job at Hafod y Llyn. Land was purchased for an eased curve at Croesor Junction, and a depot was made at that point. An access road for Ynysferlas Farm was included as works in mitigation, westbound from Croesor Junction. Stone was placed on the trackbed from Croesor Junction to Ynysfor to form a top, even so the load was limited to one truss at a time, flat, on the extended trailer. Two cranes were used, one specially lightened by 15 tonnes; both were brought to site via a Garreg - Hylldrem access. The loads for UB199 were delivered on Saturday February 17th, 2007. It was a long business, as the lorry had to be reversed out, and then go back to Caernarfon for the second span. It returned in the early evening, and the span was unloaded and placed in position before nightfall. There was a minor glitch. Whilst the lorry was away it was noticed that the first truss that had been lifted into place and bolted up to the end transoms wasn't seating properly on its bearings. It was realised that it was the wrong way round, since the ends are asymmetric, to allow for the 1 in 150 gradient. So before the lorry came

*UB 199 The bridge over the Afon Dylif, a much lesser stream, but perhaps not when roused. The spans are in position and have been fixed. The cross beams and other structural members are now being fitted in this splendid view of 18th February 2007.* **John Sreeves**

# The Afon Dylif and Afon Nanmor bridges

*Left:* On 24th March 2007 the decked Afon Dylif bridge has done its job, acting as the conduit for all the construction materials, including the trusses and beams of its sibling a half-mile back. Soon it will be ready for track. Look at the large amount of material needed to make the embankment to the correct width.

*Below:* A week before, on 17th March 2007, the trusses for the Afon Nanmor bridge are eased gently over the Afon Dylif bridge. Up at the Nanmor the crane will lift and install the two spans, as soon as they arrive, and in a few days, all the parts will be bolted together. This is major engineering on any scale, and the proud achievement of massive co-operation.                                                      **John Sreeves**

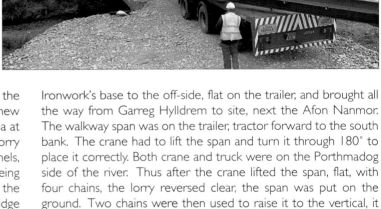

back, the transoms were unbolted and the truss reversed to the other side, to achieve a perfect fit. The following day, the intermediate cross members, waybeams, and bracing pieces were fitted. Mr John Sreeves was accommodated in the matter of taking pictures by being hoisted skywards by the crane, as can be seen in the picture on the previous page. As soon as the bridge was all bolted together, and the painting was finished, a timber deck was fitted, to allow the passage of road vehicles, and more importantly ,the crane and lorry with the spans for UB196, the Afon Nanmor bridge.

Two spans were loaded on the one trailer for this bridge. There was by this time a consolidated roadway all the way along the trackbed from Ynysfor, over the Dylif by the new bridge, and on the half mile or so to a prepared ballasted area at the side of the Nanmor, to allow the rig to turn round. The lorry crossed the new bridge on specially prepared deck infill panels, with only 200mm to spare on either side, despite the trusses being laid flat on the extended trailer. The Glaslyn-side truss was the heaviest single item to be lifted in place in the whole river bridge programme. It had a side extension with the pedestrian walkway, for the public footpath. The Afon Nanmor is 3.5m deep at the crossing, so as a precaution a rescue boat was available whilst work was taking place. This was used by one of Brunswick Ironwork's workmen to get across, prior to the bridge being in place. Upon stepping out of the boat, he lost his footing, the boat flipped upside down, and he was deposited into some extremely cold water. The boat's popularity waned somewhat after this.

The transoms, cross members, and waybeams were brought to site, with the trusses to follow. On the morning of Saturday 17th March, the trusses were loaded on to the lorry at Brunswick

Ironwork's base to the off-side, flat on the trailer, and brought all the way from Garreg Hylldrem to site, next the Afon Nanmor. The walkway span was on the trailer, tractor forward to the south bank. The crane had to lift the span and turn it through 180° to place it correctly. Both crane and truck were on the Porthmadog side of the river. Thus after the crane lifted the span, flat, with four chains, the lorry reversed clear, the span was put on the ground. Two chains were then used to raise it to the vertical, it was traversed through 180° over the river, lowered into position and married to the transoms. The lorry then returned for a similar manoeuvre to be carried out with the upstream truss. The work was completed on the two bridges, on 24th March 2007. The way was then clear for various access, roadway and drainage works to be performed before the laying of track could begin by the tracklaying gangs in August 2007.

During the weekend that the Nanmor bridge was being erected (17-18 March 2007) members of the Osprey project were seen busy installing CCTV cameras and transmitters ready for the Ospreys' return. That year they came back on 26 March and had laid three eggs by 16 April.

*UB196 (**UB51.98**) over the Afon Nanmor with the north span being installed on 17th March 2007. The south span, with the walkway beams is already in position. The components of the bridge were fastened together rapidly. It was a very neat job and was a particular credit to Brunswick Ironworks, and to John Sreeves, the designer. These are the bridges you'd want on your model railway!*                                      **Peter Johnson**

244

*At Croesor Junction the PB&SSR/WHR left the Croesor Tramway to run towards the Aberglaslyn Pass. The Tramway headed for the Croesor Valley. Dr John Prideaux (L) and Mike Hart (R) examine the remains of the old WHR bridge on 23 April 2007 during a Trustee's Visit. The Landrover pauses on the old Croesor trackbed, used for access through Garreg Hylldrem Farm. The curve was eased for the reconstruction. The new alignment is some way away but will allow for 25mph running.*

It was a job completed just in time.

The line of railway from the Afon Dylif bridge to Pont Croesor is practically level, for one and a half miles, apart from a couple of areas of 1:500 gradient. The curve at Croesor Junction was eased considerably to allow eventual 25mph running, and the line was built outside the Limits of Deviation, with land purchased for the purpose.

The line straightens out, and then curves to an open level crossing (LC112), Ynysfor Level Crossing. One feature of this area is the feeding station for dairy cattle at Ty Newydd Morfa farm. The agricultural atmosphere is so pressing, that the curve has been named Pooh Corner. Towards the Afon Glaslyn, there is a flood relief channel UB209 that needed major work.

The first job that took place here was in 2005 on the embankment between Ynysfor Level Crossing and Pont Croesor. The thick gorse was removed, and replaced immediately

*Surely a sign with a spectacular view. Ynysfor level crossing (**LC54.67**) in glorious weather. There is but one problem to make the photographer change location, the pressing agricultural smell - this is Pooh Corner.* **Peter Johnson**

with a fence, or live stock would have escaped. The flood relief channels UB209 and adjacent UB210 were to be replaced by removing the structure, and then letting in pipes, constructing side walls, filling over the top, and then building the formation back up, so that ballast could be placed and then track laid. There were six pipe sections, and they looked extremely neat, flanked in vernacular stone. The construction was complete by 19th February 2008. There was just a small pipe culvert to be completed near to Ynysfor level crossing, and then the track could be laid. This was laid over the Afon Dylif Bridge by 10th February 2008. The straight section south of Ynysfor allows stunning views to be taken with a video camera, in a car on the road running in parallel with the train.

The next 'civils' job south was the restoration of the longest bridge on the line, the eight-span Pont Croesor over the Afon Glaslyn.

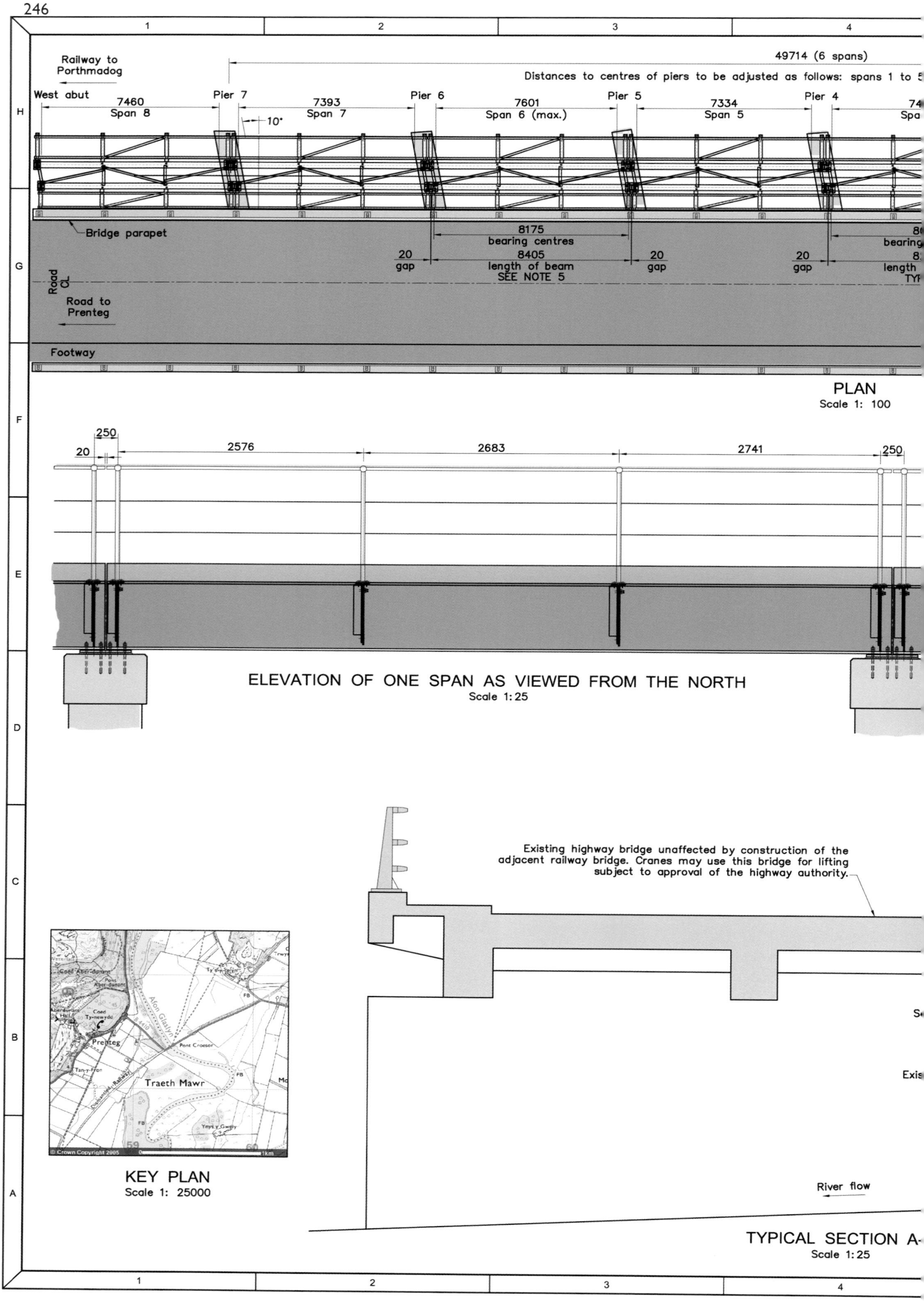

| | 1 | 2 | 3 | 4 |
|---|---|---|---|---|

Railway to
Porthmadog

49714 (6 spans)

Distances to centres of piers to be adjusted as follows: spans 1 to 5

West abut | 7460 | Pier 7 | 7393 | Pier 6 | 7601 | Pier 5 | 7334 | Pier 4 | 74
Span 8 | | Span 7 | | Span 6 (max.) | | Span 5 | | Spa

10°

Bridge parapet

8175
bearing centres
8405
length of beam
SEE NOTE 5

8
bearing
8
length
TY

20
gap

20
gap

20
gap

Road CL

Road to
Prenteg

Footway

**PLAN**
Scale 1: 100

250
20

2576

2683

2741

250

**ELEVATION OF ONE SPAN AS VIEWED FROM THE NORTH**
Scale 1:25

Existing highway bridge unaffected by construction of the
adjacent railway bridge. Cranes may use this bridge for lifting
subject to approval of the highway authority.

Se

Exis

River flow

**TYPICAL SECTION A-**
Scale 1:25

**KEY PLAN**
Scale 1: 25000

| | 1 | 2 | 3 | 4 |
|---|---|---|---|---|

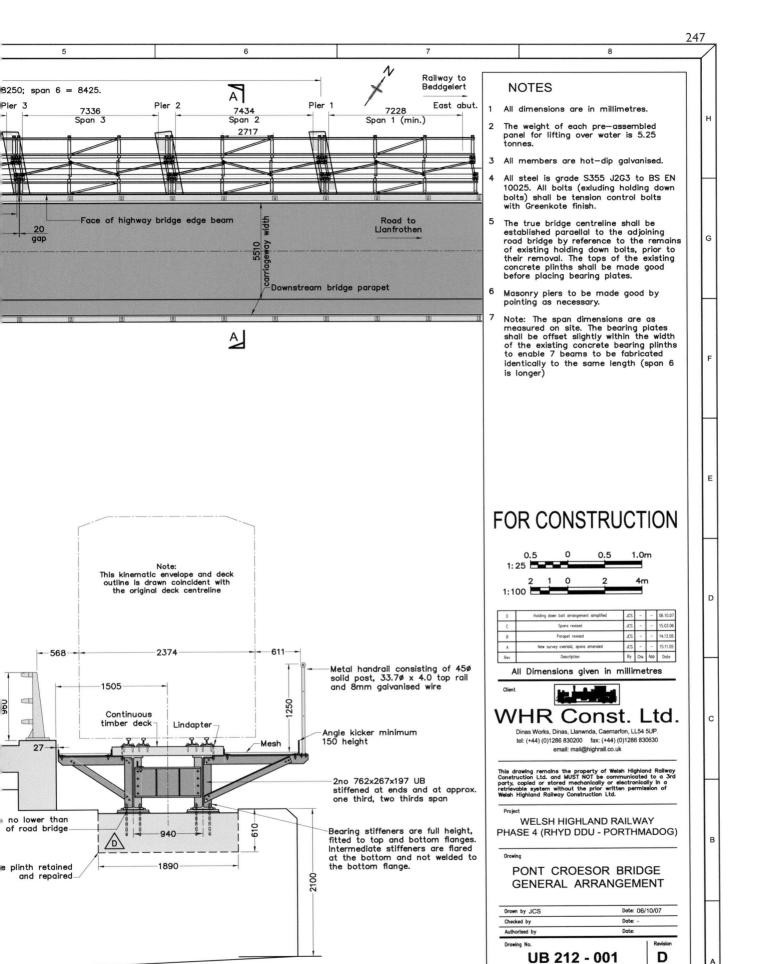

| 5 | 6 | 7 | 8 |

8250; span 6 = 8425.

Pier 3  |  7336  |  Pier 2  |  7434  |  Pier 1  |  7228  |  East abut.
Span 3         Span 2         Span 1 (min.)

2717

N

Railway to
Beddgelert

— Face of highway bridge edge beam

20
gap

5510
carriageway width

Road to
Llanfrothen →

Downstream bridge parapet

A⌐
A⌐

### NOTES

1   All dimensions are in millimetres.

2   The weight of each pre-assembled panel for lifting over water is 5.25 tonnes.

3   All members are hot-dip galvanised.

4   All steel is grade S355 J2G3 to BS EN 10025. All bolts (exluding holding down bolts) shall be tension control bolts with Greenkote finish.

5   The true bridge centreline shall be established paraellal to the adjoining road bridge by reference to the remains of existing holding down bolts, prior to their removal. The tops of the existing concrete plinths shall be made good before placing bearing plates.

6   Masonry piers to be made good by pointing as necessary.

7   Note: The span dimensions are as measured on site. The bearing plates shall be offset slightly within the width of the existing concrete bearing plinths to enable 7 beams to be fabricated identically to the same length (span 6 is longer)

Note:
This kinematic envelope and deck outline is drawn coincident with the original deck centreline

568 — 2374 — 611

1505

Continuous
timber deck     Lindapter

27

Mesh

960

1250

— Metal handrail consisting of 45⌀ solid post, 33.7⌀ x 4.0 top rail and 8mm galvanised wire

Angle kicker minimum 150 height

— 2no 762x267x197 UB stiffened at ends and at approx. one third, two thirds span

no lower than of road bridge

940

610

e plinth retained and repaired

1890

2100

Bearing stiffeners are full height, fitted to top and bottom flanges. Intermediate stiffeners are flared at the bottom and not welded to the bottom flange.

## FOR CONSTRUCTION

| 0.5 | 0 | 0.5 | 1.0m |
1:25

| 2 | 1 | 0 | 2 | 4m |
1:100

| D | Holding down bolt arrangement simplified | JCS | – | – | 06.10.07 |
| C | Spans revised | JCS | – | – | 15.03.06 |
| B | Parapet revised | JCS | – | – | 14.12.05 |
| A | New survey overlaid, spans amended | JCS | – | – | 15.11.05 |
| Rev | Description | By | Chk | App | Date |

**All Dimensions given in millimetres**

Client

## WHR Const. Ltd.

Dinas Works, Dinas, Llanwnda, Caernarfon, LL54 5UP.
tel: (+44) (0)1286 830200   fax: (+44) (0)1286 830630
email: mail@highrail.co.uk

This drawing remains the property of Welsh Highland Railway Construction Ltd. and MUST NOT be communicated to a 3rd party, copied or stored mechanically or electronically in a retrievable system without the prior written permission of Welsh Highland Railway Construction Ltd.

Project

WELSH HIGHLAND RAILWAY
PHASE 4 (RHYD DDU - PORTHMADOG)

Drawing

### PONT CROESOR BRIDGE
### GENERAL ARRANGEMENT

| Drawn by JCS | Date: 06/10/07 |
| Checked by | Date: - |
| Authorised by | Date: |

| Drawing No. | | Revision |
| **UB 212 - 001** | | **D** |

| Drawing Scale: 1:100, 1:25 | Original Size: A1 |
| CAD Filename: | Plot Scale: 1:1 |

| 5 | 6 | 7 | 8 |

FILE STORAGE PATH =
XREF STORAGE PATH =

ORIGINATING DEPT =
PLOT DATE = 06/10/07

*Right: Pont Croesor as it once was, empty of the railway, with the thick gorse growing on the embankment that stretched away towards those sunlit mountains. Unless you knew about WHR, it was difficult to know that there had ever been a railway here. This picture was taken on 18th April 2004.*

*Below: The new spans are being laid on to plates that are placed on top of the refurbished piers. There have been holes drilled exactly in the abutments to bolt the plates down and anchor them in place. Note that the spans are slightly skewed, and this is seen with the first cross-member. This picture was taken on 2nd January 2008.* **WHRCL**

## Pont Croesor UB212

Pont Croesor (UB212 - **UB55.54**) carries the railway and the B4410 Prenteg-Llanfrothen road across the Afon Glaslyn, with the railway on the upstream side. The river is broad at this point, and the bridge length of 65.25m is carried on seven masonry piers that required remedial work. The bridge, was built in wood for the Croesor Tramway in 1864, and heavily rebuilt in 1922-3 for the WHR. The rail deck was removed in 1948-9, and the road deck was extensively refurbished and strengthened in 1994. After this work it encroached slightly on the railway side of the bridge, but not enough to cause a problem. The eight spans, fabricated in 2007 by the Brunswick Ironworks in Caernarfon, vary between 7.210 and 7.565m, and the piers are not at right angles to the decks, but are on a ten degree skew.

The new deck was designed by John Sreeves. The design follows that of the 1922 version, but the twin steel beams are 770mm deep, instead of the previous 508mm, as a result of the much heavier loading to be carried. Transverse and diagonal bracing are similar, and sleepers were laid to form a continuous deck, following the practice established on Phase 3 bridges. The track level is now higher than the original. Flanking walkways and a handrail on the upstream side only were provided, to comply with current standards. The piers were repaired by re-pointing where necessary, and the existing concrete plinths were reused, with new holes drilled for the holding down bolts. Irregularities in the pier spacing prevented making all of the beams the same length. Nevertheless, in order to rationalise the fabrication work, the sixth span from the north has beams 8.405m long and the remainder are 8.230m long, with the bearings offset very slightly from the pier centre-lines. All steelwork

*Above: The spans are being delivered from Brunswick Ironworks after being galvanised and reassembled. This is another picture from 2nd January 2008. Indeed the whole bridge was delivered that day and at the end of work, all the spans were in position on their plates.* **WHRCL**

*Right: On 24th January 2008 the concrete lorry is pouring a mix into the shuttering prepared for the bridge's north retaining wall. This will be flush with the main longitudinal girders. Note that the vegetation visible in the picture above has gone, the fence is in and the trackbed base is laid and firmed.* **WHRCL**

*On 4th June 2008 the finished 65 metre bridge was visited by retired railway grandees, who were fascinated by the project and the progress that had been made. Gordon Pettitt OBE, formerly GM Southern Region, and Managing Director of Regional Railways, casts a questing eye from Span 8, towards the camera from the finished bridge, which by now has deck and track, and awaits the completion of the complex, adjacent B4410 level crossing before trains may run.*

was galvanised to achieve long-term corrosion protection, and the pre-assembled deck panels were made light enough to be lifted by a crane positioned on the road deck without damaging the highway.

On 3rd January, after installation of the spans on the previous day, fine adjustment took place to achieve optimum line and level, by packing with shims. Greased rubber pads were inserted, the handrail was completed, and then bolts and baseplates were grouted into position. After, some strengthening work was done on the abutments; the walkway was completed, and the handrails were adjusted. Ballast retaining walls were cast adjoining the ends of the deck on 24th January, and the decking timbers were laid on 29th January - but not fixed. There was work to be done to link the bridge on the southern side, but the level crossings needed to be installed first, before the connection was made. It was a surprisingly quick transformation. One minute it seemed there was no bridge - then there was! The track was laid

*Construction is still not yet complete in this view of 20th December 2008, looking towards Porthmadog. To the left, and to the right, walls had to be constructed. The tarmac has now been made up to the level of the rails. Then will come the control system, the road furniture, with light and horrible yodel alarm.*

across on the bridge itself on 2nd February 2008, but at that time the continuous track was still at the Afon Dylif. The track from the north reached the bridge on 10th April 2008.

## Pont Croesor AOCL to Cae Pawb

There was a change to what was first envisaged at this point. The popularity of the Ospreys led to the opening of an RSPB Centre, and this generated seasonal road traffic for the accommodation crossing. It was complex:

o The B4410 crossing (LC114A - **LC55.58**), needed to be built.

o The road level needed to be raised, thus supporting walls had to be constructed.

o A second level crossing to reach the Osprey Centre on the east side of the line (LC114B), also included in the lights of the B4410 crossing, and some 60ft to the south of it had to be incorporated,

o Adjacent, to that, a footpath crossing (LC114C) was to be built.

o Points also had to be laid a few yards further on, to

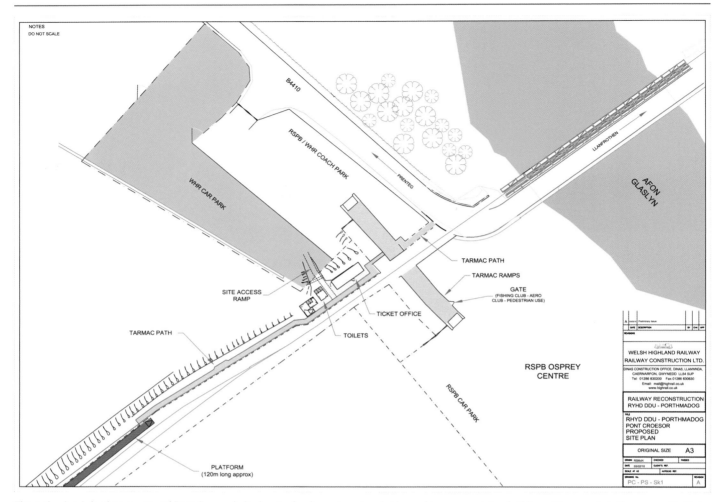

NOTES
DO NOT SCALE

B4410

RSPB / WHR COACH PARK

PRENTEG

LLANFROTHEN

AFON GLASLYN

WHR CAR PARK

SITE ACCESS RAMP

TARMAC PATH

TARMAC RAMPS

GATE
(FISHING CLUB - AERO CLUB - PEDESTRIAN USE)

TICKET OFFICE

TARMAC PATH

TOILETS

RSPB OSPREY CENTRE

RSPB CAR PARK

PLATFORM
(120m long approx)

WELSH HIGHLAND RAILWAY
RAILWAY CONSTRUCTION LTD.

DINAS CONSTRUCTION OFFICE, DINAS, LLANWNDA,
CAERNARFON, GWYNEDD, LL54 5UP
Tel: 01286 830200    Fax 01286 830630
Email: mail@highrail.co.uk
www.highrail.co.uk

RAILWAY RECONSTRUCTION
RYHD DDU - PORTHMADOG

RHYD DDU - PORTHMADOG
PONT CROESOR
PROPOSED
SITE PLAN

ORIGINAL SIZE    A3

PC - PS - Sk1    A

*This is the sketch for the area around Pont Croesor halt, showing level crossing, river, bridge and temporary station buildings. The second platform was added later.*

facilitate the passing loop. Clearance work had been done in October 2006. Level crossing works started on 20th July 2008. The shallow embankment of the station area and loop footprint needed widening. When the formation was made, a point and track was laid in to facilitate construction onward. The station arrangements at Pont Croesor displayed a considerable amount of forethought. It was to be an autoloop, but it was recognised that until two-train (FR/WHR) acceptance at Porthmadog was organised, it would likely have a 'frontier' role. There was the opportunity to offer generous parking space at this location. It is outside the National Park, and has the benefit of the Osprey Centre adjacent. There was no telling just how popular the station would remain after Porthmadog was 'sorted', but whilst trains at first terminated at Pont Croesor in May 2010, and then enjoyed a limited 'run through', with only certain services to and from Porthmadog, it was a wise precaution to plan for a fairly busy time. Thus a second platform was added. The normal temporary ticket

office and loos were provided, and a splendid 'tin' building in the WHR 1922 'vernacular' style. When the station opened for business, and the trains started to roll, large coaches appeared full of people. The positioning of Pont Croesor is ideal as a coach embarkation point. Of course this was negotiated by the Commercial Department and they began taking full advantage of the potential by selling the station.

Before opening, the level crossing controls had to be designed and installed, such that trains could approach in the normal manner, but also depart the halt from either line. When the control system was installed, the walls were made up, and ARMCO barriers were in place, then testing was conducted. This took place in early May of 2010, ready for the start of passenger service.

The CP Notices for the trackbed through to Traeth Mawr, the limit of the WHR(P) line, and beyond, were issued far back on 14th May 2004. This was the last section of trackbed to be cleared, in late October 2006. G.H. James Cyf. won the construction contract and

*This photograph is a clear illustration of why the Croesor Tramway was built on an embankment here. Taken on 5th October 2008.*
**R. Woods**

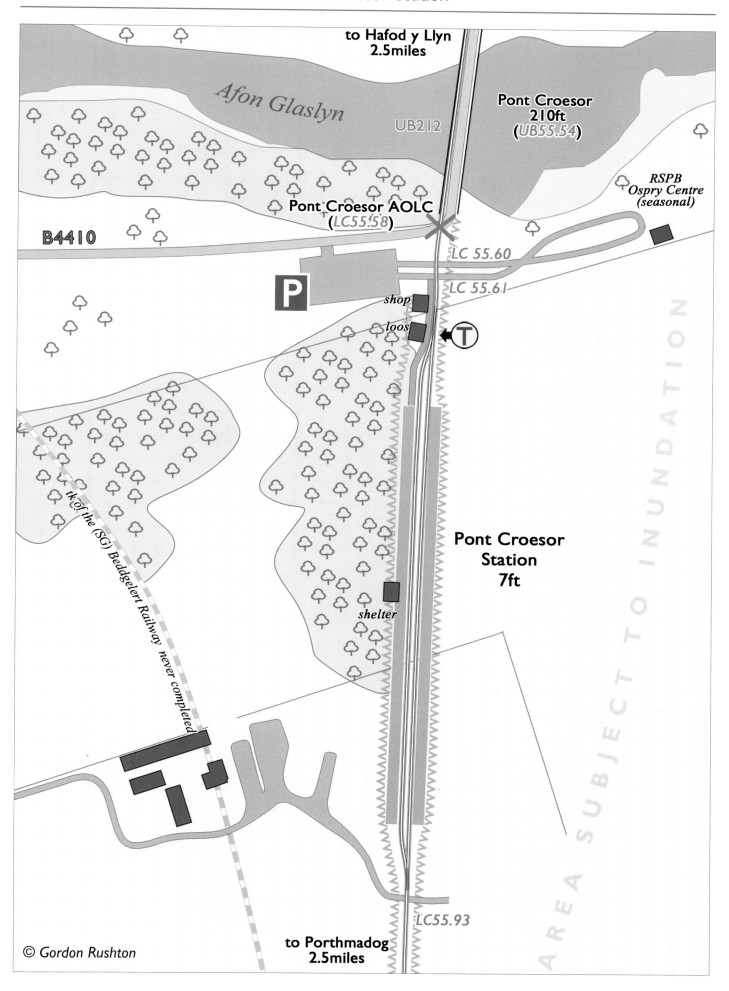

to Hafod y Llyn
2.5miles

*Afon Glaslyn*

UB212

Pont Croesor
210ft
(*UB55.54*)

RSPB
*Ospry Centre
(seasonal)*

Pont Croesor AOLC
(*LC55.58*)

B4410

LC 55.60

P

LC 55.61

shop

loos

T

*Trk of the (SG) Beddgelert Railway never completed*

Pont Croesor
Station
7ft

shelter

A R E A   S U B J E C T   T O   I N U N D A T I O N

LC55.93

to Porthmadog
2.5miles

© Gordon Rushton

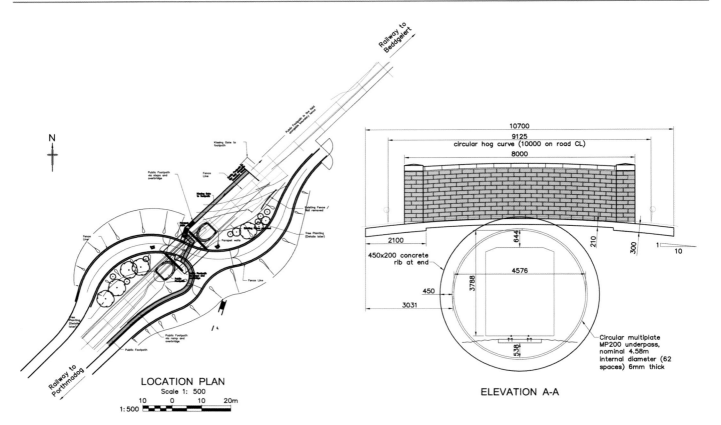

**LOCATION PLAN**
Scale 1: 500
10    0    10    20m
1:500

© *John Sreeves: extract from preliminary drawing 07.11.07 - OB217*

**ELEVATION A-A**

Circular multiplate
MP200 underpass,
nominal 4.58m
internal diameter (62
spaces) 6mm thick

# ARMCO BRIDGES - OB216 and OB217
## Locations:    OB56.83        OB57.26

the reconstruction work began in the middle of April 2008. This was not an easy section of line, as there were mitigation measures to construct two, large ARMCO bridges. The concept of these bridges is that the tube is placed in a trench on a firm, earth bed. Earth is piled up around and on top for the roadway, and the voussoirs of the bridge are cast in concrete, and faced in slate (or brick). The roadway is made on top, with fencing and parapet, and the ballast is made up underneath. Then the track is laid through. There were also areas of embankment to restore, and a culvert to build - all in all it was an expensive stretch of railway.

However, very rapidly work advanced. The corrugated sections for the ARMCO bridges were delivered to James's compound on 15th April. The survey posts were all out by 28th April 2008. Soil was being scraped, and a firm base was being laid rapidly, using the ubiquitous ground slate waste.

In June the first ARMCO tube was being assembled, OB216. The second tube was erected a couple of days later. The banks either side of OB217 were rising rapidly by the end of June, reaching full height by 15th July 2008.

The large footprint

of the construction gave a large area of elevated ground from the floodplain - to permit animals to find sanctuary in the large standing area. In addition, the gently inclined bridge approaches were suitable for vehicles and trailers to cross, facilitating the two farmers and avoiding occupation crossings.

About 100 yards or so on the Porthmadog side of Pont Croesor station, the Environment Agency had declared it prudent to carry the embankment on a bridge of 14 longitudinal pipes (UB214). Known as the 100 year culvert, it protects the embankment from build up of water on the landward side of the

***Above:*** *Both of the ARMCO bridges can be seen in Peter Johnson's view, taken on 5th September 2008. Cnicht stands in the background, masquerading as Snowdon. It is a rather indulgent backdrop for two such austere bridges.*
**Peter Johnson**

Traeth. Unfortunately the information of this requirement had not been passed on from the aspirant railway builders. It was another expensive challenge to face as the formation at that spot had long been completed and the track had been laid.

In mid-September 2008, GH James began work on the flood culverts. They had to remove the track and ballast, then dig out the embankment, and put in a binding slab. 14 pipes were laid in, then the voids between them were filled with concrete. The

**Right:** *It wasn't known by FR Co. that it had been agreed to construct this large flood relief culvert - so it had to be done after the line had been completed. However, it was done rapidly, and it was doing its job immediately on completion in the floods of October 2008.* **WHRCL**

**Below:** *This is a WHHR train, hauled by Bagnall 0-4-2T locomotive Gelert, that came from the Rustenberg Platinum Mines in South Africa. although construction of the 800m extension began in 2005, it opened in April 2007. The loop portion was removed, so push-pull operation continued until 'join-up'.* **Alasdair Stewart**

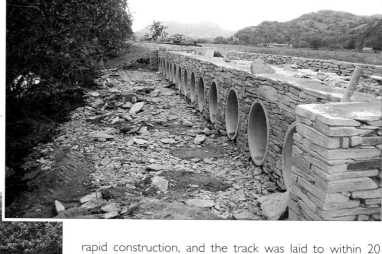

fronts, round the pipes were faced with stone, a slab was cast on the top, the ballast put back and the two lengths of rail restored on 1st November. The construction job was all done in a month. The culvert was operating during the October floods.

The WHHR extension to Pont Croesor, Phase 1, was from Pen y Mount to Traeth Mawr, where there was to be a loop line constructed. The points out on to the WHR main line were put in position in August 2002. By March 2003, the course of the line as far as Traeth Mawr had been fenced, vegetation cut back, and a 'haul road' had been made. In November 2003 the loop foundations were put in. In June 2006 track was laid. The extension was opened in March 2007 and passenger trains were using the extension in April 2007. Passengers did not get on or off at Traeth Mawr, the locomotive ran round the train and it then returned to Pen y Mount.

Alas the end, loop line section, with its big dip, had to be removed on 28th October 2007 to give contractors access to the trackbed to Pont Croesor. WHHR trains continued to run in push-pull mode. On 24th May 2008 an additional four track panels had to be lifted to allow the whole embankment in that area to be brought up to level, and the dip to be filled in - so the whole formation was on top of the flood embankment. Both ARMCO bridges were completed in August 2008. This was extremely

rapid construction, and the track was laid to within 20 yards of the WHRL Traeth Mawr Loop by 30th August 2008. The join was made the following day. Thus the WHRL was connected right through to Dinas and to Caernarfon. Relations between the companies were good at this time. Alas the WHHR were then obliged to cease service on this line, and it is a pity that resource problems had prevented them from completing the line through to Pont Croesor, as had been their aim.

The TWO assumption was that the course of the restored track would follow the Croesor Tramway. Pen y Mount was another point where the track was laid outside the Limits of Deviation. However, through Pen y Mount there were three items to be taken into account:

1. A footpath diversion over the WHRL platform
2. A TRANSCO gas pipeline manhole
3. Laying in the Pen y Mount Junction point.

WHRL placed the point connecting the main line such that the rails were off the Croesor Tramway to the west, with the fenceline on WHRL land. This was agreed because the public footpath could then take the line of the old Croesor Tramway and run straight up the right hand side of the railway, without diversion, and the TRANSCO manhole cover could stay where it was.

Construction was now complete from Pont Croesor, right through the site of Traeth Mawr Loop, as far as Pen y Mount. Work was needed on the approach to the Cambrian Coast line. Gabions were installed to stabilise the sandy embankment behind the caravans at Gelerts Farm.

The next big challenge was the Cambrian Crossing (Cae Pawb) and the Cross Town Link - CTRL - that had been progressing simultaneously with the advance from the north.

*The points at Pen y Mount give on to the main line. They are kept clamped and locked now until needed for something to run in or out from WHHR. The position of the track is not where shown on the TWA drawing.* **Steve Broomfield**

A journey on the Welsh Highland Heritage Railway is rather different from a trip from Porthmadog to Blaenau Ffestiniog or Caernarfon. People begin their experience in a heritage train, normally pulled by steam but it doesn't last for very long. The hour-long visit includes a visit to the Engine Sheds where visitors find out about the narrow gauge railways of Porthmadog. There's a miniature railway on the site, a cafe and the place is particularly welcoming for kids. This is the friendly face of railway heritage, and it shows, by David Allan.

Obviously restoring the WHR was something that the 64 Co. very much wanted to be able to do. This book tells of the struggle, and of how events were shaped. All that is now past, and the WHR tracks pass Pen y Mount reaching a full 40 miles from Caernarfon to Blaenau Ffestiniog. Our railway is still very much in place, and has a particular function, as well as a bright future.

The 64 Co. people offered their help to restore the WHR and they served their time on tracklaying in various places. Concurrently, activity was still going on to build up and maintain the WHHR site from Tremadog Road through to Pen y Mount. It was clear that we needed to develop activities that would differentiate us from the big passenger carrying railway that would gradually develop as our neighbour. It was clear to us that huge Garratt locomotives and twelve corridor coaches with loo on board and service of tea, coffee, buns and cakes was more than slightly removed from the little three coach trains that used to chug up and down the old WHR. We have those old trains, we have spent a lot of time collecting them and putting them back into museum condition. It is clear therefore that if we want to be different, to attract an audience, then the right way to go about it is to blaze the heritage trail, as there is nothing at all in Porthmadog that does a good job to explain the large railway heritage of the port and all that went with it.

In the cradle of the narrow gauge, the very place that such railways were invented, there was nothing to explain the why's and the wherefores. So this led us to another good idea, which was to put in place a proper museum of Slate, Steam and Sail. Such things are not done without time and effort, so this had the effect of promoting a proper development programme for the Welsh Highland Heritage Railway. Of course this in some way offered an alternative course of evolution for our team, now it was no longer down to us to restore the WHR main line. At least, among the Garratts and the new shiny coaches, there would be someone who was going to keep the charming heritage of this railway alive and available to enjoy.

There was already the nucleus of a quite splendid collection of narrow gauge delights. We had saved and restored to

*Running out from Pen y Mount on to the WHR main line is something that WHHR would very much like to do. Currently the ride ends at Pen y Mount but the thought of a heritage ride to somewhere like Beddgelert, or even from time to time further still, is something to be worked on.*
**David Allan**

operation the handsome Hunslet 2-6-2 tank locomotive Russell, built for the ill-fated Porthmadog Beddgelert and South Snowdon Railway. We had found dismembered carriage bodies occasionally scattered in fields in the locality. They had been brought back and lovingly restored to be reborn as top-quality survivors from the past. The 26 foot long Gladstone Car, for example, No.8, was constructed by the Metropolitan Carriage and Wagon Co. in 1891 as a tourist car for the North Wales Narrow Gauge Railway. It was rescued in 1989, and it is a miracle that it has survived - even more so, that we can offer people the chance to experience it. Prime Minister Gladstone travelled in it on the way to a holiday in the Nant Gwynant, thus it got its name.

There are other carriages from the 19th century, a shed with working steam locomotives in it, and we have managed to obtain one of the old celebrities of the WHR, one of the ex War Department Baldwin, American made, 4-6-0 tank locomotives. The old WHR was never a star performer commercially - it was a very hand to mouth affair. When 'bargain' steam locomotives were available from WWI war surplus, No. 590 came to the WHR. Cordially hated by its crews, but featured many times in photographs, and adored by today's enthusiasts, we shall restore the Baldwin No. 794, that came from India and was loaned to us by the Imperial War Museum. Alas No. 590 was cut up and scrapped when the WHR closed in 1937. The idea of one day being able to see her puffing uphill through the Aberglaslyn Pass, with an original train behind her makes all that sacrifice and expense worthwhile!

Today the concept of recreating the past has been made possible by a lot of people working together to harness their expertise. The fact that the public are entertained and interested by a professional presentation of the past, together with an understandable explanation of how things work means that our ideas have promise. To be able not only to show people and interpret these rare trains from the past, but to invite the visitor to ride on them as well makes us even more attractive as a proposition - one can see, and more than touch.

It is satisfying to know from visitor feedback that the WHHR

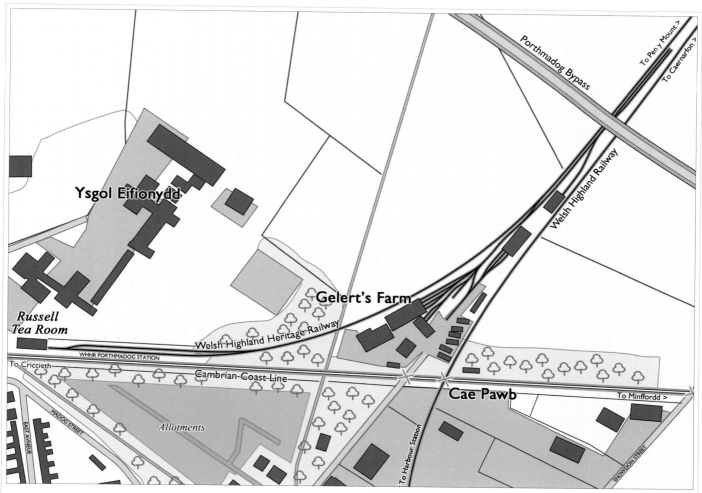

*The WHHR line shown from the Russell Tea Rooms, nearly as far as the terminal platform, short of Pen y Mount. The WHHR line is laid on the old Beddgelert Siding, an exchange spur with the former WHR, but the smooth curve in fact is one of the last remnants of a standard gauge branch to Beddgelert, only part constructed, and lost in the collapse of Overend Gurney's Bank in 1866.*

offers a high degree of satisfaction for children. The younger members of society are vital to our interests. If we fail to interest them in the past, then the future is uncertain.

Our search for a differentiated future for the WHHR from our big-railway neighbours is accomplished. The FR has been kind in lending us its artefacts, and a combined museum will complement our railways and the visitor experience that is there to be gained from them. There are exciting times to come as the newly restored WHR settles in, as the Slate, Steam and Sail concept develops, and as we get ready for and introduce some heritage train experiences up the WHR with the original equipment. This truly will be the co-operation that works for all.

*Gelert and Prince at Traeth Mawr with a long train of heritage rolling stock. It is these sights that thrill the enthusiast and holidaymaker alike, and the WHHR can lay on heritage trains for people to experience what it was like to take a trip in days gone by. When the weather is like this, it is railway Heaven on earth.*

**David Allan**

## Cae Pawb Cambrian Crossing and the Cross Town Rail Link

During the FR Co. bidding for the trackbed, and the thinking to lease the trackbed for the 64 Co. to construct the WHR, the question of how to get across the Cambrian Coast Line was hardly considered. Then when it was, preliminary thoughts as part of the feasibility study, considered the provision of a bridge would be both expensive and impractical. It was stated at that time, that crossing the Cambrian was impossible, and that the Cross Town Rail Link was in consequence impractical. When serious inquiries were made with Railtrack about the crossing, it was pleasing to find that it was not a problem to arrange, provided that FR Co. would bear the expense of the installation, and that HMRI approved it.

There was discussion over whether the CTRL would receive assent for a TWO, and there were some anxious moments on the way. The question of wether it was built was never in doubt, but there was a time when it was thought that the CTRL would only have been used for stock movements. From that there was a passing thought that everything would turn into the 64 Co. station, at Tremadog Road, to make a sort of Porthmadog Grand Central, and that FR/WHR/WHHR trains would come together. This looked practical, as the massive car park next the National Rail station was a boon, and having all together in Porthmadog, including the Cambrian Coast Line was quite a sensible idea. However, it was forestalled by the incompatibility of the philosophies of the two companies. FR Co. fought the link through the TWO public Inquiry, and this set the proposal to terminate WHR and FR trains at Porthmadog Harbour.

Thus Cae Pawb was assured, and technical volunteers took over the task of designing the crossing, the only one of its kind in UK. The crossing track was manufactured by Corus Cogifer in Scunthorpe, as a fabricated piece of trackwork, designed and made specially for the application. The components were delivered to adjacent, private land in Porthmadog on 25th October 2006. They arrived dismantled, and were put together within crane-reach of the installation site, to await possessions of the Cambrian Coast Line from October 31st - November 2nd 2006. The installation was by Carillion Rail. After it was all placed into position and tamped, the standard gauge resumed service.

The narrow gauge side took a lot longer. First the approach tracks were connected with 'pinch' type trap points to protect the standard gauge. It was decided that the Cambrian Coast Line would have precedence. The plan was to have the narrow gauge tracks ready to coincide with the completion of the CTRL. Meanwhile, the standard gauge ran the first steam train across the crossing on 31st July 2007. The best reply made was that *Jack Lane*, a new quarry Hunslet delivered ballast by steam on 7th August 2008.

Eventually all the tracks were installed, with the physical track route being made across the Cambrian, and awaiting the electrical installations by August 2008. Then the CTRL was completed, and there was a period when the track was all in, but the electronics were not connected and operating. The reason for this was that Britannia Bridge, Snowdon Street, and Cae Pawb, all required complex and expensive electronics to make them work. There was a pause, to collect the funds to pay for this.

However, the crossing was useful, as it was particularly convenient to be able to move rolling stock and locomotives by rail, rather than by road. Once the physical track connection was made of course, on 28th February 2009, it was possible to make arrangements for narrow gauge trains to cross, by manual means, by clamping and flagging, and this obviated further cumbersome road movements of rolling stock. Network Rail were minded to agree with this, at times when there was no traffic on the Cambrian Coast. The first narrow gauge train across was on 12th March 2009, with *Vale of Ffestiniog* ; the first narrow gauge steam locomotive to cross was NGG16 No.87 on 23rd March 2009. Then came the installation and testing of the complex electronics. Fortunately, it was possible with skilled volunteers and design work from Roland Doyle to do the job for a lot less than the £1.5m Network Rail price.

*Above: The crossing assembly is seen here at the Corus Works in Scunthorpe on 20th October 2006. This was a 'dry run' assembly, and examination, to make sure all the bits fitted, prior to dispatch to site.*
**WHRCL**

*Right: On 31st July 2007, the first steam train to cross the installed crossing was the 'Pocket Rocket' hauling the Cambrian Coast Express, the famous steam train name revived for specials to run regularly between Machynlleth and Porthmadog.*
**Bruce Brayne**

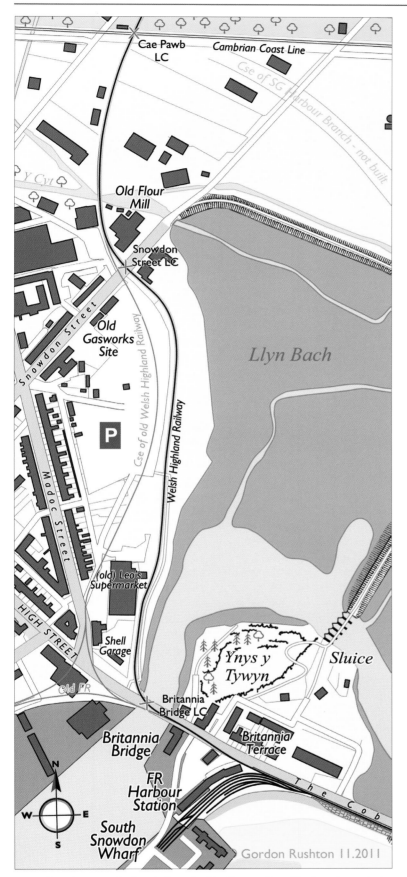

*It is only a short stretch of track, but a bit like German Re-unification - it was 'going to happen'. Quite right too. It made it possible for WHR trains to have either direct exchange with the FR, or to run trains through between the two railways. The extra economic wealth that it is generating for everyone in the region is impressive. There were those who opposed it, but now it is built is the time to enjoy the success. It was expensive, but now it is there, everyone is enjoying the spectacle. 'When does the train come?' is the top Tourist Inquiry Kiosk request!*

There was no doubt in the minds of all on the FR that if the WHR was to be restored, then it should be connected to the FR. If the strategy of complementing FR was to work properly, then it was better to run the two railways in combination. That way, the traffic drawn from Caernarfon to Porthmadog could better be combined with new destinations for traffic on the FR. Through trains had always been part of the plan.

A cross-town line was in place from 1864, when Croesor Tramway was built. The Tramway went along Llyn Bach, across Snowdon Street, and the Cambrian Railways line to Pwllheli was built across it in 1867. The grey line on the map represents the old course of the line. When the WHR was built in 1922, through trains were loaded and unloaded standing in the road at Harbour station, rather than reversing in and out. As Porthmadog Harbour Station was unsuitable for WHR trains, a station on the CTRL called Porthmadog New was opened. Later, to escape the cost of the Cambrian crossing, the old company changed its arrangements to suit its pocket, but not its passengers. When they terminated trains without crossing the Cambrian, and made people walk between trains, this was not popular. Here was food for thought in the 1990s when planning the arrangements to be made.

As far as the CTRL route was concerned, it was clear that a lesser disruption of road traffic would be caused by making a sharp right off Britannia Bridge, and heading up the side of Llyn Bach closer to the water's edge. The old Croesor Tramway/WHR course would be rejoined at the old flour mill. To do this meant taking some parking spaces from the municipal Llyn Bach car park, and returning them from the old gasworks site. The arrangements for doing this have become prolonged.

WHR exits to the north, along the wall of the council depot, crosses Snowdon Street on an AOCL, and rejoins the original course past Snowdon Mill. It crosses Y Cyt, and runs through the old site of Porthmadog New to traverse the Cambrian Coast Line at Cae Pawb. Not only do the passengers enjoy this busy glide through the fringes of the town, but spectators gather to view the event from the road, though no one enjoys the horrible yodel-alarms.

As the restoration approached Porthmadog, reports of alleged opposition from the Town Council, and the Chamber of Commerce filtered through. There were concerns expressed about the crossing, and the disruption it would cause to the town. These persisted until after trains began to run, but then subsided. Bypass opening has stilled delay concerns entirely.

Harbour Station was not designed for a Garratt +10. Therefore the choice was either a shunting move, involving an extra locomotive, or a loop line and extra platform. There was no space for that without significant track alterations that required widening of the Cob. This solution (marked orange on the seaward side of the fan of sidings) cost an additional £1m, but it allowed Harbour Station to be expanded to accept a train from each railway together. The Cob widening gained planning permission, but finding the £1m was problematic. The detailed story of the project is told later. The management contract for the CTRL went to Arup, and the contract for construction was awarded to Carillion Rail, who had put in Cae Pawb.

## Cross Town Rail Link

Autumn 2005 saw the start of the clearance of vegetation between Snowdon Mill and the Cambrian Crossing. A start was made in the main car park, and the Gas Works site was cleared. Chartered Engineer David High joined the team to manage the project. Long-term FR stalwart, David High worked formerly for consultants Posford-Datrys. The section from Snowdon Mill to Harbour Station was treated like a tramway. There were two AOCLs, one at Snowdon Street, and the other across Britannia Bridge. There were plans for a siding part way along the Llyn Bach. The two sections of rails set into the road would be of the tramway type. Before work proper started, a problem arose. The course of the line was to swing from the centre of the Britannia Bridge on a 50m radius curve to cross close by the western, upstream abutment, then to follow the footpath along the Llyn Bach, hard up against the wall, to leave room for both. A short length of the training wall on the upstream left bank collapsed on 6th February 2007. Work began on it almost straight away, as it needed strengthening work in the neighbourhood of the railway. Work also began to convert the gas works site into car park, to compensate for the spaces that were being taken by the railway's run along Llyn Bach. There was a small

boundary adjustment to the former Leo's supermarket, (now Wilkinson's Hardware), to ease the passage of the line. There had been consideration about buying the store when it closed, and even of making it a terminal station, but this was too expensive. It was later decided that the expedient course was just to run everything to Harbour, and to deal with the problems raised by altering that site to cope.

The special tramway rail for the CTRL was delivered in June 2007. Made in Austria, the rail came pre-curved, with a shallow profile, compatible with installation over Britannia Bridge without excavation into the bridge deck concrete reinforcing layer. It also has a flangeway capable of accepting NG15 and NGG16 locomotives on the 50m radius curve off the Bridge. The tramway rails were laid on baseplates, with tiebars, and were continuously welded. The rail was encased in a plastic boot, and after fixing in position, concrete was poured in to rail level. The two tramway rail sections are on the Britannia Bridge, and across Snowdon Street to just past the Mill; between is plain track.

The car park, altered and surfaced, was ready for the Whitsun Bank Holiday, 2007. Carillion then set up their base in August 2007, enclosing an area for their site compound. A service duct trench was cut for the crossing at Snowdon Mill; works from the Mill to Cae Pawb were conducted in September 2007. Gabions were placed along the embankment sides to strengthen it. The bridge over Maddocks canal Y Cyt was repaired, and a few bits of old FR bullhead rail and some 'S' chairs were recovered from the former flour mill loop. The footpath from car park to Britannia Bridge was closed for the works, and this allowed that whole stretch to be worked on. The wall with Wilkinson's land was rebuilt in its new location, the footpath was altered to suit along Llyn Bach, and

*Above: The tramway rail was specially ordered to fit, pre-cut and curved, with some straight bits added. It was stacked in the Carillion compound, and this view of 5th April 2008 shows the plastic boot fitted and the baseplates and clamps.*

*On 5th April 2008 tramway rail has been installed on the base-slab past the Snowdon Mill. You can see the baseplates set to the right height to receive the next two rail lengths, and the reinforcing mesh ready to bind with the top layer of concrete, so that the tramway rail is flush to the road surface.*

suitable work was carried out to protect a parallel outfall sewer pipe. This was to be sure that no train weight could damage the pipe, and it included the installation of a reserve sewer pipe. The civils work to Cae Pawb was finished by the end of December, and so ballasting began in January 2008.

The railway exit from the Britannia Bridge to run north was a sub-project in itself, as to make the minimum 50m curve, and to achieve the right alignment with the footpath, linkspans were required. In February major work was carried out to sheet-pile the training wall, then after the interlocking piles were trimmed, a concrete capping beam was added, with a masonry face built below.

At the other end of the CTRL, towards the end of February 2008, the disturbance at Snowdon Mill was rapidly taking shape. The service trench was filled, the road kerbs for the junction and level crossing were laid, pavement was installed, and the course of the railway past the Mill was visible between buttressed, upstanding kerb stones. By

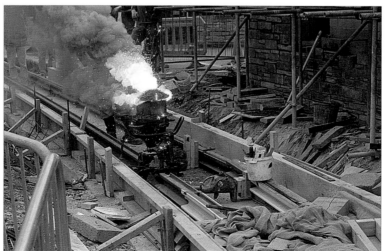

*On 12th June 2008 a Thermit pot crackles as it produces the weld-metal required to join tramway rail at the western exit of Britannia Bridge. This method takes time to set up but it is time well spent, for a cost of £50 the strongest join was made.* **John Peduzzi**

March, the sewer protection works could be seen as what looked like continuous concrete slab, all along Llyn Bach. The parapet walls, bounding the Council depot adjacent to Snowdon Street were completed in early March, and the trackbed by the Mill was receiving reinforcing rods, ready for concrete to be poured for the tramway track, and affixing of tie bars. The pouring started in the second week of March. Carillion brought in staff who had suitable expertise from the construction of the Nottingham tram system, to assist in the complexities of fitting the special tramway track into position. Once the concrete slab was laid on the trackbed, baseplates were fitted. These were supported on two height-adjustable studs, grouted into the concrete slab beneath. The pre-curved track was lodged on the baseplates, adjusted to the correct height, and the whole thing was welded length to length, then a plastic boot was applied. Slotted retaining clips on the threaded studs were tightened over the boot to keep all secure, and after careful check to see that the track was precisely in

*Members of the Railway Study Association and RROS listen to explanation from David High at the start of the lazy 'S' from Harbour Station on to Britannia Bridge. The pre-curved track has been adjusted for height and gauge, and sits on the baseplates, outside the re-profiled Cob Records store. It awaits fitment of the plastic boot, and most of the shuttering is in place for the enveloping concrete to be poured. Just one more length of tramway track has to be welded on to the end of this one, and then there is plain track to the WHR points at Harbour Station. 14th February 2009.*

the correct position, the tram track was concreted to rail level.

By April 2008 the track slab was being prepared to cross Snowdon Street, and agreement had been reached with the Trunk Roads Agency to install new bridge beams for the tramway track across the Britannia Bridge westbound in May. This was between the two bank holidays (May Day and Whitsun), whereupon the work would start again for the eastbound carriageway during June. The whole tramway track had to be installed in the road by the last week of June.

Traffic was diverted to single-line working on the river side of the Britannia Bridge, so that the westbound part of the road could be excavated, with Carillion working a seven day week to make sure the work was done within the critical time slot. The rebar was made up, installed, and fitted, and the first section of slab was cast on 8th April. Two lengths of pre-curved rail were put in position on their baseplates by 13th April, and were welded to a second, straight pair, that

*The 50m curve has begun, but has been paused half-way across the carriageway. The whole road was opened for Whitsun 2008, and here it is seen with traffic control back, just before the rest of the curve was completed. Taken 4th June 2008.*

were then pulled into the gentle curve they were to assume, and the clips fastened. These two lengths were what it took to bridge the east pavement, and the road exit to south Snowdon Wharf and Harbour Station. One more length swung the railway in an arc to the middle of the westbound carriageway, not quite on to the Bridge. The first two lengths on the east seaward side were concreted to rail level, the centre slab was poured, the rails fitted, boot attached, and all was concreted to rail level. It was completed for the traffic control to be removed for the May Day bank holiday.

Work on the rails across the Britannia Bridge proper started on 6th May 2008, with the re-establishment of single-line working, and the removal of the tarmac top off the short length of seaward side road, ready for the track to be attached directly to the bridge strengthening beams cast a few years earlier. On 12th May a pair of short, straight rails was placed in position on the tiebars, and base plates were grouted

*Above: The first stage slab for the track over the Snowdon Street AOCL is about to be poured, in this view taken on 28th May 2008. Work is taking place all along the CTRL* **R Cooper**

*Left: Rebar and shuttering are in place for the linkspan upstand on 4th June 2008. This is the first of three structures designed to support the linkspans. The linkspans do not support the track, but they do strengthen and stabilise the ground adjacent to the waterway, without which the track would not bear the weight of a Garratt.* **R Cooper**

into the bridge beams. A pre-curved section was welded on to these on 14th May, the whole was positioned and ready, with a protrusion into the river side carriageway on 15th May 2008, followed by concrete pouring on 16th May.

At other work sites on the tramway, at Snowdon Mill the concrete was poured to bring it up to track level on 1st May. At the same time, the concrete linkspan upstand on the Llyn Bach shore was being poured, and this had to be scheduled round the tidal flow. The first half of Snowdon street level crossing was being excavated ready for the slab that would connect it with the track from Cae Pawb. The work on the section between Snowdon Street and Britannia Bridge, along Llyn Bach was being readied for plain track to be laid. The footpath was realigned and relaid at this spot in readiness for its reinstatement.

Towards Harbour Station, solid rock was reached a few inches below the road surface near the Cob Records store. This needed to be excavated, to find a satisfactory foundation for a concrete base, to extend the track across the face of the store building. The building had been cut back on the 'road' side, and extended on the FR 'car park' side to make room for the railway.

On 21st May 2008 BT contractors dug up the pavement on the seaward side of Britannia Bridge, to lay telecoms ducting. On 23rd May two-way traffic working was again reinstated for the Whitsun Bank Holiday.

On 29th May the slab was cast in front of the Cob Records store, for a further two sections of gently curving tramway rail heading towards Spooner's in the old FR Goods Shed. The course of the line here was now blocked by a telegraph pole that was taken out on 2nd June.

On the Britannia Bridge, the short remaining section of the 50m curve off the Britannia Bridge, across the eastbound carriageway, awaited the completion of the link span works.

During this time the second stretch of tramway track at Snowdon Mill had made progress. The first half of the Snowdon Street AOCL had been excavated and the track laid by 22nd May 2008. The rest of the slab was cast on 29th May. The final lengths of this street tramway were laid in place on 4/5th June and the slab was cast round the rails on 6th June completing this section of tramway track.

The second part of the link span upstand had been cast ready to receive the spans later. Behind them the line of the track curved from the Britannia Bridge to the footpath at the side of Llyn Bach. The spans were put in to support the track at the landward end, and to provide the foundation to stabilise the ground at the edge of the waterway.

*A week after the picture opposite, on 12th May, the short length of the centre of the 50m curve has been laid, taking the track to the end of the bridge. Note evidence of the BT service duct, left, and the shallow, surface concrete pour awaited, right.* **John Peduzzi**

*Right: This view of 27th May 2008 shows the primary slab of the last part of the tramway track, in front of the Cob Record store, which is being remodelled. Progress requires the removal of the telegraph pole, and this was done on 2nd June 2008.*            **R Cooper**

*Below: On 18th June 2008 the link spans arrived. This picture shows the first of the three beams being lowered into position on its upstand. When the link spans were fixed and covered with a deck, then the track across the bridge could be connected with that along Llyn Bach*
**Roger Dimmick**

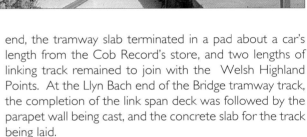

end, the tramway slab terminated in a pad about a car's length from the Cob Record's store, and two lengths of linking track remained to join with the Welsh Highland Points. At the Llyn Bach end of the Bridge tramway track, the completion of the link span deck was followed by the parapet wall being cast, and the concrete slab for the track being laid.

On 14th July the rails were put in place over the linkspans, and welded on 15th July. The concrete was poured by 18th July, and traffic control came off the Britannia Bridge. By 26th July a lot of cladding work was proceeding, and the coping stones for the Britannia Bridge parapet were being finished. The last section of slab track was cast on 30th July, completing the Britannia Bridge section. Over the whole CTRL completion works were proceeding. The footpath was tarmacadamed, and access to the Llyn Bach shore was restored. All the necessary road furniture was placed in position: ribbed tactile paving, and deterrent paving, to warn and to deter people from crossing on to the rails when trains are in transit on the crossing. Tarmac was also laid to fill the gaps in walkways, and all assumed a neat and ordered appearance.

Wooden sleepers came for the plain track to link the tramway sections, and with the Cambrian Coast crossing at Cae Pawb. Tracklaying was taking place in August. The poles for

On the Britannia Bridge the traffic lights were re-installed, directing the line of traffic to the seaward side. The tarmac top was removed from the eastbound carriageway on 6th June to reveal the bridge slab. The link span preparatory works were coming to an end with the joining together of the upstands that sat on top of a capping beam. Whilst the first pour of the far upstand took place on 9th June 2008, the pavement was being removed from the Britannia Bridge, with the first stage slab being cast on 10th June. The trackwork on the bridge was quite quick, as there was no excavation, just the removal of tarmac. Then the baseplates needed installation, the track was placed in position, welded, booted, and the mesh for the concrete installed on 12th June. Fill was brought to the link span site to make up the ground and this provided hard standing for a concrete crane to fill all the mesh in the Britannia Bridge roadway, enclosing the tramway rails and bringing the road surface up to the correct height. The track now curved towards the Shell garage, stopping at the road's edge.

Next, the link spans needed to be installed. The three beams arrived on 18th June 2008, and were installed the same day. Once fitted, on the following day, a start was made on the slab to go on top of the beams. When the rebar core was complete the slab was poured on 26th June.

At the Harbour Station

the many signs required for the two AOCLs were installed appropriately. Part of the completion works was the stone cladding of the steel sheet piling, and an attractive drum feature was added to the end of the Britannia bridge parapet, where the track went off up the side of Llyn Bach. A more eclectic choice were the ARMCO barriers around Snowdon Mill, to separate track and walking space. The barriers, the new fencing that appeared at the lineside, the neat slate

*By 24th June 2008 this close-up shows the stub-end of the track from off the Britannia Bridge and the rebar cage for the link span slab. On top of the slab the track will be laid in the normal way.*
**Andrew Thomas**

*Left:* Once the track was in, then the 'furnishing' began. Surfaces needed to be made continuous, with tarmac, various pavements types needed to be laid, here deterrent paving, the uncomfortable pyramids, and ribbed paving.  Also the signage poles needed to be planted in the appropriate places.  **WHRCL**

*Below:* The day of the Golden Bolt, 28th February 2009 - a celebration with head-to-head motive power on the WHR spur, like the Golden spike in the USA, with the proud track gangs gathered.  There was satisfaction that although it could not yet all be used, the rails from here were now continuous to Caernarfon.

walling, the separation with deterrent paving, offered a neat and ordered appearance.  Soon the new railway began to look as if it had always been there, it was so ringed around with formal 'acknowledgements' of its presence.

The transitional rails separating the tramway and plain track took longer than normal to install, the separations needed to be well supported.  The sections were all connected together by February 2009, so there was continuous 600mm gauge railway now for 40 miles.

Thus a special Golden Bolt ceremony was held to celebrate the connection on 28th February 2009.  Now it had become possible to make stock movements by rail.  This needed road closure notices, and the co-operation of the Police.  The first was at 05.00 on 12th March 2009.  The three crossings still needed to be commissioned, with the necessary electronics to be installed and made to work.  There was a pause in expenditure at this late stage in the project, but work went on across the summer, such that on 15th October  the HMRI inspected the crossings and passed them fit. The Sponsors train, the first public passenger train (there were a number of first trains) ran on 30th October 2009, and at least that train had come right through from Caernarfon, so perhaps that was 'first' enough?

## Britannia Bridge AOCL

Despite opposition and concern, the Britannia Bridge AOCL went ahead. Of course it was vital to the railway's interests, and street running was considered to be a draw for passengers. The crossing was properly commissioned under a level crossing order. A rational look at this crossing, and comparisons with the large selection of level crossings across UK, revealed no greater risks from the Britannia bridge AOCL than for others.

On 7th July 2011 the return service from Caernarfon steams across the Britannia Bridge AOCL, with a queue of 7 cars and a lorry, eastbound. The sprinkling of visitors watching this manoeuvre is constant, there are about a dozen; four are in view.

Before installation there was great concern about the traffic congestion that would be caused. Yet the assessment foresaw no distinguishing reason that singled out this crossing for particular prohibition:

**1.** It would carry trains at walking pace, thus they were quite capable of stopping 'on sight' and if required, likely to do so in a very short distance.

**2.** Road congestion might be inconvenient, but if the Cob was congested, trains already stopped before crossing the road. If there were cars in the way, then the train would be obliged to wait until they cleared.  Besides, a bypass was likely soon, and thus congestion would not be a problem.

Yet there was complaint focussed on cyclists. Before the crossing was commissioned there were some incidents, and this called forth police concerns.  The remedy was temporarily to fill the flangeways with tarmac, until the crossing was inspected and commissioned with lights and alarms, with a safe cycle path to follow westbound.  Like many AOCLs, evidential CCTV is now installed, so that all incidents may be checked. This is not a level crossing for any motorist game of chicken, but from time to time motorists seem to stray into the path of trains.  Trains  just stop and wait. There are few rail movements across the crossing,  and each one

*Left: The Britannia Bridge AOCL westbound flashing head is centre-right. Cyclists are guided to turn left, to cross the tracks at 90° Considerable flashing of red lights takes place upon crossing initiation, and a major noise is created by the yodel alarms. When the sequence is complete, a continuous white light allows the train to proceed.*

*Below: This is the temporary layout arranged to handle WHR trains in 2011 and 2012. The second platform to be added with a loop, for the WHR trains will cause the track in the foreground to be displaced to seaward with another line added. In order to do this the Cob must be widened.*

blocks the crossing for about 90 seconds. One of the main questions for the Porthmadog Tourist Information Centre, adjacent to the Britannia Bridge, is for the timetable of movements, as visitors are most keen to see the famous little steam train that goes down the road.

As far as the congestion is concerned, the opening of the Porthmadog Bypass in 2011 removed all of that. A surge of traffic on the Ffestiniog and Welsh Highland Railways is likely to compensate for those that now drive by the town. It is now more likely that cars will be parked in Porthmadog for people to go on the train, as the charges in the Llyn Bach car park have been moderated. All this will be very good for business in Porthmadog.

## Porthmadog Harbour Station

Harbour Station was never called upon, nor ever needed to handle more than one train in the platform at once. on a regular basis until 1993. Then, as an experiment, to attract traffic that was time and cost constrained, a series of summer, Minffordd Shuttle trains was run. These were able to use the long, single platform without incident. There was a realisation by FR Co. that Harbour Station would be problematic for Garratts and long trains up the WHR, and Fairlies and long trains up the FR, both at the same time. A number of schemes were considered.

1. Termination at Tremadog Road (WHHR). It was difficult to reach agreement over ownership of assets and security of tenure, but the changes to the site and the need for more land made it impractical.

2. The Porthmadog Gateway. A station would have been fed from the Bypass. This was rejected, but could happen as an intermediate stop in the future.

3. Minffordd Yard. This had promise from

proximity to the Bypass, the avoidance of elevated parking charges, lots of room for locomotive and carriage servicing and storage. The emergence of a practical Porthmadog scheme with funding, and the moderation of parking charges handed the advantage to Porthmadog Harbour.

The Harbour Station scheme received main funding from the National Station Improvement Project, and matched funding came from the Phase 5 Appeal in Steam Railway Magazine. This scheme includes a long WHR second platform with loop. To accommodate this, the Cob was widened from the South Snowdon Wharf outstand at No.6 Road, to beyond the king points on the Cob. With this arrangement an FR and a WHR train may be in the station at one time, and the locomotive from each can go for fuel and water and run round its train. When through trains are operated, then the Ffestiniog locomotive can be replaced by a Garratt and *vice versa*. This is an outstanding use of a limited space. The only thing that cannot be done is to pass two WHR trains, without running one of them into the FR platform, and reversing out after. Note that 11 of the 13m WHR cars can be fitted down Nos 3&4 Road for berthing. The complexity of the new layout and the moves that can be made will lead to the establishment of a raised signal box, with permanent, fixed signalling for the station area.

*A footpath along the Cob runs on the left-hand side. This will remain. Another two tracks will be laid, so the existing ones will be displaced in a seaward direction. The platform will be in between. The widened section will go almost as far as the starting signal, seen just to the right/rear of the cab of* Castell Caernarfon.

## LAYOUT K1

**KEY**
- ⬜ HARBOUR STATION PLATFORMS
- ▨ COB FOOTPATH
- ⬜ EXISTING TRACKS SHOWN GREY

THE TRAIN ILLUSTRATED IS WHR SET (12No 13m COACHES)
SKETCH SHOWS WELSH HIGHLAND RAILWAY TRAIN IN THE
PLATFORM AS ARRIVED.

PROBLEMS:-
1) Difficulties servicing WHR Loco.
2) Similar to Layout (c) but more versatile
3) WHR Trains arrive using turn out.
4) FR Trains arrive using turn out.
5) Access to signal box
6) WHR loop designed as run round. Not a passing loop.
7) 1in8 Points except to under water tower.

*Right: Harbour Station has only ever had one platform. However to allow a train from each railway to be in the station at the same time, a second platform is needed. The addition of a loop line allows the WHR locomotive to reach the Caernarfon end of the train for departure. After patient work, Stuart McNair drew together all the elements of what was needed into this sketch that also shows siding capacity.*

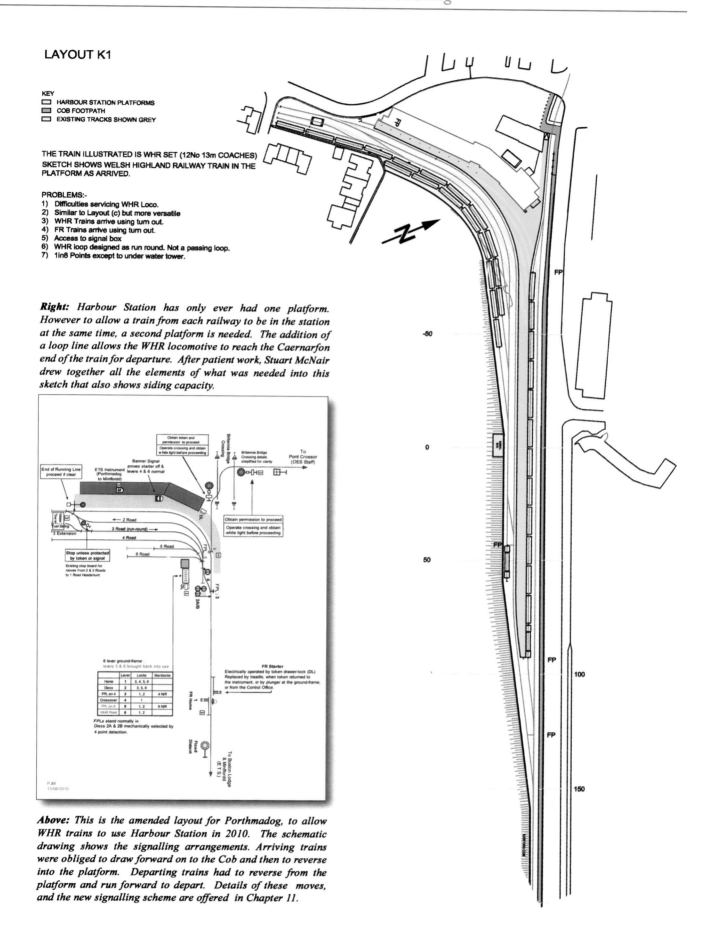

*Above: This is the amended layout for Porthmadog, to allow WHR trains to use Harbour Station in 2010. The schematic drawing shows the signalling arrangements. Arriving trains were obliged to draw forward on to the Cob and then to reverse into the platform. Departing trains had to reverse from the platform and run forward to depart. Details of these moves, and the new signalling scheme are offered in Chapter 11.*

*The locoshed at Dinas was the former WHR carriage shed. The title of the land passed to the National Rivers Authority (Dŵr Cymru) and it was bought by FR Co. The sale included the old loco shed (out of sight behind the camera), and spare land behind that, but it did not include the second part of the old carriage shed building (seen in the picture). The remainder of that was purchased in 2011, thus a further two 'Garratt' spaces have been created here, giving more room for maintaining and overhauling these necessary locomotives. Photograph taken 8th August 2006 of K1 (L) and NGG 16 No. 143 (R)*

As the 1922 WHR was not built as an integrated whole, then the portfolio of land titles held was confused and sometimes difficult. As it was assembled to begin construction this became apparent. Matters had (thankfully) been eased in anticipation by the granting of compulsory purchase powers in the TWO. A segment of the reasoning for that concession was due to the potential for someone gaining a ransom strip that they refused to sell, but the exercise of CP powers allowed no relief from dispute over title. Despite what people may think, the law in Britain is unclear in many areas, even if it is supposed that this should not be so by reading the statutes applicable. The result of this lack of clarity can be prolonged court appearances, sometimes with an unsatisfactory outcome. CP powers did not resolve all the issues of title, although they did resolve the question of who the title holder was going to be ultimately - the FR Co.

Part of the problem was the differing statutory instruments that applied to the route. The 1922 WHR was built by LRO from Croesor Junction to Rhyd Ddu, but there had already been powers for this. The Croesor Tramway, from Porthmadog to Croesor Junction was built by wayleave, but amending Acts were made later, and the powers were sold to the PB&SSR with embodiment into the WHR in 1901. This made life complicated. To cap it all, the title holder, the OR, during closure, deliberately withheld acts of ownership upon the land, increasing expectation by the new users that they could claim title. Finally, when the deeds were handed over, there were places were title appeared to be uncertain. This may have been an end to the WHR legal

tangle, but the iteration of some of the effects of it did little to help solve all the problems. The following set of circumstances shows some of the certainty and some of the confusion:

### Caernarfon Dinas

The standard gauge railway from Caernarfon to Afon Wen closed in 1964. The GCC obtained title, and offered FR Co. a 999 year lease from Caernarfon to Dinas. That left the first three miles without any problems over land title. However, there were problems at Dinas on former NWNG/WHR land, as the OR had sold title to two sections of land. The station yard was in the hands of the GCC Engineers Dept, and the old WHR Car shed and loco shed were owned by the Environment Agency (National Rivers Authority). Both had been acquired from the OR properly, but of course the FR Co. interpretation of the residuary powers, from the 1896 Light Railways Act LRO, was that a sale of land may not obstruct the 'statutory purpose', and it was supposed that a strip of land sufficient for the railway through the property, following the trackbed would not have been included on the sale. However, this was not put to the test, as both landowners agreed to sell. The importance of the 'interpretation' is significant for what followed on Phases 2-4.

### Dinas - Rhyd Ddu

The whole of the 1922 WHR 22 mile route was included in the TWO application, made on 27th March 1997, though the funding from the Millennium Commission only took construction as far as Rhyd Ddu. The OR held title to the trackbed land. Some of

*Below: This area of Porthmadog car park also has unfinished business, but the railway has been rebuilt.*

this was quite clear, but not all. Title was transferred to FR Co. on 3rd February 1999 for £1. There were no serious title arguments between Dinas and Rhyd Ddu, though there were a number of problems from people who had occupied the land, and were reluctant to leave it. The TWO conditions required FR Co. to mitigate the problems caused to landowners who had become dependent upon the trackbed. This was by negotiation, and there were those who would, and those who would not talk to the negotiators. Looking back, it seems that those who did talk came off best, however for a the time life became difficult. Some could not see how land used for fifty years should be given up for a tourist railway, at great inconvenience and financial detriment to themselves. To get the TWO powers, it was mandatory to have made fair offer of a settlement to objectors. The objector was not required to agree to the mitigation terms, but if there was consistent refusal of a 'fair' offer, bearing in mind that title was now vested in FR Co., then there could be no mitigation. There were some who insisted that as they had occupied the land for fifty years, then they had acquired title to it by Adverse Possession. This was disputed, as there is a clear AP procedure, action has to be taken to get it. The TWO powers came on 21 July 1999. Regardless of mitigation, all frontage landowners were issued with CP notices at appropriate times between Dinas and Porthmadog. The game had changed subtly - the railway could be built, and when work started anyone with valid title to the trackbed land would need to be paid a value for that land within one month of the start of work.

The places where the trackbed was enjoying use by others were easy to see. The whole of the exit embankment from Dinas under the main road was filled in. The line at Bryn Gloch, just south of the road across the railway, Pont Betws Garmon, was in use to serve the caravan site there. Just beyond, the trackbed had been narrowed by land take, notably on the site of the Dŵr Cymru water processing plant. Beyond Castell Cidwm bridge, the trackbed had been absorbed back into a farm, and in several instances on the remaining route to Rhyd Ddu, it was used regularly to facilitate access. Rhyd Ddu station site had been turned into a car park to serve the path up Snowdon. So there was a great deal of change to handle, some of it with willing participants some unwilling.

## Rhyd Ddu - Porthmadog
More radical use had been made of the vacant trackbed on this

section, which began to be tackled in 2004. It was easier for the reason that the frontage landowners had seen how people had fared on the earlier sections, yet there were particular differences. There were a couple of landowners who claimed that the Adverse Possession proceedings had been dealt with correctly - though this process was disputed by FR Co. However, a dispute about land value alone in this area would hardly break the bank. Even if one allowed the claim to title, without prejudice, and paid the land value, this farmland was not expensive. The compulsory purchase procedure took precedence. The FR Co. could enter on the land after Notices to Enter, and Notices to Treat had been issued. If the value or other factors were not in contention, then within a month FR Co. must pay 80% of the agreed value. If there were other factors in contention, then wrangles had to be settled by the Lands Tribunal, but building the railway was still permitted to proceed, as this was not an argument about title, it was about value or compensation.

The first major alternative use of the trackbed on Phase 4 was at Meillionen in the Forestry Commission run camp site. This was settled and mitigation factors agreed - a bridge and new road was built to enable access to parts of the camp. Meillionen Halt was constructed and now this large camp site has a station.

There was a land dispute to be settled at Beddgelert, and this has been achieved. There was dispute over title of trackbed land between Pont Croesor and Traeth Mawr that took much longer to settle. However this too was achieved. There were a number of requests for mitigation on the Phase 4 portion of the trackbed. Most visible mitigations are the new roads next the railway at Hafod y Llyn, and from Pont Ynysferlas towards Pont Dylif.

Not everything can be settled in the short term. There is a dispute in Porthmadog that has been long-running. However the railway is built, and there is likely to be a conclusion to this problem too in the fullness of time. Thanks to CP powers, problems over land have not threatened the project as they did in the past. The legal tangle has been thoroughly unravelled.

How can a newly rebuilt railway terminate in a Victorian station by the sea that is already short of space, and considers itself to be seriously cramped? Circumstances have brought the restored WHR to a termination at Porthmadog Harbour Station. An ingenious solution has been found that offers the room for this to happen. For Harbour Station this is the first major rebuild in almost 150 years. Project Engineer, Ian Hartill explains how the Cob has been widened to offer the extra space needed.

Widening the Cob has been planned for a great deal of time, as the overall authority for the work was obtained in the TWO. The planning work to obtain the various specific permissions began in 2006/7. Consents had to be obtained from a wide range of bodies, and during 2007/8 detailed designs were needed of the proposal, such that consultant engineers were employed. Particular work was necessary to obtain the marine licence, and with all the permissions falling in to place, then to find the funds. The National Station Improvement Project offered a grant of some 66% of the £1m project cost, leaving the FR Trust to find the balance from the Phase 5 Sustainable Railway Appeal, to which was added Gift Aid, and the FR sponsor's additional 10%. Thus with permissions and funds, the job went out to tender and was won by Jones Bros, of Ruthin.

The first part of the plan involved the delivery of some 27,000 tonnes of granite rock from the nearby Minffordd Quarry to enable the westernmost 260 metres of the 200 year old Cob embankment to be widened. This was necessary to allow the construction of a new platform and loop line for use by Welsh Highland trains, and also enables a complete rework of the station layout.

Materials for the Cob Widening came from the Tarmac Minffordd Quarry. The delivery route to Harbour Station used the new Porthmadog Bypass, with the lorries running along the High Street, across the Britannia Bridge, and then making a right turn on to a purpose made site access past Spooners. The block paving from outside Spooners was carefully lifted and taken by train to Minffordd where it has been stored for re-use. Tarmac was then laid to form the haul road across the station. A proportion of the core fill material was recovered from the bypass construction site compound, and laid as a protective roadway across the fan of the station tracks. The concrete was surfaced with tarmac, and matters were arranged so that regular deliveries could be made by multiple vehicles, carrying the appropriate grade of granite material for the works.

The core fill of mixed, small stones, was the first material imported to the site. Each successive lorry load was placed

*The first phase of Cob Widening was to get the fill from Minffordd Quarry across the tracks to the seaward side. The work proceeded quickly, seen here on 26th January 2012. A coat of stones was placed first, covered with larger rocks on top, to break up the waves and absorb their energy. The work began at the Porthmadog end and moved towards Boston Lodge. The job had a narrow time window whilst no trains ran. After consolidation and settlement tracks can be laid.*

**Left:** *In this wintry scene looking east to the snow covered Rhinogs, the fill is seen tapering towards the north beyond the machine. This is stone from Minffordd Quarry forming the core fill, reaching out 9m from the wave wall on the left of the picture.*

**Both Photos David High**

**Below:** *These stones are the rock armour, to be placed on the outside of the core fill. Some rocks weigh up to a tonne, and they are the first defence against the wave action, breaking them up and dissipating their energy without allowing erosion.*

against the base of the existing Cob, working from west to east, in a layer of 450mm depth. The stone fill was levelled by machine to form a haul road over the 250m length of the working area. As quickly as practical the road was increased in depth and width to create a working platform raised far enough to be out of reach of the tides. The core fill was extended seaward to 9m from the original WW2 Cob wave wall. The extension was built up in three bands of 3m width, to give sufficient room for the continued hauling of the core fill material. As it was laid, areas were used for storage, for the machines to continue to work outside lorry delivery times and during high tide levels. The layers were compacted and consolidated by being passing over by a large bulldozer used on the site.

When the haul road had reached a height of one metre, a PC210 excavator was positioned on the core fill, and used to excavate the toe. The excavated material from the bed was placed beyond the construction site, to be redistributed later against the base of the new Cob formation. During this excavation the 1:2.25 slope from the toe needed for the wave surface was created in sections up 20m long . This slope was lined with a geotextile sheet on which the first layer of rock armour was placed as the sea wave defence.

The granite rocks used as armour vary between 300Kg and 1000Kg. Some of these are quite large rocks, and all were delivered to site from Minffordd Quarry by 20 tonne tipper wagons, and either stored or tipped to be placed in their precise location as required by the excavator located on the haul road. Storage of the armour rock was necessary as the work was done in co-ordinated stages.

The method of working was that after the haul road had been raised, the core fill was added, then a new layer of geotextile was placed,

with up to one metre of overlap on the previous. This was followed firstly by placement of the next band of rock armour, and then the process was repeated to work up the batter towards the top layer.

The operation was carried out eastwards, gradually widening and raising the new section of Cob towards the level required.

The structure will need three months or so to settle before any construction work can be done on top of it. Settlement will be determined by a number of survey points, returned to on a regular basis for 'level' readings. When settlement ceases the construction of the new perimeter wave wall may begin. A wave wall of mass concrete and any other structures would suffer badly from any subsidence of the ground.

The new 350m wave wall will be built to replace that removed during the widening works. The details of this must satisfy the Environment Agency – Wales, responsible for all coastal flood defence. After the successful completion of the construction works, the road access will be removed, and the site prepared for the new platform, station layout and signalling. All of this work is expected to take most of 2013, with the new trackwork and signal box, planned for installation ready for the 2014 season.

*The simplest/cheapest way of getting the stone across the tracks at Harbour Station was to tarmac across the tracks. This provided a suitable road surface and still allowed the tracks to be used if needed (February Half-term 2012). The strategy was effective.*

**WHRCL**

**J**ohn Sreeves first came to Ffestiniog in the 1970s, and is a clear example of why one should always encourage the young. He was inspired by his adventures, and chose a career in civil engineering. He was able to repay the experiences of those early days by returning to the WHR project. He began surveying and tracklaying, until the urgent task of designing bridges came his way - he then designed nine for the WHR. John is an Associate Director, Bridges with the international engineering consultants Halcrow Group Ltd.

**I** volunteered on the Ffestiniog Railway Deviation in May 1974 at 16. My first journey to North Wales from Redditch took five hours on a moped, at an average speed of 23 mph! Working with the Midland and Northern group led by Tony Baker and Chris Chitty followed, and the Deviation experience determined my future career in civil engineering, with power stations, drainage, and highways on the CV, but very little railway work.

My first involvement with the WHR project was in 1994, with survey work for the TWO application. During weekends, and a remarkable week of a searing heat wave in August 1995, the entire length of line was surveyed, with Stuart McNair and others. The result was a gradient profile, complete with all structures and obstructions identified and measured. Land surveys were also conducted at Dinas, Waunfawr, Rhyd-Ddu, Beddgelert, Porthmadog, and some other areas of interest.

From 1997 I regularly worked with the track gangs, earning a reputation for laying out many sleepers singlehandedly in advance of the head of steel. However the nature of voluntary effort changed when an e-mail from Andy Savage in January 2003 asked whether I could design a bridge for Betws Garmon, using some scrap beams from Sheffield. This was the first steel bridge in my career, as reinforced and pre-stressed concrete was my only previous experience. As HRH Prince Charles had been booked for the opening, requiring the Afon Gwyrfai to be bridged urgently, much late night work was needed for modifications to the beams. So it was with relief that the bridge fitted the gap on 5 June 2003, and carried Prince Charles safely across eight weeks later.

The Phase 4 challenge had to be accepted, so I designed another eight bridges, and was fortunate in receiving much advice from colleagues in the office.

Nevertheless, the design and draughtsmanship required was to occupy 1786 hours of spare time over three years. It was with immense pride that I enjoyed the reward of seeing the prominent landmark of Bryn y Felin Bridge successfully constructed on 11-12 March 2006. As a modern structure that was almost indistinguishable from the original, it remains the greatest highlight of my entire career. The following year, I half-heartedly entered the bridge in a competition at the Institution of Structural Engineers, and we achieved third place in the heritage category, out of 10 entries received, beaten only by Dresden and St Pancras Stations!

The other bridges soon followed; Nantmor Road on 29 October 2006, Dylif River on 17 February 2007, Nanmor River on 17 March 2007 and Pont Croesor on 2 January 2008. Much credit is due to the fabricators at Brunswick Ironworks who constructed all of the bridges to great accuracy, and without any errors or rework. After that, two overbridges remained which became a pair of Armco tunnels carrying farm tracks over the line near Traeth Mawr. My other works have included a small culvert at Pont Cae'r Gors, scour repairs at Meillionen Bridge in Beddgelert Forest, Beddgelert Station water crane, and a condition survey of Tryfan Junction station building. There have been two papers for the Institution of Civil Engineers Proceedings to promote the railway.

The whole project has been magnificent!

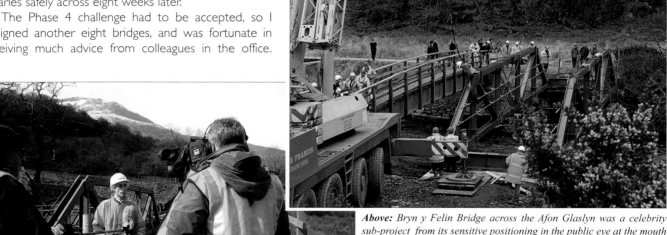

**Above:** *Bryn y Felin Bridge across the Afon Glaslyn was a celebrity sub-project from its sensitive positioning in the public eye at the mouth of the famous Aberglaslyn Pass, and for its modern construction that conformed exactly to its predecessor. John is to the bottom-centre of the photograph, behind the gorse, looking concernedly at the installation, like a modern-day Brunel.*

**Left:** *Next came the interview; the television was interested in the achievement - it really sprang the WHR into the public eye. So John was being asked how it was done and other associated questions. This bridge was the second of his nine.* **John Sreeves**

# Chapter 9
## Locomotives
## 1995 - 2011

Part of the problem with the North Wales Narrow Gauge Railways (NWNG) was that the promoters did not envision big loads being carried - and in that, indeed they were right! The locomotives were rather clever, and of the Spooner genre, rather than sloggers. It was rugged territory, and the minerals they sought to carry were impoverished ores, or slates that were expensive to work. They did not know when they built the railway that the world was changing, such that the enterprise proved to be fruitless in a short while; the mining activity was vulnerable to competition. The demand for minerals led to more easily obtainable supplies of more concentrated ores from elsewhere, and the development slate deposits more cheaply exploited in neighbouring valleys eclipsed them. The sources of traffic on the branch to Rhyd Ddu eventually failed, and the railway was never extended to Caernarfon. The finances were parlous, the traffic was thin, and the locomotives were hardly overworked.

*Prince is expected to pull 6 cars on the FR, but he is shown here at Waunfawr with only two cars. Three might be possible, but only the vintage cars.*

The WHR enterprise exploited the failed NWNG in the 1920s. Government unemployment relief had been combined with shiny optimism to complete the railway from Dinas to Portmadoc, as employment relief, but it was unfounded. However, the electric Portmadoc, Beddgelert and South Snowdon Railway plans were not proceeded with. In the 1930s, steam locomotives were expected to pull only three or four carriages, and tourists were wooed - but not in numbers enough for the railway to prosper. The enterprise closed in 1937 and the locos were either scrapped or sold. The lessons of the past were clear to most of those wishing to set up the new Welsh Highland Railway. An enterprise based on the logic of the old was unlikely to succeed. If the line

was reinstated throughout its length, and only three car trains were run over it, the outcome would be profitless. A terminus at Caernarfon was deemed essential. This was the major weak point of the NWNG; it could not be competitive with mandatory transhipment at Dinas. The new Ffestiniog promoters considered that decent length trains, to transport visitors on a grand scale as on the FR, were a key element of success. There were some difficulties executing this determination. The WHR has gradients of 1:40, in comparison with the 1:70 of its FR neighbour. If FR style locomotives were used, then the train length must diminish to the three or four cars of old, rendering the operation financially non-viable. Even dinky vintage puffers with people jammed into a short train were likely to repeat the financial failure that befell the WHR in the 1930s.

The answer was not hard to find. Tough two-foot gauge railways, with 1:40 gradients and sharp curves, were operated extensively in the Republic of South Africa. To haul paying loads they had resorted to and perfected the ultimate Beyer-Garratt, 2-6-2+2-6-2, articulated design, the NGG16. Many were now idle, as the carefully regulated transport system in RSA disappeared, and the 2ft gauge lines in Natal and elsewhere were closing. Thus NGG16 locomotives were available, and kind friends of Ffestiniog were around in South Africa to help make reasonable and secure purchases.

Even before it was clear that Caernarfon to Dinas would become the first part of the WHR to be restored, negotiations were going on for the locomotives needed to make the sure that the railway had suitable motive power. The strategy devised for restoration of running large trains from the Caernarfon end was

*Here is the first train to work from FR to Welsh Highland in the late afternoon of 31st October 2010, returning from Rhyd Ddu, driven by F&WHR GM Paul Lewin. Lyd, the re-recreated Lynton and Barnstaple Railway, Manning Wardle 2-6-2T, heads the Tracklayer's Train, double headed, with single Fairlie 0-4-4T Taliesn. Two smaller locos are needed to bring a decent sized train up the 1:40 gradients and 55m reverse curves on this uncompromising railway. It's ever so much fun, as long as you aren't expecting to do this in commercial service, and are expecting to pay all the bills afterwards. Lyd is hardly small, as she will take 8 unaided up the FR - but that's 1:70, and although it has curvaceous moments, there isn't the concentrated nastiness to locomotives that the WHR can summon. So the smaller locomotives are run for fun; thus they hardly appear in these pages. The one that does, would be a giant on the FR - the NG 15. That 2-8-2 tender engine is written up later. So when you travel on WHR and FR, enjoy the fact that the two railways will forever be separated, though their tracks may join. A Garratt is not likely to work to Blaenau without exceptional expenditure, and the small locos are likely to stay mainly on the FR. Vive la différence! Hir yn byw y gwahaniaeth.*

*The NGG16 design delivers a standard gauge punch on a 2ft gauge railway. A large boiler is slung between two power bogies, with the fuel and water carried on them. The bogies have a six-wheeled power unit, with pony wheels each side, to guide the driving wheels through sharp curves in either direction. The boiler is short and fat, the right shape for making steam, and the least affected by steep gradients. These 14.75m long Garratts are hardly a thing of beauty; they really do pull the loads, and the restored WHR would be lost without them.*

possible as the powerful locomotives were evidently to be had.

In June 1993, Mike Hart and Mike Schumann went to see ex-Boston Lodge engineer Phil Girdlestone, then the Mechanical Engineer of the 610mm gauge, Alfred County Railway from Port Shepstone to Harding in KwaZulu-Natal. He knew where there were locomotives no longer needed for the service, that could be made available for sale. He was also aware of their service histories, and of the state they were in. As a demonstration, he provided NGG 16, No.141, that he had modified with producer gas coal consumption, to haul a train equivalent to 15 cars. The two Mikes pronounced themselves satisfied with the way that the locomotive pulled the train up average grades of 1:60, with a ruling grade of 1:37. This led to purchase 'reservations' for two NGG16s, at £90k each, with an option of a third, and the purchase of a dozen, braked, empty flat wagons. Nos 138 and 143 (the last built Beyer-Garratt) were the ones chosen. The price included overhaul to working condition. Three other Garratts stored at Paddock were also identified for possible purchase. No sale was confirmed until after the result of the Transfer Order inquiry was known.

At the Portland Cement works at Port Elizabeth. SAR Class 91 diesel-electrics had taken over the workings of the B+B Funkey diesel locomotives on their connecting line. Two idle locomotives were purchased for a bargain £11k each on that visit.

At one stroke the WHR had been furnished with its immediate requirement for motive power, and it set the scene for what was to follow. For various delightful reasons, all to be explained in the text to follow, by 2010 the railway had acquired four of these ideal steam locomotives. It was clear from the work that had gone on in preparation for the public inquiry that the ideal number to have ought to be five. Favourable circumstance offered additional NGG16s 87 and 140 that came into ownership, and 109 may indeed follow. The four are certainly enough for the moment; five will be needed for a three-train service, however for anyone with an NGG16 that they wish to run, then finding a suitable railway is difficult. The WHR is similar to the Natal narrow gauge, in gradient and curve, though not length; Wales is wetter, with slippier rails. So more Garratts might yet find their way to the WHR.

K1, the first Garratt, owned by the FR Co. was an obvious choice to restore, as the wide stage that was now becoming available was tempting. But the WHR story is not just about Garratts. The powerful 2ft gauge, 2-8-2 African tender engines, the Kalaharis are also on the scene. Built in 1953, NG15 Class 133 and 134 also come from Belgium (like NGG No. 87). Their eight-coupled driving wheels are guided by a Krauss-Helmholtz arrangement between the pony truck and the leading driving axle, to permit the eight coupled wheels to traverse sharp curves. They are reputed to offer the equivalent of 75% of a Garratt in power output. No. 134 is under overhaul, for completion in 2014.

The remaining expressed wish is a powerful diesel locomotive. The Funkeys have proved to be invaluable. So much so that it is clear that a unit of more than 350hp is needed. Their replacements, the SAR Class 91 would be ideal, except that they are cut down, metre gauge locomotives, and as a result are too massive. WHR is inventive, and a bigger, 5-600hp diesel is on the shopping list, either to buy in or if necessary to build.

*So you never knew that K1 did a secret trip up the FR to Blaenau in works grey with the 'green set'? Wickedly, to deceive, there was a quick morning trip up to Minffordd with the carriages and* Conway Castle. *Then a bit of manoeuvring to set it all up, and after, some work in Adobe Photoshop, designed to confuse. Effective though?*

## K1 The First Garratt

Herbert Garratt was an artist; he sketched out an articulated locomotive design that came to him whilst observing the transit of a bogie wagon through points. He showed this to directors of Beyer, Peacock in 1907, and got interest from a locomotive builder and exporter who was searching for any design that would offer superiority over competitors. Tasmanian Government Railways were going to buy a Mallet design for their 2ft gauge, 17 mile, North East Dundas Tramway, from Zeehan to Williamsford. The route was tough, with 1:25 gradients and 1½ chain radius (30m)

curves. Garratt designed K1, based on the Mallet specification, and used this design in his patent application of 26th July 1907. He painted oil pictures of Garratts before any were ever built, and one of an 0-6-0+0-6-0 shows the cylinders on the outside ends. K1 and K2 were built in 1909 as compounds; the customer insisted. This might have been a throwback to the Mallet design that the Garratt supplanted. To shorten the receiver pipe between high and low pressure cylinders, he designed them facing inwards. Future Garratts would be simple locomotives, there were no more compounds, either across the cylinders or between the

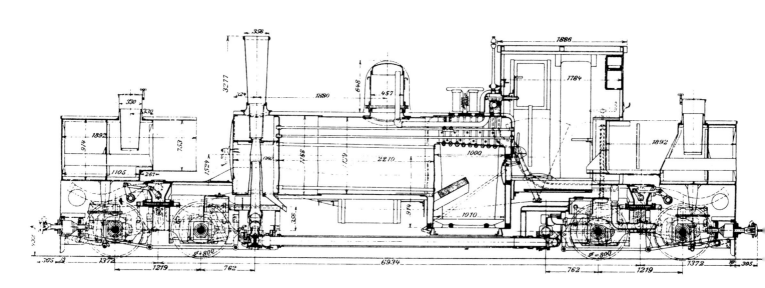

*Celebration time on the 8th of September 2006, in bright afternoon sun at the Super-Power Weekend. K1 is at Dinas, with a lineup of five coaches, the same as the Minffordd Weighbridge photo opposite - but this time for real! K1 can be thrashed up the railway and keep time with more cars than the Funkey - but this might not be good news for the old girl. She is cherished, and many want her to have a quiet life - but after all these years, she can still do it!*

power units (save for the 1925 built Burma GA Class). Little fuss was made about this revolutionary articulated design, as it probably took Beyer's time to find out the principle's capability.

The tramway remained open until 1925*. The locomotive was bought back by Beyer, Peacock in 1947. The loco that exists is a blend of K1 and K2; the boiler was apparently from K2, and the switch seems to have taken place whilst still in service. K1's boiler apparently was sold to a sawmill, so there wasn't much choice in the matter. Beyer, Peacock closed in 1966; although K1 was offered to the Narrow Gauge Railway Museum at Tywyn in 1961,

*sources do not agree, some say 5th July 1932

it could not be stored under cover, and that was not acceptable. Festiniog Railway Company Director Bill Broadbent, working in Manchester, managed to pick up the K1 at a knockdown price in 1966 of £1,400 (£1k to buy, £400 to move). On the face of it this seems to have been a wonderful bargain, and there was much enthusiasm. However, internally one can see the writhings in the Society Magazine, that the purchase was a 'venture of faith' and that the *'Company has not budgeted for such an expenditure and does not have the financial resources to meet an additional commitment of this magnitude'.*

***Above:*** *Not in any shape of the imagination does a front on view of a Garratt look pretty, and K1 started the trend! On the Super Power Weekend, in September 2006 she lifts a light train through the site of Tryfan Junction.*

***Below:*** *On 8th September 2006 K1 is at Dinas being prepared for duty. The loco simmers quietly, gathering strength from the rising steam pressure. She is still in non-solo mode, until someone paints out the yellow stripe, as she has now been 'passed fit to run'.*

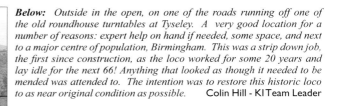

**Above:** *Double Fairlie* Earl of Merioneth *shunts the locomotive, minus boiler, into No6 Road at Porthmadog in early October 2000, on the occasion of the FR Vintage Weekend. The disparity in loading gauge size is apparent from this photograph. K1's footplate is about level with Earl's nameplates! The changes to make K1 run up the FR would have eclipsed those to* Moel Tryfan *and* Russell *- and those were considered to be vandalism! So it is easy to understand why the cash-strapped FR directorials were so narked with Director Broadbent - we are all glad he did it though. Thanks Bill!* **Ben Fisher**

**left:** *The FR loves things like this - it gives great glee. Here is K1, on Porthmadog No.6 Road, and of course this is right where it was parked in 1966, when it was rescued from the doomed Beyer, Peacock plant at Gorton, Manchester. It's a tiny point of detail, but in 1966, the siding ran along the top of the wall - that would have been difficult to replicate. K1 stayed up there all season until the waiting tarpaulin claimed her at Glan-y-Mor. In 2000 she went back to BL for completion.* **Ben Fisher Website**

The FR Co. Board was furious with Broadbent, and hoped the Society could pull the chestnut from the fire for them. They were in luck, as enthusiasm ran very high, and there was a good response to the K1 Appeal. K1 was enormous, dwarfing FR stock - and there was no chance at all of it running up the Festiniog without the most savage butchery - and no one was going to do that with the world's first Garratt. It was a white elephant, but fortunately the flush of enthusiasm meant it was a popular white elephant, and it had been saved. K1 was covered by a tarpaulin in Glan y Mor Yard for ten years, until eventually it went to the NRM at York in 1976. During much of the 1980s it was there, on display. It got an attractive coat of works grey which looked very nice. It could be seen in a prime spot, on the turntable, mounted on a standard gauge well wagon. Lots and lots of people enjoyed the view, which was useful later.

Eventually K1's time came up. The WHR revival offered somewhere for her to run again, albeit with a slight gauge reduction of the wheelsets from 610mm to 597mm. The K1 Group was formed under the leadership of Colin Hill. In 1995 K1 went to Tyseley. There she was stripped right down. It was decided that the locomotive would be restored 'as original', as superheating with 'simple' cylinders would require drastic alterations that were not acceptable to such an historic machine.

The boiler needed to be renewed. At first Winson Engineering took this on, but the job was completed in 2002 by Israel Newton. In April 2000 The loco frames went to Dinas, and the power units to Boston Lodge. The loco (minus boiler) was displayed at the October 2000 FR Vintage Weekend in Porthmadog, the place where she had last been 34 years earlier.

The new boiler arrived at Boston Lodge on 15th August 2002; and was prepared for its steam test, with K2's chimney attached. This took place on 15th September 2002, and the boiler passed the official steam test on 7th October 2002. Four days later, it was placed in the frames and the cab was attached. Then the maze of copper piping had to be cut, installed and fitted, a major job. There was a special oil burner to be made, and all the fittings had to be installed. Before the cladding could go on, a temporary halt was called to construction to wait for some more funds.

By January 2004 Roland Doyle, was appointed to project manage the completion. This followed his work on *Palmerston* and *Taliesin*. Roland was in the interregnum of the WHLR General Manager's job. The volunteers and staff worked together to finish the project. The tanks were patched, and not replaced. The front one was on by May16th; the brick arch was in by June 19th, and the rear tank was on by July 17th. The 'ten year ticket' for the boiler started with the successful cold test on July 12th. On July 23rd 2004 the boiler inspector granted full approval, and K1 was back in business, 95 years old, and inactive for 75 years. The snagging list of faults was gradually worked through, and the locomotive is the only working compound in Britain (apart from models). Both modes were tried with intrigue, but of course the locomotive could not go far. It was found that with care it could be moved by rail to Minffordd for road transport, minus chimney, dome and cab. Thus K1 went off by road to Dinas on October 2nd 2004, to take up residence in the goods shed. The next job was a clearance trial up the WHR as far as Castell Cidwm, and the locomotive was passed by HMRI on 8th November 2004. Following that, various snags had to be sorted. Trials with

*Above:* The overhaul of this vintage locomotive was undertaken with great attention to detail. The temptation to make it a simple rather than a compound was rejected. The book has various drawings, and is open at the cladding page as that was the activity in progress.

*Below:* On 08.09.04 K1 outside the erecting shop at Boston Lodge, in fine September sunshine. The chimney's off because if it's on, the loco cannot go in and out of the shop - it is just too big. At this time the locomotive is fitted with oil burning rig. It was under test, and had steamed successfully.

6 cars took place, but hot axleboxes recurred. In May 2005 this problem was 'nailed' by beams that can be used to jack the loco off the wheelsets to get at the bearings. With smoother oil ways and underfeed lubrication, the problems with hot axle boxes ceased for a while, until returning later with alignment problems. The year 2005 wasn't a very good one for this locomotive.

On 8th September 2006 K1 was permitted to haul its first passenger train, solo. More work followed in mid-October, and some of the foibles were now better understood, like driving her as a compound. In January 2007, work started on converting the locomotive to coal firing. This involved a lot of work, like a new ashpan and brick arch, a rocking grate, effective spark arrestor, and a bunker. By the end of the year the locomotive was working the 'all day' service. She cannot handle 7 cars up the hill, which is a pity. However, it is early days yet, and it may be that if K1 cannot be thrashed she could last a long time!.

K1 in Boston Lodge Erecting Shop on 14th February 2003, with work in progress by volunteers as the funds had run low. Pipework is not complete, and so the cladding cannot be fitted. No one lost hope, they just spent time raising funds, and as soon as these were available, paid work resumed.

*In the early 'imagination' days there was a concept that the WHR Garratts would be red, indeed the 'Make Your Dreams Come True' poster shows a red locomotive with green and cream carriages. In fact the locomotives were anything but red for many years. These things take time. Eventually NGG16 No.138 appeared in a spectacular crimson livery, seen here in afternoon light at Caernarfon on 9th August 2010.*

## NGG16 The Little Giant

The NGG16 is the final form of the Garratt locomotive, and as chance will have it, with K1 and No 143, the WHR has the first Garratt and the last Beyer-Garratt built in Britain. These articulated machines of 2-6-2 + 2-6-2 wheel arrangement, are the practical expression of the greatest available power for sharply curved and steeply graded 2ft (610mm) gauge lines. This type was built over a 40 year period from 1937, in gradually improving form, and gave excellent service to South African Railways until they were retired from service as the narrow gauge lines were first dieselised, and then closed by the traffic moving to road. There were 34 NGG16s built, distributed among the 2ft gauge lines in South Africa. The long wheelbase keeps the axle load down, and the pony trucks either side of the driving wheels punish the tracks less. For the operators, they have in one machine, the power of almost two locomotives, and for the train crew, one squat boiler produces large amounts of superheated steam, in quantities that can supply any demand from the cylinders. Fuel and water provision offers a sufficient range before replenishment, but the Namibian Garratts hauled an additional bogie tank car of water.

Their attraction for the WHR lay in the fact that it is a line somewhat like those in Natal, and the power and reliability of the NGG 16 was highly desirable to haul a paying load. Two things have been proved to everyone's satisfaction. The first is that the locomotives have done what was expected of them. They are good for over ten carriages on the WHR. (They were not tested in service on more, as the WHR in 2010 did not have more carriages to place on a train.) Efficient, working sanding gear is essential for work in Wales. On a wet and greasy rail , the climb

| NGG 16 Garratts built | | | |
|---|---|---|---|
| Nos | No | Year | Builder |
| 85 - 88 | 4 | 1937 | Cockerill, Seraing, Belge |
| 109 - 116 | 8 | 1939 | Beyer, Peacock, UK |
| 125 - 131 | 7 | 1951 | Beyer, Peacock, UK |
| 137- 143 | 7 | 1958 | Beyer, Peacock UK* |
| 149 - 156 | 8 | 1967/8 | Hunslet-Taylor, RSA |

All locos built for SAR/SAS, except for *. These for Tsumeb Corp., went to SAR/SAS as the Otavi Rly was regauged from 610-1067mm

up out of Beddgelert, up Cwm Gloch and through Cutting Mawr is a severe test of traction. Adhesion might be the limiting factor for these locomotives, as they have plenty of power. At 48ft 6ins (14.8m) long, they exceed the length of a WHR carriage, but this long length is helpful to bridges, as is the maximum axle load of just under 7 tonnes. The FR converted locomotives to oil firing, and so the Garratts also began with that mode. This was satisfactory, but expensive. Now firing by coal has been introduced, and of course this is cheaper, as powerful, but dirtier. However, the Lempor-Girdlestone exhaust, and loads that do not overtax the locomotives means that they do not throw sparks.

The second thing is that the WHR is such a splendid canvass for such splendid machines, that when they became available to buy, those that bought them found a hearty welcome. Thus the WHR now has four NGG16 locomotives, with three working; the largest regularly working contingent of these locomotives left.

*On the left one of the 'really useful locomotives' of preservation, an Ivatt Class 2, 2-6-2T (Seen here at Sheffield Park, Bluebell Railway). There were tender and tank versions built, and the design was repeated in the 84XXX and 78XXX Standard Class locomotives. On the right is NGG16 No. 143, as working on the WHR (Seen here at Dinas). In the table below, compare the dimensions - it makes interesting reading!*

| Ivatt Class 2, 2-6-2T - Standard Gauge | |
|---|---|
| Heating Surface | 1025 sq ft |
| Superheater | 124 sq ft |
| Grate area | 17.5 sq ft |
| Length between tubeplates | 10'10½" |
| Cylinders (2) | 16"dia x 24½"stroke |
| Driving wheel diameter | 5'0" |
| Weight (full) | 66.25 tonnes |
| Tractive effort (boiler 200lbs) | 18,513 lbs |
| Length | 38'9½" |

| NGG16 2-6-2+2-6-2 Beyer-Garratt - 2ft Gauge | |
|---|---|
| Heating Surface | 921.1 sq ft |
| Superheater | 149 sq ft |
| Grate area | 19.5 sq ft |
| Length between tubeplates | 9'3½" |
| Cylinders (4) | 12"dia x 16"stroke |
| Driving wheel diameter | 2'9" |
| Weight (full) | 59.1 tonnes |
| Tractive effort (boiler 180lbs) | 21,553 lbs |
| Length | 48'6" |

*Comparisons shouldn't get out of hand! Both machines were designed and constructed for specific (different) jobs. The interesting detail is to show that boiler sizes were similar, and that the narrow gauge power output is greater. On the 2ft gauge, the largest example eventually managed to reach standard gauge outputs.*

*Below: Boston Lodge Works, on 6th July 2010. The boiler from NGG16 No.140 is in the frame of loco No.143. All are standard boilers,(with detail differences) and it's what SAR/SAS did on a regular basis. Locomotives can be placed back in service quickly, whilst boilers get an extended overhaul. The NGG16 boiler is large, good at steaming - as it is short and fat - and more able to resist the tendency on steep gradients for the boiler water level to disappear out of the sight glass. It was one of the Beyer-Garratt advantages over long, thin, Mallet boilers. There is space for plenty of superheater elements on the Garratt, which makes for more fuel-efficient, more economic operation. The large distribution manifold sits on top of the firebox. In front of it is the high dome, that guards against priming on steep gradients by making the steam take-off as far as possible away from the water surface. It is a good and well tried and tested design - and the WHR has four of them!*

*Above: Boston Lodge Works, on 5th June 2007. One of the 2-6-2 outside, bar framed, power bogies from NGG16 No.87 is in the Erecting Shop being overhauled. This detailed view shows the rear pony-truck, with its roller bearing housings, Above is the compensated springing lever. This is adjusted to carry just under 4 tonnes of the bogie's weight. Together the pony-trucks guide the bogies smoothly round curves in either direction. The balance weights on the three driving axle cranks can be seen clearly. To the right of the centre balance weight is the bogie pivot. High-pressure steam from the regulator is fed to the cylinders through steam-tight ball joints. This whole segment of the machine is most carefully designed and put together, to give trouble-free operation, despite its complexity. Boston Lodge is enjoying the fruits of having eight of these bogies for three NGG16s in service - although there are some differences between them.*

*Double-headed Garratts wait at Dinas for departure with the first public steam train through the Aberglaslyn Pass to Hafod y Llyn, on 21st May 2009. A number of these special trains were run for the various stages of opening of Phase 4. The opportunity was taken to invite various dignitarios, and to make full use of the goodwill generated. Garratt No, 87 leads, assisted by No. 143, hauling nine carriages.*

*A Garratt at Porthmadog was still a rare event at the Golden Bolt ceremony on the 28th February 2009. The comparison in scale with* Merddin Emrys *remains quite a surprise. Official policy says that light grey is an impractical livery - but it looked superb. The cock being snooked with the prochronism of a web address is delightful. It is a subtle indication that whilst all is serious, a sense of wry humour can still be maintained.*

## NGG16 - No. 87

NGG16 No. 87 was built as the second-to-last of a batch of four locomotives, made by Cockerill, Belgium. Garratt's joint patent with Beyer, Peacock ran out when, after his early death, Beyer's were unable to renew it. Hanomag were in there quick, and freed from the tie with Beyers, SAR/SAS gave them an order for the 12 excellent NGG13 Garratts. The design was developed jointly and was what SAR/SAS wanted. However, Hanomag sold out to Henschel, and SAR/SAS went back to Beyer, Peacock, who were too busy. So the job went to Cockerill for the first order of the new class of machine. They differed little from the NGG13 - but perhaps the auspices of the return to Beyer,

*There will be many photographs from here in the future, right down by the River Glaslyn, in the gorge, with the railway running by above. No. 87 is now in blue, and is fired with coal. She passes by with the 12.10 train from Caernarfon to Pont Croesor, on 27 May 2010. The service will shortly run right through to Porthmadog.*

Peacock led to the new class number of NGG16! However the objective was to eliminate a number of NGG13 faults, like bogie bar frame cracking, small cab, poor sanding, sub-optimal boiler mounts, and lack of fuel and water capacity. The round tank top of Nos 85-88 distinguishes them from their later siblings - see this on No. 87.

The locomotive was delivered to Port Shepstone, Natal to work the line to Harding. It spent its last days on the Umzinto-Donnybrook line, ultimately being left cold outside Donnybrook shed. It was brought back to UK for a Yorkshire railway scheme that did not go ahead, and it moved to the Exmoor Steam Railway. Donations from a private sponsor brought the locomotive to Porthmadog on 3rd February 2006, and paid for its overhaul. During the next three years it was thoroughly overhauled at the Ffestiniog Railway's Boston Lodge Works. A huge amount of work was done on the locomotive, some of which you will see in the following illustrations. After taking part in the Golden Bolt ceremony at Porthmadog, it took up service on the Welsh Highland Railway in April 2009. It managed to steam solo, all the

**Left** : The sheer size of this firebox is a bit big on a narrow gauge engine! There were many stays to work on. The general condition of the boiler was good, but it was still a great deal of work. October 2007.

**Right:** Here, one of the 15 superheater flues is being fitted into the boiler. All the tubes were changed on No. 87, as a matter of course. October 2007.

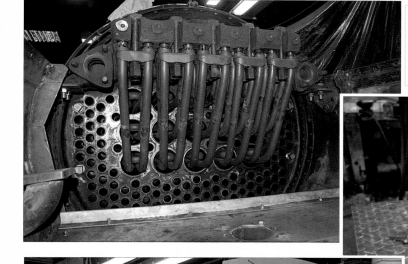

**Left :** The superheater elements are now connected to the 'header' and have been fitted into the flues. This much superheating will really have an effect on the long runs achieved on the WHR. NGG16 Class are modern engines. June 2008.

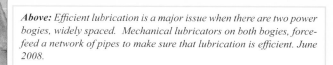

**Above:** Efficient lubrication is a major issue when there are two power bogies, widely spaced. Mechanical lubricators on both bogies, force-feed a network of pipes to make sure that lubrication is efficient. June 2008.

**Left :** The original buildings at Boston Lodge served the horse-drawn railway from 1832. Steam began in 1863, and construction of steam locomotives in 1879. No one ever envisaged a locomotive of this size being overhauled here - it dwarfs the place, and has an air of Gulliver visiting Lilliput. The chimney has be off to get the engine out of the building into the Yard.

*Left: A kit of parts for the Walschaerts valve gear is laid out on the bench in Boston Lodge, on 14th November 2008, all shiny and clean, and re-bushed, ready to go on to the bogies. This is not all the gear, it is just a part.*
**Peter Johnson**

*Below: Oooh-er! No.87 makes an unauthorised excursion 'off-rail' in 1972. One can well appreciate from this view that lurking in there was a bogie frame crack from the experience! They were on the Umzinto to Donnybrook line in Natal, when herself made a break for freedom near Highflats. One hopes that subsequent action removed any taste this locomotive may have for such excursions. Yet please note that much of the rail from this line was relaid on the WHR after it closed.*
**Terry Hutson collection**

way to Dinas. The first delivery of steam by rail! Dark blue livery has been applied, and the locomotive runs on coal.

The story of the overhaul of No. 87 is of the largest locomotive project ever undertaken by Boston Lodge. The building of locomotives is not new: two double Fairlies, one single Fairlie, and a L&B 2-6-2T, in recent times attest to that. Yet the rebuilding of an NGG16 in this pint-sized workshop is another thing. Such a large locomotive offered logistical problems from the start. The inwards delivery was made to Minffordd Yard on Saturday 4th February 2006. A pair of ambulance bogies and power by *Moelwyn* got the boiler unit to Boston Lodge, after a squeeze through Rhiw Plas bridge. The two power units were brought down by *Moelwyn* the following day. Fortunately, a set of the proper drawings were obtained from the Transnet Heritage Library in Johannesburg, including 60 boiler drawings of a HANOMAG boiler for an NGG13. Now the little surprises began to be discovered. The boiler on 87 was from an NGG13, although it had received new inner and outer fireboxes ten years before withdrawal, which had rather skewed the choice in favour of No. 87 as a restoration candidate. The NGG13 v NGG16 similarities are greater than the differences, but the drawings came in handy. All the non-ferrous fitments had gone, so new had to be made - but this was to be expected. The bogies were power-washed and dismantled, but it was spotted that the frames from this early batch have less substantial horn guides than for the later locos - thus they are not interchangeable with 138, 140 and 143; components are however. A bogie frame crack was welded up; this was said to have been damage caused by an excursion into the cess in 1972. A new rear bunker was made by the Brunswick Ironworks in Caernarfon, and a new cab was fabricated. A new boiler backhead and firebox rear was made by Israel Newton.

A new chimney pattern was made; the chimney was cast, and new superheater elements were obtained. Some bits were borrowed from sister No. 140, but this is now normal practice. It will be interesting to see the barter when No. 140 is being recommissioned as itself.

By early May 2008 the boiler was coming together to culminate in successful test steamings in early June. In December the locomotive was reassembled, and the complete engine was test steamed in Boston Lodge Yard on January 21st 2009. By the time of the Golden Bolt ceremony at the end of February, No. 87 had run around Harbour Station, and was ready to go to Dinas. This it did on March 23rd 2009; the first steam locomotive to use the cross-town link, to cross the Cambrian, and to run between Traeth Mawr and Hafod y Llyn. Its first public duties on the WHR were to double-head the opening trains to Beddgelert on April 7th 2009. It ran a successful season in 2009 in grey, a colour that everyone liked unless they had to clean it - and it was repainted in time to enter service at Easter 2010, resplendent in dark blue. It enjoyed its finest hour as a Royal Locomotive on the occasion of Her Majesty, The Queen's visit to the railway on 27th April 2010, when No. 87 took Her Majesty from Caernarfon to Dinas.

*On the delivery run, No. 87 slips quietly across the Cambrian - the first steam locomotive to do so. It then made its way in a relaxed manner to Dinas under clouds of steamy contentment.*
**Andrew Thomas**

# NGG16 - No. 109

No. 109 was the first locomotive of the second order of the 34 member, NGG16 class. This order went to Beyer, Peacock and 109 was shipped to South Africa before the outbreak of the Second World War in 1939. This locomotive is the first narrow gauge Garratt that Beyers produced for SAR/SAS since the NGG11 class in 1920. There were 8 locomotives in this order. They followed the previous Belgian order, maintaining their excellent reputation, and were placed on the principal narrow gauge lines. No. 109 is thought to have been both on the Avontuur and Port Shepstone to Harding lines. At the time of closure of the Umzinto - Donnybrook line in 1986, No. 109 was at Ixopo. Thereafter it was taken to Donnybrook. A preservation project in RSA caused the locomotive's removal to the east of Johannesburg. This project failed, and 109 was declared redundant and available for sale.

The Stirland Family, owners of the Exmoor Steam Centre, rescued No. 109 from South Africa. The loco arrived at Tilbury, split into its three major components, and was shipped to Exmoor, arriving on 3rd July 1995. This was the first of the NGG16 locomotives to leave Africa. The locomotive remained at the Exmoor Steam Centre for four years.

Remarkable things now happened. Pete Waterman OBE, famed music entrepreneur and lifelong railway enthusiast, is a person not inclined to offer a meek exterior. Not at all! He has done as much for railway enthusiasm as Thomas the Tank Engine, as he is a celebrity who is totally unafraid to say what he thinks. He likes trains, he says so clearly, and more to the point, he does things about it. He set up the London and North Western Heritage Railway Company in Crewe, and anticipated the 'Noughties' move to rediscover apprenticeships.

An interesting and challenging project for the apprentices is essential. Pete bought No. 109 entire, and it is possible that arrangements will be made with the FR Co. to run it for 10 years on the WHR.

His blog (**www.pete.railnuts.com**) says what needs to be said:

*No 109 stands at the Exmoor Steam Centre. The loco was chosen as, although it looks forlorn, the external appearance concealed a boiler in good condition.*

**Peter Johnson**

### Archive - October 2009

*'As first announced on this site last March, the 2 ft Beyer-Garratt has arrived today (Friday October 16th 2009) at Crewe. Number SAR 109 will be fast tracked so that it can join the Welsh Highlands' Garratts. It was built in 1939 in Manchester for SAR and numbered SAR 109. The work is part of a project for training. Over the next year, in unique partnership involving national and local government, 20 young unemployed local people will be employed by the Waterman Railway Heritage Trust completely to re-build the engine. Working as a team, these young people will learn valuable engineering skills through a structured program of practical on the job training supplemented by off-site training provided by a local college. This is a real community initiative, involving many local companies. A full update will be posted in the near future and you will be able to keep up-to-date with the project through regular updates and photos.'*

Of course such schemes have their ups and downs, as reports circulated that the 2011 'cuts' had their effects and work had slowed to a trickle. However, Pete doesn't give up on a thing like this, and Philip Hammond MP, then the Secretary of State for Transport was soon enjoying a visit to the place, whilst Pete told him just exactly how much heritage trains plough back into the economy. However, ups and downs and all, this project will progress and it will get there, and it will be done by young people as their personal achievement. The general suggestion is that if it all takes longer - then it takes longer.

*A great start was made at Pete's works on a show that was ideal for the Apprentices. Things have been less good after the 'cuts' - but Pete is an up-beat fighter, and does not give in.*

**courtesy Pete's Blog**

The wonderful thing about a project like this is how well the concept of training young people as apprentices ties in with the general policy of the FR/WHR to encourage young people to be involved with every part of the railway. If the locomotive works on the WHR, after the overhaul is completed, it will be there for all those who worked on it to see. They can also learn to fire it, learn to drive it and look after it, and its stable mates, as well as be involved with its engineering and maintenance. Nothing could be more encouraging!

*NGG 16 No. 138 in the down platform at Dinas, double-heading No. 143 on 3rd October 2007. Not everyone liked the green livery, but it was distinctive, and no one likes every livery. The good thing is that they change from time to time. The locomotive was named* **Mileniwm/Millennium** *- but that has since been removed.*

## NGG16 - No. 138

NGG 16 No. 138 was the second of a batch of seven locomotives built by Beyer, Peacock & Co. in 1958/59 for the Tsumeb Corporation of Namibia (formerly German South West Africa). In 1961 the 600mm gauge (*sic*) line from Swakopmund to Tsumeb was regauged to 1067 mm (3'6") before the engines could be delivered. They were employed on SAR 610mm narrow gauge lines instead. No. 138 went to Port Shepstone to work the line to Harding, in Kwazulu-Natal, which later became the Alfred County Railway. In March 1996, the visit to South Africa to see former colleague Phil Girdlestone, by Mikes Schumann and Hart, was about proving that NGG16 Garratts would perform on the WHR, and seeking two for possible purchase.

*NGG 16 No.138 on the Alfred County Railway under test in 1996.* **Mike Schumann**

The ACR people managed to convince them that NGG16s had the capability that WHR needed by taking No 138 up the Harding line under test, and a purchase price was negotiated of £100k for each locomotive, both of which would be overhauled before dispatch from South Africa.

No. 138 arrived at the FR in January 1997. There was dissatisfaction with the state of the locomotive, and Boston Lodge felt it advisable to do work on her to bring her up to the engineering standards that the FR was required to maintain, and cosmetic work, needed after the sea journey in an open sided container. The stripping for testing by the volunteer team *'Mission Beyer-Garratt'* suggested the boiler work to be done, for which the experts from the Severn Valley Railway rendered valuable service. The loco was reassembled at the FR depot at Glan y Pwll, steam tested in April 1997, and then formed the main attraction at the May Gala in Blaenau Ffestiniog. The locomotive was demonstrated in steam across the Gala period, with people even having the great fun of being able to take the controls. Colleague locomotive No. 140 was also there at this time, but in a non-working condition.

No. 138 moved by Alleleys low-loader from Dinas (Blaenau), to Dinas (Caernarfon) on 23rd September 1997. She was painted in FR dark green, with the illuminated letters WHR on the rear bunker. Service began on the Caernarfon to Dinas section of the WHR on 13th October 1997, though the railway closed for winter in early November. No. 138 worked most trains until October 1998, when sister locomotive No. 143 arrived to share the work. In 1999 No. 138 saw little service, and *Mountaineer* came to the railway in time for the 2000 season, replacing *Blanche.* Two Garratts out on the line was overkill. She worked before and at the September 2000 Gala, but over the winter was repainted in a lighter shade of green, with black borders, lined out in yellow. This was further modified in 2002, when the loco was also named *Mileniwm/Millennium* to commemorate the Millennium Commission funding, and the participation of Edison Mission Energy as sponsors.

In early October 2003, the loco was split into its three constituents, so that

*Worth repeating this view - newly arrived 138 at Dinas, undergoing examination*
**Mike Schumann**

across the winter of 2003-4 she had a substantial overhaul. This was carried out at Dinas, as Boston Lodge was so busy - though some pieces had to go as individual bits to Boston Lodge for machining etc. Both power units were back on their wheels by April 6th 2004; the locomotive steamed on April 21st, and returned to traffic at the start of May, with reports of radical improvements in fuel efficiency. A leaky fuel tank was substituted, and then refitted after repair at Boston Lodge. Declining steaming performance was traced to leaking superheater elements and misalignment of the blast pipe. Service performance from the second week in August 2004 was much better as a result of the work.

In spring 2008 the 'ten year' ticket expired for the boiler. Generally with Fairlies and Garratts the custom, more in line with 'fleet' thinking, is to do work when it is needed, rather than try to save it all for the major overhaul, as a number of parts are either interchangeable, or can fit with minor alteration. Thus it was planned that 138 should receive the boiler of sister No. 140. The volunteer Team Wylfa did major work in stripping the boiler, and getting on with the remedial work, removing the tubes etc. Brunswick Ironworks built a new water tank for the locomotive that was ready for fitting in September 2008. Boiler Inspection revealed the need for the replacement of a few firebox stays, a number of dome rivets, and rivets on the pad for the blow-down valve, as well as the obligatory retubing. The boiler unit was

*Superpower Weekend, 10th September 2006, when odd things happen! NGG 16 No. 138 drifts down the gradient into Tryfan Junction, hauling a 'mixed' train, that includes as the Observation Car a vehicle borrowed from the FR, and others besides. Behind the engine four of those 'free' SAR goods wagons.*

*NGG1 16 No. 138 runs down, past Hafod y Llyn loop, now rusty, on its way to Pont Croesor on 12th September 2010. Behind, FR Car 119 offers a low roof, and ex-Romania Car 2060 a high one. The train is now on the WHR 'flatlands' where wide views and rapid progress is the norm.*

being worked on in the loco shed with the new tubes being fitted in October, and the unit was complete by November. Both power units were installed under loco No. 143, and concurrent with the boiler work, No. 143's rear power unit was being overhauled. The front was released, refurbished, and stored in the carriage shed. Eventually both power units (ex143) went into service with No. 138. The policy is now to use parts commonality, and to remove confusion the locomotive shall be identified by the number of the frame unit. The boiler/frame and both power bogies went to Boston Lodge on March 16th 2009. The boiler cladding was replaced with nice, neat, new plates in December, and each unit was painted red in the paint shop after reassembly. On 5th May 2010 the boiler unit went to Dinas; a by the end of May the three units were put together, ready

*Red, oil fired, NGG 16 No.138 outside Dinas depot, in steam on 27th May 2010, just before it was passed fit to haul its first solo train after overhaul.*

for testing. On 29th May the loco, still fired by oil, had its first solo duty on the WHR.

The locomotive looks quite splendid in its red livery, and it stands out extremely well in that colour. (The same was said of *Prince* when it transformed from green.) But the high cost of

oil fuel means that wherever practical, a coal fired locomotive is rostered, indeed in 2012 it will be converted to burn coal.

Coal is now significantly cheaper than oil. Although the question is less clear on what the secondary costs are of coal versus oil, the purchase price is much less. The reason oil was first used on FR was the incidence of lineside fires. Perhaps the locomotives in most danger from that are *Linda* and *Blanche*. Locomotives with larger fireboxes do not offer the same risk. A double Fairlie can be fired on coal without ejecting sparks that cause lineside fires, as fire screens and ashpan protection are effective. The Lempor-Girdlestone exhaust makes Garratts 'safe'. Perhaps the oil era was somewhat overdone? However, it was probably cheaper at one time. Oil costs are at unaffordable levels, and coal is cheaper. It is likely that the Penrhyn sisters will remain on oil, but probably the rest of the fleet that can burn coal will do so, as it is calculated to make the best commercial sense. Perhaps in the future, a more efficient oil burner might be developed, or there may be a drop in price. Currently coal is king and FR are confident that the right decision has been made..

*A carpet of steam is laid down by 138 as she leaves the Phase 4 subscribers' inspection train at Rhyd Ddu on 24th March 2007, hence the special headboard, as the restoration was extending, with track nearly to Beddgelert by this time.*

*No. 138 at Caernarfon in glossy red on 9th August 2010. The size and appearance of a Beyer-Garratt is evidently having impact on the youthful audience, watching with rapt attention.*

## NGG16 - No.140

Fourth of a batch of 75 locomotives built by Beyer, Peacock & Co. in 1958/59 for the Tsumeb Corporation of Namibia (formerly German South West Africa) was NGG 16 No. 140. In 1961 the line from Swakopmund to Tsumeb was regauged to 1067mm (3'6") before the engines could be delivered. They were employed on SAR 610mm narrow gauge lines instead. No. 140 went to Port Shepstone to work the line to Harding, in Kwazulu-Natal, which later became the Alfred County Railway. Sister Tsumeb loco 138 went to the same railway at the same time.

When that line became the Alfred County Railway, the loco was repainted to red, and was known as the Red Devil, being something of a celebrity. Phil Girdlestone was experimenting successfully with the Porta System (including the Gas Producer Combustion system) and the locomotives chosen for this were generally painted red. Sadly she suffered from sudden theft of her non-ferrous fittings, and was taken out of service. When she was out of use a band of German enthusiasts bought her. That in itself is a great thing, but finding somewhere to repair and then run your NGG16 is a bit of a problem. No. 140 was bought by WHR for a small price, and was shipped to Wales for a large price! At first she went to the FR Dinas, at Glan y Pwll Depot in April 1997 and sat. She was shown not in working order at a Gala where No. 138 paraded up and down.

*Formerly the WHR Dinas engine shed and now converted to a workshop, on 9th April 2006, the 'front' bogie of NGG16 No. 140 is being overhauled in this useful space. This bogie has since found use under No. 138*

In late 2002, she was moved out of the carriage shed at Glan y Pwll and into the yard, moving to WHR Dinas in early 2005. The duty for No 140. has been to donate parts to other locomotives undergoing restoration, such as 138 and 143. Her time will come. There are now four NGG16 class Beyer-Garratts destined for work on the WHR. In the future No. 140 will take up her identity once more. There might even come a time when all 4 locomotives are available for work together, but that may never be a practical proposition.

*No. 140's boiler has been used, its bogies have has been used. The cab and tanks are available as spares if needed, or may well be re-incorporated into the loco itself when it is reincarnated in the future. Time will tell. Dinas, 9th September 2006.*

*No. 143 leaves Dinas, bound for the terminus at Waunfawr on 11th September 2002. The locomotive is in SAR black livery, complete with the overhead electrification warning - most relevant, as out of Umzinto there was dual gauge (1067mm and 610mm gauges) trackage that was electrified!*

## NGG16 - No. 143

NGG 16 No. 143 was the last of a batch of seven locomotives built by Beyer, Peacock & Co. in 1958/59 for the Tsumeb Corporation of Namibia (formerly German South West Africa). It was therefore the last Garratt built by Beyer, Peacock in Manchester. A further 8 Garratts, 149-156, were built by Hunslet- Taylor in South Africa in 1967/8, but 143 is the last Beyer-Garratt that was built at Gorton.

In 1961 the 600mm gauge line from Swakopmund to Tsumeb was regauged to 1067mm (3'6") before the engines could be delivered. They were employed on SAR, 610mm narrow gauge lines instead. No. 143 went to Humewood Road to work the line from Port Elizabeth to Avontuur, which later became the Apple Express. The loco ended its working life on the Umzinto to Donnybrook line.

In March 1996, there was a visit to South Africa to see former colleague Phil Girdlestone, by Mikes Schumann and Hart. During the trip, Mike Schumann agreed to buy 143, and arrangements were made for Alfred County to overhaul her. She arrived in Wales in early 1997, with her companion No. 138, but all was not considered to be well, and the boiler was sent to Riley's at Bury for significant attention. Riley's also attended to the two power units at the same time. Thus, 143 entered service on the Caernarfon-Dinas section, a year later than 138. The locomotive worked the short 3 mile line to Dinas, until it was extended to Waunfawr in 2000. The locomotive worked turn and about with No. 138 until the public opening to Rhyd Ddu, and then the mileage of the line increased to 12. The following year, the increase in mileage was apparent and loads were greater over the increased distance with two trains in service for most of the time.

Maintenance often requires the separation of the boiler and power units, and both Boston Lodge and Dinas are equipped with co-ordinated, screw lifting jacks, to enable them to do this. The loco was separated in December 2002, and was back in service after reassembly in February 2003, sporting a new main steam pipe - quite a complex item.

No. 143 ran on through 2004/5. After the end of the steam service in 2006, she was taken out of traffic. This time the front power unit was removed to be taken to Boston Lodge, in order for the cylinders to be rebored and the wheels to be turned. The overhauled power unit was returned to Dinas on March 26th 2007, and was moved back into the loco shed to be placed under the frames, and then to have the water and oil tanks put back on to complete the locomotive. Steam testing took place on May 2nd 2007, and after running shuttles on test for a real ale festival, the locomotive went back into public service in May 2007. The numberplate backgrounds shifted from red to blue. On a black locomotive this is surprisingly noticeable. The blue is said to be authentic for SAR, and looked good.

The construction mileage had increased again, from the railway's extension to Beddgelert, and on through the Aberglaslyn Pass. Trains could not yet terminate at Beddgelert, as the park boundary on the Afon Dylif had not been reached. Although No. 143 worked a Subscribers' train to Hafod y Llyn on 5th April 2008, the line couldn't be opened for public service that year.

The rear power unit gave trouble, and failed in 2008 with a damaged crankpin. This was a major problem, as No. 138 was 'out of ticket' and undergoing overhaul, and No. 87 had not yet

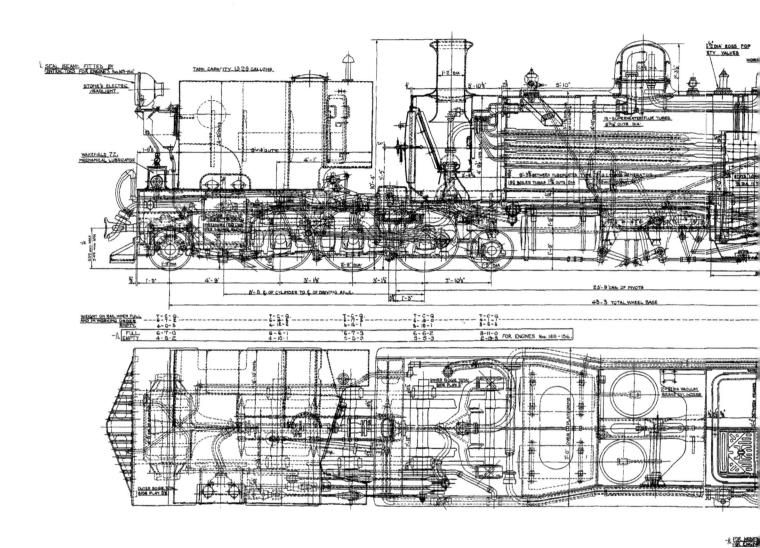

# BEYER, PEACOCK'S GA DRAWING OF THE NGG 16 CLASS

Courtesy FR Co. - Boston Lodge

\* Tsumeb engines had no water in back tank; 87 did, but it has been taken out. So no WHR NGG16s currently have water on back tanks. Tsumeb front tanks were 1,340galls.
Tsumeb engines were fitted with Wakefield lubricators and adjustable bogie pivots, but movements of components cause changes, and on FR mechanical lubricators are standard.

| NGG16 2-6-2+2-6-2T Beyer-Garratt - 2ft Gauge | | Bogie wheelbase (coupled) | 6'3" |
|---|---|---|---|
| Heating Surface | 921.1 sq ft | Bogie wheelbase (total) | 13'10½" |
| Superheater | 149 sq ft | Tractive effort | 21,553 lbs |
| Boiler pressure | 180lb (12.4 bar) | Length | 48'5" |
| Grate area | 19.5 sq ft | max. axle load | 6 ton 8 cwt |
| Length between tubeplates | 9'3½" | Front tank (water)* | 1,325 galls |
| Cylinders (4) | 12"dia x 16"stroke | Back tank (water)* | 540 galls |
| Driving wheel dia' | 2'9" | Back tank (oil) | tba galls |
| Outer carrying wheel dia' | 1'9" | Bunker | 6 tons 5 cwt |
| Inner carrying wheel dia' | 1'9"+ | Boiler outer dia' | 4'10" |
| Weight (full) | 61 tons 8 cwt | Max height and width | 10'4" x 6'10" |

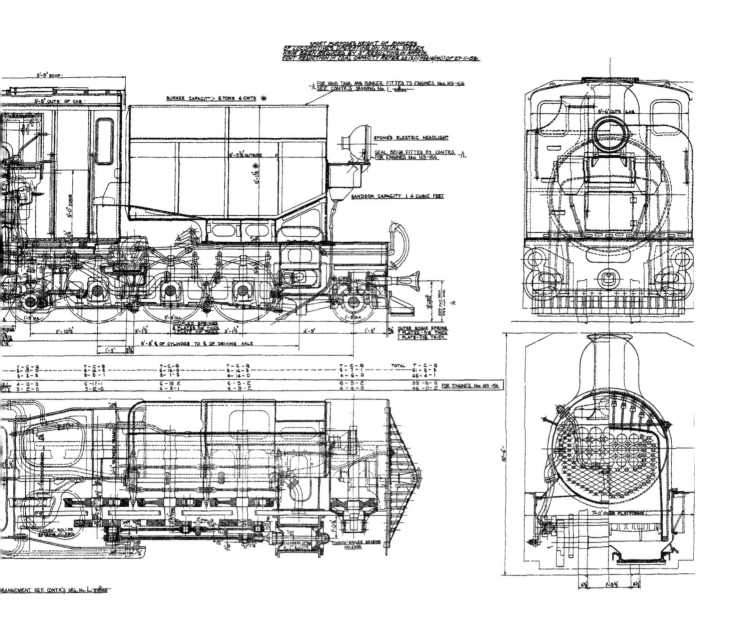

# AS USED BY SAR/SAS

| Garratt service summary WHR | | | | | | | | | | | | | | |
|---|---|---|---|---|---|---|---|---|---|---|---|---|---|---|
| Loco | 1997 | 1998 | 1999 | 2000 | 2001 | 2002 | 2003 | 2004 | 2005 | 2006 | 2007 | 2008 | 2009 | 2010 |
| KI | KI GROUP TYSELEY 4.00 | | | BOSTON LODGE | | | | | | 9.06 | | | | |
| 87 | | EXMOOR STEAM CENTRE | | | | | | | | 2.06 | | | 4.09 | |
| 109 | | | E X M O O R | | S T E A M | | | C E N T R E | | | | | 10.09 | L&NWR |
| 138 | 9.97 | | | | | | 10.03 | 5.04 | | | | 4.08 | 5.09 | |
| 140 | 4.97 | STORED IN GLAN Y PWLL, BLAENAU | | | | | | | 1.05 | OVERHAULED AS 'PARTS' ‡ | | | | |
| 143 | | 9.98 | | | | | | | | 10.06 | 5.07 | 10.08 | | |
| | | | | | | | | | | | | | | |

*Yellow line - out of service, blue line - under overhaul, red line - in service (note: 143 came back in service in 2011)*
*‡ Boiler from 140 is now in frames of 143, and this method of 'swap round' will become normal, loco is 143 as frames designate number of loco.*

*The picture shows the bogie power unit pivot point of an NGG16, located between the second and third driving axles, with its cover removed. This bogie is an older Belgian built example, off No. 87. Beyer, Peacock's patent design takes up wear through an ingenious combination of fixed and floating baseplates, plus four floating semi-circular sections. This partly accounts for how they were able to reverse the disadvantage of the Beyer's inability to renew Herbert Garratts patents through his untimely death, by inventing cause for a new patent. So the bogies are 'interchangeable' - but not quite, as amongst other items the pivots are different.*

entered service. This was the first real WHR motive power crisis and it was decided that the rear power unit from sister No. 138 would be used in exchange, under 143, which would allow the failed bogie to be sent away to Boston Lodge for repair. Interchangeability of these major components was achieved satisfactorily, and the loco went back into service on July 9th 2008. The damaged bogie went to Boston Lodge to be mended. In fact two wheelsets had to be sent away, and one had a new crankpin fitted

The locomotive ran the services in 2008, working the last train of the season.

At the end of 2009 NGG16 No. 143 had reached the end of its ticket, and so it was withdrawn for overhaul. However, the component parts could still be shared. Two locomotives were waiting to begin service. No. 87, which before taking up service would enjoy its debut at the Golden Bolt ceremony in Porthmadog on 28th February 2009,

*The rebored, wheel turned, overhauled front bogie of No. 143 waits in Dinas Yard to be reunited with the rest of the locomotive on 26th March 2007. It was the the rear bogie that failed in 2008.* **WHRCL**

after, running on its own to Dinas, and No. 138, which emerged in May 2009, ready for service. Thus there were again, two NGG16s on offer for work, on the by now extended railway. A third Garratt locomotive is needed for a timetabled service of two train sets. The question of making the best use of the potentially interchangeable component parts was now being thoroughly exploited, with Boston Lodge able to recognise and adapt for the minor differences between the sub-types of the NGG16s. At the same time it was decided that the way to keep tabs on 'what locomotive is what' is to declare that it is the frame that decides the locomotive's identity.

No. 143 emerged from Boston Lodge after overhaul in June 2011, converted to run on coal, painted in lined out green and was engaged in test running until it was able to enter service. So now there is a red (138), a green (143) and a blue (87) Garratt in service. Passengers like this.

*The first passenger train through the Aberglaslyn Pass to Hafod y Llyn was the Sponsors Train, hauled by No. 143, assisted by Castell Caernarfon, seen here pausing to take water at Rhyd Ddu on 5th April 2008. At this time there was no run-round facility south of Beddgelert, thus the need for the diesel. The rain was free.*

*No. 143 emerged from overhaul on 11th June 2011. Here she is crossing the town on 30th June 2011, doing some running in after her overhaul, preparatory to going into service. The locomotive now burns coal, so 138 was left as the only Garratt burning oil in 2011.*

*Simon Bowden's photo of NG15 No.119 at Sandstone Estates, Orange Free State, shows what handsome little locomotives the Kalaharis actually are. These are by far the most powerful single engines on the 2ft gauge in UK, and seeing one put back to work will be a pleasure.*

**Simon Bowden**

## NG15 - Nos. 133 and 134

The NG 15 class are a conventional answer to the difficulty of employing enough power on the 2ft gauge to haul economic loads over long distances. These sturdy 2-8-2 locos are reputed to have 75% of the hauling power of a Garratt. Their articulated (Krauss-Helmholtz) front truck and front axle is a way of laying down the power to the rail, through sharp curves, with good potential adhesion, with a maximum axle load of 6 tons 15¼ cwt, but with a tender to pull. Thus for an extra 7 cwt (355kg) per axle, a single engine with such power is available. Adhesion does not decline with the use of fuel and water.

They were built for German South West Africa, to bring trains of copper ore along the Otavi Railway, 214 miles, from Tsumeb to Karibib. Built under the Kaiser and run by the Germans until after WWI, the line runs through the arid Namib and Kalahari deserts and the locos (generally knows as Kalaharis) were equipped with a massive tender, capable of carrying 5½ tons of coal and 2,860 gals of water. [This was why the NGG16s ordered by Tsumeb had no water tank under the back bunker, as they were expected to trail a tank car with over 3,000 galls of water in it.] Three NG15s went to the Otavi Railway from Henschel in 1931, three from Anglo-Belge in 1939. Five more went in 1950, and a further five in 1953, of which the two on WHR were included. The last order was from Henschel, for the Tsumeb Corporation in 1958, when a final five locomotives were built. The line was regauged to 3'6" in 1961, and both No. 133 and 134 went to the 2ft gauge SAR line to Avontuur. They were spotted at Humewood Road Shed in 1991, with 133 out of use and 134 still active.

Both 133 and 134 were brought to Britain in 1998 for a railway scheme on the Yorkshire coast; when it fell through they were bought by Mike Schumann for WHR. Loco 133 is in store at Dinas in 2012. Loco 134 is under restoration by volunteers at Dinas. They are well on with the job, are equipping the locomotive with a more modest and a more elegant tender, with tender-cab that is practical for working on the WHR. There are hopes for the NG15 on the WHR. It might be that its power and economy is particularly suited for the line, but, like all tender locos, having arrived at the terminal, it will be obliged to return tender-first, unless there is some provision for turning. This oughtn't to be a big problem for visibility, with a well-balanced bogie tender. It might be that one day turntables, or triangles will be available - though this is problematic. But here is the rub in the comparison between NG15 and NGG16. If the 2-8-2 were to be made into a 2-8-4T, that required no turning, the extra axle load would be well over the acceptable limit, even for a reduced 1000 gals of water in side-tanks, and 3 tons of coal in an extended bunker (even the cut down tender will likely accommodate 4.5 tons of coal and 2000 gallons of water).

They are magnificent 2ft gauge locomotives, and might well turn out to be economic and useful in a way that, alas, K1 has not been able to be. However until one is tried, this is more speculative than recommissioning Garratts, and enjoying the 'fleet' benefits of doing that. The restoration of No.134 is proceeding, with a hope that the locomotive will be available for service in 2014. In 2012 No. 133 still waits. The availability of Garratts has rather eclipsed these potentially useful engines for the moment. The hope is that once one of them is in service, people will wonder why they had such small priority. We shall see.

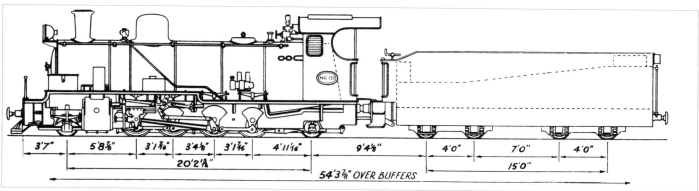

| NG15 2-8-2 - 2ft Gauge | |
|---|---|
| Heating Surface | 796 sq ft |
| Superheater | 180 sq ft |
| Boiler pressure | 171b (11.8 bar) |
| Grate area | 16.7 sq ft |
| Length between tubeplates | 13'1½" |
| Cylinders (2) | 15¾"dia x 17¾"stroke |
| Driving wheel dia' | 2'9" |
| Outer carrying wheel dia' | 1'9" |
| Inner carrying wheel dia' | 1'9" |
| Weight (full, with tender) | 67 tons 16 cwt |

| | |
|---|---|
| Wheelbase (coupled) | 9'7" |
| Wheelbase (total) | 20'3" |
| Tractive effort | 16,610 lbs |
| Length (+tender) | 54'4" |
| max. axle load | 6 ton 15 cwt |
| SAR Tender (water) | 2,860 galls |
| WHR Tender | 1500 galls |
| Oil Tank | n/a |
| SAR Coal | 5 tons 10 cwt |
| Boiler outer dia' | 4'2" |
| Max height and width | 10'5" x 6'10" |

*Left : This is NG15 No 136 in her natural setting, Hulmewood Road Shed, Port Elizabeth, South Africa. The picture was taken in August 1971, when trains were worked right through to Avontuur, 178 miles (285km) from Port Elizabeth. The loco's massive tender from Namibia days carries 2,860 gals of water, and she looks in pretty good shape.* **Leith Paxton**

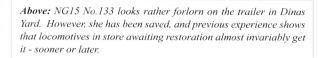

*Above: NG15 No.133 looks rather forlorn on the trailer in Dinas Yard. However, she has been saved, and previous experience shows that locomotives in store awaiting restoration almost invariably get it - sooner or later.*

*Left : The chassis of NG15 No. 134 being stripped by Team Wylfa on 26th October 2008. The volunteer group is steadily bring back the engine, with much hard work.* **Team Wylfa**

*There was extreme enthusiasm, when the two Funkey locomotives arrived, to try one out. Steve Coulson and volunteers stripped off what was needed for Funkey 1 to work up the FR. The locomotive is seen here at the completion of a test in Harbour Station, Porthmadog in 1995. Travelling on this locomotive turbo-super-coupé was a never to be forgotten experience. It was more powerful than anything else that had ever been run!*

## Castell Caernarfon

Pretoria Portland Cement Ltd in Port Elizabeth had a branch line upon which two graceful Baldwin Pacfics worked. One of these has since found its way to the Brecon Mountain Railway. The replacements were two diesel hydraulic locomotives, made in 1967 by C.H. Funkey and Co (Pty) Ltd, Alberton, Johannesburg, built formerly for a diamond mine. These were replaced by SAR Class 91 diesel locos running through from the main 2ft gauge line, and the Funkey locos were declared 'spare'. Two locos were examined by Messrs Hart and Schumann on their visit to RSA in 1995, and Mike Hart bought them for FR Co. for £22k. They arrived at Minffordd Yard in 1994, and with 335hp to offer, from a turbocharged, Cummins, 6cyl diesel, (similar to the engine in the Sprinter DMU) they represented something of

*Both Funkeys just after arrival in Mifffordd Yard, with Fred Howes and Jon Whalley in triumphal pose. For £22k a pair, these were a good buy, and 'just what was needed'. Of course they couldn't go anywhere on FR, they were far too big!*

a revolution in FR diesel power. The idea was to place one on

each railway. Saying you had a Funkey diesel was lots of fun to start with, whilst the joke was still fresh. For the FR, these locos represented the chance of a diesel that could rescue or work a full-size train. The FR was rather caught 'on the hop', as 0-6-0DH *Criccieth Castle* was being built with a 204hp power unit at the time, but a bogie diesel with 335hp was too good an offer to miss, and the WHR would most certainly want one. There was a mismatch in size for the FR Funkey. It needed a new body to comply with the FR loading gauge. Experiments started quickly to try a locomotive out. The cab was dismantled, and the Funkey1 was made able to test run, at first between Boston Lodge and Porthmadog. The performance was impressive. There was no doubt that the locomotive had the power to rescue a 12 car FR train, plus the steam loco - and that's what FR was looking for. Likewise WHR wanted a powerful and economic unit capable of working trains. Much

Castell Caernarfon *(Funkey 2) in all its glory, at Dinas on 12th October 2010. There is no doubt at all that this locomotive was a 'good buy' for £11,000. It has been invaluable, although it has a hard life, and has had to be repaired several times as a result of it. It is reasonably comfortable to drive, although rather noisy and a bit slow, but it is solid and reliable - just not powerful enough for what is now expected of it.*

work was needed on Funkey2, and the overhaul took place at Boston Lodge in July 1996. The loco was on view in the Maes at the Caernarfon Festival, where it was named by Dafydd Wigley MP, *Castell Caernarfon*. It was in Dinas in January 1997 for the construction launch ceremony. The loco's power was not needed on Phase 1 construction trains, indeed the smaller locomotives were often preferred. However when the section to Dinas was placed in passenger service *Castell Caernarfon* performed on the first five cars with ease and excellent economy. The locomotive was in service throughout the construction period. Heavy maintenance was given in January - April 2005. Alas the idea was excellent but the locomotive evidently had its own mind, as one of the final drives failed, and between May and early 2008 the locomotive borrowed the bogies of its sister locomotive, whilst the final drives were away having a lengthy overhaul.

It must be said at this point that this diesel locomotive plays a central role on the WHR. Its instant availability makes it suitable for rescue missions, its economy makes it suitable for more lightly loaded trains, and for large works trains. It will do what is asked of it, but of course it wasn't designed for this work and is underpowered. It manages to take six WHR cars up the hill from Pont Croesor to Rhyd Ddu. It will do this willingly enough, but the engine temperature rises towards the maximum, and there is speculation in the cab over whether or not it will get over the top without turning into a steam locomotive. Thus it spends much of its time being thrashed, so the railway really needs a more powerful unit. The FR has 'form' for overexerting its diesels. Perhaps one day something suitably powerful will be possible.

The engine was stripped out in 2009 and its sister was sent to deputise. Now the CTRL

*Funkey 1 - Vale of Ffestiniog, helps out on WHR when needed. This is a common occurrence, and will become more so, as all the loco needs to do now is to roll across the town of Porthmadog. There is no difference in power between the two locomotives, but obviously the FR loco conforms to the kinematic envelope of the FR. The two will not work in multiple. Vale of Ffestiniog is seen here at Beddgelert on 7th April 2009.*

is in place this is not a problem. The locomotive returned to service to continue to do what diesels do. The sister locomotive, *Vale of Ffestiniog* is to be seen on the WHR quite frequently, deputising for *Castell Caernarfon*. It is interesting that on the FR, with its 1:70 gradients the Funkeys have no problem with 10 cars, but the limit is 6 on the WHR.

The data table for the Funkeys is adjacent.

*Upnor Castle*, a real slogger of a Planet Locomotive, had given faithful service on the FR for years, even hauling passenger trains of up to six cars at a vibrating 17½mph, from Porthmadog to Blaenau Ffestiniog. It was moved from the FR to the WHR in 1997, after being overhauled and fitted with a reconditioned Gardner engine.

| *Castell Caernarfon* B-B diesel mechanical locomotive | |
|---|---|
| Length over frames | 31ft |
| Wheel arrangement | B-B |
| Total wheelbase | 22ft 6ins |
| Bogie wheelbase | 5ft 2ins |
| Bogie centres | 17ft 4ins |
| Prime mover | Cummins NT855L4 - 6cyl, turbo-diesel |
| Power output | 335HP at 2,100rpm |
| Transmission | mechanical, via cardan shaft |
| Gears (each way) | 3 |
| Max speed | 20mph/32kph |

On the WHR there was the job to do that the locomotive was suited for. It was based at Dinas to haul construction materials about, and then was sent up to Wernlas Ddu to act as the locomotive on site at that location. When the sites joined, and Phase 2 was completed, *Upnor* was to be seen lurking beyond Waunfawr for a while, until eventually it was liberated on to the Phase 3 railway construction.

*Upnor* had a major role in the construction of Phase 4, carrying rails from the various depots, and being involved in a most interesting process that *Upnor's* excellent slow speed performance permitted it to perform. As pictured below, left, the locomotive would haul the rail carriers to the place where the rails were needed, then the train would be uncoupled, *Upnor Castle* would be attached to a rail by a stout chain, and it would draw forward, sliding the rail off the wagon and dropping it in the two-foot. Two rails were dropped side-by-side, and then the process would be repeated a little further on, until the train had been unloaded. After this process, when tracklaying started, an RRM pair would be brought to pick up the rail to be taken to the location in which it was to be laid.

The faithful *Upnor Castle* was badly in need of a major overhaul after the construction was completed. In April 2010 she went in to Boston Lodge for this, and came out with a new gearbox. The locomotive returned to traffic

*Above:* **Upnor Castle** *on the WHR construction work was a very useful unit. This gives a clue as to why it was worked until it was worn out, as everyone will tell you that it was this locomotive that 'built' the WHR. Here she is carefully extracting a rail from the stack on the 'flat' wagon south of Pont Cae'r Gors, on 18th August 2006, ready for being picked up by RRMs to be laid at Tro Cwm Du.* **Graham Whistler**

*Above:* Upnor Castle *used to work passenger trains on the FR, and would go past, engine roaring fit to burst. It was exceedingly rare to see it do this on the WHR, but the absence of* Castell Caernarfon *forced the issue, and* Upnor *and* Conway *are seen working a passenger train on 27th June 2006.* **John Peduzzi**

*Left: This is the conflab to explain what had been achieved at Boston Lodge, now the old diesel has come in and had her overhaul after such faithful service in rebuilding WHR. This picture was taken on 8th July 2010. The locomotive was soon back in service.*

*Left:* Conway Castle *stands at the mouth of No. 4 Tunnel (the long one) with the Trustees' inspection train on 3rd October 2007. It is pouring with rain, and the Great Men are deliberating over the finer points of detail of the new piece of track through the Aberglaslyn Pass. No one minds the weather, as this occasion has been waited for so long by all.*

*Below:* Conway Castle *attending the Black Hand Gang's efforts (they laid 11 lengths across the weekend) on 4th February 2007 at the top end of the Cwm Cloch site. The locomotive has the SAR NGV[16] brake van behind it. This vehicle was restored in 2006. Behind that is the mess van, old FR Obs Car 100.* **D. Waldren**

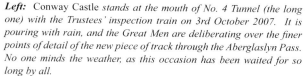

*Below:* Dolgarrog *standing in Minffordd Yard, flanked by Mr Ewing on the left and Mr Thomas on the right. It might be that the locomotive is a tad apprehensive, with those two gentlemen holding such purposeful spanners. Truth is that this loco was nimble and able, and just what the tracklayers needed to help them to be productive. The picture was taken on 13th July 2008* **A Thomas**

in July and the cycle of abuse started all over again. This diesel is truly a workhorse and has never been pampered, but of course that is what it is for - to work..

Upnor Castle's sister locomotive was another superannuated shunting locomotive, that had its years of glory trashing gearboxes from the strain of heaving six-car trains up the FR at unsuitable speeds. Conway Castle had the distinction of being able to work in push-pull mode. It was the chosen locomotive to work the 'Green Set', created with the INCA grant. Apart from its push-pull mode, and electrically worked gearbox shift, the basic locomotive was the same as for Upnor, but with some very swish body styling on top. All of this glamorous lifestyle went by the wayside when it came to do proper shunting on the WHR during construction time. Effectively it was a spare locomotive, and so suffered less abuse from this activity than in its former role. In 2011 it remained as the last reminder of the green and cream FR, INCA livery.

The 28hp Motor Rail Simplex locomotive Dolgarrog was loaned to WHR in 2002 by RWE npower. It had been appearing on the FR with some wagons before, and it proved most useful on the WHR tracklaying task. It was built in 1962 to run on the three mile Cowlyd Reservoir Railway. The dammed lake provides

water for Conway and Colwyn Bay. However, the railway closed after a derailment in 1968, and although the loco was used on the Llanberis Lake Railway for a cabling contract, it was consigned to a museum role. This loco brought with it the squaring of an intriguing historic circle, especially as it was employed on Phase 4 work. In 1903 the North Wales Power and Traction Company were the promoters of the PB&SSR. In 1918 the organisation was bought by the Aluminium Corporation of Dolgarrog, eventually acquiring a majority interest in both WHR and FR under the chairmanship of H.J.Jack. It is a particularly convoluted story tied up with the development of the electric power and distribution industry in its infancy, in which the PB&SSR (more about this company in Appendix 'A') was but a pawn. Jack resigned in 1924 accepting blame for the lack of success of the 1922 WHR. Only a year later disaster struck when on 2nd November 1925 the Eigiau and Coedty dams failed, releasing a huge volume of water that flooded Dolgarrog in the Conwy Valley, killing 16 people. This time, in the 21st century, the association with Dolgarrog was a happy one, as the little locomotive was popular with the tracklaying volunteers, and did an excellent job, first on the Rhyd Ddu to Glanrafon section, and then on the works for Phase 4. It needed repair in Dinas during 2008, and again in 2009 with engine bearing problems however these problems were solved by substituting other locos.

There were other small diesels that worked on the restoration of the WHR. Brian Faulkner's Lister Rail truck covered for Dolgarrog in 2008, Harold, the Hunslet shunter from Boston Lodge, Criccieth Castle the 250hp Baguley 0-6-0DH from the FR in early March 2009, and the Barclay 30hp locos Taxi 1, and Taxi 2 and others, kindly loaned by WHRL when their work gangs came across to join with laying track.

## WHR steam locomotives, old and modern

| No. | Date | Builder | Type | Gone | Notes |
|---|---|---|---|---|---|
| Wks 738 No.11 | 1875 | Vulcan Foundry Ltd | *Moel Tryfan* NWNG 0-6-4-T single -Fairlie | 1937 scrap | The first 0-6-4T in Britain. In a parlous state when WHR was completed in 1922, it went to the FR in 'payment' in 1937, was scrapped by Garraway in 1954 as a necessity to raise money, and no one has yet had the courage to build a replica - but they will! |
| Wks 739 | 1875 | Vulcan Foundry Ltd | *Snowdon Ranger* NWNG 0-6-4-T single -Fairlie | 1912-13 rebuilt | It succumbed when the best features of both sisters (Sister to *Moel Tryfan*) were combined in about 1912-13 to keep one of them running. |
| Wks 206 | 1878 | Hunslet Engine Co. | *Beddgelert* NWNG 0-6-4ST (rigid wheelbase) | 1906 scrap | Power with as little mass as possible for working the Bryngwyn Branch, this locomotive was 80% more powerful than a (single) Fairlie. (says Boyd) It was worn out and replaced in 1906, after the peak of mineral traffic in 1897. |
| Wks 979 | 1908 | Hunslet Engine Co. | *Gowrie* NWNG 0-6-4Tsingle-Fairlie | 1918 sold | An up-to-date version of the Spooner Fairlie, in anticipation of the extension to Portmadoc, it was not considered a success, with a smaller boiler than the others and the same size cylinders. She was sold in 1918 for further service elsewhere. |
| Wks 901 No.12 | 1906 | Hunslet Engine Co. | *Russell* PB&SSR 2-6-2T | - | Ordered by the PB&SSR as an adjunct to their electric locos which never came; the railway failed and Russell passed to what became the WHR. It was cut down to run on FR, and was sold at the end of the WHR in 1937, had a further career until rescued, and is now preserved by WHHR. Under overhaul in 2012. |
| Wks 45172 No.13 | 1917 | Baldwin | WHR 4-6-0T | 1942 scrap | WW1 WD loco, bought as a 'bargain' by Col. Stephens, the locomotive was unpopular with the crews, was unreliable and rode atrociously, neither did it pull much! It staggered on until closure, was incarcerated in Dinas, and then scrapped. |
| Wks 5292 K1 | 1909 | Beyer, Peacock | Tasmanian Gov. Rys 0-4-0+0-4-0 Garratt Compound loco | | This was the first Garratt; it worked on the NE Dundas Tramway, Tasmania. It was brought back to Beyer's upon the closure of the line, and bought by FR on the closure of Beyer's. Said to be an amalgam of Nos 1 and 2, it was restored in 2006 by a team led by Colin Hill, later by Roland Doyle, to 'as was' condition: a saturated steam, compound locomotive. (Hot water and steam to those who know no better.) Active 2012 - Burning coal. |
| SAR 87 | 1937 | Société Anonyme John Cockerill, Seraing, Belgium | SAR NGG 16 2-6-2+2-6-2 Garratt | | One of the first batch of NGG 16s, this locomotive was delivered to the Port Shepstone to Harding line in 1937. It left service from the Umzinto-Donnybrook Line in 1987. The WHR bought it from the Exmoor Steam Railway, with a grant for purchase and overhaul from a private individual. It was overhauled at Boston Lodge and entered service in 2009, initially in grey, but then in midnight blue. Active 2012 - Burning coal. |
| SAR 109 | 1939 | Beyer, Peacock | SAR NGG 16 2-6-2+2-6-2 Garratt | | This locomotive worked on the SAR NG lines, ending its days on Umzinto-Donnybrook in the 1980s. It was the first NGG16 to come back to UK, to the Exmoor Steam centre in 1995. It has been obtained by the generosity of Pete Waterman OBE, and is being restored at the L&NWR premises at Crewe, as an apprentices scheme. When finished it will go to WHR. |
| SAR 138 | 1958 | Beyer, Peacock | *Millennium* SAR NGG 16 2-6-2+2-6-2 Garratt | | Ex Tsumeb Copper Corporation, and then SAR (Natal). Bought from Alfred County and overhauled, arriving in Wales 1997, named in 2002. Carried a variety of colours but in 2010, de-named, resplendent in red. Burning oil in 2012, going to coal. |
| SAR 140 | 1958 | Beyer, Peacock | SAR NGG 16 2-6-2+2-6-2 Garratt | | Ex Tsumeb Copper Corporation, and then SAR (Natal). Bought by a private buyer, the locomotive will work on the WHR, but is currently donating its parts to allow other NGG 16s to run - a normal practice. The bits not in use are at Dinas and Boston Lodge. One day it will run again as itself! |
| SAR 143 | 1958 | Beyer, Peacock | SAR NGG 16 2-6-2+2-6-2 Garratt | | This was the last Garratt made by Beyer's. Ex Tsumeb Copper Corporation, and then SAR (Midland). Bought from Alfred County and overhauled, arriving in Wales 1998, it was painted in SAR black and gave sterling service. In 2011, returned to service with bits from No. 140. Now painted green and burns coal. |
| SAR 133 | 1953 | Société Anglo-Franco-Belge, Belgium | SAR NG 15 2-8-2 *Kalahari* Class | | Worked on the Otavi Branch in South West Africa (now Namibia) under the Tsumeb Corporation, and when that was regauged to 3'6" the loco went to the 2ft gauge SAR line to Avontuur. Loco 133 is in store at Dinas in 2011. Both funded by MS for £35k |
| SAR 134 | 1953 | Société Anglo-Franco-Belge, Belgium | SAR NG 15 2-8-2 *Kalahari* Class | | Both 133 and 134 were brought to Britain in 1998 for a planned railway scheme but when that was not possible, they were bought by FR for WHR. NG15s have a Kraus-Helmholz truck to help curving and a massive tender (which has been reduced in size for WHR working). In 2012, No. 134 is being overhauled for service in Dinas by a group of volunteers. Hoped to be in service in 2014. |

## WHR diesel locomotives, old and modern

| No. | Date | Builder | Type | Gone | Notes |
|---|---|---|---|---|---|
| 8 | 1928 | Kerr Stuart KS 4415 | 0-6-0DM McLaren-Benz 4cyl diesel | 1929 back again 1997 | One of the earliest diesels to be built, with a McLaren-Benz 4 cyl engine, with a JAP aux. engine for starting. 2ft dia. wheels on a 5'6" wheelbase. It worked the Bryngwyn Branch on test for a while and went to the FR for trials in 1929. It wandered off, via Ireland (converted to 3' gauge) and ended up in Mauritius in 1934, working until 1971, and then being plinthed. It came back (courtesy Greenwich & District NGS) and is under restoration as the oldest surviving British-built diesel. |
| | 1954 | Hibberd, 'Planet' | ***Upnor Castle*** 0-4-0DM 180hp Gardner 6LXB diesel | 2010 to FR | ***Upnor Castle*** was built for the Admiralty and worked the 760mm gauge Chattenden (Lodge Hill) and Upnor Railway. Sold to the Welshpool and Llanfair in 1961, where it was named. It came to the FR in 1968, (for £600)was regauged, re-engined (Foden FD6 126bhp removed) and ran there until 1997. ***Upnor Castle*** was the locomotive that 'built' the WHR. Its throaty Gardner 6LXB 180hp diesel could be clearly identified all over the line, as it was institutionally misused (as all construction vehicles are). An extensive rebuild in 2010 will allow its misuse again. What are diesels for? It's a great machine. |
| | 1958 | Hibberd, Planet | ***Conway Castle/Castell Conwy*** - detail as above - | | This locomotive had a quite different body built for working push-pull trains on the FR. It was displaced to work on the WHR construction of Phase 2. This is in fact more the sort of work that they were designed for, and their rugged nature has allowed ***Conway Castle*** to slug it out for years |
| | 1967 | CH Funkey & Sons, Johannes-burg | ***Castell Caernarfon*** B-B diesel mechanical 335hp Cummins 6 cyl diesel | | Bought from the Pretoria Portland Cement Co in 1993 and overhauled in Boston Lodge in 1995-6 this 27 ton loco (Funkey 2) has proved invaluable for 15 years. The opening of the through route with the steep grades and curves up from Croesor Jn to Pitt's Head is asking too much. CC cannot pull a full load of 10 cars over this section. Sister locomotive to ***Vale of Ffestiniog*** on the FR, which works on WHR as well, as required, and to whom these notes also apply . |
| | 1962 | Motor Rail Ltd, Bedford (Sim-plex) | ***Dolgarrog*** 22154, with Dorman 2LB 28hp engine | | On loan to WHR from RWE npower, ***Dolgarrog*** was originally employed on the Llyn Cowlyd Tramway. It came to work on Phase 3 in May 2002 and was employed in trackwork, where it was used nimbly moving in and out with RRMs, delivering supplies to the Head of Steel between Rhyd Ddu and Glanrafon. Later it worked on Phase 4, and became a firm favourite. |

*The end of the line! On the 9th of August 2010 Castell Caernarfon stands at the head of the 19.20 from Pont Croesor to Caernarfon. This bright August evening illuminates the flatland beauty of this quiet spot. The loco has a long climb ahead with 6 cars.*

*Left:* NGG 16 No. 140 on its way to Izotsha hauling a Banana Express. This train ran on the line from Port Shepstone to Harding, the Alfred County Railway. The train operated between Port Shepstone and Paddock (29km), with stop at Izotsha (13km). After the bankruptcy of ACR in 2004, Patons County Narrow Gauge Railway ran the service most successfully until Spoornet pulled the plug in December 2005. Loco No. 140 is now on the WHR in Wales, circulating its various parts to other locomotives, pending resuming its identity one day as a whole locomotive.

**THIS PAGE: ALL PHOTOS**
**Hannes Palling**

*Right:* Arriving at Izotsha NGG 16 No. 140 hauls a Banana Express from Port Shepstone, 13km away. By the mid-1990s (when this series of photos were taken) the 2ft gauge was in decline by competition from unregulated road transport. However, there was a brisk tourist trade established, as many people visiting the area heard of the Banana Express and wanted to travel on it. It was an expanding business, adding to the prosperity of the area and creating jobs. Alas for reasons of political correctness, the story of why the tourist business was lost is an own-goal that someone might one day describe when talking plainly comes back into fashion. There are sad echoes of it on area web sites, lamenting its loss - evidently the executioners knew little of the regional economic effects of tourist trains. The gain to the prosperity of Gwynedd has been most welcome.

*Left:* Locomotive NGG 16 No. 140 in the station at Izotsha, over the pit before hauling a Banana Express towards the start depot of Port Shepstone. The withdrawal of this expanding and potentially prosperous tourist train in 2005 left the tourist trade much the poorer, plus the same has happened to the famous George to Knysna, Garden Route 3'6" gauge steam train. However, this locomotive and others, plus the sleepers and rails relocated to serve the WHR from the Umzinto-Donnybrook line further along the coast was a gain to Wales. Wales has certainly had its tourism business stimulated by the repatriation of these engines.

*Right:* In 1970, SAR NGG16, No. 87, stands on the pit, outside the locoshed at Umzinto, the end-station of the 2ft gauge line to Donnybrook. There was a 3'6" gauge, electrified line at Umzinto. It all began closure in parts from 1985, some the rails and sleepers went to the WHR, so 87 is still rolling over them.

This locomotive was built in 1937 in Belgium by Cockerill, one of only four out of a total of 34 in the class. This was because at the time Beyer, Peacock were too busy with orders. 87 found its way to Porthmadog from Exmoor, and it was bought, overhauled and runs on WHR courtesy of a kind donor, to whom thanks are due.

**Photo: Peter Bagshawe**

*Left:* Port Shepstone loco shed, Alfred County Railway, showing NGG 16 Locos, Nos 138, 125 and 116, from left to right. Loco No. 138 was one that went to Wales after overhaul by ACR. The reason why it had extensive remedial works done on it before entering service perhaps lies in the fact that ACR believed that they could perform an overhaul on it of sufficient quality to satisfy European standards, despite the fact that they were working in far from idea conditions, sometimes in the open, and without full workshop facilities. Perhaps their aspirations were led by the purchasers pleasure in the reduced purchase and overhaul price. Both parties might have been rather too hopeful, but it most certainly did not make for harmonious relations. However, both 138 and 143 were placed in WHR service, eventually, and would be joined by 87, 140 and ?109..

**Photo: Peter Bagshawe**

*Right:* Locomotive NGG 16 No. 140 brews up ready to leave the terminus at Port Shepstone with a Banana Express. This was a delightful scenic trip, along the coast and then inland past sugar cane fields and banana plantations. It is a view we are unlikely ever to see again, as in 2008 the bridges were badly damaged and the loco is now on the Welsh Highland Railway. It is a shame that an operation with such tourism potential is now lost to us, but that damage was so severe to the trackbed that these scenes will remain in the past. It's a pity that the coaches could not come too, but unfortunately they were not suitable for duty in Wales.

**Photo: Hannes Paling**

*Left: In March 1996 an FR group went to the Alfred County Railway that had taken over the 76 mile 2ft (610 mm gauge) line from Port Shepstone to Harding in 1987, after SAR had closed it. These are Mike Schumann's photos of NGG16 No.143 that he was looking to buy. Here the locomotive is at Harding, in the yard, with the resident diesel shunter, on the front of a wood train, but surrounded by wood. The railway was immaculate when run by SAR, but as these railways were run down, so they became unkempt.*

*Right: NGG16 No.143 was purchased and brought to the Welsh Highland Railway. Here is the same locomotive now working on a train of SAR wagons, awaiting departure from Dinas in 2000. Alas in South Africa matters did not going so well for the Alfred County Railway. It closed in 2004 by the termination of the lease by Spoornet. Subsequently the line was badly damaged by storms along the coast in 2008 and it is unlikely to run again. However, South Africa's loss was Wales's gain. No.143 has been well looked after, and as the WHR has opened, piece by piece, she has had harder and harder work to do. In 2012 she was working ten car trains up the five-miles of 1:40 gradients through Beddgelert, traversing 53m radius curves, climbing up the hill to Point Cae'r Gors, and so she is doing the job she is designed to do. She has been overhauled twice in the last ten years and so is in good condition. Furthermore the locomotive is now working as one in a group of similar locomotives, thus the facility of interchanging parts is taken full advantage of. This is what the concept of re-opening the Welsh Highland Railway very much hoped for with its motive power.*

*Left: Locomotive NGG 16 No. 143 in the station at Harding in March 1996. It has the letters WHR placed on the rear bunker and she is shortly to set off on a test train. Mike Schumann paid £100k for this locomotive, overhauled, which is a great deal of locomotive for the money. The FR Co. got to South Africa and acquired these engines at just the right time. The credit for this goes to former Boston Lodge resident Phil Girdlestone, who was the Chief Mechanical Engineer of the Alfred County Railway. He provided the contacts within Spoornet for the sale of 138 and 143, the pair, that came to WHR, and it was he who arranged to overhaul the locos in RSA.*

**Right:** *In March 1996 NGG 16 No.143 stands in Harding Station, at the head of the 76 mile Alfred County Railway from the Natal coast. There is a certain activity going on at the other end of the locomotive. When this is complete No.143 will head the train. Mike Schumann, who took the photograph, is visiting to buy locomotives for the WHR. Two will be bought, Nos 138 and 143, both ex-Tsumeb locos, the last built by Beyer, Peacock in Gorton, Manchester. However, from other sources three other NGG16s will also come to the WHR, nos 87, 109 and 140.*

**Left:** *Locomotive NGG16 No.143 steams out of Dinas on to the Welsh Highland Railway proper, sounding the whistle for the foot crossing passing Dinas loco shed. Behind No. 143 are South African Railways wagons. The middle one is a hopper wagon, much needed to lay ballast for the track of the newly restored Welsh Highland Railway. Behind the locomotive and the third wagon in the train are SAR gondola wagons that by great fortune were used to contain all the various track bits that came over when track from the recovered Donnybrook line was bought for further use on the WHR. It made most sense just to place these in a wagon and ship them over to Wales. Delightfully, when the wagons arrived, they were 'runners' and they have been used ever since, in various forms from partly knocked down to complete. The picture is of the first Superpower Weekend. It was a matter of great delight to see these locomotives, the most powerful 610mm gauge steam locomotives in existence, at work again on the 597mm gauge WHR. The scene looks remarkably similar to that on the Alfred County Railway. The marked difference is that the old loco shed at Dinas is of course roofed in slate - well it would be, as it is in Wales.*

**Right:** *Locomotive NGG 16 No. 143 simmers, ready to leave the terminus at Harding with a train. Next to the locomotive, only just in the picture, is one of the bogie water carriers that these engines were designed to work with in their Tsumeb days. Nos 137-143 were built to work in Namibia but they never did, as the railway was regauged to 1067mm. So the locos all came to work on the Umzinto, Port Shepstone and Avontuur lines. The back bunker has no water space, so on longer runs, the water carrier will increase the operating range. In the front there is 1,340 galls, OK for the WHR but it wouldn't have got you from Izingolweni to Bongwana.*

*NGG16 No.143 in sparkling new green livery takes the  token at*
*Porthmadog for Pont Croesor, to go for a test run, on  20th June 2011.*

# Chapter 10
## Carriages
## 1995 - 2011

Carriages are the forgotten arm of heritage railways; though carriages earn the money, engines get the glory. There are the 'sporties' among us, who appear to believe that comfort rots the mind and weakens purpose, and that unreconstructed 'original' is good. When combined with the devout heritage believer, this accounts for those railways that proudly offer today's ride in a rattly vehicle with slatted wooden seats. Unfortunately the British are normally polite about this. The FR used to squeeze eight large, elderly ladies from coach tours into one of the compartments of a vintage coach; they probably had to take it in turns to breathe. It is in fact the case that the British standard posterior has undergone expansion during the last 60 years. People are larger today than quarrymen were in the days of old. FR heard the message loud and clear, when the keensies, who had assembled a beautiful train of unrivalled historic accuracy and elegance, placed it in normal service. They were surprised by the reaction of the public, who far from being enraptured, complained that they wanted to go in those corridor carriages with toilet and buffet car. This was the problem of satisfying the wider market. There were people who sat in open carriages with evident glee during gale force winds and horizontal rains, wrapped in anoraks and waterproofs, whilst crossing the spray-blasted Cob. There were a small number of vintage enthusiasts, who gloried in a train consist with no vehicle newer than 1880. The majority though, plainly looked for more comfort.

This was the main talking factor when Mikes Hart and Schumann were deliberating with the FR General Manager in 1993, setting plans for the future. The key question was whether to make all the new build of coaches capable of traversing Blaenau to Caernarfon throughout, or should the WHR carriages be confined to the WHR, so that they could take full advantage of the more generous loading gauge planned for the restored railway? As it turns out, the restored FR dimensions are shy of permitting WHR carriages to travel up the line by only a few centimetres, and that in a handful of places. Unfortunately, one

*FR No 18: elegant carriage, impeccable Victorian pedigree, fabulous to look at - but not to ride in at 8 per compartment, and with no access to services. Nice in first though!*

of those places is Garnedd Tunnel. A million tons of rock above militate against the remedial works needed to pass all stock. Garratts of course were always out of the question - larger by far that the carriages, they are simply too big to fit, and much remedial work was needed lowering the track on NWNG bridges. Thus it seems the FR is highly unlikely to have its individuality eroded - the living rock is its guardian!

At the time, the GM was clear in his view that all carriages should be capable of running on both railways - fearing operational disaster if they could not. The counsel of the two Michaels prevailed, and a longer, wider design was chosen for WHR. The extra room meant that reduced knee interlock with one's neighbour required less negotiation for any shifting of position. Also, the increased internal width offered that extra inch or so, to support the overhanging 'cheek'; comfort levels rose. The differences were so important that Norman Bond and his team of FR carriage builders found ways to stretch the envelope on the FR, to achieve similar improved standards of comfort - and with the rebuild of Car 103, they were successful. Now the two railways are connected, and the era of through running has begun, new FR carriages offer similar comfort levels to WHR carriages. That magical and Chimerical named train **The Snowdonian**, from Blaenau Ffestiniog to Caernarfon, may now run with the new FR carriages.

In 1993, strategic thinking indicated that the new railway would only work if everyone thought 'big'. This led to the original proposal for 15 car trains hauled by Garratts. Service experience has tended to make this a lesser figure, but the reasoning, and all those business plans at the inquiries, showing the movement of large numbers of people, sprang from these thoughts. It was believed in 1993 that some 40 new carriages would eventually be needed to do the job - and it was clear then that at least four types were required: Observation, guard/catering, saloon and open saloon. Such an undertaking needed some bold designs, but the one which the GM's spare moments on the computer first produced was for a Pullman. This was a pipe dream indeed, and hardly

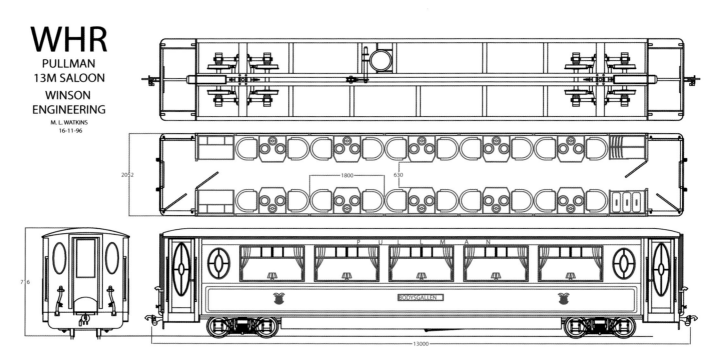

**WHR**

PULLMAN
13M SALOON

WINSON
ENGINEERING

M. L. WATKINS
16-11-96

*The concept in design and build for this carriage followed the same innovative design concept as for the more humble saloons also built by Winson Engineering. The 13m underframe supports a 2052mm wide body, allowing seating for 20 people, arranged 1+1 in loose seats. Marvellous!*

fitted the requirement for a hard working, high earning, tourist railway, but it showed the areas to which minds were going. The Pullman idea glowed in the dark from the statement it made to all the detractors, the critics, and the way it faced down the strife everyone had to bear. As a grand vehicle for delighting and entertaining visiting dignitarios, and for enchanting those who took comfort in scenic excursions really seriously, the Pullman concept had no equal. The reason WHR has one is due to the vision and generosity of the one who funded it. Implementing the concept offered a few problems to be overcome. *Bodysgallen*, Car 2115, was built by Winson Engineering, and it was delivered in 1998. They were a local engineering firm in Penrhydeudraeth who won the order for the first set of five WHR carriages. The 'as built' interior included plastic panels. Boston Lodge was requested to upgrade the vehicle at little cost. Fortunately the solution was to use some walnut veneered panels that had already been donated by the sponsor. These were decorated by inlaid, laser cut marquetry, which looks very nice indeed. Beautiful little armchairs were specially made; they are very comfortable to sit in,

*Above: Inside Car 2115 **Bodysgallen**, the surfaces covered with fabric deaden the noise, so one glides along. Individual chairs were purpose built for this carriages and no expense was spared. The GWR designed an excellent hard wearing moquette that it used to cover its carriage seats known as Fruit Bowl. This can still be bought from a manufacturer who kept the original loom pattern, so the interior looks wonderfully 'retro', complete with polished wood and marquetry panel decorations. It is lovely.*

**Below:** *Car 2115 is named after Bodysgallen Hall, near Llandudno, built on the site of the fifth century stronghold of Cadwallon Lawhir, King of Gwynedd, and now a superb hotel. This comfortable carriage has allowed the WHR to receive its patrons in style. This was necessary when the enterprise was trying hard to raise funds and to convince everyone of its clear intent to build back to Porthmadog. In service it offers paying passenger the real extra luxury they are looking for - and it is very popular.*

*Car 2115 stands at Caernarfon on 9th August 2010, at the rear of the 17.05 service to Pont Croesor, looking good after overhaul.*

and the big windows allow an excellent view of the splendid panorama that unfolds along the line. The vehicle is suitable for light refreshment service, like cream teas, adding value, and making the WHR experience even better. In 2009/2010 winter the interior was completely rebuilt at the Boston Lodge Carriage Works, ridding the car of the MDF doors that had deteriorated. In service the 20 seat *Bodysgallen* is extremely popular, and its sumptuous interior set the tone for the Welsh Highland Railway. It is the first 2 ft gauge Pullman car ever to be built, an elegant and comfortable vehicle, and when combined with the Pullman Observation Car *Glaslyn* (described later), it shows what could be done for a luxury **Snowdonian** train, as the WHR establishes itself as a world tourist attraction.

The FR/WHR is exceedingly low speed railway. The idea of a stout metal underframe, supporting a wooden or steel body, is acceptable, as the FR centre, chopper coupling will retain the coaches together in alignment, in the unlikely event of a collision or derailment.

The urgent need for FR carriages in the 1970s coincided with new metal skills at Boston Lodge, and salvaged old Isle of Man carriage underframes were given simple steel bodies - the Tin Cars. These temporary 'stop-gaps' suffered from short seat bays which it is difficult to remedy, and makes them less comfortable to ride in than more recent types. They work on the WHR as relief vehicles, but the simplicity of their construction was echoed in the new WHR cars, by mounting a welded, tubular steel body framework upon a new, strong, metal underframe. This is filled with insulation and covered with best quality, marine plywood panels, with a decorative wood finish inside. The results are excellent. The design method is strong, economical, and furthermore, lends itself to the minimum of corrosion, but with the maximum ease of panel replacement. Doors, windows and interior fitments follow, and these continually change over the years, according to the advancements in understanding and experience in workmanship. Likewise if changes to the body are needed, to permit a disabled loo to be installed, or to facilitate a service car type, then the

*Below: Inside an FR (Carnforth) saloon shows it would be better if the smaller type of person travelled in this vehicle. These cars find use on the WHR pending more carriages being built. Alas the smaller type of person is no longer universally available in Britain.*

*Above: A 'tin car' at Tan-y-Bwlch. Though they are now a bit rattly, and with interiors that are difficult to modify, they are being left behind by the general improvement in other coaches in the fleet and so are being refurbished one by one.*

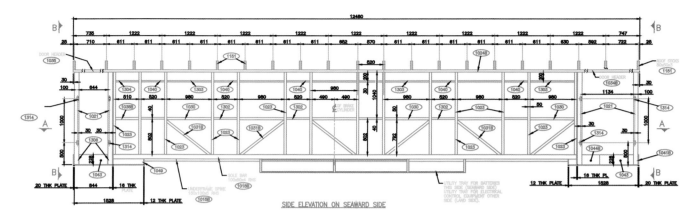

*The concept in design and build for this carriage was based on a tubular, stainless steel framework, built on a stout steel underframe. It makes for an economical build, good insulation properties, and panels that can be reached for maintenance purposes. In addition, should the car body need to be changed, this is not the problem that it would be, were it welded steel or monocoque.*

tubular steel framework can be repositioned, and the car rebuilt economically.

Winson Engineering did a good job in delivering 5 carriages for the Caernarfon to Dinas service, followed by the Pullman. They are large and comfortable carriages built for the economical price of £50k each. There was much thought about what type of bogie to use, to mount these cars upon. The FR designed a quite complex bogie for its modern carriages, using 'Metacone' rubber suspension. This was rejected, as there was an alternative source of cheap, redundant narrow gauge, diamond frame, freight bogies available from South Africa. These were tried out with the Winson coaches, with new, softer springs, and the carriages rode acceptably well. Thus more of these simple bogies were obtained, and they have been put under carriages on the Welsh Highland, though they have been found to require remedial work because of their poor condition. Then some Romanian, roller bearing bogies were regauged from 760mm to 600mm, and these require less maintenance than the SAR, plain bearing bogies. Thus the South African bogies have been modified to accept roller bearings, which will significantly reduce maintenance demands by eliminating daily oiling.

The first five WHR carriages were 12m (39ft) long vehicles: a semi-open 2020 of 36 seats, three saloons 2040/41/42 of 36 seats, and 2090, a guard/saloon of 22 seats. They were delivered to Dinas in 1997, with a sixth, the Pullman, *Bodysgallen* of 20 seats, and 13m (42ft) length, being delivered in 1998. The train capacity was 166 3rd, and 20 1st. A full list of carriages is shown in the panel, later in the chapter. These carriages carried the load until Phase 2, Caernarfon-Waunfawr, 7 miles from Caernarfon opened, and two train sets were needed; the extra carriages were borrowed from the FR.

In 2002 Alan Keef delivered two 36 seater, 13m, semi-open saloons, 2021 and 2022, raising the home total to 8 cars, with third capacity of 238. The price for these two vehicles was £50k each; this shows what a bargain the Winson cars were! The open saloons are popular, but the inspired feature of the design is the corridor connection, that enables movement from closed to open carriages. On a lovely day it is difficult to find a space in an open car. It is easy for those familiar with the railway and its surrounds to forget just how beautiful a ride on the WHR is. The WHR in all

*Above: Car 2041 in BL Carriage Shops for maintenance in July 2007, after ten years in service. Items have lasted well, and you can see the construction methods used for the body, together with BR window droplight mechanisms as used in Mk1 coaches.* **Peter Johnson**

*Below: All five of the Winson built cars are seen in this 1997 view of Dinas. How things have changed. Photographs of the early days are quite difficult to find, unlike today, when everyone has a digital camera of exceptional quality. The carriages worked together as a rake for some time and riding in them showed a marked space improvement compared with those on the FR* **Ben Fisher**

*Snowdon Ranger Halt on 14 September 2003, one of those lovely afternoons where the choice of a corridor semi-open carriages is inspired, despite the slatted wooden seats. The well patronised 2020 looks well in a passable imitation of early BR livery. This has never bothered the WHR/FR, the livery looks strikingly good across the hillside. These carriages are a good design and evidence of the 'think big' policy of the WHR strategists. 2020 has been rebuilt into 2011, a service car.*

its scenic variety surpasses the FR in almost every way, except that the FR offers exhilaration from the way in which its trains seem to move rapidly along. The Welsh Highland trains feel slow-paced in comparison. Travelling the superb scenery is extremely pleasurable. When it is wet, there are still takers for the open cars, as the roof keeps off most of the rain. If it gets too wet or cold, people may take shelter in the closed cars. It is the photographers who derive the most pleasure from these vehicles. For them the endless curves, look-downs, and general scenic beauty of the ride, allows great volumes of excellent shots to be taken. This is something that cannot be done in the same way today on the standard gauge, and people love the narrow gauge as a result.

*A donor's gift allowed a replica NWNG Ashbury 'summer' coach to be built, though its doors are fully glazed. It is beautiful work by Boston Lodge, but its 56 wooden seats are character-forming, so it is loaded only to 48!*

The veteran NWNG car, No 23, built by Ashbury in 1894, one of the first cars restored to FR revenue earning service under the new regime, was refitted in the 1990s and rather provocatively (given the then current brouhaha), restored to green WHR livery. It went back to its former railway in 2002, as an historic supplement to the loading problem. It was joined the same year by replica carriage No. 24, in NWNG livery, so one car runs in each train set as a safeguard against crush loading. A trip in it is pleasant enough, though when filled to capacity the journey is rather matey.

In 2003, the construction of Phase 3 delivered a further 5 mile stretch of railway to Rhyd Ddu. The line was now 12 miles long. The FR had some 32 carriages for a line only a mile-and-a-half longer, and the WHR had only eight vehicles! There were 6 carriages borrowed from the FR, and with only 14 carriages in two trainsets of 7, the bookings rose to some 60,000 people - it was a problem. More carriages were needed urgently. The line would double in length over the next five years. There was a requirement for at least two, 10 car sets by that time, and this was to cause major difficulties.

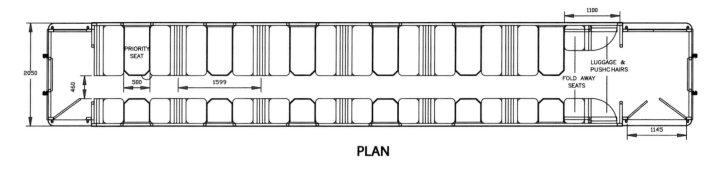

**PLAN**

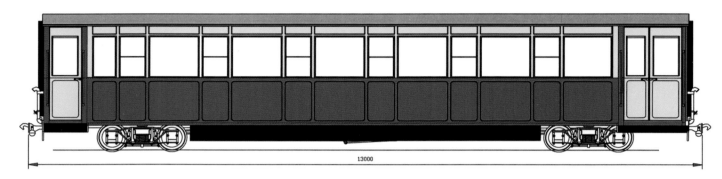

*The detailed WHR design changed across the years, although the principles remained the same. The 35 seat interior is here modified to accept, luggage, pushchairs and wheelchairs. Cars 2043 - 2045 were constructed at Boston Lodge in 2006/7. At 13m, a bit longer than the Winson cars, they sported the big double doors. The SAR bogies' plain bearings need constant attention. Romanian roller bearing axle-boxes bogies were coveted, and certain bogies were installed.*

In 2006 there was a major fund raising drive, to try to assist in finding the money to build new carriages. Carriages are not as popular as locomotives when fund raising, but despite this, £350k was raised, enough to build and equip a further three cars.

Boston Lodge Works built and delivered three more cars in 2007: 2043/2045, and an observation in 2009. These carriages, 13m (42ft) long are the largest ever built for FR/WHR. The same basic principles were applied as to the shorter Winson cars: a stout underframe, tubular steel body framework, and infill panels. The third class cars were fitted out with well upholstered seats and wood-lined interiors, with 6 droplight windows and

35 seats, in 6 bays at 1.6m pitch (5'3''), the sixth bay being 3 fixed and two folding seats, to allow space for wheelchairs to berth, or pushchairs and luggage to be stored. At one end, each vehicle is fitted with a set of large double doors. When a ramp is presented to the doors, a wheelchair may gain access, and be berthed next to a window. This offers a much better facility for the mobility impaired.

The cost of these cars was £90k each - rather a steep rise from the original Winson quote. However, quality carriages sustain a higher fare. The original cars were 'built to a price'; experience since supports the more expensive 'do everything you have to do

*Below: Here is Car 2043 in service in a train at Dinas on 3rd October 2007. It rides on SAR freight bogies, with softer springs with shock absorbers fitted. Plain bearings reside in the axleboxes, and these most be examined and oiled regularly. They are gradually being replaced with roller bearings.*

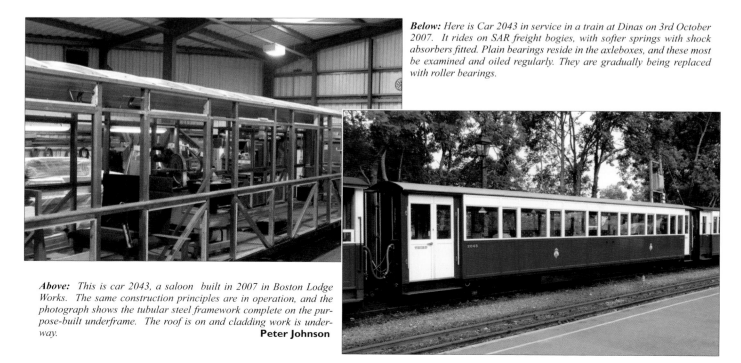

*Above: This is car 2043, a saloon built in 2007 in Boston Lodge Works. The same construction principles are in operation, and the photograph shows the tubular steel framework complete on the purpose-built underframe. The roof is on and cladding work is underway.*
**Peter Johnson**

*Left: Daron defends his little cakes in the ample galley of Car 2010. The presence of this car, with kitchen, 'prep space and the fitment of a loo in the other end, plus a space for the guard and the emergency equipment, with a neat little generator for power, is a massive advancement, and makes catering on board a reality. No more the curly edged sandwiches - welcome the cream teas in Pullman splendour. Apparently this car has already acquired a rare reputation for a splendid bacon butty - this can only be good.*

*Below: The layout plan for Car 2010 showing how it is packed with goodies that more than justify its inclusion in a train, especially a 'long distance' one.* **Drawing, FR Co.**

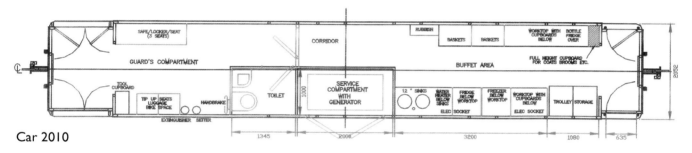

Car 2010

now' method, as this favours cars remaining in service to take their remedial work at the appointed service intervals.

A new type of carriage was built in 2008, a car embodying loo, buffet, guard compartment, and a generator capable of supplying power to the kitchen equipment. Construction of the frame for Car 2010 was sent out to DWJ Welding, a local fabricator in the old Ferodo factory outside Caernarfon. When this came back complete in January 2008, it was placed on roller bearing, Romanian bogies that had been regauged and adapted for the purpose. It was taken by rail to be skinned and equipped by the FR Carriage Works at Boston Lodge. The interior fitment deliberately did not include any passenger accommodation. The car is 'seatless', apart from that required by any operating personnel. The advance is the provision of a diesel driven electric generator, with its 'hush kit'. Electric power allows chill cabinet, fridge, grill, microwave, and independent

lighting to be provided.

The vehicle was moved by road to Dinas in September 2008. No. 2010 entered service in October 2008. It now mounts catering and buffet service down the train, and will allow light meals to be offered in a Pullman car. It is important to provide the service of food and beverage on the continually lengthening WHR journey. Also the provision of a decent toilet is really necessary, as the throughout journey time has risen to two hours and thirty-five minutes. Car 2010 contains the toilet, together with a suitable retention tank.

A further initiative was to convert the 22 seat, 1997 Winson built, Guard/saloon Car 2090 during the winter of 2008/9 to include a toilet. This made similar facilities on offer on both WHR sets. What's available on Car 2010 is better and so a second service car, Car 2011 was created. Vehicles of this type are not cheap, however the increase in amenity, and the add-on

*Car 2010 on clearance test at Harbour Station, on August 27th, 2008. The yellow roller bearing axle box covers of the Romanian bogies may be seen. This car has retention tanks for the toilet, in common with all others on FR/WHR.* **Ben Fisher**

service that can be offered makes them vital additions to the fleet. Thus Boston Lodge converted Winson semi-open 2002 to match Car 2010. The FR too is investing in these vehicles.

Through working over the full 40 miles between Blaenau Ffestiniog and Caernarfon length is a new and exciting concept on the narrow gauge. In April 2011 the first **Snowdonian** train was run. This train paves the way for the possibility of new equipment for the future, to allow new markets to be exploited successfully. The economics of trading seat space in higher class vehicles, for higher value tickets with meals is a difficult area to manage. Through running with will provide an opportunity to explore it, and will reveal sources of traffic not yet tapped.

Information passes continually between all the heritage railways - staff are always talking and comparing notes. Thus the kindly intervention of Terry Turner, GM of the Welshpool and Llanfair Railway, came the suggestion to Mike Hart that the WHR could source reasonably priced, painted and overhauled body-shells from redundant CFR (Romanian State Railways) 760mm gauge carriages. The W&L has benefitted from its attention in this area, as Romania has joined the EU, and this has tended to herald closure for steam powered little narrow gauge railways - thus there was equipment available at reasonable prices.

It appeared at the time that the price fitted out would be less than building the car in the workshop at Boston Lodge, as well as taking less workshop time - money and time being two items in short supply. The Romanians tendered for overhauling the bodywork, stripping the car, regauging the bogies, fitting vacuum brakes and couplers, a wooden floor, and then shipping the painted shell to Boston Lodge to be equipped for the WHR. The price for this was calculated to be £25k for the unfitted shell and then £15k for final fit, offering a refurbished vehicle complete for £40k per car. One car was authorised, to

try out the system, to see if satisfactory vehicles at reasonable prices could be obtained this way. Thus it was that Car 2060 arrived at Boston Lodge on 19th August 2007, by indirect means. The height of the CFR carriage, bearing in mind it was formerly a 760mm gauge vehicle, meant that transit by rail from Minffordd Yard to Boston Lodge was blocked by the height restricted Rhiw Plas road bridge. Instead, in the early morning, the delivery lorry pulled in to Rhiw-Plas road lay-by, and a crane lifted Car 2060 on to blocks, before it was lowered on to its bogies and taken to the Carriage works. The interior fit is smart, and whoever organised those large, drop windows was inspired! The same 2+1 seating was installed as in Cars 2043/45. The job included electrics, seating, heating, floor covering, walls and ceiling covering. There are 6 bays of 6 seats, 36 in all. Inside, the car sides are vertically planked in wood and the ceiling is panelled in white. It is an airy and comfortable car to ride in, with lots of headroom. It makes a Tin Car look like something from the London Tube. Though it looks rather strange in a rake of WHR carriages, the roof line matches a Garratt very well, as there's still car headroom in the improved NWNG loading gauge. Alas, the price comparison with a home-built vehicle was subsequently skewed by the steady drop in the value of the Pound Sterling. Taken together with a general

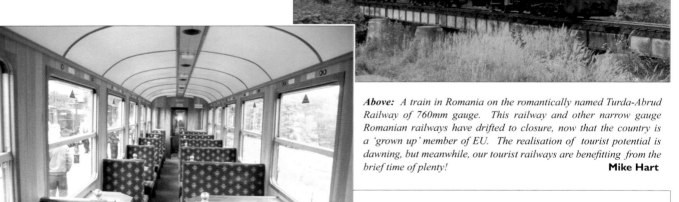

*Above: A train in Romania on the romantically named Turda-Abrud Railway of 760mm gauge. This railway and other narrow gauge Romanian railways have drifted to closure, now that the country is a 'grown up' member of EU. The realisation of tourist potential is dawning, but meanwhile, our tourist railways are benefitting from the brief time of plenty!*                                        **Mike Hart**

*Above: The pleasant and airy interior of Car 2060. When the sun re-ally does get on with shining, the fact that the windows can offer such a large opening to keep cool air blowing through firmly seals this car into the affections of the public!*

*Right: In fact Car 2060 looks well in proportion. It is only the comparison when alongside an NWNG car that suggests that this is in fact the norm, and the old FR cars are sub-miniature!*

shortage of funds for carriages, options on other Romanian vehicles have not yet been taken up. Thus 2060 is one of a kind, but if circumstances change, the option of the running 'shell' from Romania, and final fit in Wales might yet be repeated.

There are of course plans for other types and styles of vehicles, but finding funds for construction is an unavoidable requirement. Phase 5 has this as one of its main tasks. Innovation is alive and well in Boston Lodge, where the frontiers of carriage design and

*The saloon in Glaslyn is similar to that of Bodysgallen, with bespoke, comfortable arm-chairs and the genuine 'club' atmosphere of a Pullman car, but this time all in miniature. It is plain from the loadings that people like this - but they do not expect it. You can see that this is Mr McNair's (C/R) natural environment.*

and made steady progress to delivery into service on March 10th, 2009. The price tag exceeded £100k - but the magnificence is breathtaking, as it is undoubtedly the most glorious 2ft gauge vehicle in the world. But then the Welsh Highland Railway in its 25 miles offers changing vistas without parallel in Britain, and as good as the best on the globe. It isn't dizzying heights or depths that people enjoy; it is the prospect of rolling mountains, glistening rivers, attractive little dwellings, lush grass and mountain

build are being pushed ever outwards. It was the need for an observation car that drove the frontiers forward. Hitherto FR cars had been borrowed. The WHR need was answered by money made available for the purpose in 2008. Design work went ahead, using the same basic tubular steel frame on underframe principle of the other WHR cars. The licence to use the Pullman name was obtained from BRB Residuary. Inspiration was drawn from the legendary Caledonian Railway Pullman Car *Maid of Morven,* built by Cravens of Sheffield in 1914, that ran as an observation car, during the season, between Glasgow and Oban. It had something quite revolutionary at the time, an observation end fitted with curved glass in three panels. The idea of curved windows is excellent, as it reduces internal reflection and makes it easier for the occupants to enjoy the view to the outside. Norman Bond, who runs the Boston Lodge Carriage Works, originated this design, and he and his colleagues created a vehicle of striking appearance, utility and comfort. Like *Maid of Morven* it has three, curved glass panels at the end. Today the safety-glass was more easily obtainable, and the size and shape used allows replacement, as they are in effect 'off the shelf' items. The underframe of this car, No. 2100, was delivered from the fabricators in April 2008

prospects - and from this observation car, you can see it all!

The glory was added to by HM The Queen, who on 27th May 2010, travelled in Car 2100 between Caernarfon and Dinas, where she named it *Glaslyn*. This vehicle faces those who join the train at Caernarfon, and all who see it want to travel in it. For a little train to offer the choice of a first class journey in *Bodysgallen*, or the stylish *Glaslyn*, makes quite sure that the first class product is differentiated from third class. The prestige cars reinforce the view that the Welsh Highland Railway is a major business force, and a top visitor attraction.

A the end of 2011 two 9 car rakes were available for service, offering appx. 251 third and 20 first seats each. The extra distance to Porthmadog created by Phase 4 has the effect of lowering the number of trips that might be run in a day. Yet different markets open up, offering more traffic. Through service from the FR and a greater number of WHR trips is awaited from the alterations to Harbour Station. Another train set will then be needed to FR loading gauge dimensions. Raising the funds to construct the new train set is a problem of a different order. However with the fare levels and the numbers being carried it's a paying proposition.

*Below: Here is proof that curved glass does not reflect flash back into cameras. That means that the 'nobs' sitting in Glaslyn can take all the shots of the 'other' people they want, and get good results - beats going into an open car, doesn't it?*

*Above: There really isn't a hope if this car is parked at the end of the platform of avoiding the clear comment 'I want to go on that!' This is the effect this magical carriage has on people. Everybody is very proud.*

The need for Glaslyn is obvious looking at the nature of the WHR. David Sumner left this world, but before his departure Bodysgallen got to him in a big way. His legacy was generous, and stipulated it should be used to create a Pullman car. Alas it was entailed, something not known in time to do anything about it! However, all were content with the Pullman car concept, so much so that the money for it was found. When Her Majesty made the delightful suggestion that a visit to the area ought to include a trip on the Welsh Highland Railway, the idea of her naming the new carriage came naturally, and so HM The Queen unveiled Car No 2100, Glaslyn. The vibrant body colour came from the L&Y Ry based livery used on the Ffestiniog Railway's Victorian carriages. When urged to adopt Pullman colours to match Bodysgallen, Norman commented 'I'm not painting it s - - t brown like that one!' - and that was that. No one's complaining. The car is heated by a Eberspacher Space Heater - an electrically powered, diesel fuelled device of startling efficiency, adopted now throughout the fleet.

*Below*: The Maid of Morven had end doors at the front, that were used for normal entrance and egress. It was decided to do the same for Glaslyn, but not to make them usable in normal service except by the staff. Thus to get in the car, the approach is via the twelve-seat saloon behind, and the 'observers' are not disturbed. However, to enable full access for the mobility impaired, the large door can be swung open, using a carriage key. The ramp may then be put in place for wheelchair loading. It is also possible to get the furniture in and out this way, as required. The old FR 'Barn' Observations had full Pullman armchairs installed - to get them out, the side of the coach had to come off!

*Above*: Inside Car 2100 Glaslyn, the curved end can be seen doing its stuff. Outside the car is just entering the Aberglaslyn Tunnel; inside the elegant lights are on already in anticipation. Note the ceiling rose, centre of the curved end. The ceiling arches inside, independently of the flat roof of the curved end section. Rather than have fixed, swivel chairs in the 12/14 seat observation end, low-back, individual, bucket seats allow the passengers freedom to point the way they wish. The upholstery is again 'Fruit Bowl', to match the seating in Bodysgallen. This feature offers all the conformity needed between the two carriages. This is a carriage that simply has to be travelled in.

# WHR Carriages - the modern fleet 1997-2009

| No. | Date | Builder | Type | Seats | Notes |
|---|---|---|---|---|---|
| 2010 | 2008 | FR Co Boston Lodge | Service Car | 0 | A car with a kitchen, guard's compartment, toilet - fitted with a generator. |
| 2020/ 2011 | 1997/ 2010 | Winson Engineering/ Boston Lodge | Semi-open/ service car | 36/ 0 | One of the first 5 - Caernarfon - Dinas, converted in 2010 to Car 2011 a service car to match Car 2010's amenities. |
| 2021 | 2002 | Alan Keef | Semi-open | 36 | It was decided that one semi-open car is needed in each set - their corridor connection allows access by choice. |
| 2022 | 2002 | Alan Keef | Semi-open | 36 | |
| 2040 | 1997 | Winson Engineering | Saloon | 36 | Three 12m 'standard' WHR 3rd Class saloons were made. |
| 2041 | 1997 | Winson Engineering | Saloon | 36 | |
| 2042 | 1997 | Winson Engineering | Saloon | 36 | |
| 2043 | 2007* | FR Co Boston Lodge | Saloon | 35 | The first of the double-door cars for easier disabled access. |
| 2044 | 2007* | FR Co Boston Lodge | Saloon | 35 | These vehicles are 13m long. |
| 2045 | 2007* | FR Co Boston Lodge | Saloon | 35 | *Conditions of a Visit Wales Grant required all three vehicles to be delivered in 6 months - this was done with hired help - quite an achievement for a small organisation- phew! |
| 2060 | 2008 | FR Co Boston Lodge | Saloon | 36 | Romanian carriage formerly of CFR - see text for description |
| 2090 | 1997 | Winson Engineering | Guard/saloon | 22 | The last of the first 5 - In 2008-9 fitted with wide door for wheelchairs, a guard's compartment and a loo |
| 2100 | 2009 | FR Co Boston Lodge | Pullman Obs | 20 | The magnificent *Glaslyn*, named by HM The Queen |
| 2115 | 1998 | Winson Engineering | Pullman Saloon | 20 | The *Bodysgallen* Pullman saloon, the pioneer 2ft gauge Pullman |
| 23 | 1894 | Ashbury | NWNG Summer coach | 56/42 | Coach 23 passed to the FR when the WHR closed, it's roof was lowered to fit the FR. After much refurbishment and rebuilding it found its way back to the WHR in 2002, it is generally in service on WHR but visits the FR too |
| 24 | 2002 | FR Co Boston Lodge | NWNG Summer coach | 56/42 | Coach 24 was built in 2002 as a replica NWNG car by those who should have known better - but fortunately did not. This glorious, cramped little vehicle in NWNG livery acts as a valuable space supplement on trains, and runs opposite No 23 |

*Notes: There are not enough carriages for the traffic demand, which saw surges from the opening of each new frontier, like Beddgelert, Hafod-y-llyn and Pont Croesor, and the effect of events, like the visit of HM The Queen in April 2010. As soon as the track was laid over the Cambrian Coast line, and connected to Harbour Station, stock exchanges became possible at nominated intervals. Today FR carriages on the WHR are subject to frequent changes. During the summer of 2009, FR carriages 119 and 120 supplemented the WHR fleet - it varies and as the two railways integrate they will be seen as one.*

*Ffestiniog watch out! It's views like these that the people have discovered abound on the WHR for. It's a railway where look up and look down are both impressive, with mighty vistas everywhere to be seen. Large, comfortable carriages are just what's needed in this game. Both railways are quite different and that's good.*

*The dream view! Seen from the road both of the Glaslyns look impressive. The car is above; the river is below.*

*Norman Bond seen in the rebuilt FR Car No. 103. Norman and the team - **Team 'X'** - have managed to move the art of narrow gauge carriage building to new heights. Never before have so many carriages been built and refurbished in Boston Lodge Carriage Works in so short a time. Norman is a retired electronics engineer, and without his particular skills and flair, together with the team of people around him, the combined carriage fleet would not be what it is today. Boston Lodge is now a significant carriage builder in UK - the largest for narrow gauge.*

*Car No. 123 rolls on to the WHR at Harbour Station, in this view that we are all so delighted to get used to. It is 20th April 2011, and the Cross Town Link is now a common feature for Porthmadog townsfolk. So a Top End, 3rd Class Observation Car slips into the scene almost un-noticed. We saw it!*

## Lazarus & the Super-Barns

Years ago, when Gordon Rushton was the GM, the old Garraway Obs, Car No. 11 was turned round, so that for the first time there was a 'Top End 'Obs' on the FR. In fact the vehicle was used to entertain William Hague MP, then Secretary of State for Wales, to an excellent lunch, by Maes y Neuadd, whilst riding up and down the Ffestiniog Railway. The Car was also used as an Inspection Saloon for the FR Trust, propelled up the line by *Sgt Murphy*. However, the top end 'Obs was not persisted with, although the idea never quite went away.

The Barn Observation Carriages Nos 100 and 101 were built in 1970, the parts being fabricated by Watsons of Birkenhead, and erected in Boston Lodge Works. The series was based loosely on Car No. 14 ex Lynton and Barnstaple Railway. They were designed by Fred Boughey as steel underframed, wooden bodied carriages, economic to build, easy to assemble, and comfortable to travel in. It was their great roominess, when compared with the old Festiniog Railway carriages, that earned them the nickname Barns.

In 2003, the Welsh Highland Railway needed a second train set; the old Barn Observation, Car No. 100 was transferred for use as a guard's van, but was looking really tired. (In truth it was not too healthy when it left FR metals, but there was nothing else available to do this important job). In February of 2006, Barn Observation Car 101 was sent to the WHR to replace the exhausted Car 100 on the second set. The Car 101 swivel seats had been re-covered with some donated airline upholstery, and the saloon had been fitted out with first class seats temporarily removed from Carnforth Car 113 whilst it was under overhaul (It was known as the Tart's Parlour.). This arrangement lasted until the new observation car *Glaslyn* was finished and delivered to

the WHR in March 2009. By then Car 101 was looking decidedly sad. Car 113 finished overhaul and returned about the same time to the FR, and its first class compartments were restored using the seats taken back from Car 101. Thus 101 had no seats in the saloon area, and decidedly threadbare seats in the 'Obs end. The last outing of Car 101 in public service was in September 2009, when the saloon was fitted out with plastic garden seats for the occasion. It was then left in the sidings at Dinas, as there was no use identified for it, but there was obviously life left in the body.

Car 101 had entered service in March 1970. Much celebrated, it has been refurbished a number of times; abandoned, it would have quietly rotted away to firewood after 40 years of service. As the bodywork was in reasonable condition, a scheme was put forward to turn it to make a third class, top end observation carriage. Various schemes were examined, but for modern, larger humans, it is now necessary to offer more leg room than the original Barns and Tin Cars.

The number 101 was retained for a new Observation Car., yet to be constructed. The old 101 was therefore re-numbered to 123. The observation end now has a bay of seven seats, the guard's area has been retained, but the partition has been moved in, to allow the double doors to become part of the mobility impaired passenger seating area. This accommodates two wheel chairs, when the seats are tipped up, offering an official sized footprint for the wheelchairs. There is now an excellent ambience in this car, with modern seating, and a clean sweep in the interior. Steve Morris, the FR cabinet maker, made a kit of parts that formed the new seats. All of the refurbishments were done by volunteers, and the finished painting was completed by the Boston Lodge professional team..

This carriage now has thirty seats, with a number of unique

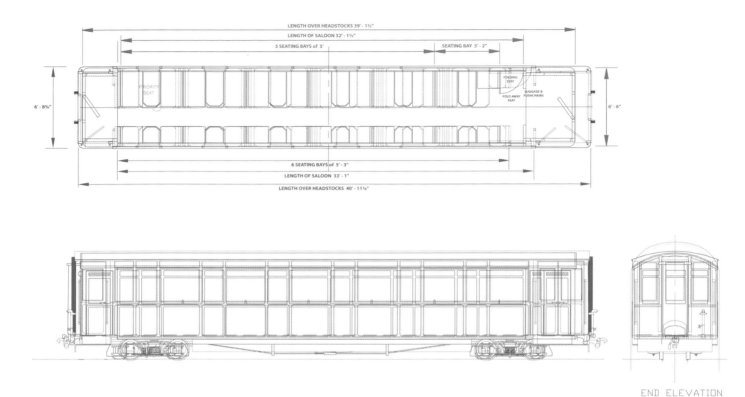

LENGTH OVER HEADSTOCKS 39' - 1½"
LENGTH OF SALOON 32' - 1½"
5 SEATING BAYS of 5'
SEATING BAY 5' - 2"
PRIORITY SEAT
FOLDING SEAT
FOLD AWAY SEAT
BUGGAGE & PUSHCHAIRS
6' - 8¾"
6' - 6"
6 SEATING BAYS of 5' - 3"
LENGTH OF SALOON 33' - 1"
LENGTH OVER HEADSTOCKS 40' - 11¼"

END ELEVATION

**COMPARISON CARRIAGE DIMENSIONS** - FR SUPERBARN
- WHR 13M CARRIAGE

features, but most of all it provides extra capacity for very little cost. So Car 101 was not left to rot. It has come back from the grave like Lazarus, and in 2011 when it took to the rails and filled with its first, rather delighted passengers, it felt like it was a miracle.

Super-Barns, with 6 seating bays of 5ft, to the drawing shown above, with 36 seats, are now being built for service on the combined railway. Car 121, paid for by the Ffestiniog Railway Society, will be rolling on the combined railways in 2012. Car 108, another Super-Barn, will follow close behind, and assuming that the funds are available, more will follow. In all some eight more carriages are needed.

## Dyfodol

Carriages are the key to earning for any passenger railway. Comfortable seats are a plank of maintaining a decent revenue per seat, and planks to sit on are amusing for a short time only. Few spend a short time on WHR trains. It is clear that the amount of time that people could dwell in an WHR/FR carriage now theoretically exceeds that from Kings Cross to Aberdeen. Plus, a railway with unique vehicles stretching back to the 1860s really ought

not to be relying on them for daily service in 2012; there is an obligation to cherish them, and keep them for special occasions as befits their glorious antiquity (and aching discomfort).

There is a need for a strengthening of the current WHR gauge sets, with a couple more third class saloons. This will make two train sets, one of 9 cars and one of 10 - possibly a further third saloon will be needed. The frequency of service with only two sets, and a round trip that takes over 5 hours, is a bit light. Three sets at least are needed to offer five trips per day on WHR, and even now the afternoon train doesn't get back to Caernarfon until 19.00. Yet the third set must be flexible enough to be able to venture up the Ffestiniog, and thus must be FR gauge. And here is unknown territory.

There might yet one day be the Welsh version of the Glacier Express. In 2011, it cost £180 first, £120 second for the 8hr, 290km one-way trip. This is the way the market is going. There are flights of fancy that imagine a set of luxury, Pullman, clerestory coaches, a true train of 'varnish', for the very special world tourist market. Who would have imagined *Glaslyn* when Allan Garraway converted No. 11 to an 'obs, and who thought in 1959 a 40 mile FR would become a reality? **Hyn yn y dyfodol.**

*It's that man again! Norman Bond leans out of new Super-Barn Car No. 121, paid for by the Ffestiniog Railway Society - another in the series of new comfortable carriages. At 12m, No.121 is the longest carriage to be built for FR, able to work across both railways, with unrivalled comfort in third class. 2nd November 2011*

# Chapter 11
## The Track, Operations, and Train Service

Railway track on the 2ft gauge has been undergoing steady development over the last 50 years. Not the changes needed for high speed operation, but narrow gauge track has a number of new and useful criteria, developed on the FR and applied when the WHR was restored. The materials and the methods have changed radically during the time that the FR has been running its railway. The FR was fascinated with its own cuteness during the Victorian Era. In the 1860s it installed and maintained doublehead rail, as a replacement to the 'T' rail of the horse tramway days. Afterwards this was replaced with bullhead rail, well suited to 3 chain curves. Mr Vignoles's solution, of a flat bottom rail, with plain spikes into the sleeper, was held at bay. Recovered rail from the Penrhyn Railway offered bullhead 2ft gauge rail in the early preservation era of the 1960s, but the bullhead materials were gradually eclipsed by heavier flat bottomed rail, and bullhead was specifically confined to stations and other places where 'cute' matters.

The NWNG adopted flat bottomed track, as did the WHR, which was built under austere circumstances in the 1920s; simplicity was the rule. During the period of restoration and operation of FR, and when the restoration of WHR came about, the restorers with experience were quite clear that the nearer track could approach the 'fit and forget' system, the better life would be.

The 60lb/yard flat-bottomed rail of the FR preservation era

Lilla, *the FR's pet, runs up into Minffordd ,over what is the only double-tracked piece of 2ft gauge bullhead railway in the world. Probably the FR isn't very impressed with this, as it has a railway to maintain, and infrastructure offers enough potential difficulties without encouraging the presence of track with radical differences. It looks nice though!*

was screwed straight to the sleepers, and had no 1:20 inclination, or toe-in. Later, experience led to 60lbs per yard, flat bottomed rail, screwed on to baseplates fitted to suitable sleepers. The rail with the metric equivalent to 60lbs/yard is 30kg/ metre (*Please tolerate mixed units, as track gauge is measured in millimetres and weights will be in kg and lbs.*). Amounts of standard gauge siding and branch line rail had been on the market at various times when FR was restoring to Blaenau. Alas the ideal 60lbs rail was rare and 75lbs occasionally came on the market from old MoD sidings that were recovered. The 75lbs per yard rail was tried as sources of it became available that were cheap. However, in the end it was more expensive and bigger than needed for the 2ft gauge, and so whenever possible the FR bought 60 lb rail. An over-heavy rail section (such as 75lb) did not lie easily on the sharp, canted curves of the FR. New 60lb rail was purchased at an economic price from British Steel's rolling mill at Workington, as a result of the Rhodesia embargo; the FR was constantly on the lookout for more sources of economic, second-hand supply.

In the late 1990s, when the demand arose for rail for the Phase 1 Caernarfon - Dinas construction work, still there were few UK sources available for 60lb rail. The Channel Tunnel Railway (CTR), all 60lb rail, was being dismantled and there was a great deal of it for sale. However this rail was unsuitable, as it was in six and nine metre lengths only. Some sleepers and fastenings were bought. However, the unfortunate demise of the South African narrow gauge came at the right time to shape the future of the restored WHR. The South Africans no longer considered their narrow gauge was viable, and that decision has helped the WHR to be restored at a lower cost.

South African Railways (SAR) were pulling up 2ft gauge branchlines in Natal, all laid in 30kg per metre rail, and this was eagerly grasped, as it was from similar sources to the locomotives that were being purchased. The SAR rail was excellent; it came

The description of the WHR track has a more human dimension, and carries sufficient technical complication to warrant being separated out in its own right. The risks of doing this are to create duplication There is good and bad in consolidation and separation, but as the decision was taken to separate, please forgive the duplication.
                                                                    Author

*The track gang returns to continue laying track in the Aberglasyn Pass, on 15th September 2007, during Phase 4. Behind the camera is Tunnel No 2. The Indian steel sleepers hold ERC Clips, and the track rests on a nylon pad. There are 24 sleepers to a 60ft length, sleeper centres are at 2'6" feet intervals (closer at the ends). There were problems with the ERC clips to start with, so they were replaced with a new batch. Shown here is S30 (30kg/m) rail purchased new from Poland.*

from the recently relaid Donnybrook line, that was closed prematurely due to flood damage. It had been laid to 610mm gauge, was only lightly used, and came with a matching stock of steel sleepers and fittings. The original decision was made to ship this across in panels. It was cheaper for SAR to recover the rail this way, and it was thought that it would be easier to lay. Caernarfon - Dinas was a railway with space around it. Putting the track down in panels was thought to be the most economic and rapid method of doing the job. The rails, sleepers and fastenings that came, supplemented the NGG16 Garratts, NG15 Kalaharis, and wagons that were also obtained - the passenger coaches might have come too, except that they were not suitable.

Clive Briscoe's picture in Chapter 4 shows stacks of track panels waiting at Immingham for transport to the WHR. Some 1200 tonnes of materials came in during Phase 1, and within it was coiled the first of those hateful little reverses that fate always has waiting. For your delectation this will be revealed gradually.

With 2ft gauge materials from SAR there was the question of gauge. FR and WHR gauge is set at 597mm track gauge‡ but of course there is widening of gauge on curves. The narrow gauge curves a lot - that's normally why narrow gauge is chosen; it fits into tighter places than wider gauges, and railways with

sharper curves and steeper gradients are cheaper to build. The SAR gauge is 610mm - so any track panel had to have its gauge adjusted to 597mm for WHR plain track, and it would need to be widened to a preset formula for curves.

The rather advanced decision was taken to create a splendid machine for laying the track panels, and in Chapter 4 the Forth Bridge was described - the machine for doing just that. It was related there, that unknown to the innocents in Britain, there were two lengths for SAR steel sleepers. The drawing sent showed the shorter one; alas the track panels were all of the longer! So for a start the machine was hampered. Yet the worm of fate was more deeply embedded than this. It is probably time for some technical information:

**1.** The gauge generally had to be reduced by 13mm, and adjusted appropriately for curvature, by means of rearranging the position of the different rail clip types.

**2.** That was possible, as the SAR steel sleepers can accommodate clips of various sizes. For each panel of track with 24 sleepers there are: 96 clips, 96 bolts, 96 nuts and 96 washers, offering a total of 384 bits of small steel. To reset the gauge, the clips are unfastened, and one or more of appropriate size inserted, then the fastenings are tightened up again to hold the gauge set.

**3.** Curvature will inevitably cause the inner rail to protrude, as the distance on the inside of the curve is shorter than the outer. The difference is called the 'lead' and 'lag' on curves. If ignored, the rail joints will move out of parallel (or not be 'square')as panel

‡ For the pedant, note that 597mm gauge is more like 23¹⁷/₃₂", perhaps you may allow 1'11½", as ¹/₃₂ is only 0.03125mm? At any rate, the point is that this isn't 1'11⅝", that's 600mm gauge. If you want 'real' 2ft, that's 610mm gauge. Do you give in?

is added to panel.

**4.** In UK it is thought desirable to have rail joints square. Rail joints dip in traffic, (even when supported) and unless they are square, vehicles will roll from side to side, and the bogies will have to negotiate twist in the track. Twist in the track can offer the means for the wheel flange to climb the inside of a rail and cause a derailment. (Staggered (non-square) rail joints were allowed in later Phases, but under special conditions. They were not laid in on Phases 1-3, but introduced subsequently as needed.)

**5.** With jointed track, it is not possible to keep rail joints exactly square. Nor can a little be taken off each rail to keep them so, as the smallest cut can only coincide with the mid-point between first and second fishplate-bolt hole (and you then drill the second one again). This means that the joints are allowed to move out of square with accumulated lag or lead, but only as far as about 2 inches. (This varied slightly with the rail type: SAR rail has fishplates with 4" hole centres, thus 2" is the minimum; Polish rail fishplates have 5" centres, thus the minimum is 2½".)

**6.** Thus, if using panels, each length of rail has to be adjusted individually, to fit the exact place where it is laid.

**7.** One may now see that panel fittings had to be fastened and unfastened a number of times, in order for it to fit the precise curvature and gauge requirement of the place where it is laid. Frequent adjustment of the rail position up and down an SAR track panel is likely to bring on the early onset of suicidal tendencies.

**8.** One might be prepared to accept panels along miles and miles of straight (or nearly straight) track, where adjustments would be negligible. However, this description does not fit most of the WHR, Phases 1-3. SAR

*West Coast Main Line : A different world to the WHR. At the same time (29th April 2006) the WCML was being relaid and upgraded, shown here at Hartshill, Warks. Huge rails, (UIC 60 - 121lb/yd) concrete sleepers, big heaps of ballast - not the same thing at all.*

track panels, with 384 fittings, were not the easy solution they had seemed. It was a cost-effective solution that was sought. Compromise was necessary, as time was limited, (Millennium Commission was pressing) and money was tight. Much thought went into the changes that came about in Phase 4.

One might ask why not remove these problems and just weld the track as on the 'big railway'? The answer to that is that the UIC 60 rail on main lines is held in large concrete sleepers of great mass. The rails are tensioned to a set ambient temperature, and the forces of expansion and contraction are then constrained within the mass of the track, which is further confined by a ballast shoulder, within the mass of stones 'locked' together. On the narrow gauge the track mass is less, the line curves much more, and it would be difficult to lay in an effective ballast shoulder. Thus welded track would carry unacceptable risk of distortion during too narrow a range of temperature conditions.

The demise of the 'panel' method required some careful reasoning, resulting in sensible conclusions on the standards that were applied to the second hand SAR track..

## Standards

For Phases 2 & 3, track from South Africa would be sent to Wales as individual parts. The advantage of this was that although it was less convenient for the demolition people, larger amounts of air were no longer being shipped; the rail, fittings and sleepers could be stacked densely, with more weight being fitted into expensive containers. It was because of this switch that wagons began to be shipped as deck-cargo, to contain the broken-down track stuff. The wagons were scrap to SAR; they were 'free' to WHR, but as they still actually worked, they were a Godsend! A disadvantage to 'de-panelling' was that rails then needed to be carefully 'sorted' for wear, and length (as most of the rails had previously been laid on curves).

o The Roland Rail Mover was invented by Roland Doyle. Hence a new method of laying the track was introduced. The RRM really is an excellent piece of kit. Simple and easy to use, suited exactly to the volunteer track gangs. It has the excellent simplicity of being compact, thus you can get round it in a confined space - something that a narrow gauge, single-line railway like the WHR specialises in. Thus track could be laid more easily, almost everywhere, in rapid time.

o Supply was arranged by a system of rail stacks.

o The required sleepers, rail, and fastenings, were brought to site, so that the sleepers could be carried off rail wagons, the bags of fastenings could be distributed, and the rails dragged off the wagon to lie inside track already laid, ready to be suspended under the RRMs, to be pushed to site.

o The sleepers were ported to be placed at prearranged spacings on the compacted and prepared roadbed.

o The correct clips for gauge and the fastenings were placed within the sleepers, ready for the rails to be slotted in.

o The RRM rollers were laid out, and the rails next to be laid were brought to the railhead, suspended under the RRMs.

o The rails were lowered on to the rollers, extended into position, then barred into the fastenings, situated in the slots in the sleepers.

o The fastenings were tightened, thus setting the rails to the appropriate gauge.

This was a really good tracklaying method used for Phases 1,2 and 3, whilst the SAR rail and sleepers were available. It could allow up to ten lengths to be laid in a day in ideal conditions, with a big track gang. Most of all, it allowed tracklaying to be done by staff and volunteers. This wasn't only nice from the good feeling it gave everyone, the volunteers' time was measured and included in the grant claim - the FR Co. got money for it.

Phase 4 saw a considerable change. New S30 (30kg/m) rail was bought from Poland, and new steel sleepers and elastic rail clips (ERCs), that looked like Pandrol clips, were bought from India.

*1 Left:* John Ewing waves the magic wand over the track in the Aberglaslyn Pass. This was the moment the track was about to reach from Caernarfon, for 18½ miles into Tunnel No.2. The 32yd tunnel represents a challenge. The track must be placed precisely. Unfortunately the wand does not build the railway in an instant, it is used to ensure a precise distance between sleepers. The layout of the steel sleepers includes the ERC fastenings at the side, and the nylon pad that sits under the rail. Note that the spades at the end of the sleepers are not steeply inclined, but they dig in to the ballast, plus it rises up inside the sleeper, and thus when interlocked with all the other surrounding pieces of ballast, it serves to fix the sleeper firmly in place. This is the reason why there is such emphasis with this type of track in making sure that the sleepers are put in the right place to start with.
**This series of photographs was taken on 15th September 2007, to describe Phase 4 tracklaying methods. The Aberglaslyn Pass is used as the example.**

*2 Right:* A couple of right-hand (low side) rails have already been laid in; the ERC fasteners are in their slots and driven home. The track will now be aligned, as with only one rail in the slot, it is easier to move it about into precisely the position wanted.
The rollers have been used to move the rails into place, and then the rails were barred into the slots, on top of the nylon pads.
Looking south towards No.2 Tunnel, you can see the wooden profile boards, 1m above the finished formation level. There are some wooden sleeper stacks - it was first proposed to lay this track on wood sleepers, but this was later changed to steel - and leaning against the rock wall are the well used bars that are used to adjust the track into the correct alignment. Note also the greased fishplated joint in the right-foreground.

*3 Left:* the previous caption explained why and how this track was being installed one rail at a time. Here the companion rail is rolled in to the Head of Steel on a pair of RRMs. Rail is usually moved in pairs in RRMs. These simple appliances make it easy to pick the rail up from the middle of the track, and then to transport it with a minimum number of people. When they are ready, the rail is lowered from the front RRM on to the rollers, rolled into part-position, and then the front RRM may let go and the rail can be manoeuvred into the right spot, and barred on to the nylon pads in the exactly the position required. It is all so much easier than having to carry the rail manually. This is not to indicate that the gangs are full of wimps; the advantage is that it allows is a longer day before people get really tired. In the picture is some of the new 30 kg/m rail from Poland.

*4 Right:* In action here is the Partner K1250 Active, petrol power cutter. It was worthwhile investing in machinery like this. It offers a rapid, precise cut, and is much better than the old hacksaw based alternative. The rail was being cut at this point to bring the rail joints back into square, as the line here is relatively straight, whereas before there were many curves. The saw is always attached securely to the rail, which is quite heavy enough to stay put until it is cut. All the ERC fastenings were not in position at this time.
After the cut it was necessary to use the drilling machine to bore the appropriate bolt holes in the rail to attach the fishplates.
Then the precise gap in the rail is adjusted by bar, according to the temperature, the fishplate is bolted on, and all the fastenings are placed in position and tightened up.
This is skilled work, and mistakes can be expensive, however the volunteers quickly learned how to do things properly and the work was completed smoothly and rapidly.

**5 Left:** *The tool for pulling the ERC fastenings into their housing comprises a long lever, with a hinged hook, and a fixed stop on the shaft - very simple. Placed correctly, it pulls the clip into its socket with an audible crunch. The forces, even with this manual method, are quite massive. There were instances of the clips breaking. They were replaced with clips made from new material which did not fail - the problem may have been temperature during manufacture, however the replacements were satisfactory. Clips take little time to install, and this method of laying track is quick. The maximum laid in a day by one gang, on to a prepared trackbed was 24 lengths, some 480m of track. That was a rare occurrence, but the subtle method was to let the contractors extend the ballast bed in the week, and the volunteer tracklayers to catch up with laid track at the weekends.*

**6 Right:** *The bolt-holes have all been drilled, and the fishplates have been greased, and then fitted by power wrench, but here you see the final touches with a torque wrench, to make sure that the bolts are all tightened to the same tension. Note that the fishplate bolts are on the outside. Also note that before placing all the ERC clips, the rail gap was adjusted to the optimum by barring.*
*The track will now be run over to deliver supplies to the next lengths, and the process will be repeated, beyond. Great care is taken over running on this track at this time. The works locomotive are permitted, at very slow speed. This is less through natural caution, and more about avoiding building-in a permanent vertical distortion. Incautious and prolonged running over track in this state will cause real damage. The track will be bent vertically, and will acquire a 'memory' of the distortion, so that when it is in service it will tend to return to the distorted state. This is expensive in maintenance.*

**7 Left:** *In the sidings at Rhyd Ddu are two of the WHR's bogie ballast wagons. The far one is No. 4023, a specialised drop wagon, designed to allow the placement of precise quantities of ballast in precise locations, and was built in Romania in 2006 for service on the railway. It will discharge from either the side or underneath, between the rails. The nearest vehicle is one of the ex-South African Railways 'Y' type ballast hopper wagons. Two (4021/2) came to WHR in 2000. These vehicles, all vacuum braked, are needed to permit the placement of the thin extra layer of stones needed to bring the ballast up to the level of the tops of the sleepers, and to effect the correct gradient of ballast at the side of the track to the level of the trackbed. The track needs ballast support to allow it properly to 'float' on the top of the ballast bed, and to remain in place. Thus the track offers a flexible but static support to the vehicles that run over it.*

**8 Right:** *Each sleeper must have the proper ballast support underneath it, to align the railway accurately, and to set the track at the right vertical level. This had traditionally been done by hand and by eye; the process takes time and requires much skill. The objective is a smooth ride, the maintenance of the set radius on curves, cant and the track alignment set to kinematic envelope. The position of the track must not lead to any contact with trackside objects. The machine opposite is the FRAMAFER KMX95 CM, tamper-lifter-liner, that can perform all the above duties mechanically, under computer control. This unit is similar to main line units, and was designed for gauges from 1m - 600mm. It is a 1995 built machine, and was found in the Lorraine coalfields. It was on offer at an affordable price, and was acquired in 2005. After repair, adaptation, and commissioning, it went to Dinas in 2006. Of course it's a complex machine, and requires careful attention but it saves a good deal of time, and produces a quality job. The KMX can work on the FR and on the WHR.*

*Left: The Roland Rail Mover works on simple principles. The rail is lifted (two at a time) from the centre of the track, where it had been placed from off the supply wagon. It is pushed with the two RRMs to the head of steel, and the rail is let down on to rollers to be placed in position. The RRM could be pushed by hand, it could be attached to a locomotive, or even form part of a train. Picture taken 15th September 2007.*

*Below: The tramway rail on the Cross Town Rail Link (CTRL) is here out of square from its curving past the old flour mill. What will happen in this case is that as it is the end of the section of tramway rail, it will be cut off square after crossing a short transition panel, and it will be joined with the conventional rail to continue north to the Cae Pawb crossing. Picture taken on 20th December 2008, with Stuart McNair casting a critical eye.*

The first batch of ERCs from India had to be replaced. The ERC fitted sleepers are set to gauge, thus two types are used, one at 597mm for straight track, and the other at 610mm, for gauge widened curves. To handle the gauge transition, a number of gauge adjustable SAR sleepers were laid. This can be seen on the sharp curves on Phase 4, where a continuous run of ERC type Indian sleepers is suddenly punctuated by some SAR sleepers as the gauge is varied appropriately.

Standard SAR fishplates were used for SAR rail. For Phase 4, the rails were drilled to a different hole spacing, so SAR fishplates would not fit. Polish fishplates were used, but they were not strong enough on curves to resist the lateral force exerted by the rails. To prevent 'threepenny bitting' on the affected curves, stronger fishplates were purchased from Darlington with CRhE funds, and fitted between Pont Cae'r Gors and Croesor Junction, and a 'stagger' was introduced into the rail joints. On sharp curves, like those above Beddgelert that are 53m radius, parallel joints induce 'threepenny bitting' even with the strong fishplates, and rail pre-bending was needed (rails were sent away for 'curving'). So rails were laid with the joints 9m out of square. The tendency of the rail to straighten the curve could not then be exerted at the weak point of two fishplates together. The rules on the straight applied to this staggered rail on the curve. It was not allowed to move out of square by more than the practical cutting distance for a rail-end drilled for fishplate

bolts for Polish fishplates.

Steel sleepers were chosen as they were easily available. Steel sleepers are cheap, light, easy to store and transport, easy to lay, and if they are fitted correctly, they stay where they are put.

*Above: Some of the curves on the line are severe, such as this one of 53m radius at Cwm Cloch, above Beddgelert. It is also on a 1:43 gradient, thus the locomotives are working hard ascending and braking hard descending. This causes the tracks to try to 'straighten out' on curves and strain the fishplates. Thus the need for tough, strong examples. Here is 'The Tracklayers' Train' on 31st October 2010 - it was quite a celebration.*

*Left: Wooden sleepers were used strategically. Here they are grouped closely together to form a deck on Pont Croesor. Note they are also used in transition to steel, in running off the bridge. Most big bridges used a sleeper deck, except for the steel bridge across the A4085 just south of Nantmor - that was ballasted.*

It is this final condition that can cause problems. Once fitted they can be difficult to move, and although track that stays where it is laid is desirable, correct installation is essential. Railtrack donated wooden sleepers that were available for certain locations that demanded them - across bridges, where some sleeper thickness was needed, in stations, where 'cuteness' was preferred, and so on.

The art of laying new railway in 2ft gauge had mostly been forgotten by the volunteers. The last time it was done in quantity was on the Ffestiniog

*The last extensive tracklaying experience was gained on the FR between Dduallt and Blaenau Ffestiniog, and this was a four-mile section, rather more modest than Caernarfon to Porthmadog. The picture here is of the Archer Dam, from the footplate of Vale of Ffestiniog taken on 27th March 2003, and showing the rails running north along Llyn Ystradau towards Tanygrisiau .*

The process of laying the track on WHR differed widely between Phases. On Phase 1, the track started from the Dinas end and progressed steadily in one wave to Caernarfon. On Phase 2 and 3, the tracklaying started from more than one place, because bridges could not be completed at the same rate as trackbed. Tracklaying was discontinuous, much to the frustration of some. It was necessary to port materials, to establish depots, and this was a nuisance. On Phase 4 the track construction swept in a continuous wave from

Railway Deviation, and Building Back to Blaenau in the late 1970s and early 1980s. The WHR railway restoration was on a rather different scale, as there was 25 miles to put down, not just a few. To begin with the job was intended for contractors, not because volunteers were thought unable to do it, but merely for convenience and speed, to get the Caernarfon to Dinas line laid. However, it became clear very early on, that this job was going to be done by volunteers as well as by the paid staff. Not only did the staff teach the volunteers how to do the work to the highest standards, in the best FR traditions, but the use of volunteers allowed much more to be done with less, and it earned cash from the grant schemes. The pace after Caernarfon to Dinas slackened, giving time for organisation. It was discovered how many people were interested - just like the Deviation. As the tracklaying tasks returned, and demand for volunteers rose, so did the supply. The supply continued to mount, and the system to deal with it expanded. The track laying system, once established, never let the project down. In fact so good did the track gangs become that they were often champing at the bit, waiting for the engineers and trackbed preparers to finish so that they could get the track laid.

Rhyd Ddu to Traeth Mawr, to meet the WHRL-laid track, and then to connect with the crossing of the Cambrian Coast line at Cae Pawb, and the tramway of the Cross Town Link.

SAR materials were used as far as Rhyd Ddu. By then it was necessary to get more materials, and there was a reappraisal of the system to use Indian sleepers with ERC fasteners, with the remaining SAR equipment was kept for transition to gauge widening on curves. It is this system that has been exampled in the adjacent pictures. It all ran very smoothly, with an excellent volunteer organisation, largely due to the work of Paul Bradshaw, Dafydd Thomas, and their teams, and later Alasdair Stewart and Stuart McNair who calculated the alignments.

***Above:*** *Putting in Canal Curve, between Pont Cae'r Gors and Meillionen Halt, on 12 October 2006. This was sharp, and so was the learning curve on how to install and maintain such track.*
**Jane Ewing**

***Left:*** *Here is the same bit of track from the train, descending towards Beddgelert, showing how sharp this curve is, and there are a number of these '50m' radius curves in the forest section. This picture reinforces the point that when trains go round them, with a speed limit of 15mph, the fishplates have to be strong, and the track well prepared and laid, in order for everything to stay in place.*

## The track - Points

Points (turnouts) on WHR were required in some quantity. Initially the availability of points from the dismantled SAR narrow gauge system drove the key decision to adopt SAR standards, and to acquire points from that source. Points are expensive: they require a specialised sleeper layout; the crossing is a complex fabrication of rails and 'spacer' blocks; point blades require much work to achieve the precise machining of the blade, and the blades have to be tied together with an actuation and locking mechanism. Thus, being able to purchase this precision piece of kit at a fraction of the manufactured price made a lot of sense, even though the point assemblies could not be used 'as delivered'. Work was needed on each point, as the gauge of 610mm has a different 'back to back' measurement from FR standards. 'Back to back' is a critical distance between the wheel backs; it is 21 inches on FR. This and the 'back to front' measurement must be set correctly, as derailment or damage may occur if it is not. A set of new cast WHR marked, iron 'spacer' block was needed to ensure that diamonds and check rails had the correct clearances when bolted together.

The first sets of points came from parts assembled in Minffordd Yard. These were used on Phase 1 at Dinas and Caernarfon. Later, points were pre-assembled at Dinas, ready to be dropped into position at loops and sidings. Twelve sets of points were employed at Dinas itself. Later additions to the layout increased that number to fourteen, and it ius likely that the layout will alter in the future as necessary.

On Phase 2, points were needed at Waunfawr. By the start of December 2002, Phase 3, three more sets of points were completed, one for Rhyd Ddu, and two for Plas y Nant siding (The loop was never installed, and the siding was removed after restoration). The 2003/4 season, short loop at Rhyd Ddu was lengthened in 2005/6, and that included laying in sidings that were south facing, ready for Phase 4 construction. During the time that Rhyd Ddu was the terminus, there were two passing places, Waunfawr and Dinas.

Phase 4 construction had need of points at the first passing

### Point installations - WHR

| Place | Hand | Lever | Comments |
|---|---|---|---|
| Caernarfon | 2 | 1 | One was later removed |
| Dinas | 8 | 6 | 2x2 GF, N and S end 2 auto loop for station |
| Waunfawr | - | 2 | Auto loop |
| Plas y Nant | 1 | - | 2 delivered, one used. Siding gone after const. |
| Rhyd Ddu | 1 | 4 | 2 auto loop, 2 GF (not yet-2012) (1 trap) |
| Beddgelert | 1 | 2 | 2 auto loop, one token locked hand point |
| Hafod y Llyn | 2 | - | Clamped & locked, emergency loop/PW siding |
| Pont Croesor | - | 2 | Auto loop |
| Pen y Mount | 1 | - | Clamped and locked |
| Cae Pawb | - | - | Flat crossing std/narrow |
| Llyn Bach* | 1 | - | OOU |
| Porthmadog* | - | 1 | GF worked 'WHR point' |

\* Until resignalling in 2013-4

## WHR - Schematic

AL auto loop : GF ground frame : HP hand points, L = token locked

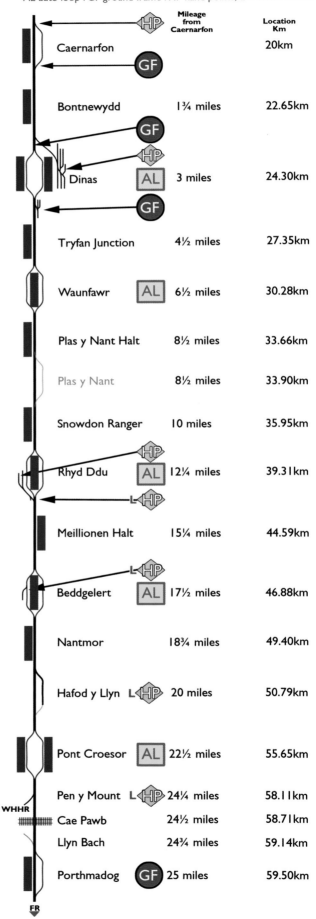

| | Mileage from Caernarfon | Location Km |
|---|---|---|
| Caernarfon | | 20km |
| Bontnewydd | 1¾ miles | 22.65km |
| Dinas | 3 miles | 24.30km |
| Tryfan Junction | 4½ miles | 27.35km |
| Waunfawr | 6½ miles | 30.28km |
| Plas y Nant Halt | 8½ miles | 33.66km |
| Plas y Nant | 8½ miles | 33.90km |
| Snowdon Ranger | 10 miles | 35.95km |
| Rhyd Ddu | 12¼ miles | 39.31km |
| Meillionen Halt | 15¼ miles | 44.59km |
| Beddgelert | 17½ miles | 46.88km |
| Nantmor | 18¾ miles | 49.40km |
| Hafod y Llyn | 20 miles | 50.79km |
| Pont Croesor | 22½ miles | 55.65km |
| Pen y Mount | 24¼ miles | 58.11km |
| Cae Pawb | 24½ miles | 58.71km |
| Llyn Bach | 24¾ miles | 59.14km |
| Porthmadog | 25 miles | 59.50km |

*Left:* This view looks south towards Porthmadog, and shows the bottom end point of the loop line at Pont Croesor. A location cabinet will cover the installation. The detection (not yet fitted) sits on the long timber ends, opposite the mechanism. On the right hand side of the track, at the end of the fence, there is the pole, upon which will be mounted the points indicator. Currently the points are clamped in the reverse position.

**Both photos: Andrew Thomas**

*Bottom:* Adjustments are being made to the weighted lever, a magnificent piece of machinery, constructed by Boston Lodge. The lever is tempered in its movement by the diagonally mounted hydraulic damper, seen mid way along the red lever arm. The lever is in the normal position. It will rise when the points are deflected, and the damper will govern the speed of the return. The default position of the lever is down, with points normal.

place, Beddgelert. An autoloop was installed here, together with a clamped and locked hand-worked point on the up side, leading to a siding. The Hafod y Llyn (first a siding) loop line was used as a temporary run round, with hand points (clamped and locked when not needed). There was a short platform there, so people could alight, but the public were never encouraged to do so.

After the next passing place at Pont Croesor was opened, it was no longer used as a loop. Pont Croesor was fitted with an autoloop. The two-platform layout assumes right-hand running. In the event of a 'turnback' south, then a logical game (authorised by Control) has to be played, to make a departure in the wrong direction.

The next set of points is at Pen y Mount; these are kept clamped and locked until needed. Provision was made for a siding at Llyn Bach, next the car park on the CTRL at Porthmadog. The point was laid in, but has not been used yet. The final points on the WHR were the 'Welsh Highland Points' at Porthmadog. These join to the platform line, and they date back to the first days of the FR (as the continuation to the Harbour and Milepost '0'). When Porthmadog Harbour Station layout is rebuilt, a two-point run round loop will be installed.

There was a gradual realisation in service that the turnout standards chosen were a little sharper than was desirable. This led to new, longer, turnouts being made and installed towards the end of Phase 4.

Autoloops were a handy combination for loop lines tried and tested in South Wales. The standard gauge lines opted for more expensive hydrostatic point actuation machinery. On

WHR it was decided that a weighted lever, fitted with hydraulic damping, would do the job. The points are detected in the same way as their standard gauge cousins. Approaching trains receive a lit point indication to confirm that the points are detected in the 'normal' position. Trains run into the loop on the right hand. The movement in is made at restricted speed. Once passing formalities have been completed, and the driver has the token for the next section, the train leaves through the exit point, displacing them from 'normal' to 'reversed'. The slow speed obviates undue wear; the damping prevents the rapid, automatic return of the points to the normal position. When the train has passed, the points will revert to normal, and the detection will be made, to light the point indicator, ready for the next movement. Autoloops provided a simple and cost-effective crossing point that requires no ground frame. The slow speed and simplicity of design means that wear is at a minimum, and reliability is very high.

## WHR STANDARD TURNOUT

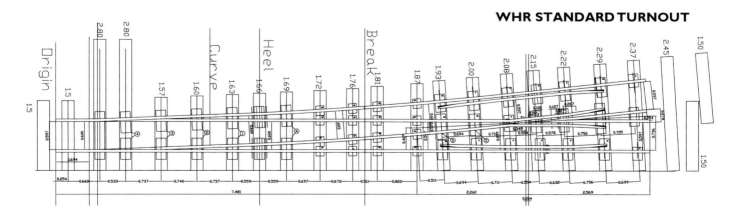

*Left: The 'Forth Bridge' paused near the Pant Road overbridge in August 1997. The idea was that the grilles were removed and a trolley equipped with a winch ran out on the girder extension, lifted a panel from the wagon, then ran out on the forward section and lowered it into place. There were two snags to this labour saving boon. It was unable to pass track panels with the SAR wider sleepers through its innards, flat - so they had to be tilted to be carried, and there were some 80 of these. Plus the massive erection would not fit through the NWNG bridges. After Phase 1, it languished until broken up. Chapter 4, Phase 1 tells more.*

**Ben Fisher**

*Below: A slightly blurry, hazy photo from 1997, shows the track advancing on to the station site at Caernarfon, with the point laid into what will become the water tower road that was removed in 2005.*

**Ben Fisher**

## Phase 1 - the track

Caernarfon to Dinas was only three miles, and it was not considered that there would be much of a challenge to lay track on that. However, as you will have seen from the descriptions, the SAR track hardly conformed with anything that had been laid before on the FR. The first job was to get a yard laid at Dinas, the HQ and starting point for the action. This happened on 28th-29th December 1996, when the first two lengths went down in the goods shed. Mowlem had the £750k contract to build the railway. At first it was 'contractor only', and the track was laid in panels.

There were 80 panels brought from South Africa, adjusted to the 597mm gauge and gradually laid in, by the ill-fated 'Forth Bridge'. The introduction of RRMs speeded up the construction of track from components, and this method became the main method, as well as the introduction of tracklaying volunteers, such as the CRhE Black Hand Gang, along with teams from other railways. The volunteers were made welcome once Mowlem had laid the ballast bed, as it was obvious that staff and competent volunteers could handle the job. In September 1997 the track reached Caernarfon Station. Service began on 11th October and the official opening was 13th October 1997.

## Phase 2 - the track

Phase 1 track had been laid from Dinas to Caernarfon in a continuous sweep, following on the preparation of the trackbed and the laying of the ballast bed. This would not be possible for the next two phases for the simple reason that the bridges could not be built and completed at the same rate as the trackbed could be prepared for track. The Millennium Commission was urging that the railway be completed. The TWO proceedings had taken a year and work did not start until November 1999. No matter how hard the tracklayers laid track, there was no way that it would be in place for a completed railway party at Rhyd Ddu. In fact it did not get there until 2003.

The first track on the old Welsh Highland Railway trackbed was laid at by the CRhE West Midlands Group at Plas Bodaden in November 1999.* A construction siding was laid in at Cae Wernlas Ddu, and a large rail stack was established. *Upnor Castle*

(with a temporary engine shed), DZ wagon no. 1424, and sets of RRM (Roland's Rail Movers) rail grab trolleys were moved there. In addition, the railway's ballast tamper and the pair of self-discharging ballast wagons from South Africa came to the site in early June 2000, followed in 2003 by the FR's Stefcomatic tamper, although it experienced difficulties with the 1:40 grades when operating downhill; if humoured it was effective.

The section between the Rhostryfan Road (**UB25.84**) and Tryfan Junction was the first place where main line track was laid on Phase 2., with 650 metres of track laid in the second week of April by crews working in both directions from Cae Wernlas Ddu. Two gangs of employed tracklayers were at work for about 11 or 12 hours each day. Within a month there was track in place from close to Rhostryfan Road almost as far as Tryfan Junction. Material was brought by road from Dinas to the Dinas side of Rhostryfan Road, so that tracklaying could proceed towards Cae Moel, OB6. The first section of Phase 2 to have its ballast laid was from UB19 back to Cae Wernlas Ddu, followed shortly afterwards, in the opposite direction, by the stretch from Rhostryfan Road to Cae Wernlas Ddu. In each case Jones Bros laid the ballast-bed from the extremities of the section back towards the Cae Wernlas Ddu construction base. The first train through OB14 was on 21st June 2000. The track then stretched from the landslip area just beyond UB27, some 5¼ miles from Caernarfon, two miles to Cae Moel. It was at Cae Moel where the stream was removed from under the bridge, under the track to its own separate culvert.

The connection was made from Dinas when the track joined on 15th July 2000. In the meantime, the railhead was advancing through the landslip area to the temporary ballast stockpile at

---

* **Note:** The 'knowing' will point out correctly, that the old WHR trackbed was joined just outside the old engine shed at Dinas. This was laid in Phase 1.

Cyrnant, about 6 miles from Caernarfon.

Wooden sleepers, donated by Railtrack, were used for the track in Waunfawr Station, the track there was being laid in July 2000. The station opened on 7th August 2000, with only one platform face, and a siding. It was necessary to keep an engine at Waunfawr to shunt the trains. When the loop was installed in September, normal operations began. On 21st September 2000, HMRI gave formal approval of the line Dinas-Waunfawr.

## Phase 3 - the track

There was a pause in tracklaying at the end of Phase 2. Although the Millennium Commission was still urging early completion upon the FR Co., and materials flowed to the next jobs, these were bridgeworks. The first track on Phase 3 was the extension from Waunfawr to UB51, the bridge over the Afon Gwyrfai that lost its NWNG hogsback girder bridge, in favour of a 'pre-owned' BR bridge. There was a stop at that point, first the work in the Aberglasyn Pass had to be completed before any work could start within the National Park boundary at Betws Garmon, secondly tracklaying could not be linear, as UB51, OB53 the road bridge, the work at Bryn Gloch campsite and the moving of a water main, had to be done first, and all that took time. Thirdly an outbreak of foot and mouth disease in February lasted until April, and caused much delay to construction. It was not until November 2001 that more track was laid, and this time it was south to north, from a work base established at Rhyd Ddu.

Phase 3 offered more of a problem to using the trackbed for access. NWNG overbridges required heavy rebuilding: the track had to be lowered to take Garratts; underbridges were obliged to be rebuilt over rivers, for reasons of the age and condition of the abutments, and in order to carry the heavier loads of the 60 tonne Garratts. The time it took to do these jobs regulated where the track could be laid, and when. In addition, in an area where the railway became more remote, and track was not deliverable by rail direct from the rail stack at Dinas, incidental road access became more difficult to arrange. There was always the risk throughout the whole project that if the use of the trackbed for road vehicles was misjudged, with too great a frequency of too heavy loads, then the damage could make tracklaying impossible before it was repaired. A system of depots, fed by the main rail stack at Dinas by road, and careful planning, was the key to the trackwork placement, and in order in which it was done. This was quite unlike the second half of the railway, from Rhyd Ddu to Porthmadog, as will be described later.

Materials needed adding to. The materials available from the Umzinto - Donnybrook line had been delivered to make an impressive 'track mountain' at Dinas. This now needed refreshment. Some 13,500 more sleepers with fasteners were purchased, to supplement the store that had diminished to 2000. The addition offered enough material to reach Rhyd Ddu. A large stock of SAR 'high-inertia' fishplates were obtained, enough to go to Beddgelert. New 30kg/metre rail was rolled in South Africa, enough to reach Rhyd Ddu - 400 lengths of this was delivered to Waunfawr during the last week of April. This was followed by a further consignment of 640 new rails in August 2002, and that was enough to complete Phase 3. Half of the rails in this shipment were bent, because they were not handled properly in RSA. Jan Woods arranged for the damaged rails to be re-rolled in the Midlands, at the shipper's expense. When these rails were returned they went to the appropriate depots for installation.

By early November 2001 a little track was laid from Rhyd Ddu, north, round the corner. This progressed steadily, so that by the end of March the northbound Head of Steel was past the Rhos Clogwyn incline. There was a pause, but at the end of June 2002, tracklaying reached the Glanrafon sidings site, which was then taken over as the work base for Jones Bros to refurbish the Glan yr Afon Bridge.

A work base was established at Snowdon Ranger in late April 2002. In March 2003 the Simplex diesel *Dolgarrog* and its locoshed, made from a container, were moved to Snowdon

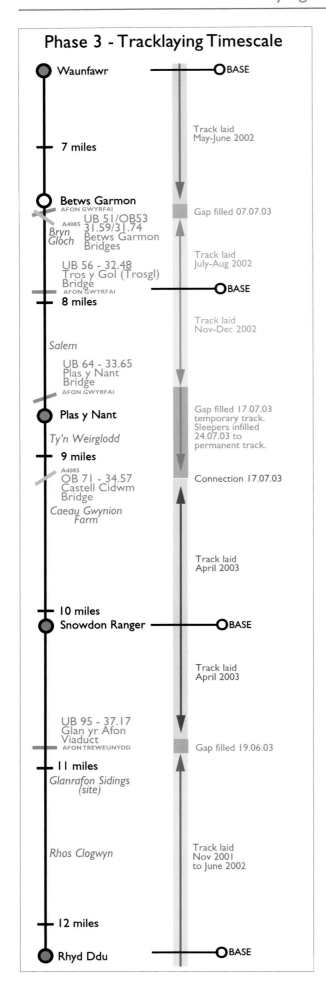

**Phase 3 - Tracklaying Timescale**

Waunfawr — BASE

7 miles

Track laid
May-June 2002

Gap filled 07.07.03

Betws Garmon
AFON GWYRFAI
UB 51/OB53
A4085 31.59/31.74
Bryn Betws Garmon
Gloch Bridges

Track laid
July-Aug 2002

UB 56 - 32.48
Tros y Gol (Trosgl)
Bridge
AFON GWYRFAI — BASE

8 miles

Track laid
Nov-Dec 2002

Salem
UB 64 - 33.65
Plas y Nant
Bridge
AFON GWYRFAI

Plas y Nant

Gap filled 17.07.03
temporary track.
Sleepers infilled
24.07.03 to
permanent track.

Ty'n Weirglodd

9 miles

A4085
OB 71 - 34.57
Castell Cidwm
Bridge

Connection 17.07.03

Caeau Gwynion
Farm

Track laid
April 2003

10 miles
Snowdon Ranger — BASE

Track laid
April 2003

UB 95 - 37.17
Glan yr Afon
Viaduct
AFON TREWEUNYDD

Gap filled 19.06.03

11 miles

Glanrafon Sidings
(site)

Rhos Clogwyn

Track laid
Nov 2001
to June 2002

12 miles

Rhyd Ddu — BASE

Ranger, together with a braked flat wagon. Tracklaying began southwards towards Glan yr Afon in April 2003, using materials from a rail stack established there. The ballast train was moved to Rhyd Ddu in May 2003, with *Conway Castle* and ballast hoppers, ready to bring the ballast up to the correct level for opening as each stage of track was laid and then became available for finishing.

In the second week of April the track reached Glan yr Afon Bridge. The bridge was completed in mid-June 2003 and track was laid across it by June 19th. Tracklaying also began northwards to link up with Castell Cidwm, and by early May the Head of Steel was within sight of Castell Cidwm, and activity switched elsewhere pending the completion of the bridge works at Plas y Nant. Once the track was down on the Castell Cidwm - Rhyd Ddu section there were many jobs to be done that took full advantage of it. *Dolgarrog* was supplemented by the arrival of the WHRL locomotive *Taxi 2*, a Barclay locomotive of 1970.

Meanwhile, further north, the site at Tros y Gol (Trsogl\*), where the NWNG hogsback girder bridge crossing the Afon Gwyrfai (UB56 - ***UB32.48***) was being upgraded and refurbished, provided a good place to work on an intermediate section of tracklaying. The section of track that was laid, in July and early August 2002 north from Tros y Gol through OB54, lay fallow for almost ten months until it made connection with the Waunfawr to Betws Garmon section in early July 2003. Track was laid south towards Plas y Nant bridge as soon as Jones Bros had completed the laying of the ballast, and a rail store south of the bridge was established. Another isolated section of track was then laid in November and December of 2002, whilst the two hogsback bridges were being refurbished. By 6th January 2003, the track had reached the approaches to UB64, the bridge at Plas y Nant. Tros y Gol bridge was finished on 28th March 2003. The tracklaying south from Rhyd Ddu halted near to bridge OB71 (***OB34.57***) at Castell Cidwm in April 2003. On 17th July 2003, the two sections were joined completing the route, and the first train went through on 18th July. Any sleeper gaps were filled in, and the track was made permanent throughout by 24th July 2003.

Excitement rose to fever pitch when it was announced that HRH The Prince of Wales was coming to travel on the railway. So rapid was progress that HMRI was welcomed on 'The Inspector's Train', to make the third of the inspections from Waunfawr to Ty'n Weirglodd Isaf cutting on Saturday 26th July. This train was made up with England locomotive *Prince*, carriages WHR No.23 and FR No.10 The sight was what one would have expected to see on the old WHR - though not in such fine condition. The train proceeded from Waunfawr. It was an excellent photographic opportunity for those who had been tipped off.

The railway was passed, and some snagging work needed to be done. Thus on 30th July 2003, 'The Prince's Train' ran with the same train, and No.24. HRH went on the footplate from Snowdon Ranger on the journey up from Waunfawr to Rhyd Ddu and did some driving. He was rather taken with 'The Old Gent', it having been explained that he was named after his forebear in 1863! The atmosphere was affable, with congratulations for the tasks achieved. Of course the run round loop at Rhyd Ddu had not been finished, and there were a host of other jobs to be done before the railway opened for service. The loop was made short, and the station had one platform face. All deficiencies were attended to later. Public service started on 18th August 2003; the NWNG was open for business again. All that was needed was the simple matter of another 13 miles Porthmadog. This required a few 'bob' to arrange, and would give a mere 13 miles to lay - but until it was arranged, not much new happened, just 'sorting out'.

---

\* Note: Our impeccable Welsh correspondent states: 'The name Tros y Gol is not right. Trosgl the location is correctly 'rough ground' not Tros y Gol, as this would make no sense - literally 'over the Gol' - the river here is the Gwyrfai. The wrong name has arisen from a typo at some time or other.'

*Left*: This is early on 27th October 2001, at the start of Phase 3, with preparations in hand, and the rail stack by the big boulder (Graig Rhwygo Blwmar), outside the Rhyd Ddu station site. The RRM's are ready to go, rails and materials are on site, and the track laying will soon begin at a modest pace towards Rhos Clogwyn, to reach Glan yr Afon Viaduct by June 2002. Note that the NWNG route ran right of the Knicker Ripping Rock, whereas to miss the car park, the restored WHR runs to the left of the rock.
**Andy Keene**

*Right*: Around the corner, you cannot see it, is the reclusive OB62, the road to Pen y Gaer. Behind the camera is the level crossing access to Bryn Afon, back towards Betws Garmon, and the quarry at Salem. This is the last of the light on 6th January 2003, it's winter, and its cold with a darkling sky - excellent for character forming tracklaying.
**WHLR**

*Left*: Tracklaying peeps round the corner, through the Bryn Gloch site. This did not happen until 7th September 2002, and the track came from the Tros y Gol site to the south. This was the effect of the bridge rebuilds, (three within a mile) preventing the job being 'linear'.
**Ben Fisher**

*Right*: The extremely useful little Simplex *Dolgarrog* peeps out of its container 'shed' at Snowdon Ranger. This is a depot, and the arrangements for loading rail can be seen clearly in the left-foreground. The track is running now to the south in this view taken on 12th March 2003.
**WHLR**

*Left*: These things sort of happen by chance, but in suitably horrid weather the track was linked between Rhyd Ddu and Caernarfon by the fixing of these fishplates on 17th July 2003. The job had now to be neatened up with the sleepers put in on the Plas y Nant bridge just down the road. It it was a nice little occasion, perhaps tempered slightly by the water trickling down the back of the neck. But, this is Wales - and all that green doesn't exist with no 'charge'. Now, at least, a rail vehicle could get all the way through to Caernarfon, as required.
**Jan Woods - WHLR**

*The first steam to run over Phase 3 was* Prince, *hauling 'The Inspector's Train', comprising WHR No.23 and FR No. 10. This delightful period piece chuffed up from Waunfawr at a slow speed, stopping as directed by the Inspector. Quite unexpectedly for a July Saturday in this part of Wales, it rained! Somehow this added to the atmosphere of this brand new railway. Plas y Nant bridge hosts its first steam train since 1937.*

*This is some of the first track to be laid on Phase 4, on 22nd January 2006. Behind, the rising flanks of Snowdon; all around are the big hills, cloaked in autumn colours. The gang are working out from Rhyd Ddu with RRM's, with the next lengths of rail ready to be heaved on to the waiting rollers. However, it's 15.00 now and the light is beginning to go. Also it's cold, and rather damp. But they're on the way to Porthmadog!*

## Phase 4 - the track

Phase 4 construction took place from early 2005, and the track was down by the end of 2009. The 13 miles was built steadily enough, with a great deal of variety of track to be put down - including the tramway section through the town of Porthmadog. The Phase 4 section was constructed 'continuously'. This allowed the track to be laid from one end to the other. There were some interruptions , but mostly the gangs were able to keep going. It was here that the major tracklaying records were achieved.

The materials used on Phase 4 were different. Indian sleepers, Polish rail, nylon pads, elastic rail clips (ERC) and the fishplates have all been described. The work began in December 2005, by now there was no namby-pamby notions about foul December weather - everyone knew what it was like. The lengths of rail were spreading outwards on to the ample ballast bed in January 2006. By now the volunteer gangs

*It was important to bring the newly laid track up to the standard that enabled works train to run. The Matisa tamper is seen here on 6th May 2003, near to Pitt's Head, with the ballast plough and ballast hopper wagons.* **WHLR**

were an indispensable feature. They continued to improve in expertise and achievement as time moved on and the Head of Steel progressed. East Anglian Group specialised in providing specialised equipment to make life easier. A piece about them and the equipment follows, but one of their overhauled and converted wagons was already in use on this first section of track, to carry the sleepers to the place they were needed. *Dolgarrog* the diesel was used to head these excursions, as the rail extended out and over the Summit The Rhyd Ddu station layout had also to be completed. By May 2006 tracklaying had curved through Pitt's Head. The recently laid track was top-ballasted and tamped to bring it up to a standard where works trains could run on it. Leaving track 'as laid' invites distortion if run over by all but the lightest weights. The rails, so distorted, acquire a 'memory' from the experience, and become a maintenance nightmare.

The Summit was reached over the weekend

*Left:The FRAMAFER KMX tamper at work at Hafod Ruffydd on 4th May 2007. This machine with its high work capacity is able to tamp 650m of track per day, and does a superb lining and tamping job. Afterwards the track is well consolidated, well supported, and may be run over with confidence.* **WHLR**

*Below The Rest of the World Gang return to the site to install safety fencing at UB133 The McAlpine Bridge. The view looks north up the hill. Under the bridge is the Afon Hafod Ruffyd Isaf. Picture taken on 27th July 2008, after the track had been laid through the site.* **Andrew Thomas**

of June 17-18th. The Rest of the World Gang laid 14 lengths of track over the weekend of July 29-30th, extending the railhead beyond Pont Cae'r Gors cutting. On August 11th, the first pre-curved rails were brought up by train for the sharp Tro Cwm Du, and of course on the sharp curves, the SAR sleepers with gauge widening fastenings were used. On 3rd September 2006, the Tuesday Gang were almost within sight of Hafod Ruffydd, laying in a 180m radius curve that, although it did not require SAR sleepers, was fitted with joints staggered by 9m to ease the strain on the fishplates, thus to keep the curve stable. By September 30th, tracklaying south of Hafod Ruffydd was in progress, reaching the edge of the forest in early October, and negotiating Canal Curve by 14th October 2006, heading north to Weirglodd Isaf. The tracklaying proceeded in wet and cold autumn weather, moving towards the Forest Campsite in late November. The sharp curve past Weirglodd Isaf was recognised as having a critically thin embankment, which was rectified later in 2009. News came back about what a wonderful piece of tourist railway this was, with wide vistas of Snowdon, alternating with deep deciduous forest, and the train snaking over the sharp curves to gain height. Since no one had ever seen it, all had to wait a long while before services could be reinstated. The weather put no one off; as the ballast bed was released, plans were made to lay track on it as soon as possible. The supplies organisation worked smoothly to see that trains of rails, sleepers and fastening were in position for when they

*Above: The Rest of the World Gang, supported by a group from Imperial College Railway Society, grin damply for the camera on the curve they are laying near to Weirglodd Isaf. No one actually believed that this activity is natural behaviour, but it is so much fun that people love to do it! Taken on 22nd October 2006.* **K. Winter**

*Right: Here the Rest of the World Gang preside over the emergence of the track, just over 15 miles from Caernarfon. Behind the camera is UB150 and LC77, and the lead-in to Meillionen Halt. Above is the sharp curve across UB145 and past the level crossing at Weirglodd isaf. This is remote country.* **Jane Ewing**

*Right:On 26th November 2006* Dolgarrog *descends towards Meillionen Halt, having just passed over Coed Mawr level crossing. Rail is being transported slung under a couple of RRMs. As the head of steel advanced, rails laid ready in the 2ft had to be recovered for use, and transported over the newly laid track, ready to be rolled out on to the prepared sleepers. Depending on how rapid the advance was, the distance for* Dolgarrog *to travel may be quite great. She was an invaluable little engine.*        **WHLR**

*Below: Jonathan Hall telephones from Meillionen Halt to describe the extraordinary scene of track returning to a platform, instead of it being the other way round.*        **P. Nock**

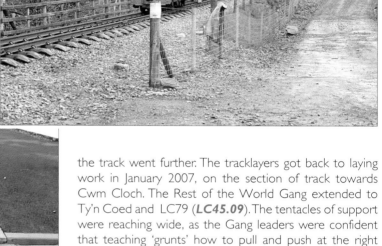

were needed. The track came into the camp site at the end of November, when there was a working party including Permanent Way Institution officials, no less. This would have been a pleasant change for some of the standard gauge members of the group. The track crept steadily over Coed Mawr Crossing and Meillionen Crossing (**LC44.39**) and came on down into the Halt. This was the unofficial target for the year, and it was exceeded by a few rail lengths. Thus some 3½ miles of new track had been restored in one year, which is a good record. However, there would be no services run on the track until the National Park boundary had been reached at Pont Dylif; that was the agreement.

There were many consolidation jobs to be done before

the track went further. The tracklayers got back to laying work in January 2007, on the section of track towards Cwm Cloch. The Rest of the World Gang extended to Ty'n Coed and LC79 (**LC45.09**). The tentacles of support were reaching wide, as the Gang leaders were confident that teaching 'grunts' how to pull and push at the right time was practical. Thus Imperial College Railway Society, and Newcastle University Railway Society, supported the fight against the adversity of Welsh weather to lay lengths of track. It was deeply satisfying work, with the immediate reward of being able to see what had been achieved. The tracklaying pushed on steadily to Cwm Cloch, where pre-curved rails became a necessity. The rails for the 53m curves round the head of Cwm Cloch were sent away to Wolverhampton for

*Above: On 4th February 2007, both works trains bask in bright winter sunshine at the top end of Cwm Cloch Uchaf. Behind the figure on the right can be found the end of the PB&SSR formation, excavated but not used, as its steepness was too much for steam locomotives.*        **D. Waldren**

*Left: The is the end of the straight at Cwm Cloch Uchaf, just before LC82. The Rest of the World Gang are doing their stuff on 11th February 2007, and as can be seen the fine weather has gone After crossing the Afon Nant Cwm Cloch the line curves once more before the steep curve, and deep cutting of Cutting Mawr.*        **Ben Fisher**

*Above: R. Cooper's brilliant stitched panorama of the track as it descends through Cwm Cloch Uchaf shows the whole scene, from the short straight above the level crossing (LC82 - now LC45.70), the bridge over the stream, and the sinuous sweep of the rails descending towards Cutting Mawr. This panorama was taken in July 2007, to illustrate the fence work that had been erected to protect the crossing.*  **R.Cooper**

factory bending. The lead-in, up to LC82 (**LC45.70**), the top level crossing of the site was reached by early February and the track was over stream and level crossing by 17-18th February. The next part was very curvaceous. In a bold move, the railway builders had turned the downhill course of the line through 180°, cutting through the contours, still dropping at 1:48 on the 53m radius part of the curve. The line went from embankment to cutting and back to embankment. The southernmost part of the loop was level with the Goat tunnel entrance. This section needed the pre-curved rails that took up a lot of wagon space, and could not easily be popped into the 2ft, ready for the RRMs. Correct cant and gauge widening was also necessary, so SAR sleepers were used with their fittings that made the gauge adjustable. Special care was given to fishplates and staggered joints, and seating the track firmly. Locomotives ascending would use full power, so this area of track would take a beating.

On 24th March 2007 the Subscribers, who had shelled out £1m so far, visited the works in the first passenger train that had travelled the section on a 'Forest Train' from Rhyd Ddu to the mouth of Cutting Mawr. Push-pull car 1001 on the end of the train allowed it to propel back up the hill to Tro Elain, where No. 138 was attached, for the first steam hauled passenger train over the Summit. Subscriber satisfaction was expressed in the massive collection of funds, and they went away delighted from the first passenger train that had managed to penetrate that far. One should note in passing, the thoughtful process of proceeding at reduced speed, of using the twist tolerant heritage FR stock, employing a light train so as not to distort vertically the newly laid rails, and applying the safety measures of locking people in, and the prohibition at anyone dismounting at the end of the run at Cutting Mawr. Of course the advice of the HMRI was sought before carrying out the operation. The two railways were separated by a locked stop-block in normal course, and train movements were managed most

*Above: The curve into Cutting Mawr needed gauge widening. All the track knowledge gained hitherto was now brought to bear. So the Indian sleepers were substituted by SAR ones, with the fiddly bits involved, and the track was laid with the pre-curved rails from Wolverhampton. This view was taken on 25th February 2007.*  **WHRCL**

*Right: The railway emerges from the depths of cutting Mawr, on to the 53m radius curve that together with the 1:43/1:48 gradient makes even Garratts chuff a lot when climbing this section of track. This view was taken on 18th March 2007.*  **J. Comerford**

carefully in the construction section by operating staff on the ground.

The tracklaying continued over that weekend, and the Black Hand Gang reached through Cwm Cloch Canol on the weekend of April 14-15, followed by a drive to reach Beddgelert. The tracklayers were right up with the laying of the ballast at this point. In the third week of April, deliveries from Dinas included the turnouts for the Station loop and siding. The top end points were placed in position and the track was extended through the station on the eastern (Down) side. The bottom points were laid in, and the first two lengths of track on the Up side were laid on 22nd July 2007. The track was laid through the

*Above: Three trains ran on 24th March 2007. Such an indulgence sprang from the minds of the fundraisers, Andy Savage and Gordon Rushton. There was objection from Paul Bradshaw of the tracklayers, and nervousness from Paul Lewin the General Manager of the railway. This was overcome with negotiation, and promises from the fundraisers that the inconvenience and the lost time of the tracklayers would be more than compensated by the extra money that would be raised from excited punters offered such an immense privilege. This was indeed the case. Not only were subscribers persuaded to extend their periods of subscription, but they gave generously. Much money was raised that day - enough for a few lengths of track!* **Peter Johnson**

*Above: The top points were put in on 23rd April 2007, followed by the bottom points two days later, as the Down side track was laid through the station. The track was laid on wooden sleepers, partly because people thought it looked nicer, partly because they were in stock, through the kindness of Railtrack, who had donated them.* **D. Waldren**

*Left: The KMX tamper is in Beddgelert on 15th May 2007, fettling the track after the top ballast had been put on. There was a particular job for it in the station, it set the precise track alignment so that the contractors could put in the platform edging relative to the track. This was the easy way of dealing with the curved Beddgelert Station site. The turnout in the foreground will be fitted as the siding points.* **WHRCL**

Goat Tunnel on wooden sleepers and round the curve, past the 'bridge to nowhere', but the test train with the SAR van would not fit. There were expensive sounding noises from the roof of the SAR van. A minor amount of rock or concrete shaving was required. As the tunnel roof at this particular point is a bit thin, rather than try to remove shotcrete, it was both easier and safer that the trackbed be scraped out. In addition, some loose rock was removed from beneath, to lower the level of the trackbed in the tunnel. A thinner layer of ballast was put back, and over the weekend of 30th June - 1st July 2007 the line was relaid on the thinner, steel sleepers, with the SAR 'gauge adjustable' sleepers laid appropriately, to allow for the sharp curves beyond the tunnel mouth, and the correct roof clearance was achieved, but as a result the drainage channels were foul of gauge. To bring them 'to gauge', 100mm was removed from the trackside upstand. This was possible without permitting any flooding when it rained. Meanwhile the track was being laid onwards to Bryn y Felin. Outside, there was a necessary rail length puzzle to be solved when it came to joining up the re-sleepered track with the onward laying. The Rest of the World Gang sorted matters out on 14th July 2007. They needed to balance the rail lengths by up to 18 inches (over three lengths), and to avoid a rail join within the transition between different types of sleeper. This was completed on 15th July. By 28th July the Head of Steel reached the roadside at Bryn y Felin,

*Right: On 27th August, the Head of Steel is in the pass. Dolgarrog has just brought down another pair of rails slung under the RRMs. walkers strolling past on the Fisherman's Path looked on with benign curiosity as rails return to this prized part of the Welsh Highland Railway. It is the afternoon of 28th August 2007.* **WHRCL**

*Below: On the previous day, the rails were quite a lot further back. Here the track is being placed in the glittering sunshine of the late afternoon. The faithful Dolgarrog is waiting with more supplies as the rails are cajoled to curve by the experienced tracklayers. In the distance, behind the locomotive is where the railway was planned to go, further up the river side - but never did.* **Peter Johnson**

18 miles from Caernarfon.

## Aberglaslyn - Gatws Bach

By 11th August the tracks were on the bridge over the Glaslyn - this was quite a moment. Crossing the Glaslyn meant entering the Pass of Aberglaslyn, and this was a culmination of purpose. People felt very good. There was a certain amount of hand rubbing with glee about having entered the Aberglaslyn Pass. This was the essence of the WHR, the bit that everyone said they'd come to see. It was 'forbidden' too - but if anyone felt unease about that, they only had to look across at the road. If they had a conscience about spoiling 'quiet enjoyment', they had but to listen to the roar of the river to confirm how it drowned out the groaning traffic.

On Bank Holiday Monday, the tracks were stretching out down the Pass. The rest of the World Gang laid the track steadily right through the Aberglaslyn. The Black Hand Gang reached the first tunnel in the Pass, the 32 yds, Tunnel No.2, on 15th September,. The track was laid through the much shorter 10 yds, Tunnel No. 3 and it was taken onwards by the Territorial Army, and then into T4 on 22nd September by the Rest of the World Gang. The track was just poking out of southern portal of the 306yds Tunnel No. 4 on 10th October 2007, in time for the Trustees train. It poured on the day, but no one minded getting soaked to see progress like this. It had only been

*continued on page 352*

*Above: The track has now entered Tunnel No. 4, 306 yards. All impediment to its replacement has now been removed in this view of 22nd September 2007. Wood sleepers have now given way to steel, and the tracklayers intend to push on as fast as they can, but the ballast has not been prepared very far in front, their rate of working is so rapid.* **WHRCL**

*Left: On the occasion of the visit of the Trustees on 3rd October 2007, the track has been laid through Tunnel No. 4 and is about to poke out of the southern end. A pair of Rail Movers marks the Head of Steel. The railway is now restored right through the Aberglaslyn Pass.*

**H**ow does it happen that human beings become so comprehensively infected with deep and glowing passion for such a little bit of railway in Wales? It has to start somewhere, and here is a clear account of how another poor innocent fell willing victim to those dragons and their beguiling influence. He's trapped now into enjoying the railway and it's beautiful setting for the rest of his days. This is the magic of the Welsh Highland Railway - or perhaps it's a small part of it. Let Jonathan Hall charm you.

**A** dark December day in 2006, the sky the colour of rain washed ink; the sort of day that never gets beyond a kind of murky twilight. And I'm stood by the side of a railway track, in a place I now know as Cwm Cloch, but back then was 'Some Hillside Near Beddgelert'. Some wet hillside. A sudden gust of icy rain has soaked through every single weak point of my new, but no longer clean clothing; my toes are squelching in the new steel toe capped boots, my tee shirt's in a thick clammy ball, somewhere in the small of my back (subsequently it turns out my pants have dyed my nether regions a sinister shade of tangerine; even the few fivers in my wallet are soggy). It's Saturday - Saturday! The time I'm normally sat in the local 'deli on the second cappuccino, doing nothing more stretching than deciding between the book and the big crossword (easy clues). So here I am, one of eight, lifting a rail with these big pincers, realizing for the first time in my life how devilishly heavy a length of narrow gauge rail can be - terrified beyond measure that someone's going to ask me to do something with one of the sinister looking chipped yellow tools, piled up by the track. Cold, wet nervous, and so far out of my comfort zone that I cannot even conceive of what comfort is. But there's something else as well; something totally unexpected, exhilaration. And long ago memories of an old lady I'd met for some five short days, some 36 years previously.

Summer 1970: someone's relative's died, and there's some money. This being 1970, and us being a middle class family, it's spent (partially) on a few days in a 'Nice But Not Outrageous' hotel in Beddgelert, North Wales. In my memory it's one of those enamelled childhood summers, with ladybird book, blue skies and the grass bleached greeny-brown. I'm sure it must have rained, this being North Wales, but I don't remember it. And just a short walk from the hotel in this rocky valley with a bridge across a river - just like the Airfix bridge I'd got the previous Christmas. Also, there's a bump in the land; a long, smooth bump, that went one way under the road into weedy nothingness, and the other up the rocky valley.

'Trains used to run there', I was told in the lovely soft Welsh voice of Jane the Chambermaid.

She seemed very old at the time but was probably no more than sixty. I liked Jane - I remember that too. I remember her candy pink plastic dustpan and brush, her beige housecoat, and her plastic apron with blue anchors on it. And her voice. The voice that taught me how to say the Welsh for 'good morning' and 'thank you' and 'Wales for ever'. She told me about this railway; how

trains ran there when she was little. Short, rocking, stumpy trains, that went so slow the boys used to jump off them, and race them, and jump back on again. Trains that disappeared up that rocky valley or down into a big long tunnel and away to the big town of Portmadoc.

That was the start of it. Over the next thirty-six years I found out more, and more, and more: more facts, more knowledge, overlain book by book, photo by photo, black and white pictures of short stumpy engines on wonky, weedy tracks. My favourite was the Baldwin - the easiest to draw. I still come across Biroed images of it when I'm throwing out – it steams forever on those wonky weedy tracks; school jotters, uni-notebooks, staff meeting files, production notes, OFSTED folders. Underneath all of that, under those books and plans and slide shows and drawings: there's a river bridge with the rails leading up the valley and a soft Welsh voice whispers 'Trains used to run there.' A lost world - gone forever.

Amazingly, unbelievably, I heard that they'd started to rebuild it!

*Jonathan and Co. rolling down to the Head of Steel, with all materials in tow.*
**Ynys Bersen**

Of course I had to go there; I had to be a part of that. This notion emerged, like going to the gym, learning Spanish, really reading the Sunday papers - comfortable, pleasant intention, nothing more. I couldn't imagine doing anything more than logging on to the websites, maybe watching from the side of the road (if it wasn't raining). Laying actual railway track? I don't think so; surely you needed to be something for that- have some qualification of some kind? What this would be I wasn't sure, but some level above fitting light bulbs and putting up shelves (I did it once. They sagged at both ends, and subsequently in the middle.).

The first thing I did at work was log onto Ben and Barrie's website. So I saw all these places from my mind's library of black and white photographs slowly transformed from jungle, to mud, to building site, to railway track - Dinas, Tryfan (totally the opposite way round to how I'd always imagine it) Waunfawr. I knew the days of that mythical grassy bump in the ground were numbered.

Here I'd love to be able to say there was some moment, some epiphany, but it wasn't like that. The kindness of a lady from the ticket office at Porthmadog in delivering my Superpower tickets (driving out to Beddgelert on her way home) allowed me to see Palmerston gently steaming under the trees at Cwm Cloch. I stood at Rhyd-Ddu staring at the newly gravelled trackbed, stretching off to Pitts Head and the love stealthily took a firmer hold.

One night sat in a pub with my mate Nocky, he said something like 'Do you fancy having a go one weekend?', and I said something like 'Yes'. So we went.

Not just like that - not at all. Stepping out of your comfort zone takes a fair amount of nerve and organization, buying suitable clothing, phoning people, arranging accommodation. But on one weekend we were in the car and driving to North Wales. Me, fully expecting to be sent back before the end of Saturday as incompetent. But I didn't; I ended up on 'Some Hillside Near Beddgelert', in the pouring rain, aligning rail joints. And a whole raft of weekends followed on from that one in cold, wet December. In my memory they all merge into each other- wet ones, dry ones, ones where they couldn't start *Upnor Castle*, ones where we ran out of rail clips. It's hard to single them out now but I think of three things:

## 1. The wonderful team of people.

Of course no one laughed at me. No one even noticed - or if they did they weren't bothered. There were plenty of people all raring and eager to use those sinister tools; they were more than happy for me to lift and shove and push, as directed, working together as a team. Corporations pay huge sums of money to send their staff on team building weekends; they missed a trick with the Welsh Highland. After 20 of us laid down seventeen lengths of track in one weekend, I was ready to put those people in my will!

I remember fragments of the conversations as we pushed, and dragged, and clipped, and greased. The one way system in Stafford (a joke apparently) 'Last of the Summer Wine', any good since Compo died?: discuss. Whether *Merddin Emrys* would explode the minute she hit the gradients above Beddgelert.

Coming from a working life where every conversation seem to be focused, high powered, important: SATs, budgets, data and test results, coming from an environment when every time I entered a room someone expected me to be in charge and to know what was happening, and what they should be doing - it was bliss. I was so used to opening a door, striding in with purpose, and saying 'right' in cheerful yet purposeful tones; now I was the lowest of the low, pushing and clipping and lifting as directed. When I wasn't needed, I either chatted, or sat on a pile of sleepers and read my book, or ate midget gems, or looked at the hills, until I was needed, and someone told me what to do. And then I did it, and when it was done, I sat down on my pile of sleepers again. I never realised how blissful a hot shower and thick medicated shampoo could be. I never realised how good it was to have aching limbs because I'd been using them all day; how good it was sitting in a pub with a pint, talking about nothing much, putting the world to rights. Being in a team - we're designed for it.

## 2. The moving Head of Steel

That first time, when there were only eight of us, we were just aligning joints (I can use phrases like that now, and know what they mean. I like to do it at parties and impress people.) On the Sunday, when we'd done, someone said 'let's go down to the Head of Steel'. I remember I felt a thrill at the words. That phrase - there was something about it, a mystic sort of ring, like it'd be guarded by Orcs, or elves, or something. So we all piled into the 2 wagons behind *Dolgarrog*, and rattled and jolted our way down, through curves and 'S' bends, through trees and across hillsides, along that track that I'd only ever know as a bump in the earth, or a line in

a book. Somewhere by Beddgelert Forest camp site we stopped. A primrose yellow triangle was bolted to the track, looking flimsy and toy-like (but was in fact steel, and heavy, and meant finger squashing business). Beyond that, padlocked together, were yellow trolleys; things I now know of as Rail Movers (and can now be added to my list of light bulbs and paint brushes as things I can operate.) And after that, the rusty track lost its 2 foot symmetry, and widened; one track stretched beyond the other - and it all stopped. It came to an end. Off into the distance along the side of the camp site was a neat track of gravel, and an isolated station platform.

This was the Head of Steel - and now there was an important point to Ben and Barries' websites. Monday morning, log on and find out: where had the Head of Steel advanced to? How many lengths had the other teams managed to lay? And on John Sreeves's map I watched, week by week, as the line turned from red (disused railway), to blue (prepared trackbed), to green (track). It was like a very slow Blue Peter Totaliser.

*The head of Steel in December 2007 - of course it was in a different place on most days - that was the fun of it!*

Leaving the track on Sunday teatime I'd take a moment to see how far we'd come. How much railway line was there, where before there'd been a gravelly track? And think - there was only ever going to be that brief moment in time- that week- when the Head of Steel would be where it was.

## 3. The rides of joy along the new line.

That first time, when we all piled on those two wagons - it was like being a kid- I mean surely, surely, someone was going to come and stop us? They couldn't really let eight men clamber into two wagons behind a diesel that reminded me a bit of my Mother's old sewing machine? But they did, and every chance I got I rode on that train.

I'm lucky; I know. For most people, their first- maybe their only- trip on the Welsh Highland will be on a comfy padded seat, or a wooden slatted one, possibly with someone selling them a guide book, maybe with a plastic cup of tea and a wrapped piece of cake. They'll see the places, the views; identify them in the book, perhaps photograph them or film them. But they won't know them like I do: the corner where the sleepers fell off the wagon; the straight where *Dolgarrog* slipped to a stand, and had to be pushed; the curve through the trees where the rail movers went AWOL. They won't know the exhilaration of clinging to a pile of elastic rail clips, bumping down (or up) a hill as an engine coughs and barks and chokes, and the wind slaps your face. You've never known a railway 'till you've worked on it: 'till you've aligned its rails, clipped its track, cut its vegetation, and unclogged its drains. I know the Welsh Highland; I know its curves and ditches, its views and shelters, its cuttings and gradients. I've seen the sun set over its autumn colours, and a deep, silver frost turn its rails white. Those names, the marks on the map in Boyd, are now overlaid with views and memories. And somewhere under all this wonderful, unbelievable new world of *Lyd* at Beddgelert, K1 on Britannia Bridge, Fairlies at Bryn y Felin and photo specials to Rhyd-Ddu - somewhere under all of that, there's this soft Welsh voice telling me: 'Trains used to run there'. ∎

**K**nowledge is a wonderful thing - and the techniques needed to lay 25 miles of narrow gauge track were not available before the restoration began. The story here is that these people found out how to do it, as part of a wonderfully loose organisation with extremely clear aims. Volunteers were instrumental in relaying the track of the WHR. They did it rapidly and efficiently in two major gangs, that drew their members from all walks of life. Mike Fisher offers a few stories from the Rest of the World Gang.

**A**lthough the Rest of the World Gang (ROWG) first appeared during the initial stage of track laying at Rhyd Ddu, once Phase 4 got off the ground, its roots lay in the experience and knowledge of the techniques used in the laying of narrow gauge railway track gained by individuals in the earlier phases of construction. Some of these early members were FR Deviationists. Perhaps the term Deviationist should be explained since the facts are important in understanding the ethic of this new Welsh Highland track laying team. "Deviationist" was the name given to the individuals who in the '60s designed and started building to bypass the old Moelwyn Tunnel which had been severed at its top end by the new power station lake. They included the civil engineering earthworks, initially with little or no mechanisation. Typically these individuals were young, often undergraduates, who came for the fresh mountain air, the work, but perhaps above all, the camaraderie associated with a seemingly impossible objective. I won't mention the remote bunk house which they also constructed! Quite a few had no interest in railways or the FR in particular. So, when the news of the grant of money for Phase 4 construction became public there was a core of volunteers with the Deviationists' ethic ready for work. However, the money came with strings, a time limit for completing the steel through to Porthmadog, and more volunteers were needed, thus ROWG came into being, led by Paul Bradshaw. They worked every alternate weekend with the Black Hand Gang. Later, working weeks became established for the benefit of those who came from further afield.

Volunteer time sheets contributed to the matched funding and volunteers came forward in their hundreds. Attendance was open to all (with a minimum age limit), subject to completion of a registration and health form, with attendance at a very thorough safety briefing, invariably given on the morning of first appearance. There are 596 registration forms on file, though 459 have actually had briefings, and have by implication worked. The attractions for the work were in many ways similar to those of the earlier pioneers, but there was one startling difference.

Whilst the Deviationists were young adults, Phase 4 volunteers were on average much older. ROWG was not affiliated to the CRhE and the group was not formally constituted in any way. Like the Deviationists before them, some recruits had no railway interest at all.

ROWG participants did, as the name suggests, come from all over the world as well as all over the UK. They were new to the project in the majority of cases. Travel to North Wales and the need for accommodation represented a considerable financial commitment, so there was always an unstated but demonstrable wish to get things done, so as not to waste this investment. Thus the reputation for long hours and hard work was realised as panels of track laid, and the good natured grumbling when occasionally the logistics failed, or alternative work was required. Often, it was the seemingly slower progress of the contractors working ahead preparing the formation and laying ballast that stopped work. On one occasion sleepers were being placed one by one, as each new metre of levelled ballast appeared behind the retreating JCB, just to get that extra panel. The volunteers never let the Project down.

Working above Beddgelert brought a number of problems as the track advanced; the 1 in 40 gradient was one, with its risk of run-aways. Stop blocks were used above all critical crossings, and unbraked wagons were always placed uphill of

*The ROWG laying in the loop at Hafod y Llyn on 3rd May 2009. Although there was to be a 'supply' depot set up here, the loop needed to be laid to expedite it, thus stuff still had to come from afar, but not for much longer/*     S. Melhuish

the loco, usually *Dolgarrog*. Then there was the longer and longer distance travelled every day from Rhyd Ddu, taking up precious construction time, though riding on the wagons on top of boxes of equipment or more uncomfortable bags of clips was always considered one of the perks of the job. Finally there were the struggles laying the curved track, initially using straight rail, sometimes with the free end protruding over the edge of the embankment before the pre-curved rails appeared. Where there may be staggered joints there is only one way that we know of in this situation to get the job done. That is to get the sleepers roughly in position, pull out a rail, then mark the correct sleeper positions with chalk; jack the rail, and get the sleepers into correct spacing. Then insert the ERC) and try to get alignment. For the uninitiated, the track is laid to surveyor's marks, nails on the top of wooden pegs set every 10m to the

*The Rest of the World Gang outside T1, the Goat Tunnel, at Beddgelert on 26th April 2007, on the first time this track was laid!*

watching the curious passengers, when a cry was heard from the open coach "Look! There's a woman!" I think the woman in question was pleased to be recognised as such, as she is usually found well-disguised with track grease.

The working week, taking the steel through Beddgelert station, was arguably one of the most incident packed weeks. We started by extending the track down from the lower Cwm Cloch crossing, and the day was blessed with persistent heavy rain. Water had to be emptied from our boots at the day's end. Then at the station approach we entered the worksite of William Hughes, the construction company contracted to build the station infrastructure. Their site, their rules! So a large cardboard box arrived, containing hard hats, a requirement of the site's strict safety regime. Riding on wagons was not allowed and I think the mixed-sex gang was regarded with some suspicion, as a sort of loose cannon. In the end, though, I think we earned the foreman's respect. There was a little added pressure to the proceedings as the General Manager had arranged for a visiting steam locomotive, the "quarry Hunslet" *Velinheli* to appear for a publicity event, and we had to have the track in place for this to happen - all of this on wooden sleepers not used by the gang before. Paul had (unwisely?) made a promise, back at the top of the hill that he would buy everyone an ice cream when we reached Beddgelert, and he was a good as his word. I think the villagers were a little surprised by the large contingent of individuals queuing at the shop dressed in very dirty HiViz clothing. *Velinheli* duly arrived on cue, and the station took on a festival atmosphere with local school children and parents invited to see the first steam engine in the station for 65 years, and to listen to a welcome from Lord Dafydd Elis Thomas. At the end of the week we reached the site where the bottom station point was waiting for us, having been craned in. It was in the wrong place and there was considerable discussion about how to move it. A mass crowbar event had failed. In the end it was the toppling jack trick that got it in place correctly. Both gangs have since become experts at moving points, but that is another story. Finally we reached the Goat Tunnel entrance.

side of the track, and an offset from those to the edge of the nearest rail. All this to the nearest millimetre. You try this on a tight curve! Get one point right against the peg and the others drift. There was in consequence a frequent, but slightly unpopular call for "Everyone on crowbars please", from Paul, going back and forward over the newly laid track. Get it wrong and the problems multiply rapidly.

All this said, ROWG was notorious for innovation. Once past Nantmor and its reinforced earth embankment, the track straightens out and many of the difficulties disappear. The construction base moved to Hafod y Llyn. Time was getting short to completion, and with the grant money at risk, extra working weeks were organised. ROWG carried out experiments to improve the daily panel rate by carrying out a process review and eliminating unnecessary steps, in short adopting a "Get it right first time" approach. Various odd items of homemade equipment served to this end, including builder's line, a sleeper spacing chain, a laser with sighting boards, and finally an accurate steel wire with sleeper spacing marks, to place sleepers exactly where they needed to be, so that rails could just be dropped in and clipped up. Job done! This approach was why the daily count of panels continued to rise, up to the last push to Traeth Mawr, when an observer remarked that he had timed one panel every 15 minutes - then we ran out of rail.

A project like this will obviously have had a big impact on some memories, none more so than the characters themselves coming as they did from all walks of life, near and far. The comedians, the back room experts, professionals, tradesmen, the quiet ones with responsible jobs that just welcomed a chance at a manual job requiring no brain power, or responsibility as relaxation, some out of work but wanting to keep their hand in, and of course the ladies. Little incidents stand out, like the time we were working trackside with the trains in service. Clearing the track for a slow, passing train, we were leaning on our tools,

It has been stated that permanent way is far from permanent. Constant maintenance is required, and ROWG, now much slimmed down, is still involved with that maintenance. Above all for those taking part in this project, it has been great fun, and many good friends have been made. New volunteers are always welcome. There's so much to do, even more track to put down one day perhaps! ■

The Ffestiniog family of Society Area Groups enjoys a long history of organising homework projects. These enable members who find it difficult to visit the railway to contribute in a practical way, and in keeping with this tradition, the East Anglian Group (EAG) of the Welsh Highland Railway Society formed a project group with exactly the same aim.

The East Anglian Group became involved in homework projects in a rather unusual way. Committee member Richard Watson lives not far from the Mid Norfolk Railway station at Yaxham, the location of a steam engine repair business based in the former goods shed. In 2002 he asked permission to look around, and when inspecting the traction engines and a Kerr Stuart "Joffre" 0-6-0T spotted a strangely familiar boiler in the brambles. When he asked about it he found that it was part of a Baldwin 4-6-0T belonging to the Imperial War Museum (IWM).

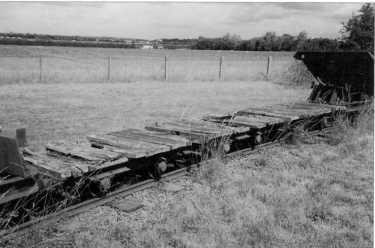

*How it all started (1). The boiler in the undergrowth*

The boiler had been sent by the IWM for assessment but unfortunately was found to be beyond repair. As the IWM had no funds available for a replacement work on the locomotive had stopped. The engine was the same type as 'old WHR' No. 590, so Richard's interest was aroused particularly as he knew that work had been done to restore the chassis. He contacted the museum with an offer to buy the engine for private preservation, but was met with a polite refusal as an agreement had already been made to lend it to the Welsh Highland Heritage Railway at Gelert's Farm! The museum said however that it was minded to dispose of its 2 foot gauge railway, and would be prepared to dispose of it to a bona fide organisation completely free of charge. The IWM had originally planned to re-create a Word War I trench railway at Duxford, complete with Baldwin but this had come to a halt due to a change of policy, one of the factors being that an aviation fuel tank farm had been built across the trackbed.

This was a most unusual offer so Richard lost no time in arranging a visit to assess what was available. The railway itself comprised about 400 yards of light rail with ERC clips, in the form of a plain line ending in a balloon loop. The working Simplex locomo-

tives had already departed for pastures new, but there were some home built passenger coaches, a number of skips and several flat wagons.

The offer was of course very generous, but on reporting our assessment to the FR Co it was decided that the majority of the materials were not really suitable for further use. Four small Hudson flat wagons had potential, however, so they were acquired for use on Phase 4 Construction. We contacted the local area group at the Lynton & Barnstaple, who said they'd be pleased to receive the remaining track and rolling stock, so a joint working party was set up with the L&B. The track lifting and vehicle recovery exercise must count among the more unusual in preservation history. The railway at Duxford was located on an operational airfield so our party needed special permission to work "Air Side". Richard as party leader was responsible for safety and was given a 2-way radio (Call Sign: "Railway One") to allow contact with the Control Tower. During work to recover rails and sleepers, we often looked up from our labours to watch vintage aircraft such as the B-17 Flying Fortress ("Sally B"), and Spitfires taking off and landing. Wonderful stuff! We also investigated a stack of rails only to find an enormous badger sett right under the stockpile.

Thus began a project group known as the "EAGles"

*How it all started (2). The Duxford wagons 'as found'.*

(ouch), and our small band of volunteers has been meeting at monthly intervals ever since. We've been very fortunate as our member, Rob Blackmore, very generously allows us the use of his premises at Mill Green, near Cambridge for our project work. Camaraderie with friendly banter, sparkling wit and repartee are the order of the day, and are to us (nearly) as important as actual work......

*Left: The Beddgelert station sign, and this together with signs at Meillionen (Forest Camp Site), Nantmor and Waunfawr, are all proud products of group projects.*

*Below: No.5003 the day it was completed, 22nd August 2011. It stands under cover - probably the last time it will be pampered until it is rebuilt again!*

Following a degree of head scratching we set to, restoring and modifying the trucks, raising the chassis level and converting them from side to centre buffers. Four neat little wagons emerged, and these were taken to the railway in good time for the start of track laying on Phase 4 beyond Rhyd Ddu. The vehicles carried people, sleepers and a multitude of other materials and were used extensively with the Simplex diesel *Dolgarrog* over nearly the whole line between Rhyd Ddu and Britannia Bridge.

In 2005 we were asked to make a number of station name boards for locations between Waunfawr and Pont Croesor. The initial request for nine signs expanded to thirteen in all, and many hundreds of man hours were spent in our workshops at Mill Green and Colkirk, near Fakenham. (The last named was quite literally, "homework") The specification called for a box section of treated timber battens, with a facing of a commercial polystyrene sheet material known as Foamalux. The initial signs were covered on both sides with signmakers' black vinyl, but as self-coloured black Foamalux became available the need for vinyl was eliminated.

Soon after we moved in at Mill Green, one of our members went around the back of the building to answer a 'call of nature'. He was confronted by the completely coincidental, and amazing sight of four large ex-Royal Navy 2'6" gauge flat wagons in storage. The neighbouring timber merchant had bought them on a whim at auction, and we later found they were available for sale. They still bore signs of their former ownership, the Royal Naval Armaments Depot at Beith in Ayrshire, and were of nominal 5-ton capacity. Though much modified by their previous owners – we believe they had once been covered vans – they were nevertheless in fair condition. With the approval of the FR Co. we negotiated their purchase and the first task was to have the wheel sets re-gauged and profiled to FR standards. This was done by the Talyllyn Railway at Pendre, and Roger Thacker kindly

*5001, the tamper runner, with the KMX at Dinas.*

provided transport in both directions. When he returned to pick them up they were brought down to Tywyn Wharf by a double headed diesel 'special' with our wheels safely inside a wagon. A Bobcat loader made short work of transferring them to his van and they returned safely to Mill Green. The railway asked for the first wagon to be completed as a runner vehicle for the KMX tamper-liner. Designated no. 5001, the vehicle is used for carrying tools and other items as the tamper itself has no significant spaces for stowage. It is also important to keep the operating cabs and their electronics free from clutter and grease.

The rebuild of No. 5001 was relatively straightforward as frame widening and vacuum brakes were not required, though chopper couplings did form part of the specification. The wagon left our site for the WHR in October 2006 brightly painted in 'digger' yellow (to complement the KMX), and has been in use ever since with the tamper. It lacks continuous brakes so has special dispensation to run with the KMX – on condition safety chains are used in addition to the normal chopper couplings.

At the time of writing we had just completed a two-car Lineside Clearance train for use on the 40-mile railway. Close consultation with the Outdoor Engineering Department of the FR resulted in the design, intended to help removal of overhanging trees and boscage. This involves two of the Royal Navy flat wagons, rebuilt

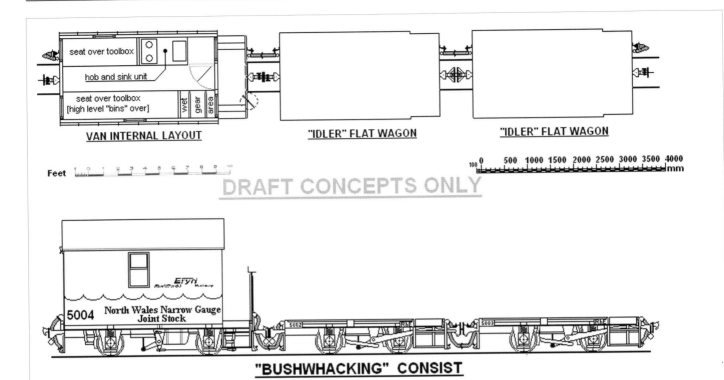

VAN INTERNAL LAYOUT     "IDLER" FLAT WAGON     "IDLER" FLAT WAGON

seat over toolbox

hob and sink unit

seat over toolbox [high level "bins" over]

wet gear area

Feet

DRAFT CONCEPTS ONLY

"BUSHWHACKING" CONSIST

5004   North Wales Narrow Gauge Joint Stock

Eryri

Rev C: 18/03/09 trainpipe now to "Snowdon" side, 5003 'mirrored'
Rev B: 17/09/08 To current thoughts
Rev A: 08/06/08 wagon numbers corrected to build sequence     Rev D : 26/03/09 updated to current requirements
TRH 13/02/07
© EAG CRhE    Was EAG Sk/07/HH/001L - renumbered 07/05/08    *Drawing: Roger Hornsby*

Sk/des/bw/016D

with widened frames, to enable the deck to be built out to the full width of the FR loading gauge.

The trucks are the first of their type to be equipped with vacuum brakes. Modifications were necessary to permit former FR vacuum cylinders to be shoehorned between the frames, with through train pipes and hoses fitted for running as a matched pair. The vehicles are equipped with universal couplings between the wagons, to enable them to 'sandwich' specialist FR stock such as the 'Cherry Picker'. The couplings were built from scratch by Roger Hornsby; the outer ones being normal FR chopper type, fabricated from parts supplied by the railway. As the original drawbars were missing, the opportunity was taken to make and fit new drag boxes below frame level to bring them to the standard FR/WHR coupling height.

The final vehicle will be rebuilt as a mess van at the original suggestion of Mike Hart, and we will naturally consult closely with the end users on its final design. This project will be even more ambitious as the frames and wheelbase are to be lengthened by about two feet with an enclosed body fitted. A balcony is likely

*The two idler flat wagons at Dinas during the 2011 Superpower. Braked, roller bearing, modern wagons like this are a real asset on the WHR.*

to be included to allow tree pruning, and we expect to provide storage spaces beneath seats to allow for strimmers and long handled loppers. There will be places to hang wet waterproofs to allow them to dry off.

The drawing above shows how the mess van might look. We are learning fast about carriage construction – if the FR Society Midland Group did it in 1964 with van No.51, then so can we...... the East Anglian 'can do' attitude is, we think, proving useful to the Welsh Highland Railway and we hope to achieve even more in future. Thus the two wagons will have a running mate, ready for the time when the boscage needs to be cut back - it's already growing! ■

**EAGLes Past and Present**
**Nobby Clark**, retired automotive engineer, K1 a speciality
**John Edgar**, man with a land rover and trailer
**Roger Hornsby**, retired construction engineer and welder extraordinaire
**Mark Neilson**, EAG chairman and scrap metal cash converter
**Tom Skinner**, Boston Lodger, sometime Prince rebuilder, and metal shaper
**Micky Smith**, man of many skills and luxuriant beard
**Roger Thacker**, a man with a van and transporter of bits
**Keith Thomson**, IT expert, photographer and all rounder
**Bob Turner**, Transport planner and painter-in-chief
**Richard Watson**, organiser and general gopher.

*The track on steel sleepers advances steadily southwards to the Tunnel No. 2 on 15th September 2007 - a nice panoramic view!* **Martins Kreicis**

*Left: The Railway drops from the hills on to the flatlands. It does so in dramatic fashion. Here's the bit on the uphill journey where the locomotives are first called upon to exert their power, a short piece of 1:70, that stiffens almost immediately to 1:40. For the most part, that gradient obtains for the next four miles. This is the transit from 'easy' to 'hard' times. The groves of trees, naked in winter have survived the reinstatement of the railway. It already looks a mature scene, and on 21st December 2007 it hadn't yet even been tamped.*

*Below: Further down the hill the telephoto lens reveals the differences in the levels of the freshly laid tracks that would not be tamped until the attentions of the KMX Tamper came to them on February 13th 2008. The siding can be seen clearly, with a wagon of supplies, and 'Plas Dolgarrog', for the locomotive that was, alas, out of service. This picture was taken on the same day as the previous one.*

on August 10th that G H James Cyf, the contractor, had taken over the tunnel and had laid the ballast bed just after the floor had been lowered. The nice thing about this work was how much the volunteer gangs were enjoying doing it, and the friendly rivalry between them to get lengths of track laid down. Plus the time all counted in the grant claim. Soon the Pass was completed and the ballast hopper came down to put the top ballast in. The Welsh Highland Railway had returned to recreate its most famous view, and that was a fine thing indeed.

The track was across the Cwm Bychan bridge and into Nantmor Cutting, up as far as the limit of ballast near the crossing on 6-7th October 2007. The KMX tamper was there, later, consolidating the track for use. The track was laid over the Nantmor OLC (Open Level Crossing) and through the site of the 'halt to be' by 10th October. They were down the hill and almost on to the flat by the end of the weekend of 17-18th November. This abrupt change from the Welsh Flatland Railway to the Welsh Highland Railway has always been remarked, especially as the sudden rise of the embankment, first 1:70 and then to 1:40 could be viewed from the snaking A4085 as it comes over the hump from Garreg. Here was the track now, approaching Hafod y Llyn, a place that was to be used as a temporary turnback loop for services right through from Caernarfon, nearly 20 miles back. There was no intention to make Hafod y Llyn a halt, other than to turn back trains on a temporary basis. This was not intended for public service. That would be better at Pont Croesor, with its road crossing and at

*Above: At Hafod y Llyn, Mr Dafydd Thomas gets down to it whilst track-laying. They are joining two lengths of rail: lining them up; adjusting the gap to the correct value; greasing the rail behind where the fishplate will go, and then bolting on the fishplates.* **J Comerford**

*Right: By the year end, the Head of Steel had moved on to Hafod y Llyn Isaf, next to Ynys Ferlas. Behind the camera after another squiggle, the road finally turns in to the farm and the line curves on to the Ynysferlas bridge (UB51.98) over the Afon Nanmor. The picture was taken in 21st December 2007.*

Upnor Castle *brings a ballast train to 'top-fill' the track, in preparation for tamping. Behind, glorious in the wan, winter sunshine on 10th February 2008, is the impostor Cnicht on the left, and Moelwyn Mawr on the right. Behind* Upnor Castle *is the Romanian ballast wagon that permits ballast to be dropped with precision. Following, are two ballast wagons for dropping ballast either side of the rails, the SAR tool van, and push-pull trailer 1001.*
**Ben Fisher**

Nantmor, with the village nearby. Hafod y Llyn was to enjoy a brief moment of glory, and then to become a siding-loop. It was also useful as a depot for storing materials, temporarily, as while the track progressed southward, all was being hauled in either from Rhyd Ddu or Dinas. On 23rd November the siding was put in, and the track surged onwards. Once it was in, then the trains started arriving with supplies to this location, that was also road served, and out of the way.

Sadly the much loved and very much used *Dolgarrog* suffered serious mechanical failure, and had to go to Dinas. *Upnor Castle* returned from repair in December to be based at Hafod y Llyn. There was a working party over the festive season that happened to be blessed with good weather. The turkey-fuelled effort was to propel the track to the Afon Nanmor bridge. The method used was to lay the rails in across the bridges first, then connect the track to them. This made sure the bridge track was where it should be. The bridge was duly renamed Pont Ynysferlas, (UB196 - **UB51.98**). This avoids mis-identification between Nanmor and Nantmor. On Saturday 26th January the Rest of the World Gang, together with the Imperial College Railway Society, and the FR Dee and Mersey Group, managed to lay fourteen track panels. This moved the tracklaying through the old Ynysferlas Halt, and that weekend the all-time record of 21½ panels was

made, with the track reaching a point 18m short of the Afon Dylif bridge. The achievement was all the more impressive as there was no *Dolgarrog*, it was still poorly, and *Upnor Castle* was not as yet permitted to cross Pont Ynysferlas. So there was much humping by hand and RRMs. The track had then to be laid on the bridge and connected back to the Head of Steel.

On the next working party, 4th February 2008, a neat little Lister diesel locomotive had been borrowed for the track to reach another milestone. The railway was finally laid out of the Snowdonia National Park, and this triggered the possibility of running service to Beddgelert from Caernarfon. The Tuesday Gang were busy, erecting signs on the level crossings that had

*Above*: The track makes a curve to the south, on to Pont Dylif (**UB52.63**) on 27th January 2008. The track went down at the weekend, the contractors advanced the trackbed ballast in the week, as though it were symbiosis.
**Ben Fisher**

*Right*: The land-take on the curve past Croesor Junction was just outside the limits of deviation. Land was purchased to accommodate a wide, sweeping curve, that will eventually allow trains round with no reduction of speed. This picture shows the gangs at work on 9th March

**Left:** *Ever hopeful, the sterling test over crocks of gold at the end of rainbows was conducted at Pont Croesor using professional equipment in March 2008, alas the dig was fruitless, though a drain was found and repaired.* Upnor Castle *and works train stands on the curve. It is a nice alignment, with full line speed expected. The purchase of the extra bit of land to allow this was money well spent.* **T Evans**

**Below:** *Ynysfor Level Crossing roadway was laid in on 31st March as an isolated piece of track. As a simple installation it got its LC Order first on Phase 4 in November 2008. Construction revealed evidence of the old WHR, with sleeper marks in the roadway. The new track reached it in the first week of April, and then swept past into the distance.*

**WHRCL**

been created, and then they concentrated on laying track. on 12th February, onwards from Pont Afon Dylif. The Black Hand and Rest of the World Gangs advanced the track over the next two weekends to the start of the diversion past Croesor Junction. By the beginning of March, the track had come round the curve and on Monday 10th March a new daily record of fifteen panels was made, taking the track to Gatws Bach (**53.96**). They were closing in on the contractor's ballast work, when there was a stop for Easter 2008.

## Ynysfor - Traeth Mawr

Ynysfor Level Crossing, LC112 (**LC54.67**), had track laid in by the Rest of the World Gang on 31st March 2008. Brief reminiscences were on hand when excavation of the road revealed old WHR sleepers at a level corresponding with the new ballast bed level. James had stripped the organic matter from the trackbed in January, and a piece of embankment had to be replaced near to Pont Croesor. The gaps in the ballast either side of this crossing were filled in as far as Pont Croesor and this facilitated the April 2008 tracklaying week.

For perhaps the first time on the restoration project some sort of normality was achieved in tracklaying, in that the route here was flat and nearly straight! Ten lengths were laid on Monday April 7th 2008, the first day of the April tracklaying week - one length in the morning and nine after a rail delivery from Dinas arrived at 12.15. Sleepers were brought down from Hafod y Llyn by the Lister, and contractors James Cyf were also placing sleeper bundles further south. There was a danger with this competent gang that they would run out of track materials, and so it was ensured that further sleeper and rail deliveries made to the site on the 8th provided all the main materials needed for the week.

The daily tracklaying record was broken on Tuesday, 8th April 2008, with 20 panels laid in a day. This took the Head of Steel to within sight (and smell) of Pooh Corner. Ten panels had half their clips fitted on the day, as these ran short and deliveries were awaited. Forty volunteers were present in total for this massive 'rail bash'. The extremely productive gang included apprentices from Network Rail and graduates from Grant Rail. They certainly got on with the job.

Fencing between the road and railway also started on the 8th April 2008, and James Cyf were in the process of tidying and vacating the LC112 compound. By the end of the day the fencing contractors had installed all the fence posts on the roadside session, and wire was being strung.

The remaining ERC clips were added to the track on the 9th, and the gang went on to lay another fifteen lengths, which almost brought the rails as far as Pont Croesor. The final length to connect with the bridge was laid on April 10th 2008, and just before lunchtime, the Lister became the first loco to venture on to the structure.

*The Rest of the World Gang laying track towards Ynysfor Level Crossing on 6th April 2008. Overnight the mountains have been coated in snow, to make them look even better, and Cnicht on the left is doing its best as a Snowdon impostor. The guys are all ready for action, having laid a few lengths of sleepers. Here the next two rails are being run off the RRMs on to rollers, ready for fastening down.*

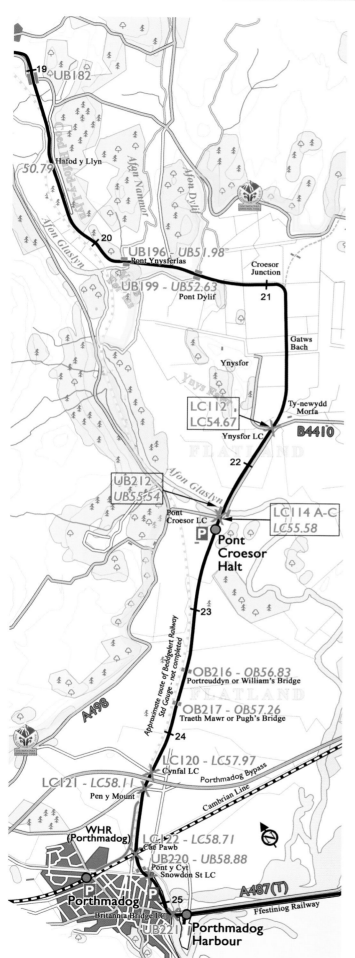

*The gap in the rails seen above was temporary, forming part of a process of moving rails around to put joints in the best possible positions at either end of the bridge and between the level crossings. This one was remedied by replacing the 14 metre closure rail at the North end with a longer one, and the removed rail was adapted to form the closure rail required between crossings LC114A & B.* **WHRCL**

*This is the gap at the south end of the bridge. From here the rail joins had to fall in the right places between the level crossings. The wooden sleepers at either end of the bridge provided the best transit between the wooden sleeper deck on the bridge and the steel sleeps bordering it. This tracklaying job had to be done quickly and accurately across the road on 23rd July 2008.* **WHRCL**

The level crossing panel was installed on 22nd July 2008, so that the road surface on either side of it could then be built up. With the rails on the bridge screwed back in place, *Upnor Castle* was able to push the panel into position, with an excavator jib supporting the south end. Given the nature of the job, with the closure of the road to traffic the correct level of the track had to be established quickly, and hydraulic pan jacks were brought along to make sure this happened.

The object of the exercise at this time was to 'finish' the railway as soon as possible, to connect it with the FR across the CTRL. So pending work to create the station was laid aside, and the points and left had side of the loop were put in, the track was laid through the station site and even the south end point was left out until later, as the track was laid towards Porthmadog. This left the three adjacent level crossings to be equipped and commissioned, the loop to be laid, the platforms to be built and the place to be furnished for receiving trains as a temporary terminus - but service was not intended until May 2010, service to Beddgelert/Hafod y Llyn came first.

Ballasting throughout the section was completed on August 22nd 2008; the southwards tracklaying push got off to a flying start on August 23rd 2008; fifteen lengths were laid, taking the Head of Steel as far as the site compound, next to LC115 (**LC55.93**), some 2½ miles from Porthmadog. Another fifteen lengths were laid on August 24th 2008, quickly exhausting the Pont Croesor rail stack; *Upnor Castle* therefore made runs back to collect more from the larger stack at Hafod y Llyn. The rail bolsters were back at Dinas, and having had a bogie swap, were due to deliver the final load of rails on the evening of August 25th, clearing the Dinas rail stockpile. Tracklaying on August 26th 2008 did not get going until after lunch; despite this

twelve panels were laid, taking the Head of Steel to within a kilometre of the WHR(P) track at Traeth Mawr - where a start was made on recovering the rails and sleepers that had been left there earlier in the year, their having been lifted to allow correction of the dip through the site of the former loop. Sleepers were laid on the ballast between the limit of WHR(P) working and OB217 (**OB57.26**). By the end of the day eighteen panels had been laid, exhausting the supply of rails, and taking the Head of Steel to a point immediately north of OB217, and very close to the location of the previous buffer stops at the end of Traeth Mawr loop. All sleepers were laid out to connect with the WHHR track from the south, and the last of the rails placed on the bank at that end of the section were extracted. The next day's work would switch to the section of the CTRL between Cae Pawb and Snowdon Mill, while rail would be delivered from Minffordd to Rhyd Ddu by road, for tracklaying to continue at Traeth Mawr at the weekend. Then on 31st August 2008, there would be rail continuous for 24 miles from Caernarfon to the Cambrian Coast Line at Cae Pawb.

*The arrival of the 'Caernarfon Connection' at Traeth Mawr was a moment for celebration with the 'Golden Clip'. It was a sad moment for WHR(P), as it was an end to their dreams of an autonomous railway to Pont Croesor. Despite that there was a welcoming 'chin-up' atmosphere as the scene of the union on 31st August 2008 shows.* **S Macfarlane**

*Right*: On 25th May 2010 the work is still going on to finish various details on this complex crossing. This view is taken looking south, from the edge of the B4410 crossing, looking into the station, across the RSPB level crossing, and less distinctly the adjacent foot crossing. The official opening of the station was 26th May 2010, but trains had been running since 22nd May.

*Left:* Neatness now prevails on this view of Pont Croesor AOLC, across the B4410 on 25th May 2010. Pont Croesor itself points to the glorious mountains. The railway is running trains from Caernarfon to Pont Croesor on a 'shakedown' service, all is now ready for the official opening the following day.

*Right:* The train from Caernarfon has arrived in this mid-morning view at Pont Croesor. The second platform has not yet been built, but one is enough for one train. NGG16 N0. 87 brought the eight carriages in and a large party decanted to waiting road coaches - amazing on only the fourth day of operation.

*Left:* The second platform has now been added, and here is a through train from Blaenau Ffestiniog hauled by two double Fairlie locomotives, with Merddin Emrys as pilot loco. Things change fast on this railway. On 2nd April 2011 the Snowdonian train ran from Porthmadog to Blaenau Ffestiniog to Caernarfon and back to Porthmadog. It was full at £130 per ticket. This was just a sample of the growing popularity that the WHR enjoyed immediately. The prospect of maintaining Pont Croesor as a railhead was short lived. Expansion of the service to Porthmadog was arranged as soon as it was possible.

*Here's as historic scene as any, there's not much ceremony, but the Black Hand Gang are fetching the last rail to be fastened in to the WHR, making continuous track from Porthmadog to Caernarfon, and restoring the Welsh Highland Railway. It is 14th February 2009 and work has been going on this project since 1997. It's not a bad result, but it will be a while before trains run. However, it all needs to be complete for the famous Golden Bolt ceremony on 28th February 2009.*

## Cae Pawb to Harbour Station

CTRL work was done as a series of separate tasks that eventually all came together. Obviously, the civil engineering work needed to be completed before the track was laid. The Cae Pawb crossing was relatively straightforward. The crossing and transition tracks came together, and the trap points to guard the crossing were installed at the appropriate distance. To the north the track to Pen y Mount was connected, on the CTRL, it was plain track in the south, after passing through the site of the old Porthmadog New, and crossing Y Cyt, there was a join with tramway track close to the Snowdon Mill. Plain track resumed at the car park, after the Snowdon St AOCL until the approach to the Britannia Bridge. Tramway track was laid until just past the Cob Records store, with a couple of plain lengths connecting to the Welsh Highland Points in Harbour Station. In each case when abutting tramway and plain track, there needed to be a pad, and a connecting transition length.

Work had gone on to put the Welsh Highland Points back, a year previously, so there was something to connect to. Those points had been left there without the blade on the seaward side, until it was fitted during tests in November 2008. The last rails were laid in towards the junction on 27th February 2009.

The next job was to refurbish the ground frame and connect that up to the points. The Golden Bolt ceremony was held, on 29th February 2009, a sort of polite re-run of the celebration at Promontory Utah, but with a victory for temperance.

Thereafter trains could cross under special arrangements, until the lights and control gear were installed. The track gangs still had 'finishing' work to do across the whole system, like the upgrading of fishplates on curves. The first passenger trains ran on 30th October 2010.

*On 15th February 2009, this shot shows the installation of the connecting lengths of track and also reveals the transition pad and flangeways needed for smooth change between standard flat-bottomed rail and the newer tramway rail. Note that before trains can run, a slice of Spooners (the beer store no less) has to be removed.* **Ben Fisher**

This is the famous Golden Bolt ceremony on 28th February 2009, Merddyn Emrys was brought with NGG16 No.87 to be the first steam locomotives to run over the WHR Points. They were come together with a number of those who worked hard to lay the track, in a sort of 2009 Promontory Utah, Union Pacific -v- Central Pacific scene. Missing this time are the bottles of booze, not concealed from temptation by the Temperance Society, but totally banned by Health and Safety - a more compete job. It was a happy day - the railway was now through from Caernarfon to Porthmadog, and that's what everyone wanted.

**Above:** There are the points, now connected and run over in this view from 3rd November 2011. It's a little bit strange to think that the track on the right runs all the way to Caernarfon, and rolling along it is fun. However for the tracklayers putting the railway in is one things, setting it up and maintaining it is entirely another.

**Left:** Paul Lewin, General Manager, displays the specially prepared golden bolts, to make the last rail join in the track between Caernarfon and Porthmadog. The bolts have heads, to celebrate the effort that the tracklaying gangs made, volunteering on the railway. See the inset above. One bolt-head celebrates the Black Hand Gang, and the other the Rest of the World Gang, but all who were there recognises the immense amount of effort put in on this railway from so many sources. Also present in Paul's hand is the original silver trowel, used at Creua to inaugurate the construction of the Festiniog Railway in 1833.

**M**any people thought that the crossing of the Cambrian Coast Line by the Welsh Highland Railway would be impossible except by bridge. Early negotiations with Railtrack had established that provided FR Co. were paying, then the items that remained to be discussed were the mechanisms to make it safe operationally. It's the construction and operation which will be described now, by CTRL Project Manager David High who used his professional knowledge as a Civil Engineer, together with experience as an F&WHR driver to bring the WHR into Porthmadog.

**T**he WHR has a bouquet of interesting geographical features which account for its popularity, but among the more interesting technical features is the flat crossing of the Network Rail, Cambrian Coast Line at Cae Pawb. To the visitor, clattering across the standard gauge Coast railway is a novel experience. It is one of the last of such crossings in existence today. However this introduction of a short section of 597mm track into the national rail network is also unique, as the only point in the UK where an independent railway company bisects Network Rail (NR).

Bisection of lines we can all live with, the really important issue which had to be addressed when this arrangement was proposed is how to avoid the bisection of trains, one by another! In times of strife Winston Churchill always knew how to throw a few words together, and when I started as Project Manager of the CTRL it was clear that Churchill had been there before when he said "It is a riddle, wrapped in a mystery, inside an enigma". If we take the permanent way as the riddle, the signalling infrastructure is the mystery; how to operate it must be an enigma.

Starting with the riddle, if you travel from Caernarfon to the up home signal at Cae Pawb you cover 24½miles (38.71km) of track using two rail profiles, the ex SAR 60lb/yard rail and S30, a metric rail, which is very similar. Before the flat crossing was installed the Cambrian line was laid in standard, 95lb/yard bullhead rail. Cae Pawb may appear to be short (at either 597mm or 1435mm depending on your perspective) but its complex construction involved 5 different rail sections.

The standard gauge rail in the crossing is an unusual profile, with the head and foot dimensions of 113lb/yard flat-bottomed rail, but no web. Rail like this is used in turnout construction to give strength. The standard gauge is continuous through the crossing, with notches appropriately machined in its head, to allow for the passage of the narrow gauge flanges across it. To match the height of this rail the narrow gauge needed to be a 113lb/ yard profile. Just in case this massive construction is not man enough, each standard gauge rail is supported by a large piece of steel which also serves to locate the narrow gauge rails

in the right location relative to the flangeway slots.

Completion of the standard gauge track is made using 113lb/ yd twist rails before transferring back to the bullhead rail with a transition fishplate. On the narrow gauge side the difference between the 113lb/yd rail and the S30 rail is enormous and requires transition fish plates, first to a panel of 80lb/yd flat-bottomed rail, before ultimately connecting in to the S30 profile.

This leads neatly to the mysteries of signalling. In September 2010 a new signalling system came in on the Cambrian line. This was the pilot installation (in the UK) of ERTMS (European Rail Traffic Management System). Cae Pawb interfaces with the ERTMS signalling and it is no coincidence that the first narrow gauge train carrying passengers did not run until 31st October 2010. On the Cambrian route protection is provided by 'Nodes', effectively home or stop signals, provided either side of the crossing. These are normally at danger, unless an NR train is due. The trap points on the WHR line stop the narrow gauge trains broadsiding their standard gauge counterparts.

A frequently asked question is 'who controls Cae Pawb'? The answer curiously is that it depends whose train it is. Under normal circumstances NR have control of the crossing. For a WHR train to cross, the Cae Pawb signaller must request the use of the crossing from NR Signaller at Machynlleth, by depressing a button on the panel. If the Cambrian Line is clear, an electronic release is given that allows the Cae Pawb panel to be operated by the WHR signaller. Having obtained control of the crossing the trap points are set to plain line, and the approach signal cleared. Once the WHR train is across, the signal is returned to danger, the trap points open and the release is returned to the NR signaller.

Cae Pawb is between two level crossings on the Cambrian line, Traeth Mawr ABC(L), an automatic barrier, and Porthmadog Station, full barrier level crossing. The operation of these crossings relies on the use of track circuits, one of which runs through the site of Cae Pawb. Joining the two running rails together with the narrow gauge rail will clearly complete the track circuit, so the flat crossing itself is isolated to prevent this short by the introduction of insulated block joints (IBJs).

*This view on 1st November 2006 shows the crossing at Cae Pawb being laid in and connected to the Network Rail Cambrian Coast Line during a 3day possession. There was a long way to go yet before any narrow gauge trains would run, but the Cambrian Coast had to be back in business quickly.* **Arup Rail**

*Left: The numerous rail profiles and types leading up to this crossing. Here, on the narrow gauge side, S30 rail butts with 80lbs/yd transition rail as a lead in to the much heavier 113lbs/yard flat bottomed rail. Yes, it does like what they do in model trains, but it's the same job that needs to be done, whatever the scale.* **WHRCL**

*Below: The trap point from the northern direction sits adjacent to the fence to Gelert's Farm. When fitted and in operation, if the route is not set and clear, both blades will be held in, away from the running rails. Thus, an approaching train that fails to stop will be deposited on the sleepers, expensive, messy, but safer than a collision.*

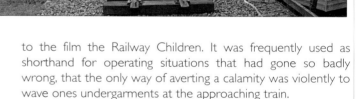

Thus, effectively there is a hole in the NR track circuit, and should a class 08 shunter ever reach Porthmadog is will be briefly be 'lost'. The WHR line is also track circuited to cover the trap points and approaches to Cae Pawb. Clearly there is a similar 'hole' in the WHR track circuits and there is the very real potential for FR locomotives to be 'lost' in this hole when straddling the NR line. The solution to this is quite simple and known as sequential locking. The sequence for (say) a light engine movement across the crossing is: approach track circuit occupied, approach track circuit vacant (loco 'in hole' as it traverses the crossing), trailing track circuit occupied, trailing track circuit vacant. Once a route is set on the WHR panel (in normal circumstances) it cannot be re-set until the full sequence has taken place, thus providing an acceptable guarantee that the NR line is clear.

This leads on neatly to the enigma of operating. The operating rules define who does what at Cae Pawb. One of the fundamentals is that the staff of one railway has no jurisdiction in the operation of the other. This is fine when all goes well (as outlined above), but there needed to be a plan for operating during adverse situations. Meetings took place with NR to discuss the issues and develop operating instructions. These took place in unusual locations to suit the NR representatives work programme: London, Porthmadog, Birmingham, Hereford and Highley all come to mind. The recollection of sitting in the kitchen of the station house at Highley discussing how to avoid 'the red petticoat scenario', with a glimpse of passing Severn Valley trains visible via the mirror, is a lasting memory of my involvement with the CTRL project. The red petticoat scenario of course was a reference to the film the Railway Children. It was frequently used as shorthand for operating situations that had gone so badly wrong, that the only way of averting a calamity was violently to wave ones undergarments at the approaching train.

Another interesting aside in the operating discussion is the name 'Cae Pawb'. To the WHR it was 'Cambrian Crossing', and this name went back into history, as the Croesor Tramway, and then the old WHR had a crossing here, but the NR team did not like use of the word 'Cambrian'. To them it covered most places west of Shrewsbury, and was therefore too general for use as a specific location name. They suggested Croesor Crossing, but the WHR already had Pont Croesor and Croesor Junction, and so confusion could result. Cae Pawb was the compromise. As it translates as 'everyone's field' there is some poetic crossover to the site's function, especially if you are familiar with the old railroading term 'a cornfield meet', the latter being a euphemism for a collision of two trains. I thought it was a lot better to keep my limited knowledge of both Welsh and old railroad slang to myself when making the Cae Pawb suggestion.

*This is the view looking west when crossing at Cae Pawb. The flat bottomed rail leading to the crossing is only one length before bullhead rail resumes. Next door is a gated occupation crossing. Sharp eyes may see an Arriva 158 train waiting at Porthmadog Station, ready to set off.*

# Operations

Much careful thought went into planning the restored WHR before any rails were laid. The decisions made had a profound effect on subsequent operations. The fundamentals were as follows:

**1.** A loading gauge capable of accepting NGG16 Garratts would be installed.

**2.** The railway would follow the FR in principle, adopting the FR Rule Book and the vacuum brake.

**3.** The WHR would use the same Control arrangements as the FR.

**4.** The principal motive power would be steam.

**5.** Long trains of between 10 and 15 cars would be operated - thus minimum crossing loop length would be 195m.

**6.** Inter-operability and the running of through trains was desirable, hence the FR loading gauge would gradually be expanded to accept Garratts.

**7.** WHR coaches would be wider, longer and taller than FR coaches.

**8.** Signalling would be 'basic', to begin with using staff and ticket, but perhaps moving on to a radio/computer Dispatcher system.

**9.** This would require 'auto-loops'

There were a number of commercial considerations that drove

*Vacuum brake connections between the cars. The larger pipe than for air brakes advertises that a lower working (non) pressure of 0.7Bar (10Lbs/sq.inch) is in use. Almost unbelievably the unit of measurement is Inches of Mercury! And we need 19 of those to move on this 'metric' railway.*

the operation. The railway's objective was to generate large amounts of traffic from the Caernarfon area, which would then be brought to Beddgelert and Porthmadog, to join with the Ffestiniog Railway. The aim was to complement the Ffestiniog Railway, and to pay its way. In combination the two railways would aim to regain market share, (lost by the Ffestiniog over the years) and to become together a world class tourist attraction.

To pay its way it was considered necessary for it to follow the FR by running long trains. Of course this decision had immediate feedback into motive power. The FR ruling gradient is 1:70; the WHR ruling gradient is 1:40. Upon the former, the double-Fairlie can manage 12 car trains; the only locomotive capable of matching that on a 1:40 is an NGG16 Garratt.

The original idea to widen the FR loading gauge for the SAR Garratts, depended on gauge easement through a number of 'pinch points' like Garnedd Tunnel that would cost much. WHR carriages can pass under Rhiw Plas bridge (except Car 2060 the Romanian car), yet it would be expensive to widen the loop for clearance at Minffordd Station loop - there needs to be a good reason to do this. The original policy of increasing the FR loading gauge is currently not affordable.

The WHR cars reflect the need for more room for a population grown in dimensions. Vintage FR cars were built in an age when people were smaller. FR trains may run through onto the WHR, but not the other way round. It has been possible to increase the FR carriage internal width for passengers, yet to remain within the kinematic envelope, and this has led to today's new FR stock, the super-Barn series. These carriages are now being built to 13m length, the longest FR cars ever. Thus as the two railways come together, the through running aspiration has been achieved by the FR stock, with the WHR stock

**Above**: *Car 24 is built to the NWNG loading gauge, but beyond, the rest of the rake are to the new WHR standard. Note that after the doors are pinched in, the open car's bodywork is wider. This gives more room internally. Please note that Car 24 is limited to 42 seats, not 56 as it was is the past*

**Right**: *The Waunfawr - Rhyd Ddu train staff is placed momentarily on the running plate of* Castell Caernarfon *to be photographed. Attached to it are keys for particular items in the section, like the train staff cabinet. This is not an ETS token.*

turning back at Porthmadog. All WHR stock can work to Boston Lodge, for servicing and maintenance, including Garratts.

The original plan was to have three sets of coaches for the WHR, and to build the necessary passing loops to permit a frequency of service similar to that on the FR. Restoring the WHR has been a long process, and the plans have been subject to change.

There is no mobile phone signal in many places along the WHR. Thus communications, especially during operational difficulties, can pose problems. So the original idea for a sophisticated, hi-tech, wireless operating system was unachievable without large expense.

Caernarfon - Dinas was simple enough to operate on the system of 'one engine in steam'. As soon as there was a railway, then a baton, was designated the train staff or token. As sections of railway were built and brought into service added, then by 2009, five sections were in operation, each with a token unique to the section:

1. Caernarfon to Dinas -
2. Dinas to Waunfawr -
3. Waunfawr to Rhyd Ddu -
4. Rhyd Ddu to Beddgelert -
5. Beddgelert to Pont Croesor -
6. Pont Croesor to Porthmadog -

The tokens are suitably inscribed, and kept in a secure place until used. Only with the token may the train enter the section to which it applies.

It took from 1997 to 2009 to restore service to the 25 mile line throughout, with various operating changes being made as need dictated.

A locked, yellow-painted stop-block protected with a red flag was mounted at the start of engineering works, Trains required permission from a Responsible Person (PICOP) in order to make any move inside the possession for the engineering works. It all worked well and was safe, but immediately the HMRI

*In an echo of the 1860s the 'Ladybird' acts as Beddgelert's Home Board. To pass it the two yellow lights - the proceed indicators - must be illuminated .*

| yellow |
| blue |
| red |
| green |
| purple |
| orange |

permitted passenger trains to run, the train movements were authorised and regulated by FR Control in Porthmadog. Matters were ordered simply at first. If a passenger train was out, no engineering movements were permitted without a possession. Later, when construction was proceeding (as in Phase 2) then any new works were separated from the passenger line by a locked stop-block; the key for that was held by the PICOP.

The rules were already in the Ffestiniog Rule Book - and that had been refined during the engineering works for the Deviation.

One token for the one section became a limiting factor, as it was irksome at Dinas, that when a passenger train was on the line at Caernarfon, no movement was possible between the South Yard and the North Yard. After the Waunfawr section was added in 2000, then a locomotive was (notionally) trapped in the shed when a train was between Dinas and Waunfawr. Signals were installed, and the concept of the Shunt Token was introduced to provide the flexibility needed within station limits. The removal of a Shunt Token extinguishes the home signal, proceed aspects, and train movement within the limited station area inside the 'limit of shunt' boards is thus permitted. Shunt Tokens are currently provided at Dinas, Rhyd Ddu and Beddgelert. The moment two passenger trains were required in service, then a more flexible system was needed on the main line.

## Signals, Sections and ETS

Signals on the FR had originated from the old GWR disc and crossbar signals. Both Brown, Marshalls of Birmingham and McKenzie & Holland of Worcester had supplied examples of a three-foot, slotted disc, the former in 1864. These have been adopted in the modern era as a distinctive shape, and have evolved for universal use on the WHR in lieu of semaphore signals. The general name for them is a 'ladybird', which is obvious from their shape and colour. The signals are painted boards or discs, yellow for distant, and red for stop signals.

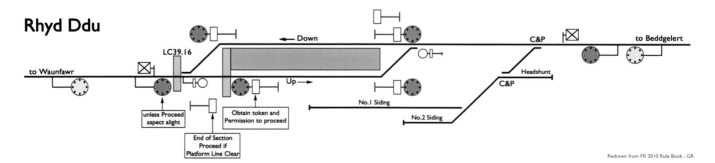

*The FR Rule Book has station diagrams that show the signalling. The 'ladybirds' are shown, the 'limit of shunt' boards are the white squares with black cross, the small white circles on stands are point indicators and the 'end of section' and 'obtain token' notices are clearly marked. Trains treat the red 'ladybirds' as stop signals unless they have lit aspect lights. These are significant as they prove that the 'shunt' token is not in use if they are lit.*

# Dinas

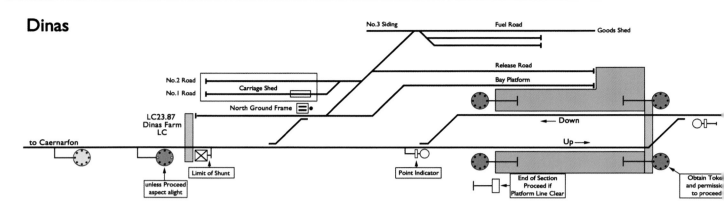

*Autoloop fitted stations require brains to marshal trains. Visualise a locomotive coming off shed to take a train to Caernarfon and you will find out why. In order not to 'freeze' Dinas when a train is in either section, a shunt Token may be taken out to allow movement between Shunt Limits. This has the key to unlock the ground frames - but having manoeuvred the empty stock for Caernarfon into the Up loop, by use of the release road, then the stock must be run round in the Up side; so in order to go to Caernarfon, a wrong line departure must be made without more fiddling. Not the same as FR where all is either panels or levers.*

Movements on the single line, Ffestiniog Railway are governed by the Electric Train Staff (ETS). Connected token issuing instruments govern each section. The Ffestiniog system is complex and expensive, but flexible and versatile. Loop lines at intermediate stations permit trains to pass one another. All regular moves are signalled, and signals are connected with the points. Thus loop lines at Minffordd and Tan y Bwlch have shunting panels to control the movements of signals and points.

An ETS token instrument will only ever issue one token for one section - once a token for the section is withdrawn at any of the connected instruments, all are locked, and another may not be issued until the withdrawn token is replaced in any one. The action of taking a token from the instrument also clears the section signal. The level of safety that this system offers is much respected.

No ETS machines are installed on the WHR. The tokens lie in a locked cabinet. The train crew ask for permission from Control to take the token and to enter the section. If the token is not there, then the train must wait for the incoming service to make an exchange of tokens; each train in possession of a new token must confirm with Control permission to enter the section ahead.

This is a safe system, even without the guarantee of a section signal locked to the issue of a token from an ETS machine. The limitations of single section tokens began to be felt when by 2003 there were three sections, Caernarfon-Dinas, Dinas-Waunfawr and Waunfawr-Rhyd Ddu.

Commercial demand required a second train from Caernarfon to run through to Rhyd Ddu, to join the preceding train. As there would be a train already at Rhyd Ddu, there could be no token at Waunfawr, and even though the first train would be safely locked in the loop at Rhyd Ddu, there was no way the second train could join it, without the token being brought from Rhyd Ddu to Waunfawr by car. Yet railways have long found a solution to this problem. The Divisible Staff, or Staff and Ticket system, allows extra flexibility, with the possibility of more tickets to be issued with the permission of the controller if needs be. Thus this system was introduced on the Welsh Highland Railway.

If a second train is to follow the first train through the section, after the driver and guard of the first train formally see token for the section, Control may authorise a metal 'ticket' to be taken from the cabinet, and the token is left where it is. The first train that has uplifted a 'ticket'

*Above: This is the cabinet at Minffordd Station containing (R) the Porthmadog section instrument and (L) the Tan y Bwlch section instrument. With Control's permission, and when properly prompted, the instrument will deliver one miniature train staff as permission to proceed, and it will clear the section signal. Very safe!*

*Right: Lyd on test waits in Rhiw Goch Loop, on 8th August 2010, outside perhaps the greatest manifestation of FR garden shed technology. But, hard up against the signal box are living examples of the FR pole route, rare survivor from the 19th century, and bearer of the wires connecting the ETS machines.*

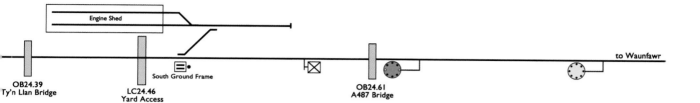

OB24.39
Ty'n Llan Bridge

LC24.46
Yard Access

South Ground Frame

OB24.61
A487 Bridge

to Waunfawr

proceeds in the normal way and reports its safe arrival at the end of the section. This having being accomplished the Controller may allow a following train to enter the section, uplifting the token proper.

Undoubtedly the ETS system is safer and more flexible. If the section signal is also locked to the token instrument, so that it will clear only when a token has been issued, this offers an additional safeguard. However, electrically connected ETS machines are rare today. Such complex electro-mechanical instruments are hard to find and are no longer manufactured. They are also expensive to install and maintain, and the two railway were, until 2010, run separately with no physical connection. That changed with the completion of the CTRL.

It had been thought in the early days, that the right way forward was a computer dispatch system. All of this was achievable in the Hi-tech 'Noughties'. The operators were not in favour of differing systems. They argued that the FR system should be extended from Porthmadog to Caernarfon, with suitable ETS instruments installed to dispense tokens. To help this to happen they obtained a supply of instruments from Ireland. Installation of the ETS system on WHR was now inhibited by the means of connection.

The FR has a pole route, carrying bare conductors in the traditional manner (over most of the 13 mile FR route). Tended by volunteers, these wires are the means by which communication is maintained between ETS token instruments. No such infrastructure exists on the WHR. HMRI were satisfied that the 'Rheilffordd Eryri Block System' offers adequate safeguards for the demands placed upon it. The priorities of the construction periods militated against weighty discussions of the finer merits of

ETS -v- Staff and Ticket, if the system installed was satisfactory for the job to be done. However ETS became possible by another route. Roland Doyle, was considering how to establish a reliable Micro-ETS system, to permit one ETS instruments to be connected via national telephone line and Internet. In this elegant system, a coded message is sent and suitably verified from one section ETS machine to another. If no token is already out the issuing machine will permit a token to be withdrawn. It might not be long before a section signal can be added to this, thus enabling the same safe system as on the Ffestiniog to be extended to the WHR. This will mean that the whole 40 mile system is working with same style of ETS staffs. Further enhancements are also under consideration to increase flexibility and decrease the costs of autoloops on both railways. Meanwhile, the 'Rheilffordd Eryri Block System' continues, and the equilibrium in the workings was restored by the service extension to Porthmadog. The lower number of trains, and the greater simplicity of the WHR, makes less demands on the system. Staff and Ticket working is there to provide a safe extension of flexible working. As usual, innovations are taking place, leading to advances all the time.

*Above: On 6th August 2005,* Prince *repositions to join his train in the Tan y Bwlch Up platform, to make a Down departure. The signalling is organised to do this, with the local control panel open, with the loco having been called forward by the subsidiary signal. The main signal would clear unless the 'inhibit' plunger was depressed when withdrawing the token. This is the complex FR system.*

*Left: The train staff ticket is a more robust affair when created in metal. The words engraved on it are clear, the authority for any move comes from the Controller. All is well from a safety point of view provided the procedures are observed properly. That of course applies universally on railways.*

### TRAIN STAFF TICKET

PONTCROESOR – PORTHMADOG HARBOUR STATION SECTION

TICKET NUMBER : PHS63

AFTER SEEING THE TRAIN STAFF COLOURED ORANGE YOU ARE
AUTHORISED TO PROCEED AS INSTRUCTED BY CONTROL

## Autoloops

Another innovation, imported by volunteers working on the National Network is the autoloop. This had two complex forms that have now been simplified. Originally track circuits or treadles indicated the approach of trains, and point motors set the loop to accept an incoming train, with the signals governed by points detection, and the safety of track circuits installed within the station crossing loop. This electromechanical system is over provision for five crossings per day on a single line worked with tokens and a traffic Control. On WHR trailable, hydraulically damped points that auto-restored to 'normal' were installed with lit point indicators, that detect the lie of the points. Points are set 'normal' for right hand running facing the direction of travel. This assumes the practice (hitherto strictly prohibited) of trains on departure trailing the inward set of points set to 'normal' when making an exit to the loop. All trains use all the autoloops, each train has a train staff, and the controller permits all movements. Loops of this type are cheaper than the electromechanical system. There is some wear caused on the backs of loop exit point blades, but the lowered expense of installation more than offsets this.

The latest installations use a 'slower' hydraulic damper to prolong the return movement of the exit point blades, obviating the striking of it by each wheel flange. It is possible that electric points may soon be offered in a simpler, cheaper form. Autoloops permit the crossing of trains in a safe, and easy to use manner, as well as being economic to install. The diagram of Rhyd Ddu on the previous page shows the current signalling installation. Autoloops were installed at Dinas, Waunfawr, Rhyd Ddu, Beddgelert and Pont Croesor. These work well when there are two train sets out on the line. If traffic grows to the point where a third set is needed in order to enhance service levels, then more loops will be required, and this will be affordable. Additional loop placements have been designated at: Plas y Nant, Hafod Ruffydd, Hafod y Llyn, and Llyn Bach. The absence of control panels means that shunting at Autoloops can be complex..

*In 2011 the Porthmadog Harbour Ground Frame was enhanced to deal with the WHR Points, Lever No.5 and disc signals were added for the exit from the station yard and the entrance to the WHR. Porthmadog is not fully signalled and is at the limit of what can be accomplished safely, given all the movements. The restrictive arrangement will suffice until the completion of the Cob Widening in 2013, and then it must change.*

so the inadequate site has been a pint pot into which the FR has constantly poured its quart. Working it has in living memory depended upon a six-lever ground frame at the Station throat.

With the advent of the WHR, and the successful establishment of the Cross Town Rail Link, the situation has become much worse. To permit trains from the WHR to access PHS, the only method was to run the train out on to the Cob, to place a locomotive on the rear, and then to haul it back into the PHS platform. A departure requires the procedure in reverse. Garratts and WHR trains are cleared into Boston Lodge, but no further. This immediately ruled out an FR and a WHR train occupying the station at the same time - though through trains were possible. A second platform was clearly indicated but the large traffic potential of the combined railways threatens to swamp the place, and of course it is expensive to make the alterations needed. The new loop, extending onto the Cob, will permit a WHR train to arrive and run round, and at the same time to allow an FR train to approach and run in to the adjacent platform. This could mean that up to 500 people are on the station at one time,

## Porthmadog

It wasn't until the modern era that the FR was wholly dependent on passengers. Even so Porthmadog Harbour Station (PHS) has never had more than one platform face. At the time when the Tremadoc Estate was up for grabs, the FR Co. could have had the freehold of the whole wharf, but it could only find the funds to buy its own site. The extension across Britannia Bridge round to the wharves beyond Pen Cei was lost; the wharf beyond the PHS was sold off for holiday homes, and so having completed the necessary arrangements for operating two trains at once in the station, there will be a considerable priority to deal with the people, with pressure for enhanced retailing and catering facilities. However what will still be a problem is two trains wishing to pass each other at Porthmadog, one coming off WHR, one going on to WHR. If this is required it will be better to make the crossing at Minffordd, or Pont Croesor. There will be thrills for the timetable planners for years, as it is not clear in 2012 what the commercial results will

*Pont Croesor Loop, Porthmadog end points, actuating lever, with weight. The weight keeps the points 'normal' - Down trains to loop line - and the hydraulic cylinder ensures slow but steady points replacement to normal, after the displacement by the passage of a Porthmadog bound train.* **Andrew Thomas**

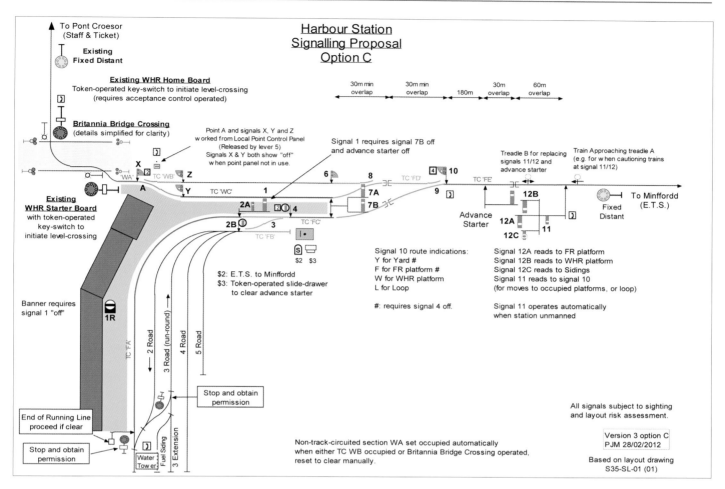

**Harbour Station
Signalling Proposal
Option C**

To Pont Croesor
(Staff & Ticket)

Existing
Fixed Distant

**Existing WHR Home Board**
Token-operated key-switch to initiate level-crossing
(requires acceptance control operated)

**Britannia Bridge Crossing**
(details simplified for clarity)

Point A and signals X, Y and Z
worked from Local Point Control Panel
(Released by lever 5)
Signals X & Y both show "off"
when point panel not in use.

Signal 1 requires signal 7B off
and advance starter off

Treadle B for replacing
signals 11/12 and
advance starter

Train Approaching treadle A
(e.g. for when cautioning trains
at signal 11/12)

30m min overlap   30m min overlap   180m   30m overlap   60m overlap

**Existing
WHR Starter Board**
with token-operated
key-switch to
initiate level-crossing

Advance Starter

To Minffordd
(E.T.S.)

Fixed Distant

$2: E.T.S. to Minffordd
$3: Token-operated slide-drawer
to clear advance starter

Banner requires
signal 1 "off"

2 Road
3 Road (run-round)
4 Road
5 Road

Signal 10 route indications:
Y for Yard #
F for FR platform #
W for WHR platform
L for Loop

#: requires signal 4 off.

Signal 12A reads to FR platform
Signal 12B reads to WHR platform
Signal 12C reads to Sidings
Signal 11 reads to signal 10
(for moves to occupied platforms, or loop)

Signal 11 operates automatically
when station unmanned

End of Running Line
proceed if clear

Stop and obtain
permission

Stop and obtain
permission

Water Tower
Fuel Siding
3 Extension

All signals subject to sighting
and layout risk assessment.

Non-track-circuited section WA set occupied automatically
when either TC WB occupied or Britannia Bridge Crossing operated,
reset to clear manually.

Version 3 option C
PJM 28/02/2012

Based on layout drawing
S35-SL-01 (01)

be of a full WHR service arriving and departing from Porthmadog Harbour, nor the operational reliability for FR of co-ordinating both lines to occupy platform space with tight time restrictions. The basic commercial strategic plan for the WHR 'runs out' when it reaches Porthmadog and full service starts, as the process of large market access to WHR being only from Caernarfon ceases. So far, until 2011, the market grew from Caernarfon, with new traffic, and the FR did not lose business. WHR trains lengths were gradually increased to take the traffic.

The differentiation between the two railways is strong in the public's mind, and it seems that people are persuaded to try both. Prospects look good in 2012, with the unknown factors of how flows like Porthmadog to Beddgelert and through travel from Blaenau Ffestiniog to destinations beyond Porthmadog will grow. In addition Beddgelert has not been accessible by railway from Porthmadog since 1937. Here is the biggest change in Porthmadog Harbour Station for some 150 years.

# The Cross Town Rail Link (CTRL)

The original FR ran from the other side of the harbour basin, across the Britannia Bridge to the old WHR points. The '0' point was a little beyond Pen Cei. Porthmadog Harbour Station had tracks through it on to the quays beyond, and when passenger trains began in 1865, the station was built where it is today, and not across the Britannia Bridge. The Croesor Tramway connected directly into the tracks around the basin, and the WHR when built in 1922 used the connection across Britannia Bridge.

*The two yellow lights shine out clearly on the Ladybird (now changed) that acts at the northern home signal in this photograph taken of the first passenger train to cross Cae Pawb and the Cross Town Rail Link into Porthmadog on 30th October 2010. Thus the line is clear, and the route has been set across the Cambrian and on to the CTRL.*

All cross-town connections gradually faded, until extinguished by closure of WHR in 1937. The Croesor track was not lifted, and so occasional unofficial use was made, but it had ceased to be a working railway, and the Cambrian crossing was taken out. WHR restoration saw the whole railway put back on a more convenient route along the side of Llyn Bach, to minimise street running, with AOCL's to cross Snowdon Street and the Britannia Bridge, and a crossing of the Cambrian Coast Line protected by narrow gauge signals and trap points.

*Left: The token has been taken out of the keyswitch and is now handed to the driver, who may drive on to the Britannia Bridge AOCL if the flashing white light is showing. The limit here is 5mph, rising to 10mph on the crossing and along the side of Llyn Bach.*

*Below: This is Cae Pawb crossing control panel, with the crossing keeper (Mr Phil Brown) and acolytes (Mr David Davies, and Mr Martin Neeves), in attendance to learn the panel. They were indeed learning, as this is taken from the first passenger train to cross the Cambrian Coast Line, on 30th October 2010.*

Operating this piece of line is unlike any other section on either railway. As already described, Cae Pawb has been specially designed for the job and is unique in Britain.

The crossing keeper contacts the Network Rail Signaller at Machynlleth, to get permission to 'power up' the panel. When starting from Harbour Station, the WHR train is currently pulled out of the platform, with a pilot engine on the front. When clear of the WHR points, the pilot locomotive is detached, the train locomotive is attached, and the train is run forward. The token switch is operated at the appropriate moment to engage the Britannia Bridge crossing sequence, and the token is handed to the locomotive crew. The starting signal clears after the AOCL warning sequence has been operating for some time, allowing the train to cross at 5 mph. There is a closed right of way along Llyn Bach, with a 10mph speed limit, and the train strikes in to the Snowdon St AOCL at a treadle after Gas Works Siding points. An annunciator also sounds to warn the crossing keeper, waiting at Cae Pawb, who then asks Machynlleth for a release. Whilst the train approaches, the crossing keeper sets the crossing for the WHR train. After the Snowdon St AOCL sequence has been made correctly, the train may cross it at 10 mph.

A LED signal just after Y Cyt indicates a red or green aspect, to show the status of Cae Pawb. The train may cross on green. After it has passed, and signal and points have returned to their normal position, the crossing keeper hands back the release to Machynlleth. This is a complex stretch of railway, much enjoyed by passengers, and with a unique narrow gauge flavour.

misplaced. In default all may feel innocent, until a rescue outfit steams round the corner and runs into the halted train, because it was not where they thought it was. Things have changed since Ffestiniog revival The WHR had to be measured in kilometres, whether the locomotives had speedometers measured in miles per hour or not - the EU says so. The Ffestiniog is all neatly laid out in miles; the question of changing this does not arise. However, new kilometre posts went out on to the WHR, and all structures were allocated a kilometric positioning number from the 'zero' point. This is simple enough, as was the decision to make the 'zero' point for the WHR Caernarfon. However the potential confusion of having the same locational number on both railways needed to be addressed. Thus the Caernarfon 'zero' point was made 20. Waunfawr is therefore '30' (approx 10kms out) and Dduallt remains '10'(miles). There are no WHR distance numbers corresponding with FR distance numbers, whatever the unit.

Of course there are those who still swear blind that the '20' leaves enough room for the extension to Bangor.

## Units and Measurements

There has to be agreement on what measurements are being used, or when trains stop, the descriptions of where the train crew are can be dangerously

*On the left is a kilometre marker, and on the right is a kilometric location plate. Bearing in mind that Caernarfon is at Km20, this must be close by - it is the St Helen's Road brick underbridge.*

**Andy Savage**

## Speed limits and running times

There were plans for running times on WHR that have not been achieved. The original timetables for the Business

Plan produced in the 1990s assumed that a 97 minute transit would be possible, achievable with a maximum of 25mph and an average speed of 19mph. In 2012, nowhere on the WHR does the speed exceed 20mph. The average running speed is 10.3mph, with a transit time of 155 minutes - not one of the faster trains in Britain! The list of speed restrictions is long, and in comparison FR trains seem like greyhounds. Yet the FR covers its distance at an average of 10.4mph. There is a direct relationship with increase of costs and increase of speeds, however everywhere on the consolidating WHR, there is activity to improve 5mph speed limits to 10mph, 10mph to 15mph, etc., as experience shows that incremental increases of speed all sum as significant reductions in journey time. It is a long and worthwhile process, as although these are not meant to be rapid trains, there are operating and commercial advantages to be had from reduced journey times, from staff duty hours, more commercially convenient times, and even (when significant reductions in transit times are achieved), better productivity from the locomotives and rolling stock.

## Names

Standing aside from any language differences over what things are called in either Welsh or English, it is clarity not confusion that is needed with locations. It was announced with gravity, in 1995 or thereabouts, that this railway would not use names, but numbers. However as it is operated by humans and not by machines this was wishful thinking. Following on from kilometric positioning, Those Welsh place names derived from physical characteristics are translatable - Ffridd Isaf/Lower Pasture, Clogwyn y Gwin/Wine (coloured) Crag - but there can be name repeats. There are two places with the name Hafod y Llyn (Summer pasture by the Lake). As one is on the FR and the other on WHR, the locational number (**LC50.79**) is also a necessity, as it defines the railway and the position. The previous Pont Nanmor (**UB51.98**) has been renamed Pont Ynysferlas, to avoid Nanmor being confused with Nantmor at **UB50.00**. Some names are idiosyncratic, like Keay's Culvert or Tro Camlas/Canal Curve. The lowland nature of the part of the WHR on the Traeth Mawr brings proximity to cows. The curve next to Ynysfor level crossing (**LC50.79**) is unofficially called Pooh Corner, from the olfactory effect of the activity of cattle in the immediate area.

It is easy enough to 'call' things, but how are they spelt? Convention has moved the spelling of Welsh place names towards accepted Welsh Language norms. On place names, current practice means the removal of all hyphens, and the application of Welsh spelling, but of course there are traps for the unwary. Consider that alphabets differ: Welsh has no J, K, Q, V, X, or Z. English has no combinations like Ch, Dd, Ff, Ng, Ll, Ph, Rh, or Th. Train crews on FR or WHR need to master Welsh pronunciation in order to state position, though if you say you are at 'Bedelgert', the name will still come through!

This book attempts to

address the title current to the context. For example in 1922, when WHR was built, the Carnarvonshire County Council was involved (1889-1926). From 1926 to 1974 the Caernarvonshire County Council existed, thereafter becoming Gwynedd County Council and the town became Caernarfon. The Welsh Highland Railway Society was styled Cymdeithas Rheilffordd Eryri and the initials for that are strictly CRhE. Indeed the 64 Co. styled themselves Rheilffordd Ucheldir Cymru, the literal translation - thought by FR types to be decidedly unromantic, thus FR opted for Rheilffordd Eryri - as the only highland around was Snowdonia, and calling it the Snowdonia Railway, it was thought, showed glowing imagination; apparently locally it's 'lein bach 'Stiniog' and 'lein bach Beddgelert'. The Festiniog Railway Company with one letter 'F' instead of two arose because that is how it was spelled in 1832, and the name is incorporated within an Act of Parliament. In this volume FR Co. refers to that name. There are those who insist that FR should be FfR. If you wish to offer Welsh capitalisation, it should be RhFf. Now there's thinking for you!

## Control

Since the modern Ffestiniog started serious operation there has been a Control Office. The railway grew in sophistication, developing the BR standard Rulebook, augmenting it to conform to the peculiarities of operations of narrow gauge, single line, steam railways. During passenger operations there needs to be a qualified person available, to oversee the activities on the ground. This supervision ranges from timekeeping through safety, to acting as the first response to the media. Keeping track of trains and safety on a day-to-day basis is the responsibility of the Control Office. There is no distinction between paid staff and volunteers; the key criterion is the qualification of the person who is Controller. Guards, drivers, signallers and those with transferable skills from the big railway, often gravitate to be a Controller. The duty involves logging every movement, giving permission for trains to take tokens to enter sections, making arrangements in the event of lateness or disruption, on FR, on WHR, and on other transport providers, and making sure that the staff (volunteer or paid) are in place for the duties assigned to them. A 40 mile railway has meant major expansion.

Control exercises choice on timetables and arranges staffing. There is liaison with Boston Lodge over loco crews, and the general carriage capacity, timely and safe running of the railway is considered paramount. Control personnel test train crew on the Rulebook, and pass out operating staff for service. Thus it was obvious that WHR would be included under the management of Porthmadog FR Control. The result has been long co-ordination between the two railways, in standards and staffing. Operations on the two railways are now seamless; that's good for business, and for profits. It is also a good feature of FR/WHR that young people are well represented. This extends into the Control Office.

*The Control Office has a strategic view (behind them) over Harbour Station and the Cob. It is a good place to put such an office, and such a necessary service.*

**T**oday you can mention a diesel with confidence on the FR, as a number of heads will rise in interest. Few 'steamists' would be with you, but a quiet revolution is going on, and the two 'big' diesels that were undreamably large in the 1990s are generally approved of. The prospect of a proper big diesel with loads of 'grunt' is beginning to excite people, so this volume makes no apology for including account of something that steam cannot do. If you want to run nonstop from one end terminal to the other, you need a diesel; let Bob Cable tell you why.

**T**he Ffestiniog Railway has long been well known for it's ability to field extraordinary Galas and special events. With the completion of the Welsh Highland Railway, a whole new raft of possibilities have opened up, as witnessed by the glorious *Snowdonian* in March 2011 - seen elsewhere. However the FR family has also been adept at quietly doing the extraordinary with little or no publicity. Thus it was at the 'Spring Thing' event in 2011 that the eagle eyed might have noticed a 'NONSTOP' run from Blaenau Ffestiniog to Caernarfon, inserted almost apologetically on Sunday 1st May 2011. This train would surely be notable as the longest non-stop run ever achieved on a preserved railway in Britain.

Perhaps because no one quite believed it could be done, or because it had to be diesel hauled (even the FR has yet to perfect 2ft gauge water troughs), the train ran with little fanfare.

So it was that FR Funkey diesel Vale of Ffestiniog set off with 7 carriages at the unusually early hour of 08.40, 10 minutes late as it happened, for what was an unremarkable run to Blaenau. However once at Blaenau, the Vale and her crew of two, Messrs Bob Cable and David Davies, crept off

arrangements except at Rhiw Goch and Harbour Station. A 'mobile' signalman in the person of Mike Baker, who had ably co-ordinated the arrangements for the train, would race (carefully by road) from station to station where ever the train was not scheduled to cross another or where there was no resident signalman.

Thus six minutes after departure, the train inched through Tanygrisiau, and off at a very gentle pace to allow the signalman to get ahead of the train. Indeed the order of the day was for the drivers to be patient and to roll along gently. Giving in to temptation and romping though any sections would lead to a wait in a loop somewhere and ruin the day.

Tan y Bwlch was passed at 10.36, 5 minutes later than the working timetable, before continuing onward through the woods to Rhiw Goch. Here the 'Express' comfortably passed the 10.15 from Porthmadog to Blaenau behind the Earl of Merionydd.

Onward past Penrhyn, the train slipped passed Minffordd, still 5 late, with the General Manager manning the signalling arrangements. Swinging round Boston Lodge curve the down home was seen to be clear but the discs beyond, controlling the points to the WHR, were firmly 'on' as they should be. After passing the home, the signal could be returned to danger and the points set for the WHR, so the train edged forward gently towards Porthmadog. When the WHR Points disc signal cleared, the engine swung on to the WHR, passing Harbour station 58 minutes after leaving Blaenau.

Exchanging the token for the Pont Croesor staff, the ensemble rumbled at the prescribed 5mph over Britannia Bridge, round the back of Wilkinsons, over Snowdon Street, and finally we clattered over the Cambrian Coast line at Cae Pawb. The Welsh Highland Heritage Railway were in fine form, with no

*Above: Actually at the Blaenau buffer stops - on record.*
**All pictures - both pages  Bob Cable**
*Right: Rolling into Rhiw Goch, ready for a dignified run through the Loop, the picture from the co-pilot's seat.*

round the corner, out of sight, to 'kiss' the buffer stops. The Vale would truly become the only engine to have covered the combined railway every inch of the way!

Departure time was set at 10.05 and departure was (almost) deliberately a little late at 10.08. Now as those in the know will appreciate the FR, and now the WHR, are NOT well set up for nonstop working as traincrews operate all the token and staff

less than 3 engines saluting the train with a chorus of whistling and waving, responded to with much blowing of the Vale's horn, and waving in return. Who says there is any animosity between the two organisations?

Due to an anomaly in the working timetable the train was now two minutes early, so progress was pedestrian to spill a little time. Mike Baker appeared for the third time at Pont Croesor, activating the crossing with the staff before exchanging it with the loco crew. From here we have to admit that there was a little cheating going on, or at least those involved were making use of technology that was unavailable to our forebears. A mobile call from Control warned the crew that the 10.00 from Caernarfon was running a bit late and that an arrival at Beddgelert at 11.42 was needed to guarantee a nonstop transit. A splendid dawdle ensued, hardly a hardship on a wonderful sunny day with the mountains of Snowdonia filling the windows ahead of the train. Having given the passengers plenty of time to enjoy the delights of the Aberglaslyn Pass, the train nosed rather tentatively into Beddgelert. With no mobile signal hereabouts were we still too early? There were lots of people on the platform but was No 87 round the corner out of sight? Happily the 10.00 from Caernarfon was comfortably in the platform, and the special could surge away up into Beddgelert Forest, with this potential obstacle behind it.

The next excitement was whether or not the Vale would overheat on the 1 in 40. Due for a new radiator last winter, an unfulfilled ambition, the engine had given trouble though much of 2010 with overheating, although in fairness this was often when double heading with the K1. The latter did not have a good year in 2010 either, and the practice of pushing a sulking K1 in front, as well as hauling 9 carriages, became known amongst some diesel drivers as 'pushing the Pram' up the hill! No wonder the Vale was often nearly on the boil. Careful handling however got us to the top of the hill this time, with the temperature gauge just hovering at the 100 degrees mark. Our mobile signalman offered appropriate token exchanges, to see the train past Rhyd Ddu, and Waunfawr for the 5th and final time. Still the train was forced to amble, with the prospect in mind of crossing the 12.30 from Caernarfon at Dinas. Suddenly, just before Tryfan Junction, a call from Control confirmed that the Up train was safely in the loop at Dinas. The Vale was able to surge away with her train.

The 'Express' now rattled down the bank, past Plas Bodaden, exchanged staffs with the crew of the waiting 138 at Dinas, and had a burst of line speed running down the bank into Caernarfon. Clattering out from under St Helen's Road Bridge the real Caernarfon Castle hove into sight and, now checked to the required 5mph, the train drew to a stand in Caernarfon Station, exactly on schedule at 13.00.

With just a tad under 40 miles under it's belt, the Nonstop Special had indeed done it nonstop in a time of 2 hours and 52 minutes.

After a few photos for the record the crew drew the Vale forward to 'kiss' the stops at Caernarfon. Every inch of the railway had been covered.

In the same time we might have gone from Paddington to Port Talbot or Euston nearly to Penrith, but we wouldn't have had so much fun. Was it the longest nonstop run, in terms of time that is, anywhere on Britain's railways that day or month or even year? The FR and WHR can be proud to have set a time and distance record for any nonstop run on a preserved railway.

Who will beat it?

*Above: Thumbs up for a 40 mile run non stop. Who will beat it?*

*Above: A celebration from the first non-stop team at Caenarfon*

*Below: Proof positive - the buffers at Caernarfon!*

nderstanding how the tokens work offers the key to how the WHR hopes to extend the ETS system across the whole Ffestiniog and Welsh Highland Railway, so they have a similar method of operation. The FR has a proper pole route, almost unique today and unaffordable on the 25 mile WHR, now that electrical connections by bare conductors are superseded by Internet and radio communication. Thus inventiveness was brought to bear, to see if in the 21st century a mix of old and new was possible says Roland Doyle.

olliding trains are not good for business, but security for multiple, bi-directional train running on single lines was difficult to arrange. At one time safety was achieved by putting a policeman on duty on each single line section of a railway. The train was not allowed to enter the single line section until the policeman was aboard the locomotive. After a while, the policeman's baton became the symbol for the movement authority. Called the 'token', it was placed on the hands of the driver, as the sole authority for a train to occupy the section to which it applied.

In 1888 the L&NWR invented an electrically worked instrument the Electric Train Staff (ETS) from which one token could be withdrawn at any time, from any instrument connected into the circuit. In 1912, the Festiniog Railway installed the Electric Train Staff system. Engineers provided token machines at both ends of the single line section, with a magazine of tokens, locked inside the machine, issued one at a time..

The machines at either end of a section are connected electrically, and function by means of a changeover switch, or commutator, which reverses polarity when a token is either taken out, or put in. If the polarity is the same on both machines, then a token may be taken out, and a train may pass through the section. Meanwhile, should it be attempted to take out another token from any instrument anywhere on the circuit, because the polarity in the circuit has been inverted on one of the instruments, both instruments will remain locked, denying the issue of any further token. Immediately the absent token is replaced in the instrument at the other end of the section, the polarity will agree and both the instruments are unlocked, to permit another, one token, to be removed. It will be seen that this system has the versatility to permit trains to pass either following one another through the section, or bi-directionally.

The electrical connection depends upon a pair of copper wires connecting the instruments together. The signaller wishing to release a token will ask the colleague at the other end of the section for a 'release'; the remote signaller would then hold down a key on the instrument, which applies a low voltage across the two wires, with a polarity set by his ETS machine. If both ETS machines are the same polarity, the local signalman will be able to extract a token, but in so doing will invert the polarity of his machine thus locking it. This also has the effect of locking the machine at the remote end. The train may then travel along the single line section and the token would be placed in the ETS instrument at the other end, inverting its polarity, so that both machines are now the same polarity (but both inverted from the original polarity). Since both machines are the same polarity, it is again possible to extract one token from either machine.

The need for the signaller was reduced by using the locomotive crews to operate the ETS system. A small generator handle on the 'remote operator' is wound to energise a relay at the remote end, which applies the remote instrument polarity to the line back to the local machine for comparison. Coincidence of polarity permits a token to be withdrawn. This system has been in use for many years now, and has worked very well indeed. However, a new 25 mile pole route

*Above: Two trains at Waunfawr, one each side of the loop. In the old days, the Policeman would get off one and go to the other, so it could return to Dinas. The Rhyd Ddu Policeman would be waiting to return to Rhyd Ddu, and to conduct the train there safely. Expensive in manpower, yet secure and convenient until an unbalanced service was desired - then there were problems.*

*Right: Countless train crews wind the little handle (which gives a most satisfying 'whirr') and observing the little signal go to CLEAR, they may then gently negotiate a token from the instrument, only to find if they take too long, that the relay un-latches and they have to wind again. If the polarity of the Minffordd instrument differs from this, then there's a token out, the relay will not latch, the little signal dips into the red LOCKED area and the instrument will not give you a token, no matter how gentle or kind you are.*

up the WHR would be unaffordable at today's prices. There is another potential problem – both the FR and WHR traverse the Snowdonia National Park which has strict planning rules for obvious reasons. The FR's pole route can stay because it has 'grandfather rights' but a new pole route up the WHR is unlikely to be acceptable.

Currently some drivers drive only on one part of the F&WHR. To make better commercial use of the rolling stock, it is planned for trains to run on both parts of the railway during a day. So train crews are more useful if they are signed for the whole of the 40 mile railway. Thus it follows that the same collision avoidance system, the ETS, is desirable on both parts of the railway; so how can it be done?

The FR obtained a batch of 17 ETS machines which had been made redundant from Iarnród Éireann, Irish Railways. These machines are now rare, so it was a good bit of luck to be able to get them. The practicality of fitting ETS all the way up the WHR

*The ETS machine at Porthmadog, connecting with the other end of this section, Minffordd. It is here as an 'end of line' instrument, but of course it isn't the end of the line anymore! There will be changes soon no doubt.*

was now possible, but the cabling cost was still an obstacle. There was a Doyle inspiration to use a novel method of linking the machines at an affordable price. There is a pre-existing, cabled infrastructure, available on demand anywhere along the WHR route - the public telephone. It would be possible to connect the instruments over the public phone system. Yet today there is something more subtle than that rather public affair - the Internet. The Doyle inspiration was to obtain the remote machine's polarity by using secure double-encrypted communications, with a view to keeping out unwanted third parties. This new connection method is called MicroETS.

At a token station equipped with the MicroETS system, each ETS machine has a MicroETS Outstation, a box about a foot square containing 4 purpose-made computers (microcontrollers).Each micro controller has independent access to the Internet but sits behind a firewall. Three of these computers are channel cards and communicate with three cards in the outstation at the remote end. The system would function with just one channel card at each end, but nowadays we are required to build in 'redundancy' . When comparing remote polarity with local

polarity, each of the 3 channel cards must agree that the polarities are the same before the machine is unlocked. The fourth computer in an outstation is an Event Recorder which keeps a record of events against time.

To prevent miscreant intervention, the channel cards generate a 'Magic Number' which is only used once. Each channel card in an outstation generates a different magic number. The corresponding channel card at the remote end is able to generate the same magic number, and so is able to check that it receives the right one with each communication. The magic number is very large. Statistically, the chances of someone guessing the magic number correctly is equivalent to someone winning the National Lottery three weekends in a row. But there are three of them. (It hasn't proved possible yet to persuade the cards to win the Lottery.)

The 'feel' of the system is the same as the original system - it's just 100 years newer and obviates the need to wire instruments together permanently. However, there is a major enhancement to the original system, and that is the MicroETS Management Server system, which collects data from all the Event recorders in all the outstations, and will show a mimic diagram of the railway in Control to show where tokens are in or out, and the direction of any movement authority. An engineer tasked with maintaining the MicroETS system can also run a PC with the MicroETS Maintenance Manager software which allows remote diagnostics without leaving the comfort of the office. If an outside visit is called for, the nature of the fault and the spare parts needed will be indicated.

Highrail Systems Ltd are currently preparing for a system trial, on the WHR, with linked ETS machines being installed at Beddgelert and Pont Croesor. Railway operators like to use equipment with a solid safety record, thus the new equipment is setting out to generate a safety history, by the shadow issue of ETS tokens between those two points.

During the trial, the system will be 'offline' from train operation so that it does not interfere with the extremely complex, current 19th century system of a piece of metal hanging on a hook with string.

*Purpose-made, channel cards by Highrail Systems Ltd ensure a properly checked and secure remote operator 'request' from one ETS instrument to another. Assuming polarities are the same, then a token may be withdrawn.*

**S**ignalling is a visible demonstration of the workings of a railway. Ian Rudd has long been a signalman on the FR, and has demonstrated his commitment by heading a team to rebuild the signal box at Rhiw Goch. When the word went out that it was now time to re-equip Porthmadog Harbour Station, with signalling for the large increase in activity needed to serve the terminus of two railways, the chance was taken to instal equipment in keeping with the wonderful narrow gauge atmosphere. Ian has volunteered to team-lead the task.

**D**uring 2011, the Welsh Highland Railway was finally connected to the Ffestiniog Railway again and services ran after a gap of seventy four years. The trains which did run through to Porthmadog had to be pulled back into the Harbour Station platform with a separate engine provided for the purpose. As there was either a Ffestiniog or a Welsh Highland train in the station - there could not be both - passengers could not transfer from Ffestiniog to the Welsh Highland trains.

So plans were drawn up for an island platform with the Welsh Highland trains on one side and the Ffestiniog trains on the other. To do this it was decided that the present Harbour station layout together with the signalling would have to be completely redesigned and rebuilt.

The last time this happened was just before the reopening to Dduallt in 1968. A six-lever Great Western ground frame was installed, along with Great Northern somersault signals. from Holloway Sidings in north London. They had been in use for about 60 years and, after refurbishment have had a further 40 or so year's faithful and reliable service out on the cob at Porthmadog. The ground frame came from Long Dyke Junction near to Roath on the east side of Cardiff on the South Wales main line. It provided access to Cardiff docks and Roath running shed. The locking configuration required at Porthmadog was the same at Long Dyke as that: 2 signals and 2 turnouts with locks. Thus it fitted the requirements at Porthmadog neatly, Later the Welsh Highland Points were taken out. Thus the second of the two points and locking levers on the frame, formerly the main line to the harbour proper, and the FR '0' was made redundant. All was put back in 2011 for reopening, and WHR ran again.

In 1968, as the work was taking place, the emotive and distinctive trident signal, which had been erected by the old Company on the Cob, blew down in a strong gale. The resignalling that took place in the late 1960's did not restore it but has served the FR well - now all must change.

At the other end of the FR, at Tanygrisiau, a group of signalling volunteers led by Bob de Wardt and Derek Winter started a scheme, in the 1990's, to signal Tanygrisiau Loop. with motor worked points and signals controlled from a Midland frame. Despite the work being on the brink of completion a decision was made to throw out the manual concept and make it simplified auto-loop. All the equipment which had been laboriously tailor-made for the scheme was taken down and carefully put into store for many years. However, the two bracket platform starters at Tanygrisiau were sold to the Isle of Man Railways. One of these signals now graces the end of the platforms at Douglas Station so at least someone benefitted from the carefully created narrow gauge appearance intended for Tanygrisiau. Both of the home signals posts are still where they were erected at Tanygrisiau, sentinels to the failed signal splendour.

So semaphore signalling on FR has had a chequered careers, as a grand scheme for Tan y Bwlch in the 1960s was also abandoned. When the requirements for resignalling Porthmadog were studied the simplest case seemed to be all electric with point motors and colour light signals. This would indicate a nice modern

**Above:** *Two trains at Waunfawr, one each side of the loop. In the old days, the Policeman would get off one and go to the other, so it could return to Dinas. The Rhyd Ddu Policeman would be waiting to return to Rhyd Ddu, and to conduct the train there safely. Expensive in manpower, yet secure and convenient until an unbalanced service was desired - then there were problems.*

**Right:** *Isle of Man Railway No. 4 Loch, has the honour of receiving a clear signal from an ex-Tanygrisiau bracket signal, mounted at the platform end of Douglas station. We can forgive their 3ft gauge hearts for acquiring and making good use of our signals. Yet there is a dark place that rankles against the forces of reaction who could not perceive the value of this homogenous sight of a Victorian locomotive passing a Victorian signal. Now the FR has changed, we give thanks - and go to the business of getting it all set up, ready.*
Peter Matthews

railway, not unlike London Transport, but without the tube trains. The Semaphorites sensed that here was necessity seeking invention! The option put forward to the Directors used the redundant material from the Tanygrisiau scheme and added to it with immaculate adherence to visual historical accuracy. The genius was to employ the same equipment that would have to have been bought for the London Transport style colour light scheme, but altered subtly with beautiful semaphore signals in place of immutable colour lights. heads. Of course the Directors were hooked by this proposal. It was right in line with FR philosophy - do things hi-tech, but make 'em look antique. Things such as a new signal cabin, new cable, a new relay room, and signal heads were common to both proposals. The big advantage of the 'retro-scheme' was that it grabbed the collective imagination, and did 'more for less'. So, with the promised sponsorship and volunteer offers, the fully signalled semaphore scheme looks like costing less than re-creating Ealing Broadway.

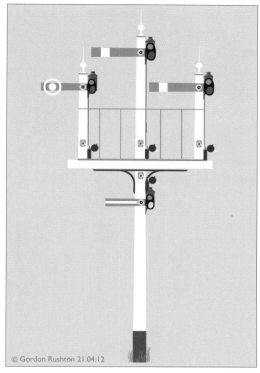

*The concept of what the Cob Trident signal may look like if it is taken 'retro' to Mckenzie and Holland, but with 2-colour spectacles (it could be LEDs). Whatever the detail, this is one impressive signal!*

© Gordon Rushton 21.04.12

A long, long time ago, when Doctor Beeching was wreaking destruction on our much loved branch lines, there were volunteer expeditions to Bala Junction to rescue the extensive signalling equipment, made redundant by the extinction of the entire system. It was an impressive collection, which was added to over the years, most of it GWR in origin, and it was always intended for the great signalling schemes 'to be', at Blaenau Ffestiniog and Porthmadog. Bits of the collection were used over the years, but experience indicated that standard gauge stuff in general was not well suited to large narrow gauge arrays. So it was gradually sold to those railways who needed it, and proved to have been a useful investment. However, now the time for which the old equipment was originally intended has come, we need some new equipment to do the job.

To give an idea: 5 new point machines, are needed of a type which is fully approved and has been tested; these will cost something like £3,000 each; 2 new Douglas fir signal posts will be in the region of £500 each; two new LED route indicators, about £350 each; 12 new track circuit boxes, about £300 each for the materials,

then the time and labour to assemble all the parts to make a working track circuit. Fortunately we have in stock all of the 200 or so relays which will be able to make the whole thing work. However each relay will need wiring up and the whole scheme will take something like 9 months to wire completely. The wiring diagrams and cross checking will take many months to prepare. It all has to be completed by April 2014. It's a real challenge.

The scheme, when completed will be worked by a Westinghouse 'L' frame. Peter Burke has donated the frame and he intends to help to install it.. Such is the power of this scheme.

The frame was installed at Darlington south in 1939, and was replaced in 1972. It has been in store since then and is in excellent condition only awaiting resetting to the Porthmadog's configuration.

A new signal cabin and a separate relay room will be required. at the end of the cross over from the FR sidings to the main line. The cabin will be long and thin and will be constructed on a similar style to the down platform shelter at Minffordd and the old signal room at Tan y Bwlch. As with the other buildings, it will be made out of timber but will be strengthened to withstand the winds and rain in the exposed location of the Cob. A team of volunteers, many of whom assisted in the construction of the new signal box at Rhiw Goch, have indicated that they would like to do the same again. This time the framework will be constructed in-house, and hopefully erected during the late autumn and the winter of 2012/13. The relay room will be erected first, to allow the wiring up to begin. Each of the buildings will have slated roofs, and modern standards of insulation. The Operating Manager has requested that provision is made in the signal cabin for a control desk so, during quieter times, the railways Controller may also operate the signals.

When the scheme is completed, it will give the Ffestiniog and Welsh Highland Railway's Porthmadog station a traditional appearance with Mackenzie and Holland style semaphore signals to be installed, including replacement of the trident signal. It will provide miniature shunt signals, all of which will be worked with an electric frame operating electric point and signal motors.

It will look so good!

*Discreet and neat, these point motors are installed unobtrusively by the trackside, quietly doing their job. If you prefer the unsightly point rodding to these, then you have missed the point of the FR/WHR. The objective is do it the best way possible - that's this way!*

Quality support was a priority in restoring the WHR. In 1992 CRhE was set up to achieve this. With some cash support via the FR Trust, members were recruited to the attractive and exciting WHR restoration project, and were soon busy. CRhE membership and their input shot upward. There were few politics, just a determination to enjoy and get on with the restoration. They quickly became, and remain principal, tracklayers and providers of a host of wanted items, with massive help, and expertise. CRhE Chairman Dafydd Thomas explains.

This is a story of a needed society, with support for a massive and exciting task. The directors are volunteers, drawn mostly from local people who have made a huge impact on the Welsh Highland Railway's restoration - after all it was volunteers who first sought to restore the railway.

The Society has raised funds and provided volunteers on an industrial scale, which has matched valuable grant funds as well as enabling all the work performed. Support, especially in the local area, has led to appearance at public events and the distribution of lots of publicity. All this activity has helped to create the conditions for the enterprise to prosper..

The members never had any doubt about what needed to be done, as the CRhE journal, Snowdon Ranger, kept everyone up to date with the news. The Millennium Fund grant required matching funds and CRhE started a Track Appeal to help. Early schemes raised £40k, and the later Track Metres project gained 450 sponsors to raise £300k. Success here stimulated the Phase 4 Appeal later.

Whatever the jobs that needed doing, CRhE would seek people with the skills to do them. Volunteers were involved with surveys of trackbed usage, assisting with the public enquiries, and preparations for tracklaying. Society volunteers trained so that there would be guards when the railway opened in 1997. The K1 Group, began their work at the Birmingham Railway Museum's Tyseley depot. The locomotive was moved to Boston Lodge for completion. The K1 Group still meets regularly to work on improving and maintaining that locomotive.

Society volunteers work on carriages, restoration of buildings, creation and maintenance of gardens, lineside clearance, restoration of non-passenger vehicles, building and installing water tanks; fabricating station running-in boards, lineside walls and fencing, clearing trackside ditches, building level crossings, restoring bridges, assembling turnouts, manning the buffet trolleys, driving and firing locomotives, cleaning locomotives and carriages, guarding trains, selling tickets, and helping with marketing, as well as a whole range of other tasks. They are active in the organisation of the ever popular Santa Trains, the real ale festival – Cwrw ar y Cledrau / Railale and

'Superpower', around the Society's AGM weekend.

The Society funded Snowdon Ranger and Nantmor Halts and the shelters were erected and painted by volunteers. The Society has funded, commissioned, erected, and painted platform shelters at Beddgelert, Meillionen and Waunfawr, fencing at Caernarfon and Dinas stations. CRhE Area groups have funded and given practical assistance with:
- Wagons for use on the reconstruction of the railway and others for use in maintaining the operating railway.
- The crossing gates at Cae Pawb.
- The summit sign at Pitt's Head.
- The replica Lamp Hut at Beddgelert.

*The 'crinkly tin' hut may not be the most elegant building in the world but it is very much 'in period' for the 1922 WHR. This is what they built at halts, and it is not the sort of detail that the FR Co. funded 'basic railway' could manage to provide. CRhE could, and did. Buildings like this add atmosphere and amenity to the WHR, and together with the adjacent Pont Croesor announce to the customer that the place is cared for.*

The Society provided the majority of the funding for the purchase and fit out of the former Welsh Water building at Dinas, that will allow the locomotive shed's space to be more than doubled. The Society has also taken on the task of restoring No.134, one of two NG15 class 2-8-2 locomotives that the railway has. There are working parties throughout the year, possessed of a determination that it will be ready for work in 2015. Progress is on time but funds are welcome.

The Society wishes to raise cash to provide hostel facilities for volunteers in the vicinity of Dinas, and this will make life easier, cheaper and more practical for those who are actively involved with the continuing tasks on the WHR.

It was CRhE volunteers who laid the first lengths of track at Dinas. The tracklaying volunteers did their apprenticeship at Glan y Pwll on the Ffestiniog Railway, laying No.6 road, the first place that NGG16 No.138 was steamed upon arrival from South Africa. It was CRhE volunteers who were involved with the assembly of No.138 after its arrival. Those who made the fortnightly trip to Blaenau Ffestiniog were joined by others from further afield, but essentially it was people who lived within about thirty mile radius of Blaenau. Many were first language Welsh speakers, and Welsh was more often than not to be heard above the clamour of the tracklaying. We made friendships which have endured, and formed the nucleus of a gang that still continues in 2012. This North Wales Gang soon got the name The Back Hand Gang, not from any political affiliation, but simply because of the staying properties of the thick, black, grease used to lubricate the fishplates, in which everyone's hands became covered.

By May 1997 the volunteers came to join employed staff laying the track going north from Dinas towards Caernarfon. By October 1997 the track had been completed on Phase 1, which enabled trains to be run for a period of three weeks. Christmas 1998 saw us lay the track into the newly constructed Carriage Shed at Dinas on our own. We experimented with Roland Rail Movers and Ed Lloyd Hughes took a roller conveyor, cut it up into its individual rollers and welded in some cross pieces, so that we had rollers of the right height and width to place in the middle of the track. All we now had to do was put these rollers at every fifth sleeper, starting from the end of track and roll in the rail. It was a tracklaying breakthrough. Fred Howes the Ffestiniog Railway's Civil Engineer pronounced our work fit enough to run the carriages on, and Roland Doyle, WHLR's GM congratulated us on a job well done. We had won our spurs. From now on we were permitted to run our own weekends without the need for a Company supervisor.

The Christmas 1999 task was refurbishing one of the original North Wales Narrow Gauge Railway's culverts, UB27, now **UB28.62**. We had no works train as there was no track, and only a 4 tonne dumper to carry the tools, etc. The nearest mess facilities were at Waunfawr, a twenty minute trudge along the muddy trackbed, so it was tea and lunch *al fresco*. All we had was a kettle, a teapot and some cups. It was not ideal, especially when it rained, cold December rain and sleet. Again Ed Lloyd Hughes came to the rescue, and rigged up a tarpaulin, slung between trees, just in the nick of time, for as we settled down to eat our sandwiches, huddled together under the make-do shelter for warmth, the heaviest hail storm in years let rip. We must have looked a pretty glum lot under that tarpaulin, for this spot became known as and always will be Camp Despair.

In the summer of 2000 tracklaying was able to continue beyond the stop blocks at Waunfawr. The first section, of approximately one kilometre beyond Waunfawr, the start of Phase Three, was laid by volunteers. This took us to the site of Betws Garmon station beyond which there was a small local difficulty. The difficulty was the need to get across Afon Gwyrfai; the original bridge had been removed. We stopped.

In order that track laying could proceed a 'leap-frog' was carried out, as had been done on Phase 2, with rail now being delivered to Rhyd Ddu. Sleepers were laid out ready in packs at predetermined locations by the staff that did the ballasting. We soon had new rail from South Africa (it cost less to purchase

it and transport it from there than to purchase new rail in the UK). The track was laid going north towards Glanrafon. As we got further from Rhyd Ddu we were given the Simplex diesel loco *Dolgarrog*. This gave a number of volunteers the opportunity to become Construction Train Drivers, which was an advantage later, when we needed to cover greater distances with rails and tools, as well as a crew of volunteers. Again on this section the volunteers gave a location an unofficial name. There was a small pond between Clogwyn y Gwin and Ffridd Isaf curve, in which a volunteer had strategically placed some yellow plastic ducks; this location became known simply as 'The Ducks'.

Once track was complete to Rhyd Ddu, and a train service was established, attention turned to track maintenance of the 12½ miles of the operating railway. Some of the tasks were irksome, such as the removal of ash saplings from the ballast, which the permitted herbicide had no effect on; most were fun.

In 2004, as soon as the contractors had prepared a ballasted trackbed, we commenced to lay the track south from Rhyd Ddu, starting Phase 4. We now had different materials, the rail and fish plates were from Poland; the sleepers were from India, with Elastic Rail Clips (ERCs) to secure the rail to the sleepers. Once we got the hang of inserting the ERCs, it made a great difference to the amount of time it took to secure a rail to the sleepers. The only annoyance we had with this system was requirement to have a plastic pad between the rail and the sleeper. They were fine most of the time, however if there was anything more than a gentle breeze they would fly off before the rail had been put in place on the sleepers. This would involve track volunteers chasing small, red plastic squares along the trackbed, in culverts, over fences, and into lineside bushes. It looked strange.

*The Black Hand Gang is hard at work laying in the track for Pont Croesor Loop. This photograph was taken on 7th June 2009, when a, engineer's siding was being laid. Later came the bottom points of the loop, and first one, and then two platforms. The view is taken looking south. Behind are the level crossings and the Afon Glaslyn.*

**Andrew Thomas**

For the track laying south from Rhyd Ddu, a second gang was set up, led by Paul Bradshaw. Working on the 'other' weekends, they became known as the Rest of the World Gang. On occasions those 'jacks of all trades', the Tuesday Gang would also be tracklaying; they specialised in the gauge widening necessary on tight curves using left-over SAR sleepers with adjustable fastenings.

We now had a proper works train, which consisted of diesel loco *Upnor Castle*, an ex-South African brake van, which acted as our toolvan, and a mess coach (former FR Observation Car100). The mess coach was a welcome haven on cold wet days. There were also two flat DZ wagons that had been semi-permanently joined as rail carriers.

We would often be hot on the heels of the contractors as they prepared the track bed ahead of us. In this Phase there was no leap-frogging, as the bridges were being worked on well in advance. There were five major bridges on this section; all were designed by Society volunteer John Sreeves, who just happened to be a bridge engineer. A portaloo was installed in the South African toolvan, to accommodate mixed work gangs. This did not always make it to the designated point to be emptied and cleaned out; in the summer months the toolvan became known as the 'carriage of many flies'!

Phase 4 also involved a new experience for us, tunnels; there are four. One volunteer, with less knowledge of the line than many, was heard to comment, "It can rain now as we'll be inside in the dry". He soon realised how wrong he was. We had just completed laying the track through this tunnel when I asked Dave Kent, who happened to be the works train driver that day, to try the train for size, as we both had a sneaking suspicion that the height clearance looked a bit tight. Dave duly eased the train towards the tunnel and although *Upnor Castle* made it into the tunnel, within less than a half-metre, it became obvious that the ex-South African Railways brake van would not. So the track was taken up, the tunnel floor was lowered, a slightly thinner layer of ballast was installed and the track was re-instated on steel sleepers to give the clearance wanted.

Once out of the south end of Tunnel 4 work progressed quickly to Nantmor and beyond. Rail for this section had been stored in the 'two foot' north of Tunnel 4, and involved a run with *Upnor Castle* and a pair of RRMs through the tunnel to collect the rail. At this time the loco was starting so show the signs of the amount of work it had done. It was unable to maintain enough air pressure to keep systems going. On one occasion blowing up air took so long that two of the track gang, working south of Tunnel 4 began to think something was amiss. A mobile signal in this area is at best erratic, so they felt they had no alternative but to come looking. However the train had got air and was proceeding. When the train rounded the small curve towards the north end of the tunnel they saw two persons hurriedly exiting the south end of the tunnel at a remarkable speed.

Once down on the flatlands of the Glaslyn estuary, with its long straight sections, tracklaying progressed

*This was the meeting of the two 'Welsh Highlands' at Traeth Mawr near to* **OB52.76** *on 31st August 2008. The WHR from Caernarfon met the WHR from Tremadog Rd at Traeth Mawr, near to Pugh's Bridge. The Black Hand Gang, who stand together with the WHHR crew. Barrie Clark installs the Golden Clip.* **Ben Fisher**

and we had a makeshift 'Golden Clip' ceremony. The WHHR train had come up from Tremadog Road, and our Works Train was parked not far from the Head of Steel. Veteran volunteer, Barrie Clark pulled the gold painted ERC into place followed by applause from the assembled audience of North Wales/Black Hand Gang volunteers, WHHR train crew; the few passengers, craning their necks out of the coaches and a couple of dog walkers on the nearby footpath.

Eventually all sections of track were joined up, leaving just that final short piece at Harbour station. The turnout from the FR line been installed in February 2008. The actual last fishplate was fitted in the dark on 27th February 2009, with the aid of light from two wind-up torches, from the Harbour station shop and a mobile telephone. The next day we tidied up and had the by now famous 'Golden Bolt Ceremony'. What the majority never saw was that both Paul Bradshaw and I somehow, initially managed put the bolts in with the inscription upside down in the dark. Needless to say it was corrected!

So there we were, a completed line of steel from Caernarfon, 25 miles to Porthmadog. However we were far from finished; there was the loop to be put in at Pont Croesor, and much of the track needed to be fettled to bring it up to a good standard for running passenger trains.

Eventually service began from Caernarfon through to Porthmadog, and the Society's volunteers still continue to come together regularly to 'finish', improve, and maintain the track, as well as the infrastructure of the now restored and magnificent WHR.

at a swift pace with not only the North Wales/Black Hand Gang and the Rest of the World Gang working alternate weekends, but also input from other groups.

We had a preview of what it would be like when we would finally join up with the Ffestiniog Railway as the tracklaying reached Traeth Mawr and the limit that the Welsh Highland Heritage Railway had laid track to. Although it was not immediately possible to join both lines together, due to height and alignment differences, they were still very close

*Here are two great 'men of the track', CRhE Chairman Dafydd Thomas on the left and Paul Bradshaw on the right. They survey the scene at the ceremony of the Golden Bolt that took place at Porthmadog on 28th February 2009.* **Roger Dimmick**

# Chapter 12
# The Money,
# & The People

12

There was concern in FR Co. when the news filtered through that the Official Receiver was intending to sell the WHR trackbed to the GCC for £1. There was worry that this would not be good for FR; yet it was difficult to see how to protect against competition. 'Building Back to Blaenau' may have been glorious, but it was not a financial success. The FR was struggling, and was not making significant profits that it could plough back into the business. So there was no money available for extravagant gestures. The general FR view, often expressed, was that WHR restoration could only be considered when the FR was finished - and it certainly wasn't in 1988. The FR Co. Board view at the time was to search for an affordable way for some sort of protection against competition. Thus the bid for the trackbed of £16k was launched. The concept not to 'buy to shut', as there wasn't the money for that, but to get a slice of the action, without spending money that wasn't there. The approach to GCC was seen as a move to stop competitive railway development. The arguments have been rehearsed elsewhere in this volume, and the facts about the action are in the public domain. The point is that FR Co. did not have the funds to do other than intervene 'on the cheap' to protect their interests, and that is what they did. If they had wished to stop railway development totally, then an Abandonment Order could have been funded, possibly for less.

The mighty reaction against them took FR by surprise. If there hadn't been a major threat, then there was now. There was also a stated competitor. The FR response was not to back down, but to go looking for ideas to counter the threat, and to find the resources to implement those ideas. It didn't take very long for FR to embrace the concept of restoring the whole WHR. This was the reciprocal of the idea of protecting against competition by acquiring the trackbed to control development. It was clear, and expected, that FR would attend the High Court to contest

the sale to GCC. That would be expensive, but it was considered necessary. As pressure rose, it became obvious that the option to back down, and to withdraw the FR bid was now pressing. It was really irksome and humiliating to have to back down - but it looked likely. Until the offer came from TCL for reconstructing the 1922 Company the idea of the Grand Slam was ruled out from a lack of money. Acceptance of the idea was enabled by a sponsor providing the funds to be present in the High Court with the TCL proposal. The process now became like a ratchet; once a step was taken and the money was committed, the only option was to go forward to the next step.

*The ERDF INCA project included a new locomotive, the* David Lloyd George *and the Blaenau scheme included expansion and augmentation of the station. All of this 'happened' and so FR had a good reputation in receiving grants. This was helpful with the Millennium Fund application. Here* DLG *is being attached at Blaenau, to the 14.25 departure on 5th June 2008.*

The outcome of the High Court caught GCC rather by surprise. Some on the 64 Co. side reported that FR Co had 'lost' the case, as they didn't get the stay of the sale they asked for. However the outcome was not good for GCC. It seemed as though one moment they had a small outfit asking to restore a little railway track to Pont Croesor; next minute the High Court outcome was about restoring 25 miles of railway from Caernarfon through to Porthmadog. They were by no means sure they wanted such a thing. Not long ago FR had been pleading with them to prevent commercial development of a railway on the trackbed. Now it seemed they wanted to restore the WHR, extend it into Caernarfon, and cross the Cambrian to join with the FR in Porthmadog. And they were proposing to begin this by means of a Transfer Order (TO); meanwhile the sale was stopped! That was the surprise. Costs had been within the realms of the 'normal' so far, and justified to GCC by the prize of the trackbed in public ownership. The cost implications now began to be a big potential problem. Ironically it looked as though to buy and not to permit railway development was something that had passed as a concept to the GCC.

The FR three-point, Grand Slam strategy of 1991 was so good, that the resources had to be found to do it. This proposal

## AN INDICATION OF WHERE MONEY CAME FROM - WHR PHASES 1 - 4

| Segment | Date | Description | Agency | £m | Notes |
|---|---|---|---|---|---|
| High Court | 1991 | 1922 Co. reconstruction | Sponsor | 0.110 | High Court led to TO application and inquiry. |
| Transfer Order | 1993 | TO Application and Public Inquiry | Sponsor | 0.240 | Competitive application, that the FR Co. gained by Ministerial decision. |
| Phase 1 | 1993 | Rolling stock | Sponsor | 0.200 | Payment for 138 and 143 NNG 16 Garratts and wagons |
| Phases 1 - 3 | 1996 | Caernarfon - Rhyd Ddu | ERDF | 3.3 | The ERDF component for Phase 1 was £0.75m |
| Phase 1 - 3 | 1996 | Caernarfon - Rhyd Ddu | Private partnership | 1.28 | These are 'own funds' administered by FR Trust |
| Phase 1 | 1997 | Rails | Sponsor | 0.250 | Advanced purchase of rail |
| Phase 1 | 1997 | Phase 1 Construction | Sponsor | 0.500 | Matched funding of 15% of the Caern- Dinas construction |
| Phase 1-3 | 1996/9 | Caernarfon - Rhy Ddu | Wales Tourist Board | 0.445 | |
| TWA | 1997 1998 | Dinas - Porthmadog | Sponsor | 1 | These are the costs for: Caerns-Dinas LRO, TO and Public Inquiry, TWO application and the Public Inquiry that followed, then the SNPA inquiry arising, plus the bill on taking possession of the trackbed. |
| Phases 1 - 3 | 1995 1999 | Caernarfon - Rhyd Ddu | Millennium Commission | 4.58 | The total capital cost was stated as £9.16m The MC figure incl. Derelict Land Grant of which £4,266,690 (42%) was MC Phase 1 |
| Phase 4 | 2001 | Aberglaslyn Pass, remedial works against rock falls | FR Trust | 0.250 | Paid for by the Festiniog Railway Trust. £250k work, £35k supervision, description Chapter 7 |
| Phase 4 | 2004 | Rhyd Ddu - Porthmadog | WAG | 5.2 | Representing 37.5% Objective 1, WAG 9.4%. WDA 2%. The total cost estimate was £10.77m |
| Phase 4 | 2004 2010 | Rhyd Ddu - Porthmadog | Private donations | 4.6 | Generous gifts by individuals |
| Phase 4 | 2004 2014 | Rhyd Ddu - Porthmadog | Public subscription - FRT | 2.2 | A scheme set up by Messrs Savage and Rushton for public subscription - see text |
| Phase 4 | 2004 2010 | Rhyd Ddu - Porthmadog | CRhE fundraising and donations | 0.150 | The result of much effort from CRhE to support the project |
| Phase 4 | 2004 2010 | Rhyd Ddu - Porthmadog | CRhE and Volunteers | 0.500 | The immense effort of volunteers, particularly in tracklaying, that counted as 'cash' towards the project. |
| Phase 5 | 2011 | FR &WHR | Public subscription Appeal | 0.600 | The Phase 5 Appeal set up to support the Sustainable Railway. |
| Phase 5 | 2011 | FR Co. | National Stations Improvement Project | 0.600 | To improve Harbour Station, by adding a second loop and platform (for the WHR trains). To do this the Cob needed widening. |

*Some of these figures are included in totals elsewhere in the table - do not attempt to total the amounts in columns and this is **not** a full list..*
*Sponsor total: £2.3m, add loans to FR Trust (gifts) and miscellaneous, totalling a contribution of approximately £3.25m*

*WARNING: looking across these tabulations and in the text, some of the figures do not agree. It is impossible to get the 'books' to balance, and the reader is going to have to be content with the information that has been gleaned, as much of this is information is not in the public domain.*

was one that snatched the FR out of its narrowing customer base, and thrust it into a ten-year development plan that, if it was successful, would change it out of all recognition to become a major tourist initiative that could reach out to world markets. It was the dawning of this idea that offered the force necessary to find the money. It left the clamour of the petty squabbles behind. It was the grand design that mattered, and this concept grabbed people's imagination.

Pretty well the whole railway enthusiast community thought full restoration was a good idea, but how was it to be funded? The old way, to sell shares to raise money, would not work as the business model could not offer a return of profit for investment. The restoration costs from Caernarfon to Porthmadog were thought to be in the order of £19m. There was no way one sponsor could fund that. Clearly the matter was dependent on grants. Full restoration of 25 miles would be unlikely to be

affordable in 'one go'. Thus the only way to proceed was to divide the WHR into stages, and to have a 'punt' with the grant bodies, and then get on with the business of raising matching funds. The risk at each stage was to fail to come up with the money for the next stage, leading to inability to proceed, and failure of the task.

## Phases 1-3: Caernarfon to Rhyd Ddu

The chosen strategy was to begin reconstruction of the 3 mile Caernarfon to Dinas section as soon as possible, to prove that the FR 'meant business'. No grant was earmarked until one of those surprising opportunities so common to the history of narrow gauge railway restoration suddenly presented itself.

Society member Bob Gartside lived in Beddgelert in the

| **T1 Phases 1-3 FUNDS - all £k   As est'd in 1996** | | | | | |
|---|---|---|---|---|---|
| Sources of funds | 1996 | 1997 | 1998 | 1999 | Total |
| ERDF | 888 | 1224 | 538 | 650 | 3300 |
| Partnership | 500 | 260 | 260 | 260 | 1280 |
| Derelict Land* | 100 | 250 | 250 | 0 | 600 |
| Millennium | 1072 | 1479 | 645 | 784 | 3980 |
| | | | | | |
| Total | 2560 | 3213 | 1693 | 1694 | 9160 |

\* Derelict Land Grant - a special fund for rehabilitating unused land

| **T2 Phases 1-3 COSTS - all £k   As est'd in 1996** | | | | | |
|---|---|---|---|---|---|
| Expenditure | 1996 | 1997 | 1998 | 1999 | Total |
| Land Purchase | 160 | 40 | 0 | 0 | 200 |
| CEng, Wks etc | 1,165 | 2,145 | 1,250 | 1,162 | 5,722 |
| Loco & stock | 798 | 860 | 320 | 260 | 2,238 |
| Admin | 206 | 205 | 177 | 162 | 750 |
| Professional | 135 | 95 | 10 | 10 | 200 |
| | | | | | |
| Totals | 2,464 | 3,345 | 1,757 | 1,594 | 9,160 |

1990s, and he was the Chairman of the Royal Pharmaceutical Society in Wales. Whilst campaigning to retain the local post office, a fellow campaigner happened to mention to Bob that she had met someone from the Millennium Commission (MC) who was looking for suitable projects, why didn't the railway apply?

The Conservatives had created the MC in 1993 by the National Lottery Act, to administer a fund to celebrate the coming Millennium. It was one of the bodies that had an official hand in the golden pot of the National Lottery - it could 'win' a prize every week. They sought hallmark endeavours: and gave £10m to the Eden Project in Cornwall; £22m to the National Botanic Gardens of Wales; £23m to the Changing Places programme, and so forth.

Apparently there was no candidate for funding in North Wales. It was decided that although it made sense to obtain a TWO for the whole distance from Dinas to Porthmadog, the MC application would be to fund the section from Caernarfon to Rhyd Ddu, Phases 1-3. It was considered that there would be little chance of their funding restoration of the whole WHR for the reason that it was not possible to guarantee completion of the project by the Year 2000.

To apply for this grant required detailed cost information. FR was a late applicant. Trying to produce a cost estimate for rebuilding 12 miles of railway and fully equipping it in the time available before the application round closed was no easy task, bearing in mind that a lot of the trackbed was barely accessible at the time, and some landowners were hostile. Fortunately, the Scott Handley report had scheduled most of the work to be done, and had produced a cost estimate that only needed updating and expanding. The approach from FR Co. was favourably received, by MC, and helpful discussions took place. The preliminary offer of a grant was made in May 1995, coupled with a request for a more detailed analysis of costs. This was produced by consultants Symonds in Colwyn Bay. A submission of considerable detail was made and was broken down into the following:

## Overview
1. Design and Drawings
2. Estimates of Capital Costs
3. Technical Specifications
4. Names and Responsibilities of all Consultants
5. Details of any Contracts
6. Details of Planning Consents
7. Technical Surveys
8. Formal Valuation of Assets
9&10. Business Plans
11. Sources of Funding
12. Expenditure and Income Cashflows

The information in this document is complex, but it does two things outside the MC application:

**a.** It records with clarity and detail, what the FR Co. will do with the grant. There were many other projects vying for funds. If Millennium offered a grant there is no room for any accusations by detractors that the FR Co. 'doesn't mean what it says', this is a 'contract' to rebuild the railway from Caernarfon to Rhyd Ddu.

**b.** If this grant is given, then it is a message in 'clear' to all in authority that this project is 'approved'. Indeed it must change to accommodate objections; FR Co. must be expected to mitigate problems, and to serve those affected by the works, but such a grant acted as a seal of approval that complemented the High Court judgement. This bore witness to all in the area.

Later, Bob Gartside hosted Rhodri Morgan at an RPS dinner, and in conversation, as soon as Mr Morgan became acquainted with Bob's connection to the WHR, Bob was thoroughly mined for information all about the railway and its intentions. It was therefore clear that there was real interest in the project.

The estimates of capital cost for Phases 1-3 are set out in the tables **T1 & T2**. This neat schedule would undergo a certain amount of rude distortion from the length of time the TWO took to gain, and the problems following with the SNPA. This caused the MC to threaten to withdraw finance later, in June 1999.

There was a great deal of explaining to do in the application document, and not all of it was satisfactory. For example: there was no signed lease for Caernarfon - Dinas; no trains would run for two years; there was no FR Co. ownership of the trackbed, nor any permission to reinstate the railway between the two points for which FR Co. was applying for funds. The detailed estimates of capital costs hung together, but they were not immune from the changes that occur when doing the job.

The Technical Specification, prepared by Posford Duvivier in Caernarfon, contained the management 'spec, the organisational diagram, and a Gantt Chart of progress, showing termination at Rhyd Ddu at the end of September 1999. Looking at the Gantt Chart today, it seems optimistic, but it indicated clear thought about what must be done, and it passed the criteria of the MC.

The Section 6 on Planning Consent contained a great deal of conditional material. The TO was already dealt with, and there had already been a pre-meeting with the Department of Transport over the TWO application in November 1994. So it was possible to claim that the TWO process was at least being actively pursued, as the TO was made on 14 March 1995. However nothing could disguise the fact that the TWO application was only 'applied for'. Yet this was evidently such a good project, and well positioned geographically, that it still received a firm offer of funding.

On the commercial side, the Business Plans were well

rehearsed from the recent public inquiry over the TO. First of all, the railway between Caernarfon and Rhyd Ddu was forecast to be profitable, with an annual surplus of £54k. The passenger numbers between Caernarfon and Dinas were estimated at a respectable 80k per year. In fact this was never achieved - the railway moved on too soon, and there was no co-operation with the idea of a Caernarfon Park and Ride scheme. The proposal of 130k passengers to Rhyd Ddu was also never achieved. The predicted, hourly High Season service

*The basic railway ends at a basic station, with a headshunt and one siding. Water was at the far end, and to begin with there was no building, until a wooden temporary one was built later. The longer loop, twin platform face, and Porthmadog facing sidings for construction were left out of the scheme to save money. Still, a railway almost the length of the FR had been constructed for about £10m - quite an achievement.*

that this project happened. Caernarfon to Dinas was 85% funded by the MC. To bridge the 15% difference, the sponsor provided funds. The total count up of money put in to WHR by comes to approximately £3.25m, and it isn't over yet!

In case it should be thought boastful to reveal such sums, please be aware that the detail comes from the author and not from the donor, who would rather have remained discreet. Other sponsors put in even larger sums but they demanded anonymity. It was the author's insistence that the

too has never been possible, though the local and regional economic effect of the railway, that was not mentioned in the application, has been considerable.

The sources of funding document cited the ERDF application, an application to Regional Challenge, Arfon Borough, WDA and WTB. FR had previously enjoyed grant funding from ERDF (European Regional Development Fund). INCA (INcreased CApacity) and Blaenau Ffestiniog development had benefitted greatly from it - the Blaenau scheme was at 100% funding. It seems that these were favourable considerations, as the Millennium Fund agreed to grant 45% of the estimated restoration costs of

reader should see in one instance at least, what was gathered from a private sources and how it was disbursed.

Until 1996, all the costs had been accounted by the FR team in Porthmadog Harbour Station. Under the Routly regime, promises had been given that WHR and FR were to be separate entities. However when the 'lease and build' deal had not been taken up by 64 Co., and had instead been replaced after the TO Inquiry with the 'restore the lot' policy of the new regime under Mike Hart, then matters were different.

Part of the rationale of WHR was that the overheads of the FR would be shared across the new railway. Thus the promises

£9.4m for the whole 12 mile section between Caernarfon and Rhyd Ddu. So the MC contributed 43.4%, ERDF 36%, (including Phase 1 ERDF grant of £750k) Partnership 14% and the Derelict Land Grant 6.6% - a total of £9.16m. The Phase 1 funding problem had largely disappeared. The sponsor, who had borne all the project costs up to that point, agreed to make such funds as were needed available to cover the gap, to get things going. He very much wanted to see the WHR restored, and he was prepared to back the project, and to offer his professional expertise as a qualified civil engineer. Everyone did their bit to propel the project forward. Some, like Jeremy Sullivan QC, kindly gave his advocacy on a pro-bono basis for the TO Public Inquiry. More people joined together by lending their expertise to make sure

about complete financial separation were rescinded. FR stood to benefit from WHR, especially as it was starting from Caernarfon and tapping new markets. Although separate accounts were kept, there was 'crossover' as necessary between the two organisations, with the Festiniog Railway Trust being prepared to allocate funds to either railway, or as directed by the donor. Dinas (WHLR) dealt exclusively in WHR matters, subsidiary to the FR Trust. Mike Hart was in overall charge of the project as 'leader'; Mike Schumann, as a qualified civil engineer was the Project Engineer of WHLR, with control of contract work via consultants. Roland Doyle was WHLR General Manager, responsible to the Welsh Highland Light Railway Board for its conduct, with control of direct labour.

| T2a **Phases 1-3 Spend & Sources of funds** | | | | | |
|---|---|---|---|---|---|
| Description | Cost £m | Total £m | Fund £m | Total £m | Funded by |
| **COSTS** | | | | | **INCOME** |
| Legals* | 1.18 | 1.18 | 1.18 | 1.18 | .18 MC/1m MS |
| **Phase 1** | | | .75 | | ERDF |
| Rolling stock | .7 | | .45 | | WTB |
| Land Purchase | .2 | | 4.12 | | MC |
| 4.5km track | .6 | | 2.25 | | MS |
| Civils+admin | 1.35 | 3.25 | 2.31 | | Track Fund |
| Phase 2 | | | .25 | 10.13 | FRT (Ph2 on) |
| 6km track | .65 | | | | |
| Civils+admin | 2.01 | 2.66 | | | |
| Phase 3 | | | | | |
| Rolling Stock | .15 | | | | |
| 9km track | 1.00 | | | | |
| Civils+admin | 2.47 | 3.62 | | | |
| Non MC expense | .604 | .604 | | | |
| Grand Totals | | 11.31 | | 11.31 | |

**\* Legals: High Court, TO Inquiry, Trackbed legal fees, Caerns-Dinas LRO, SNPA Inquiry, NFU High Court, TWO application.**

# The Millennium Fund.

**Roger Dick represented the Project Monitor (Mott MacDonald) appointed by the Millennium Commission, verifying the claims for the work done and then seeing them certified for payment. It saved loads of time and trouble. He took lots of photos some of which have already been featured. Roger reveals interesting items about Phases 1-3, not generally known.**

Below are the figures certified by the Project Monitor for the WHR Millennium Commission Project.

| Phase | Expenditure | Grant |
|---|---|---|
| 1 | £3,254,067 | £1,405,800 |
| 2 | £2,655,899 | £841,046 |
| 3 | £3,620,000 | £2,053,154 |
| Total | £9,529,966 | £4,300,000 |

The total expenditure above is the MC "Baseline" expenditure. The full expenditure was reported in the final report to the MC as £10,133,981. The Baseline expenditure changed throughout the project by a system of *change requests*. The bottom line was that the MC had always planned to pay £4.3m and the so the figures and percentage grant were altered, to respond to changing conditions, to balance with that 'total' figure, and the £4.3m figure was adhered to.

The result of the *change requests* was that the project departed from the original planned extent, notably at stations, where Caernarfon and Rhyd Ddu were deleted or reduced in scale - in response to changing costs where conditions were revealed to be more onerous than originally planned for. Only some of the cost of the various Public Inquiries were included in the baseline. It cost over £1m to obtain the TWA Order, of which only (approx) £400k was eligible to be met by the MC. Furthermore none of the costs for the work required by TWA Order in the Aberglaslyn Pass were eligible for inclusion into in the MC project, even though these works were required to be completed before reinstatement commenced in the National Park.

The MC received a number of letters from people who did not entirely agree with the project, or who had genuine concerns over aspects of it. One letter asked whether it was known that the WHR were obtaining rail from South Africa, where it would have been designed for much different weather conditions. Thus it would be unsuitable for use in Wales. To be perfectly thorough it was decided to undertake an investigation of this potential problem. Unsurprisingly the outcome was not one of alarm, and it was settled that the rail was indeed perfectly acceptable for use in Wales. An anonymous letter containing various charges was received, including an accusation of the misappropriation of funds. The letter stated that it had also been copied to Gwynedd Council. The Project Monitor was requested by the MC to ascertain how Gwynedd Council handled such claims, so that a co-ordinated response could be made. I found the action that Gwynedd Council had taken was to throw the letter in the bin. They stated, in a more robust and experienced view, that they considered all anonymous correspondence as being mischievous and not worthy of any consideration. The MC were unconvinced, thinking that where there was smoke there was likely to be fire, and that some investigation was necessary. The issues were discussed with Mike Hart who took a similar view to Gwynedd Council.

In all, despite the concerns at the time to ensure that public money was spent responsibly, the MC grant was well spent. It was an indispensable contribution that made the WHR restoration to Rhyd Ddu possible, and it has proved to be one of the MC's most lasting contributions to the new Millennium. ∎

end of Phase 3 there were fears that WHLR might not be able to meet its obligations. Again this raised fears that the gap between available funds and necessary costs was too wide to meet by about £230k. Bear in mind that the project was running late, and that this was not the fault of FR Co. The all-up cost of the project was £11.31m, so a cost over-run was hardly surprising. At the same time the FR was experiencing cost difficulties, but the FR Trust was able to provide the bridging funds to complete the railway to Rhyd Ddu.

However there was a great deal left undone. Rhyd Ddu Station was not in a state of completeness, with a short loop line and almost nothing on the site. The Ffestiniog Trust was anxious to be certain that it had full disclosure of the position, and of course the matter had repercussions. Clear evidence was offered to the Trustees of no more problems waiting in the wings. The WHR was completed to Rhyd Ddu to the satisfaction of the HMRI, and some of the more costly problems to do with the 'finishing' of the station were rolled over into the Phase 4 project. For example: the loop and second platform face at Rhyd Ddu were not strictly necessary until Phase 4; only one siding was placed. As a temporary measure an FR garden shed technology building was erected at an affordable price. A temporary station building was all that could be afforded at Caernarfon, and at Waunfawr, there was nothing at all to start with.

The train service began, and it took no traffic away from the FR. Yet there was a mild hopelessness about being at Rhyd Ddu. Not much had changed since the NWNG days; there really wasn't anything there. Rhyd Ddu is not a natural destination, except for those who love to take a walk in the mountains, and more

Construction proceeded, and there were plenty of concerns. After Waunfawr it was clear that the MC grant was not enough to finish the reconstruction to Rhyd Ddu. Yet, any pause in the already late project could mean a stop that could be terminal. Costs were carefully pared to provide a basic railway. At the particularly up Snowdon, as a magnificent path leaves from Rhyd Ddu. The natural results of this geographic placement were soon to be come apparent. After a pleasant and celebrated visit from HRH The Prince of Wales, the service started to earn money on Monday 18th August 2003.

# Phase 4 : Rhyd Ddu to Porthmadog

The railway opened to Rhyd Ddu in 2003. It was wished fervently by Mike Hart and Mike Schumann that construction should continue onwards as a major priority. Most people recognised that an economic 'boom' was taking place in the country, and that the opportunity to go forward needed to be grabbed as soon as possible. To delay was to court disaster, as these booms have a clear history of fading fast. At first, Rhyd Ddu as an extension looked really successful. Before reaching Rhyd Ddu Waunfawr bookings were at just over 30k. In the first season to Rhyd Ddu, with all the publicity and excitement, this rocketed by 10k in one month, and the year 2003 saw traffic in the last five months increase to nearly 51k. The following full season saw the figures reach to 58.5k; perhaps Rhyd Ddu was going to be a successful commercial venture. Yet consideration suggested that Rhyd Ddu was not a place people in large numbers were likely to travel to, like say Beddgelert. There was precious little of sustenance, unless you walked some way into the village, and it was a fair wait between trains. It was wished therefore to move onwards. However, with the need to bridge the Phase 3 funding gap when rebuilding to Rhyd Ddu, and the fact that there were some problems on the FR at the time, Company finances were not showing surpluses. A new General Manager, Paul Lewin, a man who had been grounded in FR culture during the Eileen Clayton, Parks and Garden's era, was tasked with the job of creating stability. Though Mike Hart had stood down from the FR Co. Chair for family reasons, he was still in place to lead the WHR project. The Chairman of the FR Trust was now Dr John Prideaux, and the Chairman of FR Co. from 2003 was Michael Whitehouse. The team addressed the matter of funding and implementing Phase 4. To ensure that here was Trust agreement for the Phase 4 extension, the following needed to be arranged:

1. There must be no debt outstanding from the previous project, Phase 1-3.

2. New money could be found to fund Phase 4.

Mike Schumann had been carrying out civils cost estimates for the new phase, and had come up with a first figure of £4.4m.

This rose to £4.9m as far as Pont Croesor. When other items started to be added, like £1.5m for the CTRL the whole lot was estimated at £10.766m.

The next 13 miles had interesting engineering challenges that had a major effect on costs. It was clear from previous performance that the right way to do the job was to employ contractors, and that trackwork could be done by volunteers. It was equally clear that the right way to keep costs to a minimum was to build the 'basic', no-frills railway, as the bells and whistles could be added later, when it was in operation.

There was also strong pressure to manage the costs down to a price; a difficult thing to do when you cannot be sure what surprises lie underneath the surface of the railway to be constructed. To manage the costs more closely, a 'collegiate ' system of management was proposed within a new construction company, Welsh Highland Railway Construction Ltd. (WHRCL). Phases 1-3 had been reconstructed at a cost of £780k/mile - £487k/km. The proposal was to reconstruct Phase 4 for £860k/mile - £535k/km. Bearing in mind the cost of the first 3 miles between Caernarfon and Dinas in Phase 1-3, the first Phase 4 figures were courageous.

Table **T3** shows how the costs of the 16.6km from Rhyd Ddu to Porthmadog were separated. Note the 2.4km section from Pont Croesor was expected to be built by the 64 Co. Taking this section out of the figures removed some of the courage as the cost goes to £912k/mile - £570k/km. A a number of the estimated costs were removed later, to compensate for the extra costs incurred that emerged as construction proceeded. Costs grew to over £1200k/m - £755k/km as Phase 4 progressed.

Table **T4** shows the implications of the first funding income needed to meet **T3** costs. Just under 50% of the total could be expected in grants. To be able to start (and fulfil the Trust's requirements), the rest had to be promised, and the table shows the sources. The first estimate for public subscription (description to follow) was £300k.

Mike Hart succeeded with the Welsh Assembly Government in gaining a funding offer from the Objective 1, West Wales and Valleys 2000-2006, ERDF Programme. The completion of the

| **T3 Phase 4 - FIRST COSTING CALCULATION** | | |
|---|---|---|
| KM | | £m |
| 16.6 | All-in Civils cost @ £0.29/km | 4.814 |
| 2.4 | Civils Penymount - Pont Croesor* | 0 |
| 16.6 | Track/S&T @ £0.127k/km | 2.1082 |
| 2.4 | Track/S&T P'mt - Pont Croesor* | 0.1872 |
| 2 | Rly construct, RTrack-FR Harbr | 1.2 |
| | Modify Harbour | 0.3 |
| | Beddgelert Sta building | 0.20 |
| | Harbour Car pk | 0.15 |
| | Car pk land | 0.09 |
| | Mitigation | 0.49047 |
| | Management | 0.6471 |
| | Volunteers | 0.46656 |
| | (Ineligible costs) | 0.113 |
| | Total | 10.766 |

*Track materials - infrastructure to be built and funded by 64 Co

| **T4 Phase 4 - FIRST FUNDING INCOME** | |
|---|---|
| | £m |
| 37.546% from ERDF Obj 1 | 4 |
| 9.387% from WAG | 1 |
| 1.877% from WDA Grant | 0.2 |
| Sub Total | 5.2 |
| Cost | -10.766 |
| | |
| To find: | 5.566 |
| | |
| Private Gifts | 4.59 |
| Members + Gift Aid | 0.3 |
| WHR donations | 0.15 |
| WHR 64 Co* | 0.06 |
| Volunteer hours costs | 0.46656 |
| Total | 5.566 |

*the amount available from 64 Co to pay for track

WHR suited this programme well, it was an EU measure that was meant to encourage regional economic development, which is exactly what it did. The project timescale was originally set from August 2004 to June 2008. The grant rate was 37.15%. WAG were willing to fund an additional 12%, but this left FR with amounts to find that were rather large. Private gifts on such a scale were considered unlikely. However, Mr Hart managed to obtain agreement for funding on an astonishing scale from private sponsors. (With respect, and thanks, they remain private.)

Table **T5** shows the income side of **T4**, but later, and more refined. Note that the Phase 4 Appeal subscriptions rose to £586k (they went much higher later, in a effort to match the rising costs). Taken together with the supporters donations from generous sponsors (via the Trust) the balancing figure of £5.566m was assured. The project went ahead, contracts were let, work started and money began to flow.

From the start matters were difficult and cost over-runs began. Some examples are: Pitt's Head was difficult and awkward to drain and to stabilise; Pont Cae'r Gors Cutting also had to have expensive drainage work beyond that which was expected; the embankments at Weirglodd Isaf and two other places were costly; 64 Co. were unable to build to Pont Croesor, and the Cross Town Rail Link was expensive.

Table **T6** shows how the income was expanded to meet increases in costs. It was a particular struggle and a great strain upon the collegiate system. Mike Schumann was no longer on the team at this stage. Alas he withdrew for personal reasons over a fundamental disagreement in how matters were managed. Costs expanded steadily so that from the first estimates of £10.766m, they had reached £15.205m by 2009. The expanded funding level to meet them was achieved as follows: An increased grant of £1.4m was offered through the agency of WAG; private donors were persuaded to elevate their generosity by £703k; volunteer tracklayer credits went up by £705k, and the subscription scheme increased by £1.3m. It was a similar cost experience as in Phase 3. The extra cash was found, as the management had got smarter and more persuasive in trying to seek it out.

One factor however was not realised, and that was the potential income to the project promised by enhanced traffic. Carryings expressed the surge from novelty between Caernarfon and Rhyd Ddu after 2003 opening, but reduced rather alarmingly, bearing in mind that it was another five miles from Waunfawr,

and one would wish traffic to double to justify that - the increase was more like +50%. Although this was not as wished, even at these levels, income was substantially above working expenses. Moving on, it was desirable to be able to extend service with attendant increase in income. Alas funding the Phase 4 project from receipts was a problem, as the SNPA had expressed the undesirability of having any terminal in the Park until the railway was built to the south boundary. This meant that until the line was through the Aberglaslyn Pass, over the Afon Dylif, and on the flat, there could be no passenger service to Beddgelert. Negotiation of this rather important liability had taken second place to the problems of SNPA caused by the changing of their Plan (Policy TR16), such that there was a third public inquiry. The requirement was imposed upon the project by concern that unacceptable road congestion would be the effect of any railway terminating in Beddgelert. In the event people travelled by train from Caernarfon to Beddgelert when it opened, leaving their cars outside the Park. The arrangement prevented the wealth from some 70k railborne passengers from reaching Beddgelert a year earlier. It had the effect that there were no extra receipts available to offset increase in expenditure. This may be put aside in the exhilaration of the project's achievements, but the amounts were considerable. Receipts of some £1.4m per year were involved, and the difference lost was over £500k. Not only could the Trust have made good use of the extra money for constructing the railway, but construction may have been completed a full year earlier, also offering the economic benefit to Porthmadog.

To gather the funds, the pace of construction was slowed, and the scope was confined to a basic railway. Costs shown in **T3** were stripped out to accommodate the available income, and to meet the build timescale. Though traumatic this wasn't harmful, as experience showed that the costs of providing the 'bells and whistles' were eventually met later, after service began.

Service began from Rhyd Ddu to Beddgelert in April, to Hafod y Llyn in May 2009, to Pont Croesor a year later, and to Porthmadog in May 2011. Each time traffic surged. The civils costs continued to rise, with an £830k addition in 2009, including a provision for land purchase. Healthy income and active fund raising was able to offset this figure, initially by £500k, and then by more. However, it became clear when the full service began that the two platform option at Porthmadog was essential, and a further £1m would be needed to provide for that in Phase 5.

| **T5** Phase 4 - LATER FUNDING SOURCE ESTIMATES | |
|---|---|
| | £m |
| WAG Objective 1 Grant scheme | 4 |
| WAG | 1 |
| WDA | 0.2 |
| Supporters/donors | 4.51 |
| WHR Phase 4 Appeal | 0.586 |
| Cash equivalent volunteer tracklaying | 0.46 |
| | |
| Total | 10.76 |

This estimate is from when funding had been found. Generous donors came forward, the Phase 4 Appeal yielded more than was expected, and the CRhE volunteers tracklaying, which meant the grant bodies would offer an allowance for this. At this time WHRL had said they were not building to Pont Croesor

| **T6** Phases 4 - FINANCE 2009 - all £k | | |
|---|---|---|
| Sources of funds | at 2009 | Run tot |
| Welsh European Funding Office | 4920 | 4920 |
| Welsh Development Agency | 200 | 5120 |
| Welsh Assembly | 1271 | 6391 |
| Private donors | 5400 | 11791 |
| Trust Fundraisers* | 1892 | 13683 |
| CRhE (WHRS) | 192 | 13875 |
| Volunteers (time credit) | 1172 | 15047 |
| Miscellaneous | 158 | 15205 |
| | | |
| Total | 15205 | |

*Fundraising income is by subscription, some running to 2014, thus most of this income comes in as a stream and not all at once.

*It is a good idea to see what you've paid for, and it was this little darling that started it all. An Andy Savage/Gordon Rushton 1995 proposal to build a new locomotive by regular subscription was novel in preservation - Taliesin 2000. People like Fuzz Jordan went round flogging subscriptions and they were most successful. As the numbers grew to 250, the amount subscribed rose into the hundreds-of-thousands. Other schemes have since flattered by imitation - a major compliment. However, it was the FR who did this first - and the system worked very well. A similar subscription system worked for the Phase 4 Appeal.*

## The Phase 4 Appeal

**It is worth describing in some detail the subscriber funding for Phase 4. It was the most successful of its kind ever attempted, but more importantly it is a method that is open to anyone to try - and it works.**

A meeting was called on 26th July 2004, in Wragge's offices in Central Birmingham, to talk about funding and some fairly pithy comments were made, as the Trust wanted to be sure that the cost and income forecasts were robust. Present were Messrs Prideaux, Whitehouse, Hart, Lewin, Savage and Rushton.

The Trust was the effective 'authority' in overseeing the project, and monies passed that way in order to secure Gift Aid, the convenient add-on of basic tax, plus a rebate to the higher-rate taxpayer of the difference between high and basic rates(a popular arrangement that has secured much for charity). However the funding was not yet 'home' even with private donations at this level, as there was still a sizeable gap.

The reason Savage and Rushton

| Subscription Income Multiplier | | |
|---|---|---|
| 5 year scheme | £k | £k |
| Number of subscribers | £5/mth | £20/mth |
| 100 | 30 | 120 |
| 200 | 60 | 240 |
| 300 | 90 | 360 |
| 400 | 120 | 480 |
| Add Gift Aid at +25% | | |

*When it is seen written down of course the multiplying effect of group subscriptions is obvious - yet this system was extended to new heights to reach the £2m mark!*

were present was to rehearse their proposals for raising money from the members and the interested public in general. In 1995 they had devised the scheme to raise the money to build a replica of the single Fairlie locomotive *Taliesin*, that Roland Doyle and team then built. The principle had been to persuade 250 people to contribute a regular sum of money (£5) every month for 5 years. This subscription system worked well, financing the locomotive construction and several items of rolling stock. The WHR restoration had acquired a huge following, partly as a result of the notoriety arising from the disagreements in the 1990s between the FR Co. and the 64 Co., the intervention of the ARPS, and the wide reportage in Steam Railway Magazine and others. It was decided to try a subscription scheme on an altogether more generous scale, to see if this awareness could be tapped. The team recommended that a three-tier contributions scheme, with rising benefits for a rising subscription amount would probably serve best. The first presentation of the subscription plan was to the meeting at Wragge's on 26th July 2004. Gordon Rushton made the presentation, explaining that the subscription amounts would be Bronze £20, Silver £50

and Gold £100 per month, and that with 250 subscribers, all at the Bronze level £366k could be expected overall. The scheme was written down as contributing £300k and Andy Savage and Gordon Rushton were told to get on with it.

The pair pondered the best means of communicating with the public at large. It was rather obvious that Steam Railway were a good target. With a readership of some 40k enthusiasts per month, they would be an excellent launch platform for such a proposal. Plus of course it was they who had so criticised the FR's action in 1990. So there was a sense of irony in going back to them and asking for their support. The next question was how to get the message across as they were indeed helpful. It was clear that aside from any articles announcing the Phase 4 Appeal, some sort of exclusive avenue of approach was needed. Gordon Rushton designed an A4 leaflet, with a tear-off subscription form. The leaflet had all the chat about the project in purple prose. It was designed to stimulate interest, and then to encourage direct

response by signing up the reader as a subscriber with a Bankers' Order. The choice of Banker's Order was deliberate, as Direct Debits can be changed and change was not needed here. The public were thought to be more amenable to Banker's Orders.

The key to such schemes is of course the administration. Excellent administration, quick to respond to the generosity of the subscriber, efficient in dealing with the money, and able to make sure that benefits are acknowledged and dispatched with accuracy is great if you can get it. The scheme was fortunate in recruiting John Hopkins to administer the Phase 4 Appeal. His rapid response, and detailed and efficient spreadsheets, made sure that the administration was run smoothly, so that the subscription was taken up by the bank rapidly. He knew exactly what the contributions were, down to the individual postcode, and the information was made available quickly.

Steam Railway were generous in carrying the 40,000 leaflets designed for the purpose in their magazine, and they also

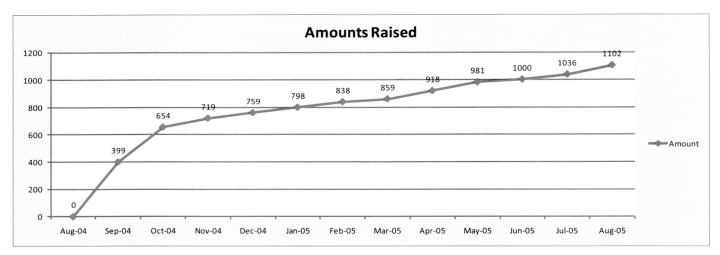

**Amounts Raised**

*Left hand side of the graph is in £k: The Steam Railway Phase 4 Appeal results were extremely good and took everyone by surprise. That first rush of £654k in September and October of 2004 was very nice. Yet it didn't stop there, it kept on rising, but at a slower rate. Within one year the cashflow income was hitting £4.5k per week.*

supported the project with articles, editorial and advertising at reduced rates. Steam Railway did as much to promote the Phase 4 project as they did to demonise the FR during the crises of the 1990s, and that had a major bearing on Phase 4 fundraising.

Results were almost unbelievably good. The Appeal went out in August 2004. The amounts coming in were huge, quite eclipsing funding requests for anything else in preservation, ever. It was clear that this initiative was switching the lights on in Steam Railway's readers' minds in an unprecedented manner. The original target was £350k. By September the subscription figure promised was £399k. The target was obviously too low, so in fine Ffestiniog tradition it was promptly raised to £500k, which in turn was surpassed in short order. In January £800k had been reached, this went to just over £1m by June 2005. It was considered that promotional activity was needed, as the amounts coming in had levelled by then. More activity was begun, this time in the Railway Magazine, and then in other publications. The basic form was the same in most cases: a leaflet included with the publication, supported by an article about the WHR, and then 'reminder' advertisements in subsequent issues.

People watched in awe as the amounts being subscribed rose and rose, and of course a steady cash stream began. After the £1m mark was passed these result began to flood the WHR team with a sense of blissful release. A result like this was a resounding vote of confidence in what FR was were trying to do. Better still, John Hopkins reported that of all the counties and regions supporting the Phase 4 Appeal, the one with the largest contribution was Gwynedd - it was such a wonderful feeling. All the misery-guts could at last be confounded, as the people who

really wanted the WHR were prepared to demonstrate their support with hard cash.

The inflow of cash and support had a number of important effects. There was an obligation to disburse the benefits that had been promised. The news of the distribution of the response to the Appeal was good news to the WAG politicians, who were supporting the project. The subscription element of the Appeal meant that people became actively interested in what was happening, and were willing to become actively involved with volunteering. They wished to be kept in touch.

Of particular note in this operation was the statistical information passed to the other members of the fund raising team by John Hopkins. It could be seen who it was that subscribed, how much they gave and where they lived. The wide geographical spread suggested universal appeal for little railways in Wales, though a number of people were well known names. These were 'members' of both the FRS and CRhE. Equally, a large component were unknown. Both societies supported the appeal, helping to sell the subscriber package, and a considerable following came from within the ranks of all supporters, in both the £20 and £100 subscription bands. This was particularly unselfish of the FRS, who gradually became uneasy that FR was no longer getting the investment it once enjoyed. This problem surfaced later on, where the story is told with the contemporary events of Phase 5.

*The same method was used to promote building new carriages. These are less popular, but even so £350k was raised - most commendable, that was three vehicles.*

When mooted, the Phase 4 subscription amounts were thought to be suicidally high. The question was asked that if the amount originally aimed for was £350k, why were they more than £5 per month, as had been set for *Taliesin*? The little team

| Subscriber Visits to WHR | |
|---|---|
| Date | Comment |
| 08.04.06 | Train Rhyd Ddu walk Hafod Ruffydd |
| 24.03.07 | Train as far as Cutting Mawr |
| 05.04.08 | First train to Hafod y Llyn |
| 16.05.09 | First train to Cae Pawb |
| 30.10.10 | First train Caernarfon - Porthmadog |

| Subscriber - Phase 4 Appeals - June 2009 | |
|---|---|
| Number | Type |
| 96 | Gold - Phase 4 and Carriage Appeals |
| 57 | Silver - Phase 4 and Carriage Appeals |
| 315 | Bronze - Phase 4 and Carriage Appeals |
| | |

stuck to its guns, (In fact for the subsequent Carriage Appeal the minimum was raised to £25.) The strategy for persuading people to give was based on the following thinking:

**1.** People will give money to a cause. It is normally on impulse, and represents what they have at that time. Selling the project demands personal contact. The best personal contact is to get out to places where the target market is present and make the pitch. This was already being done for WHR restoration, but the team determined to do something different.

**2.** It was now proven that the subscriber method worked. Consideration suggested that the Phase 4 Appeal was on a much greater scale, so it was decided to risk raising the amounts, and also broadening the approach by investing some money in it. The reasoning was that £20 represented the cost of a visit to a football match, or to the cinema, or a railway book, and that if made into a suitable package, people would subscribe.

**3.** Providing more than one choice of subscription level was to maximise the income. The £20 per minimum was a good lower limit, with £100 as the upper. The upper limit was considered to be the highest subscription amount that the team dared to visualise. It was clear that to propel people to the higher level (where many wish to aspire) an intermediate band was needed that wasn't offering quite the same interest level, but the upper band needed to have something attractive and aspirational to encourage people to go for it. So the Silver at £50 acted as a stepping stone to encourage those who could be tempted to upgrade to the Gold at £100.

**4.** The nature of the inducements was designed to be of low value, and minimum cost to deliver, but of 'unmissable' interest to the subscribers. The objective was to allow the aspirational wish of people to see behind the scenes, not something that could be bought. It offered as an attractive and innovative proposal, designed to create enthusiasm, and to offer the delight of making one's own dreams come true and it attracted subscribers.

**5.** Ideas of dreams had to persuade people to subscribe. It was not known then just how good a ride on the WHR was going to be, and so pitching to potential subscribers the 'Dream is Coming True' strap line was the best available - and it worked

very well.

By 2006 there were 72 Gold subscribers in Phase 4, who raised over half-a-million. So what was offered made sense as long it was in line with the wants and aspirations of the potential subscribers, and remained within the guidelines of HM Customs and Inland Revenue. The key factor was to steer clear of tangible benefits, available at a price, and to inhabit the area of aspirational items that could not be bought. It was most definitely the mind that mattered here, not the pocket.

Every subscriber received free travel on FR and WHR, so that they could see what it was they were subscribing to.

Tactics also indicated a yearly event, subscribers could come to the WHR to view progress. The team organised an event for 8th April 2006. The Gold and Silver subscribers were offered a train trip to Rhyd Ddu, with a walk down the trackbed as far as Hafod Ruffydd and back. This was with the specific intention of subscribers being able to come and see what their money had been spent on. Philanthropist Michael Wilkinson, keen to help, offered to sponsor trains for BRONZE subscribers. The response to this chance to see the work 'in progress' was far more popular than ever anticipated. The applications poured in and the Railway offered another train to be able to satisfy the demand. This began a tradition on what now became annual special event days. As the railway advanced into 'new' territory the annual subscribers' events were irresistible. They proved to be fertile ground for raising more funds as enthusiasm was raised to fever pitch. Of course these subscribers, sat in comfort on a nice warm train, offered the right time

*There is no doubt about the mood on this, the first passenger train to run as far as Cae Pawb, through the Aberglaslyn Pass, across Pont Croesor and through the Halt, and past the WHHR to Cae Pawb - but not across it. The enthusiasm is being shown for the view from the open car along the deep gorge of the Aberglaslyn Pass. For those running these trains (and this was the GOLD train), such a reaction was ecstatic.*

and the right place for further calls upon their generosity. On each occasion, raffles and appeals for subscription extension were effective in raising large sums. In fact, such was the atmosphere of generosity that was created and the welter of enthusiasm that the record amount collected on board, on the day the 'first' train ran was an amount in excess of £100k. That certainly made the event days worthwhile.

A 'booster' appeal was also launched to look for funds for new carriages. This too was successful, but not on the same scale. It raised £350k, enough for three vehicles to be built in Boston Lodge Carriage works.

*Delivery day was 30th October 2010, when two trains ran from Caernarfon, right through to Porthmadog. These were the first trains through, on the whole length of the new line. There was great celebration - this is what had been promised to subscribers, and it was duly delivered. Everything went perfectly operationally. Everyone was deeply charmed at the ride, the occasion, and the great sense of achievement that was present throughout the day. Any doubts that FR did not mean what it had said all those years ago were dispelled finally on this day. Everyone was very happy, and this showed in the great amounts of money promised by subscribers to the new railway. This was THE time to collect, and collect the Phase 4 Team did - they hit over £100k on a single day!*

## Phase 5 : The Sustainable Railway

Finishing the railway into Porthmadog included connecting up with the Welsh Highland Points, and that allowed a train to reverse in to the platform, with the reciprocal arrangement on departure. However, to rearrange Harbour Station to allow a WHR and an FR train to be in the platform at the same time required expensive works, as to fit all in meant widening the Cob. The good news was that powers for this work had been obtained a long while ago; it was the money that was looked for. The bad news on this was that another £1m was required, or WHR would have to be operated 'one train at a time' in Porthmadog. Although this could be lived with on a short term basis, it was desirable to arrange for a second platform as soon as

*The Glan y Mor carriage sheds were put up in the 1990s to try to protect the FR carriages from the weather. The requirement has increased now, with a WHR set of carriages that also need protection. The sheds are neither long enough, nor wide enough to shelter the vehicles now in service, and although the site is large enough for bigger sheds, they need to be built. This is one of the projects for the Sustainable Railway that benefits the FR and the WHR alike.*

possible. Thus the search for funds began again, and Mike Hart tramped the boards tirelessly in Cardiff once more.

There was a lot of sympathy, but little money. The grant bodies had spent their allocations, and priorities had shifted to new EU member states. The FR had reached its 'objective' and a huge recession had 'blown in', thus funds for little railways were in very short supply. At the same time as looking for grants, matching funding sources were also explored. The Phase 4 Appeal team were requested to act.

Unsurprisingly, the end of Phase 4 had arrived with the funding 'lemon' squeezed dry. The team believed that the generosity of the narrow base of 468 subscribers was likely to have been exhausted by the continual appeals and exhortations they had been assaulted with. In

2009, some of the subscriptions had been extended to 2014. The right thing to do was to broaden the appeal, to revisit Steam Railway and other publications in order to recruit a new base for subscribers. Of course there was nervousness about what the response would be like during the worst financial crisis to hit Europe since WW2, nevertheless it was determined to go ahead and try anyway.

Initially the determination was to try to get enough to match the funding for the Cob widening. Of course the FR is not like that, and the Phase 5 appeal came about. This sprang from the realisation that WHR was still a basic railway and there was a long list of items yet to be provided:

**1.** Carriages: there were not enough WHR cars to make 2 sets without borrowing from FR, and when things really got going after opening, 3 sets would be needed.

**2.** Stations: Caernarfon, Waunfawr, Rhyd Ddu and Beddgelert had temporary buildings. The first and last, in particular, deserved something much better.

**3.** Storage of carriages and locomotives was becoming a matter of problem, especially if more were put into service. Extension to the car shed at Dinas was required, or more accommodation at Boston Lodge.

A formula was worked out to repeat the leaflet in 2010, six years on, but this time aimed at recruiting new membership of the society of their choice, FRSL or CRhE. Accordingly an A5

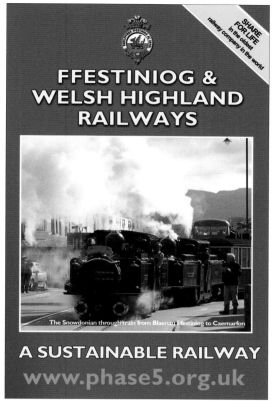

*The cover reflected the* **Snowdonian** *train of two double Fairlies run in April 2011, and puffed the Share for Life scheme.*

red leaflet went out in November 2010 Steam Railway, who supported the Phase 5 Appeal under the label 'Lets Finish the Job', and then again in Railway Magazine in 2011 as 'A Sustainable Railway'.

Phase 5 was not without controversy. There was a vigorous reaction from some in the FRS who suggested that it was high time the FR 'got something'. This led to pressure to drop the WHR 'Let's Finish the Job' branding, but a working compromise was reached when it was pointed out that FR had indeed got 'something' both from the WHR and from Phase 5. Resistance was strengthened by the fact that the leaflet was returning strongly, and some £500k in subscriptions was gained rapidly. The WHR brand was still extremely powerful and bringing in funds. The compromise was a move to the commendable suggestion that now it was necessary to address the matter of the sustainable railway. FR had still not quite been finished when WHR came along. Both railways were complementary; both railways needed improvement in order for them to be sustainable. A programme of some £8m of improvements spread across FR and WHR was assembled, and Phase 5 was gradually merged into that.

This was the first of the team's appeals that used the Internet strongly, and the response from that was excellent, as the full message plus extras was available. It was those extras that contained much entertainment.

Funding for Cob widening was found from the National Station Improvement Scheme, at 66%. The name could not be more apt.

## What was the cost?

How much the whole WHR restoration project cost is a bit difficult to pin down, especially as it cannot be said to be truly 'finished' yet. The tabulated figures are not precise, and all-embracing, they are taken from **T1,4,5&6**. Thus they generate a clear enough picture to be able to understand how the railway was financed.

At the end of the building period, and including the Harbour Station remodelling of 2011-2012, the cost amount had reached £26.5m. To that has to be added station improvements, rolling stock storage and extra rolling stock, and thus the total cost figure with confidence is £28m. In global terms this was a very cheap railway indeed. This is the first time that these figures have been assembled and published.

The component of public money in this figure, largely from Eurogrants, is 57%, an amount of £14.5m. The FR Trust managed to raise 34%, some £8.6m, with a balance of 9% from miscellaneous sources. That is a very good performance. To those who frown upon the investment of public funds, Dr Megan Williams of Prifysgol Bangor produced a proof for her Doctorate that showed for the one-off investment, the FR/WHR returned up to £14m per year to the local economy. A good deal indeed.

### The costs per mile and the total costs of WHR Restoration through the Phases.

|       | Year | Cost | Miles | Km | Cost/M | Cost/K |
|-------|------|------|-------|------|--------|--------|
|       |      | £m   |       |      | £m     | £m     |
| Ph 1  | 1999 | 3.254 | 3     | 4.83 | 1.085* | 0.673* |
| Ph 2  | 2001 | 2.656 | 3.42  | 5.45 | 0.776  | 0.487  |
| Ph 3  | 2003 | 3.620 | 5.8   | 9.28 | 0.624  | 0.390  |
| Ph 1-3 | 2003 | 9.530 | 12.22 | 19.56 | 0.780 | 0.487  |
| Ph4-1 | 2004 | 10.766 | 12.51 | 20.13 | 0.860 | 0.534 |
| Ph4-2 | 2009 | 15.205 | 12.51 | 20.13 | 1.215 | 0.755 |
| Ph4-3 | 2010 | 16.035 | 12.51 | 20.13 | 1.281 | 0.796 |
| WHR   | 2010 | 25.565 | 25.2 | 40   | 1.014  | 0.639  |
| WHR-1 | 2011 | 26.565 | 25.2 | 40   | 1.054  | 0.664  |

**Ph4-1** : **The first estimate**      ***\* inc. rolling stock***
**Ph4-2** : **The estimate in 2009**
**Ph4-3** : **The 'cost to finish'**
**WHR**  : **The 'whole' railway**
**WHR-1** : **The whole railway, plus Harbour Station, but without other Phase 5 attributes, like stations and rolling stock.**

# The Festiniog Railway Trust

The FR and WHR restorations were facilitated by the FR Trust. The pioneer Trust body was set up by Alan Pegler on 7th December 1955 to hold the shares in FR Co. John Routly, mentor to the FR pioneers, in 1954, replaced it with a charitable trust on 10th November 1964. FR conduct is vested in a Trinity: The FR Trust, The FR Company and the FR and WHR Societies. The Trust was the vehicle to hold a majority of the Festiniog Railway Company shares. This meant that the FR Co. was secure against takeover. Furthermore, as a registered charity, the Trust is a tax efficient vehicle that can reclaim gift aid. An obligation is that the actions of the Trust have to be in line with its charitable purpose. The limits on what can be paid for with funds cause inconvenience from time to time.

The Festiniog Railway Company was created by Statute in 1832. It is one of those rare Williamene, statutory companies, and is now the oldest extant railway company in the world. This has less significance than it had at one time, but it is rather special in some areas of the law, offering a status similar to a county council in certain circumstances. The FR Co. has shares, and needed the protection of a controlling interest that is vested in the Trust - that being so, any of the unsubscribed shares hold a fine caché in the order of rarity.

The Ffestiniog Railway Society (FRS) was set up before to revive the railway. FRS did not have the cash to buy a controlling interest, in consequence they accepted the arrangements for the Trust. They have patiently persisted, realising that their position in the orchestra is also determined by the strength of their fundraising, and the number of their volunteers.

The Trust collects and administers such funds as are remitted to it. Any surpluses from the FR Co. are ploughed back into the business; the Society hands funds that it raises to the Company, as it doesn't pay tax. (Although it has since become an independent charity itself.) Individuals have used the Trust as a vehicle, and appeals like Phase 4 pass the sums raised to the Trust. The funds are then disbursed for the purpose for which they were collected, as the Trustees determine.

When a bid was made for the WHR trackbed, this was by the FR Co. There were shenanigans, and the bid and all activity concerned with acquisition was declared *ultra vires* for the FR Co. The Trust set up a subsidiary, Ffestiniog Holdings, to deal with applying for the TO and to conduct

| Festiniog Railway Trust Income  - all £k | | | |
|---|---|---|---|
| Year | Legacies | Donations & Gifts | Total £k |
| 2005 | 92 | 1830 | 1922 |
| 2006 | 12 | 2238 | 2249 |
| 2007 | 76 | 1787 | 1863 |
| 2008 | 117 | 2111 | 2228 |
| 2009 | 1 | 339 | 340 |
| 2010 | 850 | 295 | 1145 |

The whole situation is more complex than this. Anyone can see the Trust accounts from the Charity Commissioners' web site. This table seeks to show the Trust 'fund raising' record in recent years.

Ffestiniog Travel.

When the TO was made for the FR Co., and construction of Caernarfon to Dinas was to begin, Welsh Highland Light Railway Ltd, was set up to conduct this activity and Cymdeithas Rheilfordd Eryri, (CRhE - Welsh Highland Railway Society Ltd) was created as a parallel to FRS. Both have a relationship with FRT.

The generosity of sponsorship allowed construction of Caernarfon to Dinas to be started before the MC grant began to pay out. Mike Schumann 'lent' the money to the Trust. When it was stated by FR Co. that money for the Ffestiniog Railway would not be used on the WHR, the separation between the two railways to observe that promise was safeguarded by the Trust. Likewise, when a legator stipulates the use to which their money should be put, it is the Trust that sees to it that their wishes are properly carried out.

Trustees are required to remain cool in a crisis, but there

*Above: Andy Savage, fundraiser and former FR Co. Director talks to Emeritus Trustee Sir William McAlpine and Trust Chairman John Prideaux. This was on a visit to Minffordd Yard to view the proposed connection to the FR main line, northbound into the Yard, and it is likely that they are talking about money, or safety.*

*Left: Secretary John Alexander, (left) and Treasurer Fuzz Jordan (right) relax in the deep comfort of the Pullman Observation Car, Glaslyn. John, as the Secretary, is forever arranging, writing and organising, Fuzz, the Treasurer, is always searching for and managing the funds, which is what the Trust is all about.*

**Right:** *On 24th March 2007 Bryn y Felin Bridge, over the Afon Glaslyn is effectively complete and ready to offer vehicle access down the Pass for trackbed refurbishment. Trustee Richard Broyd (L) and Chairman of Trustees John Prideaux (R) enjoy the spring sunshine and the achievement of bridging this river so neatly.*

**Below:** *This is MBWA - management by walking about. Trustees and a number of invited functionaries investigate the footprint of the new Tan y Bwlch footbridge that Mike Schumann is currently funding. Mike Schumann is by the signal, Trustee Robert Riddick is on the right-hand side of the picture, behind him is Treasurer Fuzz Jordan, and Chairman John Prideaux is left-of-picture.*

overwhelming. The concept of charitable giving has been a major component in providing the funds for both FR and WHR to be restored. The Trust is the vehicle by which money can be received, any rebated benefits collected from it, and the most tax-efficient handling made of it. The duty of disbursement is handled by the Trustees. The Trustees are voluntary; no one is paid for the duties they perform - the appointment is honorary. Trustees must distribute the collected funds impartially and wisely, and in accordance with the wishes of the donors, where stated. This process has been done with satisfaction over many years, as one of the features of the firm but stately progress of the FR.

Alan Pegler, as the Founder, chose who the new trustees would be. He did this with careful reference to those around him, in FR Co., FRS, and Trust, and some excellent choices were made. Eventually Alan found the process rather beyond his powers, and he transferred his authority to the trustees themselves in a Trust Deed, dated 30th September 1998. The updated Trust Deed shows a maximum of five Trustees, and includes a Company Nominee, a Society Nominee, with a balance of Independent Trustees, each of whom serves for a period of five years. An Appointing Body of Trustees, the FR Co. Chairman, and the Chairman of the FRS, replaced the Founder to appoint the Trustees by a simple majority of those attending the meeting. The FRS representative has a duty to consult with the CRhE.

This is a democratic method of appointment, and is to be preferred to the way that some little railways are

was concern over the problems that arose at the end of Phase 3, when the construction company WHLR might be unable to meet its liabilities without relief. It is typical of the FR Trust that funding was found to bridge the gap, and then to put matters in order unobtrusively. Since that time, the quality of the watching brief over the constituents' spending habits has increased; that is what trusts are supposed to do. It is instructive that Phase 4 finances, subject to much fluctuation, have been regulated most expeditiously. Lessons were learned and put into operation without fuss.

There was an amusing aside that aspersions were cast at the TO public inquiry by an opposing advocate concerning the fact that no Trustees appeared to state the case for the Festiniog Railway Company, so discreet are these learned gentlemen. It was not a matter that was pursued further, when it was instanced that no elected member of the GCC appeared to state the opposite case either.

There are a few minor snags to an otherwise excellent Trinity of Trust, Company and Society. Should the expenditure be judged not in pursuit of the 'charitable purpose', then the Trust may not disburse. Just occasionally this may be irksome, but the game must be played properly, and the benefits of having the Trust are

managed. The Trinity (Trust, Company and Society) has nearly sixty years of service to prove it. There is little doubt that Trust performance is good - it's difficult to know if this is due to the rarefied air at those heights, or to skill, dedication and experience. Junta, cabal, clique, conspiracy, tyranny, club - the Trust is none of these things. The Trustees do a good job.

# The People

**To restore such a railway there had to be the people to do it. Many of these people were not professional railway tycoons, they were just ordinary railway enthusiasts. Does this mean that anyone could have done it? Probably in general terms it does, but by now it will be clear that rather special circumstances existed for this railway to be restored. Here is an account of some of the people who were involved with the rebuilding process. The choice is random and is the privilege of the author; as to the order in which people are shown - it doesn't signify.**

## Mike Schumann BSc (Eng) MICE

Michael Alec Schumann b. January.1942, London
Father: Alec Schumann, b. Moscow 1905
Mother: Kyra Schumann neé Landsdorff, b. St Petersburg 1910 One elder brother, Andrew.

The 1955 Modern World Book of Railways by Paul Townend was Mike's first real railway inspiration. Before that there had been Sunday visits to Hadley Wood on the GN main line, and putting pennies on the line as a six-year-old near Gordon Hill on the Hertford Loop. Mike never aspired to be an engine driver, being more interested in the sense of peaceful travel behind a snorting monster, and the far-flung places to which it took it's passengers. The technology of building railways caught Mike's imagination at an early age, as well as the effects of railways on the landscape and people's lives. Narrow gauge and minor railways became a more dominant interest probably by the age twelve, in 1954, when Mike made a visit to North Wales, and first had the opportunity to walk the FR from Tan y Bwlch to Coed y Bleddiau, over an as yet unrestored section of the railway. Mike immediately became thoroughly hooked on the FR, and this spread as an interest in narrow gauge railways in general. It is remarkable how so many people coming upon little railways in

distress are so quickly focussed upon them. This has tended to be highly beneficial to distressed little railways, and for the FR, this was certainly the case with Mike Schumann.

A letter addressed to the public relations officer produced no response, as perhaps forward twelve-year-olds were considered of little use in those days, unlike the enlightened times of today! It was not until 1956 at the age of 14 that after reading an article about the FR's revival in the January Railway World that Mike joined the Festiniog Railway Society, and visited Porthmadog with two school friends for two weeks at Easter. They worked with Will Jones on relaying the throat of Harbour Station, including the WHR points. The photograph from 1956, taken by brother Andrew Schumann, shows the works proceeding. The legendary Will Jones of the FR is on the left, Paul Booth, one of Mike's school friends is in the centre, and the 14 year-old Mike is on the right. Next is mother's dog, an Alsatian (The dog may look as though it has only two legs - please accept assurances that the other two have been temporarily excluded by the exigencies of the camera).

By this time Mike was attending Oundle School, which he did from 1955-1960. He became a regular, annual volunteer to the Ffestiniog Railway (FR). Oundle School taught him the rudiments of practical engineering, and on leaving school, he went to Clare College, Cambridge, to gain a Degree in Engineering Science from 1960-1963.

His interest in narrow gauge railways deepened with time, and at university Mike joined the Cambridge Platelayers. He and Paul became members of the relatively recently founded Continental Railway Circle, and devoted themselves to narrow gauge railways, principally because they were a minority interest, and secondly as they took one to places that most other enthusiasts and even tourists never visited. They spotted Yugoslavia, where little was known about the extensive narrow gauge railway system, built by the Austro-Hungarian empire, and even less about the forestry railways. So Yugoslavia became a major interest, with a lot of time devoted to researching the political and social history of the country.

At Cambridge Mike met Gerald Fox, who was designing the Festiniog Deviation, necessary to overcome the break made in the FR caused by the flooding of the line for the Ffestiniog Pumped Storage hydro-electric scheme. Gerald was looking for assistance, but first, after leaving Cambridge, Mike spent a year in Germany, learning the language and practising civil engineering before returning home to help rebuild Kings Cross Underground Station for the Victoria Line with Balfour-Beatty from 1964-1968 and, most importantly, to join as a founder member in building the 2½ mile long Llyn Ystradau Deviation Project [1965-1978]. Gerald Fox left for America after a few years, and for the last 10 years of the project's 13 years, Mike was project engineer to its final completion in 1978.

*Porthmadog in 1956, with Will Jones (L) relaying points, Paul Booth (C) and Mike Schumann, aged 14 (R). Andrew Schumann took the photo of the works, as Mike and Paul made their goodbyes to Will Jones, after being with him for two weeks helping with the relaying. The dog is the Schumann's Alsatian. Of course a quirk of fate makes the points in the foreground those known as the Welsh Highland Points!*
**Andrew Schumann**

*Mike driving a train on his own Norton Hill Light Railway, a splendid 500m out-and-back circuit, with a magnificent Yugoslav Railways Class 73 2-6-2 and a class 83 0-8-2 as the principal motive power, built by Severn-Lamb to the 7¼" gauge. Here he is seen battling the grade with the Class 73, towing a train of scale rolling stock, well filled on one of the three open days held annually in aid of charity.*

In his career job he moved to the design office, changing to foundation engineering with Cementation from 1968-1970, In 1970 with the completion of a job in Belfast, sinking 60 metre deep by 1.4 metre diameter piles, he left Cementation for the small but largely family owned business, to establish a subsidiary and to design automatic machines for assembling aerosol valves. The company prospered and relocated to Kings Lynn to find expansion space. Now Mike's emphasis was on special projects and forward planning. Time was also spent supervising the design and construction of a similar high quality facility for the new American subsidiary of the company in North Carolina, and learning to fly an autogyro.

Merddyn Emrys, *the FR 0-4+4-0 double Fairlie locomotive, built at Boston Lodge in 1879, was a bit of an ugly duckling in its rebuilt form after FR restoration. Mike Schumann saw it restored to a Victorian glory that raised the standard for all other locomotives to follow - and that was his idea.*

In 1982 he married Angela, daughter of John Routly, then Chairman of the FR Co. and FR Trust. Then the Schumann family company became Bespak plc. Its tremendous success allowed Mike to indulge in some of the things he had always wanted to do. He moved to Snettisham in Norfolk, acquiring a property with enough space to exercise the autogyro and to construct a 500m long 7¼" gauge railway. Naturally the railway's theme was of Yugsoslavian railways, and this instantly makes it unique. Another thing was the reconstruction of Ffestiniog double Fairlie, *Merddin Emrys* in 1986, bringing it from its rather ugly and battered state, to one of Victorian splendour, with fully lined out, rich crimson lake, historic FR livery. He also established a Sponsorship Fund in support of volunteers working on infrastructure projects and the restoration of historic features of the railway, something that had hitherto been a Cinderella. This scheme offered a pound-for-pound arrangement to encourage people to choose and work on projects they liked. This novel approach has benefitted many items on the FR that add greatly to the historic value and the look of the railway, that were not justified in the terms of their financial performance.

In 1992 Mike joined the FR Co board, and became the Company nominated Trustee in 1995. At that time the foment over the controversial intervention of FR Co. in attempting to gain control of the trackbed of the WHR was in full swing. His father-in-law John Routly 'tapped' him for funds for FR Co. to be represented at the High Court to apply for a stay on the sale of the WHR trackbed by the OR to the GCC. When the results

of this indicated an application for a TO, Mike Schumann, Mike Hart and FR General manager Gordon Rushton, worked out a way of rescuing the FR's rather battered reputation, by opting for the full restoration of the WHR and its extension in to Caernarfon. He retired from Bespak plc in 1993 and became the Engineering Director of WHLR, the company charged with constructing the revived WHR from Caernarfon to Rhyd Ddu.

Mike's contribution to the restoration of the WHR has largely gone unrecognised, except to 'those in the know'. Perhaps the story here may help to set the record straight.

Mike acted as a major source of financial support from the 1991 High Court case until the completion of Phase 3 at Rhyd Ddu. Mike provided the funds needed to see the FR Co. through three public inquiries, and to permit Phase 1 to begin, before any grant money could flow back to the project.. He worked with Roland Doyle to complete of the first 12 miles of the 25 mile WHR, and was much involved with Phase 4.

He made the drawings for the Caernarfon to Dinas railway LRO, liaised with adjacent landowners and dealt with all the objectors to the LRO. He made the planning application, negotiated additional land purchase in Caernarfon to build the tunnel mouth roundabout without reducing the station area. He specified the works to produce a design brief for rebuilding the railway, supervised the consultants and monitored the contractors work to ensure that where changes were required they were highlighted in a timely fashion. All instructions to the consultants on the major contracts were made by Mike except during that period of Phase 2 when a Resident Engineer was employed.

Mike produced all the plan drawings for the TWA Order (John Sreeves surveyed and drew the vertical sections). He designed and drew works in outline for such areas as Waunfawr Station, Cae Hen access road diversion, Bryn Afon access road diversion, Rhyd Ddu station, Beddgelert Station, Snowdon Street Crossing, Britannia Bridge, and Harbour Station. Mike planned and issued most CPO Notices to Treat and Notices to Enter on Phases 1-3, and all on Phase 4. He researched the status of all adjacent landowners in Gwynedd Archives, to provide information to help refute any claims to title of the railway trackbed. He produced

*Mike points out of the open window of a vintage FR passenger coach, to a guest from Serbia (formerly Yugoslavia), the significant parts of the FR Deviation as the train runs towards Blaenau, along the shores of Llyn Ystradau*

*Mike Schumann stands by NGG15 Beyer-Garratt No. 143 that he bought from SAR, in its new guise at Caernarfon, Welsh Highland Railway on 11th September 2002. With him are two acquaintances from Yugoslavia/Serbia, Janez and Zoran. This is particularly apt, as it is a return match for a splendid little sojourn in Republika Srbska, on the famous Mokra Gora spiral. Yugoslavian 760-mm gauge railways still thrive, and Mike is helping them along too!*

three volumes concerning FR Co. title to the trackbed through the farms of the former Vaynol Estate, Beddgelert Forest, and Beddgelert Station.

It was Mike who produced drawings of standard items, such as accommodation crossings, loading gauge/structure gauge, cant tables, schedules of level crossings and their equipment. Mike obtained the Level Crossing Orders; he designed bilingual signs for level crossings, and had them approved by four different authorities.

He monitored the work of the contractors. Consultants have little experience of working on narrow gauge railways. They needed to be guided to refurbish and strengthen existing structures wherever possible to save money. It was Mike that dealt with the consultants and quantity surveyors to agree final accounts with major contractors. Mike was also concerned with the planning and the search for funding of the final 13 miles of line, Phase 4.

It was with great regret that he withdrew from Phase 4 and surrendered

his directorships of the FR Co. and WHLR Co. He says that there were changes made to the conduct and management of the enterprise that he felt unable to work with, and that in these circumstances he felt, however disappointing, that in the absence of any satisfactory resolution of the problems, the only appropriate action he could take was to withdraw.

Mike remains a trustee of the Festiniog Railway Trust, as well as being a trustee of the Little Giant Trust Ltd, and the E J Routly Will Trust. Mike also remains an interested participant in the affairs of the FR, maintaining the Sponsorship Scheme (currently engaged in Tan y Bwlch footbridge) and offering his expertise whenever it is needed to the enterprise.

No other single member of the team has offered as much money and time for so long to the FR/WHR, and it is clear that without Mike's enthusiasm, his interest, energy, and support, the FR would be a lot worse off and there would not be a restored Welsh Highland Railway, such as we have today.

*This is the Station Master at Požega in Republika Srbska, on 20th July 2001, when Mike was visiting Serbian friends and called at this splendid museum of the 760mm gauge, prior to a look at and a ride on the famous, restored, Mokra Gora spiral.*

# Dr John DCA Prideaux CBE

*John Prideaux stands in front of double Fairlie* Earl of Merioneth *at Porthmadog. John always appears from his farm, way down in Somerset, when the presence of the Chairman is needed at events, and as someone with a lifelong interest in narrow gauge, he is always in the van for flying the flag as the picture under shows.*

## John Denys Charles Anstice Prideaux  b. August 1944

The love of little railways has taken a deep hold upon John Prideaux, and he stands at the top of the Ffestiniog pile  with unique qualifications to be there. He has been associated with Ffestiniog for many years. He volunteered in the 1950s, served time as Society Archivist and whilst devoting his attention to a career on the big railway, he never lost touch. He co-wrote a book about the Lynton and Barnstaple Railway in 1964. This has been revised and reissued and complemented with books on the English, Welsh and Irish narrow gauge railways. It was standard gauge that he was determined to make his career with.

After education at St Paul's School, then in Hammersmith, he went to Nottingham University and gained a BSc in civil engineering.  He went on to do a doctorate in Operation Research and joined  British Railways in 1967. He was able to try out the theory when he became Area Manager at Newton Abbot in 1972 at the age of 28. After 2 years he was asked back into the Centre to be the  Strategic Planning Officer at BRB.  At that time he married his wife Phillipa and they subsequently had a son and a daughter.

John was evidently destined for great things as he had a spell as Divisional Manager Birmingham on the London Midland Region from 1980-83, precisely at the time when the organisational structure was moving from a geographical to a business based organisation, as there was great pressure to implement ways of reducing the high levels of subsidy. Until 1986 he was the Director of the BRB Policy Unit under BRB Chairman Sir Robert Reid's Chairmanship.  He then started what he says was his most enjoyable job in 1986, when he was appointed the Sector Director of Inter-City, with the task of transforming a loss making business into a profitable one. East Coast electrification came on stream

*Hi jinks at the opening to Porthmadog, at Pont Croesor on 20th April 2011, with Pete Waterman and Lord Elis-Thomas*

*Left: John faces the camera at Beddgelert when the WHR extended to Hafod y Llyn on 21.st May 2009. The crew are making a documentary of the railway restoration for Welsh language television, and have followed the progress for some years.*

*Below: With Chris Leah in Boston Lodge holding up the headboard for the train of eminent railway chiefs from India. There was deep diplomacy to the 'mother' narrow gauge railway from those who run the Darjeeling Himalayan Railway - FR/WHR is now twinned.*

during his time in office, he revived the Pullman brand for top-quality, prestige trains; he oversaw the introduction of a striking, and instantly recognisable train livery, the iconic Swallow emblem, and a wave of innovative and masterful marketing that was imitated around the world. He and his team enjoyed success, transforming Inter-City into a household brand, and bringing it to profitability, so that when he was asked to move into the Channel Tunnel Rail Link Project from Managing Director, Inter-City it was a sad wrench.

Yet railwaymen are expected to move when and where they are bid, and to work hard to do their jobs, so during the Bob Reid Chairmanship, as Chairman of Union Railways from 1992, he applied logic to the process, working with the DoE, DTp and Treasury, to come up with the east approach to St Pancras, that also fitted in with a government desire to regenerate Stratford. This generated a CBE for services to the rail Industry. However, at the time this result did not find universal favour, and upon John Welsby's accession to the Chairmanship it seemed that with privatisation coming there was no innovative job that appealed within the traditional core. In 1995, after a 'few' other options, he took a 'punt' by forming the joint venture that took rolling stock leasing company Angel Trains. They were extremely successful, and when they sold out to the Royal Bank of Scotland in 1997, there was the sum of £15m as a reward for all the risk. For the man for whom there seemed no job on privatisation, there was irony enough for deep satisfaction. John remained a director of Angel Trains until 2007.

John Prideaux was invited by Alan Pegler to become an FR Trustee in 1992, became Chairman of the Trust in 1998 and Chairman of the FR Co. as well in 2006. Obviously whilst earlier engaged in such high levels of ,business. the full force of his charm and intellect could not be devoted to

entirely to matters FR. However, as the WHR developed John was engaged in the debate about what should happen, when and why. He was the natural successor to John Routly leaving the Trust and took over the Chair from him. Under his leadership matters have become more studied and more logical, with a careful pick of policy, and a re-evaluation of the relationship between Trust and Company. This is just at the right time because having reconstructed the WHR, it is the time to make certain that it performs in the way it was expected, as if ill-run, it could be devastating to FR's future.

John's tenure as Chairman of both Trust and Company is seeing to that. Early he saw that the way forward depends on the emergence of the Sustainable Railway, a combined FR and WHR that concentrates its efforts on creating the wealth that it needs to remain in business and to grow. His emphasis is upon enabling the combined railways to offer the customer a product that they will continue to be satisfied with. The continuingly moving target currently has its sights on completing the railways, on providing the infrastructure needed for the service level, the comfort required on trains and the facilities expected at stations. This is Inter-City writ small, and is as enjoyable to John as it is successful. The FR/WHR is lucky to have him.

*John saying nice things to Germans when FR/WHR twin-partners came to be present at the opening of the Pont Croesor extension by Pete Waterman. Of course these guys are from the wonderful Harzquerbahn, and their train set may be considered rather better than ours, but there's great mutual respect that John was building on.*

# David Allan

David Allan collection

**David Allan  b. August 1938, Brombrough, Cheshire**

D avid's Father the was  the Chief Superintendent Engineer for Elder Dempster Lines of Liverpool.  His Grandfather had been a horse-tram driver in Aberdeen, and so David claims some rail ancestry.  His Father's was an important job, with a big shipping line, especially in war time, and though the Port of Liverpool was bombed, Bebington, where he then lived, was far enough away to escape. David first saw trains he really liked when a friend invited him to see his Trix-Twin railway, circling its 3-rail track. The irony of watching a German electric toy in 1943 escaped him, he was 5 at the time.  However the train bug was implanted and Dad managed to get him a Hornby 'O' Gauge clockwork train set in 1944, and this fixed the lifelong love of trains.  He did spend his time at the end of WW2 collecting train numbers at Bebington and New Ferry Station, but  the activity matured into more practical applications.

David worked hard at school, and when he was 11 years old, he won a place at the prestigious Birkenhead School.  Not only did this offer an excellent education, it ensured he made lifelong friends; he played Rugby, a sport he excelled at and enjoyed, and it offered an interesting journey to school every day that involved trains

*With one of these David could have access to good photographic subjects as much as his energy and time would allow.  David as a teenager at Egerton Park, Rock Ferry, Wirral in 1964.*   **David Allan collection**

- real ones.  At school he decided upon a career in farming. Accordingly, he took up a place at the Royal Agricultural College in Cirencester, Gloucestershire. The magic of farming was dulled by not having a family farm, and working for other people was not stimulating, so eventually he re-mortgaged the house and bought a garden centre in Prenton, Birkenhead, dealt in the seed trade, in selling plants, and enjoyed himself.

Of pastimes, Rugby enjoyed a major place.  He was captain of Old Birkonians in 1967 and was on the Cheshire RFU Committee, so he was well used to the social round. He became immersed in local politics, as a Wirral Councillor for eight years, and was involved with local history and environmental issues, as well as being Chairman of the Wirral Housing Committee, and the vice-chairman of four boards of school governors.

The interest in railways was kept active during his working years with annual holidays in the Isle of Man. David is particularly fond of walking along the cliff tops, and in wild, open country. Although he doesn't ride, he loves horses and maintains a close interest in them, although he is full of assurance that he does not indulge in the services of the turf accountant! The interest in flora extends to an allotment, with a particular partiality for sweet peas; the house is full of them in the early summer.

David is a lifelong camera enthusiast.  His got his first camera at the age of 10, together with an enlarger made for him by his maternal grandfather from a magic lantern.  He eventually graduated to medium format, and his speciality has always been black and white images.  Of course today he uses a digital camera, the convenience is just too great not to, but the images that please him the most are the black and white negatives he has amassed over the years, that he can delve into and enjoy. Curiously enough he did not indulge in any major photography of trains until his more recent involvement.

At home there is a large 16mm scale garden railway, that has narrow gauge trains running on '0' gauge track. Of course the whole thing is based on the 2ft gauge.  His wife Jenny, taking the interest in gardening as normal for a keen agricultural scholar, soon found out the real reason.  It has been in operation for 30 years now, and David has amassed an extensive collection of rolling stock and locomotives.

The really serious interest in railways was sparked off by the garden railway in 1981, when he decided to join the 64 Co. Restoring the Welsh Highland railway held for David the right mix of romance, of struggle and of practicality. Many skills came together for him in this new field. He spent a great deal of time walking the trackbed. He took many pictures of the derelict railway, that had comprehensively returned to nature. He joined in with the process of trying to  penetrate the thickets of bureaucracy and legal impediment that surrounded the WHR.  Of course, they were neighbours to the ever helpful FR

**Left:** *Walking the old WHR trackbed was an essential prerequisite to prepare for restoration. Here David Allan, Cedric Lodge and John Keylock are all setting out on an expedition to explore a section of trackbed that had been re-absorbed into farmland. Looks at bit like Caegwynion)* **David Allan collection**

**Below:** *A summer Saturday at Teignmouth, as Stanier 8F 48450 (82B St Philip's Marsh) hauls a 13-car ECS train along the sea wall towards Exeter, passing Parson's Tunnel Signal Box. David had arrived at this superb photographic location on his moped. Only an 18 year old could do this! He has taken a beautiful picture, perfectly framed of a rare sight. Such is the devotion of photographic enthusiasts.* **David Allan collection**

when they set up on the Beddgelert Siding in Porthmadog, acquired Gelert's Farm, and gradually began to reassemble some of the scattered remnants of the old WHR, hoping that one day they would be able to begin restoration of the real thing.

Theirs was a success story; not only did they manage to lay in a railway on the Beddgelert Siding, they also constructed workshops with the ability to restore locomotives and rolling stock. David is not an engineer, but he is an exceptionally able and experienced 'committee man', who can encourage a consensus and get things done. He was later to become the Chairman of the 64 Co. who had assembled a team of able people who courted the Gwynedd County Council, cajoling, persuading, and enticing them to endorse the restoration of the WHR. Their efforts were greeted with success in promoting a Light Railway Order between the end of the 64 Co. line at Pen y Mount and Pont Croesor. Relations with FR were going well, with the restored PB&SSR locomotive Russell visiting the FR in 1988. They were very pleased about how helpful Boston Lodge had been, and how much 'cross over' there was between the two organisations, especially in the engineering areas.

The 64 Co. were moving steadily towards a breakthrough in getting the restoration of WHR going, as by careful negotiation, the GCC had been persuaded to prepare to go to the High Court where the Official Receiver for the WHR 1922 Co. was to apply to sell the whole trackbed to GCC for £1. This would be the chance the 64 Co. had been working for - and then it happened.

The news was leaked that FR had been bidding for the trackbed anonymously and that they had offered to give the trackbed to the GCC, in exchange for agreement not to permit any railway development on it. This was a life-changing event for David Allan. The chief reason he had become involved with the WHR was to see it reopened, and he had spent some 9 years of his life striving to that end. Now as chief negotiator of the lead organisation, making progress with the GCC, and very close to breakthrough, to find in 1990 that the railway he admired, to whom

they had lent a locomotive to in 1988, was actively conspiring to prevent any railway development on the line they had for years been striving to restore was stunning. To David this was a declaration of war. In this book is the story of subsequent events, of how the nightmarish 'buy to shut' FR Co. policy changed to one of full restoration, and within 20 years the railway was restored from Porthmadog to Caernarfon.

For David the issue of trust in the FR Co. left marks large enough for him to feel unable to incorporate himself into the FR. He gradually came round to the view that although his chosen organisation was not able to assume the responsibility for restoring the whole railway, that at least it was going to be restored, all of it, and that trains would run again through that wild country that he had chosen to love. His careful assessment of the strategy and policies of the FR Co. revealed that Garratts and ten large corridor coaches were not the authentic originals that he and his colleagues had originally determined upon. Though it may be that these descendants of WHR trains would pay the bills. So together with John Keylock, Derek Lystor, Michael Davies and Cedric Lodge, he set up the Welsh Highland Heritage Group in 1997. The Group has been successful in becoming the major force for preserving original WHR heritage items, and for encouraging the delivery of the proper original trains,. It is an activity that will never be finished, as there is so much to be done. There has been co-operation with the FR Heritage Group to the point where they are now all listened to with respect. There is now a growing list of live heritage items to delight a growing audience. That is a great achievement indeed.

*David Married Jenny, and they have a son Andrew. They live in Eastham near to Brombrough, still in the Wirral that they love.*

**David Allan collection**

# John Hopkins BSc (CEng) MIEE

## John Hopkins, b. 1931 Congleton, Cheshire

John Hopkins, attended the Kings School in Macclesfield, marking up 8 pleasant years travelling daily by train by the LMS. This generated a lifetime's interest in steam locos which was encouraged when, c.1943, a young Ian Allan began publishing his "ABC"'s which opened up the subject at schoolboy level in otherwise uninspiring times for a boy of 11 or so. Many were the visits to Crewe Station, the Works, and like temples of steam.

From 1949, John trained in Manchester as an Electrical Engineer at Metropolitan-Vickers, a world-class electrical manufacturer and training company, and his fellow apprentices included several from a variety of overseas locations. His "thick sandwich" apprenticeship embedded a three-year degree course

*In 2004, John did a season's firing on this locomotive, the Manchester Museum of Science and Industry's Planet 2-2-0 replica. It just shows what these railway types get up to - John was 73 when he did that.*

at Manchester University. On coming out of time, he was fortunate to be engaged in the expanding world-interest in electron linear accelerators for cancer treatment, physics research, etc, which led to working in the factory's research department, and installing machines at Harwell and Hamburg.

He had come to concentrate on accelerator control systems thus, when a major new synchrotron was to be built in 1964 for physics research at Daresbury, Cheshire, he was again fortunate to join that project, just as its concrete foundations were invading an erstwhile potato field, and to be asked to build and equip the control room and electronics workshop. Two years in, he was informed that "his" control room was to contain a "top-line" process control computer of the day and asked he if he would kindly attend to the matter (16 kilobytes of fast memory and 200 kilobytes on one slow disc). This was only one of several career shocks to his equanimity.

When a new synchrotron was planned in about 1976, electronics, computers and process control had moved on greatly and John felt ready for a change. Fortunately again, he was able to move sideways into the site's main-frame computer operations to run the 24/7 service and this kept him going till retirement in early 1993. In the early 1980s, it had been decreed that, from middle management upwards, personal computers were becoming an essential tool and his work with them has continued to date.

Having been shown by his Professor an early post-war computer in 1953 (valves, CRT and drum memory), he reflects occasionally that his first main frame computer in 1979 had a specially-funded very large (for the day) magnetic core memory of 3 megabytes and filled a respectable building. Whereas on his desk at home are 2 PCs with a total fast memory of 8 gigabytes and disk space almost out of this World.

He found time to marry, set up house, bring up three children and to qualify as pilot of gliders and light aircraft.

His narrow gauge volunteering experience includes a weekend on the track of the Talyllyn in 1955, several weeks in all as a fitter/fireman at Boston Lodge around 1980, and a few days on the WHR track in 2002. He is a member of all WHR and FR societies and groups, holds one share in FR Co., and takes a particular interest in their AGMs. A seasoned and respected friend in WHHR has said that if he sees John in the Porthmadog area, it must be the date of a narrow gauge AGM somewhere nearby.

After retirement in early 1993, and becoming bored after six months, he obtained domestic leave of absence to attend "on spec" the Public Inquiry of 1993 into FRC's and the County Council/1964 Co's (joint) competing applications for a WHR TO.

Expecting to engage with dull matters only lightly, he took along the daily crossword, but became "hooked" within minutes, realising that such proceedings were unknown to majority of railway supporters, but vital legally before a foot could be set upon the track bed for restoration. He took what careful notes were possible, given the rapidity with which proceedings were conducted - but soon became well versed in the sequence of events, and able therefore to record intelligently what was happening. About two days into the Inquiry, after earlier slight acquaintance, Michael Schumann suggested that he might write an article on the proceedings for the new WHR Society's magazine, "Snowdon Ranger". He was taken aback by this but determined to "give it a go".

He discovered that copies of written statements of witnesses were circulated to those on the public seats but not collected up formally and that, by sitting at the end of the row, there was no concern if he dropped them into his briefcase for future reference. He discovered also that anyone who entered a written submission to the Inspector would receive a digest of his Report and the whole Decision document of the Secretary of State on the day after publication. Furthermore, the full report of the Inspector could then be obtained readily by phone call to the Ministry of Transport. John promptly drew up and made a submission.

At home afterwards, he set about digesting the heap of paperwork to write an intended two-page article. Having reached twenty pages with no end in sight, simply carried on, reaching 70; it was published in a simple manner, and well-received by the keener observers as a key to the WHR enigma.

By 1995, FRC had begun preparation for "the big one", the application for a Transport and Works Order necessary to reconstruct and operate the WHR. Starting with small spreadsheet work upon the necessary survey of footpath use, he was drawn in steadily until, by 1996, he was acting as volunteer assistant to FR Co's legal team. This led to sight of many interesting papers, being involved in support activities and working on the matter for many, many hours at home. At about that time, he joined the WHR (1964) Co (now WHHR) to become familiar with the Company, its personages, policies and problems.

The Public Inquiry into FR Co's TWO application started in December 1997, for which he was better prepared. This time, virtually no witness

### Rheilffordd Eryri
### The Welsh Highland Railway
### Recent History - 1991 to 2003

The Project of The Festiniog Railway Company
to Acquire, Reconstruct and Operate the WHR

Summaries of High Court Judgements,
Public Inquiries, Reports, Decisions
and Background Information

Compiled, written and published by John Hopkins

Version 4 - 3 December 2003

Published in aid of the funds of the Welsh Highland Railway Society

*The result of that suggestion from Mike Schumann brought the definitive work on the goings on to acquire the WHR undertaking. It is a magnificent work, of great detail and of course has been central to compiling this volume.*

*Mr and Mrs John Hopkins, suitably installed in the new Observation Car Glaslyn. This was on the WHR Subscribers' Day in 2009, and John, after the magnificent administration work he has done, was a most welcome guest on the occasion. His statistics and his efficiency in looking after the admin had made it possible for all the others to be there too!*

statement escaped "capture" by him and a significant library was collected. Delay in the final Decision by the SoS allowed comfortable time to draw up further text which, by this time, had enlarged into the "Recent History of the WHR" to cover a wider scene. Opportunity was taken to research some background, particularly of the vital roles played by TCL and the West Consortium in the 1980s. He rounded off experiences in this period by attending the National Park Planning Inquiry of 1998 and the NFU's High Court appeal of late 1999.

The final version of the "Recent History" grew to nearly 400 pages and was also received kindly by fellow supporters. He was indebted to Michael Bentley for the suggestion and support to produce hard-bound copies, and all the keen students lined up to get one, as it is the detailed history of events.

Soon after the Decision by the SoS in favour of FR Co's application to build and operate, the FR Trust began public fund raising and John was invited to act as administrator of the Phases 2 and 3 track fund to assist construction from Dinas to Rhyd Ddu, which raised some £202k. This was followed by invitation to administer the two Phase 4 appeals from Rhyd Ddu to Porthmadog, for track and train funds, which to date, have raised over £2m. Again, this involved many hours' work at home, and continues at the time of writing. He is apt to describe his Excel spreadsheets as comparable in size with a football field. However, such prodigious works of fact in all cases predict accurately exactly where the money is coming from. His immense efforts were recognised by the award of a Gold Medal in 2007.

In 2004, he did a season's firing on the coal-fired replica 1830's loco Planet at the Manchester Museum of Science and Industry, just for fun. That's John Hopkins!

# Andy Savage BSc (Eng) MBA C Eng FICE CMIOSH MCILT

### Andrew John Savage b.1952 Nottingham

Andy's parents were both in medicine, his father a doctor, his mother a nursing sister, and he is the eldest of 5, with two brothers and two sisters, now scattered around the world. He doesn't really know how or why he became interested in trains, but he is - and always has been. He thinks it's genetic.

Andy's earliest railway memories are of being taken by Dr Savage into the cab of the 'Paddy', the local service between Southwell and Rolleston Junction, which is on the Nottingham to Lincoln line. The locomotive was a Johnson 0-4-4T, the last passenger service that they ever did. The cab of course was the 'cab' of the ex-LMS push-pull carriage. This was in 1959, and the line closed in that year. An extreme fondness for 0-4-4 locomotives springs from that time, which may explain his love for *Taliesin*.

Andy attended Nottingham High school from 1960 - 1970 (8 - 18). He left as a BR sponsored scholar, to go to Leicester Uni (1971 - 74), to study engineering, and left with an engineering degree in 1974. By this time he was thoroughly railist and involved with model railways, having been to Ffestiniog in 1967 where he was hooked. His first working visit was with East Midlands Group on 6th April 1968, the day the

FR opened as far as Dduallt. Andy was a 'keensie', taking over as Working Party Organiser for the Ffestiniog Railway Society, East Midlands Group, and visiting the FR on a regular basis from 1968 onwards, eventually joining the Ffestiniog Railway Society Board in 1973.

In his career Andy was associated with British Rail through university, taking up a post as a Senior Technical Officer afterwards, and being promoted to Assistant District Civil Engineer (PW) at Gloucester in 1978.

He married in 1974 and had a son and daughter but the first marriage ended. He met his second wife Hilary Jarvis in 1987 and they married in 1991.

By 1991 Andy was Area Civil Engineer South Wales, then he moved to be Divisional Civil Engineer Watford from 1992-1994. On the Ffestiniog he was leading the project for 'Detattification', sprucing up the visual image of the railway after years of neglect, and here he formed a working partnership with Gordon Rushton, then the FR General Manager. This productive arrangement lasted and spread. At the onset of privatisation Andy was leading the restructuring of existing BR units that led to his appointment as Area Director for GTRM at Watford, and later as the Director of Engineering and Safety, a position he held and developed into the prestigious Balfour-Beatty/Carillion joint venture. At that time Andy was probably responsible for the safety of 25% of the UK rail network, as well as being responsible for 25% of England's motorway network.

Gordon and Andy worked together on fund raising Minffordd Hostel, *Taliesin* and toast rack car 39.

In 2005 Andy left Carillion to become the Deputy Chief Inspector at the Rail Accident Investigation Branch. This caused much heartache and change. He had steadily maintained his volunteer work for the Ffestiniog Railway becoming the director responsible for safety, and then the Festiniog Railway Company, Deputy-Chairman from 2003. He had been in the van of engineering matters for the FR Co., WHR restoration project, such that he championed the WHR at the 1993 TO public inquiry, and was subject to robust cross examination, in particular on the viability of the Porthmadog Cross-Town Link. The opposing advocate gained little purchase, and was obliged to leave the subject, bested over creating any doubt as to the engineering viability of the FR proposals. It was typical of Andy that he had prepared his subject so thoroughly, and in such practical detail. Andy's contribution to the WHR project continued at a great pace until 2005. He was obliged to relinquish his FR Co. directorship in order to take up the RAIB post. Thus instead he turned his mind to matters where there could be no clash of interest. At that time the Phase 4 segment of the WHR restoration project had become active. Although Andy could not have a part in this with any safety responsibility, there was nothing to prevent him working to raise funds. It was funds that were wanted urgently, and so he re-engaged

*On top of the Newport office, and the newly appointed BR Area Civil Engineer is about to 'go over the top' on an absail for charity in 1991.*

with Gordon Rushton to launch the single most successful fund raising appeal in railway preservation to date. (See text.) The results of the Phase 4 Appeal topped £2m, and this was all from ordinary citizens. This rather exceeded the £300k target placed on the scheme in 2004!

In 2009 Andy left the RAIB to become the Executive Director of the Railway Heritage Trust. For Andy he says this job was like coming home. Far from riding the Northern line from his Finchley home, to the Network Rail office at Euston, Andy prefers to cycle each day to remain trim. His new job's responsibility includes the funding of and the projects for heritage buildings chosen to be restored on the national railway system, and the small management unit is installed in Network Rail Headquarters. This job dovetailed nicely with activities on the Ffestiniog and Welsh Highland. There is still a large requirement for assistance, to bring the WHR restoration to a successful conclusion, and to fit that railway for operation throughout its length. The two railways need

*Andy fought hard and long to create Minffordd Hostel, that now has room for up to 46 people to stay in 5 modules. It was struggle to raise the money for it, and volunteers led by Eileen Clayton built it, with even a Eurogrant supporting it. No doubt at all it is a major asset, especially for the youngsters.*

to be brought together with compatible operating systems, and there is much work to be done in raising the money needed to obtain the finishing touches. So once more the dynamo was cranked up and the bulldozer started to tackle the new themes of 'Let's Finish the Job' and the 'Sustainable railway'. This time there was a full recession in swing but Andy together with Gordon Rushton battled it through, and pulled in favours to try to raise some money. In somewhere approaching six months the amount raised was moving quickly towards the half-million pound mark! So they decided to boost it further and the job will never end. 2012 will see the second year of operation of the Snowdonian, the largest grossing train of all time ever run on the Ffestiniog and Welsh Highland.

Andy is in the thick of the preservation theme, spanning the preservation and national railway worlds. This is where his energies and talents need to be. For him to accept the 2011 Heritage Heros Award for the F&WHR was as near as Heaven gets.

*Whilst great men offer their magnificent fortunes in pursuit of great projects - and the FR Co. is most grateful for the people who have done this - there are those with more modest ambitions and the means to fulfil them. Carriages have always been a sort of a Cinderella, and Andy wanted to see some of the rarer types of vehicle from back in time recreated to join the fleet now FR has the skills and the workshop to build them. Accordingly this superb 1868 Ashbury's four-wheeler he contributed to, which to ride in reminds one sharply why bogie stock was a good idea.*

## Roland Doyle TMIET AMIRSE

### Roland Doyle b. 1956 Hatfield

He says his first memory of trains was whilst out in his pram with his mother. They were up on a footbridge over Hertford station and he blew heartily on a whistle he had round his neck. The shunting engine down below immediately moved off, chuffing past, and confirming to Roland forever the power of whistles and the fascination of steam locomotives. He was totally taken and was irritatingly fond of trains from that very moment onwards.

He managed to escape to the Ffestiniog Railway (FR) at the age of 15. In 1971, he volunteered for a fortnight at Boston Lodge, together with Nigel Dant, as a cleaner. Linda had just been converted to fire on oil. At that time Blanche was also being converted from coal to oil, so everyone was enthusiastic about firing with oil, and although he had a few turns on coal he began to gain the new skill of oil firing – he also learned how to drink beer, which may have been marginally more important. In those days at Boston Lodge, the lower down the order of precedence you were, the worse you were treated. There were other skills that Roland was learning, though not about railways, and after one amorous encounter, he was 30 mins late for duty at BL and was banned from the footplate for 2 weeks by Phil Girdlestone. However, quite undaunted he became a regular volunteer increasing

his time to doing 5-6 weeks at a stretch. His studies took him to Hawker-Siddley as an undergraduate engineer. He graduated with an HND in electrical and electronic engineering, and became an engineer in the firm Hawker-Siddley Dynamic Engineering, concerned with 'systems' and machinery control, such as gas turbines on helicopters. He met and married Tricia Michelmore in 1981, and he was persuaded to move to Porthmadog. He met Tricia, who worked in the railway cafe (then known as the Greasy Spoon, ruled by a large and very stern lady) in a complex manner. The arrangement at Boston Lodge was that one could ring over to the cafe for something to eat. It would be put on the front of the next train and hurled from the locomotive as it passed on Boston Lodge Curve. On this occasion, Roland's pork pie curved off the engine at a fine rate. He managed to locate it, intact, but misshapen; relieved, he unwrapped and took a bite out of it. Before he actually consumed it he noticed that the pie was rotten, with the meat green. He went over to Harbour , to remonstrate with the Boss, who said she couldn't understand it at all. Roland pointed out that the sell-by date was nearly six months gone, but she insisted that it should have still been fresh as it had been in the freezer. Tricia provided a sweet, new, pink, fresh pork pie, and at the same time won Roland's heart.

The plan was to buy a house in Porthmadog, which they did in Chapel Street. Then Roland managed to get the promise of a job with the BBC as a broadcast engineer in Cardiff, with the cunning plan of looking for something in North Wales after he had gone through the BBC engineering training school to do another degree! This was entirely successful, and a job came up with the BBC in Bangor as a senior broadcast engineer, as they were making programmes for the then new S4C. Roland and Tricia moved to Porthmadog and got married in 1981. The job went well and Roland rose to be a supervisory engineer. He took full advantage of living in Porthmadog by volunteering on the FR, qualifying as a driver in 1983.

Roland spotted the new boiler that Mike Hart had purchased for *Palmerston*, that was sitting unused in Minffordd Yard, and decided it would be a fine idea to get together a group to reassemble the old veteran. The 'Eric the Engine' project began in 1991, and lasted until 1993, when the locomotive ran again in service on the FR. It was so enjoyable that the team looked for another project. Andy Savage offered *Taliesin* 2000 to recreate a long-lost single Fairlie. Enough funds were raised for this project to begin in 1995, with the frames being erected at Boston Lodge in 1996. Roland persuaded Boston Lodge to install and adopt the AutoCad programme to facilitate this rebuild. It was useful for other things as well, and rapidly became established for all drawings. This locomotive was worked on by the *Taliesin* Team, led by Roland and was first steamed in 1999. People had thought the old *Taliesin* was no good, as it was scrapped in 1932. Having got her going, it was soon found out that *Taliesin* was scrapped because it was so popular that

*The visit of HRH The Prince of Wales, seen here being introduced to the two General Managers, was a culmination of all the effort to get Phases 1-3 open for traffic.*

they had worn it out! The locomotive was a major success, and of course it had parts common to the double-Fairlies, and so she is much appreciated and placed firmly on the FR 'capital' list of necessary locomotives.

In December 1996 Roland was invited to become the General Manager of Welsh Highland Light Railway Ltd. At this time the Caernarfon to Dinas section, Phase I was being planned for construction. The grant from the MC and others was won, and FR was in the business of getting the railway up and running as soon as possible, if for no other reason than to demonstrate commitment and competence for the Transport and Works Order application to build the Dinas-Porthmadog section. Thus it was of the greatest importance to build the first three miles quickly and properly. The policy decided for building WHR was initially by contractor, to get a railway up and running. Thereafter to involve the volunteers with running it. However there was only 2% of volunteer input into to Phase I, and that was a disappointment to some of the volunteers. Roland's particular purpose was to manage the project work on the ground, and to protect the grant application with the proper application of funds.

Roland invented the famous Roland Rail Movers, which greatly simplified tracklaying on a single line with extremely restricted access. This was just the thing that facilitated volunteer engagement in the restoration process, and tracklaying was an area of steadily increasing volunteer involvement to such a point that in Phase 4 almost the full thirteen miles was laid principally with volunteer labour.

Roland stayed with the WHR restoration project right through Phases 1-3 until the line was reopened for service between Caernarfon and Rhyd Ddu, and was then handed over to the operators. After that, when all the snagging was complete, there was little left to do, as although the plan was to go further, this was not possible until the funds were in place to do it. So during this interregnum, Roland went back to BBC, as he was only retained on skeleton hours for WHR. He also took on some 5 months or so of contract work to finish and recommission the pioneer Garratt locomotive K1. In September 2004, the

*'Eric the Engine' passes towards Pitt's Head on 9th September 2006, on one of the Superpower events on the WHR. Though small by everyone's standards, the rebuild of* Palmerston *by Roland's team was inspired. This was the FR loco that worked often on WHR and its excellent performance and popularity means that an England engine can be seen regularly, even when* Prince *is out of service.*

extension to Porthmadog, Phase 4, received its funding, and Roland was re-engaged by the project, with as much to build again, and the money to do it. He planned the 'chop-up' into contracts and set the system in motion to get the railway constructed. All his expertise and more was needed for this piece of railway as there were large challenges to overcome, with four tunnels, four large single-span bridges and a seven-span bridge to construct, and numerous cuttings to clear and embankments to repair. Progress was going well until in March 2006 Roland was informed that there would be no further job for him as General Manager WHRCL.

Roland retired to a safe distance and began High Rail Systems in April 2006. Requests flooded in for a number of highly skilled and technical jobs for which he had the expertise, like track alignment on the computer, and the extremely complex and involved Level Crossing orders that were necessary for the WHR to operate. Roland obtained nine of these Orders for the varying crossings on the WHR, and designed the trap point actuating mechanism for the unique Cae Pawb rail on rail crossing.

There was another problem that he was grappling with. The FR is fitted with traditional, electrically connected, single-line staff instruments. These machines issue a token (or staff) to the loco driver, and then lock the instrument until the staff is returned to it, so that only one staff may be in use at one time. This assures single occupancy of the railway section. The Welsh Highland was not equipped with these instruments, thus making operations potentially inflexible. Equipping the railway would have been costly and difficult until Roland invented his MicroETS token issuing system. This uses purpose designed micro-controllers to connect instruments via the Internet, saving large amounts of money in wiring and offering the secure issue of a conventional staff, so that to the loco crew, both railways are uniform. For the WHR it offers the necessary flexibility at an affordable price. As the WHR opens for traffic, Roland is still engaged with this remarkable restoration in a unique way. He also keeps his hand in by driving on WHR and FR on a regular basis, thus continuing a driving tradition of nearly thirty years standing.

*Just before the magnificent photograph opposite, Roland's tie had been spotted to be out of line. It was immediately attended to by Pauline Holloway, so that he would be suitably 'posh' to meet HRH.*

# Gordon Rushton FCILT, MCIM

*Gordon in the cab of loco NG14a on Puffing Billy in Belgrave, Victoria, in 2009, preparatory to being ordered to drive it to Gembrook, the other end of the line. A pleasant order, but one for hot palms if you are not familiar with the railway.*

## Arthur John Gordon Rushton b. 1946 Birkenhead

Mr Rushton senior worked in Liverpool, for J Bibby and Sons, and was deeply devoted to Rugby football. Mother went to work for the British Medical Association, as a representative. The family lived in Bebington, Cheshire until 1951, and every Sunday walked down to Grandma's in Beresford Avenue for lunch. There was a major kerfuffle if Gordon was not sat in the bay window with a view out to the trains on the L&NW&GW Joint Line, entering and leaving Bebington and New Ferry Station. If the trains were out of sight, Gordon became unmanageably difficult. Thus he believes the pre-disposition to trains must be genetic.

Gordon was moderately bright at school, but always wilful; academic achievement eluded him, unless he believed the subject was interesting. To counter this unfortunate persistence, he was sent away to Rydal School in Colwyn Bay. Alas this fanned the flames, through offering vast horizons of distraction. Much time was taken with cycling, horse-riding and sailing; Gordon's passion entirely excluded Rugby. Such distractions were meant to encourage and reward high academic achievement, to complement and soothe the fevered brain, whilst working away at educating the person. Alas the distractions were not conditional. Academically, Gordon was not charmed with most subjects, though he achieved a respectable crop of 'O' levels. However, he was also able to signal trains through Colwyn Bay, not a subject offered by the Oxford and Cambridge Schools Examination Board. Qualification for this vocational achievement was obtained by long waits at the foot of the signalbox stairway, which normally led to an invitation to ascend into Colwyn Bay in No.2 Box. Long application to the passage of trains over many afternoons, eventually convinced the signalman to permit Gordon at the age of 16, to preside over the array of steam-hauled expresses on the North Wales Coast. Later, on Sundays, there was a regular slot in the No. 1 Box, at the other end of the station, whilst the signalman cleaned his car. Such encyclopaedic knowledge was expected to be reserved for physics or higher mathematics, not signalling, and there were consequences.

He first visited the Welsh railways when parents came, and the inmates were allowed out of the asylum. Mother and Father were persuaded to take the kids out in the car, looking for entertainment. In 1962 he managed to inveigle his parents to drive over the Crimea Pass to Blaenau Ffestiniog, and then down to Portmadoc, to discover the Festiniog Railway. The fact that time was short made it only possible to drive across the Cob, and have a peep in Harbour Station, and then to go on, back to Colwyn Bay via Caernarfon. This was a sore trial, and it lit the fires of want with such a bright flame, that a revisit was required. The suddenly announced, full-day holidays at Rydal, permitted impromptu visits. Thus on the May Whole Holiday in 1962, a ride in a Derby Lightweight DMU from Llandudno Junction to Blaenau Ffestiniog with 'best pal' Mike Jones, led to the harsh news that the Bala Branch was closed, so it was a walk down the FR trackbed, or wander round Blaenau. They tried the former for a while, but eventually embarked upon the walk down the FR trackbed very much by chance. The line was clear but derelict, severed at Tanygrisiau by the recently opened pump-storage, hydro scheme. It was on this five-mile walk on May 28th 1962, down the trackbed to Tan y Bwlch, to see the restored train, that the romance

*Evidently for local joyrides, this wagon was left on the track for a couple of 16 year olds to find as we walked down from Blaenau to Tan y Bwlch. One may suppose that we immediately jumped on. We knew enough about railways to understand that starting trains was the easy part of the business, and that the difficult bit was stopping them. Reluctantly we walked by.*

and delight of the idea of restoring such dereliction to active life was truly grasped for the first time. On this day there was time to go down to Porthmadog Harbour, hauled by *Prince*, and to come straight back up. Then it was necessary to run down to the main road to catch the Crosville bus up the hill from the Oakeley Arms. This was to be quite sure of making the 16.30 train down to the Junction that would permit return to Colwyn Bay, to get back to school on time. Of course, such an excursion with restricted time, on what was undoubtedly a railway chock-full of exciting and interesting opportunities, could only promote love in the heart, and as soon as possible, volunteering began. This was in 1964, just after school term. Locomotives were on coal, and Gordon spent a week shifting it about for the railway, and thought that people really didn't get a good deal when volunteering. He says he never got nearer to an engine than either cleaning it, or chucking coal onto it. The cost of such a week was very high, and no one seemed to think about any of that; you were very much on your own.

*In 1966 this was a modern railway, with Wirral electrics through to Liverpool on a 20 minute off-peak, 10 minute peak frequency. Gordon worked at Wallasey Grove Station, into which a New Brighton to Liverpool Central service is just running, on a grey day. Being a booking clerk was not exciting - the 'bin-men' theory was in demonstration. Something had to be done.*

Career thoughts of medicine were flights of fancy, communicated to his poor parents. The necessary application to this cause was not forthcoming, and 'A' level was not a success. He left Rydal to ponder the realities, oft warned about, that those who failed to achieve the requisite qualifications became bin-men. Whilst his disappointed parents were away in Jersey on holiday, Gordon signed up at the British Railways, Divisional Office at Lime Street Chambers, Liverpool to be a booking clerk. When they came back, he was being sent to Wallasey Grove Road on the Wirral electric system. After training, Port Sunlight on the Birkenhead, Woodside to Chester line was allocated as his 'permanent' station, and from time to time was left in charge of Bebington and New Ferry Station, the gas-lit palace he had so often contemplated from Nana's window. He was not entirely delighted with being a booking clerk, especially when the station master pointed out that after several years he would get used to it. Thus he managed through sleight of hand to charm himself on to the British Railways, London Midland Region, 1967, 2 year, Management Trainee course as a staff entrant. This scheme was for university people who wanted to join the Rail Industry, and there were a few staff people added. Perhaps the 'bin-man' warning had been circumvented, and one really <u>could</u> idle one's schooldays as a feckless youth?

The Management Training scheme he would willingly have

**A.J.G. RUSHTON.**

*Getting on the LMR Management Training scheme was a bit of luck in 1967. It quashed all 'bin-men' theory, and offered two years of concentrated pleasure, as well as a massive amount of experience.*

worked through for free - but given the pay and conditions, sometimes it felt that this was the case. Gordon was on the Preston Division, right at the end of steam, had a wonderful time riding on trains with an official footplate pass, and was continually amazed that he was actually meant to do this! The second placement was on the London Divison, based at Eversholt House, right at the time of the rebuilding of the West Coast Main Line, and the reconstruction of Euston Station. Volunteering on narrow gauge railways had to be subsidiary during management training, and during his first couple of jobs after that. Upon completion of the training course, Gordon's first job was Area Manager Commercial, Warrington (Central). This town in the late 1960s was a sombre place, with smoky air; everything carried a coating of grime and a rundown, rattly railway had to be run. Gordon's prime consideration was with wagon-load freight, which happened to arrive at Warrington Central in amounts that could not be handled - an interesting problem. In 1970. Gordon became a Passenger Sales Representative in London, then moving into the office at Western Towers, Reading. In 1976 he went north to Sheffield, and in 1977 joined the Sheffield Group of the Ffestiniog Railway Society (FRS). As the BR Passenger Manager in Sheffield, Gordon introduced Fuzz Jordan to a nice little earner for Society funds, running a sales stand, and then refreshments, on the Division's numerous Merrymaker trains, that ran full of punters to destinations all over UK. In 1979 Gordon was elected to the Board of the FRS, with the backing of Fuzz Jordan and the Sheffield Group. At that time the FRSL was in fairly hefty disagreement with the FR Co. on various items, as John Routly, the FR Trust and FR Co. Chairman, was an autocratic though very skilled manager, but there was still a lot of coming together on matters of joint interest, and in fund raising, at which the Sheffield Group was highly effective. Gordon was elected as Chairman of the FRSL in 1986, taking over from Gordon Caddy. Now he had the responsibility of working with John Routly. They hit it off fairly well, with Gordon and the team believing that the way to influence events was to

*FR Commercial Manager, Eammon Seddon, as the Fat Controller, speaks to Gordon's loco Sgt Murphy at one of the 1990's Gala events. It doesn't seem that Sgt Murphy was listening. The example of the sparkling appearance and nice garden at Minffordd spread throughout the railway, and the customers certainly noticed. Eammon is now the CEO of Puffing Billy in Australia. Sgt Murphy went to the Teifi Valley Railway.*

increase membership, to encourage the volunteer figures to rise, and to increase the fund-raising capabilities of the Society, such that the Company could not ignore their wishes. In fact there was no contest in this matter; the FR Co. was constructive. If there was a crowning team achievement during Gordon's time as Society Chairman, it was the relentless prosecution of Minffordd Hostel, through the planning stages, through fundraising, and to construction. To ensure that younger volunteers had affordable accommodation. Gordon and the Society were great supporters of the Parks and Gardens movement. Building Back to Blaenau had left the FR struggling, and Parks and Gardens with Eileen Clayton offered three planks: involving and empowering women, involving kids to create the future volunteers, and making the FR visually second to none. That tradition, now firm, recruited the current General Manager, and set the scene for a continuing young, vital, mixed staff on both railways, constantly renewing itself and staying bright and innovative.

Society membership topped 6000; fundraising rose, and the FRSL team was most successful. During this time, Gordon left Sheffield to work for Sealink, and ran a monthly working party to the railway with Andy Savage, driving on a Friday night from Southampton to Porthmadog, with pickup in Swindon. In 1985 Gordon was promoted to the Commercial Manager of the Sealink British Ferries, Irish Sector in London. In 1987 he went to Liverpool as General Manager of the service from Liverpool

to Dun Laoghaire. These two jobs led to his specialisation in fast ferries and trips round the world. Fortunately there were visits to Holyhead, that permitted time to be spent at Porthmadog. Reporting to Holyhead at 09.00 on a Monday morning meant an unprecedented Sunday night out in Porthmadog - that was a treat!

A hostile takeover bid for Sealink eventually led to permanent posting to Holyhead, and total disenchantment with the new Swedish, Stena Line owners. After a rigorous regime of testing, interviews, and much discussion and cross-questioning, Gordon moved from Stena Line in August 1991, to become the first General Manager who had been Society Chairman.

The FR Co. was in tumult. It was under siege from all sides for the way in which the WHR affair was being handled. The route out of this problem was found by Messrs Hart, Schumann and Rushton; it was to rebuild the Welsh Highland Railway from the Caernarfon end so that it did not compete with FR, to join it with the FR, to make the resulting railway large enough to regain its market share, and for FR to be a world attraction in its own right. It was expected that this process could be accomplished in about 20 years, provided funds could be secured. Restoration of WHR was not original thinking; the strategic plan for FR protection and redemption of market share was. A disturbingly large number of people even today seem to have problems getting their minds around this strategy; in 1992, when Gordon was one of the people proposing it, it was not thought credible.

The strains of trying to keep the FR going, manage and encourage the volunteering effort, solve the engineering problems, and to look for and gain WHR funding were intense. The High Court battle and the subsequent TO were entered into; John Routly was replaced as Chairman of the FR Co., by Mike Hart. The task was massive and Gordon was working more than 80 hours a week trying to keep the FR show on the road. The pressure was showing in the finances, and it was decided in 1996 to remove Gordon and appoint Alan Heywood in his place. Accordingly the burnt-out hulk was dispatched in February 1996, and requested to stay away. Spare no thought as to why, or of how sad this may have been. The FR decided to play it like this, and it was announced as a resignation; the Board 'wanted a change'. Three of the Board members of the time had to face crises in their association with the WHR after, and so they now know what it is like, plus there were other casualties in the organisation later - it is what it took for the WHR to be fought through to a conclusion. Gordon was just the first one to go. He went quietly and without fuss. This was good for successor Alan Heywood, who was able to ensure that there was a smooth transition, as the FR Co. moved towards getting Caernarfon to Dinas completed, and preparing the WHR Transport and Works Application.

Dan Wilson, the Snowdon Ranger Editor commented that the problems arose from 'the mice getting into the money box', but that was not the whole story. For that, complete with the pearl-handled revolver, you will have to wait for Gordon's account of his time as General Manager of the FR Co., when he will tell all. It was a mixture of innovative HR management, budgetary 'readjustment', and the immense strain of the WHR saga. The money box was sorted, and handed to Alan Heywood with a sound, workable plan. The railway did not hiccough upon Gordon's passing, as it did when the same sort of thing happened subsequently. The story of those times requires more diplomacy than can be applied this close to events, so you will have to wait for the tales of the caprice and now muted thunder of events of long ago.

Gordon became Marketing Manager of Valley Lines, one of the new Train Operating Companies, running trains from Cardiff. He was cut off from all FR dealings, and then left Valley Lines in 1998 to join Graham Whistler, a video maker. Gordon learned the new trade and enjoyed it. He also made many videos for Virgin Trains, about the new Pendolinos and Voyagers, to educate the staff by a number of informative programmes. He advised on the making of a number of videos about the FR, and reappeared on video expeditions. He was commissioned by Andy Savage to do some video work for Carillion, until at the beginning of Phase 4, Andy requested Gordon's help in setting up public fundraising, to introduce a wider element into the search for cash to complement the WEFO grant. The two set up a scheme similar to that of 1999, where by subscription they raised the money needed to construct replica single Fairlie locomotive *Taliesin(III)* over a period of ten years. They joined forces, with the splendid administrative gifts of John Hopkins added as the foundation, to raise sums exceeding £2m - more than that raised in any single railway preservation project from the public. So from being 'dumped' by FR Co., Gordon made a comeback. He says the episode was character forming, and he insists it did him no particular harm, as he had become overbearing, disagreeable and arrogant. Others too have been dragged through the hedge backwards by the WHR; it has been such a courageous, demanding and difficult strategy to follow, and the ground on the way is littered with 'corpses'. Fairness doesn't come into it, he insists; it was what was needed to get the job done. So when you enjoy a trip up the revived railway, spare a thought for all those who have striven so hard, and given their support and generosity to make it happen, only to be impaled on the fence of intempestivity. Gordon decided the sensible thing to do was to write a book in some detail about the restoration of the longest narrow gauge railway in Britain. Though far from perfect, here it is; you're reading it.

*The West Coast main Line was thoroughly rebuilt a second time to fit it for 140mph running, which turned out to be 125mph running, never mind why, and Gordon managed to be there a second time, this time to record it. Here he is taking video at Amington, standing on the Down Fast, next to the Up fast, only at the moment there isn't one - but there'll be another one along soon.*

*Looking rather fat, old and careworn in this picture, Gordon is sat in the splendour of Pullman Car Bodysgallen, on one or other of the sumptuous do's that have characterised the fundraising effort for this excellent railway. It really has been fun doing this bit, and the money raised is huge and the process continues onward as it will never be finished.*

# Mike Hart OBE

*Mike Hart sits at the side of the Afon Glasyn, in the Pass, on 1st May 2005. By now he was confident that it was a matter of time before the rails would be reinstalled, so it was no longer a gesture of hope, but of expectation, as Phase 4 funding was in the bag - thanks to his efforts!*

## Michael Clifford Hart b. April 1951 in Balham

Mike's father was in banking, working for the Midland Bank, and from time to time the family transferred home as he went to manage another branch. When Michael was 6, the family went for a holiday to Madison's Camp in Kent. Of course outside the gates of the camp is the Romney, Hythe and Dymchurch Railway, and this made a great impression on Mike, who instantly took to the miniature trains. When the family moved to Tonbridge, Mike joined the Boys Brigade, and they had summer camps in either North Wales, or on the Isle of Wight at Bembridge. He well remembers sailing from Portsmouth Harbour on the *PS Sandown*, and then travelling down the Ryde Pier tramway to the bus, observing the famous O2 0-4-4T locomotives on their trains of green vintage stock, but he was never allowed to travel on them.

The star in the firmament was the Boys Brigade camp one year in Wales on his first visit to Criccieth. For some reason, now lost in the mists of time, there was a long rail journey to the place from London Euston via Llangollen. Whilst they were there, his father took him on an all-day trip to the Ffestiniog Railway (FR) by train to Porthmadog and they travelled on the railway. Mike was instantly hooked. Later on, in 1967, at the age of 16, he managed to make his own way to the FR, and worked in Boston Lodge Works. Allocated to Fred Boughey to help with sanding down a Barn carriage, he managed to escape from this rather tedious and time consuming duty to work for the Traffic Department at Dduallt, and in the quiet times on this duty he helped by working on the track. In 1968 he was able to come up to Ffestiniog to volunteer for two weeks, and went out on the locomotive, firing for David Bascombe for several days. He came back home on the Cambrian Coast Express, insanitary and filthy, but very happy. This confirmed Mike's wish to work with locomotives and mechanical engineering, and sealed the lifelong interest he has maintained in the FR.

*Mike Hart amid the controlled chaos of Beddgelert Station rebuilding on 24th March 2007. Behind is a bank of crushed slate ready to be spread.*

Mike was not an academic giant. He preferred more practical matters, where you could see the results of your labour. After he gained an HND in engineering, he was one of the pioneers in working for the preserved railway movement, and joined the Kent and East Sussex Railway paid staff, yet he still kept his volunteer connection with the FR. He went on to work for Resco railways and eventually at Thomas Hills of Rotherham, where he bought a house and settled down. Mike is however extremely street-wise, and used his keen business brain to set up his own company Railway Wheelsets in the 1980s. He spotted the opportunity to bring in high quality components from Brazil and to offer a reliable supply to many of the emerging private railway companies. The company imports wheels and axles for Britain's modern railway stock. This business grew steadily to be one of the major suppliers in the business and it has stayed relevant for over ten years.

It was while Mike was travelling to Brazil to set up sources of supply for Railway Wheelsets that he met Heloisa on the long flight. Heloisa and Mike married, and they have two boys, Jonathan and George.

Mike also likes to keep his engineering hand in with a number of his own 'homework' projects. He has rebuilt a number of early internal combustion locomotives, including a WWI Protected Simplex locomotive, and the famous FR WWI Baldwin Locotractor *Moelwyn*. His current projects include a Sentinel steam railmotor, and a curious Sentinel shunting locomotive, *Gervase*, one of the first locomotives ever to work on the preserved Kent and East Sussex Railway. This old wheezer is something of a Cinderella, so Mike has rescued it and soon it will be back in service.

Mike's connections with Ffestiniog were strong for many years, and his evident gifts eventually led to his being appointed a

Company Director in 1990. This was at a time when Ffestiniog was embroiled in strife over the WHR. It was Mike who, with Mike Schumann and Gordon Rushton, developed the policy of rebuilding the whole railway from Caernarfon right through to Porthmadog. It was Mike who, with patient diplomacy and careful thinking, so positioned the Festiniog Railway Company that this policy could be pursued successfully. The opportunity came in 1993 for Mike to take over as Chairman of the Festiniog Railway Company. This was just at the time of the first Public Inquiry, for the Welsh Highland Railway TO. He worked hard to drive through the restoration of the WHR to Rhyd Ddu, but then was forced to withdraw from the Chair in 2001 for personal reasons. This did not stop him being a Director; nor did it stop him from pursuing and securing the necessary funding to extend the Railway all the way through to Porthmadog with the Phase 4 scheme. He retained his chairmanship of WHRCL.

Mike never allowed the WHR restoration to lie idle. His energy and dedication drove what eventually became a £28m, 25 mile project right through to fruition.

He is endlessly searching out grant aid, donors and sponsors, for the project. Thus it was well deserved that he became Michael Hart OBE in the 2009 New Years Honours List, 'for services to the Rail Industry'.

*Mike stands at Caernarfon Station in front of NGG16 No 87 on 16th May 2009 with Terry Turner (GM Welshpool & Llanfair) and Paul Ingham (Driver). This is one of the Phase 4 Subscriber Days, when the faithful gathered to celebrate their creation and to be persuaded to part with more money. Of course this is something Mike thoroughly agrees with!*

# John Routly

Ernest John Routy b.    Blackheath, London 1914
d.    4th March 2003 aged 88

**B**orn into a different age, a child of the First War, John Routly's father was a doctor. John went to Radley College near Oxford, and graduated in law from Caius College, Cambridge. He was a practising solicitor. During WW2 he was a Squadron Leader, dealing with the provision of aircraft spare parts, and after the war, he was head hunted by car and lorry manufacturer The Rootes Group as Secretary. Rootes were based in the Midlands and the south of England, and manufactured such marques of car as Hillman, Humber, and Commer vans and lorries. In 1960, by which time he had been a director for many years, he left to join William Baird as a director and travelled the world extensively buying and merging companies. He served as a Commissioner of Income Tax between 1955 and 1979. John had a healthy interest in the Conservative party, as Chairman of the Policy and Resources Committee and as Vice Chairman of the Buckinghamshire County Council from 1965. He became High Sheriff in 1972-73. Adaptable, intelligent and always active, John used his talents to be financial controller of Help the Aged, from 1975-1988, and in 1988 he co-founded and became chairman of Aids Care Education and Training.

Trevor Bailey, who was also at Radley, was interested in trains, had a sister, Jane; John was not interested trains, but he was interested in Jane. That interest had flowered into marriage in 1939, and John and Jane had two daughters, one of whom, Angela, married Mike Schumann. Alan Pegler (a chum of Trevor Bailey) was heading the takeover of the Festiniog Railway Company in 1954. They had great need of a skilled corporate lawyer, who was also financially astute, to advise them on the best legal and financial framework to create to receive this statutory company. John Routly was no railway enthusiast, and he kept a clear head, unsullied by railway dreams; he was just the man to give sensible advice to anyone contemplating the rescue of moribund little railways. He remarked later with his typical wry humour that he was not a railway enthusiast, he was a Ffestiniog Railway (FR) enthusiast.

It was his expertise that facilitated the Pegler takeover of the Festiniog Railway Company. It was John Routly who was the architect of the famous 'trinity' of Trust, Company and Society, that has proved to be so resilient and stable over the years. It was with John Routly's excellent advice that mechanisms were put in place to make sure that no individual would hold the Ffestiniog Railway (FR) assets, such that they might be vulnerable to neither domination nor asset strip by any outside agency. His mechanisms of Company, Trust and Society have offered the best governance, excellent tax efficiency, and security. Such innovation in thinking allowed the FR to survive to be in the position of gaining control of and then restoring the entire Welsh Highland Railway, and thus to grow into the longest preserved railway in Britain. Credit for these successes must go to John Routly, for although Alan Pegler may have had the money to acquire the Company, it was John Routly's legal framework that gave it the strong, stable and credible framework needed for it to prosper.

The FR had to fight hard for its survival, and John Routly's legal and financial skills were much engaged to restore the Railway back to Blaenau Ffestiniog. He took over the chairmanship of the Company in 1972, at the age of 58. The course of the line had been flooded, and he persisted with action for compensation, eventually winning a settlement of £106k, in a landmark case against the British Electricity Authority (later CEGB). The 'Deviation' line, around Llyn Ystradau, the lower lake of the hydro- electric, pump storage scheme, linked the two parts of the FR, opening the way for restoration to Blaenau Ffestiniog in 1982. The case proved to the Establishment that the restoration of tourist railways by railway enthusiasts was not something to be dismissed as of little consequence.

John Routly used his outstanding abilities and inventiveness to support the FR, and became Chairman of both Trust and Company. John never lost his contacts and associates, and maintained an active personal life away from the FR. He was a great networker and was skilful in managing to find and recruit the right people to do difficult things. He eagerly embraced and supported

*John and Jane Routly at the opening of the Railway throughout between Porthmadog and Blaenau Ffestiniog in 1984, the culmination of the railway's hopes of over thirty years. The two of them were a delightful and inseparable pair on social occasions. John would always turn out for the Ffestiniog Railway if asked; he was its constant friend.*

the opportunities offering from grants on the FR, and was a great supporter of the projects like INCA, to improve the FR's capacity, its financial performance, and its public appearance. He well understood the need for renewal, and how to use enthusiasm as a motivating tool. However, John Routly was from an earlier age, where 'top people' were what was wanted, and one only let one's guard down with 'PLU' (people like us). Some were dismayed by this, and during a period of rather uncertain staff relations, with eroded living standards, and recent redundancies, his statement that the FR was all 'Jolly Good Fun' was misplaced in the category of 'let them eat cake'. Now this phrase is a much loved FR joke, normally reserved for times when cold rain is running down the back of one's neck.

Perhaps John's social antennae were less well developed than his legal and financial aerials. He was not 'a man of the people' and so sometimes he found relations with the *hoi polloi* a trial. When in the Boston Lodge Erecting Shop with the artisans he did not radiate public warmth - but, in private he was an absolute delight to be with and he could hold an audience's attention. He was most liberal, and utterly committed to the FR; John and Jane Routly were the most gracious hosts, and John was splendid company, with an endless fund of hilarious anecdotes and a good sense of humour.

His dual occupation of the key posts of chairmanship of Trust and Company invited critical comment, that the FR was an oligarchy, and that this diminished the representation from the deserving, who worked hard for the organisation, but who had no say. Yet a Routly skill was differentiating between the deserving and the able. The FR's progress of course gave a lie to detractors; the organisation was quick on its feet, and was excellent at marshalling resources in the places that they were needed - John Routly was instrumental in this being so. He was in a dilemma about the propriety of his son-in-law being appointed as an FR Co. director, lest it be seen as nepotism. It wasn't until pressure was applied to liberate Mike's obvious skills with a seat on the Board that he eventually agreed.

He was taken to his limits by the events of 1990. The FR was struggling at this time, in an era of steadily eroding market share from other tourist attractions that were opening in the area. So when John Routly was warned that the Official Receiver (OR) was to apply to the High Court to sell the trackbed of the closed Welsh Highland Railway to Gwynedd County Council, he decided that action was needed to protect against competition arising. He was persuaded to believe,that the hitherto seemingly insignificant 64 Co. in Porthmadog, had the potential to become a significant rival to his much-loved FR. He was urged that they were capable of development into a threat, and that action should be taken to secure the FR against this. The FR Co. Board decided to make an offer to the OR larger than any other tabled for the

trackbed. John Routly wanted this to be done anonymously, as if it was done publicly, he feared a row, or the encouragement of a bidding war. He and one of his colleagues were also persuaded to speak to the County Council, to warn them that competition in Porthmadog could harm the investment they had already made in the FR, by threatening the viability of the extension to Blaenau Ffestiniog. One may well ask why he didn't just go and speak to the 64 Co. and tell them of his fears. Alas, this was not the man; his intention was to be able to control development of the WHR, and at that time no development against the struggling FR was his preferred course.

He did not anticipate the chain of events his covert action would cause, as when his machinations were made known to the 64 Co., the subsequent brouhaha was outside his corporate legal and financial skills to cope with. The most difficult time in his long career resulted. He approached the High Court hearing with the objective of gaining control of the trackbed and then allowing others to raise the funds and rebuild the railway in such a way that it was not a direct competitor to the FR. The 'misconceived' outcome of the High Court was more of a disappointment to him that to his team, but he was persuaded into acceptance by his son-in-law, Mike Schumann's delight at the opportunity that had surfaced to restore and recommission 25 miles of 2ft gauge railway.

The team around him rallied and brought round the situation to one of total reconstruction of the Welsh Highland Railway.

*John and daughter Angela Schumann at Tan y Bwlch in 1992. Angela met Mike Schumann, chief luminary of the Ffestiniog Railway Deviation and they married.*

He was persuaded to agree that a fully restored WHR could complement FR if built from Caernarfon, tapping new markets and not adversely affecting the established FR, which led to the application for a TO. The huge attendant publicity caused by the feud with the 64 Co. led to competitive applications, and that required a public inquiry. Colleagues on the Board harboured concerns that John Routly's association with the 'buy to shut' disagreement would offer a target for the opposing side, were he encouraged to give evidence at the public inquiry. Yet as the Chairman of the FR Co. he could hardly not. Accordingly John Routly stepped down from the Chair of the Festiniog Railway Company in 1993.

It was another disappointment that at the moment when a massive new challenge arose, of a potentially deeply disturbing nature to the FR, he was obliged to depart instead of being able to surmount the challenge. It was sad that someone who had given so much for so long was unable to depart on a more celebratory note, but that is the nature of the Railway.

John Routly stayed as a Festiniog Railway Trustee until 1998. Jane Routly passed away in 2000. John remained interested in the organisation he had done so much to create for the rest of his days. Too few realise John Routly's profound influence upon the foundations of today's Ffestiniog & Welsh Highland Railways.

# Michael Whitehouse LLB

**Christopher Michael Whitehouse b. October1952, in Birmingham. Lived in Harborne, Birmingham**

I f ever there was someone who had a genetic predisposition for railways it is Michael Whitehouse. His father Pat Whitehouse ran the family construction firm, specialising in public buildings. A man with a lifelong interest in trains, Pat Whitehouse sold out the business in stages to Cubitts and Tarmac, so that at the age of 50 he could indulge himself in book writing and developing his other particular hobby, Tyseley locomotive depot. Michael grew up with his father's passion for trains, and developed his own. It was difficult for a boy who's father was acquiring Castle and Jubilee Class locomotives to consider this extraordinary. Michael thought it was all run-of-the-mill, the sort of thing that fathers just 'did', and took a healthy interest. The family holidays were initially spent in Aberdyfi, Tywyn, and Dolgoch Falls, as Pat Whitehouse was a founder member of the Birmingham "railway mafia" who, with Pat Garland, John Wilkins (who owned the Fairbourne Railway) and Tom Hunt, rebuilt the Talyllyn Railway. Together, father and son, Michael and Pat rode and saw the Talyllyn, the Fairbourne and the Ffestiniog, and Michael acquired a great fund of information from asking Father, Pat, questions like why it was that

*Michael has his trains set up in Tom Rolt's back garden. The Midland Compound is Bassett-Lowke, and Father's locomotive (on loan). The little job is Michael's own Hornby 'O' Gauge clockwork favourite. Not much has changed.* **LTC Rolt**

the steam locomotive *Taliesin* that he was driving up and down the Station at Porthmadog had two regulators and not one.

The sale of B. Whitehouse and Sons resulted in an upgrading of Michael's family holidays, and in the 1960s they began to explore all parts of the world to see steam that has long since vanished starting with the Reseau Breton metre gauge system in Britanny and Chapelon pacifics and then soon ranging further afield through the Iron Curtain on the real Orient Express to Asia, and then on to Africa and South America. Michael was a willing participant in the holidays from Hallfield Prep., and then Malvern College. He left school in 1971 for Liverpool University to study law, but overseas travel to see trains in extraordinary places has become a lifelong passion. Skills learned on such trips have been applied in professional life as the law is one thing but applying it in diverse economies and working with many different characters is entirely another. These skills were to have a great bearing and benefit for the Ffestiniog & Welsh Highland Railway.

On a rainy, wet Easter in 1971, on one of those now frequent railways visits, Michael was at Boston Lodge and General Manager, Allan Garraway suggested to him that he ought to volunteer. So in the gap between school and university, the 19 year old Michael spent eight weeks at Boston Lodge, working on carriages, on *Moelwyn* on the Dduallt Shuttles and gaining some oil firing experience whilst exploring the quarries in the evenings and enjoying the annual Porthmadog carnival train with a "flower power" *Merddin Emrys* and all three buffet cars…. After Liverpool University, having attained his law degree, he needed to spend six months at law school to become a practising solicitor. He chose Guildford Law School, and whilst he was there, he spent many happy hours driving on the Spinney Light Railway, a 7¼ inch gauge line owned by Joseph Ballantine Dykes, and populated by Bassett-Lowke motive power, like a George the Fifth and a Royal Scot. He also had an invitation to run the Railway Museum at Bulawayo, Rhodesia, when sanctions were in full flow, and he replied to that by turning up for six months in 1975, and helping to manage the Easter special to Balla Balla double headed by two North British 12th class 4-8-0s as well as learning how to manage the African museum staff and joining in the high society colonial life of (the then) Salisbury capital.

Steam engines and the law started to mix well for Michael. Pat Whitehouse was invited to a lunch to recruit Friends of King George V, at that time being operated by Bulmers Cider. Pat agreed to help, and his table companion at lunch was Sir Hilary Scott, the deputy senior partner in Slaughter and May, a top UK and international law firm, who had the relationship with Bulmers. Pat asked if the firm would like to interview his son, and Michael attended an interview and was accepted for Articles.

*Michael took weekends out from Malvern College to get acquainted with "Clun Castle" when it became part of the family in 1966. He is seen here learning to drive it at Tyseley under the supervision of a regular driver. The Whitehouses simply used to call the shedmaster and ask for 7029 to be in steam on Sunday afternoon for a driving session in the yard.*
**Pat Whitehouse**

Working on international finance transactions in London for six years, Michael learned the basic essentials of being a commercial and finance lawyer and the banking requirements of his clients. These skills which assumed top service delivery and the right results were to prove a lifelong benefit to Michael in all his walks of life.

Tribal influences eventually dragged Michael back home. He he took a job with Wragge and Co. in Birmingham in 1981, and settled down to develop Tyseley as his hobby, and help his new firm develop a national and currently international practice. At this time Porthmadog was still a bit far, bearing in mind the Tyseley connections, so Michael, with a by now deep partiality for Welsh Narrow Gauge, took up as fireman on the Welshpool and Llanfair. He kept touch with the FR, attended its AGMs, and got to know John Routly. On the social front, at a party, Michael met on chance encounter a friend of a friend. Cupid's bow twanged with Helen, and her interest in mountain walking took them to Wales, where they enjoyed splendid walks, including the WHR trackbed. They were married in 1982. At that time he hardly thought trains would run again through the Aberglaslyn pass but made sure that Stuart, one of their twin boys, who shows a healthy third generation interest in steam engines and the FR in particular, took a walk

through the tunnel before track came to be relaid

When Michael heard of the likely development of the railway, he turned up at the inauguration of the Cymdeithas Rheilffordd Eryri (CRhE) in Dinas, and met Mike Hart. He had heard about the MC award, and wanted to help, so he offered to volunteer - always a dangerous thing, but he liked the new and difficult nature of the project. He suggested Tyseley as the venue for the K1 rebuild, wrote the CRhE constitution, and joined with Tony Smare in land acquisition issues. Matters became more challenging when he was asked to suggest a way of avoiding satisfying the MC need for security by taking a debenture on the Ffestiniog Railway Company which would potentially have negated the separation between the two railways so dearly desired by FR supporters in the event anything went wrong. He recommended the redesign of FR relationships, and offered only a mortgage over WHR land, and a debenture over WHRL, the WHR construction company. This was acceptable to the MC, and it avoided any risk to the FR itself. Michael joined the board of the new construction company and started work on the Caernarfon to Dinas lease and other legal and commercial matters as the project

*One may observe that Whitehouse garden railways have made ambitious strides in both size and scope over the years. Michael moves to the back of the train, whilst Stuart prepares to start locomotive* **Tryfan** *and train on their 10 ¼ inch gauge line.*

developed.

Michael was appointed the Chairman of the WHRL at the time when personal difficulties led to Mike Hart drawing back from some of his time-onerous duties. It was sensible for the WHRL Chairman to attend FR Co. Board meetings, and so he became involved with the whole strategic issue of running the FR, running the travel company, and building the WHR. Matters became complex at the end of Phase 3, as there was a shortage of funds that led to a need for the FR Trust to support the

*As an enthusiastic WHR supporter Michael attended the Subscriber's Day visits to the WHR project. In May 2009, Michael and Stuart celebrate the delights of an open car, and they are appropriately dressed for the occasion.*

Railway Trust, made sure that the basic railway could be completed to Rhyd Ddu in 2003. With the service running, attention turned to appointing a new General Manager for the Ffestiniog Railway, and ensuring that the trading position of both companies was healthy. This was achieved within three years. Attention was then given to creating a phase 4 for the completion of at least a linear WHR to Porthmadog, for Mike Hart to find the grant and key matching funds for Phase 4, and to head the new construction company

WHRL. Everyone pulled together, and the MC agreed to lower the scope of the project to cover the problems that had arisen, where parts of the job cost more than it had been possible to estimate for in the beginning (always a risk on projects of this sort.) The outcome of changes in personnel led to Michael Whitehouse being offered chairmanship of the FR Co. by George Nissen - he accepted and set about reconfiguring the FR and its finances so that it could progress on a day to day basis with gradually reducing debt and become "jolly good fun" again.

The scope of the project was trimmed back to the basic railway, with no signalling, no carriage fleet, no third Garratt and no station buildings. This, together with funds from the Ffestiniog

Welsh Highland Railway Construction Ltd. This time FRC was the decision maker and WHRCL was the implementer with FRT overseeing the capital financing

So, Phase 4 was set up and running when Michael Whitehouse handed over to a new FR Co. Chairman, John Prideaux. By this time the FR business was taking a disproportionate amount of Michael's time, bearing in mind some significant UK Ministry of Defence advisory work in warship construction and maintenance, which became all-time consuming. So Michael gradually reduced his involvement, transferring his attentions to Tyseley, until he felt his skills and time were no longer needed in Wales, and he left the WHR to surge on to successful completion.

*This is the Tyseley 'for spares' GWR Castle Class Locomotive 5043,* Earl of Mount Edgcumbe, *Pat passed to Michael and the Trustees at Tyseley three of them,* Clun Castle, Defiant *and 5043. Of all of them it was the derelict wreck of 5043 that needed most doing to restore it to the main line, and Michael wanted time to be a part of the team. Michael is in this photograph, that is his shadow on the left of mine. 5043 was powering out of Moor Street towards Marylebone shortly after.*

# Organisation
## This is a snapshot of who was doing what job within the organisations.

### 1993

**The Welsh Highland Railway Society**
Cwmdeithas Rheilffordd Eryri

| | |
|---|---|
| Chairman: | John Ewing |
| Secretary: | Cedric Lodge |
| Treas and Memb: | JE Preston |
| Committee: | EH Preston, |
| | RF Preston, |
| | JR MacGregor |
| Editorial team | PN Jarvis |
| | CC Lodge |
| | DW Lodge |

**The Festiniog Railway Society**

| | |
|---|---|
| Chairman: | PK Jordan |
| Dep Chairman: | AJ Savage |
| Financial Sec: | BWO Chicken |
| Directors: | D Burchell |
| | DJ Charlton |
| | WR Holton |
| | P Johnson |
| | TN Oulton |
| | NA Pearce |
| | IM Rudd |
| | AJG Rushton |
| | HWaters |
| President: | Alan Pegler |
| Secretary: | David Gordon |
| Assistant Sec: | Paul Harris |

**The Festiniog Railway Company**

| | |
|---|---|
| Chairman: | MC Hart |
| Dep Chairman: | CH Eaves |
| Directors: | AJ Savage |
| | MA Schumann |
| President: | Alan Pegler |
| Patrons: | J Arrivetz |
| | LA Heath-Humphrys |
| | Sir W McAlpine Bt |
| | JB Hollingsworth |
| Treasurer: | CH Eaves |
| Clerk: | M Wright |
| General Manager: | AJG Rushton |

**The Festiniog Railway Trust**

| | |
|---|---|
| Chairman: | John Routly |
| Trustees: | WB Broadbent |
| | JDCA Prideaux |
| | RJG Riddick |
| | Sir O Williams Bt MC |
| Secretary: | BWO Chicken |
| Treasurer: | PQ Treloar |

### 2002

**The Welsh Highland Railway Society**
Cwmdeithas Rheilffordd Eryri

| | |
|---|---|
| Chairman: | Dave Kent |
| Secretary: | Charles Mckenzie |
| Treasurer: | Bob Carnell |
| Membership: | Ivan Ball |
| Asst memb: | John Sweet |
| Volunteer Co: | Cedric Lodge |
| Committee: | John Ewing |
| | Elwyn Jones |
| | Dafydd Thomas |
| | Tony Williams |
| | Neil McMaster |
| Editor: | Roy Woods |

**The Festiniog Railway Society**

| | |
|---|---|
| Chairman: | PJ Hawkins |
| Dep Chairman: | RG Stibbs |
| Financial Sec: | G Bond |
| Directors: | CN Boulter |
| | RAC Buchanan |
| | DJ Charlton |
| | D J Gordon |
| | A Hayward |
| | P Johnson |
| | D Lampert |
| | H Norton |
| President: | Alan Pegler |
| Secretary: | RJH Schofield |
| Assistant Sec: | Paul Harris |

**The Festiniog Railway Company**

| | |
|---|---|
| Chairman: | G Nissen CBE |
| Directors: | MC Hart |
| | AJ Savage |
| | MA Schumann |
| | A Hayward |
| Non Exec: | M High |
| | H Waters |
| | M Whitehouse |
| President: | Alan Pegler |
| Vice presidents: | John Routly |
| | WB Broadbent |
| Patrons: | J Arrivetz |
| | Sir W McAlpine Bt |
| | Dr R Nicholls |
| | RC Black III |
| Treasurer: | M Colville FCA |
| Clerk: | Stephen Murfitt |
| General Manager: | P A Lewin |

**The Festiniog Railway Trust**

| | |
|---|---|
| Chairman: | Dr JDCA Prideaux CBE |
| Trustees: | P K Jordan |
| | RJG Riddick |
| | Sir W McAlpine Bt |
| | M A Schumann |
| Secretary: | BWO Chicken |
| Treasurer: | CM Greaves |

### 2011

**The Welsh Highland Railway Society**
Cwmdeithas Rheilffordd Eryri

| | |
|---|---|
| President: | Dave Kent |
| Chairman: | Dafydd Thomas |
| Dep Chairman: | Charles McKenzie |
| Secretary: | Alastair Wilkinson |
| Treasurer: | Ian King |
| Directors: | Dafydd Thomas |
| | Charles McKenzie |
| | Elwyn Jones |
| | Neil McMaster |
| | Peter Randall |
| | David Firth |
| | Alun Tomlinson |

**The Festiniog Railway Society**

| | |
|---|---|
| Chairman: | HRL Wilson |
| Dep Chairman: | AA Pye |
| Financial Sec: | G Bond |
| Directors: | RAC Buchanan |
| | Dr RF Buxton |
| | G Cole |
| | DJ Charlton |
| | PJ Hawkins JP |
| | SK van Lottum |
| | R Williams |
| | RJ Wilson |
| President: | Alan Pegler OBE |
| Secretary: | RJF Schofield |
| Assistant Sec: | Paul Harris |

**The Festiniog Railway Company**

| | |
|---|---|
| Chairman: | Dr JDCA Prideaux CBE |
| Directors: | MC Hart OBE |
| | N Burbidge |
| | S Murfitt |
| | Dr RF Buxton |
| Non Exec: | Dr D Gwyn |
| | C Leah |
| President: | Alan Pegler |
| Patrons: | J Arrivetz |
| | RC Black III |
| | Sir W McAlpine Bt |
| Finance: | N Burbidge |
| Clerk: | S Murfitt |
| General Manager: | PA Lewin |
| Volunteering: | Mrs PM Doyle |

**The Festiniog Railway Trust**

| | |
|---|---|
| Chairman: | Dr JDCA Prideaux CBE |
| Trustees: | R Broyd |
| | RJG Riddick |
| | MA Schumann |
| | Cllr. D Lewis |
| Secretary: | J Alexander |
| Treasurer: | PK Jordan |

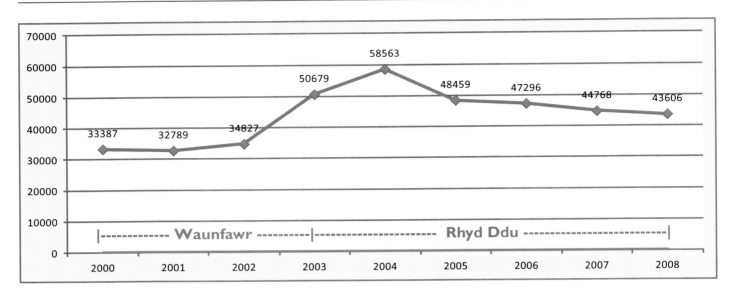

## Has the WHR damaged the FR?

I f this isn't the most important question in the book, then it should be! All that effort and expense, - what was it all about, if it was not the natural consequence of the promotion and protection of the Ffestiniog Railway? The big question therefore - and one felt deeply by those who say 'WHR - no thanks' within the FR ranks - is '**Has traffic been removed from FR by WHR?**'. See for yourself - below is a 'tell-tale' table.

With both railways set to index 100 in the year 2000, you can see the comparative rise and fall of traffic. Never has the WHR gone UP and the FR has gone DOWN on a year on year comparison until 2011, when the WHR reached Porthmadog. As each successive advance of WHR route is made, it is clear that there is a corresponding leap in traffic. It is an 'immature' market, so the traffic does not sustain. For clarity on this point the history of traffic at Rhyd Ddu is seen during the years that the WHR remained at that terminal. In the season after opening to Rhyd Ddu, there was a most satisfactory surge, that may well have convinced optimists of certain success. However, traffic steadily

declined thereafter, until the increase was only 25% on 2002. It appears as though the market responds to the curiosity value of the newly opened part, and then only some incorporate it into a repeat itinerary. Note that the FR, left to its own devices for ten years, does not advance at all. Here is the dilemma. Had FR Co. done nothing, it is likely that 'nothing' would have happened. This means the continued erosion of market share, and increased vulnerability to competition. WHR restoration has reached new markets. Traffic moved from FR to WHR in 2011 because with the bypass bridge being built at Minfford, the winter trains ran on WHR for the first time, and not on FR, otherwise the rule about FR not taking off WHR would have held good.

The challenge will be to sustain the new markets with the two railways joined, as there are a whole range of new destinations not yet tapped (like Beddgelert, and through running) and a new mix of destination choices may be offered. The greatest challenge will be to extend the concept of the Sustainable Railway to the tipping point where FR-WHR becomes a world class attraction. The Glacier Express proves that this can be done.

| Actual Bookings, WHR in k | | | |
|---|---|---|---|
| Year | TO | WHR | |
| 2000 | 65 | 33 | Waunfawr opened (Aug) |
| 2001 | - | 33 | |
| 2002 | - | 35 | |
| 2003 | - | 51 | Rhyd Ddu opened (Aug) |
| 2004 | - | 59 | |
| 2005 | - | 48 | |
| 2006 | - | 47 | |
| 2007 | - | 45 | |
| 2008 | - | 44 | |
| 2009 | 83 | 72 | Bedd & HafyLlyn opened |
| 2010 | 200 | 64 | Pont Croesor opened |
| 2011 | | 98 | Porthmadog opened |

**Clearly these numbers, based on Handley, Steer Davies and Gleave, predictions from the TO inquiry are now being achieved. (the WHR figures are bookings) What is also being achieved is a major contribution to the local economy.**

| Bookings indices, WHR -V- FR base Year 2000 | | | |
|---|---|---|---|
| Year | FR | WHR | |
| 2000 | 100 | 100 | |
| 2001 | 97 | 98 | |
| 2002 | 97 | 104 | |
| 2003 | 100 | 152 | Rhyd Ddu opened (Aug) |
| 2004 | 104 | 175 | |
| 2005 | 97 | 145 | |
| 2006 | 98 | 142 | |
| 2007 | 95 | 134 | |
| 2008 | 89 | 131 | |
| 2009 | 101 | 216 | Bedd & HafyLlyn opened |
| 2010 | 98 | 192 | Pont Croesor Opened |
| 2011 | 94 | 294 | Porthmadog Opened |

**Index year 2000: FR 131,031, WHR 33,387 bookings.**

# Appendix

Abbreviations, PB&SSR
Design Parameters, Bridge Parts, Loading
Gauge, The Future, The Legal Tangle,
The Objectors.

## Common Abbreviations

In this tale of companies and organisations there are many abbreviations, here's a list of most of them and what the letters stand for:

22 Co - Welsh Highland Railway, Light Railway (1922) Company

64 Co - Welsh Highland Railway, Light Railway (1964) Company

AIR - Association of Independent Railways

AO - Abandonment Order

AOCL - Automatic Open Level Crossing , with lights

AP -adverse possession (claim)

ARPS - Association of Railway Preservation Societies

CP -compulsory purchase

CRE - Cymdeithas Rheilffordd Eryri (Welsh Highland Railway Society)

DETR - Department of the Environment, Transport and the Regions

DfT - Department for Transport

ERDF - European Regional Development Fund

FR - The Ffestiniog Railway

FR Co. - The Festiniog Railway Company

FRHL - Ffestiniog Railway Holdings Limited

FRS(L) - Ffestiniog Railway Society (Limited)

FRT - the Ffestiniog Railway Trust

GC - Gwynedd Council

GCC - Gwynedd County Council

HMRI - Her Majesty's Railway Inspectorate

HRA - Heritage Railway Association

INCA - Increased Capacity (FR Scheme)

LC - level crossing

LRO - Light Railway Order

MANWEB - Merseyside and North Wales Electricity Board

MC - Millennium Commission

NFU - National Farmers Union

NGG - Narrow Gauge Garratt

NG - Narrow gauge as in SAR NG15 2-8-2

NIMBY - objector: **N**ot **I**n **M**y **B**ack **Y**ard

NWNG - North Wales Narrow Gauge Railways Co

OOU - **O**ut **O**f **U**se (points, lines etc.)

OLC - Open Level Crossing, no barriers or lights

PB&SSR - Porthmadog, Beddgelert and South Snowdon Railway

RhE - Rheilffordd Eryri

ROGS - **R**ly&**O**ther **G**uided Transport Sys. (**S**afety)

SAR - South African Railways

SNP - Snowdonia National Park

SNPA - Snowdonia National Park Authority

SoS - Secretary for State

TCL - Trackbed Consolidation Ltd

TO - Transfer Order

TWA - Transport and Works (order) Application

TWO - Transport and Works Order

WAG - Welsh Assembly Government

WEFO - Welsh European Funding Office

WHRCL - Welsh Highland Railway Construction Ltd

WHHR - Welsh Highland Heritage Railway

WHLR - Welsh Highland Light Railway (FR Co.)

WHRL - Welsh Highland Railway Ltd (ex 64 Co.)

WHR - Welsh Highland Railway

WHR (C) - Welsh Highland Railway (Caernarfon)

WHR (P) - Welsh Highland Railway (Porthmadog)

YHA - Youth Hostels Association

*[For more information - Google it - but put the words in full!]*

*Specially commissioned for this book is Jonathan Clay's portrayal of a Ganz - Bruce Peebles, 100hp, three-phase, electric locomotive, humming though the Aberglaslyn Pass, just past Tunnel No.3. True, the train is too long, it is doubtful if these little engines would take more than two, perhaps three cars. Also true is that the means of current collection by double trolley pole is not proven - but it's likely, as registration of the double trolley wire would be more relaxed with trolley poles, and the necessity for complex catenary would be removed. Apparently 5 engines were built, but no one ever saw such a thing, (except at an exhibition?) as the scheme collapsed in about 1906, leaving much trackbed half-completed. It is a chimera, like the Beddgelert Railway, existing specially as fuel for your imagination.*

## The Porthmadog Beddgelert & South Snowdon Railway

What an amazing little historical gem of 'might have been' to find in this corner of Wales. This railway was part of a 'package concept', to generate hydro-power, and then to distribute electricity across Snowdonia to industrial premises, like quarries, and to major consumption points, like towns. Even in the technological age of the emerging 20th century, there were restrictions about what could be built in the beautiful Snowdonian landscape. The PB&SSR project was part of a speculative, pioneering hydro-power scheme of 1901, to build Cwm Dyli Hydro Station, below the Snowdon Horseshoe, in the Nant Gwynant, in order to electrify, and then sell electric power to Blaenau Ffestiniog, Dinorwic and the Nantlle Quarries, as well as the town of Porthmadog. Power lines were not likely to be welcome. However, adding a three-phase (Ganz System), electric railway added an air of respectability to the scheme, more likely to facilitate power lines across the landscape. Although there were objections, the railway managed to penetrate the Aberglaslyn Pass. The idea was to construct the electric 2ft (597mm) gauge railway from Borth y Gest, along the Croesor Tramway, through Beddgelert to Rhyd Ddu, and down the NWNG. So the railway was a part of a rail and electric utility

scheme, akin to the American interurban and power station conglomerates. When the money ran short in 1906, the power side was completed and flourished. Any aspirations there may have been to complete the railway were lost at the outbreak of the First World War. Parts already constructed stood idle until the majority of the earthworks were incorporated into the 1922 WHR. On the parts too steep for steam working: Bryn y Felin to Beddgelert, and across Cwm Cloch, diversions were made to ease the gradient to 1:40. It was 'the bridge to nowhere' at Beddgelert that prompted childhood questions that adults could not answer. The challenge of this fascinating puzzle stimulated many an interest in the WHR, as once you had started looking in the 1960s, there was so much more to find.

Much more erudite stuff than this has been written about PB&SSR; read that to be better informed. It is a delightful speculation, that if the scheme had been successful, the crude little locomotives would soon have given way to railcars. However, the impoverished existence of the subsequent WHR probably indicates this as unlikely. The development of the land through which it ran was at such a gentle pace that a railway, even a little one, was unsustainable until our age. Instead of the PB&SSR we have Garratts and ten-car trains on a tourist railway. The logical development of the PB&SSR would have led scenes more like Switzerland than South Africa.

## WELSH HIGHLAND RAILWAY PHASE III
## DESIGN PARAMETERS: I-11-00

### 1 Kinematic Envelope.

The kinematic envelope is given on drawing FR/RE/STD/01A. This should be used for determining the dimensional clearance to be provided for new structures. Where existing structures need to be modified to accept the new kinematic envelope a minimum clearance of 150mm after allowance for curvature and cant must be provided.

The minimum acceptable clearance above locomotive chimney tops when passing through existing bridges and tunnels is related to the need to allow exhaust gasses to escape without causing back pressure within the engines smokebox.

In relation to existing bridges this should be 300mm clearance over the kinematic envelope.

### 2 Superelevation.

The amount of superelevation required on curves is detailed on the schedule - WHR track standards - superelevation - 7th June 2000

The normal design cant gradient should be 10mm in 13m track length. However where space does not permit this the cant gradient may be steepened up to but not exceeding 10mm in 8m track length.

### 3 Design Speed.

The railway should be designed to permit a maximum speed of 25mph wherever practical.

Speed may be restricted by curvature, crossings or stations.

### 4 Gradients

The maximum acceptable design gradient is 1 : 40

In matching the new formation level to the existing ground levels consideration should be given to minimising the frequency with which the gradient is changed in order to make future track alignment as easy as possible

### 5 Minimum Radius of Curves

The minimum acceptable curve radius is 60 metres

### 6 Formation Sections

The former North Wales Narrow Gauge Railway was built with a formation width of 3m with the ditches normally outside this. In a few locations it is evident that ditches/french drains were constructed within this width

The new construction formation width is 4m with ditches outside this. Where there exists a potential problem with keeping the ditches clear they may be converted to french drains.

In refurbishing the railway formation the existing 3000mm width should be considered as providing structural support to the railway track.

Wherever possible the formation should be widened to 4m utilising surplus material from the works. This extra width is purely to provide a walkway for staff and to inhibit ballast from falling off the formation.

In cuttings ditches should be 2m clear of the track centreline or either converted to french drains or a concrete lined trough with a concrete upstand to retain the ballast in place.

Conversion of open ditches to french drains is seen as very cost effective work for volunteers. French drains should therefore only be constructed where considered essential in the short term.

The formation should be levelled with a cross fall of 1 : 25. The cross fall should generally be towards a ditch or French drain and preferably towards the inside of curves.

### 7 Formation Surface Finish.

The material with which the formation is finished should be such that when either wet or dry it should not have a tendency to migrate upwards into the ballast. The formation should be finished with compacted stone or other approved finish ready to lay ballast. In appropriate circumstances a fabric filter may be employed under the ballast.

### 8 Passing Loops

Loops are to be laid out for a straight run in on the right hand track. The loops are to be of such a length as to provide 260m between fouling points. The maximum operating entry speed limit into a loop is 10mph. On exit the points are to be approached at 5mph until operated against their hydraulic mechanism and then the train speeds will rise to 10mph..

### 9 Track Standards.

**Rail:**
31kg/m SAR flat bottom in 18m lengths. Rail height 110mm
**Sleepers:**
Wooden - with cast steel baseplates - thickness 10mm
Steel       - with T bolts and clips
**Ballast:**
150mm leveled and compacted under wooden sleepers
250mm leveled and compacted under steel sleepers
Total finished depth 280mm minimum over width of sleepers
**Pointwork:**
Standard SAR 1 : 9 turnout ( See SAR and Symonds drawing)
**Track Depth:**
Typical depth rail head to formation level taken as 390mm

### 10 Accommodation and Occupation Crossings.

The gates for this type of crossing shall be placed a minimum of 2.8m clear of the centreline of the railway and a maximum of 3.8m. The closer dimension should always be used in preference.

The gates should outwards from the railway and otherwise comply with HMRI guidance.

### 11 Footpath Crossings

The decision point for this type of crossing is 2m from the railway centreline. Between this point and the gate a place of safety is required in area commensurate with the anticipated use.

HMRI prefer the use of outward opening self closing gates 1.2m wide but these do not reliably keep stock in a field. Thus where footpaths from which animals are excluded cross the railway self closing gates may be employed.

Where animals are free on the adjacent land either a stile or kissing gate should be installed. In general stiles should only be used for path crossings where the nature of the path effectively determines that people who are able to negotiate a stile are likely to use the path. The gate or stile on each side of the railway at a particular crossing should be the same.

### 12 Clearance Through Existing Bridges.

The track alignment through OB62 is straight. The track level should therefore be lowered to provide a minimum of 150 mm clearance over the kinematic envelope. The controlling point is likely to be the top shoulder positions.

A minimum of 300mm clearance above the top of locomotive chimneys is also required.

The track alignment through OB71 would ideally be curved. 150mm clearance over the kinematic envelope should be maintained at all points after making allowance for curve widening and superelevation.

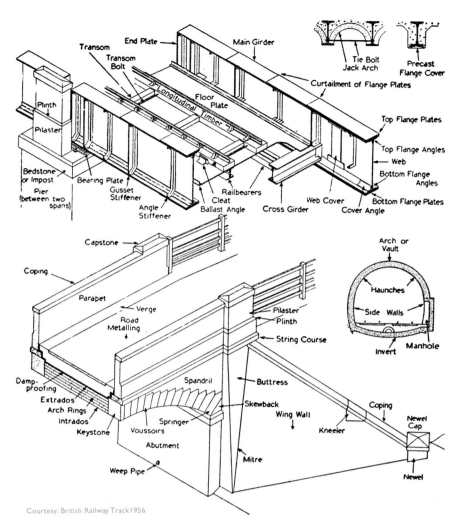

Courtesy: British Railway Track1956

This diagram from British Railway Track, of 1956 is in the book because in a volume dedicated to rebuilding a railway, there are a lot of jargon terms, and it makes sense to understand what people are on about. Some clarifications:

Not mentioned are the names of the types of girder bridges. Many call the iconic WHR curvy girder bridged Bowstring Girders, they are not. The correct term is Hogsback.

The Extrados is the outside of a bridge arch - the diagram does not make this clear.

Equally the Intrados is the inside of a bridge arch.

Spandril (also spelt Spandrel) is the space between two arches or between an arch and a rectangular enclosure.

Voussoirs are the wedge-shaped stone elements to go to making the arch or vault (and not delicate items of ladies underwear).

The Skewback is the sloping face of the abutment on which the extremity of an arch rests.

The Springer is the lowest voussoir on each side of an arch, it rests on the impost, the topmost part of the abutment from which the arch arises.

A String Course or band course is a thin projecting course of brickwork or stone that runs horizontally around a bridge, typically to emphasize the junction between deck and arch.

Any more - please 'Google it'!

This is OB 71, the A4058 overbridge at Castell Cidwm. It was built by the North Wales Narrow Gauge Railways in the 1870s, and is seen here in March 2003 in this photograph by Roger Dick, having been restored to pristine condition, ready for the track to be laid underneath it. Alas, as is the case frequently when you look for an example to aid in the naming of parts, not all the NWNG bridges are applicable. However, the Voussoirs are in brick. The Springer is a large piece of shaped stone and the bridge is on the skew. The Spandrel is incorporated into the parapet and bridge sides, and of the string course, there is no trace, as there isn't one. However, people get the general idea!.

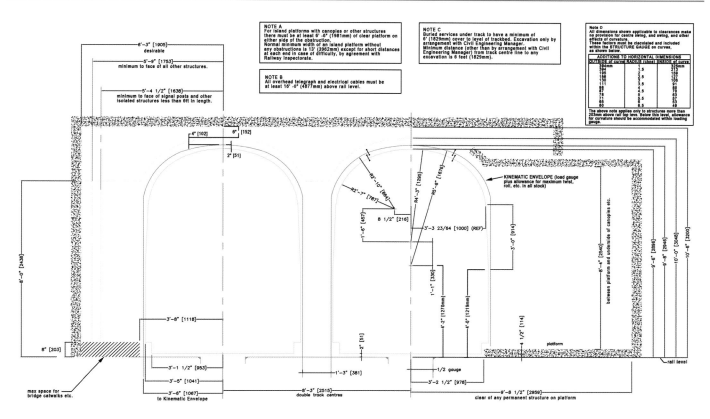

Above is the Structure gauge of the FR, and below that of the WHR - plus their respective Kinematic Envelopes (the extra bit that allows train 'wobble' factor). Above is in Imperial and Metric, below is only Metric. So, the key facts are that WHR trains may be 10'5" [3175mm] high and 7'8" [2324mm] wide, tapering to 7'2" [2134mm] at the cantrail [9'11"up]. FR trains may be 9'6" high [2540mm] and 7'0" [2134mm] wide, tapering to 6'6" [2000mm]at the cantrail [7ft up]. The WHR is approximately a foot higher and six inches wider (at the waist) than the FR.

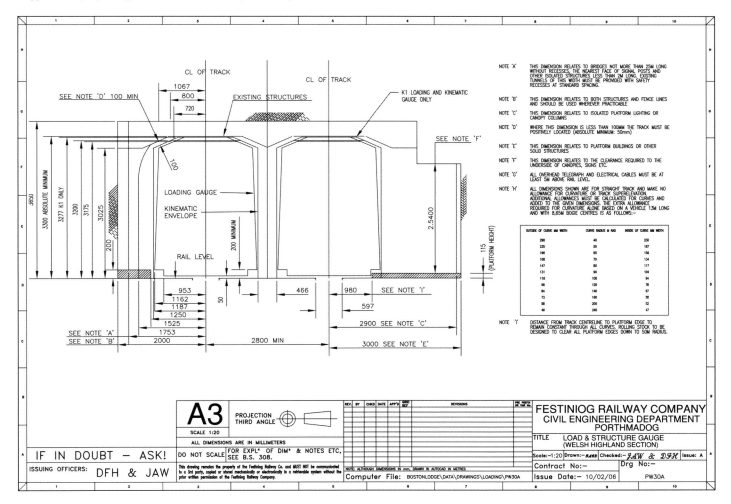

*What serious railway could bear to be without a splendid DMU vehicle like this to travel in, as a Park and Ride proposal for Caernarfon, the late-night shuttle back to Meillionen for the campers, the early morning walker's special into the hills, or that delightful coach trip with vista-vision through the ample glass? Fitted with a couple of slim diesels underneath, it may be possible to pop in two or three intermediate cars. Mmmm, when will it be delivered? Sorry to say, at the moment it is one of Jonathan Clay GRA's visual jokes - but a very good one!*

*The existence of this locomotive has always been a closely guarded secret. It is normally kept in a discreet area of Boston Lodge, disguised as a cabinet, though it has been successfully concealed at Dinas as well. The locomotive will probably remain secret until someone has worked out how to break the news to John Prideaux that it exists. At Superpower it is quite safe to use this engine as a substitute for* Taliesin, *as most people are so out of their minds that they fail to notice the difference.* Moel Tryfan *is noticeably more powerful than* Taliesin *and just as comfortable to drive. Apparently the bogie can fit under* Merddin Emrys *as companion to the Fairratt.*

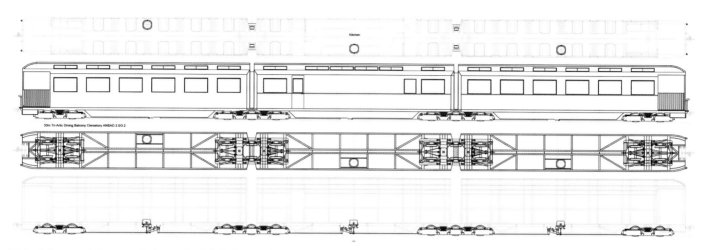

33m Tri-Artic Dining Balcony Clerestory ANSAD 2.0/3.2

*Michael Guerra indulges us with the terrific skills he has, to show what a clerestory articulated balcony diner could be like. You may think this idle speculation, but the question of how to reach the sort of tourists that inhabit the Glacier Express are amusing strategic minds now the WHR is built. The drawing may seem fanciful, but the principles might be employed in the future to provide the FR/WHR with a splendid train of Pullman 'varnish'. Anyone still laughing at the 40 mile railway?*

## The Fairratt

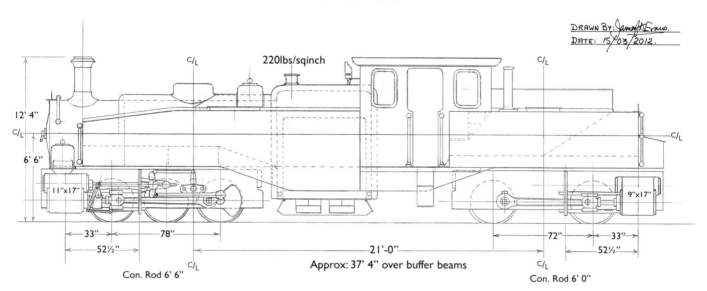

DRAWN BY: James A Evans.
DATE: 15/03/2012.

220lbs/sqinch

12' 4"

6' 6"

11"x17"

9"x17"

33"    78"    72"    33"
52½"    21'-0"    52½"
Con. Rod 6' 6"    Approx: 37' 4" over buffer beams    Con. Rod 6' 0"

Estimated weight of bogie: 10.5 tons + 12 tons load          Estimated weight of bogie: 8 tons + 7 tons load

Axle load : 7.5 tons

© James Amstrong Evans 2012

*Garratts may be seen as inefficient both due to their dated design and high maintenance. A major cause of their overall inefficiency is the dead weight which has to be lifted from sea level to 650 feet on every trip. This weight is due to all the carrying axles that were provided to allow for very large tanks/bunkers for operating lines considerably longer than 23 miles, and probably at faster speeds. A 'built for purpose' locomotive could combine the best and very different advantages of the Garratt and Fairlie concepts, with potential for considerable fuel saving, greatly reduced maintenance costs, and would produce a unique FR/WHR design. Will this get built? Would you have said that Lyd would have been built?*

## Main Features From FAIRLIE
a) All wheels driving (no dead weight)
b) Simple bogie articulation (coach-like ride)
c) Boiler/tank assembly forms mainframe (weight saving)
d) Clear sight lines for crew (safety)
e) Good bore/stroke ratio (efficiency)
f) Separate regulators (slipping control)

## Main Features From GARRATT
a) Single ended, short, large diameter boiler
b) Walk through cab (crew comfort and safety)
c) Outside frames to power bogies (stability, reduced axle box stresses)
d) Outside valve gear and springs (serviceability)
e) Piston valves (reduced friction)
f) Reasonable superheat (fuel and water saving, without increased maintenance)
g) Compensated suspension (reduced track damage)

## Main Design Requirements
a) Boiler to optimise combustion efficiency and steam raising capacity, with reasonable superheat, to work equally well on 1/40 gradients in either direction, and handle changes from one to the other. Weight considerations outweigh ultimate heat exchange efficiency.
Large fire box and advanced combustion system (deep bed gas producer, or oil fuel),
Large steam space over fire box,
Ample free gas area, and tubes not too long,
Pressure as high as possible without excessive weight (barrel plate thickness being the limiting factor), thus minimizing cylinder size and weight.
Belpaire firebox, no dome (access cover to barrel only) and high efficiency concentric element superheater.
Uniform axle load of approximately 7½ Tons, with each axle transmitting the same tractive effort. Due to the boiler weight distribution an 0-6-0 bogie would be required under that end (78"wheelbase) and an 0-4-0 bogie under the cab, bunker and auxiliary equipment (72" wheelbase)

# The Legal Tangle

The WHR assets were disposed of, save for the land. There were liabilities attendant upon that. The track was removed by requisition of the Ministry of Supply in February 1941- demolition begun by Cohens in August, was completed by early 1942. It is likely that had a viable scheme for paying the debts and restoring the line been advanced post-war the track would have been restored. However this is not a very practical speculation, WHR was in the public mind closed. It tended to be the dreamers who were asking naive questions, making ill-considered proposals, and the Official Receiver (OR) had no leisure for time wasters, and the suggestion that a bunch of amateurs should run a statutory railway was securely in that category. Thus farmers and neighbouring landowners who found its trackbed useful, apportioned for their convenience such parts that were appropriate to their needs. Statutory organisation laid pipes along it, and erected poles upon the land, all with a covenant that should the railway revert, the removal of their equipment would be at their cost. None expected anyone to collect on that. Few acts of ownership were made upon the land. This was partly as the OR had no funds, and partly as 'lying doggo' persuaded the County Council and others to assume the railway's liabilities.

## Where the OR's limits were

The OR held the assets of the 1922 Company in liquidation. Mr A. Thomas, accountant, was Liquidator until his death in 1964. From then the OR (Leslie Thomas Cramp) acted as ex-officio Liquidator.

**a.** The WHR1922 Co. was in receivership from 4th March 1927. An OR has a duty to shareholders and debenture holders to act to advantage their position within the statutory powers of the company. He may not act against their interest and the company was in liquidation, therefore there were 'no' funds.

**b.** There was a Winding Up Order of 7th February 1944, made on behalf of Caernarvonshire County Council. The 1922 Co. Receiver was discharged on 12 December 1944. The liquidation narrowed the scope of action of the OR - his job was to complete the winding up and not to run a railway.

There was no money to apply for an Abandonment Order, (AO) nor for a Transfer Order (TO) (to transfer the powers to any party interested in running a railway). There were statutory liabilities with the title to the land, and the OR could not sell such of it that would obstruct the company's statutory purpose without an AO. Thus discussions on trackbed acquisition by a third party included the condition that the purchaser fund either AO or TO, as well as paying the debenture holders, settling the debts, assuming the liabilities etc. Note that this amount was said to be in the order of £1m.

Statutory liabilities with statutory railways are not extinguished with closure or sale. So had the OR 'sold' the railway intact to a third party, the liabilities would have to be assumed by the buyer. In the event of the bankruptcy of the buyer, the liabilities would have reverted back to the OR. The only way for the OR to gain comfort was for the prospective buyer to agree to obtain an AO to dispose of the powers.

The Council could not go bust; it could obtain an AO, and it was the organisation to whom the bulk of liabilities were said to be due. Here was the ideal organisation to take title to the trackbed, and in 1981, after long negotiations, the OR saw them

as the bidder to be favoured with a bid offer of £1.

64 Co. hoped through the GCC to be able to lease portions of trackbed and to restore it to railway use. A plan discussed by GCC and 64 Co. examined the possibility of taking half the railway. A TO was thought about and discussed. The OR took counsel's opinion on it in 1979. The plan was deterred by the costs of obtaining an AO for half and a TO for the other half. It was acknowledged then that a **TO was only obtained if the applicant intended to restore the railway**.

## Why go to the High Court?

In 1989 the OR applied to the High Court to sell to the GCC for £1. Permission from the High Court was needed as the OR believed he was obliged to answer the interests of share and debenture holders, and he wasn't able to contact all of them, and there were amounts outstanding with creditors. Those who felt themselves in need of a remedy could appear in the Court to plead for it. The sale would rest upon the judgement of the Court, and if all was successful, transfer of title of the trackbed (at least all of it provably within the OR's possession) would take place after an AO (or TO). The OR offered the advice from counsel to the Court, which had a major bearing on the outcome:

**a.** Disposal of the trackbed will be *ultra vires* unless either an Abandonment Order or a Transfer Order is obtained.

**b.** The 1922 Co. is without funds and cannot do this and other matters that require an indemnity from the purchaser.

**c.** The claims of unsecured creditors and of debenture holders are now statute barred.

## The 1922 Co. Reconstruction & High Court (Dec 91)

The Judgement of the High Court was clear:

**1.** The court declined to validate either sale or transfer of the shares to FRH, and the stay was refused.

**2.** The sale to GCC was temporarily stopped, to permit FR to find ways of acquiring the residuary powers, settling the liabilities, and obtaining title to the trackbed.

**3.** GCC/OR were at liberty to restore the application, should FR fail in this respect.

**4.** The legal tangle departed. Debentures and creditors were statue barred*, liabilities were due to recent spending by GCC (of which there was none - and it was later discovered that CCC had agreed to fund overbridges anyway).

*\* Statute Barred: The Limitations Act 1980 states that when the following three conditions have all been met, then the debt cannot be pursued through the courts:*
- *That the creditor has not taken court action to recover the debt*
- *No payments on the debt have been made over the last 6 years,*
- *During the years, no one has written to the creditor acknowledging that they are owed money.*

## Adverse Possession (AP)

Parts of the trackbed were appropriated without permission. In time, with no challenges: some was reincorporated into farmland; some became access road to adjoining properties; some even became footpaths, and those who had found uses for the land, even became dependent upon it. There was a local view that after such a passage of time, the title of the land had passed to them. The land's context as a railway faded as the years rolled on. By the time restoration became a proposal there had been no track for 50 years. For someone to come and claim it was still a railway would sound strange. You may very well consider if you had made use of that land that your arrangements were secure, when in fact they were not.

Farmers, and landowners who had found the unused land useful were not challenged when they fenced it into their properties, the OR did none of the things that could be classified as 'acts of ownership'. He took the view that acts of ownership encouraged claims he could not meet.

There was a basic formula for settling matters designated by the Land Registration Act 1925, that land occupied for 12 years with no acts of ownership by the title holder may be claimed through Adverse Possession (AP). A formal process had to be followed, and an application would be unlikely to succeed if it was made after intention to develop the land was made public. 'Failure to agree' AP claims are settled by application to the Lands Tribunal.

The Land Registration Act 2002 changed the rules, to be more favourable to landowners, but in 1998 the WHR fell within the previous legislation. None of those who claimed title to the land by adverse possession had gone through the proper procedure on Phases 2 and 3, but that was not the case with Phase 4.

## Compulsory Purchase Powers (CP)

The FR Parliamentary Agent urged application for compulsory purchase powers in the TWO for Dinas to Porthmadog, to safeguard against any objector refusing sale of title to the land, and thus blocking the railway reinstatement. The DETR was not in favour of such powers being given to heritage railway restoration schemes - indeed this was the first as the powers were granted. Thus disputes over land title could not block construction, though when taking possession to do work, 90% of the land purchase price had to be paid to the title holder, and compensation could be claimed for various difficulties and disturbances.

Had reconstruction been gained by amending orders, it would have been necessary for the FR Co. to prove title to each piece of land if challenged, before reinstating the railway on it. The CP powers conferred the reverse effect. It was the granting of these powers that made it possible for such steady progress of the restoration. If title had been a 'blocking' issue, the chances of getting grants would have been remote - that would have meant little or no chance for a fully restored WHR.

## Rights of Way on the Track Bed

FR Co.'s position was that there are principles accepted in law that a public right of way cannot be created on the land of a statutory body, if such right of way would prevent the statutory body from pursuing its statutory purpose. In view of its position as the Highway Authority for the area, with the responsibility for making legal decisions on the future of footpaths on the trackbed (some were on the definitive footpath map).

GC took Counsel's advice. This made available a detailed legal analysis, and led to GC's conclusion that there could not have been valid dedication of public rights of way along the trackbed of the railway. The analysis and conclusion were put forward in a legal submission to the TWO public inquiry.

It was agreed with FR Co. that the easiest way of modifying the definitive footpath map was to use the TWO as a means of extinguishing them. The alternative methods available to GC were very time consuming. The Ramblers Association accepted that the railway trackbed should not have been made a public footpath.

Thus were rights of way extinguished where it was impossible for a reasonable alternative to be provided.

## Phase 4 Track laying Progress:

The track was laid continuously for much of Phase 4 and the gangs managed to be there to lay whenever the ballast bed was prepared and ready. It is of interest to gauge their progress.

| Date | Miles ex C | Miles built | Head of Steel Location |
|------|-----------|-------------|------------------------|
| 21.12.05 | 12 | | Rhyd Ddu |
| 03.01.06 | 12.5 | .5 | Rhyd Ddu |
| 05.02.06 | 12.75 | .25 | near Pitts Head |
| 19.06.06 | 13 | .25 | Y Copa - the Summit |
| 17.07.06 | 13.75 | .75 | LC70 - Nr Pont Cae'r Gors |
| 02.08.06 | 14 | .23 | LC70/UB131 Tro Elain |
| 04.09.06 | 14 | 0 | UB131 - McAlpine's Bridge |
| 03.10.06 | 14.6 | .6 | Hafod Ruffydd |
| 01.11.06 | 15 | .4 | Weirglodd Isaf, Nr UB148 |
| 12.12.06 | 15.5 | .5 | UB156 - Meillionen |
| 08.01.07 | 15.75 | .25 | Ty'n y Coed |
| 05.02.07 | 16.5 | .75 | UB158 - Cwm Cloch |
| 12.03.07 | 16.75 | .25 | Cutting Mawr |
| 04.04.07 | 16.9 | .15 | Cutting Mawr. |
| 06.05.07 | 17.6 | .7 | LC88 - Mynwent |
| 03.06.07 | 17.8 | .2 | OB173 - Bryn y Felin |
| 01.07.07 | 17.8 | 0 | no change |
| 01.08.07 | 17.8 | 0 | no change |
| 03.09.07 | 18 | .2 | UB174 - across the Glaslyn |
| 01.10.07 | 18.5 | .5 | between T3 and T4 |
| 11.11.07 | 19.1 | .6 | UB182 - just across A4085 |
| 13.12.07 | 19.6 | .5 | just after Hafod y Llyn |
| 07.01.08 | 20.25 | .65 | UB196 - Pont Ynysferlas |
| 03.02.08 | 20.6 | .35 | UB199 - Pont Dylif |
| 03.03.08 | 21.1 | .5 | Croesor Junction - start of curve |
| 06.04.08 | 22 | .9 | LC112 - Pooh Corner |
| 12.05.08 | 22.55 | .55 | LC114 - Pont Croesor |
| 14.06.08 | 22.55 | 0 | no change |
| 14.07.08 | 22.55 | 0 | no change |
| 03.08.08 | 22.55 | 0 | no change |
| 01.09.08 | 23.65 | 1.1 | OB217 - Traeth Mawr |
| 14.02.09 | 25 | - | Porthmadog Harbour Station Note 4 |

**Notes:**

1. Please cut some slack over exact dates and measurements as they cannot be precise.
2. Mileages are shown from Caernarfon and are approximate.
3. Chapter 11 offers the narrative, this table is just to gauge progress.
4. The bit from Traeth Mawr to Cae Pawb was built by WHHR, then from Cae Pawb to Y Cyt was laid, but the CTRL was being built at the same time. That's why it ends at Traeth Mawr.
5. The data is translated from the periodic maps of progress on Ben Fisher's website, and an attempt has been made to enter the data monthly. (As near as the maps will allow.)

# The Objectors

The inquiry objections, associated other objections, and the Secretary of State's decisions, led to an unofficial and constant barrage of minor critical comment in the local press. It meant that most times when mentioned the railway was referred to as 'controversial'. There was a continual talking down of the WHR: predictions that the WHR was not working in areas of detail; that it was harming the local interest, and so on. Handel Kardas, the late editor of Railway World made everyone laugh when he invented a fictional person called Celery Carrot, and like Dr Peter Jarvis, wrote allegorical prose and amusing verses about Celery. This caused hilarity and blunted the darts of the protests that were aimed in the Railway's direction. One of the vociferous groups gathered at the opening of trains service to Beddgelert, displaying 'white elephant' placards. It was satisfying for the railway supporters, when the train returned past the placard toters, that it had exchanged its celebrants for a full load of residents from Beddgelert, who were all enthusiastic about sampling the first train from their station since 1937. Objection diminished to vanishing point when in the first month of service some 7000 visitors came to the town by train. Yet as late as April 2011, a positive piece in the paper about the opening of service throughout evidently sought out one of the resident Beddgelert objectors, who duly trotted out the old cant, all of it provably untrue. But apparently the paper did this for 'balance'.

The farmers who suffered hardship were offered and accepted measures in mitigation. The measures taken were designed to relieve their problems. Roland Doyle and Jan Woods, when walking the trackbed found themselves facing a raised rifle from over the fence. This was followed by requests that they should remove themselves, and this they did. However, Roland walked round to the property and knocked on the door, which was rather brave. The concern expressed with the rifle arose from the claim that the fence line was wrong, and enclosed too much land. After the appearance of a substantial pile of spoil in the middle of the trackbed, which was persuaded away by more diplomacy, it was found that the landowners were correct, and the adjustment was made to the fence line in acknowledgement. The sequel to this came about when a little more land was required at the margins of their property, in order to invest a crossing, where another landowner was insisting on exclusivity. Roland had the whimsical idea to double the width of the crossing, thus permitting one narrow segment to be exclusive, but he needed a sliver of land to do it. The interview, granted from his favourite landowners to obtain this, did include the offer of being 'twatted' during the course of a mildly aggressive reception of the proposal. When it was explained that the amount of land to be taken was much less than was allowed under the powers, this receded. Roland reports that he left the premises with the agreement in place, and no more was said.

At other premises the landowner was incensed with the plans for restoration of the railway. After the compulsory purchase notice was given to fence the trackbed behind the premises, there was an altercation that escalated, when the party in question appeared with a loaded shotgun. Retreat ensued, with the police being advised. It was later noted that there was arrest, followed by the confiscation of a gun, and a restriction that no shotgun license would be issued in future to the individual involved - who later moved away. Such were the passions aroused by this change.

Occasionally the law was shown to act strangely. One co-operative farmer requested that some of the spoil being extracted from the works, to be used to fill an annoying hole on his hillside land; thus it would be much improved, and without that particular hazard. Anxious to be helpful in response to such a reasonable request, the contractor started to oblige the landowner. After a short while there came a communication from the National Park Authority no less, to desist immediately. Apparently this was some sacred spot, with much murmured poetry written about it, and so the process was obliged to be stopped. Yet there was now talk of court action against the railway company for shifting spoil from its own land, to place it on to that of another. Things began to look serious. Then it was discovered that the CP process had not in fact been completed, and that this was a landowner shifting spoil from one part of his land to another for the purposes of improvement - hence entirely legal. In the end it was decided that although the landowner had the right to place the fill in his own land, that it was better to take it elsewhere, and to cease the activity. The offending hole had a fence placed round it and was left alone again.

One landowner explained that despite TWO and CP notices, he just wanted the railway people to go away; he wished to have nothing to do with it. He was evidently a colourful character. He refused to sign a consent form to permit his land to be used as temporary access to the works, claiming heatedly that his word was his bond. When Roland retreated, obliged to be satisfied with this, the landowner did not do as he had promised. Further entreaty proved fruitless. In the end the matter went as high as the Deputy Sheriff of Gwynedd, the principal legal officer for the county. She called upon him, and he still refused to give way, whereupon he was informed that if he did not do so, he would be taken away by the two extremely large constables accompanying - he then signed. All was not over. There were works agreed in mitigation; a split field was to be piped with water for livestock, to relieve the problems brought about in crossing the reinstated tracks. The pipes were laid in, but Roland when calling found they had been ripped out. The gentleman became most agitated with Roland, shouting at him and waving his arms in the air. Red in the face, he lent over the fence to take a swipe at him and missed, but his false teeth shot out into the undergrowth. Roland said that under these circumstances, he felt obliged to maintain a straight face, apologise for the distress, and to leave.

There were objects left on the track, drainage channels were blocked, and water was diverted on to the trackbed. This happened in one area just before HRH The Prince of Wales was about to travel on the train. It was pointed out who was likely to have been responsible by 'form', and large gentlemen called to 'have a word'. It was reported that a 'satisfactory' interview took place - at any rate no such incidents recurred.

It is an interesting phenomenon with heritage railways that objectors like to denigrate the organisation with a swipe at its greed. A number of people had a go at the Festiniog Railway Company. They hadn't done their homework. All profits are ploughed back into the business, the Directors are all volunteers and all the shares are held by a charitable trust. The local newspapers pick up on the objections, and from time to time innuendo suggests that someone, somewhere is profiting at the expense of poor local folk. Yet they are not; the arithmetic is of a steady £14m returned to the local economy every year. As time moves on, like the FR, the memory of the change will fade, and apart from day to day problems the WHR will become the normal face of life in the area.

# Appendix

## Snowdon Ranger, Internet Jinks, The WHR Journal, Building to Pont Croesor & more.

## Restoring the WHR - the CRhE view

Cymdeithas Rheilffordd Eryri - Welsh Highland Railway Society

**The Snowdon Ranger No. 7**
**February 1995**

### The Gwynedd County Council Light Railways Sub-Committee.

You may have thought that by now we would be well on the way to gaining the Light Railway Order needed to get the Caernarfon - Dinas line up and running. The Gwynedd County Council Light Railways Sub-Committee, under the Chairmanship of Councillor T. O. Jones, met on 10 November 1994 and resolved:

*a) To inform the Ffestiniog Railway Company that (subject to contract) the Council are minded to grant a lease to Ffestiniog Railway Company of the necessary width of the trackbed between Caernarfon and Dinas on condition that Ffestiniog Railway allow the Welsh Highland Light Railway (1964) Ltd. to extend their existing operation in Porthmadog to Pont Croesor or beyond and that Ffestiniog Railway Company grant a lease or other interest to the (1964) Company or to the Council to enable such an extension to take place.*

*b) To welcome the appointment of consultants to look at the general development of the St. Helen's Road area.*

*c) To inspect the St. Helen's Road area and to discuss the matter further after receiving the consultant's report.*

It is hardly surprising in view of this decision that the 'other party' is not minded to accept the offer of joining in with Ffestiniog, even with the explanation that we are happy to consider extensions from Porthmadog once a railway in the North is established to generate funds for expansion. Meanwhile, until Gwynedd comes off the fence, the burghers of Caernarfon, it would seem, will have to whistle for their railway. So we went to a meeting of the Chamber of Trade and explained how the matter stood and there was something of a reaction. We shall see presently what the outcome will be. But much more is to follow - the Council and the '64 Co., co-applicants for the LRO for Caernarfon - Dinas, have been asked to lay their competing LRO application aside following the Minister's decision. Thus far they have not done so, the Council minute recording

*RESOLVED to defer consideration of the request by Ffestiniog Railway Company pending the outcome of further negotiations.*

The Minister will call another Public Inquiry to deal with the competing applications and unless Gwynedd or the '64 Co. withdraws before the Minister's call, we shall have to go through it all again. There may be some gleeful smirks among those who love us little, but it will certainly deliver a clear message about whether other aspiring railway builders want to accept our offer to join together, to live in peace and let bygones be bygones, which is the flavour of the preferred outcome desired by the preservation movement as a whole. Another outcome of the Sub-Committee was the following:

*RESOLVED to indicate to the Official Receiver that the Council wishes to see its expenditure on maintaining bridges and structures being repaid by the Official Receiver together with the debentures and interest.*

Perhaps you will conclude that such a resolution - including the repayment of a 70 year old debt incurred by a previous Council who had a Director on the Board! - is hardly encouraging. Well, we never thought it would be easy getting this railway back, did we?

---

*There was a stated feeling within FR Co. circles that 64Co. enjoyed preferment from the GCC. Perhaps this was not surprising, considering the long relationship. Perhaps it was considered by GCC that the public interest was best served by the encouragement of development of a second railway from Pen y Mount, as it was apparently not clear in the councillors mind that despite having obtained the whole trackbed, FR would restore all of the WHR. Yet the outcome of the TO Inquiry, and the clause from the High Court judgement offered them comfort if FR reneged, and the FR had been quite clear why it wished to start from Caernarfon. Knowing this therefore, the FR conclusion was that this was not a chummy set of resolutions, and it was preferment for 64 Co, as GCC seemed to have been only recent champions of the trackbed as railway. In addition, they were responsible for maintenance of the bridges, and weren't the debentures statute barred? There was more to this, as the matter rumbled on into 1995 (report in Chapter 4) and the lease was not given until mid-1996. The issues surrounding it were that GCC/64 Co. had also made an LRO application for Caernarfon to Dinas, so a charge of preferment was undesirable, and if FR co. claimed that GCC's conditions were 'unreasonable' then it may be considered that the Secretary of State's decision and the High Court Judgement were not being honoured. The matter dragged on long enough for comment to be given by David Allan in WHR Journal 117 in February 1996.*

*Following on from this was a meeting aimed at a Memorandum of Understanding, that was reported in Snowdon Ranger No.8, overleaf.*

*See also how this 'plays out' in the 64 Co. WHR Journal 117 of February 1996. You then have both views and can understand clearly what was being said.*

## Cymdeithas Rheilffordd Eryri - Welsh Highland Railway Society
### The Snowdon Ranger No. 8
### May 1995

### Joint Announcement by WHR (1964) Co. and Festiniog Railway Co.

There was a second meeting between representatives of the WHR (1964) Co. and FR on 4th April. To help to keep everyone informed of progress the following joint statement was agreed.

1. It was agreed that the WHR (1964) Company should remain autonomous, at least for the foreseeable future.
2. It was agreed that all volunteers and organisations, including the '64 Co. members, who offer support to the enterprise would be warmly welcomed to work in the reconstruction and operation of the Welsh Highland Railway.
3. The FR welcome the use of the 1964 Co. locos and stock on both WHR and FR metals and will make an agreement with the 1964 Co. which will allow its vintage trains access on a regular and equitable basis provided it is for the good of the overall enterprise.
4. In support of the whole enterprise and 3 above, '64 Co. members will put their energies into assisting with the earliest reconstruction of the whole line as well as its ongoing maintenance and operation.
5. Discussions will now continue concerning how the '64 Co. can best have a deep involvement with the whole project.

#### Additional Notes
a. The WHR Transfer Order announced last July has was finally made on the 14th March 1995. This has now cleared the way for the FR to complete the purchase of the Undertaking which will secure the trackbed.
b. Until the purchase of the WHR Undertaking is complete, work cannot commence on the trackbed. FR are keen this is resolved as soon as possible to enable work to start on arresting the deterioration of structures.

---

*The meeting was conducted at Harbour Station in a cordial and 'can do' atmosphere. The FR thought there would be more, with a 'coming together' encouraged by the opportunities created by the first meeting. Subsequent meetings did not happen for a good, long while, and as far as FR/CRhE was concerned Snowdon Ranger No. 12 records what they thought the outcome was.*

---

## Cymdeithas Rheilffordd Eryri - Welsh Highland Railway Society
### The Snowdon Ranger No. 11
### February 1996

### Editorial - Of Fish and Nets : Dan Wilson

The "Truth on The Net" piece in TSR 10 produced some divergent reactions, as you might expect. For those who didn't see it, this was something of a rant contributed in July to one of the Internet computer conferences covering UK railways, doubting the Festiniog Railway's bona fides in restoring the WHR. It was signed (if you can sign anything on a computer) "Ditchpig WHR" and emanated from an electronic address elsewhere identified as that of Andy Goodwin, the Permanent Way chief of the WHLR (1964) Ltd. To start with Mr Goodwin hotly denied any identity with "Ditchpig" but after ribald remarks on the Internet about so many friends using the same electronic address having the same awful spelling, conceded his authorship.

I published the piece partly for the entertainment and political education of readers, partly to bring out into the open for appraisal what seems to me the quite understandable resentment felt on the WHLR at the FR's success in landing the fish that has eluded them over so many years. It is a pity that events and personalities have conspired to give this feeling such a rancourous and self-destructive outlet, which as other contributors to the conference pointed out, did its originator little credit. The Snowdon Ranger has not carried, as some of the Festiniog Area Group journals have, the very frank report by Les Smith on 1994's WHLR AGM in which FR Co Chairman Mike Hart was barracked by a faction wearing T-shirts emblazoned "Death To The Festiniog Scum". I thought it best not to embarrass them. But international computer conferences are another arena altogether and call for some air to be let in.

Of course, the 1964 Co was embarrassed. I had a phone call from Dave Allan expressing "disappointment" that we had given "the Festiniog Scum" (a common WHRS name for the faction, after their T-shirts) such further prominence. Were we not hinting the material was officially inspired ?

Well, I did not think we were, at all, and was very surprised at the idea. What I was not party to at the time was the campaign the 1964 Co was running amongst County councillors to make the FR's lease of the old BR section from the County conditional on a collateral lease by the FR to the 1964 Co of the Gelerts Farm-Pont Croesor stretch of the WHR proper - the length they had been promised by the Council since the 1980s. To put the matter delicately, councillors understood (even if mistakenly) Mr Allan to be prepared to see the whole FR project sacrificed to this condition; and it was this perception which Alistair McNicol, Chairman of the 1964 Co, was at pains to correct in a Press Release in December expressing unqualified support for the greater project. It would be natural if Mr Allan thought I was tweaking his tail. Not so. It just seemed obvious to me, and I hope to readers, that we were dealing here with a loose cannon and both the material and the TSR treatment of it were in accord with that.

Now, newcomers to the WHR story will be vaguely wondering why the 1964 Co, having concluded an agreement with the FR giving its trains (conditional on operating considerations) the freedom of the whole eventual network, still cling to the idea of constructing the small piece of it they had, before the FR's intervention, been promised in the event of the County Council gaining control of the WHR trackbed. The simile of a liberated concentration camp victim clinging to his cell seems uncomfortably apt. Well, the reason is, like everything to do with the WHR, tortuous and lengthy to explain. I shall necessarily have to cut corners. The '64 Co was founded by a number of dissident Ffestiniog volunteers in the teeth of official FR opposition. On the FR the Welsh Highland was - still is in some quarters, remember - the Ffestiniog's poisoned chalice. The WHR was an irresponsible temptation, dangerous and deluded. It would render all who touched it bankrupt and mad. Thus if you turn up at Gelerts Farm to work in FR uniform, you have crashed the checkpoint, walked the bridge, gone over. It's a natural home for folk browned off with the FR. Even department heads have volunteered there rather than on the Ffestiniog. So the founding principle of the '64 Co is that it isn't the FR or anything to do with it. It isn't anti, it's just Not. Of course there are "Ditchpigs" who are anti, but that kind of thing is for simple folk who can't tell the difference and would find it boring if they could. An extremely important strand of this not-the-Festiniogness stands out in the insistence by 1964 Co members in argument on the primacy of "democracy", meaning not a great voting system every time the loo paper colour is changed but quiet influence on policy by key volunteers - a thing in which the Ffestiniog, of all volunteer-using railways (for there are some that have simply antagonised them out as a matter of policy) is historically weak. In fact volunteers do have influence on the FR but by what they choose to do rather than say, so it's invisible. An immensely long discussion could be held on this subject alone. I have to skip it, but "democracy" in this sense is highly prized by many potential volunteers, who find the distant management of a big operation like the FR intimidating and alienating. But as anyone in a big operation knows, sounding opinion is not just expensive (£800 per mailing for the FR Society) it's impossible if the operation is engaged in powerful and fast developments needing day-to-day management.

This description applies to all the larger preserved railways and it's why volunteer opinion on the smaller ones seems to that on the larger as juvenile and ignorant of business principles . Large-railway volunteers know the need for cooperation and trust; small-railway ones the need to keep romantic objectives ahead of commercial considerations. If you start off as a small railway, it is hell turning it into a big one, even if you wish to. The WHLR probably never wished to. Smallness and unadventurousness have become invisible and unacknowledged virtues because you can't easily have grass-roots influence without them. But without empire-building rhetoric, you're unlikely to pull in fresh support. As long as no real empire-builder heaves over the horizon, you can talk big and do small and no-one's going to complain. So the WHLR has always held up Porthmadog-Caernarfon as a far distant goal while actually espousing far more limited and attainable aims. Now, if you please, a real empire-builder has heaved over the horizon, and It's That Railway Again, that the WHLR has spent its life trying to get away from, with a truly nutty scheme that has no part in it other than the odd evening working for Russell or the original WHR stock. Because of its lean, mean undemocracy, the FR has been ahead of the game all along; it is simply not fair. Worse, "restoring the Welsh Highland" has suddenly been redefined as knuckling under, tailing in behind the WHRS and doing the Ffestiniog's bidding. Can you wonder that the WHLR is looking round for an escape like a cornered fox? The '64 Co hierarchy are under internal pressure to rubbish the FR and all its works, and external pressure to pay some attention to the "only Welsh Highland" rhetoric and do some serious restoring along with us. Poor folk. It's not surprising if they spring a leak and blurt out the wrong thing at times, on both sides. At the least, it behoves us to be understanding about this. I believe that the WHLR promises to add some delightful diversity to the FR/WHR network - it has some natural allies in the FR movement of whom it seems to be unaware at present - and soft talk will serve us all best right now. The Pont Croesor project is pretty irrational, spending two years building a piece of line our rehabilitation machine should be able to knock off in three weeks when it gets there - but then these railways are a little irrational anyway, are they not?

Dan Wilson

*This is some of the most advanced and prescient thinking around in 1996 - it is accurate. Dan Wilson always managed to get in among the really significant facts and winkle out the most bitingly honest and human thing to say, regardless of whether it was pro or anti the party line. So what you've got above is the brightly-lit truth, as Dan sees it. He states a view that endures through time, which is why it is said that the CRhE dumped him out for making frightening predictions, that happened to be evident to him, but not to other mortals. He sweeps aside the Internet comment (samples overleaf) as said by 'simple folk'; he knows the 64 Co. 'we're not the Ffestiniog' game, but most of all he knew well before it happened how once the FR was goaded into action, they would not stop until the entire railway had been restored. He also was of the view that the 64 Co. simply wasn't up to it, and that once they had started the behemoth moving, they'd wouldn't know how to stop it, or even to divert it. He's dead now, alas - but it was he who coined the phrase 'a feeling of creamy satisfaction'. He would have felt that, had he seen how his words came true.*

# The Internet Comments

The Internet forums were an outlet for extreme frustration even in 1995, and they were widely read. It is of interest therefore to see an extract of what was said, bearing in mind that forums are still just as active today - and just as inaccurate too. This is offered as context, to show the passions raging.

---

*Forum entry from Ian*

OK, interesting points but if you want to get picky...

At least the Fessie run a railway. Frankly, thirty years to shunt a couple of converted ammunition wagons along a slightly extended siding isn't too impressive. I'm sure they are a wonderful bunch of people, but save from some good work in restoring Russell, the WHLR (1964) have been a dead loss, and I can see why the DoT decided to give someone else a chance.

Basically the gripes seem to fall into two categories:

1) The WHR is going to be FR compatible – and if any through running, even just a coach or two – is envisaged this seems a thoroughly good idea. Of course it may mean taking the old tin opener to Russell's dome again. Also I hear of plans to increase the FR loading gauge.

2) They won't be able to do it (finance ... track quality ... locomotive patterns ... etc etc etc). I agree that they do seem to plan to raise a lot of money and I'll be intrigued to see where it comes from, but for the rest it does sound like a rather pathetic knocking.

Dear reader, visit Porthmadog and travel on the Ffestiniog, then travel on the WHLR (1964). Remember that the former have only twelve years or so head start. Who would you rather had a bash at the full length of the WHR?

By the way, I have no association with either side, but I keep in touch with both through friends.

Ian

---

*Forum entry from From Ditchpig:*

It would appear that some of my comments seem to have struck a nerve with you. Why is this I wonder? You have not stated what your interest is in this matter. Perhaps you are one of those people who support the FR and just wish that we Welsh Highlanders would shut up and go away?

> **Why don't you resign, or shut up, or (even better) stop wasting everyone's time by ceasing to churn out this unbelievable crap.**

Resign? Resign from what? The Railway? Why should I? I enjoy working at the railway, but quite frankly, I can't see what that has got to do with you. What I don't enjoy is seeing the way that Welsh Highland matters are misrepresented in certain sections of the railway press. The narrow gauge section of Steam Railway is edited by Peter Johnson (editor of the F.R. Magazine) and the narrow gauge section of the totally impartial Railway World is edited by Dan Wilson (editor of The Snowdon Ranger, the Ffestiniogs Welsh Highland society rag). Currently the only place where Welsh Highland volunteers get to air there views without them being distorted is through these pages.

Unbelievable crap? Are you suggesting that I am making up the information? I have better things to do with my time than invent lies about the Ffestiniog. The majority of the information I have reported has come from a source close to Ffestiniog, who himself has a number of doubts about the integrity of their plans. The Government's report on the Welsh Highland stated quite clearly that one of the reasons FR were given the order was that they would use a considerable amount of private funding. The four and half million pounds of lottery money that the FR have applied for is most definitely NOT PRIVATE MONEY. Actions like this can not be allowed to pass with comment being made.

> **You are so bitter, one would have expected you to leave the country by now.**

> **Alas you haven't, and we are subjected to yet more of this self-indulgent drivel.**

Bitter yes I am bitter, so are a lot of Welsh Highland volunteers, understandably so. As for leaving the country, what are you talking about?

---

*Are you mad or something???*

With regard to your comment about self-indulgent drivel, Welsh Highland supporters have had to put up with vast quantities of it in the Young Isambard column for the last couple of years.

> **Now I feel better! Thank you.**

I'm glad you feel better, I appreciate hearing your frank and forthright views and would be more than happy to discuss them with you in person next time you are in Porthmadog. You can find me in the Station Inn most Friday nights, I'll be the one wearing the Death to the FR scum T'shirt. Well ok then, one of several wearing Death to the FR scum T'shirts.

DITCHPIG

---

*Forum entry from Andrew Hughes*

Mr Johnston and Mr Webb, and anyone else out there,

I have been a member of the WHLR (1964) Co. since just before my 4th birthday, just over 20 years ago. I will try to explain here \*why\* exactly the '64 Co. has not managed to get further, and exactly why we 'hate' the FR so much......

When the original line went bust, all assets were sold off apart from the trackbed. This remained in the hands of the liquidator (I believe), and he was charged to sell the trackbed for as much money as possible, but to ensure that it would not fall back into his hands, ie he had to ensure that whoever bought it could afford to maintain it etc. The 1964 Co. set out to build a company capable of this, and it has to be said that they did damn well. Being unable to purchase the original line the Sidings at Porthmadog were bought along with Gelert's Farm. The Farm was quickly converted into a works that now boasts a superb collection of facilities, and the line was completed quickly. Trains started to be operated in 1980.

After a few years we had proved that we were running a successful operation, and that given time we would be able to rebuild the entire railway. The Liquidator was impressed, and was prepared to sell the trackbed to us. Unfortunately, he died shortly before the transfer was made, and the trackbed fell into the hands of the Official Receiver. He had no idea of what had happened at Porthmadog, or of how much had been achieved by the '64 Co., and we were forced to start the process of proving ourselves again.

During this period we made an agreement with Gwynedd County Council for the rebuilding of the line, and started making detailed plans. Around 1987 a second, anonymous bid was entered for the trackbed, once again just as we were about to make progress on this matter. It turned out a few years later that this bid had been made by the Ffestiniog Railway.

Since then a small scale 'war' has been waged in Porthmadog, over the entire issue, as I'm sure you know involving High Courts, Public inquiries, and very dubious decisions by Senior Government Officials. I believe therefore that it is unfair to say that it is just that the FR were awarded the trackbed, the '64 Co. has had a far harder time than most other railways in it's attempts to purchase the trackbed, and has also had to endure a larger neighbour using underhand (ie anonymous bid) tactics to try and prevent the rebuilding of the railway.

A few facts for public consumption....

\* The FR entered an anonymous bid to purchase the WHR trackbed, obviously not the sort of thing expected from a company that had previously been supporting the '64 Co.

\* In a meeting with GCC officials, Senior Officials from the FR made it clear that they did not want the WHR to be built, and that if they were successful in their attempts to purchase the trackbed they would NOT build the railway, and they wished GCC to refuse to allow the railway to be built should GCC purchase the trackbed.

\* The FR \*LOST\* the public inquiry, indeed they were humiliated at it, and were forced to admit that they did not want the railway to be built.

\* The FR were awarded the trackbed by the Minister for Transport, and the major reason given for this was that they would be privately funding the entire affair, and would not use \*ANY\* public money. So far they have appealed to GCC for aid, and are now hoping to get 4.5million pounds from the National Lottery.

\* The FR, and the WHRS (The FR's front company for the WHR), have

been less than honest in their public announcements and articles. They claim they are the only company to ever have wanted to rebuild the entire WHR and that they originated the idea. This is patently untrue.
*The WHR have, and have had for many years, detailed plans for the rebuilding of the railway, involving building from both ends of the track at the same time. The FR have no workable plans, indeed, they seem to think that by raising lots of money the railway will build itself. It also happens that a lot of the plans the FR have come out with were devised by the WHR many years ago.
*The FR state that they will rebuild the link through the town. This will *NEVER* happen, there are far too many obstacles in the way, not least of which is the fact that the railway would run next to a petrol station. I can imagine that Shell would be happy to have live steam locos running past that!
* In my opinion, the FR is poorly managed and run, they have spent, or rather wasted anything up to 750,000 on the WHR saga. They forced the public inquiry which cost the '64 Co. a small fortune. ALL of this money could have been far better spent on improving our respective railways.
My personal feelings for the FR can not be expressed here, but suffice to say that I have never been as furious in my life as over the last year. I have dedicated 20 years of my life to the WHR, and as far as I can tell at the moment, it is going to be wasted, as the FR have shown *NO* proof that they intend to rebuild the railway. A lot of talk, but no action.
Andrew Hughes, Journal Editor, WHLR (1964) Co. Ltd.
The above opinions are entirely my own, and are not necessarily those of the Welsh Highland Railway Company.

---

Forum entry (extract) from Ditchpig
> Ian, unconnected to either though still a biggoted little turd.
You completely failed to understand the point I was making. The 8 (not 6) incidents were not minor incidents, derailing a passenger train is not a minor incident, an engine breaking an axle coming down a steep tight curve is not a minor incident, running a steam engine out of water is not a minor incident.
The FR have set themselves up as the 'Demi-God' of narrow gauge railways, (all bow down and worship them) but basically when it comes down to it, what they have got is just an upgraded mineral line and a number of locomotives that are not suitable for the jobs they are given to do. (Earl of Merioneth, out of service for over 4 years now, Mount-anieer out of service for 2 years, Lynda out of service for 2 years etc etc). A number of major locomotive failures this summer has meant that Prince and one of the diesels have ended up double-heading trains that should have been hauled by double fairies. Running at 20 mph hauling 11 coaches is not the best way to treat a 110 year old engine that wasn't designed for working at that speed or or with that load, nomatter how many times it may have been rebuilt.
The likes of the Severn Valley, East Lancs, Bluebell railways do not have anything like the number of incidents that the FR do.
What you do not appreciate is that the Majority of the major 'improvements' that have been made on the FR have been made with public money. The new station at Bleanau was built with public money (£50,000 ish) the new 'INCA' stock coaches (Believed to be £100,000), the new double fairy
(10-20,000) the new 230hp diesel built with european money, (50-100,000), the new volunteers hostle at Minffordd (upto £100,000 of euro money.) As was shown at the WHR public inquiry, if you take the grant aid money out of the FR purse, you end up with a railway that barely makes a profit. The question has to be asked, If the FR has to apply for so many grants to improve their railway, how can they afford to waste money on the WHR project? If the kind of money they are talking about is really available then surely that money would be better spent improving their own railway and reducing their fares. Perhaps the truth of the matter is that a few money men at the top are using the FR as vehicle to put their own railway interests first rather than those of the

---

FR?? who knows.
Your comment "The WHLR(1964)Ltd shunts wagons with people sitting on them." is beneath contempt. If you've visited the railway how can you possibly make a commment like that. the WHR rolling stock is far better than a number of narrow gauge railways. Of course a couple of coaches are built on upgraded wagon chassis, in 1981 it was the quickest way the railway could get coaches into service to meet passenger demand. But to say that the railway shunts wagons with people sat on them is just total shit.
The WHR, unlike the FR, did not acquire a ready made railway with locomotives, coaches and track generally intact. It has had to build virtually everything from scratch.
Oh by the way, don't be fooled by that nice little old lady who works in the railway's shop, we're not very nice people.

---

DITCHPIG

Forum entry from Ian
Dear boy, you are playing way out of your league. Editing "bigoted turd" into your response would be more impressive if you could
a) spell it or
b) configure your Demon software properly.
The WHLR(1964)Ltd are a group of very nice people – I have visited several times and talked to them at length. Restoring Russell is an impressive achievement. Nonetheless they have been almost entirely unsuccessful at rebuilding the WHR. Their track is a siding, their rolling stock does feel like cheaply converted ammunition trucks, and is not a remote patch on FR stuff.
: The WHR, unlike the FR, did not acquire a ready made railway with
: locomotives, coaches and track generally intact. It has had to build
: virtually everything from scratch.
Just as the FR had to restore from scratch all their locomotives, almost all the rolling stock and the track – oh, and build a new bit as well. Now stop being hysterical and calm down. The WHLR(1964)Ltd and TCLtd are supposed to be friends now and I am sure that jointly they will make a better go of it than either – or worse, both – separately. Just as the WH enthusiasm for the spirit of the line should help counter the more excessively modernist TCL proposals, so should the FR expertise at securing public support and funding help the Welsh Highland get to more than three quarters of a mile within the decade.

Ian

PS I wonder if you have ever read Mann-Tram? They used to have a rather good line in hysterical illogical attacks too, and your style is very similar.
PPS To those of you fed up with the arguments, sorry. Me, I just hope that the WHR gets rebuilt by whoever can best do it.

---

This was all long, long ago when feelings ran very high. It is likely that within the circle of acquaintances, such outbursts were greeted with mirth and glee at the FR's discomfiture. A bit of consideration would have revealed that the comment, despite denial, could be taken as 'official' - otherwise why would responsible people write such stuff? But then the comments are so ill-informed and twisted they actually damage the case being made. The FR was amazed that people could be so badly informed and act to their own disadvantage in such a way. If FR supporters did this they would be 'leant on' not to. There was no official FR response, except Dan Wilson's comments in Snowdon Ranger. This may have been because FR Co. had a 'plan' and a clear strategy. Any evidence of disputatious remarks in any forum, with objectors or otherwise, was viewed by the Establishment as not 'fitting'. FR Co. depended on grants to do the restoration job, and such a label would put those at major risk - hence there was never any response. However the Internet forums were widely read, and many knew who Ditchpig was.

# What they were saying at Gelert's Farm - The WHR Journal

These extracts offer a context to understand the relations between the principals. The 64 Co. saw the 1990 FR actions as 'buy to shut', aimed directly against them, and this created a legacy of mistrust that has persisted for a long time. The extracts begin in 1995, as some earlier are included with the chapter text. Entries go up to 2000, as there was a real change in relations for the better under the David Allan Chairmanships. The history of more recent relations requires time to let it mature, did not affect WHR restoration and thus has limited relevance here. Apologies to any who see bias, none is meant.

*The following extracts are courtesy the Welsh Highland Railway Journal - Author's comment, intended to clarify, is added in italics.*
*Please note that the comments by the Author are his own surmise **and are not indications of official FR Co. policy.***

## April 1995
### Journal 114 - Dave Allan, Black and White

Well, it has not been the easiest year in the long history of our Company. To lose the trackbed in such galling circumstances was indeed a desperate blow, but it is something with which we will have to come to terms. It is something we must and will rise above. After all, the trackbed was only a means to an end, not the end in itself.

The time has come now to stop the bitterness and recriminations. There is no point in continuing some sort of Hill-Billy feud, with unthinking hatred being passed on from generation to generation, and where in the end, no-one remembers what the bloody fight was about anyway.

So let us draw a curtain over recent events, let us fulfil our destiny by completing the efforts of the last 30 years and get on with the building and the operating of the Welsh Highland Railway.

It is as well to remember what the Public Enquiry achieved. It opened the door to reconstructing the entire railway, not just to Rhyd Ddu, not just to Dinas, but to its original promoter's chosen destination - Caernarfon itself.

It is also as well to remind the world at large the major part we have played in this sensational result. It was this Company which conceived the idea, which sustained the idea and which by its grit, its determination and its enthusiasm, converted the idea to practical reality.

OK - so now we have to share the action, we're not the only player on the pitch, we're not the dominant player on the pitch and we don't even own the pitch! However, we are an integral part of the team. We have the skills, we have the determination and we have the enthusiasm. It's about time we put them to work. So where do we go from here?

The December 1994 EGM authorised negotiations with the FR. Peter Thomason and myself have recently been asked to lead those discussions. Negotiations mean sitting down and talking to the other side. They mean consolidating those areas of agreement and where there are difficulties, talking these through to see if some compromise offers itself as a solution. Compromise means that neither side will get everything it wants, but that both sides will agree on a lesser solution to the benefit of the overall enterprise. These discussions need to take place in a relaxed an cordial atmosphere. If the situation is tense, tempers flare, people become entrenched and bad decisions result. Your Company has made the first move. To create the right mood and as a gesture of goodwill it has withdrawn its objection to the FR's Caernarfon - Dinas L.R.O. application, whilst leaving our joint application, with Gwynedd, on the table in case of emergencies, and it has encouraged the Council to follow suit.

A preliminary discussion has already been held with the FR in a meeting which was as notable for its positive atmosphere as for its constructive results. Following that meeting a joint FR/WHR delegation addresses Gwynedd's LRO Sub-Committee on 8th March.

*David Allan, whose dream has always been to reconstruct the WHR in its original form, writes here in a most conciliatory tone. He has put aside any bitterness he may have felt and it seems that the two organisations will work together. The parts about negotiation and compromise were promising indeed. This did look like the start of something good. David Allan indicates his personal willingness to find a way of supporting the two organisations working together.*

## November 1995
### Journal 116 - Dave Allan, Black and White

The whole Welsh Highland situation has been transformed by the sensational news of the FR's £4.5m Millennium Fund grant towards the rebuilding of the line.

By any standards this is an excellent result. The FR have, and deserve to have, our wholehearted congratulations on their achievement. Equally sensational is that the grant is conditional on the railway being completed to Rhyd Ddu by 1999; so, unbelievably, after 30 years of talk, effort and controversy, 15 miles of track will be built in just 52 months!

It is time to sit back, draw a deep breath and let all the implications sink in. There will be mixed feelings - that is understandable. But there can be no doubt that all in all it is extremely good news for the future of the Welsh Highland Railway.

To return to practicalities, what is the role of the volunteer in all this? Not a lot it would appear. The main work will be done by contractors, leaving the track to be laid by a mixture of Welsh Highland paid labour and volunteers.

So where does this Company come in? What is our role? Not unnaturally we should like a longer length of track to extend our current operation and which would make full commercial use of the £3/4m capital which we have invested in Porthmadog. Our proposals to the FR on a northward extension, with a subsequent contribution to the overall funds, are documented elsewhere in this Journal.

What else can we offer to do?

Contractors being contractors tend to knock over every obstacle that gets in their way. Would it not be reasonable, given our agreed heritage role, to form a team to survey, document and assess every original building, part building and structure on the line, with a view to their preservation and eventual reconstruction?

This could even include old quarry lines and part of the old workings themselves. Could we ensure that all proposed new buildings are constructed in the style and spirit of the old W.H. whose heritage we are so anxious to preserve?

Could our superbly professional track laying gang, under the inspired leadership of Andrew Goodwin and Nigel Hanwell, be pressed into service for the overall benefit of the scheme? Maybe some sort of reciprocal basis could be worked out. Perhaps for each mile of track they lay south from Caernarfon they could lay another mile north from Porthmadog?

All this would enable us, indeed entitle us, to become part of a team whose role will not only be to reconstruct Welsh Highland coaches, rebuild steam and Diesel locos, operate a working museum and hopefully run heritage trains to Pont Croesor, but would also give as a major involvement in the project as a whole.

That surely is where our future lies and where our history directs us.

And finally, as they say on the News, would it not be an appropriate gesture of reconciliation if we could arrange for Russell to haul the first passenger train out of Caernarfon?

*The Millennium Grant, European Regional Development Fund application was the FR doing its thing. It knew the grant ropes, and had already won substantial sums previously. This is the breadth of vision and approach that being with the FR was about. And whilst the inspired leadership of Andrew Goodwin may be admired at Gelert's Farm, Boston Lodge knows that this was 'Ditchpig'. How was someone that said those things going to be acceptable?*

**February 1996**
**Journal 117 - Dave Allan, Black and White**
A lot seems to have happened in the three short months since this column was last penned. So to continue with a resume of events...

Following a suggestion from FR Chairman Mike Hart that our unconditional offer to build the railway to Pont Croesor (as reported in the last Journal) might hold some merit, discussions were resumed with Gordon Rushton. However from our point of view these talks were inconclusive and were interrupted at a crucial stage when Gordon had to spend some time in America.

Meanwhile Gwynedd's LRO sub-committee met to discuss amongst other things a lease of the council owned Dinas to Caernarfon trackbed to the FR. A report had been sent by this Company to all the sub-committee councillors outlining progress to date.

According to the agenda, the F.R's representatives, Messrs Hart and Schumann were to make a presentation to the Committee, but events were to take an unexpected turn. The F.R's representatives were questioned in detail on their plans and in particular their intentions for the Southern end of the route. Following some heated exchanges the Chairman took the unprecedented step of adjourning the Committee so that all parties could meet in an anteroom to discuss the problem. Unfortunately the deadlock could not be broken.

However, the Council's ever helpful solicitor, Kelvin Dent, suggested that a clause could be inserted, which would be a condition of the lease to the F.R of the Caernarfon-Dinas section. This suggestion was eventually adopted by the Committee and their final resolution read as follows:

RESOLVED In the light of the obvious threat to the sum of £4.3 million from the Millennium Fund, that we authorise the County Valuer to lease the land from Caernarfon to Dinas to the Festiniog Railway Company on condition that they use their best endeavours to enable the Welsh Highland Light Railway (1964) Company to build the railway between Porthmadog and Pont Croesor at the earliest opportunity.

Unfortunately, it must be reported that the F.R.'s principals were not, to put it mildly, best pleased with this development. But to be fair they did accept it, whereas we did not, perhaps hoping for more consideration to be given to the implications.

It must be stressed that the Council represents the interests of the Gwynedd electorate and whilst this Company may have some peripheral influence, the Councillors are rightly independent of all outside influences.

In order to underline our commitment to the enterprise and our desire not to put any of it in jeopardy, it may be as well to reveal here a further matter. An offer was made to us to put down a Notice of Motion. This would have meant that there would be a full-blown debate on the matter at the next full Council Meeting and it would also have the effect of stopping stone dead any further lease negotiations between the FR and the Council's officers. We declined the offer both in the interest of the overall enterprise and because it may have had a serious effect on the Millennium Grant.

Not only did we take this step, but following Arfon's deferment of the F.R.'s planning application for Caernarfon-Dinas in November Alisdair McNicol wrote a very strong letter of support for the application, which was then approved at the Planning Committee's December meeting. These steps follow the withdrawal of our objection to F.R.'s Caernarfon-Dinas LRO last April and our urging of the Council to follow suit.

Any suggestion that we are somehow 'dragging our feet' on the proposals is a ghost that needs to be laid now.

However, to get on to more constructive matters the Rushton/Allan talks resumed in earnest, and at last real progress seems to be starting to be made.

The Company's heritage role was agreed; its involvement and support for the F.R's Caernarfon to Dinas initiative was agreed; its support for the overall enterprise was agreed; and finally agreement was reached on the thorny problem of Pont Croesor. A memorandum of Understanding was hammered out, which is reproduced in full at the end of this report. Both negotiators agreed to recommend it to their respective Boards. This will clear the way to prepare a final agreement including access to the trackbed.

Your negotiator in his report to the Board 'strongly recommended that the Memorandum of Understanding be accepted.' The Board concurred with the recommendation and accepted the Memorandum in principle.

As this Journal closes for Press no word as yet has been received from the F.R. Although a letter from FR Chairman Mike Hart, whilst hoping for a resolution to our difference early in the New Year continues to doubt our commitment. As this article endeavours to spell out, the one thing that is not in doubt is our enthusiastic and overwhelming support for the rebuilding of the original Welsh Highland Railway as quickly as possible in accordance with the Companies Objectives.

The Welsh Highland Railway (1964) Company has pleasure in offering to The Festiniog Railway Company and its supporters active assistance and participation in the construction and operation of the Caernarfon to Dinas Railway.

The Festiniog Railway Company wishes to make known its intent, subject to land ownership and Rail Order provisions, to make a detailed agreement with the Welsh Highland Railway (1964) Company, for them to construct and operate the Pen y Mount to Pont Croesor Railway.

The two companies indicate their joint wish that their members, supporters and staff, shall work together to achieve the restoration and operation of the Welsh Highland Railway.

## MEMORANDUM OF UNDERSTANDING

The aim of the Welsh Highland Railway (1964) Company is to be the guardians and exhibitors of the heritage of the old Welsh Highland Railway, with museum and demonstration line on the Gelert's Farm site. The Festiniog Railway Company acknowledges and endorses these aims and assents to the formation of a detailed agreement to enable 64 Co. vintage trains to run on the restored WHR.

The Festiniog Railway Company will expedite the construction by 64 Co. of the Pen y Mount to Pont Croesor Railway in exchange for active 64 Co. involvement in the Caernarfon to Dinas Railway. The turning of the understanding into an agreement depends on the operation of the following factors:

The required land title and the Dinas to Porthmadog Rail Order need to be acquired to make the project possible.

The earliest start date for Pont Croesor is likely to be in 1997.

The 64 Co. assistance on Caernarfon to Dinas will be eagerly sought after lease and Light Railway Order are obtained.

The understanding gives the first priority to establishing the Caernarfon to Dinas Railway for three reasons:
- firstly that it will bring the two organisations in close working proximity to foster relations between them.
- Secondly this part of the railway will earn much needed funds to plough back into the restoration.
- And thirdly the establishment of this piece of railway will make a helpful political and economic impact on the establishment of the whole.

At the earliest practical time the two parties agree to work together to construct the cross-town link, between FR and WHR. Thereafter agreement will be sought to run Vintage Shuttle services between Minffordd and Porthmadog stations. The objective of linking Porthmadog car parks with Portmeirion shall be a major commercial aim, as well as satisfying both company's normal aspirations to serve the tourist markets.

*One may think reading this and extracts to follow that FR Co. is being either difficult or distant. If 64 Co. thought that FR Co. untrustworthy, note that FR Co. having received much rough treatment, were not over-keen in accommodating the 64 Co. either. FR Co. had a strategy based on what it knew that it could do; the TO Inquiry and the Millennium Grant were not just luck. These were FR 'calculation' and they had more, much more, ready to follow. Consider the potential outcomes here:*

*1. Before the TO Inquiry was won, the worst that could happen for FR was that **GC would win the trackbed.***

*2. Once the TO was won, the worst that could happen was that **the railway would not get built** - FR was protected from competition.*

*3. In the Journal, David Allan appears to be keen to show masterful restraint. It reads as though the FR Co. should acknowledge this. Yet have the facts in outcomes 1 and 2 been grasped?*

*4. The FR Co. could sit back and say it could do nothing now, as the Secretary of State's judgement was being frustrated, and the High Court judgement was being made invalid by GC intervention. The idea that a Notice of Motion could have been sustained is unlikely. The lease had already been waiting for over a year. To hold it up any more would require justification that the GC were unlikely to be able to provide. David Allan was revealing matters that were coming dangerously close to preferment. To imply that a Council officer 'suggested' the wording of a lease and that a Notice of Motion 'was offered' may indicate the influence of an elder statesman to the members, but it is a courageous public claim for someone who is neither an elected Council member nor an appointed Council officer.*

*5. The insertion of the conditional clause in the lease on Caernarfon to Dinas was taken by FR Co. as evidence that the 64 Co. 'peripheral' influence is only following 64 Co. self-interest, and that 'support for the overall enterprise' is to do with their Pont Croesor extension wishes.*

*6. One must now think that claiming to 'save' the Millennium Grant is opportunism. What has not been remarked on is the conflict of interests (and it's obvious today), that 64 Co. want their own railway in the south, and that the FR Co. are determined to have a 'unified' body. Right now FR are being 'nice' about this, because they want support for the TWO. If they win the TWO without 'support', they will no longer have to be 'nice'.*

*7. Looking back, it is difficult to see how GC was helpful to 64 Co. interests. Those would have been best served by their doing an old FR trick - standing on their boundaries and looking hopeful. At that time they had a strong moral case, so they would simply had to have been given 'something' significant by FR if a charm offensive had been mounted.*

*8. One could think from reading the Journal that 64 Co. was secure and likely to achieve its aspirations. Time will show that this is not the case.*

## May 1996
### Journal 118 - Alastair McNicol, Tin Hats Time

At the risk of giving undue prominence to the writings of others, wasn't it interesting to see that so prominent and well informed a commentator as Ian Allan should be casting doubts on the viability of the "Snowdonia circle" concept being promoted by the FR, with through trains from Blaenau to Caernarfon. Prepare yourself for announcements that the Southern end of the Welsh Highland is, all of a sudden, "not viable", not practical, could have been done if everyone had pulled together, but... you know the sort of thing. Incidentally let us just remind ourselves about what we are doing to help matters along. Apart from making public our wholehearted support for the whole railway, we have offered to build at our expense the two miles of railway from Porthmadog to Pont Croesor and hand it over to the FR when they link up from the north. This offer remains on the table, not having been taken up by the FR (The offer was made in August 1995.) We have offered a heritage role, including fielding our own vintage Welsh Highland transit, we have agreed a memorandum of understanding. We have offered support for rebuilding the northern end. All this, and more, has been offered. What is preventing the FR from just saying "yes?"

*The risk to crying wolf about FR intention is that if they **do** build the whole railway then it leaves you without clothes. The reason for the 64 Co. 'offer to build' being refused, even though it was made in 1995, is that FR Co. thinks that a unified structure is the only way forward, and that the application of continued pressure will either bring the 64 Co. to real negotiations for an assets merge, or if it does not they are likely to be sidelined. 'Tin Hats Time' is not demonstrating an understanding of the possible outcomes.*

## May 1996
### Journal 118 - David Allan, Black and white

Following the optimism expressed in this column in the January issue of The Journal, the inevitable pattern re-asserted itself. Gordon Rushton and myself had evolved a formulae which we both thought would be acceptable to our respective Companies, this being the Memorandum of Understanding published the last time. Both the Board and the Heads of Departments accepted it as a basis for resolving the differences between us, and this acceptance was signalled to the F.R Then four things happened:-

Gordon Rushton and the FR parted company.

The FR declined to respond to the memorandum of understanding.

The FR, who had sought our co-operation in establishing our land holding as part of the consultation process for the Transport and Works Act application, were offended to discover that we had established title to that strip of the old WHR trackbed adjacent to Gelert's Farm.

They were equally offended to discover that we had registered the name "Welsh Highland Railway" under which we have traded for over 30 years.

The series of events led to them calling off all further talks and issuing a Press Release to air their grievances to the World at large. This is extraordinary considering that so many people, including the County Council, want an agreement to be made, plus a string of promises from the FR that they would find an appropriate role for us in the enterprises so long as we complied with laid down conditions (which we did.) We responded with a series of expressions of strong support for their proposals, which I reiterate here, plus an offer to build the line to Pont Croesor and hand it over to them free of charge, plus our acceptance of the Memorandum of Understanding. It is incredible that discussions should falter on such a minor point. It is sad that not only has there been no response to the Memorandum, drawn up by the FR's own representative, but we have not even had the courtesy of a reply to our no strings offer to build to Pont Croesor. In order to try and clarify the position we have offered to convey to them free of charge that part of the WHR trackbed to which we have title as part of the agreement envisaged in the memorandum, but not even this elicited a positive response.

So where do we go from here?

It must be appreciated that the ordinary FR member does not want to see the dispute prolonged, the WHR society similarly wants a solution, we want a solution and the railway world at large must by now be heartily fed up with the whole affair. The onus is now with the FR Board, it really is about time they showed both some understanding and some magnanimity. I therefore call on them

To keep their promises to ensure that we have a major part in the enterprise (we kept our side of the bargain),

To respond to our no strings offer to build to Pont Croesor,

To accept the Memorandum of Understanding as we have done,

To show some appreciation of the huge effort which we have put in and which has made possible their plan to rebuild the Welsh Highland Railway today.

So, come on Mike Hart, Mike Schumann and the rest of the FR Board, show both us and the World your humanity.

*1. The 64 Co. claim title to a piece of trackbed, and try to register WHR as a trademark during current negotiations. They are entitled to act as they wish; FR Co. took the view that this was hardly friendly. To demonstrate that what was a minor point to the 64 Co. may not be to others, they broke off negotiations. Good or bad - let the reader judge.*

*2. David Allan appeals for the FR Co. to show humanity and understanding. Recently FRSL members were a target in the fight to get the FR Co. to back down. Deep inside some, there was a determination growing to 'stuff' them in a big way for humiliating the FR. If Mr Allan had only realised how dangerous this was to 64 Co. long term interests. A major part in the enterprise had been available from FR before the High Court. 64 Co. said no, so the door closed until FR Co. wanted something.*

*3. Why could 64 Co. not see that the battle was all about starting in Caernarfon? It was about establishing a market base there and bringing traffic south to complement FR. Why would FR Co. 'want' a railway from Pen y Mount to Pont Croesor?*

*4. Politeness and diplomacy applied at almost any juncture could have turned matters round. However, this seems to have been rejected with finger wagging demands, and accusations of lack of trust from 'buy to shut'. If lack of trust was the inhibitor, what was Journal 114 about?*

*5. It was in the FR Co mind to accept much of the Memorandum of Understanding, and that says clearly that the Dinas to Porthmadog Rail Order (TWO) must be sorted first - that bit won't change. It's the Cross Town Rail Link (CTRL) status that changed.*

*6. FR Co. has now realised that Millennium money is going to*

mean that rapid construction by contractor is more likely than relaxed construction by volunteers, whereas the Memorandum of Understanding is thinking 'old railway' - build it with volunteers.

7. Perhaps FR Co. could have been persuaded to have CTRL early, to exchange shuttles with 64 Co. The tighter timescale of getting the TWO now means FR Co. don't want it until later, as pressure from the Millennium Commission means they must attend to Caernarfon - Rhyd Ddu. Building CTRL 'at the end' removed any residual utility to FR in having a 'second' railway in the south. 64 Co. think that running on CTRL means FR Co. will bypass them and go into Harbour.

## August 1996
### Journal 119 - Alastair McNicol, Commentary
'Why I can teach thee, coz, to command The devil.'
'And I can teach thee, coz, to shame the devil.
By telling the truth; tell truth and shame the devil.
If thou hath power to raise him. bring him hither ... .'

Several withering broadsides from the vicinity of Harbour Station were directed towards the writer after the last Journal hit the mat. The offence was, apparently not being helpful....Hmm. Well let us examine what is considered helpful from the membership's viewpoint. The truth is always a good starting point for any organ which seeks to inform, and that is surely the primary reason for the existence of the Journal. To inform the membership as to what is really going on, not merely to repeat what is printed in the railway press, is surely a prime function. This organisation has always prided itself on being comfortable with the truth, and very uncomfortable with those who seek to rewrite history or skate around inconvenient facts. Sycophancy is not a commodity either much deal in, or valued very highly at Gelert's Farm. The general trend is to call a spade a spade. When the smell of rotten fish is detected people expect to start pulling up the floor boards, not to ask Harbour Station if they can smell anything amiss. So, rest assured, the pea in this writer's whistle will not be drying out.

(For those who don't know their Shakespeare please refer to Henry IV (Part 1) Act3 Scene1!

*The FR have told him that the actions of 64 Co. are not helping to gain agreement for what they want. The response is to quote Shakespeare and then make some allusions that 64 Co. has a monopoly of truth.*

*Mr McNicol's members need the chance to build their extension - writing stuff like this is most likely to achieve the opposite, as the extension is within the FR's gift - even if the members are growling. This tactic of spades, rotten fish and peas in whistles is not going to help to get it.*

## June 1997
### Journal 122 Comments from the other Side A. McNicol
I recently received a letter from Peter Booth, a long standing member from Bristol. He had attended, as an observer, a meeting of the Festiniog Railway local branch in his area. The meeting was addressed by Mike Hart, Chairman of the FR Board. While it was mostly concerned with FR matters, it was inevitable that questions relating to the WHR would be asked.

Apparently we came in for praise for our achievements at Gelert's Farm, but he was slightly more circumspect on the continuing negotiation situation. He claimed that he found it difficult to know whether the people he was speaking to were speaking for the Company or not. It was suggested the confusion was due to the fact that we are a democratic, open society while the FR are far more commercialised, and thus it is possible that many people on our side may need to talk to them. However, we did have a nominated person to speak to the FR, this being Dave Allan, so confusion on their part should have been minimal.

The other point made by Peter was about the FR's feelings on our wish to extend to Pont Croesor and beyond. When asked about it, Mr Hart said that all the indications were that we wanted to go ahead, but that they had felt very little pressure from us in that direction.

This point by Mr Hart we must take issue with. We have repeatedly told them that we want permission to extend immediately and as many people - including Mr Hart and the entire FR Board - know, we have in recent times offered to build the

railway to Pont Croesor at our own cost, and to give them the entire length once they have need of it. If they do not feel that this constitutes pressure from ourselves maybe we need to turn the heat up. We have tried almost all options, but maybe we now need to try the few remaining ones to make them hear us.

I'd like to thank Peter for sending me his letter regarding these two items. While I feel sure that most of us will be somewhat disheartened to know that the FR are still not treating us with the respect we deserve, as Peter says, it is the FR we have to deal with, and if we have to step up our action to make them listen, then we shall do so.

*FR Co. are well aware that 64 Co. want to go to Pont Croesor. However there is a TWO application in progress, and nothing can happen until that is either through or rejected. FR Co. know very well that speaking to David Allan does not make the confusion go away, as they agree things in principle with him, and then either the WHRL Board or the membership do not back him. Are the funds to build to Pont Croesor available? Are the materials needed for this piece of railway in stock, ready? Either would be an indication that the project is only being held up by waiting for the TWO. That's what Mike Hart means by pressure.*

*Is it really the case that FR MUST accept a free railway between Pen y Mount and Pont Croesor or actions will be stepped up to make them listen? This ain't going to work.*

## November 1997
### Journal 124 - Negotiations with the F.R.
### The Chairman Speaks (A. McNicol)
Members will be rightly anxious to know what is happening on the negotiation front with the F.R. Following our special mailing last time there was a clear impression that at last we were close to an agreement with them. Wrong again! By now we should really know better than that, the more cynical of you will be thinking. Well, yes, perhaps we should but optimism must have its place in the great order of things, otherwise we will all be doomed to the depths of despair. Unfortunately, matters followed a depressingly familiar pattern. Remember the tale of the man who was arrested by the Gestapo and after several weeks of interrogation was released, after it was explained that there had been a terrible misunderstanding, only to be re-arrested again as he walked out of the building. Well, so it almost occurred with us, after a meeting at which it was agreed that everyone really should be working together, and yes of course we could have our extension to Pont Croesor. Did we say Pont Croesor, is that all? Surely you'll want to go further? And running rights? No problem squire. You can have all the running rights you need. And can we use your station because we've got a bit of bother getting across town, etcetera, etcetera. Such was the enthusiasm engendered by this meeting, that we called a special meeting to endorse the broad principles. And yes I was motivated to write a piece saying how wonderful it all was. Well, that was then. But, a few seeds of doubt crept in when a letter of "clarification" arrived from the F.R. General Manger which seemed to go back on a number of points that had been agreed at the meeting with F.R. on 19th August. However, the alarm bells did not really ring too loud, because notes had been taken at the meeting by at least two people, including the Company Secretary who had taken care to check that he was getting the correct picture by querying the notes he had taken with the opposition. However, matters started to get distinctly tricky when a further meeting was held, as arranged, to take matters forward. Perhaps significantly, or not, this meeting was attended by Michael Schumann, the previous meeting having been attended by only Mike Hart and Alan Heywood (The latter of course being the F.R. General Manager). Following the first meeting our legal representative had rapidly pulled together an agreement which was sent to the F.R., but met with a resounding silence for a number of weeks. At the meeting a statement of intent was tabled, which showed a distinctly less friendly approach from the F.R. Our representatives were told how they had not understood what was being suggested, etcetera, etcetera. The meeting closed with an air of gloom and despondency (Not unknown to those associated with the Company's negotiations with F.R.). A draft agreement then followed from the F.R.'s legal representative which was a breath takingly different document to that forwarded by our side.

It contained a number of issues that were wholly unacceptable to the Board. Notably absent was an arbitration clause for resolution of disputes. To get a flavour of this draft agreement, it suggested, inter alia, that our company should build to Pont Croesor at its sole expense (No grant application allowed!), hand it over to the F.R., pay rent for its use and hand all fares revenue over to the F.R. And there was more!!! Fast Forward to E.G.M. day.

The Board was faced with a real dilemma. It had called an E.G.M. to endorse the key principals which had emerged from the initial meeting with the F.R., only to have had a much more onerous set of terms shoved under our noses at a subsequent meeting. It was therefore agreed that the meeting should be advised of the situation and a motion not to take the vote invited.

This was duly done and the formal meeting closed with commendable speed. Copies of the two agreements were made available, and an open forum held to discuss the issues raised. A variety of views were heard, and a very useful discussion took place. Members who share membership with the Society joined in what was a lively, but far from rancorous debate. Yours truly made his much quoted statement that we wanted a settlement with the F.R. and that remains our objective, but not at too high a price. Members were invited to submit comments on the agreements to Hilary Chapman our legal adviser on the matter. So, the situation remains that we did not sign an agreement in time to withdraw our technical objection to the F.R.'s T.W.A. Order, which we continue to support in principle. We shall therefore have to appear at the Public Inquiry in Caernarfon to state our case. In the meantime, the F.R., (remember, the organisation that removed the arbitration clause from the draft agreement?) has requested a meeting under the Chairmanship of the A.I.R.P.S. Yes, the same organisation we had suggested should appoint an arbitrator, but they didn't want! Confused? You should be. If time permits, an account of that meeting will follow. (Brief details below - Ed.) Who said life was dull? Meantime next time you read an enthusiastic endorsement of an agreement with the F.R. by one Alisdair McNicol, be careful to read between the lines.

### Overview of meeting held 26/11/97

As mentioned above a meeting was arranged, and took place on Thursday 26th November. David Morgan from the AIRPS chaired the meeting, but unfortunately the FR continued their original line, and no notable progress was made. Comments from them such that their use of the name was not a problem did not go down too well, neither did their request (after David Morgan had left) that we withdraw our objection. Despite the apparent unwillingness of the FR to negotiate a deal to ensure the rapid rebuilding of the line, we have arranged further meetings. Watch this space!

*Here is proof positive of just how lack of trust between the two organisations, and the need for WHRL negotiators to refer back offers keeps the two organisations apart. Yes the FR Co. is ducking and weaving; at the same time WHRL is playing to the gallery in explaining events - let me clarify.*

*The Welsh Office have caught a whiff of the opposition expressed by Porthmadog Town Council over the effect that trains will have if permitted to run over Britannia Bridge in Porthmadog. This is dangerous for FR Co., as the Welsh Office go wobbly on FR Co's wish to link the two railways then there's a real problem. So Sharpe, Pritchard, FR Co's Parliamentary Agents, advise Mike Hart to make sure no other railway company objects to the Cross Town Link, because if there's major opposition to the Britannia Bridge, then either the TWO will need to be cut back to Rhyd Ddu, or the WHR will need to use the WHRL as a terminus, with the Cross Town Rail Link (CTRL) built for stock movement, until the restrictions can be eased 'later'. So the nonchalant 'we don't need the 64 Co.' attitude undergoes an abrupt change. FR knows what WHRL wants. It is also by this time experienced enough to know that it must seek advantage for its own position, or risk real harm to its interests - remember, for the FR Co. this is all BUSINESS. So there's a love-meeting in Dinas where FR Co. offers running rights and Pont Croesor in exchange for using the WHRL station. This was what WHRL wanted to hear. They should have said 'yes', and got it on a signed bit of paper.*

*Alas the way they were structured meant that in order to say 'yes' it took until 27th September. At this moment reflect on what you have read, like Mr McNicol's note in Journal 122, and attempt to explain why*

*it was that when the offer came, after all the pressure, all the asking, instead of saying 'yes - where do we sign?', it took an EGM to decide the issue. During that time FR nailed what they were offering 'to the wall' in a letter of 26th August. This was fairly straightforward. It is evident that the FR Co. was clarifying its position - and it's an offer mind - with a view to guarding against any 'slippage' against its interests.*

*But then something else happened. The changing wind of opinion suggested that the Britannia Bridge crossing would be a runner, and the CTRL proposal was safe. So there was another meeting, this time in London, on 19th September, where the new situation and its effect was explained. The WHRL had still not had its EGM; now the FR Co. no longer wanted the facility to terminate, so its offer had changed. Yet there's something wrong with the Journal reports; cross-compare the two. Note in Journal 122 the Pont Croesor offer is:*

> 'we have in recent times offered to build the railway to Pont Croesor at our own cost, and to give them the entire length once they have need of it.'

*The FR Co. 'running rights' offer is that the fares (rent?) are collected by the operating company, with a stock (hire) payment to the operator. Now in Journal 124 the comment is critical of the FR Co proposal:*

> 'To get a flavour of this draft agreement, it suggested, inter alia, (amongst other things) that our company should build to Pont Croesor at its sole expense (No grant application allowed!), hand It over to the F.R., pay rent for its use and hand all fares revenue over to the F.R.'

*Didn't WHRL offer to build at sole expense with 'no strings'? Didn't FR say they'd collect fares and pay to use the WHRL trains?*

*The other problems here are easy enough to understand and explain.*
- *Circumstances changed - if WHRL found the original offer compelling, then allowing from 19th August until 27th September to respond positively to such an important item, is asking for trouble.*
- *And before the Morgan meeting in Warrington, on 29th November, the FR Co. had a detailed account of what had gone on at the WHRL EGM.*
- *The meeting had rejected the FR terms of 26th August, but reports of the rejection reveal a lack of reality on a breathtaking scale. The CTRL was not to be supported in any form, the Board was granted power to engage in further negotiations, and the name WHR was to be registered as a trademark for WHRL. The difficulties of going to Pont Croesor were skated over, though they were howling for 'how to do it' discussion as a major plank in WHRL expansion plans.*

*The 26th November meeting with AIRPS was to establish points of difference, and to block any attempts to say that FR would offer WHRL no deal.*

*The report above doesn't indicate any understanding by WHRL, and the fact that they still believed that their support for 'rapid rebuilding of the line' was a significant hit illustrates that fact. In the report of the EGM, in the extracts from the Journal, the theme is the wickedness of the FR. There was going to be an agreement, the 1998 Agreement. Its origins were from within this context, and its sloppiness, ill considered wording, and lack of clarity were to be its undoing.*

### April 1998
### Letter in Journal 125

Although not a working member (yet), I travelled up to Porthmadog for the February E.G.M. in order to hear the arguments before voting. I was struck at what appeared to be carelessness over the wording of the agreement, the fact that the actual text that had been signed was different from that which was mailed to the members, and the failure to provide fourteen days notice of the meeting.

At the meeting, concern was voiced by those who were against the agreement that there was a danger of volunteers being lost. I for one, however, will be more likely to get involved at Gelert's Farm if and when our company has a role in the whole W.H.R. project, by constructing northwards from Pen-y-Mount and eventually operating so-called 'heritage' trains over the whole line. While I recognise that the agreement which has been entered into in no way guarantees that this will ever happen (and the Secretary of State may well throw out the TWA application anyway), I do feel that, three and a half years after McGregor's infamous decision, it is time we moved forward. I didn't join the W.H.R.L in 1990 in order just to support a heritage centre with a less-than-three-quarters-of-a-mile running track.

I feel that the Board, albeit under pressure of time from the F.R., appear to have been careless, but if the membership had defeated the resolution in order to re-negotiate the agreement, would any future deal which the F.R. might sign be likely to be significantly better?.

Yours faithfully,
Andrew Smith.

*Here is a letter that illustrates the pressure from WHRL members: 'you'd better get us an extension; you'd better get the agreement right'. Sympathy is owed to the WHRL. Board for the position they were now in. Peoples' democracies have a problem when they are caught between a rock and a hard place like this. The WHRL cannot force FR to give them an extension - good Lord knows they have tried - and having finally pinned the FR Co. to an agreement, (See Chapter 5 for details) albeit with improvements to be made, they are already being criticised. The weak point is that Mr Smith did not join for the ¾ mile. The 'ravening beast' has alas collared the 'exciting bits', and it looks like it will build them. Opposition to the Cross Town Link was overcome in the TWO Inquiry, and Mr Meller's Proof of Evidence led to some confusion. It was made public that Mr Meller, a Director of WHRL, had withdrawn his objection to the FR's TWA application in a spirit of reconciliation, in order to further the growing co-operation between the WHRL and the FR. Yet Journal 126, to follow, seems not to take any account of this, as the 1998 Agreement was predicated on WHRL withdrawing objections to the TWO.*

*There are now mounting instances of provably 'doubtful' behaviour of 64Co./WHRL. Can FR continue to be the whipping boy? FR is now sure that 64 Co. cannot be trusted to keep agreements - and (agree with it or not) this is reflected in Mr Schumann's personal comment at the end of this section. That is a turnaround from the position before the 1988 Agreement, when it was 64 Co.'s view that FR Co. could not be trusted.*

## July 1998
## Journal 126 - The Future
The last few years have not been an easy time for this Company, but the agreement with the F.R. has opened up new opportunities for the future. There is now an undercurrent of enthusiasm building on the railway which I have not sensed for some time.

Of course, the agreement has not met with universal approval. A significant number of members voted against the resolution at the EGM, including a number of very active volunteers. Some of these, who have been very involved over recent years, have not felt able to continue to support the railway as they have done before. I can understand their feeling of disillusionment but hope that, after a period of reflection, they will realise that their contribution to the railway in the past is too great to be cast aside now, and they will return to the fold in due course. Whatever they may decide, we should all remember that it is only due to the efforts of these people, and others who have continued to support the railway since the EGM, that we are now in such a strong position. Many observers may have expected, after the 1994 decision, that we would have withered (if not died out completely) and the fact that we have survived is due to the huge commitment shown by volunteers in all aspects of the Company's activities.

The other side of the coin is however somewhat different. Over 300 members voted in favour of the resolution at the E.G.M., but only a relatively small proportion of those can have been involved in the railway's activities since the meeting. It is disappointing that so few of the 'pro-agreement' group have yet to demonstrate their commitment. I hope that they will make their contribution during the present year, and what better way could there be than by joining the hard-pressed Operating Department? We need your help too. I know that Andy Hughes will welcome any offers of support, and remember that when it comes to operating any extended railway, existing passed out staff will be at the front of the queue.

I know that many members will be thinking that the chance to get onto the trackbed is the biggest benefit arising from the

agreement, but there is much more to it than that. Under the agreement, we cannot start work on the trackbed until the F.R. have completed construction of their line from Dinas to Waunfawr. That in itself is subject to a favourable decision from the Secretary of State which, at the time of writing, is still awaited. There are however a number of opportunities which are already ours for the taking, and these can be determined from Hilary Chapman's article elsewhere in this Journal regarding the agreement.

Those aspects of the agreement which have already come into effect might be summarised as follows:
We withdraw our objection to the F.R.'s TWA application (with the exception of the compulsory purchase of our land);
We support the F.R.'s TWA application at the public inquiry;
We allow the F.R. to use our registered trade mark for its Caernarfon operation;
F.R. assists us with development of our heritage facility;
A joint steering committee is established.

Items (i) to (iii) have been implemented, item (iv) is under discussion (a report on a recent meeting with F.R. should appear elsewhere in this Journal), and item (v) should be the board's next challenge.

There should therefore be no doubt amongst the membership that these aspects of the agreement are already in place and will remain so, irrespective of whatever the Secretary of State may decide. Trackbed developments are of course dependant on that decision, and it is not worth speculating too much on what might happen. In the event of the Secretary of State deciding not to grant the F.R.'s Order, however, we will still have our existing railway, and the F.R. will still be obliged, under the agreement, to assist us in developing the heritage aspects of our operation. Certainly, if the F.R.'s application fails, it will be more difficult for anybody to build a railway on any part of the trackbed, but that is getting too far ahead with the speculation.

On the assumption that the Secretary of State will decide to make the Order, steps are being taken to dust off our plans for the Pont Croesor section and bring them up to date. In this respect, members should be aware that the documents submitted by F.R. with its application include a number of constraints in the way that the railway will be built. We already know what these are, and discussions are under way to establish what other undertakings have been given by the F.R. in their attempts to overcome objections. There are however restrictions on simple things like scrub clearance only being undertaken at certain times of the year (to avoid harming nesting birds and the like) and we are as bound by these as the F.R.. So please be patient if you do not see track being laid or bushes being cut down the day after the Secretary of State's decision. Things are not that simple - neither the decision nor the making of the Order will actually convey the land to F.R.; further procedures still have to be followed. If, however, you feel that you have expertise which would be of assistance in developing our plans, please do not hesitate to come forward.

Just because we have to wait a while before we can start physical work on the trackbed, it does not mean that there is nothing else to do. Apart from running the railway through the season, we have the heritage side of the agreement to develop. Furthermore, there will be plenty of preparation work to do as planning progresses for the extension. And not all extension work need be on the trackbed itself. To carry more passengers over a longer line will require more coaches, and trains will run greater distances at higher average speeds, meaning a greater maintenance work load and a need for better storage and repair facilities.

We already have planning permission for a large extension to the existing carriage shed. Although we might not be able to afford the high quality museum and interpretation centre originally envisaged, there is potential for building the basic structure now and using it as a combination of increased display space (including some on rails) and storage space. The internal layout could be fully developed later. We must be aware that once work starts on the extension there may not be sufficient resources to cope with this type of development as well as extending and maintaining the railway. So, don't wait any longer before getting involved, the railway needs your help - both in donations and labour - now.

Dave Meller, Chairman

It seems that in Journal 126 the Chairman is drumming up support for the extension. This is what 64 Co./WHRL have always sought. The 1998 Agreement makes provision for building and running a railway to Pont Croesor. Thus after 8 years of delay they are almost at the green light - they just have to hang on until FR Co. reaches Waunfawr. Perhaps this gives two years breathing space, assuming the TWO is awarded. Where's the money coming from? The new carriages, storage and repair facilities get a mention where's the call to rally people to the cause, to raise the cash to meet the challenges of building a new bit of railway?

In **Journal 128**, Feb 1999 (not quoted) Chairman Meller is not asking for extension funds as he wants to fund short term projects - this must raise the question about wether he and his board understood the need for really major fund raising action to have any chance at all of success of the Pont Croesor extension. In an appeal later, some £27.5k was proposed for local enhancements and extensions. The Pont Croesor job would exceed that by many times. Chairman Meller announces that the Company is poised on the brink of achieving its principal ambition. This is difficult to comprehend under the circumstances.

## November 1999
### Letter in Journal 131 - Whose Railway ?

The following letter is my own personal opinion and is no way the views of the Company or of its Board of Directors. With all the excitement going around about the Welsh Highland now being possibly rebuilt in its entirety, the comments being raised in the last Journal about the railway from the southern end have provoked the issue of finance. The implied message given in J130 [and in the earlier appeal] is that we must raise the money to build from the southern end.

May I ask -

a) why do we have to use money raised by OUR members to build a railway that we DO NOT own ?

b) why do we have to buy materials, i.e., ballast, rail, etc, again from our pockets, to build a railway that we do not own.

As it is not our railway, shouldn't we ask the FR to supply all the materials and provide the finance to build what is in effect their railway? After all, the FR would want it to be built to their specifications, whether it be conventional rails on wooden sleepers, or the oversized 'Mamod' track they have used on the northern end. Some may argue that, at least, we will be running our trains on the Welsh Highland proper. I cannot disagree with this, but we do not know how many trains we may be allowed to run, especially if the FR decide to run intensive services as per existing FR operations at Harbour Station. So we might not even get a look in. As we are always issuing appeals, the money for on-going and future projects at Gelert's Farm, the sums being talked about (up to £500,000) for extending to Pont Croesor are large. Will the members be prepared to stump up that much money, especially as we do not own the railway ? I somehow think not. So if the FR are sincere in their wish to rebuild the whole line, then they can supply the necessary finance and materials. After all, they can get grants as easy as picking apples off a tree. So, beware, in the apparent wish to build northwards, we may get a nasty sting. It would be interesting to hear how many of the members agree or disagree with my letter, but as I said at the start, it is my own personal opinion on this matter.

Mark Wigley.

*Here is a perceptive chap. FR Co. was willing to dole out 'right to run' in exchange for the construction. The construction is 'big money' but his suggestion that the FR should be allowed to build it at their own expense is what they were prepared to do anyway (and did!). For the answer to his question, look at Journal 122 extract. It simply was not 'the FR made us'. WHRL asked to do this - there was no other reason. However in November 1999 the realisation had still not yet penetrated that FR was indeed going to restore the whole WHR. So was the WHRL agreement strategy a safeguard against that, leaving Gelert's Farm with their own railway if the FR never got beyond Waunfawr or Rhyd Ddu? The sums quoted in this letter are massive - and surely no surprise, yet has there been public clarity or concern about raising them?*

*FR Co. strategy at this time is obvious. The 1998 Agreement was needed to remove TWO objection. Offering Pen y Mount - Pont Croesor to build in exchange for some 'running rights' was worthwhile for FR Co.*

For WHRL to be unable to curb its own TWO objectors and then not to complete the build to Pont Croesor was unhelpful to their cause.

*Mike Schumann's opinion in retrospect shown alongside reflects the view of the time. He may be mildly shocking with his forthrightness, but it explains how matters lay for him in the 1990s, as he was of course a director of FR Co. at that time as well as being the Managing Engineer of the restoration.*

## May 2000
### Journal 133 - Dave Allan, Black and White

The optimism expressed in the last Black & White article took a severe knock when just about anyone who knew anything about it advised me that we couldn't simply 'clear up' that section of the trackbed beyond Pen y Mount to the next crossing (Cynfal). The action of 'clearing up' would appear to be taken as having started the extension proper and would bring down upon us the wrath of every authority known to man and a few more besides! No, we have to go through the proper procedures, and these have become far more complex under recent legislation then they were even a few years ago. It is very much a far cry from the almost cavalier 'do-it-yourself' attitude which prevailed when the FR were getting their act together in the fifties!

There are two essential pre-requisites which must be completed before any physical work can be undertaken. The first of these is to update the Environmental Statement. This was produced at the public inquiry and forms a part of the Transport and Works Order. This update must satisfy at least three bodies - these are the Countryside Council for Wales (CCW), the Environment Agency (EA) and finally Gwynedd Council (GC). The FR employ an expensive firm of consultants to do this for them - we are not in that position. However, all is not lost - an approach has been made to the North Wales Wild Life Trust who have an associate company that is able to undertake this work on a professional basis. We are currently in discussion with them, and as the work involved is fairly simple, we are hoping for some positive action on this one.

The second pre-requisite is an Engineering Survey. This will establish the exact position of the track, the line of the fences, and will also identify any engineering features which must be included, - e.g. sheep creeps. This must then be agreed with Gwynedd Council who are the planning authority. It is clear that all this consultative process will take some time - and some effort!

A further difficulty may prove to be with some of the adjacent landowners along the permanent way. In spite of the authority of the Order and the provisions that it contains for land acquisition, the human factor is still involved. Some farmers remain vehemently opposed to the railway, fearing that in these difficult times for their business that their livelihood may be further affected. It will require great understanding, tact, and a personnel relations exercise to overcome this very human problem.

However, having outlined what the company must do to get even a foot on the trackbed, let there be no doubt whatsoever in anyone's mind that all these difficulties will be overcome and that the extension from Pen y Mount will be built, with a start being made this year. Let there also be no doubt that this will not be a cheap affair. The line must be built to professional standards of the same high quality adopted by the FR in their reconstruction of the northern section. We do not have the same access to the money which has allowed the FR to make such dramatic process from Dinas, but we do have access to superb in-house skills and to that enthusiasm and sheer dogged determination which has so characterised our company in the past. We will need to call on all of those latent resources and talents in the near future. Our first and most immediate need will be the cash to get us started - there is some in the reserves which has been building up slowly from those standing orders and donations but we will need an awful lot more. So please, when the appeal comes dig as deep as you can, and contribute as much as you can, using any of the various fund raising alternatives that will be presented to you.

As has been hinted in the past, the railway will not stand alone as a viable business. There are few if any preserved lines which cover their cost from the carrying of passengers alone. Balances are made up from peripheral activities, such as souvenir sales and cafe activities. Then there are 'driver experience' courses, educational opportunities, and in the case of the FR their successful travel business. Our "Unique Selling Point" could well be the sophisticated museum or 'experience' which will illustrate the history of the development of Porthmadog and the narrow gauge railways that made it what it is. All of this was explored in the last issue, to which readers should refer for a more comprehensive exposition. But there is no point in simply leaving good ideas to fester - progress has to be made. Gordon Rushton, formerly the FR's General Manager, has been retained on a professional basis to produce a business plan which will put us in the position where we can apply for grants, either European Objective One or Heritage Lottery Fund.

The town of Porthmadog has never properly exploited its prominent, and indeed unique position as the birth place of steam-driven, narrow-gauge railways. Nor has it latched on to the significant contribution that this development has made to the civilised world and to the industrial development of so many countries. Without the concept of the narrow gauge, and the articulated locomotives which provided the motive power, the mineral wealth of remote areas in many parts of the world could not have been exploited. Porthmadog was built on railways and by railways - many a larger town or city would be falling over themselves to promote such a unique heritage. There can be little doubt that Porthmadog could very easily sell itself as 'The Cradle of Narrow Gauge Railways' - this has both a national and an international appeal. It would be the town's Unique Selling Point. All other holiday towns in North Wales can wax lyrical about the scenery, the beaches and the facilities, but only Porthmadog can add its narrow gauge heritage to this general catalogue of benefits. Gwynedd has recently appointed a 'promotional executive' - perhaps it would be sensible to suggest this concept to him!

Welsh Highland Railway (Porthmadog) is in a very good position not only to tell the story of Porthmadog and the railways that made it, but also to provide a living, steaming experience of the transport involved. It is an exciting concept and one which could bring great benefit to our ambitions, as well as allowing us to give more meaning to our heritage train ride. However it is also a concept that would benefit the economy of the whole of the town and the other tourist attractions within it - including the Festiniog Railway.

So, in summary, all this is saying that we should develop a twin approach to the future development of our company. First and foremost comes the extension to Pont Croesor (and further), but this in turn will be supported by a different sort of railway experience - a novel and dramatic 'hands on' approach telling the story of the development of narrow gauge railways, and the leading role played by the town of Porthmadog.

*David Allan realises that cash is needed - indeed the FR have just told him that they will have none until someone hands them a grant to extend from Rhyd Ddu to Porthmadog. Here he is reinventing the concept of the WHRL Porthmadog site, and the twin approach of museum and railway. However, problems dogged the WHRL Pont Croesor extension, and these caused heartache that matured into a note in 2005, where FR confirms that WHRL are unable to complete to Pont Croesor, because they have not the cash and resources to do so. This is five years into the future and we are entitled to ask how WHRL thought they would achieve this dream commitment.*

*It may be that in 2000, the notion continues that FR will not build beyond Rhyd Ddu, and that the Pont Croesor extension can be catered for by volunteer means, with years to go yet, and no hurry for funds. Once more it looks like there is no realisation by WHRL of the danger of the project not being fulfilled promptly, and of what will follow. Here can be seen that the sword remains very firmly in the rock. FR is beavering away for grants, and afterwards makes a Herculean effort to get matched funding - their campaign is a frenzy of activity. The comparison is not good.*

*Hindsight reveals the problems to come - what is going to turn up in 2008 is a lot of contractor's yellow machines. The Ffestiniog work gangs will be at Pont Croesor, ready to start work in September and the WHRL will have built 800m of line, as far as Traeth Mawr Loop, only completed in 2007. This will soon be surrendered and with it went the dream.*

## Comment from Mike Schumann

Reading these entries, many of which I have never seen before, raises a number of questions in my mind that lay unanswered while we were completely taken up with trying to get the WHR restored. The effort needed to sustain the project was huge. This was costly and exhausting, and it was certainly not a fight with 64 Co. at all. They caused a fuss whilst FR was pursuing protectionist policies, but that faded after the High Court. When offers were made to 64 Co. to join, I could never understand the reasons why even if they didn't like us, they did not get themselves some insurance, with a deal for protection.

The revelation that the GCC leak filled them with such strong feelings of lack of trust explains a lot. That these feelings should persist for so long inside the organisation stripped them of opportunity later. Following the High Court case, the favoured relationship they appeared to enjoy with the Gwynedd Light Railway Sub-committee did not help them. Even after the TO was granted, there was a feeling that a significant proportion of the 64 Co. members and Directors wanted to make life difficult, and we often wondered why, as we had offered participation several times, but this never seemed to be enough.

Of course for us life was totally taken up with the real fight over WHR, to get the TWO, and to find funding. It was important not to make commitments to anyone in respect of the future, which might adversely affect the profitability of the railway operation once completed, yet we felt we must give recognition to the 64 Co./WHRL's aspiration to extend to Point Croesor, particularly if the overall WHR restoration would take years to fulfil. The FR Co. Board, once it had made a strategic decision, was happy to delegate authority to specified Directors to carry out its policy without constant referral back. 64 Co./WHRL kept having to refer back to their Board and membership for approval, which made all negotiations long winded and doubtful in outcome.

It was a matter of astonishment to us, when the 1998 Agreement was concluded, that progress in rebuilding to Pont Croesor was so slow, despite the assistance that we gave. It seemed that after 35 years of aspiration, when the green light came, preparations were incomplete. Indeed we ended up building the stretch between Pont Croesor and Traeth Mawr, but the feeling of antipathy towards the FR has persisted within the ranks of WHRL, with the reasons for this being laid at our door. There was an obvious lack of understanding of the problems that had to be overcome in rebuilding 26 miles of railway. Hopefully, the relationship problems between the FR and WHRL under present leadership are now well on the way to being resolved.

Mike Schumann
June 2011

## Building to Pont Croesor - WHRL

It took from the 'OK' of 1998 to February 2004 before 64Co./ WHRL began construction to Traeth Mawr, and progress was slow. They were hampered by lack of funds, and had been 'forbidden' to apply for Euro-grants by FR Co., who insisted that this must be done under unified control. The WHRL fundraising campaign had reached £40k out of a target of £250k. Such a long term aim ought by any standard to have commanded more support than this. CRhE in two years or so raised nearly £1m towards the WHR Track Fund with no grant assistance.

Later, WHRL Chairman James Hewett asserted that FR Co. prevented WHRL from constructing beyond Pen y Mount, as FR failed to take title to the land, that they were bound to do under the 1998 Agreement. This was also asserted by others before this time, and the matter profits from explanation.

Mike Hart wrote to David Allan requesting no contact with the landowner until FR Co.'s say-so. When compulsory purchase notices are issued, 90% of purchase price had to be handed over, and amounts (unknown) for claims in mitigation before work starts. Plus, the notices have a time limit, between issue and the start of work. In 1999 FR Co. preferred to wait until matters became clearer over title claims. Money was short, and this is why 64 Co. was asked not to precipitate any problems. The 800m section of track and loop to Traeth Mawr, with secure land title, did not open until March 2007. The 2003 internal WHRL Business Plan document states that no direct expenditure, nor changes based on a railway operating to Pont Croesor, were planned between 2004 and 2009. At a meeting on 25th August 2005 it was confirmed to FR Co. that WHRL was unable to complete reconstruction to Pont Croesor. That stretch was one of the more high-priced stretches of railway on the WHR restoration, and required some £700k to build. The 64 Co. had specially chosen Pont Croesor as their long-term aim, one much lauded over the years. There is no acknowledgement that the problems of this portion of route were understood by 64 Co. before they started declaring that they would build it. There is no viable plan yet discovered to raise the funds needed to accomplish the restoration, yet there is much written about what trains would run over it. It seems it was beyond WHRL resources to build, and that this was a matter of deep internal, political inconvenience, for which the blame had to lie elsewhere.

The FR general mood was certainly not to exclude WHRL running on the completed railway, even after FR Co. were forced to expended £700k that they had not planned for on building the section from Pont Croesor to Traeth Mawr. They did get 45% of that back from additional grant - but it still cost a lot of money.

## The 2009 Operations Proposal

There was a '2009 Operations Proposal' made by WHRL with some encouragement from FR Co. in 2008, but it proposed six timetabled trains, to Pont Croesor, November - March, with occasional heritage trains to Beddgelert, and a fares arrangement, not compliant with the 1998 Agreement. FR Co. could not accept this proposal because the regular timetabled service was 'physically impossible to operate': there was no signalling in place; there needed to be two platforms at Pont Croesor; there were problems enough to commission the section to Porthmadog before running anything, and WHRL hadn't the resources to run it anyway!. FR Co. offered instead the proposal of an occasional service, with *Russell* and two WHR carriages, working between Porthmadog FR and Beddgelert, thinking that this was affordable, practical, and could be evolved.

Opposite is a WHRL Strategy paper, the contents and potential effectiveness of which the reader may consider, as it seems to have had a profound effect on the future of the WHRL Chairman..

**Note:**\* HRA wrote to WHRL with a most serious objection over this paper.

## WHRL Strategy Paper – FR June 2010*

*Must be done FAST – say July/August this year at the latest*
1. Press – bombard local press with letters, from:
   i. WHR Ltd. staff, members, Board
   ii. Our friends and sympathisers
2. Press – bombard railway press with letters, from:
   i. WHR Ltd. staff, members, Board
   ii. Our friends and sympathisers
3. Accept offer from NG Heaven to conduct campaign, and host petition
4. Return to what we used to do - constant railway press articles – every magazine, every issue – small, medium news stories, as well as large ones. Thus keep us in the forefront of the public eye.
5. MPs, AMs, ministers - bombard with letters, from:
   i. WHR Ltd. staff, members, Board
   ii. Our friends and sympathisers
6. Chairman writes to Chairmen of all UK heritage railways, theme parks, other heritage operations, and museums, asking for support.
7. Really USE our connections with VW,TPNW, GLTW, etc. by actively pursuing our interests
8. Write to all HRA officers/board members asking for support (open letter?)
9. Write again to Charity Commission re. JP's dual role (open letter?)
10. Enlist internal support from FR members – i.e. by encouraging the democratic movement at FR
11. Pursue matter of publicly-funded railway – that it should be open access
12. Finally sort matters with David Morgan – either he supports us/works for us, or he doesn't – how long is it since we contacted him?
13. Support our own ambitions internally:
    i. Re-label our operation as "The Real WHR" (or "The Original")
    ii. Appeal to the innate sense of fair play of the British – portray ourselves as what we actually are – a downtrodden small company with the FR's jackboot on our faces – enlist sympathy
    iii. Be of one mind in fighting FR (more easily said than done)
    iv. Vigorously pursue FR on the question of their non-agreed use of our Trade Mark
*SECOND STAGE (if the above does not work)*
1. Organise demonstrations at FR openings, special occasions, etc.
2. Boycott any organisation which refuses to help us
3. Enlist the national press – quirky campaigns, news, Private Eye, etc.
4. Find unelectable councillors/AMs/MPs and enlist their public support – if they are unelectable, they'll do anything
5. Propose Board members on FR and WHR Soc boards
6. Make (more and louder) trouble at FR AGMs – Company/Society
7. Write children's books showing FR as villains
8. Pursue new media - blogs, Facebook, twitter, etc. etc. as part of an organised and concerted campaign
   But first - we must sort out whether we are serious about the Operations Proposal:
   i. Either we are, in which case we must be pro-active and not passive
   ii. Or we are not, in which case we should hang our heads in shame. If after all the (very expensive) work on our stock we really can't run our trains along one extra mile of level track at 10mph we have failed so comprehensively we might as well go home.

**BACKGROUND NOTES ON STRATEGY**
☐ We seem to be agreed (and anyway, I am totally convinced) that top management at FR Co. are, and always have been, determined to destroy WHR Ltd. as a viable, independent, entity
                        THUS
☐ There is no point in making any further concessions, because nothing will result
                        BECAUSE
☐ We cannot trust FR
                        SO
☐ It's a very bad idea to "park" the Operations Proposal, as that's playing into FR's hands, again
                        BECAUSE
☐ It will split the Company, which is what FR have always wanted
                        AND
☐ That will badly damage day-to-day operation.
                - and FURTHERMORE
☐ As we have no prospect of achieving anything useful from FR
                        AND
☐ Vetoing criticism of FR will result in a Company split (see above)
                        SO
☐ Fighting our corner will do us no damage
                        AND
☐ It will endear us to our many supporters, who want us to fight for our rights
                        AND
☐ Who knows, we might become such a thorn in FR's flesh that they concede (it's happened before)
                        AND
☐ If not, we've lost nothing
                        WHILE
☐ Retaining our integrity
                        AND
☐ Being true to ourselves by our public avowal of the righteousness of our position
                        WHILE
☐ At the same time exposing FR's evil purposes
*A thought to finish with: "No right can be lost as long as there are people still demanding it" (Egyptian proverb)*

# Map Legend

The maps have been included to improve comprehension in the text. Hopefully the symbols used do not require much cross-referring to the legend. There are two warnings, first that the maps are not meant to be strictly 'in scale', though they are not far out. If someone wishes more accuracy, then this is possible via Google Maps; these have eclipsed the OS in a fairly comprehensive manner. The second concern is that often, everything shown did not necessarily exist at the same time.

| | | | | |
|---|---|---|---|---|
| | | | | Standard Gauge Rly |
| | | | | SG only part built |
| | | | | 600mm in larger scale map |
| | | | | 600mm (LS) cutting |
| | | | | 600mm (LS) embankment |
| | Town | | Footpath (Cycleway) | 600mm in smaller scale map |
| | Buildings | | Contours (m) | Out of use/waiting for track |
| | River | | Quarry | PB&SSR route not finished |
| | Stream | | Quarry Incline (Closed) | PB&SSR route planned |
| | Sand | | Station (Open) | Old WHR layout |
| | Semi-bog | | Station (Closed) | Old SG layout - Dinas |
| | Boskage | | Gradient | Tunnel |
| | Trees (deciduous) | | Token Cabinet | Rail bridges - construction maps |
| | Trees (conifer) | LC76 | Level crossing (Public road - normally) | Road |
| | Forest (& woodland) | UB 56 32.48 | Level Crossing (construction number) | Minor road (paved) |
| | Rocky Edge | | Underbridge (construction number & kilometric location) | Path |
| | | | Boundary | SNP Boundary |
| | | | To North | Parking |

*Writing WHR Renaissance was a long haul, and sometimes extremely frustrating, however, it was evident early that to do the job justice, some detailed maps would be needed of a scope and quality that did not exist. The only way to offer comprehension to the walls of words, was either to do what Dr Ben Fisher did on his website with pictures, or to try to bridge the gaps in understanding with maps - lots of them. Ben used thousands of pictures - though his commentary is particularly satisfying to the people who did the job, it can be obscure to those (like me) who did not. A certain latent ability and underestimation of the task led to maps. The time it takes to do these maps is prodigious. There are still subjects not covered satisfactorily, as there is not the time and the aching concentration needed to do the extra maps. There is a lack of satisfaction about the quality that it is possible to achieve - yet there have to be limits. I salute JIC Boyd, and the wonderful Mr Lloyd; they broke new ground and achieved marvels, but they have been surpassed and left behind. They did not have the advantage of the TWA maps, the OS Maps, and most wonderful of all, the satellite images of Google to act as references. Best is a powerful computer with expensive software to condense the weeks and weeks it all takes into days and days. So if there is a concern about how this book became quite so expensive, the answer lies in the maps.*

# Index

Certain words occur so frequently that they have not been indexed - other minor entries have been removed. Look for people's first names, followed by their surnames.

# Afterword

When writing this story three things have become clear: the contributors have all displayed a high degree of public spiritedness, and have striven not to get their names in print, but to follow the central aim of this book, to write down the story of the largest single accomplishment of railway preservation to date; secondly, that this account's 448 pages barely scratch the surface; it is over-simplified, inaccurate and incomplete, but it has taken three years to write, and it is a start. Thirdly, there are people alienated from the achievements, who despite sharing the same aims that have now been accomplished, remain unable to share the fun. Alas, as the railway is now rebuilt, they must look for a remedy inside themselves.

The essence of what has happened, if you have read through and you think this has not been explained clearly enough, is that the Ffestiniog Railway has been joined by a companion that is profitable, complementary rather than competitive, and that declining market share has been restored and increased. In a wider context this means that the Railways contribute £14m annually to the local economy. The moral of this tale must not be the encouragement of mutual smiles of admiration; it has to be 'here is the chance of the century for FR to become a world-class attraction'. If all that has happened since 1990 leads to rapturous admiration of African Garratts pounding into the hills, then everyone has wasted their time. Yet if everyone is getting on with creating a Great Railway Journey of the World, with something delightfully Welsh, and internationally desirable, with the appropriate increase in contribution to the local economy, then the message really will have gone home. No harm in rapture for Garratts as a means to an end; much sadness if it is an end in itself.

The issue of 'Welshness' is played out on a larger stage than the FR, but the renaissance of the WHR serves to illustrate some interesting points. Whereas the initiative and the activity surrounding the restoration of the FR was predominantly 'English', that for the WHR certainly was not. The crowning glory was in the fundraising. Not only was the majority of the grant funding authorised by Cardiff, but the county that gave the 'most' in public subscriptions was Gwynedd. The future is with the young people, everywhere to be seen on the FR&WHR. To them there is no issue. Those that live there are bilingual; the railway is a social hub, and a massive window on the world. It is inclusive and not exclusive, and if you press for an explanation, the one most likely given is that everyone enjoys it in their own way.

There are divisions of activity, class and culture, as there are everywhere. Critics point to the governing structure of the enterprise as being hardly democratic. This generalisation misses the point. In good times democrats bask in the light of approval. In bad times necessary action is hard to find, if the priority of elected representatives is seeking to avoid disapproval. There have been hard times reported in this volume. To insist that FR only overcame them through good fortune, or some dark manipulation, is to fail to see the relation between good leadership, excellent organisation, and success. If you look at the FR&WHR, and you think that the charge that it is run by oligarchs is not a joke, then look again. You have only seen the exterior of the shiny engine. That Trinity of Trust, Company and Society has proved itself enough times during the renaissance for it to be effective and fair.

Of course there is a problem that this book worries some, as it has apparently been written '20 years too early.' Sorry, but this is an account that cannot be written from the grave. We have read enough of JIC Boyd to know that accounts of history in the making, whilst people are around to tell you what they did and why, are preferable to the reedy warble from the past, gleaned from dusty documents. Leave it 20 years and that'll be what you get. This is the greatest preservation project to date, and its story being made available now is an entirely justifiable compliment to all those who made it possible, plus it is an inspiration to those who would like to do such a thing. If you read this, you know that you can! The story told now should overcome the reluctance of those who cluck quietly against the mild discomfort of the revelations contained within. More importantly it claps a stopper over the chorus of 'it can't be done' - yes it can; here's how!

The account is sometimes robust, and perhaps offends, when recent opinions escape on to the page. There is a deal of shocking stuff that has not been presented, partly because it is too sensational, or it reveals a rather shameful attitude, held through prejudice or ignorance that revelation would inflame. There are people who have been left out of this account, yet they have been asked for their contribution, and for their own reasons it has not been forthcoming: some get glory due to others; some have requested to be excluded - their wishes have been respected. The book is quite unofficial, and although principal parties from all sides have been consulted, the opinions are those of the author and contributors alone.

Monetary contributions have been made by each according to their means. You will have read of staggering amounts of cash handed over by individuals in pursuit of the renaissance. It is fascinating to read about, and to understand how it was used. For that reason, not to boast, a few details have been included of who gave what. Some of it might have been 'Daddy's'; some of it massive earnings that could otherwise have been scooped by the Chancellor. Some of it is hard-earned cash, that represented the outer margin of what could be afforded - the modern-day equivalent of the widow's mite. All of it was given because the giver wanted to see the WHR restored to life. Let us say thank you and leave it at that.

The negative party began with mournful comparisons with the WHR of the 1930s. It will 'never be finished' was a cry at Rhyd Ddu. Their last refuge is that the initial surplus will soon turn to loss. It was nonsense then, and it's nonsense now!

Of course it is not over yet. - the fat lady never sings. After the re-establishment of trains between Caernarfon and Porthmadog the traffic figures were most satisfactory. The first strategy of getting to Porthmadog, bringing traffic from Caernarfon to complement and not compete with the Ffestiniog Railway, doing it without debt, and with enhanced market share with new products to be developed, has borne fruit. The strategy of the Sustainable Railway has been created for the next stage. The challenge is to expand the means for the two railways to grow, and to sustain themselves into the future. It involves finishing what was started on FR and WHR, and providing what is needed to make the enterprise prosper. This makes much sense. What has been built will now mature - but that is another story.